SAS® Language Guide for Personal Computers, Release 6.03 Edition

SAS Institute Inc.
SAS Campus Drive
Cary, NC 27513

The correct bibliographic citation for this manual is as follows: SAS Institute Inc. *SAS® Language Guide for Personal Computers, Release 6.03 Edition*. Cary, NC: SAS Institute Inc., 1988. 558 pp.

SAS® Language Guide for Personal Computers, Release 6.03 Edition

Copyright © 1988 by SAS Institute Inc., Cary, NC, USA.
ISBN 1-55544-099-1

All rights reserved. Printed in the United States of America. No part of this publication may be reproduced, stored in a retrieval system, or transmitted, in any form or by any means, electronic, mechanical, photocopying, or otherwise, without the prior written permission of the publisher, SAS Institute Inc.

1st printing, May 1988
2nd printing, September 1989
3rd printing, September 1990
4th printing, August 1991

Note that text corrections may have been made at each printing.

The SAS® System is an integrated system of software providing complete control over data access, management, analysis, and presentation. Base SAS software is the foundation of the SAS System. Products within the SAS System include SAS/ACCESS® SAS/AF® SAS/ASSIST® SAS/CPE® SAS/DMI® SAS/ETS® SAS/FSP® SAS/GRAPH® SAS/IML® SAS/IMS-DL/I® SAS/OR® SAS/QC® SAS/REPLAY-CICS® SAS/SHARE® SAS/STAT® SAS/CALC™ SAS/CONNECT™ SAS/DB2™ SAS/EIS™ SAS/INSIGHT™ SAS/PH-Clinical™ SAS/SQL-DS™ and SAS/TOOLKIT™ software. Other SAS Institute products are SYSTEM 2000® Data Management Software, with basic SYSTEM 2000, CREATE™ Multi-User™ QueX™ Screen Writer™ and CICS interface software; NeoVisuals® software; JMP® JMP IN® JMP SERVE® and JMP Ahead™ software; SAS/RTERM® software; the SAS/C® Compiler, and the SAS/CX® Compiler. MultiVendor Architecture™ and MVA™ are trademarks of SAS Institute Inc. *SAS Communications® SAS Training® SAS Views®* and the SASware Ballot® are published by SAS Institute Inc. All trademarks above are registered trademarks or trademarks, as indicated by their mark, of SAS Institute Inc.

A footnote must accompany the first use of each Institute registered trademark or trademark and must state that the referenced trademark is used to identify products or services of SAS Institute Inc.

The Institute is a private company devoted to the support and further development of its software and related services.

dBASE II and dBASE III are registered trademarks of Ashton-Tate, Inc.
Lotus and 1-2-3 are registered trademarks of Lotus Development Corporation.
VisiCalc is a trademark of VisiCorp, Inc.

Contents

List of Illustrations v

List of Tables vii

Credits ix

Acknowledgments xi

Using This Book xix

USING THE SAS LANGUAGE
1 Introduction 3

THE DATA STEP
2 Introduction 17
3 SAS Expressions 27
4 SAS Functions 39
5 SAS Statements Used in the DATA Step 107

ABORT	108	LABEL	194
ARRAY	109	Labels, Statement	195
Assignment	122	LENGTH	196
ATTRIB	124	LINK	201
BY	125	LIST	204
CALL	132	LOSTCARD	206
CARDS and CARDS4	134	MERGE	210
DATA	136	MISSING	218
DELETE	140	Null	219
DISPLAY	141	OUTPUT	220
DO	142	PUT	223
DROP	148	RENAME	235
END	149	RETAIN	236
FILE	150	RETURN	241
FORMAT	156	SELECT	243
GO TO	159	SET	246
IF	161	STOP	253
INFILE	164	Sum	254
INFORMAT	171	UPDATE	256
INPUT	173	WHERE	260
KEEP	193	WINDOW	266

THE PROC STEP

- 6 Introduction 281
- 7 SAS Statements Used in the PROC Step 283

ATTRIB	284	OUTPUT	293
BY	285	PROC	294
CLASS	287	QUIT	295
FORMAT	288	VAR	296
FREQ	290	WEIGHT	297
ID	291	WHERE	298
LABEL	292		

DATA AND PROC STEP FEATURES

- 8 Introduction 305
- 9 Starting and Running SAS Programs 307
- 10 SAS Display Manager System 317
- 11 Error Handling 395
- 12 SAS Output 399
- 13 SAS Informats and Formats 411
- 14 Missing Values 451
- 15 SAS Files 457
- 16 SAS Global Options 475
- 17 SAS Macro Facility 501
- 18 SAS Statements Used Anywhere 505

Comment	506	LIBNAME	514
DM	507	OPTIONS	516
ENDSAS	508	RUN	519
FILENAME	509	TITLE	520
FOOTNOTE	511	X	522
%INCLUDE	512		

APPENDICES

- 1 Version 6 Changes and Enhancements to Base SAS Software: Language 525
- 2 User Profile Catalog 533
- 3 SAS Micro-to-Host Link 537
- 4 SAS Installation Details 541

Index 545

Illustrations

Figures

2.1	Flow of Action within a DATA Step	23
2.2	Program Data Vector: Data from Two Sources	25
15.1	SAS Data Library Structure	451
A3.1	Example Directories for Multiple Users and Projects	416

Screens

5.1	Window with a Single Group of Fields	272
5.2	Instructions at the Beginning of a DATA Step	273
5.3	Window for Correcting Missing Data Values	274
5.4	Multiple Windows for Data Entry and Displaying Running Totals	275
5.5	Window for Creating a SAS Data Set	277
9.1	Sample Interrupt Signal Requestor Panel	309
9.2	Sample Line-Mode Session with RUN Statements	310
9.3	Sample Line-Mode Session without RUN Statements	311
10.1	Default Initial Display Manager Screen Format	319
10.2	Using the MARK CHAR Command	335
10.3	Using the MARK BLOCK Command	335
10.4	PGM Window	354
10.5	Saving Contents of PGM Window	355
10.6	Bringing a File into the PGM Window	356
10.7	LOG Window	358
10.8	OUTPUT Window	361
10.9	Executing a FIND Command	362
10.10	CATALOG Window	365
10.11	DIR Window	367
10.12	FILENAME Window	368
10.13	FOOTNOTES Window	369
10.14	TITLES Window	369
10.15	Sample Help Panel	371
10.16	KEYS Window with Default Settings	373
10.17	Defining a Function Key to Insert Text	374
10.18	LIBNAME Window	375
10.19	Displaying the DIR Window for WORK Library	376
10.20	MENU Window	377
10.21	NOTEPAD Window	380

10.22	Creating and Storing a Notepad	380
10.23	OPTIONS Window	383
10.24	SETINIT Window	384
10.25	VAR Window Displaying SAS Data Set Information	386
10.26	Default Initial Display Manager Screen Format	388
10.27	Altered Screen Format	389
10.28	Using Grow Mode	390
10.29	New PGM Window Position	391
10.30	Moving the LOG Window Position	392
11.1	Sample Requestor Panel	395

Tables

1.1	SAS Data Set Listing of Data Values	6
1.2	SAS Variable Attributes	7
1.3	SAS Variable Lists	10
4.1	Functions by Category	42
5.1	Length Produced by Various Expressions	123
5.2	Storage Length for Integers	198
5.3	How the SAS System Retains Values	237
5.4	Actions for Incompatible Variable Attributes	251
13.1	Techniques for Using SAS Informats and Formats	412
13.2	SAS Numeric and Character Informats	414
13.3	SAS Numeric and Character Formats	427
13.4	SAS Date, Time, and Datetime Informats and Formats	440

Credits

Documentation

Composition	Gail C. Freeman, Kelly W. Godfrey, Blanche W. Phillips, Craig R. Sampson, P. Darlene Watts, Penny S. Wiard
Graphics	Lisa N. Clements, Michael J. Pezzoni
Proofreading	Bruce C. Brown, Rick V. Cornell, Reid J. Hardin, Michael H. Smith, Helen F. Weeks
Technical Review	Deborah S. Blank, John H. Gough, James K. Hart, Brenda C. Kalt, Ann A. Lehman, Marian Saffer, Sandra D. Schlotzhauer, Holly S. Whittle
Writing and Editing	Alice T. Allen, David D. Baggett, Amy E. Ball, Gretel Easter, Gigi M. Hassan, Robert P. Hastings, Brenda C. Kalt, Carol Austin Linden, Gary R. Meek, Rebeccah K. Neff, Marian Saffer, John P. Sall, Harriet J. Watts, Curtis A. Yeo

Software

Implementation of Release 6.03 of the SAS System for Personal Computers was led by Robert L. Cross (Director of Core Development) and Mark W. Cates (Manager of PC Host Development). The Core Group is responsible for the core supervisor, SAS library I/O, windowing system, macro facility, procedure interface, and the DATA step. The PC Host Group is responsible for the host supervisor, DOS interfaces, display device support, and development support.

Credits for the procedures are given in the companion volume, *SAS Procedures Guide, Release 6.03 Edition*. Not listed here are other development divisions that are associated with specific products described in other manuals.

Supervisor:	Claire S. Cates, Mark W. Cates, Jeffrey A. Polzin, Carol A. Williams
I/O Systems:	Steven M. Beatrous, Edward L. McGee, Rebecca A. Perry, Jeffrey A. Polzin
Options:	Ed L. McGee, Mark V. Schaffer
Printing and Message:	Jeffrey A. Polzin, Randall K. Whitehead
Formats:	Mike R. Jones, Richard D. Langston, Jeffrey A. Polzin
Functions:	Marc-david Cohen, David M. DeLong, Mike R. Jones, Jeffrey A. Polzin, Randall K. Whitehead

Windowing System:	Malinda M. Adams, Claire S. Cates, Jeffrey C. Shaughnessy
Editor:	Jeffrey C. Shaughnessy
Parsing:	Richard D. Langston, Jeffrey A. Polzin, Bruce M. Tindall
Macro Facility:	Bruce M. Tindall
Procedure Interface:	Claire S. Cates, Richard D. Langston, Jeffrey A. Polzin
DATA Step:	Jeffrey A. Polzin, Mark V. Schaffer, Randall K. Whitehead
Communications:	Edmund B. Burnette, Cheryl Garner, David F. Kolb, Mary Ellen Toebes
Applications Facility:	Christopher D. Bailey, Yao Chen, K. Deva Kumar, Bud M. Whitmeyer
Help and Menu Systems:	Brenda S. Erikson, Gail J. Kramer
Development Support:	James H. Boone, Arthur P. Bostic, Karen L. Hoffman, John A. Toebes, Michael S. Whitcher
Development Testing:	Melissa A. Atkinson, Linda W. Binkley, Merle A. Finch, Tom C. Johnsson, Caroline C. Quinn, Deanna T. Tawiah, Linda L. Wharton, Mandy W. Womble, Ann L. Yang

Support Groups

Quality Assurance:	Pat L. Berryman, Kay D. Bydalek, Oita C. Coleman, Dianne B. Kernodle, Jeanne M. Martin, Jeff R. McDermott, Sue A. McGrath, Scott S. Sweetland
Distribution Support:	Cyndi L. Dondlinger, Bill D. Loflin, Patty P. Morgan
Technical Support:	David C. Brumitt, Linda T. Ingold, Julie A. Maddox, Janice B. Rosenbohm, Alissa R. Wilhelm

Acknowledgments

SAS Institute Inc. is unusually fortunate to have had many people make significant and continuing contributions to its development.

First among them are the chairpersons and other active members of the SAS Users Group International (SUGI). Julian Horwich, now of Arnar-Stone Laboratories, set up the first regional meetings at Abbott Laboratories in North Chicago in 1975, and organized and chaired the first international SUGI meeting in Lake Buena Vista, Florida, in 1976. Dr. Ronald W. Helms of the University of North Carolina at Chapel Hill chaired the second annual conference, held in New Orleans in 1977; Kenneth Offord of the Mayo Clinic was program chairman.

The 1978 SUGI conference in Las Vegas was co-chaired by Dr. Rodney Strand and Dr. Michael Farrell of Oak Ridge National Laboratories. Dr. Ramon C. Littell of the University of Florida and Dr. William Wilson of the University of North Florida co-chaired the 1979 SUGI meeting in Clearwater, Florida. The 1980 SUGI conference in San Antonio, Texas, was chaired by Rudolf J. Freund of Texas A&M University. Kenneth L. Koonce of Louisiana State University chaired the 1981 SUGI conference held in Lake Buena Vista, Florida. The 1982 conference held in San Francisco, California, was chaired by Helene Cavior of the Bureau of Prisons. In 1983 SUGI was in New Orleans with J. Philip Miller of Washington University School of Medicine as chairman. Hollywood Beach, Florida was the site of the 1984 SUGI conference chaired by Sally Carson of the Rand Corporation. Rodney Strand, Science Applications, Inc., and Mike Farrell of ORNL co-chaired SUGI in Reno, Nevada in 1985. In 1986 Donald Henderson of ORI, Inc. chaired SUGI in Atlanta. Pat Hermes Smith chaired SUGI in Dallas in 1987.

The University Statisticians of the Southern Experiment Stations have made numerous contributions over the years. We are especially indebted to:

Wilbert P. Byrd	Clemson University
Richard Cooper	USDA
R.J. Freund	Texas A & M University
Charles Gates	Texas A & M University
Don Henderson	ORI
David Hurst	University of Alabama at Birmingham
Kenneth Koonce	Louisiana State University
Clyde Y. Kramer (deceased)	Virginia Polytechnic Institute, University of Kentucky, and Upjohn Laboratories
Robert D. Morrison	Oklahoma State University
Richard M. Patterson	Auburn University
William L. Sanders	University of Tennessee
Glenn Ware	University of Georgia
T.J. Whatley	University of Tennessee

Acknowledgments

We are deeply grateful to our good neighbor, the Department of Statistics at North Carolina State University, and especially to these staff members:

David D. Mason	Chairman (retired)
Jolayne Service	(now at the University of California, Irvine)
Sandra Donaghy	
Carroll Perkins	(now with Westinghouse)
Francis J. Verlinden	
Evelyn Wilson	

We also wish to express our sincere gratitude to the following people who have contributed in many different ways to the success of the SAS System. See other manuals for other contributors.

Ray Barnes	Upjohn Pharmaceutical Co.
Mark Bercov	Gulf Canada
William Blair	Consultant
Dick Blocker	Washington University
George Chao	Arnar-Stone Laboratories
Daniel Chilko	University of West Virginia
Ray Danner	National Institute of Health
Paul Fingerman	Boeing Computer Services
Terry Flynn	Tymshare
Michael Foxworth	University of South Carolina
Harold Gugel	General Motors Corporation
Donald Guthrie	University of California at Los Angeles
James Guthrie	Ameritrust
Frank Harrell	Duke University
Loren Harrell	Consultant, Business Information Technology Inc.
Jim Harrington	Monsanto Research
Walter Harvey	Ohio State University
Ronald Helms	University of North Carolina at Chapel Hill
Harold Huddleston	Data Collection & Analysis, Inc., Falls Church, Virginia
Emilio A. Icaza	Louisiana State University
Ruth Ingram	Proctor & Gamble
William Kennedy	Iowa State University
Melvin Klassen	University of Victoria
John Klinkner	American Republic Insurance Company
Steve Kuekes	Consultant
Jon Mauney	Consultant
H.W. (Barry) Merrill	Merrill Consultants
J. Philip Miller	Washington University
Mario Morino	Morino Associates Inc.
Curt Mosso	University of California at Santa Barbara
Richard Nelson	Clemson University
Robert Parks	Washington University
Virginia Patterson	University of Tennessee
Jim Penny	Academic Computer Center University of North Carolina at Greensboro

Pete Rikard	Virginia Commonwealth University
John Ruth	University of Toronto
Robert Schechter	Scott Paper Company
Roger Smith	USDA
Robert Teichman	ICI Americas Inc.
John Toebes	Consultant
Jim Walker	Morino Associates Inc.
Charles Whitman	Consultant

The Version 6 project especially acknowledges the contribution of Lattice Inc., who developed the C compiler used for the PC, and Apollo Computer, which supplied us with our main development machines.

Two of the founders of SAS Institute Inc. deserve special mention.

The present SAS documentation can be traced to the work of Jane T. Helwig, now at Seasoned Systems Inc., Chapel Hill, N.C., who gathered and wrote much of the material on which this manual is based.

Finally, SAS Institute and all SAS users owe a debt of gratitude to Anthony J. Barr, Barr Systems, now of Gainesville, Florida. His work on the SAS supervisor and compiler, as well as the procedures that he wrote, help make the SAS System the useful tool it is today.

The final responsibility for the SAS System lies with SAS Institute alone. We hope that you will always let us know your feelings about the system and its documentation. It is through such communications that the progress of SAS software has been accomplished.

The Staff of SAS Institute Inc.

Using This Book

Purpose of This Book

The *SAS Language Guide for Personal Computers, Release 6.03 Edition* is one of a set of five manuals documenting Release 6.03 of base SAS software. The other books in the set are the *SAS Introductory Guide for Personal Computers, Release 6.03 Edition*, the *SAS Procedures Guide, Release 6.03 Edition*, the *SAS Guide to the Micro-to-Host Link, Version 6 Edition*, and the *SAS Guide to Macro Processing, Version 6 Edition*.

This manual contains the fundamentals of the SAS System: an introduction to the DATA and PROC steps; the syntax and use of SAS statements; and system files and options.

How This Book Is Organized

To serve as a reference for new and experienced SAS users, this manual is organized to reflect the structure of the SAS language. All SAS programs are composed of single DATA or PROC steps, or combinations of DATA and PROC steps. Similarly, the information in this manual is arranged according to where it can be used in a SAS program—in a DATA step, in a PROC step, or anywhere.

The book begins with an overview of the SAS language that describes the basics of the SAS System and defines the terms used throughout SAS literature.

The next section describes the DATA step and includes an introduction, statements used in the DATA step (in alphabetical order), SAS expressions, and SAS functions.

The PROC step is described in the next section with an introductory chapter and the statements used in the PROC step (in alphabetical order).

The next major section gives an introduction to global features, statements used anywhere in a SAS job (in alphabetical order), the SAS Display Manager System, SAS output, SAS informats and formats, missing values, SAS files, global options, and the SAS macro facility.

Finally, there are four appendices. The first appendix summarizes changes and enhancements for Version 6 base SAS software, the second appendix describes the user profile catalog, the third appendix discusses the SAS micro-to-host link, and the fourth appendix discusses SAS installation details.

How to Use This Book

If you are a new SAS user, you should read the *SAS Introductory Guide* as you begin to use SAS software. Then, after you are familiar with SAS terminology and concepts, you can quickly advance to this book and the *SAS Procedures Guide*.

As you use this book, first read "USING THE SAS LANGUAGE" to review the basics of writing SAS programs. Then turn to Chapter 2 in "THE DATA STEP" section to learn about the SAS DATA step. You can then refer to the chapters in that section for information about the expressions, functions, and statements you can use in the DATA step.

To learn about the SAS PROC step, refer to Chapter 6 in "THE PROC STEP" section. Then refer to the chapters in that section for details on the statements you can use in the PROC step. Finally, look at '"DATA AND PROC STEP FEATURES" to find out about starting and running SAS programs, error handling, and other special features of the SAS System, including the SAS Display Manager

System, SAS output and files, informats and formats, missing values, global options, and the SAS macro facility.

If you are familiar with the SAS System, first turn to Appendix 1, which summarizes the changes and enhancements to the software for Release 6.03. Next, review specific chapters to learn more about particular changes. Finally, if you want to tailor SAS software for your own needs, refer to Appendix 2 for details on the user profile catalog.

After you have become familiar with the syntax of the SAS language, you may want to use fill-in-the-blank menu screens as a shortcut to writing some of your SAS programs. See "Using the SAS Procedure Menu System" in the *SAS Introductory Guide* for more details.

Typographical Conventions

The following type styles are used in this book:

> roman type   is the basic type style used for most text.
>
> *italic type*   is used to define new terms and to indicate items in statement syntax that you need to supply.
>
> **bold type**   is used in the **SPECIFICATIONS** section to indicate that you must use the exact spelling and form shown and to refer you to other sections (either in the same or in other chapters). In addition, sentences of extreme importance are entirely in bold type.
>
> `code`   is used to show examples of SAS statements.

SAS code Examples of SAS code are shown in lowercase type. You can enter your own SAS code in lowercase, uppercase, or a mixture of the two. The SAS System always changes your variable names to uppercase, but character variable values remain in lowercase on printed or displayed output if you have entered them that way. Enter any titles and footnotes exactly as you want them to appear on your output.

Referring to Files and Directories

File and directory names are shown in lowercase type in examples of SAS code and in uppercase type in the text.

In addition, this book does not specify complete pathnames for directories and files referred to in most examples because different computing installations use different conventions for naming directories and files. Instead, most examples refer to files and subdirectories in your current directory. For example, the following LIBNAME statement assigns the libref STORE1 to the subdirectory INVENTRY in your current directory:

```
libname store1 'inventry';
```

Similarly, the following FILE statement directs output to a file named YEAR85.DAT in the MISC subdirectory of your current directory:

```
file 'misc\year85.dat';
```

If you want to refer to a file or directory that is not in your current directory, specify the complete pathname. For example, the following FILE statement directs output to a file named ACCOUNTS in the directory \USR\SMITH:

```
file '\usr\smith\accounts';
```

Note that how you specify the complete pathname depends on the conventions used at your site. See your SAS Software Consultant for more information.

Using the ENTER and Control Keys

Because keyboards differ in the number, placement, and use of their keys, you are not told exactly which keys to press as you use SAS software. However, in some chapters you are asked to type a command and press ENTER. On your keyboard, this key may be labeled with the word ENTER or RETURN or with a bent arrow. In addition, you may be asked to press the CTRL key; this key may be labeled CNTL on your keyboard.

How the Output Is Shown

Output from procedures is enclosed in boxes. Most of the programs in this book were run using the SAS global options LINESIZE=132 or LINESIZE=120 and NODATE. In some cases, if you run the examples, you will get slightly different output. This is a function of whether a floating-point processor is used in your computer, rather than a problem with the software. In all situations, the difference should be very small.

In examples that use external files, this book uses either of the following conventions:

- the italicized phrase *file-specification*. You should refer to the SAS documentation for your operating system for the rules for referencing external files on your host.
- a fileref. You should assume the fileref is assigned correctly for your host operating system.

Examples refer to SAS data libraries with one of these conventions:

- the phrase *SAS-data-library* in italics. You should refer to the SAS documentation for your operating system for the rules for assigning librefs under your host operating system.
- a two-level SAS data set name. You should assume the libref is assigned correctly for your host operating system.

Conventions for Examples and Output

Output in this book was produced using the following SAS system options:

- NODATE
- LINESIZE=76
- PAGESIZE=60
- NOSTIMER.

Programs that use only these options do not contain an OPTIONS statement. However, any program that uses other options or specifies different values for these options includes an appropriate OPTIONS statement.

Your output may differ from the output shown in the book if you run the example programs with different options or different values for those options.

ADDITIONAL DOCUMENTATION

SAS Institute provides many publications about products of the SAS System and how to use the SAS System on specific host operating systems. For a complete list of SAS publications, you should refer to the current *Publications Catalog*. The catalog is produced twice a year. You can order a free copy of the catalog by writing to

> SAS Institute Inc.
> Book Sales Department
> SAS Campus Drive
> Cary, NC 27513

Base SAS Software Documentation

You will find these other documents helpful when using base SAS software:

- *SAS Language: Reference, Version 6, First Edition* (order #A56076) provides detailed reference information about all portable aspects of the SAS language that are not procedures.
- *SAS Procedures Guide, Version 6, Third Edition* (order #A56080) provides detailed reference information about procedures in base SAS software.
- *SAS Language and Procedures: Usage, Version 6, First Edition* (order #A56075) provides task-oriented examples of the major features of base SAS software.

USING THE SAS® LANGUAGE

Introduction

Chapter 1
Introduction

INTRODUCTION 3
SAS STATEMENTS 3
　SAS Keywords 4
　SAS Names 4
　Special Characters and Operators 4
　Statement Descriptions 5
A SAS PROGRAM 5
　DATA Steps 5
　PROC Steps 5
SAS DATA SETS 6
DATA VALUES 6
OBSERVATIONS 6
VARIABLES 7
　Variable Attributes 7
　　Type 7
　　Length 8
　　Informat 8
　　Format 8
　　Label 8
PUTTING TOGETHER DATA AND PROC STEPS 8
WRITING SAS PROGRAMS 9
　Required Spacing 9
　Comments 10
　Variable Lists 10
OUTPUT FROM A SAS PROGRAM 11
NOTE 13

INTRODUCTION

Like any language, the SAS language has its own vocabulary and syntax—words and the rules for putting them together. You define your data and the questions you have about them using the SAS language, and this sequence of SAS statements is called a *SAS program*.

SAS STATEMENTS

A *SAS statement* is a string of SAS keywords, SAS names, and special characters and operators ending in a semicolon that requests SAS to perform an operation or gives SAS information.
　Here are some examples of SAS statements:

- `put X $15.;`
- `data one;`
- `format value1 abcd.;`

- `proc means data=store.supply maxdec=3;`
- `infile rawdata;`
- `do i=1 to dim(eachitem);`
- `key1: total + 1;`

In the sample SAS statements shown above,

- X, VALUE1, and TOTAL are variable names.
- ONE and STORE.SUPPLY are SAS data set names; STORE is a libref.
- the items $15. and ABCD. are format names.
- MEANS is a procedure name.
- DATA= and MAXDEC= are options in the MEANS statement.
- RAWDATA is a fileref.
- in the DO statement, DIM() is a function name, and EACHITEM is the name of an array used as the argument of the DIM function.
- KEY1 is a statement label.
- TOTAL + 1 is an expression, which includes the constant 1.

SAS Keywords

Most SAS statements begin with a keyword that identifies the kind of statement it is (special cases are assignment, sum, comment, and null statements). The SAS statements shown above do not form a SAS program but are single SAS statements referred to by their keywords as a PUT statement, a DATA statement, a FORMAT statement, a PROC statement, an INFILE statement, and an iterative DO statement. The last statement, preceded by the statement label KEY1, is a sum statement that does not have a keyword.

SAS Names

Among the kinds of names that can appear in SAS statements are the names of variables, SAS data sets, formats, procedures, options, arrays, and statement labels, as well as librefs and filerefs, which are special SAS references to files.

SAS names can be up to eight characters long. The first character must be a letter (A,B,C,...,Z) or underscore (_). Later characters can be letters, numbers (0,1,...,9), or underscores.

Blanks cannot appear in SAS names, and special characters (for example, $,@,#), except for the underscore, are not allowed. The SAS System reserves certain names that both begin and end with underscores for special variables (for example, _N_ and _ERROR_).[1]

Special Characters and Operators

Every SAS statement ends with a semicolon (;). Other special characters and operators illustrated in the statements above are parentheses (), the dollar sign $, period ., equal sign =, colon :, and the addition operator or plus sign +.

Statement Descriptions

In this manual the form of a SAS statement is specified with these conventions:

KEYWORD *parameter*...[*item* | *item* | *item*] *options*;

where

bold
   indicates that you use exactly the same spelling and form as shown.

italics
   mean that you supply your own information.

[bracketed information]
   is optional. (However, you enter brackets shown in bold as part of the statement.)

parameters not in brackets
   are not optional.

...
   means that more than one of the parameters preceding ... can be optionally specified.

vertical bar (|) separating keywords and options
   means to choose this | or this.

options
   are keyword options specific to a particular SAS statement.

For the syntax of SAS statements, see the SAS Reference Card at the back of this manual.

A SAS PROGRAM

The statements in a SAS program are divided into two kinds of steps: DATA steps and PROC steps, the building blocks of all SAS programs. Usually, DATA steps create SAS data sets, and PROC steps process SAS data sets, which are special SAS files for organizing and storing data. A SAS program is made up of either a DATA step or a PROC step, or both DATA and PROC steps. DATA and PROC steps can appear in any order, and any number of DATA or PROC steps can be used in a SAS program.

DATA Steps

The DATA step can include statements asking SAS to create one or more new SAS data sets and programming statements that perform the manipulations necessary to build the data sets. The DATA step begins with a DATA statement and can include any number of program statements. Report writing, file management, and information retrieval are all handled in DATA steps.

PROC Steps

The PROC step (or PROCEDURE step) asks SAS to call a procedure from its library and to execute that procedure, usually with a SAS data set as input. The PROC step begins with a PROC statement. Other statements in the PROC step give the program more information about the results that you want. The statements that are available for your use in each PROC step depend on the specific SAS procedure that is called. Thus, each procedure description gives the statements that can accompany the PROC statement for that procedure.

SAS DATA SETS

A *SAS data set* is a collection of data values arranged in the rectangular form shown in **Table 1.1**. The number of SAS data sets that you can use in a SAS job is limited only by space requirements.

Table 1.1 SAS Data Set Listing of Data Values

HODGES	191	36	50	5	162	60
KERR	189	37	52	2	110	60
PUTNAM	193	38	58	12	101	101
ROBERTS	162	35	62	12	105	37
BLAKE	189	35	46	13	155	58
ALLEN	182	36	56	4	101	42
HOWARD	211	38	56	8	101	38
VINCENT	167	34	60	6	125	40
STEWART	176	31	74	15	200	40
PERRY	154	33	56	17	251	250
HOWELL	169	34	50	17	120	38
ELLIS	166	33	52	13	210	115
SMITH	154	34	64	14	215	105
CROWE	147	46	50	1	50	50
CARTER	193	36	46	6	70	31
MOORE	202	37	62	12	210	120
LEE	176	37	54	4	60	25
VARNER	157	32	52	11	230	80
STONE	156	33	54	15	225	73
SCOTT	138	33	68	2	110	43

DATA VALUES

The basic unit that SAS works with is the *data value*. Consider the following example. A researcher collects data from men in an exercise program. Each man's weight, pulse, and waist measurements are recorded, as well as the number of chin-ups, sit-ups, and jumps he can do before tiring.

Each of the measurements—the first man's weight, the second man's pulse, the last man's chin-ups—is a data value.

OBSERVATIONS

The data values associated with a single entity—an individual, a record, a year, a geographic region, an experimental animal—make up an *observation*. In **Table 1.1** each row represents one observation. The first observation represents all the data values associated with the first man whose measurements were recorded. The last observation represents all the data values for the last man.

The only limit to the number of observations that a SAS data set can contain is the space available to store the observations.

VARIABLES

The set of data values that describe a given characteristic make up a *variable*. Each observation in a SAS data set contains one data value for each variable. In **Table 1.1** each column of data values is a variable. For example, the first column makes up the variable NAME and contains all the names of the men in the club, the second column makes up the variable WEIGHT and contains their weight measurements, and so on.

The maximum number of variables in a SAS data set is limited only by the maximum size of an individual observation (see "SAS Files").

Variable Attributes

SAS variables are of two types: numeric and character. In addition to their type, SAS variables have these attributes: length, informat, format, and label. Variable attributes are either explicitly specified or defined from the context at their first occurrence. See **Table 1.2** for a list of variable attributes, their values, and how to specify them.

Table 1.2 SAS Variable Attributes

Variable Attribute	Possible Values	Default Value*	Attribute Can Be Specified in...
Type	numeric character	numeric	LENGTH or ATTRIB statement**
Length numeric character	3 to 8 bytes 1 to 200 bytes	8 bytes 8 bytes	LENGTH or ATTRIB statement
Informat numeric character	(see "SAS Informats and Formats")	w. $w.	INFORMAT or ATTRIB statement
Format numeric character	(see "SAS Informats and Formats")	w. $w.	FORMAT or ATTRIB statement
Label	up to 40 characters	blank	LABEL or ATTRIB statement

* The value used if no other specification is made.
** A variable's type and length are implicitly defined by its first occurrence in any of the following statements: INPUT, PUT, ARRAY, assignment, sum, DO, RETAIN, and WINDOW.

Type Values of a numeric variable can only be numbers. In the fitness example all of the exercise values recorded are numeric; their values are measurements represented by numbers. Numeric values in the data lines can be preceded by plus or minus signs. Decimal points can be included, but commas cannot appear.

The range of acceptable numeric values is ± 10E−307 to ± 10E308 (determined by the range of your computer).

Data values can also be character; letters and special characters as well as numeric digits can make up character data values. In the fitness data, the names of the men in the NAME variable are character data values. The dollar sign ($) following the name of a variable in some SAS statements used in the DATA step indicates that the data values are character rather than numeric. Character data values in SAS can range from 1 to 200 characters long.

Length The length attribute of a variable is the number of bytes used to store each of its values in a SAS data set. The default length is 8. (To store a variable in a length different from the default and for a discussion of other length considerations, see the **LENGTH Statement**.)

Informat A variable's informat is the pattern that SAS uses to read data values into the variable. The default informat is $w.$ for numeric variables, $\$w.$ for character variables. (To use an informat other than the default, see the **INPUT Statement** and the **INFORMAT Statement**. The $w.$ and $\$w.$ informats and other SAS informats are described in "SAS Informats and Formats." To define your own informats, see "The FORMAT Procedure" in the *SAS Procedures Guide, Release 6.03 Edition*.)

Format A variable's format is the pattern SAS uses to write each value of a variable. The default format is $w.$ for numeric variables, $\$w.$ for character variables. (To use a format other than the default, see the **FORMAT Statement**. The $w.$ and $\$w.$ formats and other SAS formats are described in "SAS Informats and Formats." To define your own formats, see "The FORMAT Procedure" in the *SAS Procedures Guide, Release 6.03 Edition*.)

Label The label attribute of a variable is a descriptive label of up to forty characters that can be printed by certain procedures instead of the variable name. The default label is blank. (For information on how to specify a variable label, see the **LABEL Statement**.)

PUTTING TOGETHER DATA AND PROC STEPS

The DATA step that describes the collection of fitness data to SAS looks like this:

```
data fitness;
   input name $ weight waist pulse chins situps jumps;
   cards;
HODGES   191  36  50   5  162  60
KERR     189  37  52   2  110  60
more data lines
;
```

- The DATA statement tells SAS to create a SAS data set named FITNESS.
- The INPUT statement tells SAS to read the data and gives the order and type of the data values.
- The CARDS statement tells SAS that the lines containing the data values follow immediately.
- The null statement (;) signals the end of the data lines.

The following PROC step asks SAS to sort the observations according to the NAME variable:

```
proc sort;
   by name;
```

Since no other data set is specified, SAS uses the most recently created data set, which is the FITNESS data set.

The PROC statement that asks SAS to print a list of the data values looks like this:

```
proc print;
   title 'FITNESS DATA';
```

These statements tell SAS to use the PRINT procedure to list the data values titled FITNESS DATA.

The following PROC step asks SAS to find the mean values for the fitness measurements:

```
proc means maxdec=1;
```

This statement tells SAS to execute the MEANS procedure to get means and other summary statistics for all the numeric variables in the SAS data set. The MAXDEC=1 option specifies that the statistics should be printed with one decimal place.

These PROC step statements

```
proc corr;
   var weight waist pulse chins;
```

ask for the CORR procedure and use a VAR statement to request correlations for the four variables WEIGHT, WAIST, PULSE, and CHINS.

WRITING SAS PROGRAMS

The SAS language allows flexibility in the way SAS statements are written in a program.

Required Spacing

SAS statements can begin in any column of a line, and several statements can be written on the same line. You can begin a statement on one line and continue it to another line as long as no word is split.

You need at least one blank between each separate item in a SAS statement as in the statements above. Some special characters, such as the equal sign after a word, can take the place of a blank, although blanks are always allowed.

For example, in the statement

```
total2=total+10;
```

you do not need a blank before or after the equal sign or before or after the plus sign because the equal sign and the plus sign are special characters, but you can also have any number of extra blanks. The statement

```
total2  =  total + 10 ;
```

is equivalent to the statement above.

(Although SAS does not have rigid spacing requirements, SAS programs are easier to read if the statements are indented consistently. The examples in this manual illustrate our spacing conventions.)

Comments

Comments of the form /* COMMENTS HERE */ can appear within SAS statements wherever a single blank can appear. For example, the statement

```
proc sort /* Sort the data set */;
```

is a valid SAS statement.

Variable Lists

Variables are defined in the order in which they first appear. In the INPUT statement above, NAME is the first variable defined, followed by WEIGHT, WAIST, PULSE, CHINS, SITUPS, and JUMPS. In a DATA step with a SET, MERGE, or UPDATE statement or in a PROC step, the currently defined names are the names of the variables in the data set being processed.

After a complete list of variables has been defined in a SAS program, you can use abbreviated variable lists in many later SAS statements.

The different kinds of abbreviated lists are shown in **Table 1.3**.

Table 1.3 SAS Variable Lists

Names of the Form...	Can Be Abbreviated...	to Represent...
Numbered names of the form X1,X2,...,Xn	X1–Xn	all variables from X1 to Xn
Ranges of names of the form X P A*	X--A	all variables from X to A
	X-NUMERIC-A	all numeric variables from X to A
	X-CHARACTER-A	all character variables from X to A
Special SAS names	_NUMERIC_	all numeric variables
	CHARACTER	all character variables
	ALL	all variables

* The range is determined by the order in which the variables are defined, not alphabetically.

For example, the INPUT statement

```
input name $ weight waist pulse chins situps jumps;
```

can also be written to include a numbered variable list:

```
input name $ var1-var6;
```

Note that the character variable NAME is not included in this abbreviated list. Variables in a numbered list need not be but are usually of the same type, numeric or character.

The VAR statement for the CORR procedure

```
var weight waist pulse chins;
```

in the example can also be abbreviated as a range:

```
var weight--chins;
```

Other examples of abbreviated variable lists are shown throughout this manual. (Note: abbreviated variable lists are not allowed in the SAS data set options described in "SAS Files.")

OUTPUT FROM A SAS PROGRAM

Below is the complete SAS program for the fitness data including all the data lines and the output it produces. **Output 1.1** shows the SAS log; **Output 1.2**, **1.3**, and **1.4** show the results of the PRINT, MEANS, and CORR procedures. For a detailed discussion of SAS output features, see "SAS Output."

```
options nodate;
data fitness;
   input name $ weight waist pulse chins situps jumps;
   cards;
HODGES    191  36  50   5  162   60
KERR      189  37  52   2  110   60
PUTNAM    193  38  58  12  101  101
ROBERTS   162  35  62  12  105   37
BLAKE     189  35  46  13  155   58
ALLEN     182  36  56   4  101   42
HOWARD    211  38  56   8  101   38
VINCENT   167  34  60   6  125   40
STEWART   176  31  74  15  200   40
PERRY     154  33  56  17  251  250
HOWELL    169  34  50  17  120   38
ELLIS     166  33  52  13  210  115
SMITH     154  34  64  14  215  105
CROWE     147  46  50   1   50   50
CARTER    193  36  46   6   70   31
MOORE     202  37  62  12  210  120
LEE       176  37  54   4   60   25
VARNER    157  32  52  11  230   80
STONE     156  33  54  15  225   73
SCOTT     138  33  68   2  110   43
;
proc sort;
   by name;
proc print;
   title 'FITNESS DATA';
proc means maxdec=1;
proc corr;
   var weight waist pulse chins;
run;
```

12 Chapter 1

Output 1.1 SAS Log from Fitness Job

```
NOTE: Copyright(c) 1985,86,87 SAS Institute Inc., Cary, NC 27512-8000, U.S.A.
NOTE: SAS (r) Proprietary Software Release 6.03
      Licensed to SAS Institute Inc., Site 00000000.
   1    data fitness;
   2       input name $ weight waist pulse chins situps jumps;
   3       cards;
  24    ;
NOTE: The data set WORK.FITNESS has 20 observations and 7 variables.
NOTE: The DATA statement used 3.00 seconds.
  25    proc sort;
  26       by name;
  27    proc print;
NOTE: The data set WORK.FITNESS has 20 observations and 7 variables.
NOTE: The PROCEDURE SORT used 2.00 seconds.
  28       title 'FITNESS DATA';
  29    proc means maxdec=1;
NOTE: The PROCEDURE PRINT used 3.00 seconds.
  30    proc corr;
NOTE: The PROCEDURE MEANS used 1.00 seconds.
  31       var weight waist pulse chins;
  32    run;
NOTE: The PROCEDURE CORR used 3.00 seconds.
  33
```

Output 1.2 PROC PRINT Listing of FITNESS Data Set

```
                            FITNESS DATA                                      1

   OBS   NAME      WEIGHT   WAIST   PULSE   CHINS   SITUPS   JUMPS

    1   ALLEN       182      36      56       4      101      42
    2   BLAKE       189      35      46      13      155      58
    3   CARTER      193      36      46       6       70      31
    4   CROWE       147      46      50       1       50      50
    5   ELLIS       166      33      52      13      210     115
    6   HODGES      191      36      50       5      162      60
    7   HOWARD      211      38      56       8      101      38
    8   HOWELL      169      34      50      17      120      38
    9   KERR        189      37      52       2      110      60
   10   LEE         176      37      54       4       60      25
   11   MOORE       202      37      62      12      210     120
   12   PERRY       154      33      56      17      251     250
   13   PUTNAM      193      38      58      12      101     101
   14   ROBERTS     162      35      62      12      105      37
   15   SCOTT       138      33      68       2      110      43
   16   SMITH       154      34      64      14      215     105
   17   STEWART     176      31      74      15      200      40
   18   STONE       156      33      54      15      225      73
   19   VARNER      157      32      52      11      230      80
   20   VINCENT     167      34      60       6      125      40
```

Output 1.3 PROC MEANS Results for Fitness Data

```
                            FITNESS DATA                                      2

   N Obs   Variable    N    Minimum    Maximum     Mean    Std Dev
   -------------------------------------------------------------
      20   WEIGHT     20     138.0      211.0     173.6     19.7
           WAIST      20      31.0       46.0      35.4      3.2
           PULSE      20      46.0       74.0      56.1      7.2
           CHINS      20       1.0       17.0       9.5      5.3
           SITUPS     20      50.0      251.0     145.6     62.6
           JUMPS      20      25.0      250.0      70.3     51.3
   -------------------------------------------------------------
```

Output 1.4 PROC CORR Results for Fitness Data

```
                          FITNESS DATA                                   3
                       CORRELATION ANALYSIS

         4 'VAR' Variables:  WEIGHT   WAIST   PULSE   CHINS

                           Simple Statistics

Variable    N        Mean        Std Dev         Sum      Minimum      Maximum
WEIGHT     20    173.600000    19.738821    3472.000000  138.000000   211.000000
WAIST      20     35.400000     3.201973     708.000000   31.000000    46.000000
PULSE      20     56.100000     7.210373    1122.000000   46.000000    74.000000
CHINS      20      9.450000     5.286278     189.000000    1.000000    17.000000

        Pearson Correlation Coefficients / Prob > |R| under Ho: Rho=0 / N = 20
                    WEIGHT        WAIST         PULSE         CHINS

         WEIGHT    1.00000       0.20585      -0.23194      -0.06123
                   0.0           0.3839        0.3251        0.7976

         WAIST     0.20585       1.00000      -0.35289      -0.55223
                   0.3839        0.0           0.1270        0.0116

         PULSE    -0.23194      -0.35289       1.00000       0.15065
                   0.3251        0.1270        0.0           0.5261

         CHINS    -0.06123      -0.55223       0.15065       1.00000
                   0.7976        0.0116        0.5261        0.0
```

NOTE

1. Other examples of automatic special variables used by SAS under certain circumstances include _CMD_, _COL_, _FDBK_, _FREQ_, _IORC_, _LABEL_, _LNDET_, _MSG_, _MODEL_, _NAME_, _PRIOR_, _RBA_, _ROW_, _RRN_, _SIGMA_, _TITLES_, _TYPE_, and _WEIGHT_.

THE DATA STEP

Introduction

SAS® Expressions

SAS® Functions

SAS® Statements Used in the DATA Step

16

Chapter 2
Introduction

INTRODUCTION 17
WHAT IS A DATA STEP? 17
   Creating SAS Data Sets 18
      Data on disk 18
      In-stream data 18
      Data from other SAS data sets 19
      Writing reports 19
DATA STEP STATEMENTS 19
   File-handling statements 20
   Action statements 20
   Control statements 21
   Information statements 21
DATA STEP FLOW 22
   How Many Times Is a DATA Step Executed? 24
EXAMPLES 24
   Example 1: How SAS Executes a DATA Step 24
   Example 2: Data from Two Sources 25

INTRODUCTION

Before you can use SAS software to prepare your data for analysis or use a SAS procedure to analyze your data, you must first get them into a SAS data set. Once your data are in a SAS data set, you can combine the data set with other SAS data sets in many different ways and use any of the SAS procedures.

The DATA step includes statements asking SAS to create one or more new data sets and programming statements that perform the manipulations necessary to build the data sets. Report writing, file management, and information retrieval are all handled in DATA steps.

You can use the DATA step for these purposes:

- retrieval—getting your input data into a SAS data set
- editing—checking for errors in your data and correcting them; computing new variables
- printing reports according to your specifications and writing disk files
- producing new SAS data sets from existing ones by subsetting, merging, and updating the old data sets.

WHAT IS A DATA STEP?

A DATA step is a group of SAS statements that begins with a DATA statement and usually includes all the statements in one of these three groups:

Data on disk

DATA *statement;*
  INFILE *statement;*
  INPUT *statement;*
  other SAS statements used in the DATA step

Data in job stream

DATA *statement;*
  INPUT *statement;*
  other SAS statements used in the DATA step
  CARDS *statement;*
data lines
;

Data in existing SAS data set

DATA *statement;*
  SET | MERGE | UPDATE *statement;*
  other SAS statements used in the DATA step

In the last DATA step the bar (|) notation indicates that you can use either a SET, MERGE, or UPDATE statement.

A DATA step can also include any of the other statements introduced later in this chapter and described in "SAS Statements Used in the DATA Step."

Creating SAS Data Sets

The three types of simple DATA steps and a special DATA step for writing reports are described below.

Data on disk   The form of a DATA step for producing SAS data sets from input data on disk is

DATA *statement;*
  INFILE *statement;*
  INPUT *statement;*
  other SAS statements used in the DATA step

The statements in the DATA step above have these functions:

- The DATA statement signals the beginning of the DATA step and gives a name to the SAS data set you are creating.
- The INFILE statement describes the file that contains the data. When the INFILE statement is executed, the external file is opened.
- The INPUT statement describes your input data, giving a name to each variable and identifying its location on the disk file.
- If you are modifying the data, optional program statements give SAS directions for the changes you want.

In-stream data   The form of a DATA step for producing a SAS data set from input in the job stream with the SAS statements is

DATA *statement;*
  INPUT *statement;*
  other SAS statements used in the DATA step
  CARDS *statement;*
data lines
;

If you enter data along with your SAS statements, you still need to describe the data's format to SAS in an INPUT statement. The required statements are identical to those in the example above, except that

- no INFILE statement is needed
- a CARDS statement immediately precedes the data lines, signaling the end of the statements and the beginning of the data for the DATA step.

Data from other SAS data sets   The form of a DATA step for producing a SAS data set from one or more existing data sets is

DATA *statement;*
   SET | MERGE | UPDATE *statement;*
   other SAS statements used in the DATA step

You can create a SAS data set from one or more existing SAS data sets. For example, if you have questionnaire data stored in a SAS data set, you may want to build another data set containing only the responses for males. Rather than reading the original raw data again to produce a data set for males only, it is easier to use a SET statement to read the SAS data set, selecting only those observations where the SEX value is M.

- The DATA statement tells SAS to start this DATA step and name the new data set.
- The SET, MERGE, or UPDATE statement identifies the old SAS data sets. (Optionally, a BY statement gives the identifying variables for the SET, MERGE or UPDATE.)
- Optional program statements give SAS directions for modifying the data.

Writing reports   The form of a DATA step for producing a report is

DATA _NULL_;
   INPUT and (CARDS | INFILE) *statement;*
     or
   SET | MERGE | UPDATE *statement;*
   FILE *statement;*
   PUT *statement;*
   other SAS statements used in the DATA step

If you want to report your data values in a form different from that produced by SAS reporting procedures, you can do it in a DATA step:

- The DATA _NULL_ statement tells SAS to begin the DATA step; using the special name _NULL_ means that a SAS data set is not produced.
- To provide the input data for the report, you need either INPUT and CARDS or INFILE statements with accompanying data; or SET, MERGE, or UPDATE statements; or program statements to generate data.
- The FILE statement tells SAS where to print the report or write the file.
- Optionally, you can use program statements to compute some new values.
- One or more PUT statements write the lines of the report or file.

DATA STEP STATEMENTS

The SAS statements that can appear in a DATA step fall into several categories: file-handling statements, action statements, control statements, and information statements. Each statement is also either executable, positional, or declarative.

- Executable statements (denoted by an X in the discussion below) are programming statements that cause some action.
- Positional statements (P) cause no action at execution, but their position in the DATA step is important.
- Declarative statements (D) supply additional information to SAS. Their position in the step is not usually important.

Other statements available for use within a DATA step are introduced in the "Introduction" to DATA AND PROC STEP FEATURES.

File-handling statements File-handling statements let you work with files used as input to the data set or files to be written by the DATA step. The file-handling statements are described below:

BY	specifies that the data set is to be processed in groups defined by the BY variables. (P)
CARDS	precedes lines entered at the console—data that are part of the job stream. (P)
CARDS4	precedes in-stream data lines containing semicolons. (P)
DATA	tells SAS to begin a DATA step and to start building a SAS data set. (P)
FILE	identifies the external file where lines are to be written by the DATA step. (X)
INFILE	identifies the external file containing raw input data to be read by the DATA step. (X)
INPUT	describes the records on the external input file. (X)
MERGE	combines observations from two or more SAS data sets into a new data set. (X)
PUT	describes the format of the lines to be written by SAS. (X)
SET	reads observations from one or more existing SAS data sets. (X)
UPDATE	applies transactions to a master file. Both transaction and master file are SAS data sets. (X)

Action statements While creating a SAS data set in a DATA step, you may want to modify your data from the way they appear on the input lines, select only certain observations for the data set being created, or look for errors in the input data. Action statements allow you to work with observations as they are being created. SAS action statements are described below:

ABORT	stops the current DATA step or the session, depending on the mode of executing SAS you are using. (X)
assignment	creates and modifies variables. (X)
CALL	invokes or calls a routine. (X)
DELETE	excludes observations from the data set being created. (X)
DISPLAY	displays a window. (X)
LIST	lists input lines. (X)
LOSTCARD	corrects for lost data lines when an observation has an incorrect number of data lines. (X)

MISSING	declares that certain values in the input data represent special missing values for numeric data. (D)
null	holds a place for a label or signals the end of data lines. (P)
OUTPUT	creates new observations. (X)
STOP	stops creating the current data set. (X)
subsetting IF	selects observations for the data set being created. (X)
sum	accumulates totals. (X)
WHERE	selects observations before they are brought into the DATA step. (P)

Control statements SAS statements in a DATA step are executed one by one for each observation. In some cases, you may want to skip statements for certain observations or to change the order of the statements encountered. SAS statements that let you transfer control from one part of the program to another are called *control statements*. SAS control statements are described below:

DO iterative DO DO UNTIL DO WHILE	sets up a group of statements to be executed as one statement (DO), iteratively (iterative DO), until some condition is true (DO UNTIL), or until some condition is no longer true (DO WHILE). (X)
END	signals the end of a DO group or SELECT group. (P)
GO TO	causes SAS to jump to a labeled statement in the step and continue execution at that point. (X)
IF-THEN/ELSE	conditionally executes a SAS statement. (X)
LINK-RETURN	causes SAS to jump to a labeled statement in the step and execute statements until it encounters a RETURN statement. (X)
RETURN	when not combined with a LINK statement, causes SAS to return to the beginning of the DATA step to begin execution. When combined with a LINK statement, execution returns to the statement immediately following the most recently executed LINK. (X)
SELECT	conditionally executes one of several SAS statements. (X)

Information statements In the last category of SAS statements are information statements. These statements give SAS extra information about the data set or sets being created. Information statements are not executable and can appear anywhere in the DATA step with the same effect. The information provided in the statement takes effect either prior to the execution of the step or at the time observations are written to the SAS data set. SAS information statements are described below:

ARRAY	defines a set of variables to be processed the same way. (D)
ATTRIB	specifies a format, informat, label, and length for a variable. (D)
DROP	identifies variables to be excluded from a data set or analysis. (D)
FORMAT	specifies formats for printing variable values. (D)

INFORMAT   specifies informats for storing variable values. (D)
KEEP   identifies variables to be included in a data set or analysis. (D)
LABEL   associates descriptive labels with variable names. (D)
LENGTH   specifies the number of bytes to be used for storing SAS variables. (D)
RENAME   changes the names of the variables in a data set. (D)
RETAIN   identifies variables whose values are not to be set to missing each time the DATA step is executed and can give variables an initial value. (D)
WINDOW   defines a window for displaying text and variable values and, optionally, accepting input. (D)

DATA STEP FLOW

The DATA statement that begins each DATA step always signals the beginning of the step. The remaining statements can be called the "program" because SAS translates them to the computer's machine language and executes them each time it goes through the DATA step—usually, once for each observation in your input data.

In **Figure 2.1** you can see the normal flow of the DATA step for creating a new data set.

SAS compiles the program into machine code. All the variables mentioned in the DATA step become part of the vector of current values, also called the *program data vector*. The variables from each source of input data, together with variables created by program statements, are in the program data vector and are available to program statements in the DATA step.

The new SAS data set or data sets can contain all of these variables, or you can choose any subset of variables to be output to the data set.

Variables read with an INPUT statement or created in programming statements are set to missing before each execution of the DATA step. Variables read with a SET, MERGE, or UPDATE statement are retained. SAS executes each statement in the step, building observations for the SAS data set.

When SAS executes the last statement in the DATA step (or a RETURN statement that causes a return to the beginning of the step for a new execution), it normally writes the current values from the program data vector to the SAS data set being created.

SAS returns to the first statement after the DATA statement, initializes nonretained variables in the program data vector to missing, and begins executing statements to build the next observation.

When SAS has read and processed all the data from any of the input files, it goes on to the next DATA or PROC step.

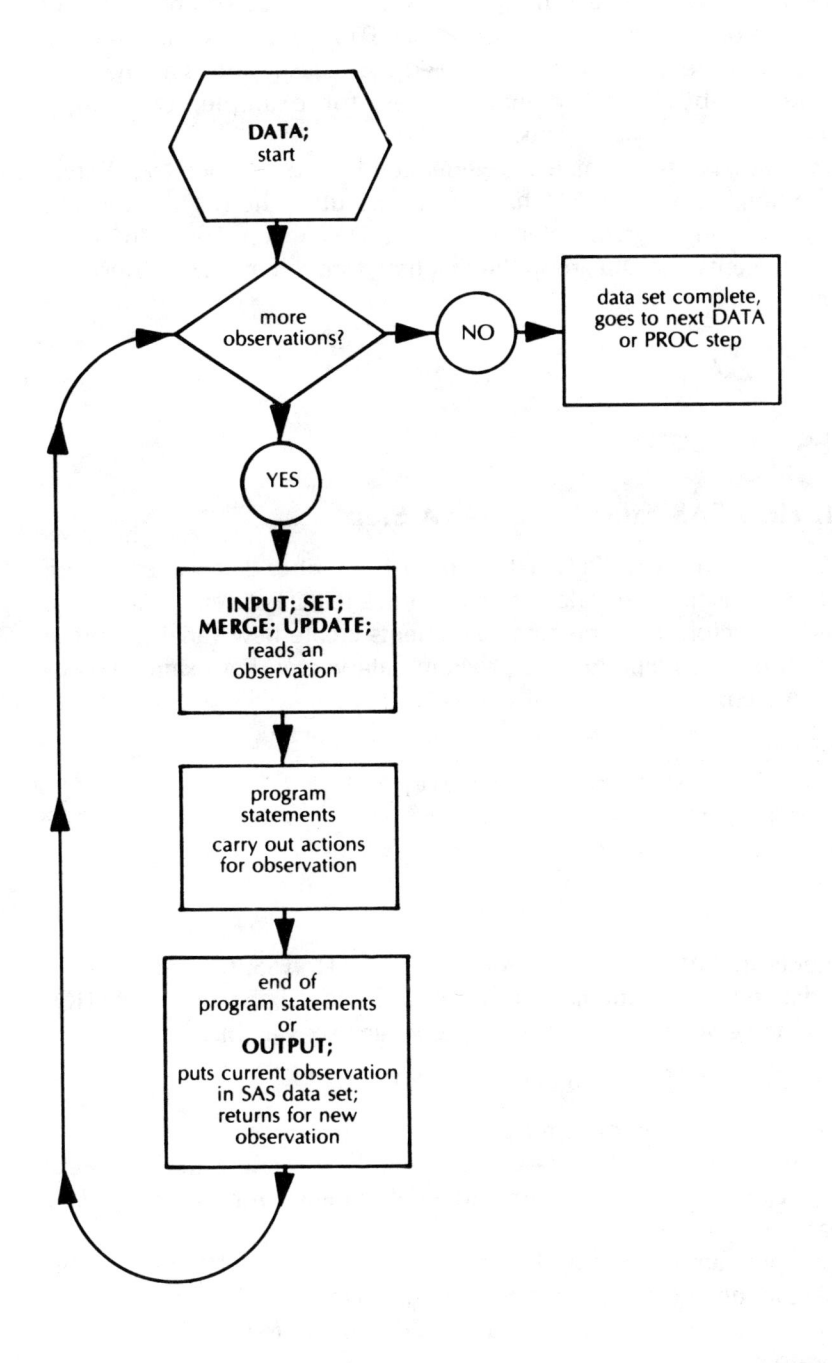

Figure 2.1 Flow of Action within a DATA Step

How Many Times Is a DATA Step Executed?

SAS goes through the statements in the DATA step for each record that it reads. Although each statement appears only once, SAS carries it out for every observation. A DATA step that does not contain an INPUT, SET, MERGE, or UPDATE statement is executed only once. Otherwise, the step is repeated until SAS runs out of data in one of the input sources or until a STOP or ABORT statement is executed. Program statements may be included that cause other statements in the DATA step to be executed many times; for example, DO loops, LINK/RETURN, or GO TO statements.

The SAS variable _N_ is automatically generated by SAS for each DATA step. Its value is the number of times SAS has begun executing the DATA step. You can use this variable in program statements in the DATA step. For example, to execute the statements in a DO group the first time through the DATA step, use the statement

```
if _n_=1 then do;
```

EXAMPLES

Example 1: How SAS Executes a DATA Step

A typical SAS job includes an INPUT statement that describes data values on disk or entered at the console. The variables given in this INPUT statement make up the program data vector. If any program statements create new variables, these new variables also become part of the program data vector. For example, consider this DATA step:

```
data fitness;
   input weight waist jumps situps pulse;
   ratio=pulse/jumps;
   cards;
data lines
;
```

These statements ask SAS to create a data set named FITNESS, to read five variables for this data set from input data lines, and to create a sixth variable, RATIO. The program data vector for this DATA step contains six variables:

WEIGHT WAIST JUMPS SITUPS PULSE RATIO

SAS executes this DATA step once for each observation.

SAS reads the current record's data values using the directions in the INPUT statement. SAS carries out the program statement, adding to the program data vector the value of RATIO.

After the last program statement, the values in the program data vector (the observation) are automatically added to the data set FITNESS being created. (This automatic outputting is equivalent to what would happen if an OUTPUT statement were present.)

SAS returns for another execution of the DATA step. (This automatic return is equivalent to what would happen if a RETURN statement were present.)

If there were twenty data lines, each containing the five input values, this DATA step would be executed twenty times; the new data set FITNESS would contain twenty observations. Each observation would contain six variables.

Example 2: Data from Two Sources

It is possible for a DATA step to contain several INPUT, SET, MERGE, or UPDATE statements. In such cases, the observations contain variables contributed by each statement. For example, consider this DATA step:

```
data fitness;
   input weight waist jumps situps pulse;
   set more;
   ratio=age/jumps;
   drop age jumps height;
   cards;
data lines
;
```

The program data vector for this DATA step is like that in the example above except that it also includes whatever variables the SAS data set MORE contains. If MORE contains the variables AGE and HEIGHT, the program data vector contains the variables shown in **Figure 2.2**. Since a DROP statement appears, observations written to the new data set FITNESS contain only these variables:

WEIGHT WAIST SITUPS PULSE RATIO

Note that when a DATA step has more than one source of input data, the step ends when all the data have been read from one of the sources. Thus, the example above is normally used only if there are an equal number of raw data records and observations in data set MORE.

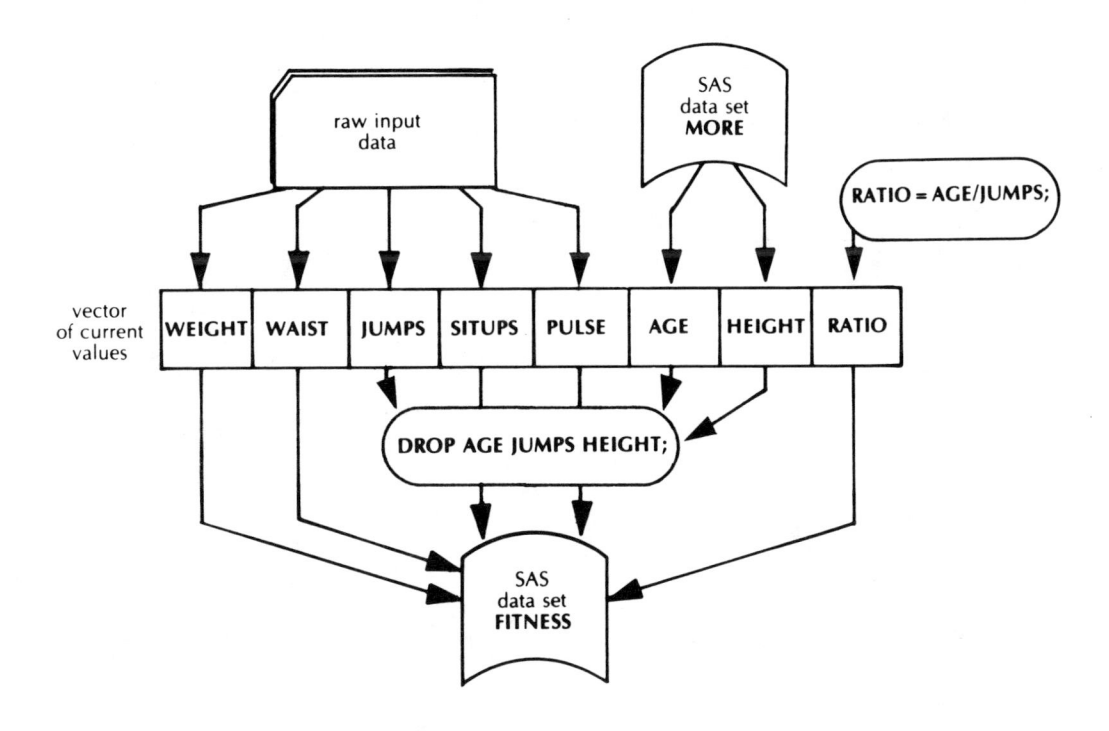

Figure 2.2 Program Data Vector: Data from Two Sources

Chapter 3
SAS® Expressions

INTRODUCTION   27
SAS CONSTANTS   28
   Numeric Constants   28
   Character Constants   28
   Date, Time, and Datetime Constants   29
SAS OPERATORS   29
   Number of Operators: Simple and Compound Expressions   29
   Order of Performing Operations   30
      Rule 1   30
      Rule 2   30
      Rule 3   31
   Arithmetic Operators   31
   Comparison Operators   31
      Character comparisons   32
   Logical Operators   33
   Other Operators   34
SPECIAL CONSTANTS AND OPERATORS   35
   Hexadecimal Constants   35
      Hexadecimal character constants   35
      Hexadecimal numeric constants   35
   Bit Testing   35
SPECIAL TOPICS   36
   Numeric-Character Conversion   36
   Working with Fractional Values and Variables   36

INTRODUCTION

An *expression* is a sequence of operators and operands forming a set of instructions that are performed to produce a result value. The operands are variable names and constants. The operators are special-character operators, functions, and grouping parentheses. (There are over 100 SAS functions that can perform a variety of roles; they are especially useful as programming shortcuts. See "SAS Functions" for a complete discussion.)

Expressions can be *simple* (using only one operator) or *compound* (using more than one operator). The following are examples of expressions:

- `x+1`
- `3`
- `log(y)`
- `part/all*100`
- `1-exp(n/(n-1))`
- `age<100`
- `state='NC' | state='SC'`
- `a=b=c`

Use expressions in DATA step programming statements for transforming variables, creating new variables, conditional processing, calculating new values, and assigning new values.

SAS CONSTANTS

A *SAS constant* is a number, or a character string in quotes or other special notation that indicates a fixed value. Constants are also called *literals*. In the assignment statement

    x=7;

the number 7 is a numeric constant, and X is a variable name.
  SAS uses five kinds of constants:

- numeric
- character
- date, time, and datetime numeric
- hexadecimal character
- hexadecimal numeric.

The hexadecimal constants are special constants discussed separately at the end of this chapter in **SPECIAL CONSTANTS AND OPERATORS**.
  Constants can be used in assignment, sum, IF, SELECT, RETAIN, PUT, and ERROR statements, and as values for certain procedure options.

Numeric Constants

A numeric constant is simply a number that appears in a SAS statement. Most numeric constants are written just as numeric data values are. The numeric constant in the expression

    part/all*100

is 100.
  Numeric constants can use a decimal point, a minus sign, and E-notation (scientific notation). For example,

- 1
- 1.23
- 01
- -5
- 1.2E23
- 0.5E-10

In E-notation, the number before the E is scaled to the power of ten indicated by the number after the E; for example, 2E4 is the same as 2×10^4 or 20000. (Numeric constants larger than $(10**32)-1$ must be specified in scientific notation.)
  A constant representing an ordinary numeric missing value is written as a single decimal point (.). A constant representing a special numeric missing value is written as two characters: a decimal point followed by either a letter (for example, .B) or an underscore (._).

Character Constants

A character constant consists of 1 to 200 characters enclosed in quotes. For example, in the statement

    if name='TOM' then do;

'TOM' is a character constant.

If a character constant includes a single quote, write it in a SAS expression as two consecutive single quotes; SAS treats it as one. For example, if you want to specify the character value TOM'S as a constant, you enter:

```
name='TOM''S'
```

You can also write:

```
name="TOM'S"
```

A constant representing a missing character value consists of a blank enclosed in quotes (for example, ' ').

Date, Time, and Datetime Constants

To express a date, time, or datetime value as a constant, use the same notation used in the informats and formats: TIME., DATE., and DATETIME. (See "SAS Informats and Formats.") Enclose the formatted value in single quotes, and follow it with a D (date), T (time), or DT (datetime). Here are some examples:

- `'1JAN1980'd`
- `'01JAN80'd`
- `'9:25't`
- `'9:25:19't`
- `'18JAN80:9:27:05'dt`

A date constant may be used in an expression like this:

```
if begin='01JAN1981'd then end='31DEC1981'd;
```

SAS OPERATORS

SAS operators are symbols that request a comparison, logical operation, or arithmetic calculation. SAS uses two major kinds of operators: prefix operators and infix operators.

A *prefix operator* is an operator that is applied to the variable, constant, function, or parenthesized expression immediately following it, for example, −6. The plus sign (+) and minus sign (−) can be used as prefix operators. The word NOT and the symbol ^ are also prefix operators (see **Logical Operators**). Some examples of prefix operators used with variables, constants, functions, and parenthesized expressions are shown below:

- `+y`
- `-25`
- `-cos(angle1)`
- `+(x*y)`

Infix operators apply to an operand on each side of an operator, for example, 6<8. There are four general kinds of infix operators: arithmetic; comparison; logical or Boolean; and others (minimum, maximum, and concatenation).

Number of Operators: Simple and Compound Expressions

When there is only one operator in an expression (for example, A/B), it is a *simple expression*. When there is more than one operator in an expression (for example, 1−EXP(N/N−1)), it is a *compound expression*.

Order of Performing Operations

The rules describing the order of evaluation for compound expressions are described below.

Rule 1 Expressions within parentheses are evaluated before those outside. 18/3*2 is the same as 6*2 or 12, but 18/(3*2) is equivalent to 18/6 or 3. Furthermore, −(X**2) is equivalent to the mathematical expression $-(X^2)$, but (−X)**2 is the same as the mathematical expression $(-X)^2$.

Rule 2 Higher priority operations are performed first. Below is a list of the priority groups:

Group I

```
**
+ prefix only
− prefix only
^ (NOT)
>< (MINIMUM)
<> (MAXIMUM)
```

Group II

```
*
/
```

Group III

```
+ infix only
− infix only
```

Group IV

| | If the symbol | is not available, use the symbol ¦ or !.

Group V

< <= = ^= >= > ^> ^<

Group VI

& (AND)

Group VII

| (OR)   If the symbol | is not available, use the symbol ¦ or !.

Note that plus (+) and minus (−) can be either prefix or infix operators. A plus or a minus is a prefix operator only when it appears at the beginning of an expression or when it is immediately preceded by a left parenthesis or another operator.

Rule 3 For operators with the same priority, the left operation is done first. There are two exceptions to this:

1. For the highest priority group (Group I), the right operation is done first.
2. When two comparison operators surround a quantity, the expression is evaluated as if an AND is present. For example, the expression:

    12<age<20

    is evaluated as if it is written:

    12<age & age<20

Arithmetic Operators

Arithmetic operators indicate that an arithmetic calculation is performed. The arithmetic operators are

- ** raise to a power
- * multiplication
- / division
- \+ addition
- − subtraction

For example, A**3 means raise the value of A to the power 3. The expression 2*Y means multiply 2 by the value of Y.

Note: the asterisk (*) is always necessary to indicate that multiplication is performed; thus, 2Y is **not** a valid expression.

If a missing value is an operand for an arithmetic operator, the result is a missing value.

Comparison Operators

Comparison operators propose a relationship between two quantities and ask SAS to determine whether or not that relationship holds. If it does hold (in other words, if it is true), the result of carrying out the operation is the value 1; if it does not hold (in other words, if it is false), the result is the value 0. The comparison operators are

= or EQ	equal to
^= or NE	not equal to
> or GT	greater than
< or LT	less than
>= or GE	greater than or equal to
<= or LE	less than or equal to
IN	equal to one of a list

Consider the expression A<=B. If A has the value 4 and B has the value 3, then A<=B has the value 0 (false). If A is 5 and B is 9, then the expression has the value 1 (true). If A and B each have the value 47, then again the relationship holds and the expression assumes the value 1.

Comparison operators appear frequently in IF statements. For example,

    if x<y then c=5;
       else c=12;

Comparisons are also used in expressions in assignment statements. For example, the above statements could be recoded:

```
c=5*(x<y)+12*(x>=y);
```

Since quantities inside parentheses are evaluated before any operations are performed on them, the expressions (X<Y) and (X>=Y) are evaluated first, and the result (1 or 0) is substituted for the parenthesized expression. Therefore, if X=6 and Y=8:

```
c=5*(1)+12*(0)
c=5
```

Note: in a comparison operation a missing value of any kind compares smaller than any other numeric value.

You can use the IN operator to compare a value produced by an expression on the left to a list of values given on the right. The result is 1 if the left-hand value matches a value in the list and 0 otherwise. The form of the comparison is

expression **IN** (*value*[,]. . .)

where *expression* is a SAS expression, usually a variable name, and *value* is a constant.

The following is an example of use of the IN operator:

```
if state in ('NY','NJ','PA')
   then region2+1;
```

This shorthand form is equivalent to the form

```
if state='NY' or state='NJ' or state='PA'
   then region2+1;
```

Character comparisons Comparisons are performed on character-valued as well as numeric operands, although the comparison always yields a numeric result (1 or 0). Character operands are compared character-by-character from left to right. Character order is determined by machine-collating sequence. (See "The SORT Procedure" in the *SAS Procedures Guide, Release 6.03 Edition*.)

The expression 'GRAY'>'ADAMS' is true, as is the expression 'JONES, C.'<'JONES, CLYDE'.

Two character values of unequal length are compared as if blanks are attached to the end of the shorter value before the comparison is made. So, 'FOX' is equivalent to 'FOX   '. (However, 'FOX' is not equivalent to '   FOX' because blanks at the beginning and in the middle of a character value are meaningful to SAS.)

For example, say you want to create a data set that includes a variable called NAME. You only want to include observations for which the NAME value begins with the letters S through Z. The statement

```
if name>='S';
```

is equivalent to

```
if name>='S
```

where blanks are extended after the S to the length of the variable NAME. Thus, the data set being created contains all observations with NAME values beginning with S through Z, that is, all values alphabetically greater than 'S

To compare only the first letter of the NAME values to the letter S, you can use a colon (:) after the comparison operator. SAS then truncates the longer value to the length of the shorter value for the comparison. For example, the SAS statement

```
if name>:'S';
```

compares the first character of NAME values with S. Any observations having NAME values beginning with T or later in the alphabet are included in the data set being created.

Note that SAS truncates and extends values only during the comparison. The values themselves keep their lengths. Any of the eight comparison operators listed above can be used with the colon in this way.

Logical Operators

Logical operators, also called *Boolean operators*, are usually used in expressions to link sequences of comparisons. The logical operators are

    &   AND
    | OR
    ^   NOT

If **both** of the quantities surrounding an AND are 1 (true), then the result of the AND operation produces a 1; otherwise, the result is 0. For example, the expression

```
a<b & c>0
```

is true (has the value 1) only when **both** A<B is 1 (true) **and** C>0 is 1 (true), that is, when A is less than B **and** C is positive.

If **either** of the quantities surrounding an OR is 1 (true), then the result of the OR operation is 1 (true); otherwise, the OR operation produces a 0. For example, the expression

```
a<b | c>0
```

is true (has the value 1) when A<B is 1 (true) regardless of the value of C. It is also true when the value of C>0 is 1 (true), regardless of the values of A and B. It is true, then, when either or both of those relationships hold.

Be careful when using the OR operator with IF statements:

```
if x=1 or 2;
```

The IF statement above is not the same as

```
if x=1 or x=2;
```

The first IF statement is always true because X=1 is evaluated first, and the result can be 1 or 0; however, the 2 is evaluated as 2=2, and since 2=2 is always true, the whole expression is true. The second IF statement is not necessarily true.

The prefix operator NOT is also a logical operator. The result of putting NOT in front of a quantity whose value is 0 (false) is 1 (true). That is, the result of negating a false statement is 1 (true). For example, if X=Y is 0 (false), then NOT(X=Y) is 1 (true). The result of NOT in front of a quantity whose value is missing is also 1 (true). The result of NOT in front of a quantity with a nonzero, nonmissing value is 0 (false); in other words, the result of negating a true statement is 0 (false).

For example,

```
not(name='SMITH')
```

is equivalent to

```
name ne 'SMITH' .
```

By DeMorgan's law, the NOT of an AND is the OR of the NOTs. The NOT of an OR is the AND of the NOTs. That is, ^(A&B) is equivalent to ^A|^B, and ^(A|B) is equivalent to ^A&^B. For example,

```
not(a=b & c>d)
```

is equivalent to

```
a ne b | c le d
```

Do not use the keyword NOT as a variable name.

Other Operators

The operators in this category are >< (MIN), <> (MAX), and || (concatenation).

The >< and <> operators are surrounded by two quantities. The result is the quantity that is the minimum if >< is the operator or the maximum if <> is the operator. For example, if A<B, then A><B has the value of A.

The || operator concatenates two character values. For example, if the variable COLOR has a value of BLACK and the variable NAME has a value of JACK, then

```
length game $ 9;
game=color || name;
```

results in GAME having a value of BLACKJACK.

If ALPHA='IBM' and MODEL='3270' then the statement

```
device=alpha || model;
```

results in DEVICE='IBM3270' .

You can concatenate several character variables in one expression. If A='ONE' and B='AND' and C='ONLY', then

```
d=a || b || c;
```

results in D='ONEANDONLY'. You can also concatenate character constants. For example, if OLDNUM='123', then

```
newnum=oldnum || '80';
```

causes NEWNUM to be assigned the value of '12380'.

The concatenation operator does not trim leading or trailing blanks. The expression

```
name='JOHN    '||'SMITH'
```

produces the value

```
'JOHN    SMITH'
```

Use the TRIM function (described in "SAS Functions") if you want SAS to trim trailing blanks from values before concatenating them.

SPECIAL CONSTANTS AND OPERATORS

Hexadecimal Constants

You can also represent hexadecimal character and numeric values as constants.

Hexadecimal character constants A character hex constant is a string of an even number of hex characters enclosed in single quotes, followed immediately by an X. For example,

```
'534153'x
```

A comma can be used to make the string more readable, but it is not part of, and does not alter, the hex value. If the string contains a comma, the comma must separate an even number of hex characters within the string. For example,

```
if value='3132,3334'x then do;
```

Hexadecimal numeric constants Hexadecimal numeric constants can be specified in SAS statements. A numeric hex constant starts with a numeric digit (usually a zero), can be followed by more hexadecimal digits, and ends with the letter X. If the constant does not begin with a numeric digit, SAS can treat it as a variable name. The constant can contain no more than 16 valid hexadecimal digits (0-9, A-F). Here are some examples of numeric hex constants:

```
0c1x 0b37x 322x 0c4x 9x
```

Numeric hex constants can be used in a DATA step like this:

```
data;
   input abend pib2.;
   if abend=0c1x or abend=0b0ax then do;
```

Bit Testing

Bit testing is a special comparison operation that tests internal bits in a value's representation. The general form of the operation is

expression = bitmask

You use a bit mask to test bits. The bit mask is a string of 0s, 1s, and periods in quotes that is immediately followed by a B. 0s test for whether the bit is off, 1s test for whether the bit is on, and periods ignore the bit. Commas and blanks can be inserted in the bit mask for readability without affecting its meaning.

Both character and numeric variables can be the subject of bit testing. When testing a character value, the SAS System aligns the leftmost bit of the mask with the leftmost bit of the string; the test proceeds through the corresponding bits, moving to the right. When the SAS System tests a numeric value, the value is truncated from a floating point number to a 32-bit integer. The rightmost bit of the mask is aligned with the rightmost bit of the number, and the test proceeds through the corresponding bits, moving to the left.

Here is an example of a test of a character variable:

```
if a='..1.0000'b then do;
```

36   Chapter 3

If the third bit, A (counting from the left), is on, and the fifth through eighth bits are off, the comparison is true and the expression results in 1. Otherwise, the comparison is false and the expression results in 0. Here is another example:

```
data;
   input @88 bits $char1.;
   if bits='10000000'b then category='a';
   else if bits='01000000'b then category='b';
   else if bits='00100000'b then category='c';
```

Note that bit masks are a special convention used with the equal sign comparison operator. They cannot be used as bit literals in expressions. For example, the statement

```
x='0101'b;
```

is not valid.

SPECIAL TOPICS

Numeric-Character Conversion

SAS automatically converts character variables to numeric variables and numeric variables to character variables, according to these rules:

- If you use a character variable with an operator that requires numeric operands (for example, the plus sign), SAS converts the character variable to numeric.
- If you use a comparison operator to compare a character variable and a numeric variable, the character variable is converted to numeric.
- If you use a numeric variable with an operator that requires a character value (for example, the concatenation operator), the numeric value is converted to character using the BEST12. format.
- If you use a numeric variable on the left side of an assignment statement and a character variable on the right, the character variable is converted to numeric. In the opposite situation, where the character variable is on the left and the numeric is on the right, SAS converts the numeric variable to character using the BEST*n*. format, where *n* is the length of the variable on the left.

Whenever SAS performs an automatic conversion, it prints a message on the SAS log warning that the conversion took place.

If converting a character variable to numeric produces invalid numeric values, SAS assigns a missing value to the result, prints an error message on the log, and sets the value of the automatic variable _ERROR_ to 1.

Working with Fractional Values and Variables

A common error with calculations involves fractional values. SAS uses the floating point instructions provided by the hardware for all numeric variable calculations. The machine stores floating point numbers only to a fixed precision. Fractional values that cannot be represented exactly in binary or hexadecimal are not stored exactly.

Even if only a fractional difference exists, the values of fractions may not be identical, and the value stored varies according to the hardware used. You can check the hexadecimal representation of numbers on your machine by displaying them with the SAS format HEX.

Because SAS is used for diverse applications, there is no best way to round or "fuzz" values that would satisfy all users. In cases where fractional values are critical, use the INT or ROUND function to tell SAS the precision you need.

You should also be careful when working with calculated fractional variables. For example, the MEANS, SUMMARY, TABULATE, and UNIVARIATE procedures with the FREQ statement always use integers, and if not supplied with an integer value, the FREQ statement truncates the value supplied.

Suppose you have a variable that was calculated using the following formula:

```
x=0.3*100;
```

The value of X is not exactly 30, as you would expect, but it is close enough for most applications. However, if used as a frequency variable, only the integer portion 29 is used. In this case, round the frequency variable before using it. If you want 29 used with values such as 29.6 or 29.556, then use a smaller unit for rounding.

These precautions do not affect most applications. When working with integer values, you can store values exactly, and no precautions are needed.

Chapter 4
SAS® Functions

INTRODUCTION 39
FUNCTION ARGUMENTS 40
FUNCTION RESULTS 41
FUNCTION CATEGORIES 42
   Notes on Sample Statistic Functions 46
   Notes on Random Number Functions 46
     CALL subroutines 47
   Notes on Financial Functions 49
FUNCTION DESCRIPTIONS 49
REFERENCES 106

INTRODUCTION

A *SAS function* is a routine that returns a value resulting from zero or more *arguments*. Each SAS function has a keyword name. To invoke a function, write its name and then the argument or arguments for which the function is to be performed enclosed in parentheses:

   `functionname(argument,argument)`

Here are some examples of functions and arguments:

- The INT function yields the integer value of the variable CASH:

   `int(cash)`

- The SUM function adds the values of the variables CASH and CREDIT:

   `sum(cash,credit)`

- In this example, the result of one function (SUM) is an argument of another function (MIN):

   `min(sum(cash,credit),1000)`

   The MIN function compares the value of the first argument to that of the second argument and returns the smaller of the two values. The first argument is the result of the SUM function, which adds the variables CASH and CREDIT. The second argument is a constant, 1000.

   SAS functions are used in DATA step programming statements and in some statistical procedures as expressions or parts of expressions. Consider the preceding examples; they must be entered as parts of SAS statements in order to have any effect. The INT function may be used as follows:

```
data income;
   input store data date7. cash 8.2 credit 8.2;
   dollars = int(cash);
   cards;
data lines
;
```

A new variable, DOLLARS, is assigned the value that is the result of the INT function.

You can use a SAS function anywhere you would use a SAS expression, not just in assignment statements. The next example uses the SUM function in an IF/THEN statement:

```
data _null_;
   set income;
   if sum(cash,credit) > 1000 then
      put store ' is an Outstanding ACME Company Store';
```

Remember as you read the function descriptions in this chapter that SAS functions must always be used in SAS programming statements.

SAS functions are especially useful as programming shortcuts for many numeric calculations and manipulations of character and numeric data. They are also useful for creating new variables from existing data. For example, say that you want to create a variable called LEAST whose value is the smaller of

- the sum of ten variables (X1, X2, ..., X10)
- a variable called Y.

You could create the variable LEAST by writing:

```
totx=x1+x2+x3+x4+x5+x6+x7+x8+x9+x10;
if totx<y then least=totx;
else least=y;
```

It is faster, however, to write:

```
least=min(sum(of x1-x10),y);
```

SAS functions fall into a number of categories: arithmetic, truncation, mathematical, trigonometric and hyperbolic, probability, quantile, sample statistics, random number, financial, character, date and time, state and ZIP code, and special. **Table 4.1**, later in this chapter, lists the functions by category.

FUNCTION ARGUMENTS

Function arguments can be simply variable names

```
max(cash,credit)
```

or constants

```
sqrt(1500)
repeat('----+',16)
```

or they can be expressions, including expressions involving other functions:

```
min((enroll-drop),(enroll-fail))
```

Some functions require no argument, some only one argument, and some operate on several arguments. (No function allows more than 2000 arguments.) All expression arguments are evaluated before a function is called. For example, 2*LOG(X+Y) is twice the natural logarithm of the sum of the value of X and the value of Y. The addition is performed first, then the logarithm of the sum is calculated, and that result is multiplied by 2.

Normally, when there is more than one argument, they must be separated by commas. However, if the arguments of a function are all variables and are in a sequence (for example, X1 through X5, or X, Y, and Z), the function can also be written in one of these two forms:

> *functionname*(**OF** *variable1-variablen*)
> *functionname*(**OF** *variable variable variable ...*)

For example, any of these forms is correct:

```
sum(of x1-x100 y1-y100)
sum(of x  y  z)
sum(x1,x2,x3,x4)
```

You **cannot** use these forms to list sequential variable arguments of a function:

> *functionname*(*variable1 variable2 ...*)
> *functionname*(*variable1variable2...*)
> *functionname*(*variable1-variablen*)

Each of these statements produces an error message:

```
y=sum(x1 x2 x3);
y=sum(xyz);
```

Any function that can accept a variable number of arguments can use this form.

You can write the special array subscript asterisk (*) enclosed in braces, brackets, or parentheses to use all elements of an array as a variable list in a function argument, for example,

```
array y{10} y1-y10;
x=sum(of y{*});
z=sum(of y1-y10);
```

The two SUM statements above are equivalent.

You can use both explicitly and implicitly subscripted arrays in this way. (You cannot use the asterisk specification with _TEMPORARY_ arrays. See the **Array Statement** in Chapter 5 for more information on array processing.)

Some functions require that their arguments have values only in a certain range; for example, the argument of the LOG function must be greater than zero. Most functions (with the exception of those producing sample statistics) do not permit missing values as arguments. If the value of a function's argument is inadmissible (that is, missing or outside a certain range), SAS prints an error message and sets the result to a missing value. If an argument of a function that produces sample statistics is missing, that value is not included in the calculation of the statistic.

In general, the allowed range of the arguments is machine-dependent (as is true, for example, with the EXP function). Note also that for some probability functions, combinations of extreme values in the arguments can cause convergence problems. When this occurs, a missing value is returned and an error message is issued.

FUNCTION RESULTS

The resulting or *target* variable for a function is usually character if the arguments are character and numeric if the arguments are numeric. The PUT function is an exception as its result is a character value regardless of the type of argument.

By default, the length of the target variable for most functions is 8 for numeric target variables and 200 for character target variables. For example,

```
least=(min(sum of x1-x10),y);
```

LEAST, the target variable, is a numeric variable of length 8. Functions to which the default target variable lengths do not apply are shown below:

Function	Target Variable Type	Target Variable Length
INPUT	character	width of informat
	numeric	8
PUT	character	width of format
SUBSTR	character	length of first argument
TRIM	character	length of argument

FUNCTION CATEGORIES

Table 4.1 Functions by Category

Arithmetic functions

ABS	returns absolute value
DIM	returns the number of elements in an array
HBOUND	returns the upper bound of an array
LBOUND	returns the lower bound of an array
MAX	returns the largest value
MIN	returns the smallest value
MOD	calculates the remainder
SIGN	returns the sign of the argument or 0
SQRT	calculates the square root

Truncation functions

CEIL	returns the smallest integer>=argument
FLOOR	returns the largest integer<=argument
FUZZ	returns the integer if the argument is within 1E−12
INT	returns the integer value (truncates)
ROUND	rounds a value to the nearest roundoff unit
TRUNC	returns a truncated numeric value of a specified length

Mathematical functions

DIGAMMA	computes the derivative of the log of the GAMMA function
ERF	is the error function
ERFC	returns the complement of the ERF function
EXP	raises e (~2.71828) to a specified power
GAMMA	produces the complete gamma function
LGAMMA	calculates the natural logarithm of the GAMMA function of a value
LOG	produces the natural logarithm (base e)
LOG2	calculates the logarithm to the base 2
LOG10	produces the common logarithm

Trigonometric and hyperbolic functions

ARCOS	calculates the arc cosine
ARSIN	calculates the arc sine
ATAN	calculates the arc tangent
COS	calculates the cosine
COSH	calculates the hyperbolic cosine
SIN	calculates the sine
SINH	calculates the hyperbolic sine
TAN	calculates the tangent
TANH	calculates the hyperbolic tangent

Probability functions

POISSON	Poisson probability distribution function
PROBBETA	beta probability distribution function
PROBBNML	binomial probability distribution function
PROBCHI	chi-squared probability distribution function
PROBF	F distribution function
PROBGAM	gamma probability distribution function
PROBHYPR	hypergeometric probability distribution function
PROBNEGB	negative binomial probability distribution function
PROBNORM	standard normal probability distribution function
PROBT	Student's t distribution function

Quantile functions

BETAINV	inverse beta distribution function
CINV	the quantile for the chi-square distribution
FINV	the quantile for the F distribution
GAMINV	inverse gamma distribution function
PROBIT	inverse normal distribution function
TINV	the quantile for the t distribution

Sample statistic functions

CSS	calculates the corrected sum of squares
CV	calculates the coefficient of variation
KURTOSIS	gives the kurtosis
MAX	returns the largest value
MIN	returns the smallest value
MEAN	computes the arithmetic mean (average)
N	returns the number of nonmissing arguments
NMISS	returns the number of missing values
RANGE	returns the range

SKEWNESS	gives the skewness
STD	calculates the standard deviation
STDERR	calculates the standard error of the mean
SUM	calculates the sum of the arguments
USS	calculates the uncorrected sum of squares
VAR	calculates the variance

Random number functions

NORMAL	generates a normally distributed pseudo-random variate
RANBIN	generates an observation from a binomial distribution
RANCAU	generates a Cauchy deviate
RANEXP	generates an exponential deviate
RANGAM	generates an observation from a gamma distribution
RANNOR	generates a normal deviate
RANPOI	generates an observation from a Poisson distribution
RANTBL	generates deviates from a tabled probability mass function
RANTRI	generates an observation from a triangular distribution
RANUNI	generates a uniform deviate
UNIFORM	generates a pseudo-random variate uniformly distributed on the interval (0,1)

Financial functions

COMPOUND	calculates compounded value parameters
DACCDB	calculates accumulated declining balance depreciation
DACCDBSL	calculates accumulated declining balance converting to straight-line depreciation
DACCSL	calculates accumulated straight-line depreciation
DACCSYD	calculates accumulated sum-of-years'-digits depreciation
DACCTAB	calculates accumulated depreciation from specified tables
DEPDB	calculates declining balance depreciation
DEPDBSL	calculates declining balance converting to straight-line depreciation
DEPSL	calculates straight-line depreciation
DEPSYD	calculates sum-of-years'-digits depreciation
DEPTAB	calculates depreciation from specified tables
INTRR	calculates internal rate of return as a fraction
IRR	calculates internal rate of return as a percentage
MORT	calculates mortgage loans
NETPV	calculates net present value as a fraction
NPV	calculates net present value with rate expressed as a percentage
SAVING	calculates future value of periodic saving

SAS Functions

Character functions

BYTE	returns a character in the ASCII collating sequence
COLLATE	generates a string of characters in collating sequence
COMPRESS	removes characters from a character variable argument
INDEX	searches for a pattern of characters
INDEXC	finds the first occurrence of any one of a set of characters
LEFT	left-aligns a character string
LENGTH	returns the length of a character argument
RANK	returns the position of a character in the ASCII collating sequence
REPEAT	repeats characters
REVERSE	reverses characters
RIGHT	right-aligns a character string
SCAN	scans for words
SUBSTR	extracts a substring
TRANSLATE	changes characters
TRIM	removes trailing blanks
UPCASE	converts to uppercase
VERIFY	validates a character value

Date and time functions

DATE	returns today's date as a SAS date value
DATEJUL	converts a Julian date to a SAS date value
DATEPART	extracts the date part of a SAS datetime value or literal
DATETIME	returns the current date and time of day
DAY	returns the day of the month from a SAS date value
DHMS	returns a SAS datetime value from date, hour, minute, and second
HMS	returns a SAS time value from hour, minute, and second
HOUR	returns the hour from a SAS datetime or time value or literal
INTCK	returns the number of time intervals
INTNX	advances a date, time, or datetime value by a given interval
JULDATE	returns the Julian date from a SAS date value or literal
MDY	returns a SAS date value from month, day, and year
MINUTE	returns the minute from a SAS time or datetime value or literal
MONTH	returns the month from a SAS date value or literal
QTR	returns the quarter from a SAS date value or literal
SECOND	returns the second from a SAS time or datetime value or literal

46   Chapter 4

TIME	returns the current time of day
TIMEPART	extracts the time part of a SAS datetime value or literal
TODAY	returns the current date as a SAS date value
WEEKDAY	returns the day of the week from a SAS date value or literal
YEAR	returns the year from a SAS date value
YYQ	returns a SAS date value from the year and quarter

State and ZIP code functions

FIPNAME	converts FIPS code to state name (all uppercase)
FIPNAMEL	converts FIPS code to state name in upper- and lowercase
FIPSTATE	converts FIPS state codes to two-character postal code
STFIPS	converts state postal codes to FIPS state codes
STNAME	converts state postal codes to state names (all uppercase)
STNAMEL	converts state postal codes to state names (upper- and lowercase)
ZIPFIPS	converts ZIP codes to FIPS state codes
ZIPNAME	converts ZIP codes to state names (all uppercase)
ZIPNAMEL	converts ZIP codes to state names (upper- and lowercase)
ZIPSTATE	converts ZIP codes to two-letter state codes

Special functions

DIFn	calculates the first difference for the nth lag
INPUT	defines an informat for a character value
LAGn	calculates the nth lagged value
PUT	specifies an output format for a value
SOUND	generates a sound
SYMGET	returns the value of a macro variable

Notes on Sample Statistic Functions

There are fifteen functions whose results are sample statistics of the values of the arguments. The functions correspond to the statistics produced by the MEANS procedure and the computing method for each statistic is discussed in Chapter 1, "SAS Elementary Statistics Procedures," in the *SAS Procedures Guide, Release 6.03 Edition*. In each case, the statistic is calculated for the nonmissing values of the arguments.

Notes on Random Number Functions

You can generate random numbers for various distributions using the random number functions. The random number functions use an argument to select an initial seed value, which initializes the random number stream. Depending on the value of the argument, one of two types of initialization is used:

Argument	Type of Initialization
≤0	On the first execution of a function, giving 0 for an argument initializes the stream with a seed equal to a computer clock observation and returns an observation generated with this seed. On subsequent executions the function returns an observation generated with the current seed.
>0	On the first execution of the function, the argument is used as the current seed to initialize the stream and return an observation. On subsequent executions, an observation generated with the current seed is returned.

Although the current seed changes each time the function is executed, the value of the argument remains unchanged. You cannot control seed values, and therefore, random numbers, after the initialization. If you want more control of the number streams, use the CALL subroutine corresponding to the random number function (see **CALL subroutines**) rather than the function itself.

CALL subroutines SAS provides a series of subroutines that give you more control over the seed stream and the random number stream than is possible with the random-number-generating functions. There is a subroutine corresponding to every random number function except NORMAL and UNIFORM. In addition, there is a subroutine called SOUND that produces a sound of a specified frequency and duration.

The random-number-generating subroutines are invoked with CALL statements. The general form of a CALL statement is

CALL subroutine(seed,variate);

where subroutine is the name of any SAS random-number-generating function (except NORMAL or UNIFORM), seed is the name of a variable to hold the current seed values, and variate is the name of a variable to hold the generated variates. The seed variable should be initialized prior to the first execution of the CALL statement, for example, in an assignment or RETAIN statement.

After an execution of the CALL statement, seed contains the current seed in the stream (that is, the seed that will generate the next number), and variate contains the generated number.

Using the CALL subroutines rather than the random number functions allows you to initialize more than one random number stream in a DATA step. By comparison, more than one set of random numbers can be created with the random number functions, but they all come from one stream (only one stream is initialized). The example below illustrates this:

```
data a;
   retain seed1 seed2 1613218064;
   di i=1 to 5;
      x1=ranuni(seed1);
      x2=ranuni(seed2);
      output;
      end;
proc print;
   title 'USING A RANDOM NUMBER FUNCTION';
```

The output produced by these statements is shown in **Output 4.1**.

Output 4.1 Random Number Functions Can Initialize Only One Stream

```
                         USING A RANDOM NUMBER FUNCTION                        1

           OBS      SEED1          SEED2         I        X1         X2

            1    1613218064     1613218064       1     0.800831   0.770936
            2    1613218064     1613218064       2     0.009603   0.498510
            3    1613218064     1613218064       3     0.442188   0.646033
            4    1613218064     1613218064       4     0.500457   0.731599
            5    1613218064     1613218064       5     0.558058   0.500674
```

Notice that although the initial values of SEED1 and SEED2 are the same (1613218064), the numbers generated and held in X1 and X2 are different. This is because only one stream was initialized; the program ignores the value given for SEED2 and uses the current seed in the stream begun by the first RANUNI statement instead. Thus, the first value of X2 is not the result of a seed value of 1613218064; it is the result of an unknown seed.

Below is an example that shows that more than one stream can be initialized if a CALL subroutine is used rather than a function:

```
data;
   retain seed4 seed5 1613218064;
   do i=1 to 5;
      call ranuni(seed4,x4);
      call ranuni(seed5,x5);
      output;
      end;
proc print;
   title 'USING A CALL SUBROUTINE INSTEAD OF A FUNCTION';
```

The output produced by these statements is shown in **Output 4.2**.

Output 4.2 A CALL Subroutine Can Initialize More Than One Stream

```
                    USING A CALL SUBROUTINE INSTEAD OF A FUNCTION              1

           OBS      SEED4          SEED5         I        X4         X5

            1    1719772190     1719772190       1     0.800831   0.800831
            2    1655573359     1655573359       2     0.770936   0.770936
            3      20623105       20623105       3     0.009603   0.009603
            4    1070543076     1070543076       4     0.498510   0.498510
            5     949591638      949591638       5     0.442188   0.442188
```

After the DATA step is completed, the values of X4 and X5 are identical for each observation because the CALL statement initialized a second seed stream that began with the same value as the first stream. By initializing SEED4 and SEED5 with different seeds, you can obtain observations from independent streams. Notice that with the CALL subroutines it is possible to see what the current seed is at any time; this is not possible with the random number functions.

Notes on Financial Functions

There are ten functions to compute depreciation. Each DEPxxx function computes depreciation for a single time period, from the beginning of the period (*time1*) to the end of the period specified. Each DACCxxx function computes the accumulated depreciation for all time periods up to the period specified.

For all of the functions except DEPDBSL and DACCDBSL, the *period* argument can be fractional. For fractional arguments, the depreciation is prorated between the two consecutive time periods preceding and following the fractional period. You should be sure that this is the appropriate method for you to use with fractional periods. In particular, many depreciation schedules specified as tables have special rules for fractional periods.

FUNCTION DESCRIPTIONS

ABS: returns the absolute value

```
abs(argument)
```

The *argument* must be a numeric value. This function returns a positive number of the same magnitude as the original value of the argument.
Examples:

```
data;
   x=abs(2.4);
   put x;
run;
```

The value returned is 2.4.

```
x=abs(-3);
```

The value returned is 3.

ARCOS: calculates the arccosine

```
arcos(argument)
```

The *argument* for this function must be a numeric value between −1 and +1. The function returns the arccosine (inverse cosine) of the value of the argument. The result is in radians.

For the examples

```
x=arcos(1);
x=arcos(0);
x=arcos(-.5);
```

the values returned are 0, 1.570796, and 2.094395, respectively.

ARSIN: calculates the arcsine

```
arsin(argument)
```

The *argument* for this function must be a numeric value between −1 and +1. The function returns the arcsine (inverse sine) of the value of the argument. The result is in radians.

For the examples

```
x=arsin(0);
x=arsin(1);
x=arsin(-.5);
```

the following values are returned: 0, 1.570796, and −0.523599, respectively.

ATAN: calculates the arctangent

```
atan(argument)
```

The *argument* for this function must be a numeric value. The result is the arctangent (inverse tangent) of the value of the argument. The result is in radians.
Examples:

```
x=atan(1);
x=atan(0);
x=atan(-9);
```

The values returned for these examples are 0.7853982, 0, and −1.46014, respectively.

BETAINV: computes the inverse of the cumulative beta distribution

```
betainv(p,a,b)
```

where

$$0 \leq p \leq 1, a > 0, \text{ and } b > 0 \quad .$$

The function BETAINV returns the *p*th quantile from a beta distribution with density:

$$\Gamma(a + b)x^{a-1}(1 - x)^{b-1} / \Gamma(a)\Gamma(b) \quad .$$

For example,

```
betainv(.001,2,4);
```

returns a value of .0101. The beta distribution is related to many common statistical distributions including the *F* distribution (Abramowitz and Stegun 1964).

BYTE: returns one character in the ASCII collating sequence

```
byte(n)
```

The BYTE function returns the *n*th character in the ASCII collating sequence. The value of *n* must be $0 \leq n \leq 127$. For example, the statement

```
x=byte(65);
```

gives X the value 'A'.
The ASCII collating sequence, from 32 to 126, is

blank!"#$%&'()*+,-./0123456789:;<=>?@
ABCDEFGHIJKLMNOPQRSTUVWXYZ[\]^_`
abcdefghijklmnopqrstuvwxyz{|}~

The ASCII characters 0 through 31 and 127 are control characters that do not print on your screen.

CEIL: returns the smallest integer ≥ argument

```
ceil(argument)
```

The *argument* must be a numeric value. This function returns the smallest integer that is greater than or equal to the value of the argument. If the argument's value is within 10^{-12} of an integer, the function results in that integer. Examples:

```
data;
   x=ceil(2.1);
   put x;
run;
```

The value returned is 3.

```
x=ceil(3);
```

The value returned is 3.

```
x=ceil(-2.4);
```

The value returned is -2.

```
x=ceil(4.000000000001);
```

The value returned is 4.

CINV: the quantile for the chi-square distribution

```
cinv(p,df,nc)
```

where

$0 \leq p < 1$, $0 < df$, $0 \leq nc$.

The CINV function computes the quantile for the chi-square distribution with degrees of freedom, *df*, and noncentrality parameter, *nc*, such that the probability that an observation from this distribution is less than the quantile is *p*. If the optional parameter, *nc*, is not specified or is zero, the central chi-square distribution is used. Otherwise, the noncentral chi-square distribution is used. The parameter *df* does not have to be an integer. The noncentrality parameter, *nc*, is defined such that if X is a normal random variable with mean μ and variance 1., X^2 has a noncentral chi-square distribution with $df=1$ and $nc=\mu^2$. For large values of *nc* the algorithm used may fail. In these cases a missing value is returned. This function is derived from the functions contributed by Hardison, Quade, and Langston (1983).

Example:

```
data;
   q1=cinv(.95,3); put q1=;
   q2=cinv(.95,3.5,4.5); put q2=;
run;
```

results in

```
Q1=7.8147
Q2=17.505
```

COLLATE: generates a collating sequence character string

```
collate(n,m,l)
```

COLLATE returns a string of characters, beginning with the *n*th character, from the ASCII collating sequence. The COLLATE function returns a maximum of 128 characters. If the string requested is longer, COLLATE returns only the first 128 characters from the collating sequence.

Define the length of the string by specifying either *m*, the last character in the sequence you want, or *l*, the number of characters you want. For example, the statements

```
x=collate(48,,10);
x=collate(48,57);
```

both give X the value 0123456789.

If neither *m* nor *l* is specified, the default length is 128. If both *m* and *l* are specified, *l* is ignored.

The COLLATE function returns characters from the ASCII collating sequence, which has values from 0 through 127. The returned string ends, or truncates, with the character having a value of 127 if you request a string length that would contain characters exceeding this value.

COMPOUND: calculates compounded value parameters

compound(*amount,future,rate,number*)

This function computes parameters for an amount that earns compound interest. The formula is

$$F = A*(1 + R)^N$$

where *F* is the future value, *A* is the initial value, *R* is the rate expressed as a fraction, and *N* is the number of periods. This function computes any one of the four parameters, given the other three parameters as arguments.

The arguments follow:

- *amount*   the amount at the beginning of the term.
- *future*   the amount at the end of the term.
- *rate*   the interest rate per period expressed as a fraction, not as a percentage. For example, 12% per year would be written 0.01 per month.
- *number*   the number of payments.

To use the COMPOUND function, specify values for three of the arguments and a missing value for the parameter you want. The function calculates a value for the argument specified by a missing value. No adjustment is made to convert the results to round numbers.

To illustrate, suppose that you invest $2000 at an annual interest rate of 9% compounded monthly. After thirty months, how much will your investment be worth?

```
data cash;
   future=compound(2000, . ,.09/12,30);
   put future=;
```

The value returned is 2502.54. Notice that the second argument is set to missing, indicating that a future value is to be calculated and that the *rate* argument must be expressed in terms of the period of compounding. That is, the 9% annual rate is expressed on a monthly basis as 0.09/12.

COMPRESS: removes specific characters from a character expression

```
compress(argument)
compress(argument1,argument2)
```

When only one argument is specified, COMPRESS returns it after removing all the blanks. When two arguments are specified, the COMPRESS function returns the first argument after removing from it all characters specified in the second argument.

For example, the following statements eliminate the blanks from the value of A:

```
a='AB C D ';
b=compress(a);
```

B's value is ABCD.

The statements below remove the special characters .;( ) from the value of X:

```
x='A.B (C=D);';
y=compress(x,'.;()');
```

Y's value is AB C=D.

COS: calculates the cosine

```
cos(argument)
```

The *argument* for this function must be a numeric value. The result is the cosine of the value of the argument. The value of the argument is assumed to be in radians.

The examples

```
x=cos(.5);
x=cos(0);
x=cos(3.14159/3);
```

return 0.8775826, 1, and .5, respectively.

COSH: calculates the hyperbolic cosine

```
cosh(argument)
```

The *argument* for this function must be a numeric value. The result is the hyperbolic cosine of the value of the argument. The result is equivalent to

```
(exp(argument)+exp(-argument))/2
```

For the examples

```
x=cosh(0);
x=cosh(-5);
x=cosh(.5);
```

the values returned are 1, 74.20995, and 1.1276259, respectively.

CSS: calculates the corrected sum of squares

```
css(argument,argument, ...)
```

The *arguments* for this function must be numeric values. For two or more nonmissing arguments, the function calculates the corrected sum of squares of the nonmissing arguments.

For the examples

```
x=css(4,2,3.5,6);
```

and

```
x=css(4,2,3.5,6,.);
```

the value returned in either case is 8.1875.

You can use an abbreviated argument list preceded by OF:

```
x=css(of y1-y30);
```

The variable names Y1 to Y30 represent numeric values used to calculate the result.

See Chapter 1, "SAS Elementary Statistics Procedures," in the *SAS Procedures Guide, Release 6.03 Edition* for a definition of this statistic.

CV: calculates the coefficient of variation

```
cv(argument,argument, ...)
```

The *arguments* for this function must be numeric values. The function calculates the coefficient of variation for the two or more nonmissing arguments that you give.

For example,

```
x=cv(5,8,9,3,6);
```

returns the value 38.50754. You can use an abbreviated argument list preceded by OF.

See Chapter 1, "SAS Elementary Statistics Procedures," in the *SAS Procedures Guide, Release 6.03 Edition* for a definition of this statistic.

DACCDB: calculates accumulated declining balance depreciation

```
daccdb(period,value,years,rate)
```

The declining balance accumulated depreciation function, $a = \text{DACCDB}(p,v,y,r)$, is computed as

$$a = 0 \quad \text{if } p \leq 0$$

$$a = v(1 - (1 - r/y)^{\text{int}(10)(1 - r/y(p - \text{int}(p)))}) \quad \text{if } p > 0$$

where a is the amount of depreciation, p is the period for which the calculation is to be done, v is the depreciable value of the asset, y is the lifetime of the asset in years, and r is the rate of depreciation expressed as a fraction. A double declining balance is obtained by setting r equal to 2. The expression int(p) denotes the integer part of p. The p argument can be fractional. For fractional arguments, the depreciation is prorated between the two consecutive time periods preceding and following the fractional period.

For example, if an asset acquired on January 1 has a depreciable basis of $1000 and a fifteen-year lifetime, then, using a 200% declining balance, the depreciation throughout the first ten years is expressed as

```
a=daccdb(10,1000,15,2);
```

This results in a value of 760.932.

DACCDBSL: calculates accumulated declining balance converting to straight-line depreciation

    daccdbsl(period,value,years,rate)

The accumulated declining balance converting to straight-line depreciation function, $a=\text{DACCDBSL}(p,v,y,r)$, is computed as

    a=depdbsl(1,v,y,r)+depdbsl(2,v,y,r)+...+depdbsl(p,v,y,r)

where a is the amount of depreciation, p is the period, v is the depreciable value, y is the lifetime, and r is the rate, expressed as a fraction, for the declining balance portion of the depreciation. The p and y arguments must be integers. Noninteger values are treated as erroneous input. The declining balance changing to a straight-line depreciation chooses for each time period the method of depreciation (declining balance or straight-line on the remaining balance) that gives the larger current depreciation.

For example, suppose you have an asset with a depreciable basis of $1000, a declining balance rate of 150%, and a ten-year lifetime. The accumulated depreciation of that asset in its fifth year would be computed as

    y5=daccdbsl(5,1000,10,1.5);

resulting in a value of 564.995.

DACCSL: calculates accumulated straight-line depreciation

    daccsl(period,value,years)

The accumulated straight-line depreciation function, $a=\text{DACCSL}(p,v,y)$, is computed as

$a = 0$ if $p<0$
$a = v^*p/y$ if $0 \leq p \leq y$
$a = v$ if $p>y$

where a is the amount of depreciation, p is the period, v is the depreciable value, and y is the asset lifetime. The p argument can be fractional. For fractional arguments, the depreciation is prorated between the two consecutive time periods preceding and following the fractional period.

For example, consider purchasing some equipment on 01APR86 that has a lifetime of ten years and a depreciable basis of $1000. The accumulated depreciation through 31DEC87 would be calculated as

    a=daccsl(1.75,1000,10);

resulting in a value of 175.00.

DACCSYD: calculates accumulated sum-of-years'-digits depreciation

    daccsyd(period,value,years)

The sum-of-years'-digits accumulated depreciation function, $a=\text{DACCSYD}(p,v,y)$, is computed as

$a = 0$ if $p<0$

$$a = v \frac{(\text{int}(p)(y - (\text{int}(p) - 1)/2) + (p - \text{int}(p))(y - \text{int}(p)))}{(\text{int}(y)(y - (\text{int}(y) - 1)/2) + (y - \text{int}(y))^2)} \quad \text{if } 0 \leq p \leq y$$

$a = v$ if $p>y$

where a is the amount of depreciation, p is the period, v is the depreciable value, y is the lifetime and where int(y) indicates the integer part of y. The p argument can be fractional. For fractional arguments, the depreciation is prorated between the two consecutive time periods preceding and following the fractional period.

For example, if an asset acquired on October 1 has a depreciable basis of $1000 and a lifetime of five years, then the accumulated depreciation at the end of the asset's second year would be computed as

```
y2=daccsyd(1.25,1000,5);
```

resulting in a value of 400.00.

DACCTAB: calculates accumulated depreciation from specified tables

```
dacctab(period,value,tab1,...,tabn)
```

The accumulated depreciation using specified tables,

$$a = DACCTAB(p, v, tab1, \ldots, tabn)$$

is computed as

$a = 0$ if $p \leq 0$
$a = v^*(tab1 + tab2 + \ldots + tab(int(p)) + tab(int(p + 1))^*(p - int(p)))$ if $0 < p < n$
$a = v$ if $p \geq n$

where a is the amount of depreciation, p is the period, v is the depreciable value, and $tab1, \ldots, tabn$ are the fractions of depreciation for each time period. The p argument can be fractional. For fractional arguments, the depreciation is prorated between the two consecutive time periods preceding and following the fractional period.

Suppose an asset that has a lifetime of five years and a depreciable basis of $1000 is acquired on 01JAN80. Using the depreciation tables as specified below, the accumulated depreciation throughout the third year is computed as

```
y3=dacctab(3,1000,.15,.22,.21,.21,.21);
```

resulting in a value of 580.00.

You do not need to specify the entire table if the *period* argument is of limited range.

DATE: returns today's date as a SAS date value

```
date()
```

The DATE function, which may also be written:

```
today()
```

produces today's date as a SAS date value.

For example, suppose that you work in a company's billing office and are responsible for preparing a list of customers whose bills are more than 15 days overdue. You maintain a SAS data set containing customer information, including the variable DATEDUE. DATEDUE contains the date a payment was due as a SAS date value. The following DATA step prepares the list of overdue accounts:

```
data _null_;
   set customer;
   tday=date();
   if (tday-datedue)> 15 then do:
      put 'As of ' tday date7. ' Account ' account
      ' is more than 15 days overdue.';
```

Note that the TDAY variable is output in DATE7. format. If a format is not assigned to TDAY, the value printed will be a SAS date value (the number of days since January 1, 1960).

See **USING SAS DATE, TIME, AND DATETIME INFORMATS AND FORMATS** in Chapter 13, "SAS Informats and Formats," for a discussion of date and time values, informats, formats, and literals.

DATEJUL: converts a Julian date to a SAS date value

```
datejul(juliandate)
```

The DATEJUL function converts a Julian date to a SAS date value. A Julian date has the form *yyddd*, where *yy* is the year 19*yy* and *ddd* is the day of the year. The DATEJUL function is useful any time you want to represent values stored as Julian dates in some other form. For example, the SAS data set SUBSCRIB contains information on a newspaper's customers. Beginning subscription dates are stored in the variable BEGIN in Julian form. You want to print a report for each newspaper route showing the date each customer began receiving the paper in WORDDATE.format. First, you must convert the BEGIN value to a SAS date value.

```
data _null_;
   set subscrib;
   start=datejul(begin);
   put a1 customer a30 start worddate20.;
```

If the last three digits of the argument's value represent a value less than 1 or greater than 366, the function prints an "invalid argument" message.

See **USING SAS DATE, TIME, AND DATETIME INFORMATS AND FORMATS** in Chapter 13, "SAS Informats and Formats," for a discussion of date and time values, informats, formats, and literals.

DATEPART: extracts the date part of a SAS datetime value

```
datepart(datetime)
```

The DATEPART function extracts the date part of a SAS *datetime* value or datetime literal. The date returned is a SAS date value. For positive dates, the statement

```
date=datepart(datetime);
```

is equivalent to

```
date=int(datetime/(24*60*60));
```

For example, say that a computing center's accounting office issues statements that list charges for each day. A billing program keeps track of connect time used and stores the information as SAS datetime values. The variable CONN shows when a user's computer session began. To create a SAS data set of charges by date, use the DATEPART function.

```
data daily;
   set accounts;
   keep user charges servdate;
   servdate=datepart(conn);
```

The value of the new variable SERVDATE is a SAS date value. To print SERVDATE in readable form, you must use a SAS date format.

See **USING SAS DATE, TIME, AND DATETIME INFORMATS AND FORMATS** in Chapter 13, "SAS Informats and Formats," for a discussion of date and time values, informats, formats, and literals.

DATETIME: returns the current date and time of day

datetime()

The DATETIME function produces the current time of day and date as a SAS datetime value. Suppose you are writing a program that will execute whenever a bank customer uses an automatic teller machine. The program must record the transaction for the bank's data base and show the date and time value of the transaction, as well as the deposit or withdrawal information. Your program may include these statements:

```
data _null_;
   when=datetime();
   more SAS statements
   put @1 id @30 when datetime17.;
```

Note that the value of WHEN is formatted with the DATETIME. format in order to print in readable form. If no format is used, the value printed is a SAS datetime value (the number of seconds since midnight, January 1, 1960).

See **USING SAS DATE, TIME, AND DATETIME INFORMATS AND FORMATS** in Chapter 13, "SAS Informats and Formats," for a discussion of date and time values, informats, formats, and literals.

DAY: returns the day of the month from a SAS date value

day(date)

The DAY function produces the day of the month from a SAS date value or date literal. Suppose you need a DATA step that updates a large SAS data set on odd-numbered days. The program is run every day, and you want it to print a notice saying "NO UPDATE TODAY" on even-numbered days. The DATA step may look like this:

```
data invntry;
   tday=date();
   dom=day(tday);
   daynum=mod(dom,2);
   if daynum>0 then do;
   update invntry newdata;
   more SAS statements
   else put tday date7. 'NO UPDATE TODAY';
```

First, the DATE function is used to assign the current date to the variable TDAY. Then the day of the month is extracted from TDAY by the DAY function and assigned to the target variable DOM. Next, the MOD function is used to find the remainder of DOM divided by 2. On odd-numbered days, the remainder is greater than 0, so the DO group updating the master data set executes. On even-numbered days, the remainder is 0, so the message is printed instead.

See **USING SAS DATE, TIME, AND DATETIME INFORMATS AND FORMATS** in Chapter 13, "SAS Informats and Formats," for a discussion of date and time values, informats, formats, and literals.

DEPDB: calculates declining balance depreciation

`depdb(period,value,years,rate)`

The declining balance depreciation function, $d=\text{DEPDB}(p,v,y,r)$, is computed as

`a=daccdb(p,v,y,r)-daccdb(p-1,v,y,r)`

where a is the amount of depreciation, p is the period for which the depreciation is to be calculated, v is the depreciable value of the asset, y is the lifetime of the asset, and r is the rate of depreciation expressed as a fraction. A double declining balance is obtained by setting r equal to 2. The p argument can be fractional. For fractional arguments, the depreciation is prorated between the two consecutive time periods preceding and following the fractional period.

For example, if an asset acquired on January 1 has a depreciable basis of $1000 and a fifteen-year lifetime, then, using a 200% declining balance, the depreciation in the tenth year of the life of the asset is expressed as

`y10=depdb(10,1000,15,2);`

The result is 36.7796.

DEPDBSL: calculates declining balance converting to straight-line depreciation

`depdbsl(period,value,years,rate)`

The declining balance changing to a straight-line depreciation function, $a=\text{DEPDBSL}(p,v,y,r)$, is computed as

$$a = 0 \quad \text{if } p \leq 0$$

$$a = v(r/y)(1 - r/y)^{(p-1)} \quad \text{if } p < t$$

$$a = v(1 - r/y)^{(t-1)/(y-t+1)} \quad \text{if } p \geq t$$

$$a = 0 \quad \text{if } p > y$$

where a is the amount of depreciation, p is the period, v is the depreciable value, y is the lifetime, and r is the rate, expressed as a fraction, for the declining balance portion of the depreciation. The value of t is $\text{int}(y - y/r+1)$ where int( ) denotes the integer part. The p and y arguments must be integers. Noninteger values are treated as erroneous input. The declining balance changing to a straight-line depreciation chooses for each time period the method of depreciation, declining balance or straight-line on the remaining balance, that gives the larger current depreciation.

For example, suppose you have an asset with a depreciable basis of $1000, a declining balance rate of 150%, and a ten-year lifetime. The depreciation of that asset in its fifth year would be computed as

`y5=depdbsl(5,1000,10,1.5);`

resulting in a value of 87.001.

DEPSL: calculates straight-line depreciation

    depsl(period,value,years)

The straight-line depreciation function, $d=\text{DEPSL}(p,v,y)$, is computed as

    a=daccsl(p,v,y)-daccsl(p-1,v,y)

where a is the amount of depreciation, p is the period, v is the depreciable value, and y is the asset lifetime. The p argument can be fractional. For fractional arguments, the depreciation is prorated between the two consecutive time periods preceding and following the fractional period.

For example, consider purchasing some equipment on 01APR86 that has a lifetime of ten years and a depreciable basis of $1000. The depreciation as of 31DEC86 is calculated using the following statement:

    d=depsl(9/12,1000,10);

The resulting value is 75.00.

DEPSYD: calculates sum-of-years'-digits depreciation

    depsyd(period,value,years)

The sum-of-years'-digits depreciation function, $d=\text{DEPSYD}(p,v,y)$, is computed as

    a=daccsyd(p,v,y)-daccsyd(p-1,v,y)

where a is the amount of depreciation, p is the period, v is the depreciable value, and y is the lifetime of the asset. The p argument can be fractional. For fractional arguments, the depreciation is prorated between the two consecutive time periods preceding and following the fractional period.

For example, if an asset acquired on October 1 has a depreciable basis of $1000 and a lifetime of five years, then the depreciation at the end of the first year and at the end of the second year would be computed as

    y1=depsyd(3/12,1000,5);
    y2=depsyd(1.25,1000,5);

and the results would be 83.333 and 316.67, respectively.

DEPTAB: calculates depreciation from specified tables

    deptab(period,value,tab1,...,tabn)

The depreciation from specified tables function, $d=\text{DEPTAB}(p,v,tab1,\ldots,tabn)$, is computed as

    a=dacctab(p,v,tab1,...,tabn)-dacctab(p-1,v,tab1,...,tabn)

where a is the amount of depreciation, p is the period, v is the depreciable value, and $tab1, \ldots, tabn$ are the fractions of depreciation for each time period. The p argument can be fractional. For fractional arguments, the depreciation is prorated between the two consecutive time periods preceding and following the fractional period.

Suppose an asset that has a lifetime of five years and a depreciable basis of $1000 is acquired on 01JAN80. Using the depreciation tables as specified below, the depreciation in the third year is computed as

```
y3=deptab(3,1000,.15,.22,.21,.21,.21);
```

resulting in a value of 210.00.

You do not need to specify the entire table if the *period* argument is of limited range.

DHMS: returns a SAS datetime value from date, hour, minute, and second

dhms(*date,hour,minute,second*)

The DHMS function produces a SAS datetime value from *date, hour, minute,* and *second* values. The date argument can be either a variable or a SAS date literal. For example, a utility company samples electricity usage at 100 residences for six months. On selected days, data are recorded every second. The company wants to analyze the data by date, hour, minute, and second across all households, so they need a data set that can be sorted by a datetime variable. The DHMS function helps them create the data set.

```
data usage;
   infile readings;
   input date date7. hour 2. minute 2. second 2. kw 10.1 house 4.;
   dtid= dhms(date,hour,minute,second);
   keep dtid kw house;
```

See **USING SAS DATE, TIME, AND DATETIME INFORMATS AND FORMATS** in Chapter 13, "SAS Informats and Formats," for a discussion of date and time values, informats, formats, and literals.

DIF: calculates the first difference for the *n*th lag

dif*n*(*argument*)

A family of DIF functions, named DIF1, DIF2, ..., DIF100 is available for numerical arguments only. (DIF1 can also be written DIF.) The result of the DIF*n* function is the current value of *argument* minus the current LAG*n* value of *argument*, that is

```
difn(x)=x-lagn(x)   .
```

Consider this DATA step:

```
data two;
   input x aa;
   z=lag(x);
   d=dif(x);
   cards;
1 2 6 4 7
;
proc print;
   title 'Differences and Lags';
run;
```

This data set is shown in **Output 4.3**.

62 Chapter 4

Output 4.3 DIF Function Results

```
                Differences and Lags                       1

         OBS     X     Z     D

          1      1     .     .
          2      2     1     1
          3      6     2     4
          4      4     6    -2
          5      7     4     3
```

Note: the function DIF2(X) is not equivalent to the second difference DIF(DIF(X)).

Note: differences are only generated when a DIF function executes; they are not automatically generated for each observation. If the DIF function executes conditionally in an IF-THEN statement, only values from those observations meeting the IF condition are used for differencing. The following example demonstrates this:

```
data a;
   input y aa;
   if _n_>1 then x=y*2+dif(x);
      else x=y*2;
   cards;
1 2 3 4
;
proc print;
   title 'Conditional Differences';
run;
```

The DATA step causes this note:

```
NOTE: Missing values were generated as a result of performing
      an operation on missing values.
```

Data set A contains the values shown in **Output 4.4**.

Output 4.4 Differences

```
                Conditional Differences                    1

         OBS     Y     X

          1      1     2
          2      2     .
          3      3     .
          4      4     .
```

X is always missing except in the first observation because DIF1(X) returns a value based on the current value of LAG(X), which in all first observations is a missing value. (See the LAG function later in this chapter.) The first time the DATA step executes, $\_N\_=1$, so the conditions of the IF statement are not met. The ELSE statement executes, and X has a value of 2. The first time the DIF function executes, the value is a missing value which causes X to be missing and all succeeding X values to be missing.

If the argument is an array name, each array element is differenced separately.

DIGAMMA: computes the digamma function

```
digamma(x)
```

The DIGAMMA function computes the derivative of the log of the gamma function, that is, DIGAMMA(x)=$\Gamma'(x)/\Gamma(x)$. The value of this function is not defined for negative integers and zero.

Example:

```
y=digamma(1);
```

returns

```
y= -.5772
```

which is the negative of Euler's constant.

DIM: returns the number of elements in an array

```
dimn(arrayname)
dim(arrayname,arraybound)
```

where n is the dimension for which you want to know the number of elements.

The DIM function returns the number of elements in a one-dimensional array or the number of elements in a specified dimension of a multidimensional array.

If the array is one-dimensional, or if you want the first dimension of a multidimensional array, no n value need be specified. For example, suppose you define this multidimensional array:

```
array mult{5,10,2} mult1-mult100;
```

The value of DIM(MULT) is 5, while DIM2(MULT) is 10, and DIM3(MULT) is 2.

The DIM function is convenient because you can use it to avoid having to change the upper bound of the iterative DO group each time you change the number of elements in the array. Here is an example for a one-dimensional array. The statements

```
data new;
   input weight sex height state city;
   array big{5} weight sex height state city;
   do i=1 to dim(big);
      put 'The value of big{i} for i=' i 'is ' big{i};
      end;
   cards;
83 2 64 14 6230
;
```

produce this output:

```
The value of big{i} for i=1 is 83
The value of big{i} for i=2 is 2
The value of big{i} for i=3 is 64
The value of big{i} for i=4 is 14
The value of big{i} for i=5 is 6230
```

ERF: error function

    erf(x)

The result of this function is $2/\sqrt{\pi} \int_0^x e^{-z^2} dz$.

The ERF function can be used to find the probability (P) that a normally distributed random variable with mean 0 and standard deviation 1 will take on a value less than X. For example,

    p=.5+.5*erf(x/sqrt(2)) .

This is equivalent to PROBNORM(X).

Examples:

    data;
       y=erf(1);
       put y;
    run;

returns the value .842701.

    y=erf(-1);

returns the value $-.842701$.

ERFC: returns the complement of the ERF function

    erfc(argument)

The function ERFC represents the complement to the ERF function (that is, 1−ERF).

EXP: raises e (∼2.71828) to a specified power

    exp(argument)

The value of the argument is limited by the machine that you use. For example, if you are using an IBM PC the value of the argument must be less than 709.78, approximately. This function raises e to the power specified by the argument. The base of natural logarithms, e, is approximately 2.71828. Using an argument greater than 709.78 will result in a number greater than the maximum allowable value for the PC.

Examples:

    y=exp(1);

returns the value 2.71828.

    y=exp(0);

returns the value 1.

FINV: the quantile for the F distribution

    finv (p,ndf,ddf,nc)

where

   $0 \leq p < 1$, $0 < ndf$, $0 < ddf$, $0 \leq nc$.

The FINV function computes the quantile for the F distribution with *ndf* numerator degrees of freedom, *ddf* denominator degrees of freedom, and *nc* noncentrality parameter. The quantile is such that the probability that an observation from this distribution is less than the quantile is *p*. If the optional parameter, *nc*, is not specified or is zero, the central distribution is used. Otherwise, the noncentral distribution is used. The parameters *ndf* and *ddf* do not have to be integers. The noncentrality parameter, *nc*, is defined such that if X and Y are normal random variables with means μ and 0, respectively, and variance 1, then X^2/Y^2 has a noncentral F distribution with $nc=\mu^2$. For large values of *nc* the algorithm used can fail. In these cases a missing value will be returned. This function is derived from the functions contributed by Hardison, Quade, and Langston (1983).

Examples:

```
data;
   q1=finv(.95,2,10); put q1=;
   q2=finv(.95,2,10.3,2); put q2=;
```

results in

```
Q1=4.1028
Q2=7.5838
```

FIPNAME: converts FIPS code to state name (uppercase)

fipname(*fips*)

The FIPNAME function takes a numeric FIPS code and returns the corresponding twenty-character state name in uppercase. For example,

```
x=fipname(37);
put x=;
```

produces the line

```
X=NORTH CAROLINA
```

FIPNAMEL: converts FIPS code to state name in upper- and lowercase

fipnamel(*fips*)

The FIPNAMEL function takes a numeric FIPS code and returns a twenty-character state name in upper- and lowercase. For example,

```
x=fipnamel(37);
put x=;
```

produces the line

```
X=North Carolina
```

FIPSTATE: converts FIPS code to two-character postal code

fipstate(*fips*)

The FIPSTATE function takes the numeric FIPS state code and returns the two-character postal code. For example,

```
x=fipstate(37);
put x=;
```

produces the line

```
X=NC
```

FLOOR: returns the largest integer≤argument

```
floor(argument)
```

This function results in the largest integer less than or equal to the value of the argument. If the argument's value is within 10^{-12} of an integer, the function results in that integer.

Examples:

```
data;
   x=floor(2.1);
   put x;
run;
```

returns the value 2.

```
x=floor(-2.4);
```

returns the value −3.

```
x=floor(3);
```

returns the value 3.

```
x=floor(-2.0000000000001);
```

returns the value −2.

FUZZ: returns the integer if the argument is within 1E−12

```
fuzz(argument)
```

The FUZZ function returns an integer value if the *argument* is within 1E−12 of the integer (that is, if the difference between the integer and argument is less than 1E−12). For example, these statements:

```
data _null_;
   x=5.9999999999999;
   y=fuzz(x);
   put y= 15.13;
```

produce this line:

```
Y=6.0000000000000
```

GAMINV: inverse of the PROBGAM function

```
gaminv(p,a)
```

where

$0 \leq p < 1$, and a>0 .

The GAMINV function computes a value of x such that

$P = \int_0^x t^{a-1} e^{-t} dt / \Gamma(a)$.

GAMMA: produces the complete gamma function

```
gamma(x)
```

The result of this function is the definite integral:

$\int_0^\infty t^{x-1} e^{-t} dt$.

The value of x must be a number less than 171.63, approximately. If it is an integer, then it must be positive and GAMMA(x) is (x-1)!. This function is commonly denoted by $\Gamma(x)$.

Example:

```
data;
   x=gamma(6);
   put x;
run;
```

produces a value of 120.

HBOUND: the upper bound of an array

```
hboundn(arrayname)
hbound (arrayname,boundn)
```

where *n* is the dimension for which you want to know the upper bound, or *n* may be omitted and *boundn* will be used.

The HBOUND function returns the upper bound of a one-dimensional array or the upper bound of a specified dimension of a multidimensional array.

If the array is one-dimensional or if you want the first dimension of a multidimensional array, you can omit the *n* value. For example, suppose you define this multidimensional array

```
array mult{5,10,2} mult1-mult100;
```

The value of HBOUND(MULT) is 5, while HBOUND2(MULT) is 10, and HBOUND3(MULT) is 2.

The HBOUND function is convenient because you can use it to avoid having to change the upper bound of the iterative DO group each time you change the bounds of the array. The following is an example for a one-dimensional array. The statements

```
data new;
   input weight sex height state city;
   array big{5} weight sex height state city;
   do i = 1 to hbound(big);
      put 'The value of big{i} for i=' i 'is ' big{i};
   end;
   cards;
83 2 64 14 6230
;
```

produce the output

```
The value of big{i} for i=1 is 83
The value of big{i} for i=2 is 2
The value of big{i} for i=3 is 64
The value of big{i} for i=4 is 14
The value of big{i} for i=5 is 6230
```

HMS: returns a SAS time value from hour, minute, and second

```
hms(hour,minute,second)
```

The HMS function produces a SAS time value from *hour*, *minute*, and *second* values. Suppose that the utility company in the example for the DHMS function (above) wanted to determine what time of day is, on the average, the time of peak electrical usage. The HMS function helps them set up the results so they can find the average.

```
data USAGE;
   infile readings;
   input date date7. hour 2. minute 2. second 2. kw 10.1 house 4.;
   hrid= hms(hour,minute,second);
   keep hrid date kw house;
   more SAS statements
```

The result is printed as a SAS time value (the number of seconds since 12:00 midnight).

See **USING SAS DATE, TIME, AND DATETIME INFORMATS AND FORMATS** in Chapter 13, "SAS Informats and Formats," for a discussion of date and time values, informats, formats, and literals.

HOUR: returns the hour from a SAS datetime or time value or literal

```
hour(time)
hour(datetime)
```

The HOUR function operates on a SAS *time* or *datetime* value, or a SAS time or datetime literal, to produce a numeric value containing the hour. For example, suppose employees in your department often run a large SAS job that prints between 200 and 300 pages of output. The information is valuable, but the printer is tied up for nearly an hour every time someone runs the job. The HOUR function allows you to display a message any time someone begins to run the job between 7 a.m and 5 p.m.

```
data _null_;
   h=hour(time());
   if 7≤h≤17 then do;
   put 'PLEASE WAIT UNTIL AFTER 5 P.M. TO RUN THIS JOB.';
```

See **USING SAS DATE, TIME, AND DATETIME INFORMATS AND FORMATS** in Chapter 13, "SAS Informats and Formats," for a discussion of date and time values, informats, formats, and literals.

INDEX: searches the first argument for the character string specified by the second argument

```
index(argument1,argument2)
```

The INDEX function searches *argument1*, from left to right, for the first occurrence of the string specified in the second argument, and returns the position in argument1 of the string's first character. If the string is not found in argument1, INDEX returns a value of 0. For example,

```
a='ABC.DEF (X=Y)';
b='X=Y';
x=index(a,b);
```

The value of X is 10, the starting position in A of the string specified by B, X=Y.

INDEXC: finds the first occurrence in the first argument of any character present in any of the remaining arguments

```
indexc(argument1,argument2,...argumentn)
```

The INDEXC function searches the first argument, from left to right, for the first occurrence of any character present in any of the other arguments. INDEXC returns the position in argument1 of the character found. INDEXC returns a value of 0 if none of the characters in argument2 through argument*n* are found in argument1.

For example, the following statements find the first numeric or special character in the character string assigned to the variable, A.

```
a='ABC.DEP (X2=Y1)';
x=indexc(a,'0123456789',';()=. ');
```

The value of X is 4 because the period (.), the fourth character in A, is the first character from the remaining arguments that INDEXC finds in A.

INPUT: defines an informat for a value

```
input(argument,informat)
```

This function allows you to "read" *argument* using any informat specified by the second argument. The informat specified determines whether the result is numeric or character. For example,

```
release='6.03';
nrelease=input(release,4.2);
```

results in NRELEASE having the numeric value 6.03.

The variable or constant specified for *argument* can be character or numeric. By specifying a character informat with a numeric value, it is possible to convert numeric values to character; however, we do not recommend that you do this. If you use the INPUT function to convert numeric values to character, an implicit conversion takes place using the BEST12. informat. The result of the conversion is right-aligned and is padded with blanks if necessary. The conversion may result in a value you are not expecting. If you need to convert numeric values to character values, we recommend that you use the PUT function.

INT: returns the integer value (truncates)

```
int(argument)
```

This function truncates the decimal portion of the value of the argument. The integer portion of the value of the argument remains. If the argument's value is within 10^{-12} of an integer, the function results in that integer. If the value of *argument* is positive, INT(*argument*) has the same result as FLOOR(*argument*). If the value of *argument* is negative, INT(*argument*) has the same result as CEIL(*argument*).

70   Chapter 4

Examples:

```
data;
   x=int(2.1);
   put x;
run;
```

produces a value of 2.

```
x=int(-2.4);
```

produces a value of −2.

```
x=int(3);
```

produces a value of 3.

```
x=int(0.9999999999999);
```

produces a value of 1.

INTCK: returns the number of time intervals

```
intck(interval,from,to)
```

The INTCK function determines the number of time intervals that occur in a given time span. The result is always an integer value. For example, at the XYZ Company, year-end bonuses are prorated for employees who started work after December 1, the beginning of the company's fiscal year. The payroll department uses the INTCK function to calculate the number of days new employees have worked. (Paid holidays and vacation days are counted; weekends are not counted.) In the following example, the data set EMPLOYEE contains the names and starting dates for each employee:

```
data prorate;
   set employee;
   w=intck('WEEK',starting,'30NOV84'd);
   d=intck('DAY',starting,'30NOV84'd);
   wdays=d-(w*2);
   drop w d;
```

The *interval* must be a character constant or variable whose value is one of those listed below. The *from* and *to* values can be expressed as SAS date, datetime, or time values; or as SAS date, datetime, or time literals. The INTCK function cannot distinguish date, time, and datetime values from each other, so you must specify the correct type of interval:

- Use date intervals when *from* and *to* contain date values.
- Use datetime intervals when *from* and *to* contain datetime values.
- Use values listed under time intervals when *from* and *to* contain time values.

date intervals	datetime intervals	time intervals
DAY	DTDAY	HOUR
WEEK	DTWEEK	MINUTE
MONTH	DTMONTH	SECOND
QTR	DTQTR	
YEAR	DTYEAR	

See **USING SAS DATE, TIME, AND DATETIME INFORMATS AND FORMATS** in Chapter 13, "SAS Informats and Formats," for a discussion of date and time values, informats, formats, and literals.

The INTCK function counts intervals from fixed interval beginnings, not in multiples of an interval unit from the *from* value. Partial intervals are not counted. For example, WEEK intervals are counted by Sundays rather than seven-day multiples from the *from* argument. YEAR intervals are counted from 01JAN, not in 365-day multiples. The result of

```
intck('YEAR','31DEC84'd,'1JAN85'd)
```

is 1, even though only one day has elapsed. The result of

```
intck('YEAR','1JAN84'd,'31DEC84'd)
```

is 0, even though 364 days have elapsed. In the first example, an 01JAN date is counted between the *from* and *to* values, so a YEAR interval is added. In the second example 01JAN is not counted between the *from* and *to* values, so an interval is not added.

INTNX: advances a date, time, or datetime value by a given interval

```
intnx(interval,from,number)
```

The INTNX function generates a SAS date, time, or datetime value that is a given *number* of time intervals from a starting value (*from*). The *interval* must be a character constant or variable whose value is one of those listed under the INTCK description (see above). Note that the INTNX function cannot distinguish date, time, and datetime values from each other, so you must specify the correct type of interval. The *from* argument must be a SAS date, time, or datetime value, or a SAS date, time, or datetime literal; and *number* gives the number of intervals to use.

For example, the XYZ Company offers its employees medical coverage only after 30 days of full-time employment. The data set called EMPLOYEE contains the names and starting dates for each employee. The following example shows how the personnel office uses the INTNX function to find the date each employee will be eligible for medical coverage:

```
data health;
   set employee;
   benefit=intnx('DAY',start,30);
proc print;
   format start date7. benefit date7.;
```

If the *number* argument is 0, the returned value is the first value of the specified *interval* in which the *from* argument falls. For example,

```
x=intnx('MONTH','05JAN85'd,0);
put x=date.;
```

produces

```
X=01JAN85.
```

Note that you must specify a SAS date, time, or datetime format to print the result as a readable value; otherwise, results are printed as SAS date, time, or datetime values. See **USING SAS DATE, TIME, AND DATETIME INFORMATS AND FORMATS** in Chapter 13, "SAS Informats and Formats," for a discussion of date and time values, informats, formats, and literals.

INTRR: calculates internal rate of return as a fraction

```
intrr(period,cash0,cash1,...,cashn)
```

This function calculates the internal rate of return for the set of cash flows given by *cash0, cash1, ..., cashn*, with the number of cash flows per interest period given by *period*. If the cash flows are monthly and you want to calculate a yearly interest rate, *period* should be 12. If *period*=0, then continuous compounding is assumed. The internal rate of return is an interest rate such that the sequence of cash flows has a net present value (see the NETPV function) of zero when discounted at this rate.

All arguments must be numeric and *period* must be greater than or equal to zero. Abbreviated variable lists can be used for the cash flow arguments. If *period* is missing, a missing value is returned. However, if some of the cash flows are missing, the internal rate of return is calculated assuming zero for the missing cash flows. The routine uses Newton's method to look for the internal rate of return nearest to zero. If the function fails to find a meaningful value, a missing value is returned. The calculated value is returned as a fraction.

To illustrate, suppose that you make an initial outlay of $400 and expect to receive payments of $100, $200, and $300 over the next three time periods. The internal rate of return is 0.19438 per payment period and can be calculated from the following statements:

```
data invest;
   rate=intrr(1,-400,100,200,300);
   put rate=;
```

Computational Details

This routine finds the root, *x*, nearest to one, of

$$\Sigma a_i x^i = 0$$

where a_i represents cash flows and the summation over *i* goes from 0 to *n*. The value of the internal rate of return is computed from *x* as

$$\text{rate}=1/x^p - 1$$

where *p* is the value of the *period* argument.

If the value of the *period* argument is 0, then

$$\text{rate} = -\log_e(x)$$

IRR: calculates internal rate of return as a percentage

```
irr(period,cash0,cash1,...,cashn)
```

This function is identical to INTRR, described earlier, except that the rate of return is calculated as a percentage.

JULDATE: returns the Julian date from a SAS date value or literal

    juldate(date)

The JULDATE function converts a SAS *date* value or date literal to a numeric value containing the Julian representation of the date. If the date is a 20th century date, there are five digits; the first two are the year, and the next three the day of the year. If the date is not a 20th century date, there are seven digits; the first four are the year, and the next three the day of the year. Thus, 1JAN85 is 85001 in Julian representation; 31DEC1878 is 1878365.

The JULDATE function can be used to convert DATE7.–format dates (for example, 1JAN85) into Julian dates for convenience or consistency. For example, in the example for the DATEJUL function, above, a publishing company kept a data set containing the names of newspaper subscribers and the dates their subscriptions began. The dates were stored as Julian dates, but the DATEJUL function allowed the company to print a report showing the dates in WORDDATE. format. Rather than require the subscription sales department to enter the dates for new subscriptions as Julian dates in order to update the main file, the JULDATE function is used.

```
data update;
   input name $ start date7.;
   julian=juldate(start);
   drop start;
   cards;
data lines
;
```

See **USING SAS DATE, TIME, AND DATETIME INFORMATS AND FORMATS** in Chapter 13, "SAS Informats and Formats," for a discussion of date and time values, informats, formats, and literals.

KURTOSIS: calculates the kurtosis, the 4th moment

    kurtosis(argument,argument,...)

The *arguments* for this function must be numeric values. At least four nonmissing values are required. The result is the kurtosis statistic of the nonmissing arguments.

For the example

    x=kurtosis(0,1,0,1);

the value returned is -6.

You can use an abbreviated argument list preceded by OF.

See Chapter 1, "SAS Elementary Statistics Procedures," in the *SAS Procedures Guide, Release 6.03 Edition* for a definition of this statistic.

LAG: calculates lagged values

    lagn(argument)

A family of LAG functions, named LAG1, LAG2, ..., LAG100, is available for obtaining up to 100 lags of a variable's value. (LAG1 can also be written as LAG.) The LAG function can have either numeric or character arguments. It remembers values of the argument from a previous execution of the function.

Each LAG function in a program has its own stack of lag values. The stack for a LAG*n* function is initialized with *n* missing values, where *n* is the number of lags (for example, a LAG2 stack is initialized with two missing values). Each time the function executes, the value at the top of the stack is returned, and the current value of the argument is placed at the bottom of the stack. This means that missing values are returned for the first *n* executions of a LAG function, after which the lagged values of the argument are returned.

For example, consider this DATA step:

```
data one;
   input x aa;
   y=lag1(x);
   z=lag2(x);
   cards;
1 2 3 4
;
proc print;
   title 'Lag Output';
run;
```

Data set ONE contains the values for X, Y, and Z shown in **Output 4.5**.

Output 4.5   First and Second Lags

```
                    Lag Output                        1

            OBS    X    Y    Z

             1     1    .    .
             2     2    1    .
             3     3    2    1
             4     4    3    2
```

The LAG1 function returns one missing value and then the values of X (lagged once); the LAG2 function returns two missing values and then the values of X (lagged twice).

Note: values are placed in a LAG stack only when a LAG function executes; values are not automatically generated for each observation. If the LAG function executes conditionally in an IF-THEN statement, only values from those observations meeting the IF condition are used for lagging. The following example demonstrates this:

```
data a;
   input y aa;
   if _n_>1 then x=y*2+lag(x);
      else x=y*2;
   cards;
1 2 3 4
;
proc print;
   title 'Conditional Lags';
run;
```

The DATA step causes this note:

```
NOTE: Missing values were generated as a result of performing
      an operation on missing values.
```

Data set A contains the values shown in **Output 4.6**.

Output 4.6 Conditional Lags

```
        Conditional Lags                    1

         OBS    Y    X
          1     1    2
          2     2    .
          3     3    .
          4     4    .
```

X is always missing except in the first observation because LAG1(X) returns a value from the last time the LAG executed, not from the previous observation. The first time the DATA step executes, _N_=1, so the conditions of the IF statement are not met. The ELSE statement executes, and X has a value of 2. The first time the LAG function executes, the lag value is a missing value, which causes X to be missing and all succeeding X values to be missing.

If the argument to LAG is an array name, each array element is lagged separately.

LBOUND: returns the lower bound of an array

```
lboundn(arrayname)
lbound (arrayname,boundn)
```

where *n* is the dimension for which you want to know the lower bound, or *n* may be omitted and *boundn* will be used.

The LBOUND function returns the lower bound of a one-dimensional array or the lower bound of a specified dimension of a multidimensional array.

If the array is one-dimensional or if you want the first dimension of a multidimensional array, you can omit the *n* value. For example, suppose you define this multidimensional array

```
array mult{2:6,4:13,2} mult1-mult100;
```

The value of LBOUND(MULT) is 2, while LBOUND2(MULT) is 4, and LBOUND3(MULT) is 1.

The LBOUND function is convenient because you can use it to avoid having to change the lower bound of the iterative DO group each time you change the bounds of the array. The following is an example for a one-dimensional array. The statements

```
data new;
   input weight sex height state city;
   array big{2:6} weight sex height state city;
   do i = lbound(big) to hbound(big);
      put 'The value of big{i} for i=' i 'is ' big{i};
      end;
   cards;
83 2 64 14 6230
;
```

produce the output

```
The value of big{i} for i=2 is 83
The value of big{i} for i=3 is 2
The value of big{i} for i=4 is 64
The value of big{i} for i=5 is 14
The value of big{i} for i=6 is 6230
```

LEFT: left-aligns a character expression

left(*argument*)

The LEFT function returns the argument with leading blanks moved to the end of the value. The argument's length does not change. For example, the statements

```
a='   HI THERE';
b=left(a);
```

give B the value 'HI THERE   '.

LENGTH: gives the length of a character argument

length(*argument*)

The LENGTH function returns the length of the character expression specified by the argument. The result is the position of the right-most nonblank character in the argument. If the value of the argument is missing, LENGTH returns a value of 0. For example,

```
len=length('ABCDEF');
```

gives LEN a value of 6, which is the last character in the argument, F.

LGAMMA: calculates the natural logarithm of the GAMMA function of a value

lgamma(*argument*)

This function results in the natural logarithm of the GAMMA function of the value of *argument* (see GAMMA). The value of *argument* must be positive.
  Example:

```
data;
   x=lgamma(2);
   put x;
run;
```

results in a value of 0.

LOG: natural logarithm

log(*argument*)

The result of this function is the natural (Naperian) logarithm of the value of *argument*. The argument must have a positive value.
  The base of natural logarithms is e, approximately 2.71828.

Examples:

```
data;
    x=log(1);
    put x;
run;
```

results in a value of 0.

```
x=log(10);
```

results in a value of 2.30259.

LOG10: common logarithm

```
log10(argument)
```

This function results in the common logarithm (log to the base 10) of the value of the *argument*. The argument must have a positive value.
Examples:

```
x=log10(1);
```

results in a value of 0.

```
x=log10(10);
```

results in a value of 1.

```
x=log10(100);
```

results in a value of 2.

LOG2: logarithm to the base 2

```
log2(argument)
```

This function results in the logarithm to the base 2 of the value of *argument*. The argument must have a positive value.
Examples:

```
x=log2(2);
```

results in a value of 1.

```
x=log2(.5);
```

results in a value of −1.

MAX: returns the largest value

```
max(argument,argument, ...)
```

The *arguments* for this function must be numeric values. At least two nonmissing values are required. The result is the largest value among the nonmissing values of the arguments.
For the examples

```
x=max(2,6,.);
x=max(2,-3,1,-1);
x=max(3,.,-3);
```

the values returned are 6, 2, and 3, respectively.

You can use an abbreviated argument list preceded by OF.

See Chapter 1, "SAS Elementary Statistics Procedures," in the *SAS Procedures Guide, Release 6.03 Edition* for a definition of this statistic. Note that the MAX function does not necessarily return the same value as the MAX operator described in Chapter 3, "SAS Expressions."

MDY: returns a SAS date value from month, day, and year

```
mdy(month,day,year)
```

The MDY function produces a SAS date value from numeric values that represent *month*, *day*, and *year*. For example, the SAS statements

```
data a;
   m=8;
   d=27;
   y=47;
   birthday=mdy(m,d,y);
   put birthday= date7.;
```

produce the line

```
BIRTHDAY=27AUG47
```

Note that this result is printed as a SAS date value (number of days from 01JAN60) unless a date format is specified.

See **USING SAS DATE, TIME, AND DATETIME INFORMATS AND FORMATS** in Chapter 13, "SAS Informats and Formats," for a discussion of date and time values, informats, formats, and literals.

MEAN: computes the arithmetic mean (average)

```
mean(argument,argument, ...)
```

The *arguments* for this function must be numeric values. One or more nonmissing values are required. The function results in the average of the values of the nonmissing arguments.

The examples

```
x=mean(2,.,.,6);
x=mean(1,2,3,2);
```

return the results 4 and 2, respectively.

You can use an abbreviated argument list preceded by OF.

See Chapter 1, "SAS Elementary Statistics Procedures," in the *SAS Procedures Guide, Release 6.03 Edition* for a definition of this statistic.

MIN: returns the smallest value

```
min(argument,argument, ...)
```

The *arguments* for this function must be numeric values. Two or more nonmissing values are required. The result is the smallest value among the nonmissing values of the arguments.

For the examples

```
x=min(2,.,6);
x=min(2,-3,1,-1);
x=min(0,4);
```

the values returned are 2, −3, and 0, respectively.

You can use an abbreviated argument list preceded by OF.

See Chapter 1, "SAS Elementary Statistics Procedures," in the *SAS Procedures Guide, Release 6.03 Edition* for a definition of this statistic. Note that the MIN function does not necessarily return the same value as the MIN operator described in Chapter 3, "SAS Expressions."

MINUTE: returns the minute from a SAS time or datetime value or literal

```
minute(time)
minute(datetime)
```

The MINUTE function operates on a SAS *time* or *datetime* value or SAS time or datetime literal to produce a numeric value containing the minute. For example, the statements:

```
data a;
   time='3:19:24'T;
   m=minute(time);
   put m=;
```

produce the line

```
M=19
```

See **USING SAS DATE, TIME, AND DATETIME INFORMATS AND FORMATS** in Chapter 13, "SAS Informats and Formats," for a discussion of date and time values, informats, formats, and literals.

MOD: calculates the remainder

```
mod(argument1,argument2)
```

The result of this function is the remainder when the quotient of *argument1* divided by *argument2* is calculated.

Examples:

```
data;
   x=mod(6,3);
   put x;
run;
```

returns the value 0.

```
x=mod(10,3);
```

returns the value 1.

```
x=mod(11,3.5);
```

returns the value .5.

```
x=mod(10,-3);
```

returns the value 1.

MONTH: returns the month from a SAS date value or literal

```
month(date)
```

The MONTH function operates on a SAS *date* value or date literal to produce a numeric value containing the month. For example, the statements

```
data a;
   date='25DEC79'd;
   m=month(date);
   put m=;
```

produce the line

```
M=12
```

See **USING SAS DATE, TIME, AND DATETIME INFORMATS AND FORMATS** in Chapter 13, "SAS Informats and Formats," for a discussion of date and time values, informats, formats, and literals.

MORT: calculates mortgage loans

`mort(amount,payment,rate,number)`

This function calculates parameters for a mortgage loan with equal periodic payments and a fixed interest rate compounded each period. The formula relating the MORT arguments is

$$P = \frac{R A (1 + R)^N}{(1 + R)^N - 1}$$

where P is the payment, R is the rate, A is the loan amount, and N is the number of payments. The function calculates any one of the four parameters for a mortgage loan, given the other three.

The arguments are as follows:

- *amount* the amount borrowed
- *payment* the periodic payments
- *rate* the interest rate per period expressed as a fraction, not as a percentage (see the COMPOUND function earlier in this chapter)
- *number* the number of payments.

To use the MORT function, specify values for any three of the arguments and a missing value for the remaining argument. The function calculates the missing argument. The arguments must be listed in the order shown in the form example above. No adjustment is made to convert the results to round numbers.

Suppose that you want to borrow $50,000 for thirty years at an annual interest rate of 10% compounded monthly. You can use the function in a DATA step to determine the monthly payment:

```
data loan;
   payment=mort(50000, . ,.10/12,30*12);
   put payment=;
```

The *payment* argument is missing because that is the parameter of the mortgage that is to be computed. The value of PAYMENT is 438.7858.

Note that the interest rate and number of payments must correspond to the period of compounding; therefore, in the example above, the annual rate is divided by 12, and the number of years is multiplied by 12.

N: reports the number of nonmissing arguments

`n(argument,argument, ...)`

The *arguments* for this function must be numeric values. At least one argument is required. The function returns the number of nonmissing arguments.

For the example

`x=n(1,0,.,2,5,.);`

the value returned is 4.

You can use an abbreviated argument list preceded by OF.

See Chapter 1, "SAS Elementary Statistics Procedures," in the *SAS Procedures Guide, Release 6.03 Edition* for a definition of this statistic.

NETPV: calculates net present value as a fraction

```
netpv(rate,period,cash0,cash1,...,cashn)
```

The NETPV function calculates the net present value for a set of cash flows given in *cash0, cash1, ..., cashn*. The interest rate is specified by *rate*, and the number of cash flows per interest period is specified by *period*. The value of *period* should correspond to the units of the *cash* and *rate* arguments. For example, if the cash flows are monthly and a yearly interest rate is specified, *period* should be 12. If the value specified for *period* is 0, continuous compounding is assumed. Note that *rate* is specified as a fraction, not a percentage.

All arguments must be numeric. If either the *rate* or *period* argument is missing, a missing value is returned. However, if some of the cash flows are missing, the net present value is calculated ignoring the missing cash flow values.

To illustrate, assume an initial investment of $500 returns payments of $200, $300, and $200 over the succeeding three periods and a discount rate of 10% per period. The net present value of the investment is computed using the following statements:

```
data asset;
   value=netpv(.10,1,-500,200,300,200);
   put value=;
```

The net present value of the investment is 80.0150.

Computational Details

The net present value is calculated as $\Sigma a_i x^i$, where $x = 1/(1 + rate)^{(1/p)}$ and p is *period*. If the *period* argument is 0, the net present value is computed as $\Sigma a_i x^i$, where $x = \exp(-rate)$.

NMISS: reports the number of missing values

```
nmiss(argument,argument,...)
```

The *arguments* for this function must be numeric values. At least one argument is required. The function gives the number of missing values in a string of arguments.

The example

```
x=nmiss(1,10,3,.);
```

returns the value 1. You can use an abbreviated argument list preceded by OF.

See Chapter 1, "SAS Elementary Statistics Procedures," in the *SAS Procedures Guide, Release 6.03 Edition* for a definition of this statistic.

NORMAL: generates a normally distributed pseudo-random variate

```
normal(seed)
```

82 Chapter 4

The *seed* for this function must be a numeric value. It should be either zero (0) or a five-, six-, or seven-digit odd integer. The result is a pseudo-random variate; the variates generated by NORMAL appear to be normally distributed with a mean of 0 and a standard deviation of 1.

The *seed* is used only the first time the function is evaluated. Each subsequent time the function is evaluated, the result of the last evaluation is used in generating the new variate. If *seed* is 0, SAS uses a reading of the time of day from the computer's clock to generate the first variate. Otherwise, the constant specified is used to generate the first variate. An expression

```
x=m+s*normal(seed)
```

can produce variates with mean M and standard deviation S.

The NORMAL function uses a central limit theorem approximation

$$x = \Sigma_{i=1}^{12} u_i - 6$$

where the u_i are produced with the UNIFORM function. (See the RANNOR function for a better generator.)

NPV: calculates net present value with rate expressed as a percentage

```
npv(rate,period,cash0,cash1,...,cashn)
```

This function is identical to NETPV, described above, except that the rate of return is entered as a percentage.

POISSON: probability values for the Poisson distribution

```
poisson(lambda,n)
```

where

$0 \leq lambda$ and $0 \leq n$.

This function returns the probability that an observation from a Poisson distribution is less than or equal to *n*. Lambda is the value of the mean parameter. A single term of the Poisson distribution may be computed as a difference of two values of the cumulative distribution. If x=POISSON(lambda,n) then

$$p = \Sigma_{j=0}^{n} e^{-\lambda}(\lambda^j/j!) \quad .$$

Example:

```
data;
   p=poisson(1,2);
   put p;
run;
```

results in the value .9197.

PROBBETA: probability values from a beta distribution

```
probbeta(x,a,b)
```

where

$0 \leq x \leq 1$ and $0 < a,b$.

This function returns probability values from a beta distribution. The a and b values are the shape parameters of the beta distribution, and x is the value at which the distribution is to be evaluated. The density is

$$x^{a-1}(1-x)^{b-1}\Gamma(a+b)/\Gamma(a)\Gamma(b) \quad .$$

The incomplete beta function can be obtained from this function by multiplying the beta probability by values of the complete beta function, which can be computed from the GAMMA function.

This function is related to many of the common distributions of statistics and also has applications in analyzing order statistics (see Michael and Schucany 1979).

PROBBNML: probability values from a binomial distribution

```
probbnml(p,n,m)
```

where

$0 \leq p \leq 1$, $1 \leq n$, $0 \leq m \leq n$.

This function returns the probability that an observation from a binomial distribution with parameters p and n is less than or equal to m. The binomial probability parameter is p, and n is the degree of the binomial distribution. A single term in the binomial distribution can be obtained as the difference of two values of the cumulative binomial distribution.

If

```
p=probbnml(p,n,m)
```

then

$$P = \Sigma_{j=0}^{m} \binom{n}{j} p^j (1-p)^{n-j} \quad .$$

Example:

```
data;
    p=probbnml(.5,10,4);
    put p;
run;
```

results in the value .37695.

PROBCHI: computes probability values for the chi-square distributions

```
probchi(x,df,nc)
```

The PROBCHI function computes the probability that a random variable with a chi-square distribution, with df degrees of freedom, falls below the x value given. This function accepts noninteger degrees of freedom. If the optional third argument is not specified or has the value zero, the central distribution is computed. Otherwise, the nc parameter gives the noncentrality value, and the noncentral chi-square distribution is computed. The noncentral chi-square probability function is derived from the functions contributed by Hardison, Quade, and Langston (1983).

For example

```
p=1-probchi(31.264,11);
```

returns the value .001.

PROBF: the probability for the F distribution

`probf(x,ndf,ddf,nc)`

The PROBF function computes the probability that a random variable with an F distribution, with *ndf* numerator degrees of freedom and *ddf* denominator degrees of freedom, falls below the *x* value given. This function accepts noninteger degrees of freedom. If the optional fourth argument is not specified or has the value zero, the central distribution is computed. Otherwise, the *nc* parameter gives the noncentrality parameter to use in computing the noncentral F distribution. The noncentral F probability function is also derived from the functions contributed by Hardison, Quade, and Langston. To find the significance level, use

`1-probf(x,ndf,ddf)` .

For example,

`p=1-probf(3.32,2,30);`

returns the value 0.04982954.

PROBGAM: probability values for the gamma distribution

`probgam(x,a)`

The PROBGAM function computes the probability that a random variable with a gamma distribution with shape parameter η falls below the *x* value given. The GAMINV function is the inverse of the PROBGAM function.

The density is

$$x^{\eta-1}e^{-x}/\Gamma(\eta)$$

where

η is the shape parameter.

PROBHYPR: probabilities from a hypergeometric distribution

`probhypr(nn,k,n,x,or)`

where

$1 \leq nn$
$0 \leq k \leq nn$
$0 \leq n \leq nn$
$MAX(0,k+n-nn) \leq x \leq MIN(k,n)$.

This function returns the probability that an observation from a hypergeometric distribution with a total sample *nn*, margins *n* and *k*, and odds ratio *or* is less than or equal to *x*. Zero is a valid value for the margin *k*, which forces the value of *x* to also be zero, resulting in a returned value of 1 regardless of any other values.

If you omit the *or* argument, its value is assumed to be 1.

Example:

```
data;
    x=probhypr(10,5,3,2);
    put x;
run;
```

results in a value of .9167.

```
x=probhypr(10,5,3,2,1.5);
```

results in a value of .8541.

A common use of the PROBHYPR function is for computing the probability of randomly selecting an object in a subgroup, which has a hypergeomeric distribution, from a larger group. For example, if you are sampling from a population of nn objects, k of which are defective, a sample of n is drawn from the population. There are x defective in the sample, and they have a hypergeometric distribution. The default for ratio is 1 and leads to the usual hypergeometric distribution.

PROBIT: inverse normal distribution function

```
probit(argument)
```

This function is the inverse of the standard normal cumulative distribution function. The value of argument should be between 0 and 1. The result will be truncated, if necessary, to lie between -5 and $+5$. PROBIT is the function inverse of PROBNORM. If X is a normally distributed random variable with mean 0 and standard deviation 1, then z is the probability that X will take on a value less than PROBIT(z).

Example:

```
data;
    x=probit(.025);
    put x;
run;
```

results in a value of -1.96.

PROBNEGB: probability values for the negative binomial distribution

```
probnegb(p,n,m)
```

where

$0 \leq p \leq 1$, $0 < n$, and $0 \leq m$.

This function returns the probability that an observation from a negative binomial distribution with parameters p and n is less than or equal to m. The binomial probability parameter is p, and n is the degree of the negative binomial distribution. The value of a single term in the negative binomial distribution can be obtained by a difference of two values of the cumulative distribution.

If X=PROBNEGB(p,n,m) then:

$$X = \Sigma_{j=0}^{m}(1-p)^{j}p^{n}(n+j-1)!/((n-1)!j!)$$

Example:

```
data;
   x=probnegb(.5,2,1);
   put x;
run;
```

results in a value of .5.

PROBNORM: computes probabilities for normal distributions

`probnorm(x)`

The PROBNORM function computes the probability that a random variable with a normal (0,1) distribution falls below the x value given. This function is equivalent to

`.5+.5*erf(x/sqrt(2))`   .

The PROBIT function is the function inverse of PROBNORM.
Examples:

```
data;
   x=probnorm(0);
   put x;
run;
```

results in a value of .5.

`x=probnorm(1.96);`

results in a value of .975.

PROBT: the probability for the *t* distribution function

`probt(x,df,nc)`

The PROBT function computes the probability that a random variable with a student's *t* distribution with *df* degrees of freedom falls below the *x* value given. This function accepts noninteger degrees of freedom. The third argument is optional, and if it is omitted or is zero, the central *t* distribution is computed. Otherwise, the third argument is the noncentrality value for the noncentral *t* distribution. The noncentral *t* probability function is derived from the functions contributed by Hardison, Quade, and Langston (1983). For a two-tailed test, compute the significance level by

(1−PROBT(ABS(x),DF))*2   .

Example:

```
data;
   x=probt(.9,5);
   put x;
run;
```

results in a value of 0.795.

PUT: specifies an output format for a value

`put(argument,format)`

This function allows you to "write" *argument* with the format specified in the second argument. The format must be the same TYPE as the first argument. The result of the PUT function is **always** a character string. This is useful for converting a numeric value to a character value, or for changing the character format assigned to a variable or value.

For example, this statement converts the values of a numeric variable CC containing completion codes into the three-character hex representation of the codes:

```
cchex=put(cc,hex3.);
```

CCHEX's value is the same as the characters that would be written with the statement

```
put cc hex3.;
```

If the first argument is a numeric variable, the resulting string is right-aligned. If the first argument is a character variable, the result is left-aligned.

QTR: returns the quarter from a SAS date value or literal

```
qtr(date)
```

The QTR function returns a value of 1, 2, 3, or 4 from a SAS *date* value or date literal to indicate the quarter in which a date value falls.

Examples:

```
qtr(3005) = 1
qtr('20JAN82'd) = 1
```

RANBIN: generates an observation from a binomial distribution with parameters *n* and *p*

```
ranbin(seed,n,p)
```

where

$n>0$ integer, and $0<p<1$.

For any numeric *seed* value (see **Notes on Random Number Functions** earlier in this chapter for a complete discussion of *seed*) the RANBIN function generates an observation of a binomial variate with mean np and variance $np(1-p)$. If $n \leq 50$, the inverse transform method is applied to a RANUNI uniform deviate. If $n>50$, the normal approximation to the binomial distribution is used. In this case, the normal deviate is generated using the Box-Muller transformation of RANUNI uniform deviates.

The CALL RANBIN subroutine, an alternative to the RANBIN function, gives you greater control of the seed and random number streams. For more information on the use of CALL RANBIN, see **Notes on Random Number Functions** earlier in this chapter.

RANCAU: generates a Cauchy deviate

```
rancau(seed)
```

For any numeric *seed* value (see **Notes on Random Number Functions** for a complete discussion of *seed*) the RANCAU function generates an observation of a Cauchy random variable with location parameter 0 and scale parameter 1. An acceptance-rejection procedure and RANUNI uniform deviates are used for generation. The technique relies on the fact that if u and v are independent uniform $(-1/2, 1/2)$ variables and $u^2+v^2 \leq 1/4$ then u/v is a Cauchy deviate.

If

```
x=alpha+beta*rancau(seed)
```

then X is a *Cauchy variate* with location parameter ALPHA and scale parameter BETA.

The CALL RANCAU subroutine, an alternative to the RANCAU function, gives you greater control of the seed and random number streams. For details on the use of CALL RANCAU, see **Notes on Random Number Functions**.

RANEXP: generates an exponential deviate

```
ranexp(seed)
```

For any numeric *seed* value (see **Notes on Random Number Functions** for a complete discussion of *seed*) the RANEXP function generates an observation of an exponential variate with parameter 1. The inverse transform method applied to a RANUNI uniform deviate is used for generation.

If

```
x=ranexp(seed)/lambda
```

then X is an *exponential variate* with parameter LAMBDA.

If

```
x=alpha-beta*log(ranexp(seed))
```

then X is an an *extreme value variate* with location parameter ALPHA and scale parameter BETA.

If

```
x=floor(-ranexp(seed)/log(1-p))
```

then X is a *geometric variate* with parameter P.

The CALL RANEXP subroutine, an alternative to the RANEXP function, gives you greater control of the seed and random number streams. For details on the use of CALL RANEXP, see **Notes on Random Number Functions** earlier in this chapter.

RANGAM: generates an observation from a gamma distribution with shape parameter *alpha*

```
rangam(seed,alpha)
```

where

alpha>0 .

For any numeric *seed* value (see **Notes on Random Number Functions** for a complete discussion of *seed*) the RANGAM function generates an observation from a gamma distribution with density function

$$f(x) = x^{\alpha-1} e^{-x} / \Gamma(\alpha)$$

where $\alpha > 0$, and $x > 0$.

A combination of techniques is used in generating an observation. For a noninteger *alpha*, two independent gamma variates are generated: one with parameter INT(*alpha*), which is the integer part of *alpha*, and the other with parameter *alpha*−INT(*alpha*). The sum of the gamma variates has the desired distribution. For integer *alpha*, only the first of these need be generated. The inverse transformation of a RANUNI uniform deviate is used to generate the gamma variate with parameter INT(*alpha*) and an acceptance-rejection method is used to generate the other gamma variate (Fishman 1978). To expedite execution, internal variables used in generation are calculated only on initial calls (that is, with each new *alpha*).

If

```
x=beta*rangam(seed,alpha)
```

then X is a *gamma variate* with shape parameter ALPHA and scale parameter BETA.

If 2*ALPHA is an integer, and

```
x=2*rangam(seed,alpha)
```

then X is a *chi-square variate* with 2*ALPHA degrees of freedom.

If

```
x=beta*rangam(seed,n)
```

where N is a positive integer, then X is an *Erlang variate*. It has the distribution of the sum of N independent exponential variates whose means are BETA.

If

```
y1=rangam(seed,alpha)
y2=rangam(seed,beta)
x=y1/(y1+y2)
```

then X is a *beta variate* with parameters ALPHA and BETA, and density function

$$f(x) = \Gamma(\alpha + \beta)/\Gamma(\alpha)\Gamma(\beta)x^{\alpha - 1}(1 - x)^{\beta - 1}$$

where

$0 \leq x \leq 1$ and $\alpha, \beta > 0$.

The CALL RANGAM subroutine, an alternative to the RANGAM function, gives you greater control of the seed and random number streams. For details on CALL RANGAM, see **Notes on Random Number Functions** earlier in this chapter.

RANGE: reports the range of values

```
range(argument,argument, ...)
```

The *arguments* for this function must be numeric values. The function requires two or more arguments. The result is the range of the values of the nonmissing arguments.

For example

```
x=range(2,6,3);
```

or

```
x=range(2,6,3,.);
```

return the result 4.

You can use an abbreviated argument list preceded by OF.

See Chapter 1, "SAS Elementary Statistics Procedures," in the *SAS Procedures Guide, Release 6.03 Edition* for a definition of this statistic.

RANK: returns the position of a character in the ASCII collating sequence

```
rank(x)
```

The RANK function returns an integer that is x's position within the ASCII collating sequence. For example, the statement:

```
n = rank('A');
```

returns the value 65 for N.

RANNOR: generates a normal deviate

```
rannor(seed)
```

For any numeric *seed* value (see **Notes on Random Number Functions** for a complete discussion of *seed*) the RANNOR function generates an observation of a normal random variable with mean 0 and variance 1. The Box-Muller transformation of RANUNI uniform deviates is used for generation.
  If

```
x=mu+sqrt(sigmasq)*rannor(seed)
```

then X is a *normal variate* with mean MU and variance SIGMASQ.
  If

```
x=exp(mu+sqrt(sigmasq)*rannor(seed))
```

then X is a *lognormal variate* with mean

```
exp(mu+sigmasq/2)
```

and variance

```
exp(2*mu+sigmasq)*(exp(sigmasq)-1)   .
```

The CALL RANNOR subroutine, an alternative to the RANNOR function, gives you greater control of the seed and random number streams. For details on the use of CALL RANNOR, see **Notes on Random Number Functions**, earlier in this chapter.

RANPOI: generates an observation from a Poisson distribution with parameter *lambda*

```
ranpoi(seed,lambda)
```

where

```
lambda>0   .
```

For any numeric *seed* value (see **Notes on Random Number Functions** for a complete discussion of *seed*) the RANPOI function generates an observation of a Poisson variate. The inverse transform method applied to a RANUNI uniform deviate is the generating technique. The method for inverting the cumulative distribution function varies with the value of the parameter *lambda*. For a noninteger *lambda*, two independent Poisson variates are generated: one with parameter INT(*lambda*), which is the integer part of *lambda*, and the other with parameter *lambda* −INT(*lambda*). The sum of the Poisson variates is returned (Fishman 1976). For integer *lambda*, only the first of these need be generated. To expedite execution, internal variables used in generation are calculated only on initial calls (that is, with each new *lambda*).

  The CALL RANPOI subroutine, an alternative to the RANPOI function, gives you greater control of the seed and random number streams. For details on the use of CALL RANPOI, see **Notes on Random Number Functions** earlier in this chapter.

RANTBL: generates deviates from a tabled probability mass function

```
rantbl(seed,p₁,...pᵢ,...,pₙ)
```

where

$0 \leq p_i \leq 1$ for $0 < i \leq n$.

For any numeric *seed* value (see **Notes on Random Number Functions** for a complete discussion of *seed*) the RANTBL function returns an observation generated from the probability mass function defined by p_1 through p_n. In particular

RANTBL = 1 with probability p_1
2 with probability p_2
.
.
.
n with probability p_n .

The inverse transform method applied to a RANUNI uniform deviate is used in generation.

Note: if you execute

```
x=rantbl(seed,p1,...,pn);
if x=1 then x=m1;
else if x=2 then x=m2;
      .      .
      .      .
      .      .
else if a=n then x=mn;
```

then X takes the values M1 through M*n* with probabilities P1 through P*n*, respectively.

The CALL RANTBL subroutine, an alternative to the RANTBL function, gives you greater control of the seed and random number streams. For details on the use of CALL RANPOI, see **Notes on Random Number Functions** earlier in this chapter.

RANTRI: generates an observation from the triangular distribution with parameter *h*

```
rantri(seed,h)
```

where

$0 < h < 1$.

For any numeric *seed* value (see **Notes on Random Number Functions** for a complete discussion of *seed*) the RANTRI function returns an observation generated from the triangular distribution with density function

$f(x) = 2x/h$

if

$0 \leq x \leq h$

and

$f(x) = 2(1 - x)/(1 - h)$

if

$h < x \leq 1$.

92 Chapter 4

The inverse transform method applied to a RANUNI uniform deviate is used for generation.

If you execute

```
x=(b-a)*rantri(seed,(c-a)/(b-a))+a;
```

then X has a triangular distribution on the interval [A,B] with mode C ε [A,B].

The CALL RANTRI subroutine, an alternative to the RANTRI function, gives you greater control of the seed and random number streams. For details on the use of CALL RANTRI, see **Notes on Random Number Functions** earlier in this chapter.

RANUNI: generates a uniform deviate

```
ranuni(seed)
```

For any numeric *seed* value (see **Notes on Random Number Functions** for a complete discussion of *seed*) the RANUNI function returns a number generated from the uniform distribution on the interval (0,1) using a prime modulus multiplicative generator with modulus $2^{31}-1$ and multiplier 397204094 (Fishman and Moore 1982). The *seed* must be a numeric constant less than $2^{31}-1$.

REPEAT: repeats a character expression

```
repeat(argument1,n)
```

The REPEAT function returns a character value consisting of the first argument repeated *n* times. Thus, the first argument appears *n+1* times in the result. For example, the statement

```
x=repeat('ONE',2);
```

gives the value ONEONEONE.

REVERSE: reverses a character expression

```
reverse(argument)
```

The REVERSE function returns the argument's characters in reverse order. Trailing blanks are retained and therefore the argument's length does not change. For example,

```
backward=reverse('abc  ');
```

gives BACKWARD the value ' cba'.

RIGHT: right-aligns a character expression

```
right(argument)
```

The RIGHT function returns the argument with trailing blanks moved to the beginning of the value. The character expression's length does not change. For example, the statements

```
a='HI THERE   ';
b=right(a);
```

give B the value '   HI THERE'.

ROUND: rounds a value to nearest roundoff unit

   round(*argument,roundoffunit*)

The ROUND function rounds a value to the nearest roundoff unit.
  Examples:

```
data;
   x=round(223.456,1);
   put x;
run;
```

results in a value of 223.

   x=round(223.456,.01);

results in a value of 223.46.

   x=round(223.456,100);

results in a value of 200.

   x=round(223.456);

results in a value of 223.

The value of the *roundoffunit* must be greater than zero. If the *roundoffunit* is omitted, a value of 1 is used and *argument* is rounded to the nearest integer.

SAVING: calculates future value of periodic saving

   saving(*future,payment,rate,number*)

Suppose that you invest a fixed amount every period for a number of periods. The SAVING function computes any of the four parameters of the periodic savings given the other three. The formula relating the arguments is

$$F = \frac{P(1 + R)((1 + R)^N - 1)}{R}$$

where F is the future value, P is the payment, R is the interest rate, and N is the number of payments. The arguments are as follows:

future	the future value after *number* of periods
payment	the periodic payments
rate	the interest rate per period expressed as a fraction, not as a percentage
number	the number of periods.

To use this function, specify values for any three of the arguments and a missing value for the remaining argument. The function calculates the missing argument. The result is not rounded.

For example, you deposit $100 a month into a savings account that pays monthly interest on a 5% annual basis. You want to know how many months it will take to save $12,000. This is computed using the following statements:

```
data account;
   number=saving(12000,100,.05/12, . );
   put number=;
```

The value returned is 97.1813 months.

SCAN: returns a given word from a character expression

```
scan(argument1,n,delimiters)
scan(argument1,n)
```

SCAN separates the first argument, a character expression, into "words" and returns the *n*th word. The *delimiters* are characters defined as separators between words. If the *delimiters* argument is not specified, the following characters are default *delimiters*:

blank . < (+ & ! $ *) ; ^ - / , % | > \

The statements

```
arg='ABC.DEF(X=Y)';
word=scan(arg,3);
```

give WORD the value X=Y, the third "word" in the character expression, ARG. The following statement shows another way to accomplish the same thing:

```
word=scan('AB?DEF?X=Y?',3,'?');
```

Notice that in the above statement the first argument is a character literal, rather than a variable, and that the third argument specifies a question mark (?) as the delimiter. The character chosen for the delimiter argument must be enclosed in quotes.

Leading delimiters before the first word have no effect. If there are two or more contiguous delimiters, they are treated as one. If there are fewer than *n* words in the first argument, SCAN returns a blank value.

SECOND: returns the second from a SAS time or datetime value or literal

```
second(time)
second(datetime)
```

The SECOND function operates on a SAS *time* or *datetime* value or a SAS time or datetime literal to produce a numeric value containing the seconds part of the value. For example, the statements

```
data a;
   time='3:19:24'dt;
   s=second(time);
   put s=;
```

produce

S=24

See **USING SAS DATE, TIME, AND DATETIME INFORMATS AND FORMATS** in Chapter 13, "SAS Informats and Formats," for a discussion of date and time values, informats, formats, and literals.

SIGN: returns the sign of a value

```
sign(x)
```

The SIGN function, also known as the signum function, returns a value of -1 if $x<0$; a value of 0 if $x=0$; and a value of $+1$ if $x>0$. This action is similar to $x/ABS(x)$.

SIN: trigonometric sine

```
sin(argument)
```

The *argument* for this function must be a numeric value. The function results in the sine of the value of the argument. The value of the argument is assumed to be in radians.

The examples

```
x=sin(.5);
x=sin(0);
x=sin(3.14159/4);
```

return the values 0.4794255, 0, and 0.7071063, respectively.

SINH: hyperbolic sine

```
sinh(argument)
```

The *argument* for this function must be a numeric value. The result is the hyperbolic sine of the value of the *argument*. It is equivalent to:

```
(exp(argument)-exp(-argument))/2   .
```

For example,

```
x=sinh(0);
```

returns the result 0.

SKEWNESS: gives the skewness

```
skewness(argument, argument, argument,...)
```

The *arguments* for this function must be numeric values. More than two arguments are required. The result of this function is a measure of the skewness of the nonmissing argument values.

For the examples

```
x=skewness(0,1,1);  or  x=skewness(0,.,1,1);
```

and

```
x=skewness(2,4,6,3,1);
```

the values returned are −1.73205 and 0.5901287, respectively. You can use an abbreviated argument list preceded by OF.

See Chapter 1, "SAS Elementary Statistics Procedures," in the *SAS Procedures Guide, Release 6.03 Edition* for a definition of this statistic.

SOUND: generates a sound

```
call sound (freq, dur);
```

where *freq* is the desired frequency (in cycles per second), and *dur* is the desired duration (in 1/80ths of a second).

The SOUND function generates a sound of the desired frequency and duration. The frequency (in cycles per second) must be 20≤*freq*≥20000, and the duration is in 1/80ths of a second. For example, the statement:

```
call sound(523, 160);
```

produces a tone of frequency 523 cycles per second (middle C) lasting two seconds.

SQRT: returns the square root of a value

    `sqrt(argument)`

The result of the SQRT function is the square root of the value of *argument*. The value of *argument* must be nonnegative. For example, if you specify

    `x=sqrt(25);`

the value returned is 5.

STD: calculates the standard deviation

    `std(argument,argument, ...)`

The *arguments* for this function must be numeric values. At least two arguments must be provided. The function gives the standard deviation of the values of the nonmissing arguments.

    The examples

    `x=std(2,6);` or `x=std(2,6,.);`

and

    `x=std(2,4,6,3,1);`

return the values 2.828427 and 1.923538, respectively.

    You can use an abbreviated argument list preceded by OF.

    See Chapter 1, "SAS Elementary Statistics Procedures," in the *SAS Procedures Guide, Release 6.03 Edition* for a definition of this statistic.

STDERR: calculates the standard error of the mean

    `stderr(argument,argument,...)`

The *arguments* for this function must be numeric values. At least two nonmissing values are required. The function results in the standard error of the mean of the nonmissing values of the arguments.

    For example,

    `x=stderr(2,6,3,4);`

or

    `x=stderr(2,6,.,3,4);`

returns the result 0.8539126.

    You can use an abbreviated argument list preceded by OF.

    See Chapter 1, "SAS Elementary Statistics Procedures," in the *SAS Procedures Guide, Release 6.03 Edition* for a definition of this statistic.

STFIPS: converts state postal code to FIPS state code

    `stfips(postalcode)`

The STFIPS function takes a two-character state postal code (enclosed in quotes) and converts it to the corresponding numeric FIPS state code.

    Example:

    `fips=stfips ('NC');`
    `put fips=;`

produces

    `FIPS=37`

STNAME: converts state postal code to state name (all uppercase)

```
stname(postalcode)
```

The STNAME function takes a two-character state postal code (enclosed in quotes) and returns the corresponding twenty-character state name in uppercase.
  For example,

```
state=stname('NC');
put state=;
```

produces

```
STATE=NORTH CAROLINA
```

STNAMEL: converts state postal code to state name in upper- and lowercase

```
stnamel(postalcode)
```

The STNAMEL function takes a two-character state postal code (enclosed in quotes) and returns the corresponding twenty-character state name in upper- and lowercase. For example,

```
state=stnamel('NC');
put 'STATE=' state;
```

results in the value

```
STATE=North Carolina
```

SUBSTR: a dual function: substring and pseudo-variable for character insertion

The SUBSTR function serves two different purposes. They are described below.

Substring

```
substr(argument1,position,n)
```

When the SUBSTR function is used on the right side of an equal sign (=), it extracts from *argument1* a substring that is *n* characters long, beginning with the character specified by *position*. If *n* is omitted, the substring consists of the remainder of *argument*, beginning with the character specified by *position*.
  For example, the statements

```
data a;
   date='06MAY85';
   month=substr(date,3,3);
   year=substr(date,6,2);
```

produce the value MAY for MONTH and the value 85 for YEAR.
  When the SUBSTR function is on the right side of an equal sign, any of the arguments can be literal, derived, or variable character expressions.

98   Chapter 4

Pseudo-Variable For Character Insertion

When SUBSTR is used on the left side of an equal sign, it serves as a pseudo-variable function, replacing the contents of a character value.

```
substr(argument1,position,n)=x;
```

The value of the variable or constant on the right side of the equal sign is placed into the character variable specified by the first argument, starting with the character specified by *position*, and replacing the number of characters specified by *n*. Notice that the first argument **must** be a character variable. This restriction is an exception and applies only when SUBSTR is used as a pseudo-variable function. For example, the statements

```
a='KIDNAP';
substr(a,1,3)='CAT';
```

give A the value CATNAP.

If the *n* argument is omitted, characters in the first argument are replaced from *position* to the end of the first argument. In the following example, SUBSTR replaces characters from 'N', the position specified by the second argument, to the end of the character expression

```
a='CATNAP';
substr(a,4)='TY';
```

giving A the value CATTY.

SUM: calculates the sum of the arguments

```
sum(argument,argument, ...)
```

The *arguments* for this function must be numeric values. Two or more arguments are required. The result of the SUM function is the sum of the arguments.
For example,

```
x=sum(4,9,3,8);
```

returns the value 24.

You can use an abbreviated argument list preceded by OF.

See Chapter 1, "SAS Elementary Statistics Procedures," in the *SAS Procedures Guide, Release 6.03 Edition* for a definition of this statistic.

SYMGET: returns the value of a macro variable

```
symget(argument)
```

The SYMGET function returns the value of a macro variable identified by *argument*. The SAS macro facility is documented in the *SAS Guide to Macro Processing, Version 6 Edition*.

TAN: trigonometric tangent

```
tan(argument)
```

The *argument* for this function must be a numeric value. The function results in the tangent of the value of the argument. The value of the argument is assumed to be in radians; it may not be an odd multiple of $\pi/2$.
The examples

```
x=tan(.5);
x=tan(0);
x=tan(3.14159/3);
```

return the values 0.5463025, 0, and 1.732047, respectively.

TANH: hyperbolic tangent

    tanh(argument)

The *argument* for this function must be a numeric value. The result is the hyperbolic tangent of the value of the argument. It is equivalent to

    (exp(argument)-exp(-argument))

divided by

    (exp(argument)+exp(-argument)) .

For the examples

    x=tanh(-.5);
    x=tanh(0);

the values returned are -0.462117 and 0.

TIME: returns the current time of day

    time()

The TIME function produces the current time of day as a SAS time value. For example, the statements

    data a;
       current=time();
       put current= time.;

if executed at exactly 2:32 p.m., produce the line

    CURRENT=14:32:00

Refer also to the example for the HOUR function; it demonstrates the TIME function.

Note that unless a TIME. format is specified, the result is printed as a SAS time value (the number of seconds since 12:00 midnight).

See **USING SAS DATE, TIME, AND DATETIME INFORMATS AND FORMATS** in Chapter 13, "SAS Informats and Formats," for a discussion of date and time values, informats, formats, and literals.

TIMEPART: extracts the time part of a SAS datetime value or literal

    timepart(datetime)

The TIMEPART function converts a SAS *datetime* value or datetime literal into just the time part. For positive dates, the statement

    time=timepart(datetime);

is equivalent to

    time=mod(datetime,24*60*60);

For example, at 10:40:17 a.m., these statements

    datim=datetime();
    time=timepart(datim);
    put time= time.;

result in this line

    TIME=10:40:17

Note that the result is printed as a SAS time value (number of seconds since 12:00 midnight) unless a SAS time format is specified.

See **USING SAS DATE, TIME, AND DATETIME INFORMATS AND FORMATS** in Chapter 13, "SAS Informats and Formats," for a discussion of date and time values, informats, formats, and literals.

TINV: the quantile for the *t* distribution

```
tinv(p,df,nc)
```

where

$0<p<1, 0<df$.

The TINV function computes the quantile for the *t* distribution with degrees of freedom, *df*, and noncentrality parameter, *nc*. The quantile is such that the probability that an observation from this distribution is less than the quantile is *p*. If the optional parameter, *nc*, is not specified or is zero, the central distribution is used. Otherwise, the noncentral distribution is used. The parameter *df* does not have to be an integer. For values of *nc* large in absolute value, the algorithm used can fail. In these cases a missing value is returned. This function is derived from the functions contributed by Hardison, Quade, and Langston (1983).

Example:

```
data;
   q1=tinv(.95,2); put q1=;
   q2=tinv(.95,2.5,3); put q2=;
run;
```

results in

```
Q1=2.9200
Q2=11.034
```

TODAY: returns the current date as a SAS date value

```
today()
```

The TODAY function, which can also be written

```
date()
```

produces the current date as a SAS date value. For example, executing the statements below on January 20, 1985

```
data a;
   current=today();
   put current= date7.;
```

produces the line:

```
CURRENT=20JAN85
```

Note that unless you specify a date format, the result is printed as a SAS date value (the number of days since 01JAN60).

See **USING SAS DATE, TIME, AND DATETIME INFORMATS AND FORMATS** in Chapter 13, "SAS Informats and Formats," for a discussion of date and time values, informats, formats, and literals.

TRANSLATE: replaces specific characters in a character expression

`translate(argument1,to,from,...,to,from)`

Use the TRANSLATE function to replace any occurrence of a character(s) in the first *argument*, specified by *from*, with the character(s) specified by *to*. For example, the statement:

`x=translate('XYZW','AB','VW');`

gives X the value XYZB. TRANSLATE searches XYZW for the *from* characters, V and W, and finds a W. In this case, since W is the second character of the value VW, the second character of the value AB replaces W. Thus X's value becomes XYZB.

If the *to* value is shorter than the *from* value, the *to* value is padded with blanks. The result of this padding is that the "extra" *from* characters are converted to blanks. If the *to* value is longer than the *from* value, the *to* value is truncated on the right. Multiple *to* and *from* pairs can be specified.

TRIM: removes trailing blanks from a character expression

`trim(argument)`

The TRIM function returns the *argument* with trailing blanks removed. TRIM can be useful when concatenating because concatenation does not remove trailing blanks. For example, consider these statements:

```
data a;
   input first $ 1-10 last $ 12-25;
   name=trim(first)||' '||trim(last);
   cards;
JOHN      SMITH
;
```

NAME's value is 'JOHN SMITH'. (The quotes surrounding the blank between the concatenation symbols separate FIRST and LAST with a single blank.) If FIRST and LAST are concatenated without the TRIM function, as in the following statement

`name=first||last;`

NAME's value is 'JOHN   SMITH ', with six trailing blanks retained from FIRST and nine trailing blanks retained from LAST.

The length of the receiving variable is the same as that of the argument. That is, the variable returned by the TRIM function is padded with blanks to expand it to the argument's length. This is a problem only when you are doing nothing but trimming the argument. As you can see from the example above, when you are performing an additional operation such as concatenation, the length is not a problem. The following example illustrates this point:

```
first='John      ';
last='Smith';
m=first||last;
put m=;
l=trim(first)||' '||last;

put l=;
mm=length(m);
ll=length(l);
put mm= ll=;
```

The output produced is

```
M=John    Smith
L=John Smith
MM=13   LL=10
```

TRUNC: returns a *length* truncated numeric value

trunc(*number,length*)

The TRUNC function truncates a *number* to a *length* as requested and then expands the number back to full length. The truncation and subsequent expansion duplicate the effect of storing numbers in less than full length and then reading them.

For example, if the variable

x=1/5;

has been stored with a length of 3, then a comparison

if x=1/5 then...;

will fail, but the comparison

if x=trunc(1/5,3) then...;

will be true.

UNIFORM: generates a pseudo-random variate uniformly distributed on the interval (0,1)

uniform(*seed*)

The result of this function is a pseudo-random variate; the variates generated by UNIFORM appear to be uniformly distributed on the interval (0,1).

Seed must be a constant; either 0 or a five-, six-, or seven-digit odd integer. The seed is used only the first time the SAS System evaluates the function. Each subsequent time the function is evaluated, the result of the last evaluation is used in generating the new variate. If the seed is 0, SAS uses a reading of the time of day from the computer's clock to generate the first variate. Otherwise, the constant specified is used to generate the first variate.

UNIFORM is a multiplicative congruential generator with multiplier 16807, modulus 2^{31}, and a 64-value shuffle table to remove autocorrelation. The method used is documented in Lewis, Goodman, and Miller 1969; and Kennedy and Gentle 1980.

(See the RANUNI function for a better generator.)

UPCASE: converts all characters in the argument to uppercase

upcase(*argument*)

The UPCASE function converts all characters in the argument to uppercase. For example,

name=upcase('John B. Smith');

gives NAME the value 'JOHN B. SMITH'.

USS: calculates the uncorrected sum of squares

`uss(argument,argument,...)`

The *arguments* for this function must be numeric values. At least one argument is required. The result of the USS function is the uncorrected sum of squares of the nonmissing arguments.

For the examples

`x=uss(4,2,3.5,6);`

and

`x=uss(4,2,3.5,6,.);`

the value returned is 68.25.

You can use an abbreviated argument list preceded by OF.

See Chapter 1, "SAS Elementary Statistics Procedures," in the *SAS Procedures Guide, Release 6.03 Edition* for a definition of this statistic.

VAR: calculates the variance

`var(argument,argument...)`

The *arguments* for this function must be numeric values. At least two arguments are required. The VAR function calculates the variance of the nonmissing values of the arguments.

For the examples

`x=var(4,2,3.5,6);`

and

`x=var(4,2,3.5,6,.);`

the value returned is 2.729167.

You can use an abbreviated argument list preceded by OF.

See Chapter 1, "SAS Elementary Statistics Procedures," in the *SAS Procedures Guide, Release 6.03 Edition* for a definition of this statistic.

VERIFY: returns the position of the first character that is unique to the first argument.

`verify(argument1, argument2,...,argumentn)`

The VERIFY function returns the position of the first character in *argument1* that is not present in any of the other arguments. If all characters in the first argument are found in at least one of the arguments, VERIFY returns a 0. For example, consider these statements:

```
data a;
   check='ABCDE';
   input grade $ 1;
   x=verify(grade,check);
   if x ne 0 then put 'INVALID GRADE VALUE';
```

These statements read a character value from data lines and check that its characters are the letters A through E. If VERIFY finds any other characters, it prints a message on the log.

WEEKDAY: returns the day of the week from a SAS date or literal

```
weekday(date)
```

The WEEKDAY function converts a SAS *date* value or date literal into a number representing the day of the week, where 1=Sunday, 2=Monday, ..., 7=Saturday.

Example:

```
weekday('20JAN85'd) = 1
```

See **USING SAS DATE, TIME, AND DATETIME INFORMATS AND FORMATS** in Chapter 13, "SAS Informats and Formats," for a discussion of date and time values, informats, formats, and literals.

YEAR: returns the year from a SAS date value or literal

```
year(date)
```

The YEAR function operates on a SAS *date* value or date literal to produce a four-digit numeric value containing the year. For example, the statements

```
data a;
   date=mdy(12,25,84);
   y=year(date);
   put y=;
```

produce

```
Y=1984
```

See **USING SAS DATE, TIME, AND DATETIME INFORMATS AND FORMATS** in Chapter 13, "SAS Informats and Formats," for a discussion of date and time values, informats, formats, and literals.

YYQ: returns a SAS date value from the year and quarter

```
yyq(year,quarter)
```

The YYQ function returns a SAS date value corresponding to the first day of the specified quarter. The *year* value may be either a two- or four-digit year, the *quarter* value must be either 1, 2, 3, or 4. If either the year or quarter is missing, or if the quarter value is not 1, 2, 3, or 4, the result is missing.

For example, the statements

```
data dates;
   dv=yyq(85,3);
   put dv= date7.;
```

produce the line

```
DV=01JUL85
```

The result is printed as a SAS date value (number of days since 01JAN60) unless you specify a date format. See **USING SAS DATE, TIME, AND DATETIME INFORMATS AND FORMATS** in Chapter 13, "SAS Informats and Formats."

ZIPFIPS: converts ZIP code to FIPS state code

    zipfips(zipcode)

The ZIPFIPS function takes a five-character ZIP code (enclosed in quotes) and returns the corresponding numeric FIPS state code. For example, the statements

    fips=zipfips('27511');
    put 'FIPS=' fips;

produce

    FIPS=37

ZIPNAME: converts ZIP codes to state names (all uppercase)

    zipname(zipcode)

The ZIPNAME function takes a five-character ZIP code (enclosed in quotes) and returns the corresponding twenty-character state name in uppercase. For example, the statements

    state=zipname('27511');
    put 'STATE=' state;

result in the value

    STATE=NORTH CAROLINA

ZIPNAMEL: converts ZIP codes to state names in upper- and lowercase

    zipnamel(zipcode)

The ZIPNAMEL function takes a five-character ZIP code (enclosed in quotes) and returns the corresponding twenty-character state name in upper- and lowercase. For example, the statements

    state=zipnamel('27511');
    put 'STATE=' state;

produce

    STATE=North Carolina.

ZIPSTATE: converts ZIP codes to state postal codes

    zipstate(zipcode)

The ZIPSTATE function takes a five-character ZIP code (enclosed in quotes) and returns the corresponding two-character state postal code. For example, the statements

    st=zipstate('27511');
    put 'ST=' st;

produce

    ST=NC

REFERENCES

Abramowitz, M. and Stegun, I. (1964), *Handbook of Mathematical Functions with Formulas, Graphs, and Mathematical Tables,* National Bureau of Standards Applied Mathematics Series #55, Washington, D.C.: U.S. Government Printing Office.

Fishman, G.S. (1976), "Sampling from the Poisson Distribution on a Computer," *Computing,* 17, 145-156.

Fishman, G.S. (1978), *Principles of Discrete Event Simulation,* New York: John Wiley & Sons.

Fishman, G.S. and Moore, L.R. (1982), "A Statistical Evaluation of Multiplicative Congruential Generators with Modulus ($2^{31}-1$)," *Journal of the American Statistical Association,* 77, 129-136.

Hardison, C.D., Quade, D., and Langston, R.D. (1983), "Nine Functions for Probability Distributions," *SUGI Supplemental Library User's Guide, 1983 Edition.* Cary, NC: SAS Institute Inc.

Kennedy, W.S. and Gentle, J.E. (1980), *Statistical Computing,* New York: Marcel Dekker, Inc.

Lewis, P.A.W., Goodman, A.S., and Miller, J.M. (1969), "A Pseudo-Random Number Generator for the System/360," *IBM Systems Journal,* 8.

Michael, J. and Schucany, W. (1979), "A New Approach to Testing Goodness of Fit for Censored Data," *Technometrics,* 21, 435-441.

Chapter 5
SAS® Statements Used in the DATA Step

ABORT Statement   108
ARRAY Statement   109
Assignment Statement   122
ATTRIB Statement   124
BY Statement   125
CALL Statement   132
CARDS and CARDS4 Statements   134
DATA Statement   136
DELETE Statement   140
DISPLAY Statement   141
DO Statement   142
DROP Statement   148
END Statement   149
FILE Statement   150
FORMAT Statement   156
GO TO Statement   159
IF Statement   161
INFILE Statement   164
INFORMAT Statement   171
INPUT Statement   173
KEEP Statement   193
LABEL Statement   194
Labels, Statement   195
LENGTH Statement   196
LINK Statement   201
LIST Statement   204
LOSTCARD Statement   206
MERGE Statement   210
MISSING Statement   218
Null Statement   219
OUTPUT Statement   220
PUT Statement   223
RENAME Statement   235
RETAIN Statement   236
RETURN Statement   241
SELECT Statement   243
SET Statement   246
STOP Statement   253
Sum Statement   254
UPDATE Statement   256
WHERE Statement   260
WINDOW Statement   266

ABORT Statement

You can use the ABORT statement in a DATA step to cause the SAS System to cease executing the current DATA step and resume execution with the next DATA or PROC step. The SAS System may take additional action depending on the ABORT statement options you specify. When the ABORT statement is executed, SAS prints a message and creates a data set containing the observations that were processed before the ABORT statement was executed. However, if the new data set has the same name as an existing SAS data set, the existing data set is not replaced.

The form of the ABORT statement is

ABORT [ABEND [*n*] | RETURN [*n*]];

where

ABEND | RETURN   causes an immediate normal termination of the SAS job or session with the step code (condition code) indicating an error. A data set is created that includes all observations prior to the observation being processed when the ABORT statement executes.

n   returns a value of *n*, an integer, when specified following the ABEND or RETURN option. The value of *n* is returned to the operating system by SAS execution.

For example, if *n* is 255,

```
abort 255;
```

sets the step condition code to 255.

When both RETURN and *n* are specified, SAS normally terminates the job with the step return or condition code that you specify. For example,

```
abort return 16;
```

Before you perform extensive analysis on your data, you can use the ABORT statement to halt execution if the data are not error-free. For example,

```
data check;
   input ssn 1-9 paycode 11-13;
   if _error_ then abort;
   cards;
111222333 100
AAABBBCCC 200
444555666 300
;
```

The automatic variable _ERROR_ is set to 1 if errors occur in the data lines. If any errors are found, SAS stops processing observations. In this example the second data line contains invalid data for the variable SSN. When SAS reads this data line, it sets _ERROR_ to 1 and then executes the ABORT statement. Data set CHECK is created with one observation (however, if CHECK is to replace an existing SAS data set named CHECK, the existing data set is not replaced).

In Release 6.03, the RETURN and ABEND options are equivalent. However, in Version 5 SAS software, the RETURN and ABEND options produce different results. If you write programs for transfer to a machine using Version 5 SAS software, see the *SAS User's Guide: Basics, Version 5 Edition* for information on these options.

ARRAY Statement

Introduction 109
Explicitly Subscripted ARRAY Statement 109
   Referring to Explicitly Subscripted Array Elements 111
   Using Explicitly Subscripted Arrays with DO Groups 111
     Iterative DO groups 112
     DO WHILE and DO UNTIL groups 112
   Multidimensional Explicitly Subscripted Arrays 113
   Specifying Bounds for Explicitly Subscripted Arrays 114
Examples 115
   Example 1: Assigning Initial Values to an Array 115
   Example 2: Using _TEMPORARY_ Arrays 116
Implicitly Subscripted ARRAY Statement 117
   Referring to Implicit Array Elements 118
   Using Implicitly Subscripted Arrays with DO Groups 119
   Using Arrays as Elements of Other Arrays:
     Multidimensional Implicit Subscripting 120

Introduction

If you need to process many variables the same way, you can use the ARRAY statement to define the set of variables (either all numeric or all character) as elements of an array. When the array is referenced in SAS statements later in the DATA step, the SAS System substitutes one of the elements of the array for the array reference.

Explicitly Subscripted Array Statement

Explicitly subscripted arrays consist of an array name, a reference to the number of elements in the array, and a list of the elements. You refer to elements of the array by the array name and the element number (also called the *subscript*). Since you usually want to process more than one element in an array, arrays are often placed within iterative DO, DO WHILE, or DO UNTIL groups.

The form of the explicitly subscripted ARRAY statement is

ARRAY *arrayname*[{*n*}] [**$**] [*length*] [[*arrayelements*] [(*initialvalues*)]];

where

arrayname
   names the array. *Arrayname* must be a valid SAS name that is not the name of a SAS variable in the same DATA step.

{*n*}
   represents the number of elements in the array. *N* can be either a positive integer or an asterisk (*); enclose *n* in braces ({ }), brackets ([ ]), or parentheses ( ). You can use the asterisk to eliminate counting the number of elements in the array. You can also omit {*n*}. When *n* is a number, you can omit *arrayelements*. In that case, SAS creates variable names by concatenating the array name and the numbers 1, 2, 3, ... *n*. If a variable name in the series already exists, SAS uses that variable instead of creating a new one. When *n* is an asterisk, you must include *arrayelements*.

Here are examples of ARRAY statements with different numbers of elements:

```
array rain{5} janr febr marr aprr mayr;
array month{*} jan feb jul oct nov;
array x{*} _numeric_;
```

All arrays shown in these examples are one-dimensional arrays; that is, a single number is used as the subscript. In addition, the subscripts in these examples range from 1 to the number of elements in the array. See **Multidimensional Explicitly Subscripted Arrays** later in this section for information on arrays with more than one dimension, and see **Specifying Bounds for Explicitly Subscripted Arrays** for a discussion of subscripts with other ranges.

$

indicates that the elements in the array are character. The dollar sign is not necessary if the elements have been previously defined as character.

length

specifies the length of elements in the array that have not previously been assigned a length. See the **LENGTH Statement** later in this chapter for more information.

arrayelements

can be one of the following:

variables

a list of variable names or any type of SAS variable list.

TEMPORARY

creates a list of temporary data elements. Temporary data elements can be numeric or character and behave exactly like DATA step variables except that

- they do not have names; you must refer to them by the array name and subscript
- they do not appear in the output data set
- you cannot use the special subscript asterisk (*) to refer to all the elements.

You can arrange temporary data elements in dimensions just as you do variables (see **Multidimensional Explicitly Subscripted Arrays** later in this section). You can also assign the elements initial values (discussed below).

TEMPORARY arrays are useful when the only purpose for creating an array is to perform a calculation; to preserve the result of the calculation, assign it to a variable. Performing an operation on a _TEMPORARY_ array is often faster than performing it on an array composed of previously created variables because the temporary data elements are always contiguous in memory, whereas the previously created variables may or may not be contiguous. In addition, temporary data elements require less memory than do DATA step variables and therefore leave more memory available for use elsewhere by the SAS System.

initialvalues

gives a numeric or character initial value for the corresponding element in the array. Specify one or more initial values as the following:

(*initialvalue*[,] . . .)

Elements and values are matched by position. If there are more array elements than initial values, the remaining array elements receive missing values. Follow *arrayelements* with initial values enclosed in parentheses; separate the initial values with blanks or commas. The statement

```
array test(3) t1 t2 t3 (90 80 70);
```

assigns an initial value of 90 to variable T1, 80 to T2, and 70 to T3.
If you have not already specified the attributes of the elements in the array, giving a list of initial values causes the SAS System to assign attributes based on the first initial value.

Referring to Explicitly Subscripted Array Elements

You can use an array reference anywhere that you can write a SAS expression, including the following SAS statements:

- assignment
- DO WHILE(*condition*)
- DO UNTIL(*condition*)
- IF
- INPUT
- PUT
- SELECT
- WINDOW

You can also use array references in the arguments of SAS functions.

The ARRAY statement defining the array must appear in a DATA step before any references to that array. An array definition is only in effect for the duration of the DATA step. If you want to use the same array in several DATA steps, you must redefine the elements of the array in each step.

An array reference must contain the subscript. The subscript can be any valid SAS expression. Enclose the subscript in braces, brackets, or parentheses. You can use the special array subscript asterisk (*) to refer to all variables in an array in an INPUT or PUT statement or in the argument of a function; you cannot use the asterisk with _TEMPORARY_ arrays. You must refer to explicitly subscripted arrays with explicitly subscripted references; you cannot use an implicitly subscripted reference. For example, you can write the fourth and sixth elements of array TEST as follows:

```
data new;
   input qa1-qa10 qb1-qb10;
   array test(10) qa1-qa5 qb1-qb5;
   put test(4)= test(6)=;
   cards;
data lines
;
```

The PUT statement writes the values of QA4 and QB1, the fourth and sixth elements of array TEST.

Using Explicitly Subscripted Arrays with DO Groups

You can process explicitly subscripted arrays in an iterative DO, DO WHILE, or DO UNTIL group.

Iterative DO groups To process an array in an iterative DO group:

- create an iterative DO statement in which the starting and stopping values are the beginning and ending elements of the array you want to process
- use the index variable of the DO statement as the subscript of array references within the group.

In each execution of the DO group, the current value of the index variable is the subscript of the array element being processed. For example, the statements

```
array days{7} d1-d7;
do i=1 to 7;
   if days{i}=99 then days{i}=100;
   end;
```

test the value of variables D1 through D7 in order and, if any of them has a value of 99, change that value to 100.

To process particular elements of an array, specify those elements as the range of the iterative DO statement. For example, you can process selected elements of array DAYS above as follows:

```
do i=2 to 4;
do i=1 to 7 by 2;
do i=3,5;
```

You can also process two or more arrays in an iterative DO group, as in:

```
array days{7} d1-d7;
array hours{7} h1-h7;
do i=1 to 7;
   if days{i}=99 then days{i}=100;
   hours{i}=days{i}*12;
   end;
```

You can use the DIM function in the iterative DO statement to return the number of elements in an array. The DIM function is useful because it allows you to change the number of elements in an array without respecifying the upper bound of all iterative DO groups that refer to that array. You can also use it when you have specified the number of elements in the array with an asterisk. For example, you can write:

```
do i=1 to dim(days);
do i=1 to dim(days) by 2;
```

DO WHILE and DO UNTIL groups To process arrays with a DO WHILE or DO UNTIL statement:

- create an index variable for the array before the DO WHILE or DO UNTIL group
- use an array reference in the condition of the DO WHILE or DO UNTIL statement
- use program statements within the group to change the value of the index variable.

This example illustrates a DO WHILE statement:

```
data test;
   input x1-x5 y;
   array t{5} x1-x5;
   i=1;
   do while(t{i}<y);
      put t{i}= y=;
      i=i+1;
      end;
   cards;
1 2 3 4 5 3
0 2 4 6 8 6
;
```

Multidimensional Explicitly Subscripted Arrays

To create a multidimensional array, place the number of elements in each dimension after the array name in the form

   {n,...}

(You can also use brackets or parentheses). N is required for each dimension of a multidimensional array.

Reading from right to left, the rightmost dimension represents columns; the next dimension represents rows; and each position farther left represents a higher dimension. Thus, the statement

   `array x{5,3} score1-score15;`

defines a two-dimensional array with five rows and three columns.

SAS places variables into a multidimensional array by filling all rows in order, beginning at the upper-left corner of the array (known as *row-major order*). In this example variable SCORE1 is element X{1,1}; SCORE2 is X{1,2}; SCORE3 is X{1,3}; SCORE4 is X{2,1}; and SCORE15 is X{5,3}. The following example places variables into a two-dimensional array:

```
data overtime;
   informat time1-time20 time5.;
   input id time1-time20;
   array tchek{5,4} time1-time20;
   do i=1 to 5;
      if intck('HOUR',tchek{I,1},tchek{I,4})>9 then
         if intck('HOUR',tchek{I,2},tchek{I,3})<=1 then do;
            put id @10 ' IN ' tchek{I,1} time5. /
                @10 'OUT ' tchek{I,2} time5. /
                @10 ' IN ' tchek{I,3} time5. /
                @10 'OUT ' tchek{I,4} time5. ;
            output;
            end;
      end;
   cards;
129  7:49  11:53  12:01  17:30
     8:01  12:00  12:59  17:05
     8:00  11:59  13:01  17:05
     7:33  10:49  11:50  17:56
     8:00  12:00  13:00  17:00
```

Specifying Bounds for Explicitly Subscripted Arrays

In the arrays shown so far, the subscript in each dimension of the array ranges from 1 to *n*, where *n* is the number of elements in that dimension. Thus, 1 is the *lower bound* and *n* is the *upper bound* of that dimension of the array. For example, in the array

```
array new{4} power freeman weathers fussell;
```

the lower bound is 1 and the upper bound is 4. In the statement

```
array test{2,5} test1-test10;
```

the bounds of the first dimension are 1 and 2; and those of the second dimension are 1 and 5.

You can also specify the bounds of each dimension of an array as

lower:upper

where

    lower   is the lower bound of that dimension of the array.

    upper   is the upper bound of that dimension of the array.

Therefore, you can also write the ARRAY statements above as

```
array new{1:4} power freeman weathers fussell;
array test{1:2,1:5} test1-test10;
```

For most arrays, 1 is a convenient lower bound; thus, you do not need to specify the lower and upper bounds. However, specifying both bounds is useful when the array dimensions have a convenient beginning point other than 1.

For example, suppose you have ten variables named YEAR76-YEAR85. Both of these ARRAY statements place the variables into an array named YRS:

```
array yrs{10} year76-year85;
array yrs{76:85} year76-year85;
```

With the first ARRAY statement you must remember that element YRS{4} is variable YEAR79, YRS{7} is YEAR82, and so on. With the second ARRAY statement, element YRS{79} is YEAR79 and YRS{82} is YEAR82; the array references are easy to interpret.

When you process an array like the second one above in a DO group, be sure that the range of the DO group matches the range of the array. For example, you can process the second array above in both of these iterative DO groups:

```
do i=76 to 85;
   if yrs{i}=9 then yrs{i}=.;
   end;

do i=lbound(yrs) to hbound(yrs);
   if yrs{i}=9 then yrs{i}=.;
   end;
```

In each case the index variable in the iterative DO statement ranges from 76 to 85. In the second group the LBOUND function returns the lower bound of YRS, and the HBOUND function returns the upper bound. See "SAS Functions" for descriptions of the LBOUND and HBOUND functions.

This example illustrates specifying bounds in a two-dimensional array. Suppose you have forty variables named X60-X99; they represent the years 1960-1999.

You want to arrange them in an array by decades, as follows:

```
X60   X61   X62   X63   X64   X65   X66   X67   X68   X69
X70   X71   X72   X73   X74   X75   X76   X77   X78   X79
X80   X81   X82   X83   X84   X85   X86   X87   X88   X89
X90   X91   X92   X93   X94   X95   X96   X97   X98   X99
```

It is convenient to make the row range 6 through 9 and the column range 0 through 9. This ARRAY statement creates the array:

```
ARRAY X{6:9,0:9} X60-X99;
```

In array X, variable X63 is element X{6,3}, and X89 is X{8,9}. You can remember these references easily. To process array X with iterative DO groups, use one of these methods:

```
do i=6 to 9;
   do j=0 to 9;
      if x{i,j}=0 then x{i,j}=.;
      end;
   end;

do i=lbound1(x) to hbound1(x);
   do j=lbound2(x) to hbound2(x);
      if x{i,j}=0 then x{i,j}=.;
      end;
   end;
```

Both examples change all values of 0 in variables X60-X99 to missing. The first example sets the range of the DO groups explicitly, and the second example uses the LBOUND and HBOUND functions to return the bounds of each dimension of the array.

Examples

Example 1: Assigning Initial Values to an Array

In this example, you create variables in an explicitly subscripted array named TEST and assign them initial values. Then you read values into another array named SCORE and compare each element of SCORE to the corresponding element of TEST. If the value of the element in SCORE is greater than the value of the element in TEST, the variable NEWSCORE is assigned the value of SCORE and the OUTPUT statement writes the observation to the SAS data set.

```
data score1(drop=i);
   array test{3} t1-t3 (90 80 70);
   array score{3} s1-s3;
   input id score{*};
   do i=1 to 3;
      if score{i}>=test{i} then do;
         newscore=score{i};
         output;
         end;
      end;
   cards;
1234  99 60 82
5678  80 85 75
;
```

116 Chapter 5

```
proc print noobs;
   title 'Data Set Score1';
run;
```

The special subscript asterisk (*) in the INPUT statement inputs values into all members of the SCORE array. Data set SCORE1 is shown in **Output 5.1**:

Output 5.1 Data Set Produced by Assigning Initial Values to Array

```
                    Data Set Score1                              1

         T1   T2   T3   S1   S2   S3   ID     NEWSCORE
         90   80   70   99   60   82   1234      99
         90   80   70   99   60   82   1234      82
         90   80   70   80   85   75   5678      85
         90   80   70   80   85   75   5678      75
```

Example 2: Using _TEMPORARY_ Arrays

In the previous example the elements of the array TEST are constants needed only for the duration of DATA step execution. You can use _TEMPORARY_ instead of specifying variable names and assign initial values to the temporary array elements. The following statements produce **Output 5.2**:

```
data score2(drop=i);
   array test{3} _temporary_ (90 80 70);
   array score{3} s1-s3;
   input id score{*};
   do i=1 to 3;
      if score{i}>=test{i} then do;
         newscore=score{i};
         output;
         end;
      end;
   cards;
1234  99 60 82
5678  80 85 75
;
proc print noobs;
   title 'Data Set Score2';
run;
```

Output 5.2 Data Set Produced by Using Temporary Elements

```
                    Data Set Score2                              1

              S1   S2   S3   ID     NEWSCORE
              99   60   82   1234      99
              99   60   82   1234      82
              80   85   75   5678      85
              80   85   75   5678      75
```

Implicitly Subscripted ARRAY Statement

Implicitly subscripted arrays consist of an array name, an index variable (either one you supply or a default), and a list of names (either variable names or names of other implicitly subscripted arrays). They do not contain an explicit reference to the number of elements in the array. You refer to an element of the array by setting the index variable to the number of the element and using the array name in a subsequent statement. Since you usually want to process more than one element of an array, implicitly subscripted arrays are often placed within iterative DO, DO OVER, DO WHILE, or DO UNTIL groups.

The form of the implicitly subscripted ARRAY statement is

ARRAY *arrayname*[(*indexvariable*)] [**$**] [*length*] *arrayelements*;

You can specify the items below in the implicitly subscripted ARRAY statement:

arrayname
> names the array. The array name must be a valid SAS name that is not the name of a SAS variable in the same DATA step. When the array name appears in a SAS statement, one of the array elements is substituted for the array name based on the value of the index variable, which is described below.

(indexvariable)
> gives the name of a variable whose value defines the current element of the array. All implicitly subscripted arrays use an index variable even if you do not specify one in the ARRAY statement. If you do not include an index variable, the SAS System uses the automatic variable _I_ as the index variable. The value of the index variable can range from 1 to the number of elements in the array.
>
> An index variable you specify is included in the SAS data set unless it is excluded by a DROP or KEEP statement. The automatic index variable _I_ is not included in the data set.
>
> If the index variable's value is not an integer, it is truncated to an integer using the rules of the INT function.

$
> indicates that the array you are defining is composed of character elements. The dollar sign ($) is not necessary if the character variables have been previously defined as character in the step.

length
> gives a length value to array elements not previously assigned a length. For example, the following statements define a character array ITEM:

```
data a;
   input x1 $3. x2 $3.;
   array item(j) $ 12 x1-x10;
   other SAS statements;
```

The first two elements, X1 and X2, have lengths of 3, as defined in the INPUT statement. The other eight elements of ITEM are given a length of 12 by the length specification in the ARRAY statement.

arrayelements

names the elements that make up the array. Array elements can be the names of variables or other implicitly subscripted arrays and must be either all numeric or all character. You can also use numbered lists such as X1-X10 and the special variable lists _NUMERIC_, _CHARACTER_, and _ALL_ (if all the variables in the data set are the same type). You cannot use names of explicitly subscripted arrays or explicitly subscripted array element references. A variable or an implicitly subscripted array can be an element in more than one implicitly subscripted array.

You must refer to implicitly subscripted array elements with implicitly subscripted references; you cannot use explicitly subscripted references.

For example, the statement

```
array question (i) q1-q20;
```

defines an array QUESTION with 20 elements Q1 through Q20. Using the name QUESTION in a subsequent SAS statement refers to the *i*th element of QUESTION, where *i* is the current value of the index variable I.

The array elements can be listed in any order, and the names of array elements do not have to be numbered names as in the example above. In the following example, the ARRAY statement

```
array quiz (num) q10 q3-q5 test4;
```

is a valid array definition. Q10 is the first element of the array QUIZ; Q3 is the second, Q4 the third, Q5 the fourth, and TEST4 the fifth. NUM is the index variable. When NUM's value is 1, Q10 is the variable the SAS System processes when the array name QUIZ appears in a SAS statement.

Referring to Implicit Array Elements

You can use an array name in the following DATA step statements:

assignment statement
sum statement
iterative DO
DO OVER *arrayname*
DO WHILE(*condition*)
DO UNTIL(*condition*)
IF
INPUT
PUT
SELECT

You can also use array names in the arguments of SAS functions. However, an array name in a function is not a substitute for a variable list since only one element of the array is processed in any given execution of the function.

The ARRAY statement defining the array name must appear in a DATA step before any references to that array. An array definition is only in effect for the duration of the DATA step. If you want to use the same array in several DATA steps, you must redefine the elements of the array in each step.

To refer to an element of an implicitly subscripted array, set the index variable to the index of the element you want and then use the array name in a SAS statement. For example, suppose you want to print the value of the eleventh element of the array BIG:

```
data one;
   input id x1-x10 y1-y10;
   array big (i) x1-x10 y1-y10;
   i=11;
   put big;
   cards;
data lines;
;
```

The PUT statement writes the value of Y1, the eleventh element of BIG.

Using Implicitly Subscripted Arrays with DO Groups

You can process an implicitly subscripted array in an iterative DO group, a DO OVER group, a DO WHILE group, or a DO UNTIL group.

The following example processes an implicitly subscripted array with an iterative DO group:

```
data test;
   input score1-score5;
   array s score1-score5;
   do _i_=1 to 5;
      s=s*100;
      end;
   cards;
.95 .88 .57 .90 .65
;
```

In this example the value of each variable SCORE1 through SCORE5 is multiplied by 100.

The index variable of the array must also be the index variable of the iterative DO statement. If an index variable is not specified by the ARRAY statement, the automatic index variable _I_ must by used by iterative DO loops that process the array. You can process more than one array in an iterative DO group.

The DO OVER statement automatically executes the statements in the DO group for each element of the array unless you specify otherwise. It is equivalent to the statement

```
do i=1 to k;
```

where *i* is the index variable of the array, and *k* is the number of elements in the array. The statements in the DO OVER group below change all missing values in the array BIG to the value zero:

```
data two;
   input id x1-x10 y1-y10;
   array big (i) x1-x10 y1-y10;
   do over big;
      if big=. then big=0;
      end;
   cards;
```

If the implicit array subscript is out of range (less than 1 or greater than the number of elements in the array) when the array name is used, the DATA step stops and the SAS System prints an error message in the log.

You can process more than one array in a DO OVER group if the arrays have the same number of elements and the same index variable. For example, in this DATA step each ARRAY statement defines an array with 100 elements:

```
data ftoc;
   input f1-f100;
   array f f1-f100;
   array c c1-c100;
   do over f;
      c=(f-32)*5/9;
      end;
   cards;
```

Both arrays use the automatic index variable _I_. The variables in the INPUT statement make up the F array, and the elements in the C array receive values in the DO OVER group. The DO OVER statement in the example is equivalent to the statement

```
do _i_=1 to 100;
```

Either array name F or C could appear in the DO OVER statement since both arrays have the same number of elements and the same index variable.

The following example processes an implicitly subscripted array with a DO WHILE group:

```
data test;
   input x1-x5 y;
   array t x1-x5;
   _i_=1;
   do while(t<y);
      put t= y=;
      _i_=_i_+1;
      end;
   cards;
1 2 3 4 5 3
0 2 4 6 8 6
;
```

Using Arrays as Elements of Other Arrays: Multidimensional Implicit Subscripting

Since an implicitly subscripted array can be an element of another implicitly subscripted array, double and higher-level implicit subscripting is possible. For example, assume your data values consist of answers from three tests with ten questions per test. Each student's observation contains thirty answers. You can use the ARRAY statements in the DATA step below to change missing values to zeros in these thirty answers:

```
data three;
   array test1 (j) t1q1-t1q10;
   array test2 (j) t2q1-t2q10;
   array test3 (j) t3q1-t3q10;
   array answer (k) test1-test3;
   input t1q1-t1q10 t2q1-t2q10 t3q1-t3q10;
   do k=1 to 3;
      do j=1 to 10;
         if answer=. then answer=0;
         end;
      end;
   cards;
```

The outer DO loop determines which element of ANSWER (array TEST1, TEST2, or TEST3) is being processed. The inner DO loop determines which element in the current array (that is, questions 1 through 10) is being processed.

In the example above, the DO OVER statement can be used in place of the iterative DO statements. You can nest DO OVER statements only if a different index variable is defined for each array referenced by the nested DO OVER statements. Nesting DO OVER statements when arrays use the same index variable can result in looping. The following is an example of nested DO OVER statements:

```
do over answer;
   do over test1;
      if answer=. then answer=0;
      end;
   end;
```

Because TEST1, TEST2, and TEST3 have the same dimension, it makes no difference which of the three array names is specified in the inner DO OVER statement.

See the discussion of the **DO OVER Statement** in this chapter for more information.

Assignment Statement

Introduction 122
  Variables in assignment statements 122

Introduction

Assignment statements evaluate an expression and store the result in a variable. Assignment statements have the form:

variable=expression;

The terms in the assignment have these definitions:

variable   names a new variable or an existing variable.
Variable can be a variable name or an array reference. You can assign values to the special SAS variables FIRST.byvariable, LAST.byvariable, _ERROR_, and _N_; however, the SAS System resets _N_ at the beginning of the DATA step to reflect the number of the current execution of the DATA step, even if you change _N_ during the DATA step. (See the "Introduction" to USING THE SAS LANGUAGE for a discussion of SAS variables, and see the **BY Statement** later in this chapter for a discussion of FIRST. and LAST.byvariables.)

expression   is one or more variable names, constants, and function names linked by operators and by parentheses where appropriate. (See "SAS Expressions" and "SAS Functions" for more information.)

For example, the statements

```
data one;
   input a b;
   x=a+b;
   cards;
data lines
;
```

read values of A and B from input lines and create a new variable X that is the sum of A and B values in each observation. If either A or B is missing, X is missing, and the SAS System prints a note on the SAS log to warn you. (See "Missing Values" for details.)

You can modify existing variables by writing assignment statements like this:

```
a=a+b;
```

The sum of A and B replaces the original value of A. Note that the variable A appears on both sides of the statement; the original value of A on the right side is used in evaluating the expression. The result is stored in the variable A.

Variables in assignment statements   If a variable appears for the first time in a DATA step as the result variable in an assignment statement, it has the same type (character or numeric) as the result of the expression. If a variable has been defined as numeric and then used as a result variable in an assignment statement with a character expression, SAS performs character-to-numeric conversion on the expression, if possible, and executes the statement. If the conversion is not possible, SAS issues an error message. See "SAS Expressions" for further discussion.

If a variable appears for the first time on the right side of an assignment statement, SAS assumes that it is a numeric variable and that its value is missing. A note is printed on the SAS log that the variable is uninitialized. (A RETAIN statement initializes a variable and can assign it a value, even if the RETAIN statement appears after the assignment statement. See the **RETAIN Statement** later in this chapter for more information.)

The length of a variable appearing for the first time as the result variable in an assignment statement is the length resulting from the first scanning of the statement unless a LENGTH statement specifies a different length. For character variables, the LENGTH statement must come before the assignment statement; for numeric variables, the LENGTH statement can precede or follow the assignment statement. See the **LENGTH Statement** later in this chapter for more information.

Table 5.1 gives the length of a result variable produced by various types of expressions when the length is not explicitly set.

Table 5.1 Length Produced by Various Expressions

Result Variable Type	Expression	Result Variable Length	Example

Numeric	Numeric variable	Default numeric length (8 unless otherwise specified)	`length a 4;`
			`x=a;`
			`*X has length 8;`

Character	Character variable	Length of source variable	`length a $4;`
			`x=a;`
			`*X has length 4;`

Character	Character literal	Length of first literal encountered	`x='ABC';`
			`x='ABCDE';`
			`*X has length 3;`

Character	Concatenation of variables	Sum of the lengths of all variables	`length a $4 b $6 c $2;` `x=a``b``c;` `*X has length 12;`
Character	Concatenation of variables and literal	Sum of the lengths of variables and first literal encountered	`length a $4;` `x=a``'CAT';` `x=a``'CATNIP';` `*X has length 7;`

See "SAS Functions" for information on the length of values returned by SAS functions.

ATTRIB Statement

The ATTRIB statement in the DATA step allows you to specify the format, informat, label, and length of one or more variables in a single statement.

The form of the ATTRIB statement is

ATTRIB *variable* [**FORMAT**=*format*] [**INFORMAT**=*informat*] [**LABEL**='*label*'] [**LENGTH**=[$]*length*]...;

You can specify the following terms in the ATTRIB statement:

variable
: names the variable to receive the attributes. *Variable* can be a single variable name, a list of names, or one of the variable lists described in the "Introduction" to USING THE SAS LANGUAGE except for the special lists _NUMERIC_, _CHARACTER_, and _ALL_.

FORMAT=*format*
: specifies the format to associate with the preceding variable(s). The format can be either a SAS format or a format you have created with the FORMAT procedure. See the **FORMAT Statement** later in this chapter for more information on the format attribute, and see "SAS Informats and Formats" for descriptions of SAS formats.

INFORMAT=*informat*
: specifies the informat to associate with the preceding variable. The informat can be either a SAS informat or an informat you have created with the FORMAT procedure. See the **INFORMAT Statement** later in this chapter for information on the informat attribute, and see "SAS Informats and Formats" for descriptions of informats.

LABEL='*label*'
: specifies a label to be associated with the preceding variable. See the **LABEL Statement** later in this chapter for information on variable labels.

LENGTH=[$]*length*
: specifies the length of the preceding variable. If the variable is a character variable, put a dollar sign ($) in front of the length.

Using the ATTRIB statement in the DATA step permanently associates the attributes with the variables. See the **ATTRIB Statement** in "SAS Statements Used in the PROC Step" for information on assigning attributes for the current PROC step only. You can also assign variable attributes with FORMAT, INFORMAT, LABEL, and LENGTH statements. Any attribute that you have assigned with an ATTRIB statement can be changed in an individual statement and vice versa.

Here are examples of valid ATTRIB statements:

- `attrib x length=$4 label='TEST VARIABLE';`
- `attrib saleday informat=mmddyy. format=worddate.;`
- `attrib month1-month12 label='MONTHLY SALES';`

BY Statement

Introduction 125
BY Groups 126
FIRST. and LAST.byvariables 127
BY Statement with MERGE 128
BY Statement with UPDATE 128
BY Statement with SET 128
BY Statement Using GROUPFORMAT Option 129

Introduction

A BY statement is used in a DATA step to control the operation of a SET, MERGE, or UPDATE statement and to set up special grouping variables. See the **BY Statement** in "SAS Statements Used in the PROC Step" for information on using the BY statement in the PROC step.

The BY statement has the form:

BY [**DESCENDING**] [**GROUPFORMAT**] *variable* ... [**NOTSORTED**];

where

variable
: names each variable by which the data set is sorted. The list of variables defines the data set's BY groups.

DESCENDING
: specifies that the data set is sorted in descending order by the variable that follows the DESCENDING option in the BY statement.

GROUPFORMAT
: indicates that formatted values of the following BY variable are to be used when the SAS System assigns values of the FIRST. and LAST.*byvariables*. If you omit the GROUPFORMAT option, the DATA step uses unformatted values of the BY variable. Using the GROUPFORMAT option ensures that BY groups in the DATA step match BY groups in PROC steps that use a FORMAT statement.

NOTSORTED
: specifies that observations with the same BY values are grouped together, but the BY values are not necessarily sorted in alphabetical or numerical order. The NOTSORTED option can appear anywhere in the BY statement.

The BY statement, if present, must follow, not precede, a SET, MERGE, or UPDATE statement in the DATA step. Only one BY statement can accompany each SET, MERGE, or UPDATE statement. A BY statement applies only to the most recent SET, MERGE, or UPDATE statement.

For example, the statement

```
by descending x y;
```

specifies that the data set is sorted in descending order of the values of X and, within each X value, in ascending order of Y. The statement

```
by descending x descending y;
```

specifies that the data set is sorted in descending order of the values of both X and Y.

Suppose data set CLASS contains observations with a variable DAY whose values are the three-character abbreviation for the day of the week. All the observations with the same DAY value are grouped together in the data set, but the values are in calendar order rather than alphabetical order. You can use the statement

```
by day notsorted;
```

with a SET statement to read the CLASS data set.

When you use a BY statement without specifying the NOTSORTED option, the data set used as input to the step need not have been previously sorted by the SORT procedure; however, the observations must be in the same order as if the SORT procedure had sorted them.

If neither DESCENDING or NOTSORTED is specified, the observations in the data set must be arranged in ascending order of the BY variables' values.

BY Groups

These statements:

```
proc sort data=degrees;
   by state city month;
```

produced the SAS data set below using the SORT procedure. The data set DEGREES is sorted by STATE, CITY within STATE, and MONTH within CITY. The fourth variable in the data set, DEGDAY, represents winter degree days.

STATE	CITY	MONTH	DEGDAY
NC	CHARLOTTE	1	716
NC	CHARLOTTE	2	588
NC	CHARLOTTE	3	461

———————————————————————— CITY break

NC	RALEIGH	1	760
NC	RALEIGH	2	638
NC	RALEIGH	3	502

———————————————————————— STATE break-CITY break

VA	NORFOLK	1	760
VA	NORFOLK	2	661
VA	NORFOLK	3	532

———————————————————————— CITY break

VA	RICHMOND	1	853
VA	RICHMOND	2	717
VA	RICHMOND	3	569

———————————————————————— STATE break-CITY break

The BY groups in the data set, from the largest grouping to the smallest, are represented by different values for STATE, CITY within STATE, and MONTH within CITY within STATE. In the data set above, NC and VA observations break the data set into two STATE BY groups; CHARLOTTE and RALEIGH observations divide the NC observations into CITY BY groups; NORFOLK and RICHMOND observations divide VA observations into CITY BY groups; and within CITY each observation, with its different value for MONTH, is itself a MONTH BY group.

FIRST. and LAST.byvariables

You can process the data set in BY groups if you include a BY statement after the SET, MERGE, or UPDATE statement in the DATA step.

When you are processing a data set in BY groups, you may want to identify which observation is the first or the last in a particular BY group. SAS keeps track of the first and last observations in all BY groups by creating two variables, FIRST.*byvariable* and LAST.*byvariable*, for each variable in the BY statement. The FIRST. and LAST.*byvariables* let you know when you are processing the first or last observation in a BY group. For example, if you use a BY statement containing variables STATE, CITY, and MONTH, SAS creates the variables FIRST.STATE, LAST.STATE, FIRST.CITY, LAST.CITY, FIRST.MONTH, and LAST.MONTH. FIRST.*byvariables* and LAST.*byvariables* are available in the DATA step for use in program statements but are not added to the data set being created. To display the FIRST. and LAST.*byvariables*, use a PUT statement.

If an observation is the first in a BY group, then FIRST.*byvariable* has the value 1. For all observations in the BY group except the first, FIRST.*byvariable* is 0. If an observation is the last in a BY group, LAST.*byvariable* is 1. For all observations in the BY group except the last, LAST.*byvariable* is 0.

The data set DEGREES is shown with values of the FIRST. and LAST.*byvariables*:

				FIRST.byvariables			LAST.byvariables		
STATE	CITY	MONTH	DEGDAY	STATE	CITY	MONTH	STATE	CITY	MONTH
NC	CHARLOTTE	1	716	1	1	1	0	0	1
NC	CHARLOTTE	2	588	0	0	1	0	0	1
NC	CHARLOTTE	3	461	0	0	1	0	1	1

—————— CITY break

NC	RALEIGH	1	760	0	1	1	0	0	1
NC	RALEIGH	2	638	0	0	1	0	0	1
NC	RALEIGH	3	502	0	0	1	1	1	1

—————— STATE break—CITY break

VA	NORFOLK	1	760	1	1	1	0	0	1
VA	NORFOLK	2	661	0	0	1	0	0	1
VA	NORFOLK	3	532	0	0	1	0	1	1

—————— CITY break

VA	RICHMOND	1	853	0	1	1	0	0	1
VA	RICHMOND	2	717	0	0	1	0	0	1
VA	RICHMOND	3	569	0	0	1	1	1	1

—————— STATE break—CITY break

Notice that each MONTH BY group consists of 1 observation. Thus, FIRST.MONTH and LAST.MONTH are both 1 in each observation. Notice also that when the FIRST.*byvariable* is 1 for a particular variable, the FIRST.*byvariable* is also 1 for all variables following it in the BY statement. Thus, when FIRST.STATE is 1 for an observation, FIRST.CITY and FIRST.MONTH are also 1 for that observation. The same is true for LAST.*byvariables*.

For example, the data set below is sorted by WEEK and by DAY within WEEK. Notice the values of the FIRST. variables:

OBS	WEEK	DAY	FIRST.WEEK	FIRST.DAY
1	1	MONDAY	1	1
2	1	TUESDAY	0	1
3	1	TUESDAY	0	0
4	2	TUESDAY	1	1
5	2	TUESDAY	0	0
6	2	WEDNESDAY	0	1

Although in observation 4 the DAY value is not the first with the value 'TUESDAY', it is the first value of TUESDAY within WEEK=2. That is, since FIRST.WEEK is 1, FIRST.DAY is 1.

BY Statement with MERGE

When a BY statement is used in a DATA step with a MERGE statement, the data sets listed in the MERGE statement are joined by matching values of the variables listed in the BY statement. FIRST. and LAST.*byvariables* are created for each variable listed in the BY statement.

The statements below perform a match-merge, matching on STATE and CITY within STATE. SAS data sets YR84 and YR85 have been previously sorted by STATE and CITY using the SORT procedure. The LAST.CITY variable is used in the IF statement, and the last observation in each CITY BY group is output to data set SINGLE. All observations are then output to data set NEW:

```
data new single;
   merge yr84 yr85;
   by state city;
   if last.city then output single;
   output new;
```

The NOTSORTED option **cannot** be used in a BY statement in a DATA step with the MERGE statement; the DESCENDING option can be used if the observations being merged are sorted in descending order of the variables mentioned in the BY statement.

BY Statement with UPDATE

A BY statement must appear in a DATA step with an UPDATE statement to identify the matching variable or variables to be used in the update. See the **UPDATE Statement** later in this chapter for more information. FIRST. and LAST.*byvariables* are created, and the NOTSORTED option **cannot** be used.

See the **UPDATE Statement** description for more information.

BY Statement with SET

When a BY statement is used in a DATA step that includes a SET statement with one data set name, the data set being read is processed just as though a BY statement were not included. The difference is that the BY statement causes FIRST. and LAST.*byvariables* to be created and produces an error message if the data set is not sorted (and the NOTSORTED option is not present).

For example, the DATA step below creates a SAS data set named SUBSET, which includes only the first observation in each STATE BY group from data set DEGREES:

```
data subset;
   set degrees;
   by state;
   if first.state;
```

Only STATE, the primary BY group, is used in the BY statement since only the FIRST.STATE variable is needed.

When a BY statement is used in a DATA step with a SET statement, both the NOTSORTED and DESCENDING options can be used.

If a DATA step contains more than one SET statement, a BY statement can follow each SET statement. The BY statement affects only the SET statement it follows.

See the **SET Statement** description for more information.

BY Statement Using GROUPFORMAT Option

The following example creates a data set and processes it in DATA steps using BY statements with and without the GROUPFORMAT option. Then, for comparison, a PROC PRINT step also processes the data set in BY groups.

```
proc format;
   value new 1-2='low' 3-4='medium' 5-6='high';
run;
data test;
   input i @@;
   cards;
1 2 3 4 5 6
;
data one;
   set test;
   format i new.;
   by groupformat i;
   if _n_=1 then put 'With GROUPFORMAT option:' //;
   if first.i then put 'BY group begins: ' i=;
   put 'i is ' i 2.;
run;
```

Output 5.3 shows the lines written by the PUT statement. Each time the formatted value of I changes, a new BY group begins.

130   Chapter 5

Output 5.3 BY Groups in DATA Step with GROUPFORMAT Option

```
11     data one;
12        set test;
13        format i new.;
14        by groupformat i;
15        if _n_=1 then put 'With GROUPFORMAT option:' //;
16        if first.i then put 'BY group begins: ' i=;
17        put 'i is ' i 2.;
18     run;
With GROUPFORMAT option:

BY group begins: I=low
i is  1
i is  2
BY group begins: I=medium
i is  3
i is  4
BY group begins: I=high
i is  5
i is  6
```

If you do not use the GROUPFORMAT option, the DATA step begins a new BY group each time the unformatted value of I changes. **Output 5.4** shows the result.

```
data two;
   set test;
   format i new.;
   by i;
   if _n_=1 then put 'Without GROUPFORMAT option:' //;
   if first.i then put 'BY group begins: ' i=;
   put 'i is ' i 2.;
run;
```

Output 5.4 BY Groups in DATA Step Without GROUPFORMAT Option

```
20     data two;
21        set test;
22        format i new.;
23        by i;
24        if _n_=1 then put 'Without GROUPFORMAT option:' //;
25        if first.i then put 'BY group begins: ' i=;
26        put 'i is ' i 2.;
27     run;
Without GROUPFORMAT option:

BY group begins: I=low
i is  1
BY group begins: I=low
i is  2
BY group begins: I=medium
i is  3
BY group begins: I=medium
i is  4
BY group begins: I=high
i is  5
BY group begins: I=high
i is  6
```

For comparison, a PROC PRINT step begins a new BY group each time the formatted value changes, as shown in **Output 5.5**.

```
proc print data=test;
   var i;
   by i;
   format i new.;
   title 'PRINT Procedure Showing BY Groups';
run;
```

Output 5.5 BY Groups in PROC Step

```
                        PRINT Procedure Showing BY Groups                              1
----------------------------------- I=low -----------------------------------------
                          OBS     I

                           1      low
                           2      low

----------------------------------- I=medium --------------------------------------
                          OBS     I

                           3      medium
                           4      medium

----------------------------------- I=high ----------------------------------------
                          OBS     I

                           5      high
                           6      high
```

CALL Statement

The purpose of the CALL statement in the DATA step is to invoke or call a routine. The routine is called each time the CALL statement is executed.

The form of the CALL statement is

CALL *routine* (*parameter,...*);

where

- *routine* names the routine you want to call. Individual routines are described below.
- *parameter* is a piece of information, usually a SAS variable name, to be passed to the routine.

Routines that can be used with the CALL statement include:

- *randomnumber-function* specifies one of the following SAS random number functions:

RANBIN	RANPOI
RANCAU	RANTBL
RANEXP	RANTRI
RANGAM	RANUNI
RANNOR	

  See "SAS Functions" for a description of these functions.

- SOUND generates a sound. The form of the SOUND routine is

  CALL SOUND (*freq,dur*);

  where *freq* is the desired frequency (in cycles per second) and *dur* is the duration (in 1/80th of a second). See "SAS Functions" for details.

- SYMPUT allows you to create a macro variable or assign a new value to an existing one. The form of the routine is

  CALL SYMPUT (*macrovar,value*);

  where *macrovar* and *value* can be DATA step variable names, explicit character strings (in quotes), or expressions. See "SYMPUT Routine" in the *SAS Guide to Macro Processing, Version 6 Edition* for a full description.

- SYSTEM issues operating system commands. It is similar to the X command; however, it is callable and you can use expressions and macro variables as arguments. The form of the routine is

  CALL SYSTEM (*command*);

  where *command* can be

  - the name of a character variable whose value is a system command to be executed
  - the system command, enclosed in quotes (explicit character string)
  - an expression whose value is a system command.

This routine passes the command string to the operating system to be executed. The following is an example of the SYSTEM routine.

```
data _null_;
   call system('dir *.ssd');
run;
```

In most cases the SAS System blanks the display manager screen and then displays the output. The output is not routed to the OUTPUT or LOG windows. In a few cases, (for example, a cd command), the command executes, but you see nothing.

CARDS and CARDS4 Statements

If you are entering your data in the job stream with your SAS program, the CARDS statement comes before the data lines to signal to the SAS System that the data follow. The form of the CARDS statement is

    CARDS;
data lines
;

If you use a CARDS statement, it must be the last statement in your DATA step, and it must be followed immediately by data lines. Data lines following a CARDS statement have a maximum length of 80 columns.

SAS recognizes the end of the data lines when it sees a semicolon. The first line after the last data line should be either a null statement (a line containing a single semicolon) or another SAS statement ending with a semicolon on the same line:

```
    cards;
data lines
;
```

You must use an INPUT statement to read values from data lines following a CARDS statement. For example,

```
data entries;
   input x y;
   cards;
data lines
;
```

The CARDS statement is for data lines entered following a DATA step (also called *in-stream data*); if your input lines are on disk, use instead the INFILE statement described later in this chapter.

You can use INFILE statement options in reading data following a CARDS statement by using an INFILE statement with a fileref of CARDS together with a CARDS statement. For example,

```
data temp;
   infile cards missover;
   input x y z;
   cards;
1 10 100
2 20
3 30 300
;
```

Only one CARDS statement can be used in a DATA step. If you want to enter two sets of data, either use two DATA steps or two INFILE statements, one for each set of data. (See the **INFILE Statement** for an example.)

Since a semicolon signals the end of the data lines to SAS, if the data lines following the CARDS statement happen to contain semicolons, you must substitute the CARDS4 statement for the CARDS statement.

The form of the CARDS4 statement is

CARDS4;
data lines
;;;;

After the last data line, put a line consisting of four semicolons in columns 1-4 to signal the end of the data. For example,

```
data _null_;
   input number citation & $50.;
   file print;
   put number a3 citation;
   cards4;
1  SMITH, 1982
2  ALLEN ET AL., 1975; BRADY, 1983
3  BROWN, 1980; LEWIS, 1974; WILLIAMS, 1972
;;;;
another DATA or PROC statement
```

DATA Statement

Introduction 136
Choosing a Data Set Name in the DATA Statement 137
   Default data set name 137
   One-word data set name 137
   Two-word data set name 138
Using Special SAS Data Set Names 138
   *Data set name _NULL_* 138
   *Data set name _LAST_* 138
Using More Than One Data Set Name 138
   Subsets of observations 138
   Subsets of variables 139

Introduction

The DATA statement begins a DATA step and provides a name for the SAS data set or data sets being created. SAS data sets are described in detail in "SAS Files."
The form of the DATA statement is

   DATA [*SASdataset*[(*dsoptions*)]]...;

The terms in the DATA statement are described below:

SASdataset
   names one or more SAS data sets being created in the DATA step. SAS data set names must conform to the rules for SAS names as well as to the file naming rules for the PC DOS operating system. See the "Introduction" to USING THE SAS LANGUAGE for a description of SAS names.

   The data set name given in the DATA statement may be a one-word name (for example, FITNESS), a two-word name (for example, OUT.FITNESS), or one of the special SAS names _NULL_, _DATA_, or _LAST_.

   A DATA statement may name one data set:

```
data fitness;
data out.fitness;
data _null_;
```

or more than one:

```
data year1 year2 year3;
data males females;
data library.total errors;
```

You may omit the data set name entirely:

```
data;
```

Then the SAS System names the data set using the DATA*n* convention (see below). "SAS Files" gives more information on naming SAS data sets.

(*dsoptions*)
   gives the SAS System more information about the data set being created. Data set options in parentheses follow the name of the data set in the DATA statement to which they apply.

   For example, the LABEL= option allows you to specify a label of up to forty characters for the data set. To give the FITNESS data set the label HEALTH CLUB DATA, use the statement:

```
data fitness(label='HEALTH CLUB DATA');
```

The use of these options is not confined to the DATA statement. Data set options can be associated with a data set name where it occurs in other SAS statements (except the OUTPUT statement in the DATA step).

Options most commonly used in the DATA statement are summarized below:

DROP=   lists the variables not to be included in the data set.

KEEP=   lists the variables to be included in the data set.

LABEL=   provides the data set with a label that is printed along with the name in the output of the CONTENTS procedure.

RENAME=   changes variable names.

TYPE=   specifies the data set's type. Use TYPE= only when the data set contains specially structured data such as a covariance matrix.

Refer to "SAS Files" for a complete description of these and other data set options as well as further discussion of the naming conventions mentioned below.

Choosing a Data Set Name in the DATA Statement

You should name each SAS data set in a SAS program that creates several data sets. Although some SAS users omit the data set name for very simple SAS jobs, you can keep track of your data sets more easily if you give each of them a unique name.

You must include a two-word data set name when you are storing your SAS data set on disk for use in a future SAS job. (The only exception is when you define a libref of USER; see "SAS Files" for a discussion.)

Default data set name   If you omit a data set name from the DATA statement as shown below:

```
data;
```

SAS still creates a data set. The data set is named automatically: the first such data set created in a job is called DATA1, the second is called DATA2, and so on through the job. This is called the DATA*n* naming convention and is equivalent to specifying:

```
data _data_;
```

where _DATA_ is a special SAS variable indicating that SAS is to use DATA1, DATA2, and so on.

One-word data set name   All SAS data set names have two parts separated by a period. The first part (called the *first-level name* or *libref*) identifies the location where the data set is stored; the second part (the *second-level name*) identifies the particular data set. Unless you plan to store your SAS data set on disk, you can give your data set a one-word name. For example, to begin creating a SAS data set named FITNESS, you use the statement

```
data fitness;
```

When you give a one-word name like FITNESS, SAS uses that name as the second part of the data set name and uses WORK (or the USER libref) as the first part. SAS notes and messages refer to the data set as WORK.FITNESS.

When the first-level name is WORK, the data set is temporary; it is only available during the current job or session.

Two-word data set name Use a two-word data set name if you want to store your SAS data set on disk. For example,

```
data out.fitness;
```

creates a SAS data set named FITNESS in the directory referenced by the libref OUT. See "SAS Files" for details on librefs.

If you have used a two-word data set name in the DATA step to create a data set, you must continue to use the two-word name if you refer to the data set later in your SAS job. For example, if you use OUT.FITNESS as shown above to create a SAS data set on disk and you want to refer to the data set in a SET statement later in the job, use the statement

```
set out.fitness;
```

If you use the statement

```
set fitness;
```

SAS looks for WORK.FITNESS since it always attaches the name WORK to one-word names.

Using Special SAS Data Set Names

Data set name _NULL_ You can give the special SAS data set name _NULL_ in the DATA statement whenever you want to execute the statements in a DATA step but do not want to create a SAS data set. For example, if you are using a DATA step to print a report with PUT statements based on the values contained in a SAS data set, you probably do not want to create another SAS data set containing the same data. Using _NULL_ means that SAS goes through the DATA step just as if it is creating a data set, but it does not write any observations; thus, the DATA step uses fewer computer resources.

Data set name _LAST_ _LAST_ refers to the name of the most recently created SAS data set. If a DATA statement includes the name _LAST_, the data set created has the same name as the most recently created data set and replaces the earlier data set.

Using More Than One Data Set Name

Subsets of observations When you are creating several data sets in one DATA step and want each data set to include a subset of the observations that the DATA step is processing, you can use the OUTPUT statement to add the appropriate observations to each data set. For example, you may use these statements:

```
data year82 year83 year84;
   input year x1-x20;
   if year=1982 then output year82;
   else if year=1983 then output year83;
   else if year=1984 then output year84;
   cards;
data lines
;
```

The YEAR82 data set contains only those observations where the YEAR value is 1982; the YEAR83 data set contains only those observations where the YEAR value is 1983; the YEAR84 data set contains only those observations with YEAR=1984. Observations with any other year values are not written to any data set.

Subsets of variables When you want to create several data sets containing different groups of variables, you can use the KEEP= or DROP= data set options after each data set name in the DATA statement.

For example, say that you want the data set YEAR82 to include, in addition to the variable YEAR, variables X1-X5; data set YEAR83 to include YEAR and X6-X20; and data set YEAR84 to include YEAR and all of the variables X1-X20 except X13:

```
data year82(keep=year x1-x5)
     year83(keep=year x6-x20)
     year84(drop=x13);
```

You can use either the KEEP= or DROP= option. The advantage of DROP= is that you can write a shorter list when you are dropping fewer variables than you are keeping.

DELETE Statement

A DELETE statement tells the SAS System to stop processing the current observation. The observation is not automatically written to any data set being created, and the SAS System returns to the beginning of the DATA step for another execution.

The DELETE statement has the form:

DELETE;

Here is an example:

```
data jrhigh;
   input ssn 1-9 grade 10 pretest1 14-16 pretest2 18-20;
   if grade<7 then delete;
   total=pretest1+pretest2;
   cards;
data lines
;
```

In this example, observations with a GRADE value less than 7 are not written to the SAS data set JRHIGH. The assignment statement is not executed for those observations.

When a DELETE statement is executed, SAS immediately stops executing program statements for the current observation. SAS returns to the statement following the DATA statement and begins executing the statements that follow. The DELETE statement is usually used as the THEN clause in an IF statement or as part of a conditionally executed DO group. If DELETE is executed for every observation, the new data set will have no observations.

In general, use the DELETE statement when it is easier to specify a condition for excluding observations from the data set. Use the subsetting IF statement (discussed later in this chapter) when it is easier to specify a condition for including observations.

DISPLAY Statement

The DISPLAY statement displays a window you have created with the WINDOW statement. The DISPLAY statement is an executable statement. The form of the DISPLAY statement is

DISPLAY *window*[*.group*] [**NOINPUT**] [**BLANK**] [**BELL**];

where

window[*.group*] names the window and group of fields to be displayed. If the window has more than one group of fields, give the complete *window.group* specification; if a window contains a single unnamed group, specify only *window*.

NOINPUT specifies that you cannot input values into fields displayed in the window. If you do not specify NOINPUT, you can input values into unprotected fields displayed in the window. If you specify NOINPUT in all DISPLAY statements in a DATA step, you **must** include a STOP statement to stop processing the DATA step.

The NOINPUT option is useful when you want to allow values to be entered into a window at some times but not others. For example, you can display a window once for entering values and a second time for verifying them.

BLANK clears the window. Use the BLANK option when you want to display different groups of fields in a window and you do not want text from the previous group to appear in the current display.

BELL rings the computer's bell when the window is displayed, if your personal computer is equipped with a bell.

You can use the DISPLAY statement in noninteractive mode to display a window on the screen. The window does not become part of the SAS log or output file.

See **Displaying Windows** in the **WINDOW Statement** later in this chapter for information on using the DISPLAY statement.

DO Statement

Introduction 142
Simple DO Statement 142
Iterative DO Statement 142
  Array processing with the iterative DO statement 145
DO OVER Statement 145
DO WHILE Statement 146
DO UNTIL Statement 146

Introduction

The DO statement specifies that the statements following the DO are to be executed as a unit until a matching END statement appears. The statements between the DO and the END statements are called a DO group. Any number of DO groups can be nested. The SAS System has several forms of the DO statement:

- DO
- iterative DO
- DO OVER
- DO WHILE
- DO UNTIL.

The number of times the DO group is executed depends on the form used.

Simple DO Statement

The form of a simple DO statement is

DO;
  more SAS statements
END;

A simple DO statement is often used within IF-THEN/ELSE statements to designate a group of statements to be executed depending on whether the IF condition is true or false.

For example, the statements

```
if x>5 then do;
   y=x*10;
   put x= y=;
   end;
z=x+3;
```

specify that the statements between DO and the END (the DO group) are to be performed only if X is greater than 5. If X is less than or equal to 5, statements in the DO group are skipped and the next statement executed is the assignment statement.

The statements

```
if x>5 then y=x*10;
if x>5 then put x= y=;
z=x+3;
```

produce the same result, but the program is less efficient because the IF expression is evaluated twice.

Iterative DO Statement

Iterative execution of a DO group can be specified by using an index variable in the DO statement. The iterative DO statement causes the statements between the DO and the END to be executed repetitively based on the value of the index variable. The form of the iterative DO statement is

DO *indexvariable=start* [**TO** *stop* [**BY** *increment*][**WHILE** | **UNTIL**(*expression*)]]...;
   SAS statements
END;

You can use these terms in the iterative DO statement:

indexvariable
> names a variable whose value governs execution of the DO group. After the final execution of the DO group, the value of the index variable is
>
> *start* + *increment**(INT((*stop-start*)/*increment*)+1) .
>
> Unless dropped, the index variable is included in the data set being created.

start
stop
> specify numbers or expressions that yield numbers to control the number of times the statements between DO and END are executed. The DO group is executed first with *indexvariable* equal to *start*.
>
> When both *start* and *stop* are present, execution continues (based on *increment*'s value) until *indexvariable* is greater than *stop*. When only *start* is present, execution continues (based on *increment*'s value) until a statement directs execution out of the loop. If neither *stop* nor *increment* is specified, the group executes once. Values of *start* and *stop* are evaluated prior to the first execution of the loop.
>
> For example, each of these DO groups is executed ten times:
>
> ```
> do i=1 to 10;
>    SAS statements
>    end;
> ```
>
> ```
> do i=1 by 1;
>    SAS statements
>    if i=10 then go to f;
>    end;
> f:put 'FINISHED';
> ```
>
> You can also replace *start* and *stop* with a series of values separated by commas. The values can be numeric or character. For example:
>
> ```
> do count=2,3,5,7,11,13,17;
> ```
>
> executes the DO group for COUNT=2,3,5,7,11,13,17. The statement
>
> ```
> do month='JAN','FEB','MAR';
> ```
>
> executes the DO group three times, once for each value JAN, FEB, and MAR of the index variable MONTH.

increment
> specifies a number or an expression that yields a number to control incrementing of the value of *indexvariable*. The value of *increment* is evaluated prior to the execution of the loop. For example,
>
> ```
> do count=2 to 8 by 2;
> ```
>
> causes the DO group to be executed for COUNT=2,4,6,8. The value of COUNT after the final execution of the DO group is 10.

If no increment is specified, the index variable is incremented by 1. If *increment* is positive, then *start* must be the lower bound and *stop*, if present, must be the upper bound for the loop. If *increment* is negative, then *start* must be the upper bound and *stop*, if present, must be the lower bound for the loop.

expression

is any expression. The rules for using a WHILE or UNTIL clause are the same as for the DO WHILE and DO UNTIL statements described later in this section. For example,

- `do i=1 to 10 while(x<y);`
- `do i=2 to 20 by 2 until((x/3)>y);`
- `do i=10 to 0 by -1 while(month='JAN');`

A number of clauses separated by commas can be included in the statement. In an iterative DO statement with more than one clause, each clause is evaluated prior to the execution of that clause. A WHILE or UNTIL specification affects only the clause in which it is located.

For example, the statement

```
do count=2 to 8 by 2,11,13 to 16;
```

causes the DO group to be executed for the following values of COUNT: 2,4,6,8, 11,13,14,15, and 16.

Here are some other examples of valid iterative DO statements:

- `do i=5;`
- `do i=1 to n;`
- `do i=n to 1 by -1;`
- `do i=k+1 to n-1;`
- `do i=1 to k-1, k+1 to n;`
- `do i=2,3,5,7,11,13,17;`
- `do i=.1 to .9 by .1, 1 to 10 by 1, 20 to 100 by 10;`
- `do i='SATURDAY','SUNDAY';`
- `do i='01JAN85'd,'25FEB85'd,'18APR85'd;`

The values of *start*, *stop*, and *increment* are evaluated before the statements in the DO group are executed. Any changes to the upper bound or increment made within the DO group do not affect the number of iterations. For example, consider this DATA step:

```
data iterate1;
   input x;
   stop=10;
   do i=1 to stop;
      *Always 10 iterations;
      y=x*normal(0);
      output;
      *Changing value of stop does not stop execution of group;
      if y>25 then stop=i;
      end;
   cards;
```

Setting STOP to the current value of I does not stop execution of the DO loop. You can, however, change the value of the index variable. Thus, you can stop execution of the loop either by setting I to STOP's value or by using a GO TO statement to jump to a statement outside the loop. For example,

```
data iterate2;
   input x;
   stop=10;
   do i=1 to stop;
      *Number of iterations ranges from 1 to 10;
      y=x*normal(0);
      output;
      *Either statement stops execution of group when y>25;
      [if y>25 then i=stop;] or [if y>25 then go to out;]
      end;
   [out:;]
   cards;
```

Consider these statements:

```
data createx;
   input x y z;
   if x=. then do k=1 to 25;
      x=uniform(0)*100;
      output;
      end;
   cards;
```

Each time X is missing, 25 observations are output, each with the values of Y and Z from the current data line and with randomly generated values of X. Each time the value of X is not missing, no observation is output.

Array processing with the iterative DO statement You can use an iterative DO statement to execute the statements in a DO group for some or all of the variables in an array.

To process an array in an iterative DO group, create an iterative DO statement in which *start* and *stop* are the beginning and ending element numbers of the array you want to process. Within the DO group, refer to elements of the array by their index value. The following example recodes the value 99 to 100 for any of the variables D1 through D7 that have a value of 99:

```
array days{7} d1-d7;
do i=1 to 7;
   if days{i}=99 then days{i}=100;
   end;
```

See the **ARRAY Statement** earlier in this chapter for more information.

DO OVER Statement

You can execute the statements in a DO group for the elements in an implicitly subscripted array with the DO OVER statement.

The form of the DO OVER statement is

DO OVER *arrayname*;
   more SAS statements
   END;

where

arrayname
   specifies an array that has been previously defined in an implicitly subscripted ARRAY statement (see the **ARRAY Statement** earlier in this chapter for details).

The DO OVER statement automatically executes the statements in the DO group for each element of the array unless you specify otherwise. It is equivalent to the statement

```
do i=1 to k;
```

where *i* is the index variable of the array, and *k* is the number of elements in the array.

For example, in the following DATA step, the DO OVER statement causes the values of SCORE1 through SCORE5 to be multiplied by 100:

```
data test;
   input score1-score5;
   array s score1-score5;
   do over s;
     s=s*100;
     end;
   cards;
.95 .88 .57 .90 .65
;
```

DO WHILE Statement

You can execute the statements in a DO group repetitively while a condition holds using the DO WHILE statement. The form of the DO WHILE statement is

DO WHILE(*expression*);

where

expression
   is any expression (see "SAS Expressions" for details). The expression is evaluated at the top of the loop before the statements in the DO group are executed. If the expression is true, the DO group is executed.

These statements repeat the loop as long as N is less than 5. There are 5 iterations in all (0, 1, 2, 3, 4):

```
n=0;
do while(n lt 5);
   put n=;
   n+1;
   end;
```

DO UNTIL Statement

The DO UNTIL statement, like the DO WHILE statement, executes the statements in a DO loop conditionally. The DO UNTIL evaluates the condition at the bottom of the loop rather than at the top (as does DO WHILE). Thus, the statements between DO and END are always executed at least one time. The form of the DO UNTIL statement is

DO UNTIL(*expression*);

where

expression
   is any expression (see "SAS Expressions" for details). The expression is evaluated at the bottom of the loop after the statements in the DO

group have been executed. If the expression is true, the DO group is not executed again. The DO group is always executed at least once.

These statements repeat the loop until N is greater than or equal to 5. There are 5 iterations in all (0, 1, 2, 3, 4):

```
n=0;
do until(n>=5);
   put n=;
   n+1;
   end;
```

DROP Statement

You can use the DROP statement in a DATA step to specify variables that are not to be included in the SAS data set or sets being created. A DROP statement in a DATA step applies to all the SAS data sets being created in the step. To drop variables selectively when multiple data sets are being created, use the DROP= data set option with each data set name. (See "SAS Files" for more information about data set options.)

Although variables appearing in a DROP statement are not included in any SAS data set being created, these variables can be used in program statements. The DROP statement can appear anywhere in the DATA step with the same effect since it is not an executable statement.

The form of the DROP statement is

DROP *variables*;

where

> *variables* specifies the variables you want omitted from the data set(s) being created. Any form of variable list may be used (see the "Introduction" to USING THE SAS LANGUAGE for details). Do not abbreviate the variable names.

Here is an example:

```
data parts;
   input name $ parta partb;
   test=parta+partb;
   drop parta partb;
   cards;
data lines
;
```

The variable TEST is computed for each observation by adding the values of PARTA and PARTB. The DROP statement tells the SAS System not to include the variables PARTA and PARTB in the new data set.

The effect of the DROP statement is the reverse of the KEEP statement's effect. To save writing, the DROP statement is preferred if fewer variables are being dropped than kept. Do not use both DROP and KEEP statements in the same DATA step.

When both RENAME and DROP statements are used in a DATA step, the DROP statement is applied first. This means that the old name should be used in the DROP statement.

The DROP statement is available only in the DATA step. To exclude variables from a PROC step, use the DROP= data set option.

END Statement

The END statement is the last of the SAS statements that make up a DO group or a SELECT group. The form of the END statement is

END;

An END statement must end every DO group and SELECT group in your SAS job. For example, a simple DO group and a simple SELECT group are shown below:

```
do;
  more SAS statements
  end;


select(expression);
  when(expression) SAS statement;
  otherwise SAS statement;
  end;
```

See the **DO Statement** and **SELECT Statement** elsewhere in this chapter for examples using END.

FILE Statement

Introduction   150
Specifications   150
When Multiple FILE Statements Specify the Same Output File   154
Print Files   155

Introduction

The FILE statement specifies the current output file. The current output file must be an external file. PUT statements write to the current output file or to the SAS log if no FILE statement is specified.

FILE statement options allow you to control how the output file is written. You can use FILE statement options to

- define variables that keep track of the current line and column pointer location
- specify headings to be printed at the beginning of each new output page.

More than one FILE statement can be used in a DATA step. The FILE statement is executable and therefore can be used in conditional (IF-THEN) processing.

When you use the FILE statement, you may also need to use other related statements, such as PUT, RETURN, and FILENAME. The PUT statement builds and directs output lines to the external file named in the most recently executed FILE statement. You need to understand the RETURN statement if you use the HEADER= option with the FILE statement. PUT and RETURN statements are described later in this chapter. You may also need to understand how the FILENAME statement is used with the FILE statement to define external files. The FILENAME statement is described in Chapter 18, "SAS Statements Used Anywhere."

Specifications

The form of the FILE statement is

FILE *filespecification* [*options*];

where

filespecification
    identifies the file. *Filespecification* can have the following forms:

fileref
    gives the fileref of the external file to which PUT statements write output lines. Associate *fileref* with the name of the external file in a FILENAME statement. If you use a fileref in a FILE statement without having used it in a FILENAME statement, SAS creates a file named *fileref* in your current directory.

'*filename*'
    specifies the complete name of a PC DOS file. Enclose *filename* in quotes.

LOG
    writes the lines produced by PUT statements on the SAS log. Since output lines are by default written to the SAS log, a FILE LOG statement is needed only to restore the default action or to specify additional FILE statement options.

At the beginning of each execution of a DATA step, SAS sets the fileref to LOG. Thus, the first PUT statement in the following DATA step always writes a line on the SAS log; the second PUT statement writes a line to the PRINT file:

```
data _null_;
   first PUT statement
   file print;
   second PUT statement
   more SAS statements
```

PRINT
: writes the lines produced by PUT statements on the standard SAS print file along with output produced by SAS procedures. When PRINT is the fileref, the SAS System uses carriage control characters and writes the lines with characteristics given in the section entitled **Print Files**.

options
: use the following options to control how lines are written to the current output file:

COLUMN=*variable*
: defines a SAS variable whose value is the current column location of the pointer. SAS automatically assigns the current column location to the COLUMN= variable.

HEADER=*label*
: associates a label with a group of SAS statements that execute each time SAS begins a new output page. *Label* defines the first statement in the group. You must include a RETURN statement before the group and as the last statement in the group. Use the HEADER= option with print files.

The following DATA step illustrates the use of the HEADER= option:

```
data _null_;
   set sprint;
   by dept;
   file '\misc\year85.dat' print header=newpage;
   put @22 dept @34 sales;
   return;
newpage:
   put @20 'SALES FOR 1985' /
       @25 dept=;
   return;
```

The statements after the NEWPAGE label are executed when SAS begins printing a new page. You can use any SAS statement in the group of statements labeled for execution with the HEADER= option, even statements containing constants or variable names.

LINE=*variable*
: defines a SAS variable whose value is the current relative line number within the group of lines specified by the N= option (described below). Thus, this variable can have a value from 1 up to the value specified by the N= option. If N= is not specified, the LINE= variable has a value of 1.

LINESIZE=*value*
LS=*value*
> sets the maximum number of columns per line for reports and the maximum record length for data files. If PUT statements try to write a line that is longer than the value specified by the LINESIZE= option, SAS writes the line as two or more separate records. For example, if the LINESIZE= value is 80, the following PUT statement writes three separate records:
>
> ```
> put name 1-50 city 71-90 state 91-104;
> ```
>
> The value of NAME appears in the first record, CITY in the second, and STATE in the third.
>
> The default LINESIZE= value depends on the type of file. The following list gives default line sizes depending on how you specify the FILE statement:
>
> | | |
> |---|---|
> | FILE LOG | LINESIZE= system option |
> | FILE PRINT | LINESIZE= system option |
> | FILE *fileref* PRINT | LINESIZE= system option |
> | FILE *fileref* (non-print) | LRECL= value |
>
> SAS will not write a record that is longer than the LINESIZE= value. If you specify this option, the value must fall within the range 64 to 256.

LINESLEFT=*variable*
LL=*variable*
> defines a SAS variable whose value is the number of lines left on the current page. Consider the following DATA step:
>
> ```
> data _null_;
>    set info;
>    file print linesleft=l;
>    put ə10 name /
>          ə10 address1 / ə10 address2 /
>          ə20 phone //;
>    if l<7 then put _page_ ə;
> ```
>
> In this example, if there are fewer than seven lines left on the page, the PUT _PAGE_ @ statement begins a new page and positions the line pointer at line 1.
>
> You can use the PAGESIZE= option (described below) to specify the number of lines per page.

LRECL=*value*
> specifies the logical record length of the output file. If you do not specify a logical record length, SAS uses the value of the LINESIZE= option. If LINESIZE= is not specified, SAS uses a value of 80 for non-print files and 78 for print files.

MOD
> writes the output lines after any existing lines on the file.

N=PAGESIZE
N=PS
N=*value*
> gives the number of output lines available to the pointer. The value of the N= option can be a number or the keyword PAGESIZE (PS). If the N= option is not specified and no # pointer controls are used in the

current DATA step, one line is available; that is, the default value of N= is 1. If N= is not specified and you do use a # pointer control, N= has the highest value specified for a # pointer control in any PUT statement in the current DATA step. (See the **PUT Statement** description for a complete discussion of the # pointer control in the section **Pointer Controls and Format Modifiers**.)

When the value of N= is 1, the SAS System writes each line before it begins the next. When the value of N= is 3, for example, lines are available to the pointer in groups of 3. Initially, lines 1, 2, and 3 are available, and you can move the pointer from line 1 to line 3 and back to line 1; lines 1, 2, and 3 are available until you move the pointer to line 4. Then lines 4, 5, and 6 are available, and so on. The pointer advances to line 1 of a new page when the PAGESIZE= value is reached or when a PUT _PAGE_ statement is encountered.

If the current output file is a print file, N= must have a value of either 1 or PAGESIZE.

Specify N=PS if you want to arrange each page of output before writing it. The following job produces a four-column telephone book listing; each column contains a name and a phone number:

```
data _null_;
   file print n=ps;
   do c=1, 30, 60, 90;
      do l=1 to 50;
         set phone;
         put #l @c name $20. +1 phone $8;
      end;
   end;
   put _page_;
```

The N=PS option makes all lines on the page available to the pointer. The L and C variables mark the current line and column of the pointer. The SET statement reads a SAS data set containing the names and telephone numbers. The PUT statement writes the NAME and PHONE values on the current line (the L value) at the current column (the C value). L's value is incremented by one until fifty names are written.

When the inner DO loop is satisfied, C is incremented to thirty to move the pointer over to the second column, and fifty more names are written in that column. When the outer DO loop is satisfied, the report includes four columns of fifty names each.

When the last value in the last column has been written, the PUT _PAGE_ statement writes the entire page. In the next execution of the DATA step, the C and L values begin at one again.

NOPRINT
   suppresses addition of the carriage control characters to the output lines for a print file. The most frequent use of the NOPRINT option is in printing a file that already contains these carriage control characters.

NOTITLES
NOTITLE
   suppresses printing of the current TITLE lines on the pages of print files (those where the fileref is PRINT or where the PRINT option appears in the FILE statement). When NOTITLES is omitted, the SAS System prints any titles currently defined.

OLD
   writes the output lines at the beginning of the file.

PAD
NOPAD
: controls whether records written to an external file are padded with blanks to the length specified in the LRECL= option. NOPAD is the default.

PAGESIZE=*value*
PS=*value*
: sets the number of lines per page for your reports.

    The value may range from 20 to 500. If no value is specified, the value of the system option PAGESIZE= is used. See Chapter 16, "SAS Global Options," for more information.

    If any TITLE statements are currently defined, the lines they occupy are included in counting the number of lines for each page.

PRINT
: produces a printed report in which carriage control characters appear in the output lines. The PRINT option is not necessary if you are using fileref PRINT.

RECFM=*recordformat*
: specifies the record format of the output file. Values for the RECFM= option are

    - F--fixed length
    - N--no format
    - D--data sensitive
    - U--undefined.

    RECFM=N treats a file as one large record (or a recordless series of bytes) rather than as a series of records. This option permits writing binary byte-addressable files.

    The following FILE statement options cannot be used with RECFM=N:

    HEADER=
    LINE=
    LINESIZE=
    LINESLEFT=
    LRECL=
    N=
    NOPRINT
    NOTITLES
    PAGESIZE=
    PRINT

    When writing to a file specified as RECFM=N with PUT statements, you must follow each statement with the @ character. You cannot have line or page advances when writing to such a file.

When Multiple FILE Statements Specify the Same Output File

If more than one FILE statement specifies different options for the same output file, the options execute as though you specified all of them in one FILE statement. You do not have to list previously specified options in subsequent FILE statements for the same output file. If you specify an option more than once using different values, the last value that you specify is used. For example,

```
data _null_;
   infile in;
   input name $ gift $ cost;
   file shoplist linesize=50;
   put name gift cost;
   file log;
   put cost;
   file shoplist linesize=20 print;
```

In this program the first FILE statement specifies fileref SHOPLIST and the LINESIZE= option to create an output file with a line length of 50 columns. The second FILE statement writes all COST values on the SAS log. The third FILE statement again specifies SHOPLIST with an additional option and a new value for the LINESIZE= option. When this program executes, the output file referenced by fileref SHOPLIST contains carriage control characters because the PRINT option is specified and has a line length of 20 columns.

Print Files

A file that contains carriage control characters such as formfeeds (to start a new page) and carriage returns (to overprint lines) is called a **print** file.

The SAS System inserts unprintable printer control characters into print files to cause the printer to begin a new line, a new page, or overprint the preceding line. The SAS System automatically produces print files when PRINT is specified as the fileref or when the PRINT option is used in the FILE statement.

FORMAT Statement

Introduction 156
Using FORMAT for Datetime Values 157

Introduction

You can use the FORMAT statement to associate formats with variables in a DATA step. The formats can be either SAS formats or formats you have defined with PROC FORMAT. You can give the same format to several variables or different formats to different variables in a single FORMAT statement. When the SAS System prints values of the variables, it uses the associated format to print the values.

Using a FORMAT statement in the DATA step permanently associates a format with a variable; see the **FORMAT Statement** in Chapter 7, "SAS Statements Used in the PROC Step," for information on assigning a format for the current PROC step only.

You can associate formats with variables with the statement

FORMAT *variables* [*format*] [**DEFAULT=***defaultformat*]...;

These terms are included in the FORMAT statement:

variables
names the variable or variables you want to associate with a format.

format
gives the format you want SAS to use for writing values of the variable or variables in the previous variable list. Every format name ends with a period (for example, SEXFMT.) or has a period between the width value and number of decimal places (for example, DOLLAR8.2).

See Chapter 13, "SAS Informats and Formats," for more information on the types of SAS formats that are available. See Chapter 19, "The FORMAT Procedure," in the *SAS Procedures Guide, Release 6.03 Edition* for information on how to define your own formats.

DEFAULT=*defaultformat*
specifies a temporary default format (character, numeric, or both) for displaying variable values. If no default is specified, the SAS System uses the BEST. format for output variables. With the DEFAULT= option, you can declare your own default character and numeric formats. The same FORMAT statement can contain a DEFAULT= specification along with other format specifications. The DEFAULT= specification can occur in any position within the FORMAT statement and can contain either a numeric default, a character default, or both.

For example, the program statements

```
data _null_;
   format y 10.3 default=8.2;
   x=12.1;
   y=10.3;
   put x=;
   put y=;
run;
```

produce the following output in the SAS log:

```
X=12.10
Y=10.300
```

Note that the default formats are not permanently associated with variables that the DATA step creates in an output data set but apply only during the current DATA step.

If a variable appears in more than one FORMAT statement, the format given in the last FORMAT statement is used. A FORMAT statement used in a DATA step to associate one format with a variable can be overridden by a FORMAT statement in a later PROC step. The original format name remains stored with the variable in the data set. To disassociate a format from a variable, use the variable's name in a FORMAT statement with no format.

You can also assign formats with the ATTRIB statement. You can change a format assigned in a FORMAT statement with an ATTRIB statement and vice versa.

This example uses the FORMAT procedure to define a format and a FORMAT statement to associate the format with a variable:

```
proc format;
   value sexfmt 1='MALE'
                2='FEMALE';
data all;
   input name $ sex @@;
   format sex sexfmt.;
   cards;
Jane  2  Bill  1
more data lines
;
```

The FORMAT procedure defines the SEXFMT. format. The FORMAT statement in the DATA step associates SEXFMT. with the variable SEX. When the values of SEX are printed by any procedure, MALE and FEMALE are printed instead of the numbers 1 and 2.

When a FORMAT statement associating a variable or variables with a format is used in a DATA step, SAS associates the specified format with the variables in the SAS data sets being created and uses the format for printing values of the variables. The format name is stored with the data set. (Note: for permanently stored SAS data sets, if you associate a user-defined format with a variable, the format must be accessible when the data set is referenced, even if you will not be printing the variable's values. See Chapter 19, "The FORMAT Procedure," in the *SAS Procedures Guide, Release 6.03 Edition* for more information.)

When a variable that has been associated with a format in a FORMAT statement later appears in a PUT statement without a format specification, the variable's values are left aligned in the output field with leading blanks trimmed.

Using FORMAT for Datetime Values

If a variable contains SAS date, time, or datetime values, you must assign the variable a corresponding date, time, or datetime format in a FORMAT statement in order for the values to be printed in an understandable form. For example, consider this DATA step:

```
data inventory;
   input descript $ acquired date7.;
   format acquired worddate.;
   cards;
cabinet 15JAN84
desk 03MAR85
more data lines
;
```

The FORMAT statement associates the SAS format WORDDATE. with the variable ACQUIRED, which contains SAS date values. (Note that the INPUT statement uses the SAS date informat DATE7. to read the data lines properly.) Without the FORMAT statement, values of ACQUIRED are printed as the number of days between January 1, 1960 and the ACQUIRED date, a large number that is difficult to interpret. See Chapter 13, "SAS Informats and Formats," for more information on date, time, and datetime formats.

GO TO Statement

A GO TO (or GOTO) statement tells the SAS System to jump immediately to the statement indicated in the GO TO statement and begin executing statements from that point. The GO TO statement and destination must be in the same DATA step. The destination is identified by a statement label in the GO TO statement and the target statement.

The statement has the form:

GO TO *label*;
GOTO *label*;

where

> *label* specifies a statement label that identifies the GO TO destination, which must be within the same DATA step. See **Labels, Statement** later in this chapter for more information.

The difference between the GO TO and LINK statements is in the action of a subsequent RETURN statement. A RETURN after a GO TO returns SAS execution to the beginning of the DATA step, whereas a RETURN after a LINK returns SAS execution to the statement following the LINK. In addition, a GO TO statement is often used without a RETURN statement; execution continues until another GO TO statement or the end of the DATA step, which contains an implied RETURN, is reached. A LINK statement is usually used with an explicit RETURN statement.

GO TO statements usually appear as the THEN clause in IF-THEN statements. In the example below, the SAS System jumps over the assignment statements to the OK label when X is between one and five inclusive:

```
data info;
   input x y;
   if 1<=x<=5 then go to ok;
   x=3;
   count+1;
   ok: sumx+x;
   cards;
data lines
;
```

In the example above, the labeled statement is executed for every observation. Sometimes you want a labeled statement to be executed only under certain conditions. For example,

```
data record;
   input x y z;
   if 1<=x<=5 then go to ok;
   x=3;
   count+1;
   return;
   ok: sumx+x;
   cards;
data lines
;
```

The statement

```
sumx+x;
```

is executed only for observations with X values between one and five inclusive. When the RETURN statement is executed, the SAS System outputs the current observation to data set RECORD and returns to the beginning of the DATA step and a new execution.

GO TO statements can often be replaced by DO-END statements. For example, using DO-END in the first example above results in:

```
data info;
   input x y;
   if x<1 or x>5 then do;
      x=3;
      count+1;
      end;
   sumx+x;
```

The second example above with DO-END and IF-THEN-ELSE is

```
data record;
   input x y z;
   if x<1 or x>5 then do;
      x=3;
      count+1;
      end;
   else sumx+x;
```

See the **RETURN Statement** later in this chapter for other examples using the GO TO statement.

IF Statement

Introduction 161
IF-THEN and IF-THEN/ELSE Statements 161
Subsetting IF Statement 163

Introduction

In SAS processing there are two kinds of IF statements:

- Conditional IF statements, written with a THEN clause, are used to execute a SAS statement only for observations that meet the condition specified in the IF clause. An optional ELSE statement gives an alternative action if the THEN clause is not executed.
- Subsetting IF statements, without a THEN clause, are used to cause the SAS System to continue processing only those observations or records that meet the condition specified in the IF clause.

IF-THEN and IF-THEN/ELSE Statements

Use the IF-THEN statement when you want to execute a SAS statement for some but not all of the observations in the SAS data set being created. SAS evaluates the expression following the IF. When the expression is true for the observation being processed, the statement following THEN is executed. When the expression is false, SAS ignores the statement following THEN and executes the ELSE statement immediately following the IF. If no ELSE statement is present, SAS executes the next program statement.

The form of the IF-THEN statement is

IF *expression* **THEN** *statement*;

where

expression
is any valid SAS expression. SAS evaluates the expression in an IF statement to produce a result that is either nonzero, zero, or missing. A nonzero result causes the expression to be true; a result of zero or missing causes the expression to be false. For example, in the statement

```
if x=3 then statement;
```

when the variable X has a value of 3, the result of evaluating the expression 3=3 is 1, that is, true. In the statement

```
if x then statement;
```

the expression is true when variable X has a value other than 0 or missing. See "SAS Expressions" for more information on the way SAS evaluates expressions.

statement
can be any executable SAS statement or DO group. The following list identifies executable SAS statements: ABORT, assignment, CALL, DELETE, DISPLAY, DO, FILE, GO TO, IF-THEN, INPUT, INFILE, LINK, LIST, LOSTCARD, MERGE, OUTPUT, PUT, null, sum, RETURN, SELECT, SET, STOP, and UPDATE.

For example, the statement

```
if year=1984 then color='BLUE';
```

assigns the value 'BLUE' to a variable named COLOR when the value of YEAR is 1984. If the value of YEAR is not 1984, COLOR is not assigned a value; the value remains as it was before the IF statement.

In the example

```
if year<1980 then delete;
```

SAS deletes the observation when its value for YEAR is less than 1980.

The ELSE statement can immediately follow an IF-THEN statement to specify a statement that is to be executed when the condition of the IF is false.

The form of the ELSE statement is

ELSE *statement*;

where

statement
   is any executable SAS statement or DO group as described above.

The statements

```
if year=1984 then color='BLUE';
else color='RED';
```

assign 'RED' to the variable COLOR when the value of YEAR is not 1984.

Here are some other examples of IF-THEN/ELSE statements:

```
if 0<age<1 then age=1;
if response=. then delete;
if status='OK' and type=3 then count+1;
if state='CA' or state='OR'
   then region='PACIFIC COAST      ';
else if state='NC' or state='VA' or state='MD'
   then region='MID ATLANTIC COAST';
if hours>40 then link overtime;
else if 0<hours<=40 then link regular;
else put 'PROBLEM OBSERVATION' _all_;
```

To execute more than one statement for a true condition, follow THEN with a DO group:

```
if answer=9 then do;
   answer=.;
   put 'INVALID ANSWER FOR ' id=;
   end;
else do;
   answer=answer10;
   valid+1;
   end;
```

See the **DO Statement** description earlier in this chapter for more information.

IF-THEN/ELSE statements can be nested, as in this example:

```
if x=0 then
   if y^=0 then put 'X ZERO, Y NONZERO';
   else put 'X ZERO, Y ZERO';
else put 'X NONZERO';
```

The first ELSE statement pairs with the second IF statement, and the last ELSE statement pairs with the first IF statement.

In the example above you can use the SELECT statement instead of nested IF-THEN/ELSE statements, as follows:

```
select (x);
   when (0) do;
      select (y);
         when (0) put 'X ZERO, Y ZERO';
         otherwise put 'X ZERO, Y NONZERO';
         end;
      end;
   otherwise put 'X NONZERO';
   end;
```

The **SELECT Statement** is described later in this chapter.

Subsetting IF Statement

Use the subsetting IF statement to cause the SAS System to continue processing only observations from the external file or SAS data set used as input to a DATA step that meet the condition specified in the IF statement. The resulting SAS data set therefore contains a subset of the original observations.

The form of the subsetting IF is

IF *expression*;

where

expression
  is any valid SAS expression. The expression must conform to the rules in "SAS Expressions."

If the expression is true (is nonzero and nonmissing), SAS continues executing statements in the DATA step for the observation it is building. If the expression is false (0 or missing), SAS immediately returns to the beginning of the DATA step for another execution without outputting the observation. The remaining program statements in the DATA step are not executed.

For example, the statement

```
if sex='F';
```

results in a data set containing only observations with a SEX value of 'F'.

Here is an example that uses subsetting IF statements to produce new data sets that are subsets of an original data set.

```
data populace;
   input name $ sex $ age marital $;
   cards;
data lines
;
data seniors;
   set populace;
   if age>=65;
data wives;
   set populace;
   if sex='F' and marital='M';
```

Data set SENIORS contains only those observations from POPULACE with an AGE value of 65 or greater. The data set WIVES contains those observations for which the SEX value is 'F' and the MARITAL value is 'M'.

INFILE Statement

Introduction 164
  Where the INFILE statement goes 164
Specifications 165
Options 165

Introduction

An INFILE statement identifies an external file (that is, a non-SAS file) that you want to read with an INPUT statement. The external file can be on disk or can be data lines you enter at the keyboard. (SAS data sets are not read with an INFILE statement. Instead, use a SET, MERGE, or UPDATE statement to read a SAS data set in a DATA step.)

For example, suppose you want to analyze sales information in an external file with PROC TABULATE. Before invoking PROC TABULATE you need to create a SAS data set from the external file with the INFILE and INPUT statements.

INFILE statement options describe the input file's characteristics and specify how it is to be read with an INPUT statement. Using INFILE options you can:

- define variables whose values reflect the current pointer location, the length of the last line read, or whether the current line is the last in the file
- define what happens when the pointer reaches past the end of the current line
- restrict processing of the file by skipping lines at either the beginning or end of the file or both.

Where the INFILE statement goes Since the INFILE statement identifies the file to be read, the INFILE statement must execute before the INPUT statement that reads the data lines.

If you read several external files within one DATA step, each file must have a corresponding INFILE statement. The INPUT statement reads from the current input file, that is, the file pointed to by the most recently executed INFILE statement. At the beginning of each execution of the DATA step, the current input file is implicitly CARDS until an INFILE statement executes.

When you read from more than one external file in a DATA step, you can partially process one external file, go on to a different file, and return to the original file. An INFILE statement must be executed each time you want to access a file, even if you are returning to a file previously accessed.

Suppose your program reads from two files, referenced by the names EXFILE1 and EXFILE2. To access the files alternately, execute a new INFILE statement for each access:

```
data mydata;
   infile exfile1;
   input ... ;
   more SAS statements
   infile exfile2;
   input ... ;
   more SAS statements
   infile exfile1;
   input ... ;
   more SAS statements
```

Notice that to read from EXFILE1 a second time, you must execute a second INFILE statement for EXFILE1.

When you use more than one INFILE statement for the same fileref, and you specify options in each INFILE statement, the effect is additive. That is, the options specified in each INFILE statement are added to the options specified in any subsequent INFILE statement(s) for that file. To avoid confusion, you should specify all options in the first INFILE statement for a given file.

Since the INFILE statement is executable, it can be used in conditional processing (in an IF/THEN statement, for example).

Specifications

The form of the INFILE statement is

INFILE *filespecification options*;

where

filespecification
identifies the file. *Filespecification* can have the following forms:

fileref
specifies the fileref (file reference) that identifies the input file.

A *fileref* is a short name for the file you want to process. At some point prior to execution of the INFILE statement, you explicitly associate the fileref with the file's complete name in a FILENAME statement. If you use a fileref that has not been assigned in a FILENAME statement, SAS searches for a file named *'fileref'* in your current directory.

'filename'
specifies the complete name of an external file. Enclose *filename* in quotes.

CARDS
specifies that the input data immediately follow a CARDS statement in your SAS job. Use CARDS instead of a fileref when you want to use INFILE statement options to read in-stream data (entered at the keyboard). In other words, use both an INFILE statement and a CARDS statement: substitute the word CARDS for the *fileref* in the INFILE statement:

```
data exam;
    infile cards options;
    input...;
    other SAS statements
    cards;
data lines
    ;
```

options
specifies one or more INFILE statement options described in the next section.

Options

The following options can appear in the INFILE statement:

COLUMN=*variable*
COL=*variable*
defines a variable that the SAS System sets to the column location of the input pointer. For example, these statements

```
data one;
    infile '\weekly\monday.msc' column=c;
    input @5 x 3.;
    put c=;
```

produce the line

```
C=8
```

DELIMITER=*'list of delimiting characters'* | *charactervariable*
DLM=*'list of delimiting characters'* | *charactervariable*

The DELIMITER= option allows a delimiter other than the blank for list input. In the following example, input data is divided by commas. By setting the DELIMITER= option to accept commas as valid data delimiters, the input can be easily read:

```
data new;
   infile cards dlm=',';
   input a b c;
   cards;
1,2,3
4,5,6
7,8,9
;
```

Note that if you specify multiple characters as delimiters, all the specified characters are assumed to be delimiters. For example, in the statement

```
infile cards dlm='AB';
```

both A and B are assumed to be delimiters.

END=*variable*

defines a variable that the SAS System sets to 1 when the current line is the last in the input file. The value of the END= variable is 0 until the last line is processed. You cannot use the END= option for UNBUFFERED files or for files allocated to your console, including a CARDS file.

EOF=*label*

is a statement label that you specify as the object of an implicit GO TO when the INFILE statement reaches end-of-file. The SAS System jumps to the labeled statement when an INPUT statement attempts to read from a file that has no more records.

The EOF= option (and not END=) should be used when the DATA step uses

- multiple INPUT statements
- INPUT statements that read more than one data line at a time
- INPUT statements that execute within conditional (IF-THEN) constructs
- UNBUFFERED files, including a CARDS file.

The following example illustrates the EOF= option:

```
data two;
   infile input1 eof=next;
   input...;
   return;
next: infile input2 eof=last;
   input...;
   return;
last: infile input3;
   input...;
```

In this example:

- In the INFILE INPUT1 statement, EOF=NEXT directs the SAS System to the label NEXT when all data have been read from the external file INPUT1.
- NEXT labels another INFILE statement naming the external file INPUT2. The EOF=LAST specification directs the SAS System to the LAST label when all data have been read from INPUT2.
- LAST labels another INFILE statement that names another external file, INPUT3.

FIRSTOBS=*linenumber*
> indicates that you want to begin reading the input file at the line number specified, rather than beginning with the first record. For example, to start with record 100 you may use this INFILE statement:
>
> ```
> infile '\misc\june.dat' firstobs=100;
> ```

FLOWOVER
> specifies that if the INPUT statement reads past the end of the current record, the INPUT statement is to continue reading data from the next record.

LENGTH=*variable*
> defines a variable that the SAS System sets to the length of the current input line.
>
> You can reset the value of the LENGTH= variable in program statements. This is useful when copying the input file to another file with PUT _INFILE_; you can use the LENGTH= option to truncate the copied records. For example, the statements below truncate the last 20 columns from the input lines before they are copied to the output file:
>
> ```
> data _null_;
>    infile xyz length=l;
>    input;
>    l=l-20;
>    file out;
>    put _infile_;
> ```

LINE=*variable*
> defines a variable that the SAS System sets to the line location of the input pointer. The value of the LINE= variable is the current relative line number within the group of lines specified by the N= option (described below). Thus, the value of the LINE= variable ranges from 1 up to the value of the N= variable. Without the N= option, the LINE= variable has a value of 1 since by default only one line is available to the pointer. For example, the statements
>
> ```
> data test;
>    infile b n=2 line=l;
>    input name 1-10 #2 id 3-5;
>    put l=;
> ```

produce the line

```
L=2
```

LINESIZE=*linesize*
LS=*linesize*
> limits the record length available to the INPUT statement when you do not want to read the entire record.

For example, say that your data lines contain a sequence number in columns 73 through 80. You could use the INFILE statement

```
infile c linesize=72;
```

to restrict the INPUT statement to the first 72 columns of the lines and prevent inadvertently reading a sequence number as data.

If an INPUT statement attempts to read past the column specified by LINESIZE=, the action taken depends on which of the FLOWOVER, MISSOVER, and STOPOVER options is in effect.

LRECL=*logicalrecordlength*
specifies the logical record length. Valid record sizes are from 1 to 32767.

MISSOVER
prevents a SAS program from going to a new input line if it does not find values in the current line for all the INPUT statement variables. When an INPUT statement reaches the end of the current record, values that are expected but not found are set to missing.

For example, suppose you are reading temperature data. Each input line contains from 1 to 5 temperatures:

```
data weather;
   infile cards missover;
   input temp1-temp5;
   cards;
97.9 98.1 98.3
98.6 99.2 99.1 98.5 97.5
;
```

The SAS System reads the three values on the first data line as values of TEMP1, TEMP2, and TEMP3. The MISSOVER option causes the SAS System to set the values of TEMP4 and TEMP5 to missing for that observation because there are no values for those variables in the current input line.

When the MISSOVER option **is not used**, the SAS System goes to the second data line for the TEMP4 and TEMP5 values, printing the message

```
NOTE: SAS went to a new line when INPUT
      statement reached past the end of a line.
```

The SAS System reads data line 3 the next time it executes the INPUT statement.

N=*number*
defines the number of lines you want available to the input pointer.

When the N= option is not used, the number of lines available to the pointer is the highest value following a # pointer control in any INPUT statement in the DATA step. When you do not use a # pointer control, N= has a default value of 1.

The only time the N= option is necessary is when you are reading a variable number of lines per observation without a # pointer control. The N= value affects only the number of lines that the pointer can access at a time; it has no effect on the number of lines an INPUT statement reads.

OBS=*linenumber*
gives the last line that you want to read from a sequential input file. This option is especially useful when you want to test your SAS program

using just a few of the records in your file. For example, the statement below processes only the first 100 records in the file:

```
infile inb obs=100;
```

You can use the OBS= and the FIRSTOBS= options together to read records from the middle of your file. For example, the statement below begins processing with record 100 and ends with record 200:

```
infile in2 firstobs=100 obs=200;
```

PAD
NOPAD
> controls whether records read from an external file are padded with blanks to the length specified in the LRECL= option. NOPAD is the default.

RECFM=*recordformat*
> specifies the record format for a file. Values for RECFM= include

- F--fixed length
- N--no format
- D--data sensitive
- U--undefined.

The default is D.

RECFM=N treats a file as one large record (or a recordless series of bytes) rather than as a series of records. This option permits access to binary byte-addressable files. The following INFILE statement options do not work with RECFM=N and produce error messages:

FIRSTOBS=
FLOWOVER
LINE=
LINESIZE=
LRECL=
MISSOVER
N=
OBS=
START=
STOPOVER

With RECFM=N, the INPUT statement format characters trailing @ and trailing @@ produce warning messages; the format characters / and #n produce errors.

START=*variable*
> gives the first column number of the record that the PUT _INFILE_ statement is to write.
>
> For example, say that you are making a copy of the file identified with fileref ABC, but you do not want the first ten columns of the records copied. These statements copy only columns 11-80:

```
data _null_;
   infile abc start=s;
   input;
   s=11;
   file out;
   put _infile_;
```

STOPOVER
   stops processing the DATA step when an INPUT statement reaches the end of the current record without finding values for all variables in the statement.

   When the STOPOVER option is specified and an input line does not contain the expected number of values, the SAS System sets _ERROR_ to 1, stops building the data set as though a STOP statement had executed, and prints the incomplete data line. Here is an example:

```
data y;
   infile cards stopover;
   input x1-x4;
   cards;
1 2 3
5 6 7 8
9 4 0
;
```

   When the SAS System reads the first data line, it does not find an X4 value. Because STOPOVER is specified in the INFILE statement, the SAS System sets _ERROR_ to 1, stops building the data set, and prints data line 1.

   Without the STOPOVER option, the SAS System would print the message

```
NOTE: SAS went to a new line when INPUT
      statement reached past the end of a line.
```

   continue to line 2, and read 5 as the value for X4. The next time the DATA step executes, the SAS System would read a new line, in this case, line 3.

TABS
NOTABS
   expands the tab character settings to standard tab settings, which are set at eight-column intervals starting at column 9. NOTABS is the default. This is useful if you are reading binary data that contain the tab character '09'x.

UNBUFFERED
UNBUF
   tells the SAS System not to perform the usual look-ahead read. When the UNBUFFERED option is specified, the SAS System never sets the END= variable to 1.

INFORMAT Statement

The INFORMAT statement associates informats with variables. You can use it in a DATA step to specify a default informat for variables listed in an INPUT statement. You can also use it in some procedures such as the FSEDIT procedure in SAS/FSP software.

You can associate informats with variables by using the statement

INFORMAT *variables* [*informat*] [**DEFAULT**=*defaultinformat*]...;

These terms are included in the INFORMAT statement:

variables
: names the variable or variables you want to associate with an informat.

informat
: gives the informat you want SAS to use for reading values of the variable or variables in the previous variable list. When an informat is specified in an INFORMAT statement, **only** the informat type (RB., IB., $, and so on) is used. Any width or decimal specification is ignored. Every informat name ends with a period (for example, $15.) or has a period between the width value and number of decimal places (for example, 8.2). All the informats described in Chapter 13, "SAS Informats and Formats," except the $CHAR., BZ., and $VARYING. informats can be used. (You should not use the $CHAR. and BZ. informats because blanks are significant to them; however, list input mode uses blanks to indicate the end of an input field. Therefore, unexpected results may occur with embedded blanks in data lines when you use the $CHAR. and BZ. informats.)

DEFAULT= defaultinformat
: specifies a temporary default informat (numeric, character, or both) for reading variable values. You can declare a default informat for numeric and character variables. The same INFORMAT statement can contain a DEFAULT= specification along with other informat specifications. The DEFAULT= specification can occur in any position within the INFORMAT statement and can contain either a numeric default, a character default, or both.

  For example, the SAS program

```
data _null_;
   informat default=3.1;
   input x1-x10;
   put x1-x10;
   cards;
 11 22 33 44 55 66 77 88 99100
;
run;
```

  yields the following output in the SAS log:

  1.1 2.2 3.3 4.4 5.5 6.6 7.7 8.8 9.9 10

  The blank space before the first 1 in the data fills that field to its three-digit length and is assumed to be a part of the number. Note that the default informats are not permanently associated with variables that the DATA step creates in an output data set but apply only during the current DATA step.

When you use an INFORMAT statement to associate an informat with a variable and then use the variable's name without an informat in an INPUT statement,

SAS reads the value using list input mode (described with the INPUT statement later in this chapter).

For example, these statements

```
informat frstname lastname $15.;
input frstname lastname;
```

are equivalent to the statement

```
input frstname : $15. lastname : $15.;
```

The colon format modifier (:) is described with the INPUT statement later in this chapter.

INPUT Statement

Introduction 173
  Kinds of data 174
Column Input 175
  Requirements 175
  Features 176
  Missing values 176
  Blanks 176
List Input 176
  Requirements 176
  Features 177
  Order of variables 177
  Missing values 177
  Blanks 177
Formatted Input 178
  Requirements 178
  Features 178
  Grouped format lists 178
  Format modifiers 179
  Order of variables 180
  Missing values 180
  Blanks 180
  Storing informats 180
Named Input 181
  Requirements 181
  Restrictions 181
Advanced INPUT Statement Features 182
  Column pointer controls 182
  Column pointer location after reading 186
  Line pointer controls 186
  Line hold specifiers 187
  Reading past the end of a line 189
  Formatted lists with pointer controls 189
  SAS format modifiers for error reporting 189
Special Topics 190
  Numeric data: details 190
  Character data: details 191
  The INPUT statement without operands 191
  How the SAS System handles invalid data 191
  End-of-file 192
  Arrays 192

Introduction

The INPUT statement describes the arrangement of values in an input record and assigns input values to corresponding SAS variables. A simple INPUT statement can read simple input data records. You may need to use the INPUT statement's advanced features to read more complicated input data.

Use the INPUT statement **only** for values stored in an external file or values that follow a CARDS statement. If the data are already in a SAS data set, use a SET, MERGE, or UPDATE statement instead.

The general form of the INPUT statement is

INPUT [*specification*]...;

There are four ways to describe a record's values in an INPUT statement:

- column
- list, or free-format
- formatted
- named.

The following simple INPUT statements, reading the variables NAME (character) and AGE (numeric), illustrate the column, list, formatted, and named input styles. (Character and numeric data are introduced in **Kinds of data**, below.)

With **column input**, the column numbers containing a variable's value follow the INPUT statement variable:

```
input name $ 1-8 age 11-12;
```

With **list input**, the variables to be assigned data values are simply listed in the INPUT statement:

```
input name $ age;
```

With **formatted input**, you specify an *informat* after the INPUT statement variable. The informat indicates the variable's data type and field width.

```
input name $char10. age 2.;
```

With **named input**, you specify the name of the variable followed by an equal sign, and the SAS System looks for a variable name and equal sign in your input data:

```
input name = $ age =;
```

Input styles can be mixed within an INPUT statement. For example, you can read NAME with column input and AGE with formatted input:

```
input name $ 1-10 age 2.;
```

A DATA step that reads an external file can have one or many INPUT statements.

Kinds of data Data values are either *character* or *numeric*. A character value is simply a sequence of characters. It can contain letters, numbers, and all kinds of special characters—for example, underscores (_), pound signs (#), and ampersands (&). A numeric value usually contains only numbers, including numbers in E-notation, and sometimes a decimal point or minus sign. (You can use formatted input to cause SAS to read values containing certain other characters as numbers.) Character and numeric data are discussed in more detail in **Special Topics** later in this section.

Both character and numeric data can appear on data lines in *standard* or *nonstandard* form. Standard-form data are stored with one digit or character per byte. (One column on a screen or printout is equivalent to one byte.) Standard-form data can be read with all three input styles. Examples of simple standard data include:

```
ARKANSAS
1166.42
```

Data that are not in standard form can be read only with formatted input. Examples of nonstandard-form data include hexadecimal and binary values, as in

```
43415259   (a hexadecimal representation of the value CARY)
00000110   (a binary representation of the value 6)
```

A value read with an INPUT statement is assumed to be numeric unless a dollar sign follows the variable name in the INPUT statement, a character informat is used, or the variable has been previously defined as character. If you specify a data type that is incompatible with the data value, SAS takes the action described in **How the SAS System handles invalid data**.

Column Input

Requirements With column input, the column numbers containing the value follow a variable name in the INPUT statement. Column input can be used when the input values are

- in the same columns on all the input lines
- in standard numeric or character form.

For example, if the numeric variable COUNT occupies columns 7 and 8 in all lines of input data, this INPUT statement

```
input count 7-8;
```

reads the value of the variable COUNT from columns 7 and 8 of each line of input data.

The form of the INPUT statement for reading one variable with column input is

INPUT *variable* [$] *startcolumn*[−*endcolumn*] [.*decimals*];

where

variable
names the variable whose value the INPUT statement is to read.

$
indicates that the variable has a character, rather than a numeric, value. If the variable has been previously defined as character, the $ sign is not required.

startcolumn
is the first column of the input record that contains the variable's value.

−*endcolumn*
is the last column of the input record that contains the variable's value. If the variable's value occupies only one column, omit *endcolumn*. For example

```
input name $ 1-10 pulse 11-13 waist 14-15 age 16;
```

Values for the character variable NAME start in column 1 and end in column 10. Values for PULSE start in column 11 and end in column 13, and so forth. AGE occupies only column 16.

.*decimals*
gives the number of digits to the right of the decimal if the input value does not contain an explicit decimal point. An explicit decimal point in the input value overrides a decimal specification in the INPUT statement. For example, the statement

```
input number 10-15 .2;
```

reads the value of NUMBER with two decimal places. The following list shows some input data for the NUMBER variable and their values when SAS reads the data with the .2 specification:

Input	Result
2314	23.14
2	.02
400	4.00
−140	−1.40
12.234	12.234 (input decimal overrides)
12.2	12.2 (input decimal overrides)

Features   Features of column input are

- Input values can be read in any order, regardless of their position in the record. For example, the statement

    ```
    input first 73-80 second 10-12;
    ```

    first reads a value of the variable FIRST from columns 73 through 80 and then a value for the variable SECOND from columns 10 through 12.
- Character values can have embedded blanks.
- Character values can be from 1 to 200 characters long.
- Values or parts of values can be reread. For example, in

    ```
    input id 10-15 group 13;
    ```

    columns 10-15 contain an ID value; the third digit of ID, column 13, is a group number.

Missing values   Blank fields and fields containing only a period (.) are interpreted as missing values.

Blanks   Column input ignores both leading and trailing blanks within the field. Thus, if you use the INPUT statement

```
input count 7-9;
```

and the value for COUNT is in columns 7 and 8 and column 9 is blank, the value in columns 7 and 8 is used. The SAS language does not treat trailing blanks as zeros as some other languages do (for example, FORTRAN).

If numeric values contain blanks that represent zeros or if you want to retain leading and trailing blanks in character values, you must read the value with an informat. See the **Formatted Input** section for more information.

List Input

Requirements   With list input, the SAS System scans the input line for values, rather than reading from specific columns. Consider list input when

- input values are separated from each other by at least one blank
- periods, rather than blanks, represent missing values
- character input values have a maximum length of 8 bytes unless given a longer length in an earlier LENGTH, ATTRIB, or INFORMAT statement.

With list input, the values for the variables are delimited by one or more blanks or by the end of the input record, whichever comes first. Unless explicitly specified elsewhere, the length of character values is 8 bytes by default. To read longer values, use formatted input; that is, specify an informat, use column input, or define a longer length in a LENGTH, ATTRIB, or INFORMAT statement.

Features List input may be the easiest style to use since you can simply list the variables to be assigned values in the INPUT statement. It is not necessary to know what columns the data values occupy in the input record. However, this style has some restrictions on the order of variables and missing values.

The form of the INPUT statement for reading one variable with list input is

INPUT *variable* [$] [&];

where

variable
    names the variable whose value the INPUT statement is to read.

$
    indicates that the preceding variable contains a character, rather than a numeric, value. If the variable has been previously defined as character, the $ sign is not required. For example,

```
input name $;
```

&
    indicates that a character value may have one or more single embedded blanks. Because a blank normally indicates the end of a data value with list input, when you use the ampersand modifier indicate the end of the value with at least two blanks. For example, the following INPUT statement can read the values listed for the variables NAME and AGE:

```
data one;
   input name $ & age;
   cards;
J. Jones   20
J. R. J.   31
;
```

Order of variables When reading with list input, the order of the variables listed in the INPUT statement and their corresponding values in the input data must be the same.

You cannot read values selectively with simple list input, although you can ignore all values after a given point. For example, suppose each input line contains five values for the variables A, B, C, D, and E, and you want only values for A, B, and D. With simple list input you cannot skip C, but you can omit E since it is after D, the last value you want:

```
input a b c d;
```

Missing values Missing input values must be represented with a single period (.) to be read with list input.

Blanks If you want to read values that contain leading, trailing, or embedded blanks with list input, use the DELIMITER= option on the INFILE statement to specify another character to be used as a delimiter. (See **The INFILE Statement** earlier in this chapter for information.) If your input data uses blanks as delimiters and has leading, trailing, or embedded blanks, you must use either column or formatted input style. There is one exception: character values containing single embedded blanks can be read using the ampersand (&) modifier described above, but your data values must be separated by two or more blanks.

Formatted Input

Requirements An INPUT statement reading *formatted input* lists a SAS informat after the variable. An *informat* gives the data type and field width of an input value. See Chapter 13, "SAS Informats and Formats," for more information about informats.

Features With formatted input you can:

- read input values with contiguous blanks
- read data in virtually any form
- use grouped format lists
- use format modifiers.

Formatted input is often used with the pointer controls discussed later in **Advanced INPUT Statement Features** and with format modifiers. Note, however, that neither pointer controls nor format modifiers are required to use formatted input.

The form of the INPUT statement for reading one variable with simple formatted input is

INPUT *variable* [*formatmodifier*] *informat*;

where

variable
  is the variable that the INPUT statement is to read.

formatmodifier
  modifies the way the informat reads the input value. There are two format modifiers: the colon (:) and ampersand (&). They are described in **Format modifiers**, below.

informat
  gives the informat to use when reading the input value. An informat always includes or ends with a period (.), for example, 3.2 and $CHAR4. See Chapter 13, "SAS Informats and Formats," for complete descriptions of all SAS informats.

  Informats for character values begin with a dollar sign ($).

  Decimal points included in the input override decimal specifications in an informat.

Grouped format lists When input values are arranged in a pattern, they can be described with a grouped format list. A grouped format list consists of two lists, each enclosed in parentheses: the first names the variables to be read; the second gives their corresponding informats. You can write shorter INPUT statements with format lists because

- the format list is recycled until all variables have been read
- numbered variable names can be used in abbreviated form to avoid listing all the individual variables.

You can use as many format lists as necessary in an INPUT statement, but format lists cannot be nested. For example, if the values for the five variables SCORE1-SCORE5 are arranged four columns per value without intervening blanks, the following INPUT statement

```
input (score1-score5) (4. 4. 4. 4. 4.);
```

reads their values. However, if you specify more variables than informats, the format list is reused to read the remaining variables. Therefore, this shorter format list accomplishes the same thing:

```
input (score1-score5) (4.);
```

When all the values in the variable list have been read, the INPUT statement ignores any directions remaining in the informat list.

You can use commas between items in format lists to delineate separate informats. In this statement,

```
input (a b) ($,5.);
```

the comma indicates that the $ specification is associated with A and that the 5. informat is associated with B. Without the comma, as in

```
input (a b) ($ 5.);
```

the SAS System interprets the statement with a single informat, $5., and associates it with both A and B.

The $n*$ modifier in format lists specifies that the next format is to be repeated n times. For example, say that you want to read first a value of the variable NAME, followed by the five SCORE values:

```
input (name score1-score5) ($10. 5*4.);
```

This INPUT statement first reads a value of the variable NAME from columns 1 through 10; then reads the five SCORE values from the next 20 columns.

Format modifiers Format modifiers change the way an informat reads an input value. Specify a format modifier before the informat to which it applies. There are two format modifiers:

:

combines informats with the scanning feature of list input. The colon indicates that the value is to be read from the next nonblank column until

- the next blank column
- the length of the variable as previously defined has been read
- the end of the data line

whichever comes first. If the length of the variable has not been previously defined, its value is read and stored with the informat length.

For example, say that the first value on each input line is a last name that can be up to 15 characters long. Use the colon (:) format modifier before the $15. informat to indicate that the value ends at the first blank column, the end of the data line, or the end of 15 columns, **whichever comes first**. For example, the following INPUT statement

```
input lastname :$15.;
```

reads the following input data:

```
Smith 123 Highway
Longlastname 527 Avenue
```

&

indicates that a character input value may contain one or more single embedded blanks and is to be read from the next nonblank column until one of the following is encountered:

- two consecutive blanks

- the length of the variable as first defined in the DATA step
- the end of the input line

whichever comes first.

For example, the statement

```
input lastname $ state & $;
```

indicates that the input line contains first a value for the character variable LASTNAME and then a value, which can include one or more single blanks, for the character variable STATE.

Note: because the ampersand format modifier indicates that the input value may contain single embedded blanks, signify the end of the value with two blanks.

The & modifier has the same effect as the : modifier except that the terminating condition is two blanks rather than one. For example,

```
data one;
   input lastname & $15. name1 $;
   cards;
Longlastnameone  John
Mc Allister  Mike
Longlastnamethree  Jim
;
```

The colon is unnecessary in this case because the ampersand implies the colon's function. The value for LASTNAME is read from the first nonblank column up to 15 columns or until two consecutive blanks or the end of the line.

Note: using the : or & format modifier invokes the scanning feature of list input. Although the variable **value** contains only the input read from the next nonblank column until either the next blank or the defined length of the variable, the input pointer does not stop until it finds a blank. Therefore, do not use the : or the & format modifier unless

- input data values are separated by blanks (two blanks in the case of the & modifier), or
- you intend to read only the last variable in the input line using the format modifier, and therefore do not care about the input pointer location.

Order of variables Simple formatted input (that is, without pointer controls) requires that the variables be in the same order as their corresponding values in the input data. You can read variables in any order by using pointer controls.

Missing values Missing values in formatted input are generally represented by blanks or a single period for a numeric value and by blanks for a character value. However, some informats, such as $CHAR., treat blanks as valid data. See Chapter 13, "SAS Informats and Formats," for more information on how a particular informat handles data.

Blanks The informat used with formatted input determines the way blanks are interpreted. For example, the $CHAR. informat reads blanks as part of the value, whereas the BZ. informat turns blanks into zeros.

Storing informats Informat names specified in the INPUT statement are not stored with the SAS data set. Informat names specified with the INFORMAT or ATTRIB statement are stored, allowing you to input informatted values in a later DATA step without specifying the informat or to input data using PROC FSEDIT in SAS/FSP software.

Named Input

Requirements The named input style can be used when your data lines contain variable names followed by an equal sign and a value for the variable. For example, you would use named input to read an input line containing AGE=21, rather than just the value 21, for the numeric variable AGE.

The form of the INPUT statement for reading variables with named input is distinguished by the equal sign following a variable name:

INPUT {*pointercontrol*}*variable*={$}{*informat*} . . . ;

where

= indicates that the named input style is to be used.

The INPUT statement begins reading named input at the current location of the input pointer. Thus, if the input lines include some data values at the beginning of the line that cannot be read with named input, you can use another input style to read them. For example, the INPUT statement

```
input pulse waist age= sex=$;
```

reads the input line

```
80 32 AGE=35 SEX=M
```

The value of the variable AGE is assumed to end when the next variable name, SEX, or the end of the line is encountered.

Once an INPUT statement starts reading named input (initiated by an equal sign after a variable), the SAS System expects all remaining values in the input line to be in this form. The named input values can be in any order and do not all need to be specified in the INPUT statement. For example,

```
input id name=$20. sex=$ age=;
```

could be used to read the input line

```
4798 AGE=23 SEX=F NAME=JOHN SMITH
```

In this case, the variable ID is read with ordinary list input. The remaining values in the input line are read with named input.

If character values in the input lines contain an equal sign, put two blanks before and after the data value. For example, the input line

```
HEADER=  AGE=60 AND UP  NAME=JOHN DOE
```

could be read with the statements

```
format header $30. name $15.;
input header= name=;
```

because there are two blanks before and after the value for the variable HEADER, which contains an equal sign.

Restrictions When an equal sign follows an INPUT statement variable, the SAS System expects that data remaining on the input line contain only named input values. This means that

- the remaining input values must be in the form *name=value*.
  If any of the values are not in named input form, the SAS System handles them as invalid data. (See **How the SAS System handles invalid data** for more information.)

If named input values continue after the end of the current input line, a slash (/) at the end of the input line tells the SAS System to go to the next line and continue reading with named input. Note that a slash (/) in the INPUT statement has the same effect as it does in the input line with named input.

- you cannot switch to another input style for a particular input line once you start reading it with named input. All of the remaining values on the input line must be in the named input form. However, you can read input data in other forms with corresponding input styles before starting to use named input.
- if you have used a variable that appears in a line of named input in any other statement (for example, in a LENGTH, ATTRIB, FORMAT, or INFORMAT statement), the value is automatically read from the input, whether or not it is explicitly specified in an INPUT statement. Even if you explicitly read only one named input value with the INPUT statement, all of the remaining named input values in the current record are read, and the values are assigned to the corresponding variables.
- you must use an INFORMAT statement preceding the INPUT statement to read a named input variable with an informat. If you specify an informat for any variable being read with named input, you must supply an informat for all variables to be read with named input.
- you cannot use the *arrayname(*)* variable specification with named input.

Advanced INPUT Statement Features

As the SAS System reads values from the input lines, it keeps track of its position with a pointer. For example, if each observation has several data lines of input and you are reading a value that begins in the tenth column of the second line, the pointer's position is line 2, column 10.

Pointer controls reset the pointer's column and line position and tell the INPUT statement where to go to read the data value. There are two kinds of pointer controls and two line hold specifiers:

1. **column pointer controls** move the pointer to the column you specify. There are nine column pointer controls: @n, @pointvariable, @(expression), @'characterstring', @charactervariable, @(characterexpression), +n, +pointvariable, and +(expression).
2. **line pointer controls** move the pointer to the line number specified. There are four line pointer controls: #n, #pointvariable, #(expression), and /.
3. **line hold specifiers** keep the line pointer on the current input line. There are two line hold specifiers: *trailing @* and *trailing @@*.

You can also determine the pointer's current column and line location with the COLUMN= and LINE= options in the INFILE statement.

Specify pointer controls before the variable to which they apply. Line pointer controls at the end of the INPUT statement can be used to move to the next input line or define the number of input lines per observation. The sections below describe each type of column and line pointer control and line hold specifier.

Column pointer controls   Column pointer controls indicate in which column an input value starts. There are nine column pointer controls. Absolute pointer controls begin with an @ sign and can have a numeric or a character value. Numeric absolute pointer controls move the pointer to a specified column number; character absolute pointer controls locate a series of characters in the input line and move the pointer to the first nonblank column after that series. Relative pointer controls begin with a + sign and move the pointer a specified number of columns.

@n
moves the pointer to column *n*. N should be a positive integer.

@*pointvariable*
moves the pointer to the column given by the value of *pointvariable*. The *pointvariable* must be numeric.

@(*expression***)**
moves the pointer to the column given by the value of *expression*. The *expression* must evaluate to a positive integer.

To move the pointer to a specific column, use the @ followed by the column number, variable, or expression whose value is that column number. For example, the statement

```
input @15 sales 5.;
```

moves the pointer to column 15. The INPUT statement in this example

```
data one;
   a=25;
   input @a name $10.;
   more SAS statements
```

also moves the pointer to column 25, the value of A.

In this example the INPUT statement moves the pointer to position 30:

```
data one;
   b=10;
   input @(b*3) grade 2.;
   more SAS statements
```

The @*pointvariable* control is often combined with the trailing @ control described in **Line pointer controls**. In this example,

```
data one;
   input x @;
   if 1<=x<=10 then input @x city $12.;
   else input @50 county $10.;
   more SAS statements
   cards;
```

the SAS System obtains the value of X for the current observation in the first INPUT statement and uses that value to determine the column to move to in the second INPUT statement.

The pointer can go backward as well as forward. For example, this INPUT statement

```
input @26 book @1 company;
```

first reads a value for BOOK starting at column 26 and then moves back to column 1 on the same line to read a value for COMPANY. If a negative number is associated with the @ pointer control, the pointer moves to column 1.

In this example that mixes input styles,

```
input name $ 1-10 @15 pulse 3. @20 waist 2. age;
```

a value for NAME is read with column input from columns 1 through 10; the pointer moves to column 15, reads a value for PULSE from 15, 16, and 17 and for WAIST from 20 and 21, both with formatted input, and then reads a value for AGE with list input.

@'characterstring'

moves the pointer to the first nonblank column after *characterstring* in the input line. For example, suppose you are using SAS procedure output as input to a DATA step; the first line of each page contains the default title SAS and the time of day and date. To read the time value, you can use this statement:

```
input @'SAS' timevar time5.;
```

The pointer moves across the data line until it encounters the characters SAS; then the INPUT statement reads a value for TIMEVAR from the next nonblank column.

Suppose that a data line contains the value

```
size=133
```

You can read the value 133 as follows:

```
input @'size=' x 3.;
```

(This example uses the @'characterstring' pointer control to read data lines that required the named input feature available in earlier releases of the SAS System.)

@characatervariable

locates the series of characters in the input line given by the value of *charactervariable* and moves the pointer to the first nonblank column after that series of characters.

For example, the following statement reads in the WEEKDAY character variable. The second @1 is used to restore pointer control to the beginning of the input line. It then scans for the value of WEEKDAY and reads the value for SALES from the next nonblank column after the value of WEEKDAY:

```
input @1 day 1. @5 weekday $10. @1 @weekday sales 8.2;
```

As another example, suppose you have a large raw file of data whose values look like this:

```
values NEW YORK 2 more values
values RALEIGH 1 more values
values CARY 3 more values
values CHAPEL HILL 2 more values
```

You have already created a permanent SAS data set IN.SURVEY using some variables from this file. IN.SURVEY contains a character variable CITY whose values are the city names above. Now you discover that you need to add the numeric values following the city names in the file as a numeric variable named GROUP. You can use this DATA step:

```
data out.survey2;
   set in.survey;
   infile 'a:\survey85.dat';
   input @city group : 8.;
run;
```

The INPUT statement scans each data line for the series of characters in the value of CITY for that observation and reads the value of GROUP beginning in the next nonblank column. (Note: this example assumes

@(*characterexpression*)

locates the series of characters identified by *characterexpression* and moves the pointer to the first nonblank column after the series. For example, suppose that data lines in a file look like this:

```
85 values JAN values JAN85 6.2 values
84 values OCT values OCT84 11.3 values
85 values JUL values JUL85 1.6 values
85 values AUG values AUG85 1.4 values
```

You want to read a value for variable RAIN beginning at the first nonblank column following the month name and year. This DATA step locates the values:

```
data rainfall;
   infile 'weather.dat';
   input @1 year $2. @11 month $3. @;
   input @(month||year) rain : 4.1;
run;
```

The first INPUT statement reads values for YEAR and MONTH; the second INPUT statement concatenates those values to determine the location of variable RAIN in the data lines.

+*n*

moves the pointer *n* columns. *N* must be a positive integer.

+*pointvariable*

moves the pointer the number of columns given by the *pointvariable* value.

+(*expression*)

moves the pointer the number of columns given by *expression*. The expression can evaluate to a positive or negative integer.

The relative pointer control + followed by a number, variable, or expression moves the pointer the number of columns indicated. To move backward, use +*pointvariable* or +(*expression*). For example, the statement

```
input @23 length 4. +5 width;
```

moves the pointer to column 23, reads a value for LENGTH from the next four columns (23, 24, 25, and 26), and then advances the pointer five columns to read a WIDTH value in column 32.

This example moves the pointer backwards by setting a *pointvariable* in the DATA step to the number of columns you want to back up and by specifying that variable after the + pointer control. For example, say you want to back up one column:

```
data four;
   m=-1;
   input x 1-10 +m y 2.;
```

This INPUT statement reads a value for X from columns 1 through 10 and then moves the pointer back one column to read a value for Y starting in column 10. You can also use a negative expression:

```
data four
   input x 1-10 +(-1) y 2.;
```

Column pointer location after reading The pointer's location after reading depends on the input style used. When reading with **list input**, the pointer moves to the second column after the value. For example, suppose the statement

```
input x y;
```

reads a value for X from columns 1 and 2. Because the value for X was read with list input, the pointer's location is column 4, the second column after the value. The SAS System reads the Y value starting from column 4.

Exception: when the ampersand (&) modifier is used with list input, the pointer moves to the third column after the value since the ampersand requires two spaces between input values.

When reading with either **column** or **formatted input**, the pointer moves to the first column after the value. For example, consider the statement

```
input a 3-4 b;
```

or the statement

```
input @3 a 2. b;
```

The field for the A value ends in column 4 (even if the value itself occupies only column 3), and the pointer moves to column 5 after reading the value for A.

Whenever you move the pointer to a new input line, the column pointer is automatically set to 1.

Line pointer controls Line pointer controls specify the input line from which the INPUT statement is to read a value.

The following four line pointer controls are used when each observation has values on more than one input line:

#*n*
   moves the pointer to line *n*.

#*pointvariable*
   moves the pointer to the line given by the value of *pointvariable*. The *pointvariable* must be numeric.

#(*expression*)
   moves the pointer to the line given by the value of *expression*. The *expression* must evaluate to a positive integer.

   When the INPUT statement needs to read several input lines per observation, the SAS System must know from which line to read values. The number following the # pointer control specifies the line that contains the next group of values. For example, in the statement

```
input @12 name $10. #2 id 3-4;
```

the value for ID is in columns 3 and 4 of the second input line. (A #1 is implied between INPUT and the @12 pointer direction, indicating that the value for NAME begins in column 12 of the first input line.) The highest number following the # pointer control in the INPUT statement determines how many lines per observation are read, unless you override this by specifying N= in the INFILE statement. For example, in this statement,

```
input @31 age 3. #3 id 3-4 #2 @6 name $20.;
```

the highest value after the # is 3; thus, the INPUT statement reads three input lines each time it executes unless the N= option has been specified in the associated INFILE statement.

When each observation has multiple input lines, but values are not read from the last line, a # pointer control at the end of the INPUT statement must move the pointer to the last line in each observation unless the N= option has been specified in the INFILE statement. For example, if there are four lines per observation but values are read only from the first two lines, the INPUT statement may look like this:

```
input name $ 1-10 #2 age 13-14 #4;
```

/

advances the pointer to column 1 of the next input line. For example, the statement

```
input age grade / score1-score5;
```

reads values for AGE and GRADE from one input line and then skips to the next line to read values for SCORE1-SCORE5.

When you have advanced to the next line with the / pointer control, you must use the #*n* pointer control or the INFILE statement N= option to define the number of lines per observation in order to move the pointer back to an earlier line. To return to an earlier line when reading from multiline input, give the total number of lines in the input record with the #*n* pointer control at the end of the INPUT statement or the N= option in the INFILE statement. The following statement requires the #2 pointer control unless the INFILE statement has the N= option specified:

```
input a / b #1 @52 c #2;
```

The above statement reads a value for A from the first line, for B from the second, and then returns to the first line to read a value for C. The #2 pointer control identifies two input lines for each observation, so the pointer can return to the first line for the value of C.

If the number of input lines per observation varies, use the N= option in the INFILE statement to give the maximum number of lines per observation. See the **INFILE Statement** description earlier in this chapter for more information. The N= option overrides any specification implied by pointer controls.

Line hold specifiers Line hold specifiers keep the line pointer on the current input line when:

- a data line is read by more than one INPUT statement (*trailing @*)
- one input line has values for more than one observation (*trailing @@*).

Use the following line hold specifier to read an input line with more than one INPUT statement:

@, trailing
> holds a data line for the next INPUT statement in the step. The next INPUT statement for the same execution of the DATA step accesses the same data line rather than reading a new one.
>
> The @ is called a *trailing at-sign* because it must be the last item in the INPUT statement.
>
> Normally, each INPUT statement in a DATA step reads a new data line. To read values from the same data line with more than one INPUT statement, use a trailing @ at the end of each INPUT statement that is to read from that line.

For example, say that you have two kinds of input data lines. One type of data line gives information about a particular college course; the other contains information about the students taking that course.

You need two INPUT statements to read the two lines because they have different variables and different formats. Lines containing class information have a C in column 1; lines containing student information have an S in column 1. You need to check each line as it is read to know which INPUT statement to use. You need an INPUT statement that reads only the variable telling whether the line is a student or class record:

```
data schedule;
   input type $ 1 @;
   if type='C' then input course $ prof $;
   else if type='S' then input name $ id;
```

The first INPUT statement reads the TYPE value from column 1 of every line. Since this INPUT statement ends with a trailing @, the next INPUT statement in the DATA step reads the same line. The IF statements that follow check whether the line is a class or student line, and each gives an INPUT statement to read the rest of the line.

A line held with a trailing @ can be released with an INPUT statement without operands or a trailing @:

```
input;
```

This statement releases the current data line so that the next INPUT statement reads a new line.

An input line held by a trailing @ is automatically released when the DATA step executes again. Thus, a RETURN or DELETE statement releases the line. If you want to read the same input line in more than one execution of the DATA step, use the @@ symbol, described below.

Use the following line hold specifier when a single input line contains values for more than one observation:

@@, trailing
> holds an input line for further executions of the DATA step. The @@ symbol (called a *double trailing at-sign*) is useful when each input line contains values for several observations.

For example, say that you have input with each line containing several NAME and AGE values. You want to read first a NAME value, then an AGE value, then output the observation; then read another NAME and another AGE value to output, and so on until you have read and output all the input values in the line. Use a double trailing @ in your INPUT statement:

```
data three;
   input name $ age @@;
   cards;
JOHN 13 MARY 12 SUE 15 TOM 10
;
```

The SAS System releases a line held by a trailing @@ when the pointer moves past the end of the line. In addition, an INPUT statement without operands or a trailing @ releases the held line immediately, as in

```
input;
```

SAS Statements Used in the DATA Step   189

and an INPUT statement with a single trailing @ releases the held line at the end of the current iteration of the DATA step (just as if @@ had not been specified):

```
input @;
```

Reading past the end of a line   When @ or + pointer controls are used with a value that moves the pointer to or past the end of the current line and the next value is to be read from the current column, SAS goes to column 1 of the next line to read it. It also prints the message on the SAS log:

```
NOTE: SAS went to a new line when INPUT statement reached
      past the end of a line.
```

Use the STOPOVER option in the INFILE statement if you want to treat this condition as an error and stop building the data set.

You can also use the MISSOVER option in the INFILE statement to set the remaining INPUT statement variables to missing values if the pointer reaches the end of a line. See the **INFILE Statement** description in this chapter for more information.

Formatted lists with pointer controls   You can write shorter INPUT statements by using pointer controls in format lists. Format lists can contain any of the pointer controls (@, @@, #, /, and +). For example, suppose you want to read 20 LOC values and 20 AMOUNT values for each observation. The values are arranged in the input lines as a string of pairs, with the LOC value followed by an AMOUNT value. Rather than write a long INPUT statement listing all 40 variables, you can use a format list to match the LOC values in columns 1-2, 4-5, 7-8, and so on with the AMOUNT values in columns 3, 6, 9, and so on. The following INPUT statement reads the values:

```
input (loc1-loc20) (2. +1) @1 (amount1-amount20) (+2 1.);
```

After the LOC values have been read, the @ pointer control moves the pointer to column 1 in the input line to read the AMOUNT values.

SAS format modifiers for error reporting   SAS format modifiers for error reporting define the amount of information printed in the log when the SAS System encounters an error in an input value.

?

suppresses the invalid data message that the SAS System prints when it encounters an invalid data value. For example,

```
input x ? 10-12;
input (x1-x10) (? 3.1);
```

When SAS encounters an invalid character in a value for the variable X, the SAS System takes the actions described in the later section **How the SAS System handles invalid data** except that it does **not** print the invalid data message.

??

suppresses the printing of both the error messages and the input lines when invalid data values are read. The ? and ?? message modifiers both suppress the invalid data message. The ?? modifier also prevents the automatic variable _ERROR_ from being set to 1 when invalid data are read. Thus, the statement

```
input x ?? 10-12;
```

is equivalent to

```
input x ? 10-12;
_error_=0;
```

Invalid X values are still set to missing values.

Special Topics

Numeric data: details Standard numeric data can be represented in several ways: standard numeric, negative, fractions, hexadecimal, scientific notation (also called E-notation), binary (integer), floating point (real binary), blanks as zeros, and special embedded characters ($, %, (), commas, and blanks). All of these numeric data forms must be read with formatted input except standard numeric and negative. For example, the standard numeric data value 23 can be expressed in any of the following ways:

Data Description	Data	Result
input right justified	23	23
input not justified	23	23
input left justified	23	23
input with leading zeros	00023	23
input with decimal point	23.0	23
in E-notation, 2.3×10^1	2.3E1	23
in E-notation, 230×10^{-1}	230E−1	23
minus sign for negative numbers	−23	−23

Remember the following points when reading numeric data:

- a minus sign preceding the number (without an intervening blank) indicates a negative value.
- leading zeros and the placement of a value in the input field do not affect the value assigned to the variable.
- numeric data can have leading and trailing blanks, but cannot have embedded blanks (unless read with the COMMA. informat).
- to read decimal values from input lines that do not contain explicit decimal points, indicate where the decimal point belongs by a decimal parameter with column input, or an informat with formatted input. An explicit decimal point in the input data overrides any decimal specification in the INPUT statement.

The following are examples of input data that either must be read with an informat or that are invalid:

Data	Reason
2 3	embedded blank requires COMMA. informat
− 23	embedded blank requires COMMA. informat
2,341	comma requires COMMA. informat
(23)	parentheses require COMMA. informat

C4A2	hexadecimal value requires HEX. informat
1DEC84	date requires DATE. informat
23−	sign should precede the number
..	missing value is a single period
E23	not a number

See **How the SAS System handles invalid data** later in this section for information on how the SAS System handles invalid numeric input.

Character data: details   Input data can include any character. However, be careful when your input data include

- **leading blanks**. Character values beginning with blanks can cause problems with list-style input because leading and trailing blanks are trimmed from a character value before the value is assigned to a variable. You can avoid problems when reading values with leading blanks by using formatted input with the $CHAR. informat. See Chapter 13, "SAS Informats and Formats," for more information on informats.
- **semicolons** in data following a CARDS statement. See the **CARDS and CARDS4 Statements** earlier in this chapter for more information and an example of how to handle semicolons in character data.

The INPUT statement without operands   An INPUT statement without variable names (sometimes called a null INPUT statement) is a statement without operands. This type of INPUT statement has several uses:

- to bring an input data line into the DATA step without creating any SAS variables
- to copy an input record to the output file
- to release an input line held by a trailing @ or @@.

For example, the following lines copy the input file to the output file without creating any SAS variables:

```
data _null_;
   infile in;
   file out;
   input;
   put _infile_;
```

How the SAS System handles invalid data   An input value is invalid if it

- requires an informat that is not available at execution time
- does not conform to the informat specified
- cannot be read with the input style specified
- is read as standard numeric data (no $ sign or informat) and does not conform to the rules for standard SAS numbers.

When an error in an input value is encountered, the SAS System

- sets the value of the variable being read to missing.
- prints the input line and column number containing the invalid value on the SAS log.
- sets the automatic variable _ERROR_ to 1 for the current observation.
- prints an invalid data message.
- prints the input lines corresponding to the current observation. If a line

contains unprintable characters, it is printed in hexadecimal form. A scale is printed above the input line to help determine column numbers.

End-of-file End-of-file occurs when an INPUT statement reaches the end of the data. When a DATA step tries to read another record after end-of-file has been reached, the DATA step execution stops. You can detect end-of-file using the INFILE options END= or EOF= and stop executing INPUT statements for that INFILE if you want to continue executing the DATA step. See the **INFILE Statement** for more details.

Arrays An array member can be read with an INPUT statement. However, an array reference cannot be used for such things as a column pointer.

When reading an array, specify the subscript following the array name:

```
data two;
   .
   .
   .
infile array2;
input arr1(indx+2) ... ;
```

In this case the subscript can be any valid SAS expression. The expression must evaluate to a valid subscript value at the time the INPUT statement executes.

You can use the array subscript asterisk (*) to input all elements of a previously defined explicitly or implicitly subscripted array. The array can be single- or multi-dimensional, and the subscript can be enclosed in braces, brackets, or parentheses. The syntax is

INPUT *arrayname*{*};

If the array is multidimensional, elements are input in row major order (that is, the elements are filled row by row).

You can use list, column, or formatted input; you cannot input values to an array defined with _TEMPORARY_ using the asterisk subscript. For example, the statements

```
array x(100);
input x(*) 2.;
```

create variables X1 through X100 and read data values into the variables using the 2. informat.

KEEP Statement

You can use the KEEP statement in a DATA step to specify the variables that are to be included in any SAS data sets being created. The KEEP statement applies to all data sets being created in the step. To keep variables in particular data sets when more than one data set is being created in the DATA step, use the KEEP= data set option with each data set name. (See "SAS Files" for more about data set options.)

If a DATA step includes a KEEP statement, only variables appearing in the KEEP statement are included in new data sets. Variables not listed in the KEEP statement remain available for use in program statements. The KEEP statement can appear anywhere among the program statements in the DATA step; it is not an executable statement.

The form of the KEEP statement is

KEEP *variables*;

where

>*variables* specifies the variables you want included in the data set or data sets being created. Any form of variable list may be used (see the "Introduction" to USING THE SAS LANGUAGE for details). Do not abbreviate the variable names.

Here is an example:

```
data average;
    input name $ score1-score20;
    avg=mean(of score1-score20);
    keep name avg;
    cards;
data lines
;
```

The effect of the KEEP statement is the reverse of the DROP statement's effect. To save writing, the KEEP statement is preferred if fewer variables are being kept than dropped.

Do not use both KEEP and DROP statements in the same step. When both RENAME and KEEP statements are used in a DATA step, the KEEP statement is applied first. This means that the old name should be used in the KEEP statement.

The KEEP statement is available only in the DATA step. To include variables in a PROC step, use the KEEP= data set option.

LABEL Statement

You can use LABEL statements in a DATA step to give labels to variables. The label is stored with the variable name in the SAS data set and printed by many SAS procedures.

The form of the LABEL statement is

LABEL *variable*='*label*'...;

where

    variable names the variable to be labeled.

    label specifies a label of up to forty characters including blanks. The label must be enclosed in either single or double quotes. Quotes as part of the label must be written as two quotes and are counted as one character.

Any number of variable names and labels can appear. Here are examples of LABEL statements:

- `label compound='TYPE OF DRUG';`
- `label score1="GRADE ON APRIL 1 TEST"`
  `score2="GRADE ON MAY 1 TEST";`
- `label date='IF Y=0 W=DATE OF TEST';`
- `label n='MARK''S EXPERIMENT NUMBER';`

You can also assign variable labels with the ATTRIB statement.

Labels, Statement

You can use a statement label to identify a statement referred to by a GO TO or LINK statement. A statement label has the form

label: *statement*;

These terms make up the statement label:

label identifies the destination of a GO TO statement, a LINK statement, the HEADER= option in a FILE statement, or the EOF= option in an INFILE statement. The label can be any valid SAS name followed by a colon (:).

statement is any executable statement in the same DATA step as the statement or option that references it. No two statements in a DATA step should have the same label. If a statement in a DATA step is labeled, it should be referenced by a statement or option in the step.

For example,

```
data inventry order;
   input item $ stock @;
   if stock=0 then go to reordr;
   output inventry;
   retrun;
reordr: input supplier $;
   put 'ORDER ITEM # ' item 'FROM ' supplier;
   output order;
   cards;
data lines
;
```

In the example above, the first INPUT statement reads a record containing an item description (ITEM) and the number in stock (STOCK). If STOCK=0, the GO TO statement causes the SAS System to jump to the statement labeled REORDR—another INPUT statement. SAS reads the name of the supplier for that item, writes a message on the log, and outputs the record to data set ORDER. When STOCK is not zero, the record is output to data set INVENTRY, and SAS returns to the beginning of the DATA step for a new observation.

LENGTH Statement

Introduction 196
Numeric Data 196
   Truncation 197
Character Data 198
Changing Variable Lengths 199

Introduction

You can include a LENGTH statement in a DATA step to specify the number of bytes the SAS System is to use for storing values of variables in each data set being created.

Specify the LENGTH statement as

LENGTH [*variables* [**$**] *length*] ... [**DEFAULT**=*n*];

These terms are included in the LENGTH statement:

- *variables* names the variable or variables to which you want to assign a length. The variable list can include any variables in the data set; an array reference may not appear.

- **$** indicates that the variable or variables in the preceding list are character variables.

- *length* is a numeric constant that can range from 3 to 8 for numeric variables and from 1 to 200 for character variables. Note that this length value is not a format; it does not contain a period.

- **DEFAULT**=*n* optionally, changes the default number of bytes used for storing the values of newly created numeric variables from 8 to the number *n* that you specify; *n* can range from 3 to 8.

For example, the statement

```
length name $ 20;
```

sets the length of the character variable NAME to 20.

You can assign variable lengths with either a LENGTH or an ATTRIB statement. Any length assigned with a LENGTH statement can be changed in an ATTRIB statement and vice versa, subject to the rules for assigning lengths discussed later in this section.

The length of a variable depends on

- whether the variable is numeric or character
- how the variable was created
- whether a LENGTH or ATTRIB statement is present.

The following discussion describes variable lengths in general. The **Assignment Statement** earlier in this chapter contains a table that summarizes the length of variables created in assignment statements. The "SAS Functions" chapter discusses lengths of values returned by functions.

Numeric Data

Normally, numeric variables in SAS data sets have a length of 8 bytes. However, many values can be represented exactly in fewer than 8 bytes. When your data set is very large, using fewer than 8 bytes to store values that do not need that much precision can significantly decrease external storage requirements. Before you use the LENGTH statement to change the number of bytes for storing numeric values, however, note carefully the discussion below on truncation problems.

Truncation Consider the case where numeric values are represented in a base-16 number system. Exact decimal fractions, such as .3, are not necessarily exact fractions in base-16 representations. This situation can create difficulties.

For example, suppose that you use a LENGTH statement to store the values of a variable in 3 bytes:

```
length a 3;
```

Each value of A is initially moved into an 8-byte field during the DATA step. When the value is moved to the SAS data set, the last 5 bytes of the value are dropped. Then, when the value is used for processing in a later DATA or PROC step, its representation is again brought up to 8 bytes by appending nonsignificant zeros.

Unless the part of the representation originally dropped consists of all zeros, something is lost in truncation. The example below illustrates how that loss can affect the behavior of the SAS System:

```
data one;
    input a 1-4 b 6;
    length default=3;
    cards;
1.4  6
1.1  5
1.1  6
1.3  4
1.3  3
2.0  4
;
data two;
    set one;
    if a=1.3;
run;
```

Data set TWO has **no** observations. The constant 1.3 in the subsetting IF statement in the second DATA step has the full 8-byte representation of the 1.3, whereas the fourth and fifth values of A are identical to it only in the first 3 bytes of their values. Hence A will never be found equal to 1.3.

Although you should be aware of problems like these, using single-precision storage of 4 bytes does give you 6 significant digits. This storage is sufficient for most applications. Thus, using a default length of 4 to store numeric values when space is an important consideration is usually safe. See "SAS Expressions" for additional information on working with calculated fractional values.

The discussion of truncation problems applies to data values that are not whole numbers (integers). When a variable's values are all integers, you can safely use the LENGTH statement to save storage space for the data set being created. **Table 5.2** shows the lengths that can represent all integers through the magnitude indicated.

Table 5.2 Storage Length for Integers

Length	Can Represent All Integers Through	
3	8,192	2^{13}
4	2,097,152	2^{21}
5	536,870,912	2^{29}
6	137,438,953,472	2^{37}
7	35,184,372,088,832	2^{45}
8	9,007,199,254,740,992	2^{53}

Character Data

The length of a character variable is set the first time that the variable is used in a SAS DATA step. After the length has been specified, you cannot change it except in a later DATA step by using a LENGTH or ATTRIB statement. (See **Changing Variable Lengths** below.)

Since the INPUT statement can implicitly define a character variable's length, the LENGTH statement should precede the INPUT statement when it defines lengths for character variables that are different from the lengths implied in the INPUT statement.

For example, the statements

```
data one;
   input name $ 1-10;
   cards;
data lines
;
```

implicitly assign the variable NAME a length of 10. If a LENGTH statement appears before the INPUT statement, as in

```
data two;
   length name $20;
   input name $ 1-10;
   cards;
data lines
;
```

NAME's length in the output data set is 20 instead of 10.

When a character variable appears for the first time in a DATA step, its length is determined from the context of its use. For example, consider these statements:

```
data two;
   input x;
   if x=1 then a='NO';
   else a='YES';
```

A appears for the first time in the assignment A='NO'. Thus A's length is 2 in the data set, the length of the character literal 'NO'. When the value 'YES' is assigned to A, only the first two letters are saved; the 'S' is lost. To avoid this problem, use a LENGTH statement to give A the length you want:

```
data two;
   input x;
   length a $ 3;
```

```
        if x=1 then a='NO';
        else a='YES';
```

or rearrange the statements:

```
    data two;
        input x;
        if x ne 1 then a='YES';
        else a='NO';
```

A's length in both data sets is 3, and so the complete value 'YES' can be saved.

In another example, below:

```
    data three;
        length b $ 15;
        input x b;
        if x=1 then a=b;
```

The length of B is defined as 15 by the LENGTH statement. The first appearance of A in the step is in the assignment A=B. Thus A's length is 15, determined by the length of B.

When you use list input to read a character variable, a length of 8 is assumed. If any of the values are longer than 8, they are truncated to 8 unless a LENGTH statement defines a longer length, as in the previous example.

Also note that when you use a LENGTH statement for a character variable before the INPUT statement, you need not specify the dollar sign ($) in the INPUT statement since SAS knows that the variable is character by the time it encounters the INPUT statement.

Changing Variable Lengths

The contents of SAS data set FIRST show the length and type of its two variables B and X in **Output 5.6**. B is character of length 10; X is numeric of length 8.

Output 5.6 Length of a Numeric and a Character Variable

```
                              CONTENTS PROCEDURE
Data Set Name:  WORK.FIRST          Type:
Observations:   3                   Record Len: 22
Variables:      2
Label:

                       -----Alphabetic List of Variables and Attributes-----

#  Variable  Type  Len  Pos  Label
1  B         Char   10    4
2  X         Num     8   14
```

To change the length of B, a character variable, you must create a new data set and precede the SET statement with a LENGTH statement. You can also change X's length in the LENGTH statement:

```
    data second;
        length b $ 8 x 4;
        set first;
```

The variables have different lengths in data set SECOND as shown in **Output 5.7**.

Output 5.7 Different Length for Variables in the New Data Set

```
                                   CONTENTS PROCEDURE                                    1
Data Set Name:  WORK.SECOND           Type:
Observations:   3                     Record Len: 16
Variables:      2
Label:

                      -----Alphabetic List of Variables and Attributes-----

     #  Variable  Type  Len  Pos  Label
     1  B         Char    8    4
     2  X         Num     4   12
```

Although a character variable's length must be changed by placing a LENGTH statement **before** the SET, you can change X's length in a LENGTH statement placed anywhere in the step.

```
data third;
   set first;
   length x 4;
```

The result is shown in **Output 5.8**.

Output 5.8 Different Length for the Numeric Variable

```
                                   CONTENTS PROCEDURE                                    1
Data Set Name:  WORK.THIRD            Type:
Observations:   3                     Record Len: 18
Variables:      2
Label:

                      -----Alphabetic List of Variables and Attributes-----

     #  Variable  Type  Len  Pos  Label
     1  B         Char   10    4
     2  X         Num     4   14
```

The same rules apply to changing lengths of variables in any previously existing SAS data set, whether read with a SET, MERGE, or UPDATE statement.

LINK Statement

A LINK statement tells the SAS System to jump immediately to the statement label indicated in the LINK statement and to continue executing statements from that point until a RETURN statement is executed. The RETURN statement causes SAS execution to return to the statement immediately following the LINK statement and continue from there. The LINK statement and the destination must be in the same DATA step. The destination is identified by a statement label in the LINK statement and the destination statement.

The statement has the form:

LINK *label*;

where

>   *label*   specifies a statement label that identifies the LINK destination. See **Labels, Statement** earlier in this chapter for more information.

The difference between the LINK and GO TO statements is in the action of a subsequent RETURN statement. A RETURN after a LINK returns SAS execution to the statement following the LINK; a RETURN statement after a GO TO returns SAS execution to the beginning of the DATA step. In addition, a LINK statement is usually used with an explicit RETURN statement; a GO TO statement is often used without a RETURN statement. In that case execution continues until another GO TO statement or the end of the DATA step (which contains an implied RETURN) is reached.

You can place another LINK statement within a LINKed routine (called *nesting*). The maximum level of nesting is 10 (that is, 10 LINK statements with no intervening RETURN statements). When more than one LINK statement has been executed, a RETURN statement tells the SAS System to return to the statement following the last LINK statement executed.

Here is an example using one LINK statement:

```
*Study of water resources;
data hydro;
   input type $ wd station $;
   label type='STATION TYPE'
      wd='DEPTH TO WATER';
   elev=.;
   if type='ALUV' then link calcu;
   year=1985;
   return;
calcu: if station='SITE_1' then elev=6650-wd;
   if station='SITE_2' then elev=5500-wd;
   return;
   cards;
ALUV 523 SITE_1
UPPA 234 SITE_2
ALUV 666 SITE_2
more data lines
;
```

When the value of TYPE is ALUV, SAS executes the LINK statement, jumps to label CALCU, and executes that statement and the next two. The RETURN statement after the second IF statement causes SAS to return to the next statement, in this case

```
year=1985;
```

202   Chapter 5

When SAS reaches the RETURN statement after the assignment statement, SAS outputs that observation and returns to the top of the DATA step for a new data line.

If you need to execute a group of statements at only one point in a program, a DO group is simpler than a LINK-RETURN group. For example, you can write the DATA step above as

```
data hydro;
   input type $ wd station $;
   label type='STATION TYPE'
      wd='DEPTH TO WATER';
   elev=.;
   if type='ALUV' then do;
      if station='SITE_1' then elev=6650-wd;
      if station='SITE_2' then elev=5500-wd;
      end;
   year=1985;
   cards;
data lines
;
```

See the **DO Statement** description for more information.

If you need to execute a group of statements at several points in a program, a LINK statement can simplify coding the program and make it easier to understand. The example below links to a statement that recodes grades of 'E' to 'F' for grades on three tests:

```
data class;
   input id test1 $ test2 $ test3 $;
   test=test1;
   link recode;
   test1=test;
   test=test2;
   link recode;
   test2=test;
   test=test3;
   link recode;
   test3=test;
   return;
recode: if test='E' then test='F';
   return;
   cards;
data lines
;
```

To recode each test grade, SAS moves the grade to a variable TEST, links to RECODE and recodes it, and then moves the recoded value to the original variable.

You can also write this step with an ARRAY statement:

```
data class;
   array test{3} $ test1-test3;
   input id test1 $ test2 $ test3 $;
   do i=1 to dim(test);
      if test{i}='E' then test{i}='F';
      end;
   cards;
```

data lines
;

See the **ARRAY Statement** description for more information.

LIST Statement

You can use the LIST statement to list on the SAS log the input data lines for the observation being processed. When the LIST statement is executed, the SAS System causes the current input lines to be printed at the end of the current iteration of the DATA step. A ruler indicating columns appears before the first line listed.

The form of the LIST statement is

LIST;

The LIST statement is useful for printing suspicious input lines read by an INPUT statement. Here is an example:

```
data employee;
    input ssn 1-9 #3 w2amt 1-6;
    if w2amt=. then list;
    cards;
123456789
JAMES SMITH
356.79
345671234
JEFFREY THOMAS
.
;
```

Each time W2AMT is missing, SAS prints the three current input data lines on the SAS log. **Output 5.9** shows the log for the DATA step above.

Output 5.9 Listing Input Data Lines

```
NOTE: Copyright(c) 1985,86,87 SAS Institute Inc., Cary, NC 27512-8000, U.S.A.
NOTE: SAS (r) Proprietary Software Release 6.03
      Licensed to SAS Institute Inc., Site 00000000.
     1          data employee;
     2              input ssn 1-9 #3 w2amt 1-6;
     3              if w2amt=. then list;
     4              cards;
RULE:----+----1----+----2----+----3----+----4----+----5----+----6----+----7----+----8----+----9----+----0
     8  345671234
     9  JEFFREY THOMAS
    10  .
    11      .
NOTE: The data set WORK.EMPLOYEE has 2 observations and 2 variables.
NOTE: The DATA statement used 5.00 seconds.
```

The DATA step below compares how SAS prints lines from a LIST statement and a PUT statement. The step includes both a LIST statement and a PUT statement. Lines printed by the PUT statement are displayed on the log after the LIST statement in **Output 5.10**.

```
data d;
    input x y z;
    list;
    if x=y then put 'X equals Y ' x=;
    cards;
1 2 3
2 2 4
1 1 7
;
```

Output 5.10 Comparing LIST and PUT Statements

```
NOTE: Copyright(c) 1985,86,87 SAS Institute Inc., Cary, NC 27512-8000, U.S.A.
NOTE: SAS (r) Proprietary Software Release 6.03
      Licensed to SAS Institute Inc., Site 00000000.

      1          data d;
      2             input x y z;
      3             list;
      4             if x=y then put 'X equals Y ' x=;
      5             cards;
RULE:----+----1----+----2----+----3----+----4----+----5----+----6----+----7----+----8----+----9----+----0
      6 1 2 3
X equals Y X=2
      7 2 2 4
X equals Y X=1
      8 1 1 7
      9    .
NOTE: The data set WORK.D has 3 observations and 3 variables.
NOTE: The DATA statement used 3.00 seconds.
```

LOSTCARD Statement

The LOSTCARD statement is used to resynchronize the input data when the SAS System encounters a missing record in data with multiple records per observation. That is, when each observation consists of several data lines, the LOSTCARD statement prevents the SAS System from reading lines from the following observation as part of the current observation when the current observation has fewer data lines than expected. Without specific instructions such as the LOSTCARD statement, SAS does not discover that a data line is missing until it reaches the end of the data. The values for the observations in the SAS data set after the missing data line was encountered may be incorrect.

The form of the LOSTCARD statement is

LOSTCARD;

You must specify the condition that indicates a lost data line as the IF condition in an IF-THEN statement. Use the LOSTCARD statement as the THEN clause of the statement or as part of a DO group following THEN.

The LOSTCARD statement is most useful when input data have a fixed number of lines per observation and when each data line for an observation contains an identification variable with the same value.

When a LOSTCARD statement is executed, SAS takes the following steps:

1. SAS prints a lost card message, a ruler, and all the data lines read in attempting to build the current observation on the SAS log.
2. SAS does not output an observation and does not increment the automatic variable _N_. Instead, SAS discards the first data line in the group and returns to the beginning of the DATA step.
3. SAS attempts to build an observation by beginning with the second data line in the group and reading the number of lines specified in the INPUT statement.
4. If the IF condition for a lost card is still true, SAS repeats steps 1-3. To make the log easier to read, SAS prints the message and ruler only once for a given group of data lines. In addition, SAS prints each data line only once; it does not repeat a data line when it is used in successive attempts to build an observation. See the second example below for an illustration.
5. When SAS encounters a group of data lines for which the IF condition is not true, SAS builds an observation, outputs it to the SAS data set, and increments the value of the automatic variable _N_.

Here is an example:

```
data inspect;
   input id 1-3 reject 8-10 #2 idcheck 1-3 pass;
   if id ne idcheck then do;
      put 'ERROR IN DATA LINES ' id= idcheck=;
      lostcard;
      end;
   cards;
301    32
301    61432
302    53
302    83171
400    92845
411    46
411    99551
;
```

SAS Statements Used in the DATA Step 207

```
proc print;
   title 'TWO DATA LINES PER OBSERVATION';
run;
```

In this example, two input data lines make up each observation. Columns 1-3 of each line contain an identification number. You know that when the identification number in data line 1 (variable ID) does not equal the identification number in data line 2 (IDCHECK), a data line has been misplaced or left out. You specify that if a data line is missing, SAS should print the message given in the PUT statement and execute the LOSTCARD statement. Note that the first data line for the third observation (IDCHECK=400) is missing.

Output 5.11 shows the SAS log for the DATA step.

Output 5.11 LOSTCARD Statement: Two Data Lines per Observation

```
NOTE: Copyright(c) 1985,86,87 SAS Institute Inc., Cary, NC 27512-8000, U.S.A.
NOTE: SAS (r) Proprietary Software Release 6.03
      Licensed to SAS Institute Inc., Site 00000000.

    1        data inspect;
    2           input id 1-3 reject 8-10 #2 idcheck 1-3 pass;
    3           if id ne idcheck then do;
    4              put 'ERROR IN DATA LINES ' id= idcheck=;
    5              lostcard;
    6           end;
    7        cards;
   15        .
NOTE: LOST CARD.
RULE:----+----1----+----2----+----3----+----4----+----5----+----6----+----7----+----8----+----9----+----0
   14      411     99551
   15        .
ID=. REJECT=. IDCHECK=. PASS=. _ERROR_=1 _N_=4
NOTE: The data set WORK.INSPECT has 3 observations and 4 variables.
NOTE: The DATA statement used 5.00 seconds.
   16        proc print;
   17           title 'TWO DATA LINES PER OBSERVATION';
   18        run;
NOTE: The PROCEDURE PRINT used 6.00 seconds.
```

When SAS attempts to build an observation from the fifth and sixth input lines, the value read as ID (400) and the value read as IDCHECK (411) do not match. Therefore, SAS displays the lines read in attempting to build that observation, discards the first line in the group, and attempts to build an observation beginning with the second line. Since ID and IDCHECK are equal for the sixth and seventh data lines, SAS builds an observation from those lines. The resulting data set has three observations with ID values 301, 302, and 411. There is no observation for ID=400. The output of the PRINT procedure is shown in **Output 5.12**.

Output 5.12 Data Set Produced When LOSTCARD Executed

```
                    TWO DATA LINES PER OBSERVATION                    1
          OBS    ID    REJECT    IDCHECK    PASS
           1      .       .          .       301
           2      .       .          .       302
           3      .       .          .       411
```

In the example below, the DATA step reads three data lines per observation. The first observation has two missing records; the second has one; and the fourth has two. The only complete observations are the third and fifth observations.

```
data a;
   input id x $ #2 id2 y $ #3 id3 z $;
   if id ne id2 or id2 ne id3 then lostcard;
   cards;
101 A
102 B
102 B
103 C
103 C
103 C
104 D
105 E
105 E
105 E
;
proc print;
   title 'THREE DATA LINES PER OBSERVATION';
run;
```

Output 5.13 displays the log from the DATA step.

Output 5.13 LOSTCARD Statement: Three Data Lines per Observation

```
NOTE: Copyright(c) 1985,86,87 SAS Institute Inc., Cary, NC 27512-8000, U.S.A.
NOTE: SAS (r) Proprietary Software Release 6.03
      Licensed to SAS Institute Inc., Site 00000000.

      1      data a;
      2         input id x $ #2 id2 y $ #3 id3 z $;
      3         if id ne id2 or id2 ne id3 then lostcard;
      4         cards;
NOTE: LOST CARD.
RULE:----+----1----+----2----+----3----+----4----+----5----+----6----+----7----+----8----+----9----+----0
      5      101 A
      6      102 B
      7      102 B
NOTE: LOST CARD.
      8      103 C
NOTE: LOST CARD.
      9      103 C
NOTE: LOST CARD.
     11      104 D
```

(continued on next page)

```
(continued from previous page)
     12    105 E
     13    105 E
     15      .
NOTE: The data set WORK.A has 2 observations and 6 variables.
NOTE: The DATA statement used 7.00 seconds.
     16     proc print;
     17        title 'THREE DATA LINES PER OBSERVATION';
     18     run;
NOTE: The PROCEDURE PRINT used 6.00 seconds.
```

The five lines displayed after the first lost card message are the lines read in the first three attempts to build an observation. Note that the series of lines displayed looks like the series of lines in the data. This feature is helpful if you need to find those lines within the data. The three lines displayed after the second message are the lines read in attempting to build an observation from the seventh, eighth, and ninth data lines.

The resulting data set A has two observations, shown in **Output 5.14**.

Output 5.14 Data Set Produced When LOSTCARD Executed

```
                    THREE DATA LINES PER OBSERVATION                    1

              OBS    ID    X    ID2    Y    ID3    Z

               1    103    C    103    C    103    C
               2    105    E    105    E    105    E
```

MERGE Statement

Introduction 210
Merging without a BY Statement: One-to-One Merging 211
   Example 1: one-to-one merge 211
Merging with a BY Statement: Match-Merging 212
   Nonmatches 212
   Multiple observations with the same BY value in a data set 213
   Variables with the same name in more than one data set 213
   Example 2: match-merge 213
   Example 3: match-merge for table lookup 215
   Comparison of match-merge and one-to-one merge 217

Introduction

The MERGE statement joins observations from two or more SAS data sets into single observations in a new SAS data set. The way the SAS System joins the observations depends on whether a BY statement accompanies the MERGE statement.
   The form of the MERGE statement is

MERGE *SASdataset* [(*dsoptions* **IN**=*name*)]
   SASdataset [(*dsoptions* **IN**=*name*)]...[**END**=*name*];

These terms and options can appear in the MERGE statement:

SASdataset
   names two or more existing SAS data sets from which to read observations each time the MERGE statement is executed. Up to 50 data set names can appear in the MERGE statement. Here are examples of valid MERGE statements:

   - `merge males females;`
   - `merge in.fitness lib.health;`
   - `merge year1 year2 year3;`
   - `merge track save.field swim;`

   See "SAS Files" for more information on using SAS data set names.

dsoptions
   specifies any number of SAS data set options in parentheses after each SAS data set name. These options include those described in "SAS Files," as well as the following special data set options unique to the SET, MERGE, and UPDATE statements:

IN=*name*
   creates a variable with the name given after the equal sign. Within the DATA step, the value of the variable is 1 if the data set contributed data to the current observation and 0 otherwise. You can associate an IN= variable with each data set as shown below:

   ```
   data three;
      merge one(in=inone) two(in=intwo);
   ```

   INONE has the value 1 when data set ONE contributes information to the current observation; otherwise, it has the value 0. The value of INTWO is determined similarly. Both variables INONE and INTWO are equal to 1 if both data sets contribute information to the new observation. The IN= variable is not added to any SAS data set being created.

END=*name*
   creates a variable with the name given after the equal sign to contain an end-of-file indication. The variable, which is initialized to zero, is set to

1 when the MERGE statement is processing the last observation. If the input data sets have different numbers of observations, the END= variable is set to 1 when the last observation from the data set with the most observations is being processed. The END= variable is not added to any SAS data set being created.

Naming a variable from an input data set used in a merge operation in a RETAIN statement has no effect.

The MERGE statement is flexible and has a variety of uses in SAS programming. The examples in this description illustrate basic uses of the MERGE statement. Other applications include using more than one BY variable, merging more than two data sets, and merging a few observations with all observations in another data set.

Merging without a BY Statement: One-to-One Merging

When no BY statement is used, the MERGE statement joins the first observation in one data set with the first observation in another, the second observation in the data set with the second observation in another, and so forth. The number of observations in the new data set is the maximum number of observations in any of the data sets listed in the MERGE statement. When a data set being merged runs out of observations, missing values for its variables are joined with the remaining observations from the other data sets.

If a variable occurs in more than one of the data sets being merged, only one variable of that name occurs in the new data set. The value of the variable is the value in the data set listed latest (rightmost) in the MERGE statement that contains the variable and is still contributing observations.

Example 1: one-to-one merge You have two data sets, each with the same number of observations but containing different variables. One contains the name and hometown of car owners; the other contains the year and model of their cars. **Output 5.15** shows the input data sets.

```
data driver;
   input name $ city : $10.;
   cards;
CATHY PORTLAND
NANCY RALEIGH
SUE NASHVILLE
;
data vehicle;
   input year model $;
   cards;
1985 SEDAN
1952 JEEP
1978 BUS
;
proc print data=driver;
   title 'DATA SET DRIVER';
proc print data=vehicle;
   title 'DATA SET VEHICLE';
```

Output 5.15 Input Data Sets for One-to-One Merge

```
                      DATA SET DRIVER                                    1
            OBS    NAME     CITY

             1     CATHY    PORTLAND
             2     NANCY    RALEIGH
             3     SUE      NASHVILLE
```

```
                      DATA SET VEHICLE                                   2
            OBS    YEAR    MODEL

             1     1985    SEDAN
             2     1952    JEEP
             3     1978    BUS
```

You want to merge the first observation in the DRIVER data set with the first observation in the VEHICLE data set; the second observation with the second observation, and so on. The new data set (in **Output 5.16**) contains the same number of observations as each of the input data sets, but the number of variables equals the total of the variables in the two input data sets.

```
data match;
   merge driver vehicle;
proc print;
   title 'DATA SET MATCH';
```

Output 5.16 Output Data Set Produced by One-to-One Merge

```
                      DATA SET MATCH                                     3
        OBS   NAME    CITY        YEAR    MODEL

         1    CATHY   PORTLAND    1985    SEDAN
         2    NANCY   RALEIGH     1952    JEEP
         3    SUE     NASHVILLE   1978    BUS
```

Merging with a BY Statement: Match-Merging

If you want to match observations from two or more SAS data sets based on the values of some variables, then use a BY statement after the MERGE statement. Only one BY statement can accompany each MERGE statement. A BY statement applies only to the most recent MERGE statement.

In order to perform match-merging, at least one variable must be common to all data sets, and each data set must be sorted by these variables. The variables used for matching are called BY variables; the BY statement is used to identify the matching variables.

Nonmatches When nonmatching BY values occur, SAS processes all observations with the lower BY value before processing any observations with a higher BY value. The FIRST. and LAST. variables are used to detect the beginning and end of BY groups, and thus let you control whether to output, delete, or count multiple observations in a BY group. The IN= variable, described earlier, lets you

SAS Statements Used in the DATA Step 213

know if a data set contributed information to the observation being built; thus, you can use it to detect nonmatches.

Multiple observations with the same BY value in a data set The match-merge operation combines all the data from each data set that has an observation with the current BY values. That is, if a data set has more than one observation with the same BY value, the match-merge operation outputs each observation. The first observation of the BY group is combined with the first observation in the BY group from every data set with observations for that BY value; the second observation is combined with the second, and so on. The resulting data set contains as many observations for a BY group as the largest number in that BY group in any of the data sets. The total number of observations in the new data set is the sum of the largest number of observations in each BY group across all input data sets.

When an input data set exhausts the observations in a BY group, the values from the last observation in that BY group are retained and merged with the remaining observations in that BY group from other data sets. The value of 1 that was assigned to the IN= variable when the data set began to contribute information in that BY group is also retained. You can reset the IN= variable to 0 in an assignment statement before the MERGE statement if you want to detect only new information in the BY group.

If one input data set contains no observations in a particular BY group, that data set contributes missing values to its unique variables in those observations in the new data set. The value of the IN= variable is 0 for that data set throughout that BY group.

Variables with the same name in more than one data set If a variable other than a BY variable occurs in more than one data set being merged, only one variable of that name occurs in the new data set. When a BY group has only one observation in each of the data sets being joined, the value of the variable in the new observation is the value from the data set mentioned latest in the MERGE statement. When multiple observations occur within a BY group, the value in the new data set is the value from the data set mentioned latest in the MERGE statement that is still contributing information to the BY group.

Example 2: match-merge You have two data sets. Data set PERSON contains the variables NAME and SEX; data set PLACE contains the variables NAME, CITY, and REGION. **Output 5.17** displays the input data sets.

```
data person;
   input name $ sex $;
   cards;
MARY F
ANN F
TOM M
;
proc print;
   title 'DATA SET PERSON';
data place;
   input name $ city $ region;
   cards;
JOSE ERIE 5
MARY MIAMI 2
MARY TAMPA 7
ANN TAMPA 6
;
proc print;
   title 'DATA SET PLACE';
```

Output 5.17 Input Data Sets for Match-Merge

```
                    DATA SET PERSON                                    1
              OBS    NAME    SEX

               1     MARY     F
               2     ANN      F
               3     TOM      M
```

```
                    DATA SET PLACE                                     2
              OBS    NAME    CITY     REGION

               1     JOSE    ERIE       5
               2     MARY    MIAMI      2
               3     MARY    TAMPA      7
               4     ANN     TAMPA      6
```

You want to merge each observation in data set PERSON with the observation in PLACE that has a matching value of the common variable NAME. These steps perform the match-merge operation and produce the data set shown in **Output 5.18**:

```
proc sort data=person;
   by name;
proc sort data=place;
   by name;
data result;
   merge person place;
   by name;
proc print;
   title 'DATA SET RESULT';
```

Output 5.18 Output Data Set Produced by Match-Merge

```
                    DATA SET RESULT                                    3
              OBS    NAME    SEX    CITY     REGION

               1     ANN      F     TAMPA      6
               2     JOSE           ERIE       5
               3     MARY     F     MIAMI      2
               4     MARY     F     TAMPA      7
               5     TOM      M                .
```

Since data sets PERSON and PLACE are not in sorted order of the variable NAME, you must sort them before merging them. The BY group with the lowest BY value, ANN, has one observation in data set PERSON and data set PLACE, so data set RESULT contains one ANN observation with the information from the ANN observation in data sets PERSON and PLACE. The BY group with the next BY value, JOSE, has an observation only in PLACE, so in data set RESULT the JOSE observation has a missing value for SEX, the variable from data set PERSON. The next BY value, MARY, has one observation in PERSON and two observations in PLACE. Thus, the sex value of 'F' from the MARY observation in PERSON is combined with both MARY observations in PLACE to produce two observations with sex values of 'F' in RESULT. The final BY value, TOM, exists only in PERSON, so the CITY and REGION values from PLACE are missing in the TOM observation in RESULT.

Example 3: match-merge for table lookup   You have one data set that is your table; it contains an identifier variable and corresponding descriptions. You want to merge the descriptions with another data set that contains the identifier variable. For example, say the data set containing the table has two variables, NUMBER and DESCRIPT, shown in **Output 5.19**. NUMBER contains the part number, and DESCRIPT contains the part description. The other data set, shown in **Output 5.20**, contains the part number and the name of a customer. Both data sets are sorted by NUMBER, the identifier variable. The result of the merge operation is shown in **Output 5.21**.

```
data partdata;
   *The table;
   input number descript $12.;
   cards;
155 SCREWDRIVER
244 WRENCH
501 PLIERS
796 HAMMER
;
proc sort data=partdata;
   by number;
proc print data=partdata;
   title 'PARTDATA--THE ORDER FILE';
```

Output 5.19   Table Data Set for Table Lookup

```
                   PARTDATA--THE ORDER FILE                           1

              OBS    NUMBER     DESCRIPT

               1       155      SCREWDRIVER
               2       244      WRENCH
               3       501      PLIERS
               4       796      HAMMER
```

216   Chapter 5

```
data orders;
   *The list of parts that were ordered and the customers
      who ordered them;
   input number name & $16.;
   cards;
155  R. B. HOADLEY
155  G. C. FREE
244  A. T. CANNON
244  M. C. WHITE
244  Z. A. DE LA CRUZ
796  S. C. FOXX
796  M. C. WHITE
;
proc sort data=orders;
   by number;
proc print data=orders;
   title 'ORDERS--LIST OF NAMES AND ORDERS';
```

Output 5.20 List of Names and Orders to Be Looked Up

```
                    ORDERS--LIST OF NAMES AND ORDERS                    2
            OBS    NUMBER    NAME

             1       155     R. B. HOADLEY
             2       155     G. C. FREE
             3       244     A. T. CANNON
             4       244     M. C. WHITE
             5       244     Z. A. DE LA CRUZ
             6       796     S. C. FOXX
             7       796     M. C. WHITE
```

```
data complete;
   merge partdata orders;
   by number;
proc print;
   title 'COMPLETE';
```

Output 5.21 Complete Merged Data Set for Table Lookup

```
                              COMPLETE                                  3
         OBS   NUMBER   DESCRIPT      NAME

          1     155     SCREWDRIVER   R. B. HOADLEY
          2     155     SCREWDRIVER   G. C. FREE
          3     244     WRENCH        A. T. CANNON
          4     244     WRENCH        M. C. WHITE
          5     244     WRENCH        Z. A. DE LA CRUZ
          6     501     PLIERS
          7     796     HAMMER        S. C. FOXX
          8     796     HAMMER        M. C. WHITE
```

Since you combined the data sets in order to have a list of customers with a description of the part they buy, you want to delete observations from the table (PARTDATA) that have no match in ORDERS. Part number 501, PLIERS, has no match in ORDERS. You can use the IN= variable on the ORDERS data set to ensure that all observations in the result are also in the ORDERS data set:

```
data complete;
   merge partdata orders(in=a);
   by number;
   if a;
proc print;
   title 'COMPLETE (WITH IN=)';
```

Observations are only output to COMPLETE when the value of the IN= variable A is 1. See **Output 5.22**.

Output 5.22 Merged Data Set Showing Only Parts Ordered

```
                    COMPLETE (WITH IN=)                              4
     OBS    NUMBER    DESCRIPT       NAME

      1       155     SCREWDRIVER    R. B. HOADLEY
      2       155     SCREWDRIVER    G. C. FREE
      3       244     WRENCH         A. T. CANNON
      4       244     WRENCH         M. C. WHITE
      5       244     WRENCH         Z. A. DE LA CRUZ
      6       796     HAMMER         S. C. FOXX
      7       796     HAMMER         M. C. WHITE
```

Comparison of match-merge and one-to-one merge When all data sets being merged contain the same number of observations in each BY group, the result of a match-merge operation is the same as that of a one-to-one merge. However, if any input data set contains a different number of observations in a BY group (such as two observations with the BY variable value ID=3001 and no observation with ID=3002), a match-merge operation outputs all observations in the BY group for all data sets. You can detect the discrepancy in the number of observations in the BY group either with FIRST. and LAST. variables or by noting an unexpected number of observations in the output data set. In the same case a one-to-one merge operation, which joins observations sequentially, causes subsequent observations to become mismatched. You cannot detect the mismatch except by observing unusual combinations of values in the output data set (such as NAME='MARY' and SEX='M').

MISSING Statement

You can use a MISSING statement to declare that certain values in your input data represent special missing values for numeric data.

A MISSING statement has this form:

MISSING *values*;

where

> *values* are the values in your input data that you are using to represent special missing values. These special missing values may be any of the twenty-six capital letters of the alphabet (not lowercase letters) or the underscore (_). See "Missing Values" for further discussion of special missing values in the SAS System.

For example, with survey data, you want to identify certain kinds of missing data. Suppose an 'A' is coded when the respondent was absent from home at the time of the survey; an 'R' when the respondent refused to answer.

```
data surv;
   missing A R;
   input id answer1;
   cards;
1001 2
1002 R
1003 1
1004 A
1005 2
more data lines
;
```

The MISSING statement indicates that values of A and R in the input data lines are to be considered special missing values rather than invalid numeric data values.

Null Statement

The null statement is a single semicolon. The statement does not perform any action but can play the role of a placeholder. Although a null statement may be used anywhere in a SAS program, it is most useful in the DATA step. For example, in some SAS programs that include a CARDS statement you may also need a null statement to signal the end of the data lines.

The form of a null statement is

```
;
```

In the DATA step, a CARDS statement signals to the SAS System that data lines follow immediately in the job stream. SAS recognizes the end of the data lines when it sees a semicolon on a line. If the first line after the last data line already contains a semicolon, you do not need a null statement. For example,

```
data comm;
   input x y z;
   cards;
data lines
proc print;
```

However, if a semicolon does not appear in the line after the last data line, a null statement can signal the end of the data:

```
data comm;
   input x y z;
   cards;
data lines
;
proc print
   data=comm(keep=x rename=(x=visti1));
```

When your data contain semicolons and you use the CARDS4 statement, the null statement is indicated by four semicolons. For example,

```
data comm;
   input x y z;
   cards4;
data lines containing semicolons
;;;;
```

Although no action is performed by the statement, it is considered an executable statement. Thus, a label can precede it. For example,

```
data lab;
   infile in;
   input x y z;
   if x=. then go to find;
   list;
find: ;
   drop x;
```

See the section **Labels, Statement** listed alphabetically in this chapter for more information on using statement labels.

OUTPUT Statement

Introduction 220
Creating Several Observations from One Input Line 220
Creating More than One Data Set in a Single DATA Step 221
Combining Information from Several Records 221

Introduction

The OUTPUT statement tells the SAS System to write the current observation to the data set being created. The form of the OUTPUT statement is

OUTPUT [*SASdataset*]...;

where

SASdataset
> optionally specifies the data sets to which the current observation should be written. More than one SAS data set name can be given. All names specified must also appear in the DATA statement. When no SAS data set name is given, the current observation is written to all data sets being created in the step.

Simple SAS DATA steps do not need an OUTPUT statement since observations are automatically output before SAS returns to the beginning of the step for another execution. The OUTPUT statement is useful when you need to control the normal output of observations in situations like these:

- you want to create two or more observations from each line of input data
- you are creating more than one SAS data set from one input data file
- you want to combine several input observations into one observation.

When an OUTPUT statement appears among the program statements in the DATA step, SAS adds an observation to the SAS data set(s) only when the OUTPUT statement is executed. No automatic output occurs.

Creating Several Observations from One Input Line

Here is an example of creating several observations from one input line. Each line contains a subject identifier and three measurements for that subject. For each input line, you want to produce three observations. Each new observation should contain the subject identifier and one measurement.

```
data repeat;
   input subject $ measure1-measure3;
   drop measure1-measure3;
   measure=measure1;
   output;
   measure=measure2;
   output;
   measure=measure3;
   output;
   cards;
A 2 5 4
B 3 6 2
;
```

The new data set contains the observations shown in **Output 5.23**.

Output 5.23 Creating Several Observations from One Input Line

```
                    REPEAT                                              1

           OBS    SUBJECT    MEASURE

            1        A          2
            2        A          5
            3        A          4
            4        B          3
            5        B          6
            6        B          2
```

Creating More than One Data Set in a Single DATA Step

These statements create two data sets from a single input record:

```
data college hischool;
   input name $ 1-30 sex $ yrs_educ;
   if yrs_educ<=12 then output hischool;
   else output college;
   cards;
data lines
;
```

The data set HISCHOOL contains all observations with a YRS_EDUC value of 12 or less. Data set COLLEGE contains observations with a YRS_EDUC value greater than 12.

Combining Information from Several Records

These statements combine the information from several input records into one observation in the SAS data set:

```
proc sort data=payroll;
   by ssn;
data checks;
   set payroll;
   by ssn;
   if first.ssn then tot_pay=0;
   tot_pay+pay;
   drop pay;
   if last.ssn then output;
```

SAS data set PAYROLL, which has been sorted by SSN, is used as input to the DATA step. PAYROLL contains several observations for each SSN. Since the BY statement appears in the DATA step, the FIRST. and LAST. automatic variables can be used to check for the first and last observations with each SSN value. A sum statement accumulates total pay for each SSN. When an observation is the last with a particular SSN value, SAS writes the observation to the new data set. Thus, the new data set contains one observation for each SSN value in the PAYROLL data set.

The contents of data set PAYROLL after sorting are shown in **Output 5.24**.

Output 5.24 Contents of Data Set PAYROLL

```
                       PAYROLL AFTER SORTING                          1
              OBS        SSN          PAY
               1      111442222      100.00
               2      111442222       25.00
               3      333115555      160.00
               4      333115555       80.00
               5      777668888      142.66
```

The contents of data set CHECKS are shown in **Output 5.25**.

Output 5.25 Contents of Data Set CHECKS

```
                            CHECKS                                    2
              OBS        SSN         TOT_PAY
               1      111442222      125.00
               2      333115555      240.00
               3      777668888      142.66
```

PUT Statement

Introduction 223
Column Style 224
List Style 225
Formatted Style 226
Pointer Controls and Format Modifiers 227
    Pointer controls 227
    Specifying values for pointer controls 231
    Format modifiers 232
Special Topics 232
    When the pointer goes past the end of a line 232
    The pointer's location after writing a data value 232
    Grouping variables and formats 232
    Writing character constants 233
    Writing the current input line 233
    Listing values of the current variables 234
    Labeling variable values: named output 234
    Arrays 234

Introduction

The PUT statement writes lines to the SAS log, to the SAS procedure output file, or to any file that can be specified in a FILE statement. The file specified by the most recently executed FILE statement is the *current output file*. If no FILE statement executes before a PUT statement in the current execution of a DATA step, the lines are written on the SAS log.

The PUT statement can write lines containing variable values, strings of text, or both. Variable values can be labeled with the name of the variable by using named output. With specifications in the PUT statement, you list items to be written and describe their format.

You can write variable values in one of three basic output styles: column, list or free-form, or formatted style. Simple examples showing how to specify these output styles are given below. Each style is fully described in a later section.

With **column style** enter a range of numbers after the variable name; these numbers specify a range of columns into which values are written, for example,

```
put name 6-15 weight 17-19;
```

With **list style** simply list the variables in the PUT statement in the order you want to write them:

```
put name weight sex;
```

With **formatted style** specify a format after the variable name:

```
put date mmddyy8. time hhmm5.;
```

The general form of the PUT statement is

PUT [*specification*]...;

where *specification* describes how a variable's value or a text string is written in the output line. You can use the following specifications in the PUT statement:

variable
    names the variable whose value is to be written.

'characterstring'
    specifies a string of text to be written by the PUT statement. The string must be enclosed in quotes. See **Writing character constants** later in this section.

pointercontrol
: moves the output pointer to a specified line or column. See **Pointer Controls and Format Modifiers** later in this section.

INFILE
: writes the last line read either from the current input file or from lines following a CARDS statement. See **Writing the current input line** later in this section.

ALL
: writes the values of all variables, including _ERROR_ and _N_, defined in the current DATA step using named output. See **Listing values of the current variables** later in this section.

You can combine many of these features in a single PUT statement. The PUT statement writes each item in the order specified, for example,

```
put name 'weighs' weight 17-19 ' on ' date mmddyy8;
```

A PUT statement with no specifications (a null PUT statement), for example,

```
put;
```

causes the current output line to be written immediately to the current file, even if the current output line is blank. The null PUT statement releases an output line being held by a previous PUT statement with a trailing @. See **Pointer Controls and Format Modifiers** for more information on the trailing @.

Column Style

Column style describes the output lines by giving the variable's name and the columns its value is to occupy in the output line. The PUT statement writes the values of the variable in the specified columns of the output line.

If the values require fewer columns than specified, character variables are left aligned in the specified columns, and numeric variables are right aligned in the specified columns.

The form of the PUT statement for writing the value of one variable with column output is

PUT [*variable*] [=] [$] *startcolumn*[−*endcolumn*] [.*decimalplaces*];

where

variable
: names the variable whose value is to be written.

=
: specifies that the value is to be labeled with the variable name and an equal sign. See **Labeling variable values: named output** for more information.

$
: indicates that the variable contains character values rather than numeric values. If the variable has already been defined as a character variable (for example, in an INPUT statement), you can omit the $ sign.

startcolumn
: is the first column of the field where the value is to be written in the output line.

−*endcolumn*
: is the last column of the field for the value. If the value is to occupy only one column in the output line, omit the −*endcolumn* specification.

.decimalplaces
: is a period followed by a positive integer that specifies the number of digits you want on the right side of the decimal point.

There is no limit to the number of column style specifications you can specify in a single PUT statement. This PUT statement writes the values of two variables on the current output line:

```
put name $ 1-8 address $ 10-35;
```

The value of NAME is written in columns 1 through 8; then the value of ADDRESS is written in columns 10 through 35 on the same output line.

When you list more than one item, the PUT statement writes each item in the order specified. For example, the statement

```
put first 73-80 second 10-12;
```

first writes a value of the variable FIRST in columns 73-80, and then it writes a value of SECOND in columns 10 through 12 on the same output line.

The specified range of columns must provide sufficient space for the value. If you are using named output, for example, remember that the variable name, the equal sign (=), and the value must fit in the columns specified. (See **Labeling variable values: named output** below.)

If a variable has been previously defined as character, a $ is not necessary in the PUT statement. For example, in this DATA step:

```
data a;
   input name $ 1-15;
   file out;
   put name 1-15;
```

no $ is necessary in the PUT statement since the variable NAME is defined as character in the INPUT statement.

List Style

With list style you simply list the names of the variables you want written. The PUT statement writes the value of each variable listed in the PUT statement, leaves a blank, and then writes the next value.

The form of the PUT statement for writing one variable with list output is

PUT *variable*[=] [$];

where

- *variable* names the variable you want written.
- = specifies that the variable value be written using named output. See **Labeling variable values: named output** for more information.
- $ specifies that the variable is a character variable. The $ is not necessary if the variable has been previously defined as character.

In the following DATA step the PUT statement writes values of NAME, SEX, and AGE using list output style:

```
data class;
   input name $ 1-10 sex $ 12 age 14-15;
   put name sex age;
   cards;
```

```
HENRY       M   13
JOE         M   14
HENRIETTA   F   11
;
```

The following data lines are written to the SAS log by the PUT statement:

```
HENRY M 13
JOE M 14
HENRIETTA F 11
```

Notice that one blank separates the data values on the output line.

With list output, missing values for numeric variables are written as a single period (.). Character values are left aligned in the field; leading and trailing blanks are removed. To include blanks (in addition to the blank inserted after each value), use formatted instead of list style.

You can use the list output form and also specify the format to be used for writing the value if you include the colon (:) format modifier. See **Pointer Controls and Format Modifiers** below.

Formatted Style

Formatted style describes the output lines by listing variable names and formats for writing the values. With formatted style, the PUT statement writes each value using the format that follows the variable name. No blanks are automatically added between values. Formatted style, combined with the pointer controls discussed in **Pointer Controls and Format Modifiers**, makes it possible to specify the exact line and column location to write each variable.

The form of the PUT statement for writing one variable with formatted output is

PUT *variable*[=] *format.*;

where

> *variable* names the variable you want to write.
>
> = specifies that the variable value should be written using named output. See **Labeling variable values: named output** for more information.
>
> *format.* specifies a format to use when writing the data values. The format can be either a SAS format (see Chapter 13, "SAS Informats and Formats") or a format you define (see Chapter 19, "The FORMAT Procedure," in the *SAS Procedures Guide, Release 6.03 Edition*). Every format specification **must** include a period.

You can list several variables by using a format list:

PUT (*variablelist*) (*formatlist*)...;

where

(*variablelist*)
> is any valid variable list enclosed in parentheses.

(*formatlist*)
> lists the formats to be used to write the preceding list of variables. See **Grouping variables and formats** below.

The width you specify for the format must provide enough space to write the value and any commas, dollar signs, or other special characters that the format includes.

Suppose the value of X is 100. You want to write the value using the DOLLAR. format and include two decimal places for cents. This PUT statement

```
put x dollar7.2;
```

writes the formatted value, which takes 7 columns:

```
$100.00
```

If the value uses fewer columns than specified, character values are left aligned and numeric values are right aligned in the field specified by the format width.

Pointer Controls and Format Modifiers

Most of the PUT statements shown so far are examples of simple column, list, and formatted styles. Two advanced features—pointer controls and format modifiers—can add flexibility regardless of the output style you are using.

SAS keeps track of its position on each output line with a pointer. With specifications in the PUT statement, you can control pointer movement from column to column and line to line. For example, if each record requires several lines and you are writing a value that begins in the tenth column of the second line, the pointer value indicates that the current line is 2 and the current column is 10.

The pointer controls and format modifiers are described below:

Pointer controls

@*n*
> moves the pointer to column *n*.

@*pointvariable*
> moves the pointer to the column given by the value of *pointvariable*. The *pointvariable* must be numeric.

@(*expression*)
> moves the pointer to the column given by the value of *expression*. The *expression* must evaluate to a positive integer.
>
> To move the pointer to a specific column, use the @ followed by the column number, variable, or expression whose value is that column number. For example, the statement
>
> ```
> put @15 sales;
> ```
>
> moves the pointer to column 15 and writes the value of SALES using list output.
>
> The PUT statement in this example:
>
> ```
> data one;
>     input space X;
>     put @space X 5.2;
> ```
>
> moves the pointer to the column indicated by the value of SPACE and writes the value of X using the 5.2 format.
>
> The pointer can go backward as well as forward. For example, this PUT statement
>
> ```
> put @26 book @1 company;
> ```
>
> first writes BOOK's value beginning in column 26 and then returns to column 1 on the same line to write COMPANY's value.
>
> For more information see **Specifying values for pointer controls** below.

+*n*
: moves the pointer forward *n* columns.

+*pointvariable*
: moves the pointer forward or backward the number of columns indicated by the value of *pointvariable*. The pointer moves backward if the *pointvariable* has a negative value. The *pointvariable* must be numeric.

+(*expression*)
: moves the pointer the number of columns given by the value of *expression*. The *expression* must evaluate to a positive or negative integer.

The + pointer direction, followed by a number, variable name, or expression, moves the pointer the number of columns indicated. The movement is relative to where the pointer is located. For example, the statement

```
put @23 length 4. +5 width;
```

moves the pointer to column 23, writes LENGTH's value in four columns (23, 24, 25, and 26) leaving the pointer at column 27, then advances the pointer five columns and begins writing a WIDTH value in column 32.

For more information see **Specifying values for pointer controls** below.

A + can cause the SAS System to attempt to write past the current line length. See **When the pointer goes past the end of a line** for more information.

#*n*
: moves the pointer to line *n*.

#*pointvariable*
: moves the pointer to the line number indicated by the value of *pointvariable*. The *pointvariable* must be numeric.

#(*expression*)
: moves the pointer to the line given by the value of *expression*. The *expression* must evaluate to a positive integer.

When you want to write several lines of data with one PUT statement, you can use the # to indicate on which line the information is to be written. For example, the statement

```
put @12 name $10. #2 id 3-4;
```

writes the value for NAME beginning in column 12 of the first output line and then writes a value for ID in columns 3 and 4 of the second line.

The following statement:

```
put #4 id #2 name;
```

writes a value for ID on line 4 and moves back to line 2 to write the NAME value.

If the N= option of the FILE statement is not specified, the highest value used with the # pointer control in the current DATA step is the default value for N=. The N= option is described with the FILE statement.

For more information see **Specifying values for pointer controls** below.

/

moves the pointer to column 1 of the next line. For example, the statement

```
put age grade / score1-score5;
```

first writes values of AGE and GRADE on one line and then skips to the next line to write values of SCORE1-SCORE5 beginning in column 1.

@, trailing

holds a data line for another PUT statement. The @ is called a *trailing at-sign* because it must follow all other items in the PUT statement.

Usually, each PUT statement in a DATA step writes a new data line. When you want to use more than one PUT statement to write values on the same output line, you can use an @ as the last item in your PUT statement to hold the pointer at its current location. The next PUT statement executed in that DATA step then writes to the same line rather than to a new line.

For example,

```
data _null_;
   input name $ weight;
   put name @;
   if weight ne . then put @15 weight @;
   put;
```

The trailing @ in the first PUT statement holds the current output line after NAME is written; thus, if the value of WEIGHT is not missing, a WEIGHT value is written on the line with NAME. The trailing @ in the second PUT statement holds the line after WEIGHT is written. The final null PUT statement always releases the current line and positions the pointer at column one on the next line.

Suppose you have a SAS data set named DEXT containing dexterity test scores for a group of children. Each observation in the data set contains three variables: CHILD, a child's name; SCORE, a dexterity score; and TYPE, the hand (right or left) for which the score was recorded. There are two observations for each child—one for the right-hand score and one for the left-hand score. You want to print the data with the right- and left-hand scores on the same output line:

```
data _null_;
   set dext;
   by child;
   if first.child then put child @;
   if type='LEFT' then put @25 score 4.2 @;
   else if type='RIGHT' then put @35 score 4.2 @;
   if last.child then put;
```

In this example, if the observation is the first for CHILD, the child's name is written. The pointer holds that line until the left- or right-hand score is written. Still holding the line, the next record is read from DEXT and the score written; since the record is the last for a child, the line is released by the last PUT statement.

Note: the trailing @ specified in the PUT statement holds the current line for the next execution of a PUT statement even if another execution of the DATA step begins. Thus, the double trailing @ pointer control, which is required in the INPUT statement to hold the current input line, is not needed in the PUT statement.

A trailing @ holds the current output line until one of the following is encountered:

- a PUT statement without a trailing @, as shown above
- a PUT statement specifying _PAGE_ (described below)
- the end of the current line (as specified by the current LINESIZE= value)
- the end of the data.

Using a trailing @ can cause the SAS System to attempt to write past the current line length since the pointer value is unchanged when the next PUT statement executes. See **When the pointer goes past the end of a line** for more information.

PAGE

advances the pointer to the first line of a new page. The SAS System automatically begins a new page when a line exceeds the current PAGESIZE value.

If the current output file is a print file, _PAGE_ produces an output line containing the appropriate carriage control character. _PAGE_ is unnecessary in PUT statements executed by a HEADER= option in the FILE statement. Lines produced by those statements are automatically printed on a new page.

For example, suppose you want to go to the first line of a new page after printing information for the last observation in a county, as in this example:

```
data _null_;
   set states;
   by county;
   file print;
   put name 1-10 @15 pop comma9. ;
   if last.county then put _page_;
```

PUT _PAGE_ advances the pointer to line 1 of the new page when the value of LAST.COUNTY is 1. (A discussion of FIRST. and LAST. variables is given in the **BY Statement** description earlier in this chapter.)

You can specify the _PAGE_ option in the PUT statement along with variables, strings of text, and other PUT statement features. For example, suppose you want to print a footer message before exiting from the page:

```
data _null_;
   set states;
   by county;
   file print;
   put name 1-10 @15 pop comma9. ;
   if last.county then put // 'THIS IS THE LAST OF '
   county $10. _page_;
```

When an observation is the last for a county, the PUT statement skips two lines and prints the message 'THIS IS THE LAST OF ' followed by the current value of COUNTY before skipping to the next page.

OVERPRINT

prints over the previous line. You can use the OVERPRINT option when your PUT statements are directed to a print file and when the N= option of the FILE statement has a value of 1. The OVERPRINT option in the PUT statement has no effect when you are writing lines on the screen.

For example, this PUT statement underlines a title by overprinting with underscores:

```
put 'TITLE OF PAGE' overprint '_____';
```

If OVERPRINT is the first keyword in a PUT statement, the line written by that statement overprints the last line written by a previous PUT statement in the current output file. For example, the statements

```
data _null_;
   set class;
   file print;
   put name 1-10 @15 grade 2.;
   if grade >= 96 then put overprint @15 '__';
```

underline grades above 95 on the output line.

You can use the OVERPRINT option in a PUT statement with other pointer controls:

```
put @5 name $8. overprint @5 '_____'/ @20 address;
```

This PUT statement writes a value for NAME, underlines it by overprinting underscores, and then goes to the next line to write an ADDRESS value.

Specifying values for pointer controls When you specify # or @, you move the pointer to a specific line or column. Thus, the value of n or *expression* must be a positive integer. When you use a *pointvariable* with # and @, the value of the variable is truncated to a positive integer if necessary.

The + moves the pointer relative to its current location. The value specified with +n must be a positive integer. The value for the *pointvariable* or *expression* specified with + must represent a negative or positive integer. For example, after writing a value with list output, you may want to back up one column to write over the blank that the PUT statement automatically writes with list output. This DATA step shows two methods of moving the pointer backward:

```
data one;
   input a b c x y z;
   *Use an expression to move pointer backward;
   put a +(-1) b +(-1) c;
   *Use pointvariable with negative value to move pointer backward;
   m=-1;
   put x +m y +m z;
```

Since the A, B, and C and X, Y, and Z values are written using list output, a blank would normally be added after each value is written. Both the +(-1) and the +M pointer control move the pointer back one space to eliminate the blank.

The following example uses expressions and SAS functions enclosed in parentheses in a PUT statement:

```
put @(n-floor(x)) lastname +(x-sum(y,z,q)) frstname;
```

This statement first uses the FLOOR function to take the largest integer value of X and then subtracts the result from the value of N. The pointer is moved to that position on the output line to write the value of LASTNAME. The pointer is then moved to a new position that is evaluated by subtracting the sum of three variables from the value of X; then the value of FRSTNAME is written.

Format modifiers

n*

specifies that the next format in a format list is to be repeated *n* times. For example,

```
put (grades1-grades3) (3* 7.2);
```

writes GRADES1, GRADES2, and GRADES3 with the 7.2 format.

colon (:)

precedes a format and causes the SAS System to write the variable's value using the format, trimming off leading and trailing blanks, and following the value with one blank. For example, the statements

```
data a;
   x=12353.2;
   y=15;
   put x : comma10.2 y : 5.2;
```

produce the line

```
12,353.20 15.00
```

Special Topics

When the pointer goes past the end of a line SAS does not write an output line that is longer than the current line length (as specified by the LINESIZE= value). You may inadvertently send the pointer beyond the current line length with one of, or some combination of, the following specifications:

- using the @ sign to hold the current line for a value that does not fit in the remaining space
- using the + pointer control with a value that moves the pointer to a column beyond the current line length
- specifying a column range that exceeds the current line length (for example, PUT X 90-100 when the current line length is 80)
- attempting to write a variable value or text string that does not fit in the space remaining on the current output line.

When a PUT statement attempts to write past the end of the current line, SAS withholds the entire item that overflows the current line, writes the current line, then writes the overflow item on a new line.

The pointer's location after writing a data value The pointer location after a value is written depends on the output style used in the PUT statement. If list style is used, SAS sets the pointer to the second column after the value since the PUT statement automatically skips a column after writing each value. If column or formatted style is used, the pointer is set to the first column after the end of the field specified in the PUT statement.

After the PUT statement writes a character string, the pointer is located at the first column after string. After an _INFILE_ specification, the pointer is located at the next column after the record written from the current input file.

You can find the pointer's current location using the COLUMN= and LINE= options of the FILE statement. See the **FILE Statement** description earlier in this chapter for more information.

Grouping variables and formats When you want to write values in a pattern on the output lines, using format lists can shorten your coding time. A format list consists of a list of variable names, enclosed in parentheses, followed by a corresponding list of formats, also enclosed in parentheses. You can use as many format lists as necessary in a PUT statement. You can include any of the pointer controls (@, #, /, +, and OVERPRINT) in the list of formats. However, format lists cannot be nested. You must separate items in a format list either by blanks or by commas.

The following example uses a format list to write the five variables SCORE1-SCORE5, one after another, using four columns for each value with no blanks in between:

```
put (score1-score5) (4. 4. 4. 4. 4.);
```

When there are more variables than format items, SAS uses the same format list again and again until all the variables have been written. So a simpler way to write the same PUT statement is

```
put (score1-score5) (4.);
```

When the format list includes more formats and pointer controls than are needed, the PUT statement ignores any remaining specifications in the format list after all the variable values have been written. For example, the PUT statement

```
put (x y z) (2.,+1);
```

writes the value of X using the 2. format, skips the next column, writes Y's value using the 2. format, skips a column, then writes Z's value using the 2. format. The +1 pointer control remaining in the third cycle of the format list is not used.

Writing character constants You can specify any number of character strings in a PUT statement. When using list output, you can specify character strings anywhere in the PUT statement. When using column or formatted output, character strings cannot be specified between a variable and its column locations or a variable and its format.

You can repeat a character constant on the output line by using the n* format modifier or the REPEAT function.

For example, both of these PUT statements write a line of 132 underscores:

```
put 132*'_';
x=repeat('_',131);
put x;
```

After writing a character constant, the pointer is located at the first column after the constant. Thus, if you are planning to follow a character constant with a value on the output line, you may want to use a blank as the last character of the constant. For example, say that values for the variables YEAR and TOTAL are 1985 and 1000, respectively. The statement

```
put 'The profit for ' year 'is ' total;
```

writes the line

```
The profit for 1985 is 1000
```

The blank in each of the character constants prevents the values for YEAR and TOTAL from following the constants with no intervening space.

When insufficient space remains on the current line to write the entire text of a character string, SAS withholds the entire string and takes the action described in **When the pointer goes past the end of a line** above.

Writing the current input line When _INFILE_ is specified, the PUT statement writes the last record read from the file currently being used as input. The current input file can be the file specified by the most recently executed INFILE statement or data lines following a CARDS statement. Consider the following program:

```
data _null_;
   input;
   put _infile_;
   cards;
data lines
;
```

With each execution of the DATA step, the PUT _INFILE_ statement writes the next line of data following the CARDS statement on the SAS log.

If the most recent INPUT statement for the current input file read more than one line, only the last line is written by the _INFILE_ specification.

Listing values of the current variables When _ALL_ is specified, the PUT statement writes all currently defined variables using named output. For example, the statement

```
put _all_;
```

writes labeled values of all currently defined variables including the automatic variables _ERROR_ and _N_. Named output is described below.

Labeling variable values: named output The PUT statement can label values with their variable names. This form of writing values is called *named output*. You can specify named output with column, list, or formatted output by following the variable name in the PUT statement with an equal sign (=). You can label character or numeric variables. For example, this statement

```
put name= @12 height= weight=;
```

writes all three variables using named output. Thus, if the current record contains the values ANN, 63.3, and 95.1, the PUT statement writes the following line:

```
NAME=ANN    HEIGHT=63.3 WEIGHT=95.1
```

Formats following the equal sign specify an output format for the variable. For example, the statement

```
put amount=dollar8.2;
```

writes the current value of AMOUNT in named output style with the format DOLLAR8.2.

Arrays You can write an array element with the PUT statement. Do not use an array reference as a *pointvariable*. The subscript can be any SAS expression that evaluates to a valid subscript when the PUT statement executes.

You can use the array subscript asterisk (*) to write all elements of a previously defined explicitly or implicitly subscripted array to a file. The array can be single- or multidimensional, but it cannot be a _TEMPORARY_ array. You can enclose the subscript in braces, brackets, or parentheses, and you can print the array using list, column, formatted, or named output. The syntax is

PUT *arrayname*{*};

RENAME Statement

You can use the RENAME statement in a DATA step to give variables new names in any data sets being created.

The form of the RENAME statement is

RENAME *oldname=newname...;*

where

    oldname   is the name of the individual variable you want to rename.

    newname specifies the new name for the variable.

More than one set of names can appear. Since the new name takes effect in the output data set, use the old name in program statements in the current DATA step.

Here is an example:

```
data subset;
   set master;
   rename old=new x1980=x1985;
   if old>5;
   keep old x1980 y z;
proc print;
   var new x1985 z;
```

In this example, the variable OLD, a variable in data set MASTER, is given the name NEW in data set SUBSET; variable X1980 from MASTER is given the name X1985. The existing names are used in the program statements that create SUBSET; the new names are used in the PROC PRINT step that prints SUBSET. See the RENAME= data set option in "SAS Files" for another way to change variable names.

RETAIN Statement

Introduction 236
Cautions 238
Examples 238
  Example 1: Overview of the RETAIN Operation 238
  *Example 2: Selecting One Value from a Series of
      Observations* 239

Introduction

The RETAIN statement causes a variable created by an INPUT or assignment statement to retain its value from the previous iteration of the DATA step. Without a RETAIN statement, the SAS System automatically sets variables created by INPUT or assignment statements to missing before each iteration of the DATA step. Naming variables read with a SET, MERGE, or UPDATE statement, or IN= variables in these statements, in a RETAIN statement has no effect.

You can use a RETAIN statement to specify initial values for variables or members of an array. If a value appears in a RETAIN statement, variables appearing before it in the list are set to that value initially. (If you assign different initial values to the same variable by naming it more than once in a RETAIN statement, the last value is used.) You can also use a RETAIN statement to assign a sum variable an initial value other than the default value of 0.

The RETAIN statement can appear anywhere in the DATA step; its position has no effect. RETAIN is not an executable statement.

The form of the RETAIN statement is

RETAIN [*element* . . . [*initialvalue* | (*initialvalue*[,] . . .)] . . .];

where

element
  can be a variable name, a variable list, or an array name whose values you want retained. If no elements are listed, SAS retains the values of **all** variables in the DATA step (see **Cautions** below).

initialvalue
  specifies an initial value, numeric or character, for one or more of the preceding elements. If you omit *initialvalue*, the initial value is missing.

  If the initial value is not enclosed in parentheses, the SAS System assigns that initial value to the preceding elements in the list. (Therefore, all members of an array receive the same initial value.)

  If the initial value is enclosed in parentheses, the SAS System matches the first value in the list with the first variable in the list of elements, the second value with the second variable, and so on. Initial values can be separated by blank spaces or commas. If there are more variables than initial values, the remaining variables are assigned an initial value of missing and the SAS System issues a warning message. (To provide values for all members of an array with this method, you must assign a value to each individual member of the array.)

This is an example:

```
retain month1-month5 1 year 0 a b c 'ABC';
```

Variables MONTH1 through MONTH5 are set initially to a value of 1; YEAR starts out at 0; variables A, B, and C are each set to a value of 'ABC'.

Table 5.3 summarizes information on how the SAS System treats variable values with and without RETAIN statements.

Table 5.3 How the SAS System Retains Values

	Variables created in the DATA step	
	With INPUT or assignment statement	As sum statement variable
Without RETAIN statement	SAS sets all variables to missing before each iteration of the DATA step.	SAS sets the variable to zero before the first iteration of the DATA step. Thereafter, the variable retains its current value until a new value becomes available (for example, in the next iteration of the sum statement).
With RETAIN statement	SAS sets variables to missing (or to the initial values given in the RETAIN statement) only before the first iteration of the DATA step. Thereafter, variables retain their values until new values become available (for example, through an assignment statement or the next iteration of the INPUT statement).	SAS sets the variable to zero or to the value given in the RETAIN statement before the first execution of the DATA step. Thereafter, the variable retains its value until a new value becomes available (for example, in the next iteration of the sum statement). Thus, the only purpose of naming a sum variable in a RETAIN statement is to give it an initial value other than zero.

	Variables read with SET, MERGE, or UPDATE statement
Without RETAIN statement	**With BY Statement:** SAS sets variables to missing before the first iteration of the SET, MERGE, or UPDATE statement for a given data set and before the first iteration of the statement for each BY group. Thereafter, the variables retain their values until new values become available (for example, through an assignment statement or through the next iteration of the SET, MERGE, or UPDATE statement). **Without BY Statement:** SET statement: SAS sets variables to missing before the first iteration of the SET statement for a given data set. Thereafter, the variables retain their values until new values become available. MERGE statement: SAS sets variables to missing before the first iteration of the MERGE statement. Thereafter, the variables retain their values until new values become available. If a data set exhausts its observations, SAS sets variables contributed by that data set to missing.
With RETAIN statement	Naming variables read with a SET, MERGE, or UPDATE statement in a RETAIN statement has no effect.

Cautions

When just the keyword RETAIN appears without a variable list, all the variables created with INPUT or assignment statements are retained. Thus, data values can be retained in observations that should have missing values. For example, consider this program:

```
data group;
   input x;
   retain;
   if x=1 then sex='M';
   if x=2 then sex='F';
   cards;
data lines
;
```

When the value of X is either 1 or 2, all is well. But if X is 3, neither of the IF conditions is true, and SEX does not receive a new value. SEX retains its value from the preceding observation, producing an inaccuracy. Removing the RETAIN statement from this program results in SEX having a blank value when the value of X is other than 1 or 2.

Examples

Example 1: Overview of the RETAIN Operation

The following example shows the use of variable names and array names as elements in the RETAIN statement and shows assignment of initial values with and without parentheses:

```
data _null_;
   array city{3} $ city1-city3;
   array cp{3} citypop1-citypop3;
   retain year taxyear 1987 city ' ' cp (10000,50000,100000);
   file '\mydir\test.dat';
   put 'Values at beginning of DATA step:'
      / @3 _all_ /;
   input gain;
   do i=1 to 3;
      cp{i}=cp{i}+gain;
      end;
   put 'Values after adding GAIN to city populations:'
      / @3 _all_;
   cards;
5000
10000
;
```

The initial values assigned by the RETAIN statement are as follows:

- YEAR and TAXYEAR are assigned the initial value 1987.
- CITY1, CITY2, and CITY3 are assigned missing values.
- CITYPOP1 is assigned the value 10000.
- CITYPOP2 is assigned 50000.
- CITYPOP3 is assigned 100000.

Output 5.26 shows the lines written by the PUT statements.

Output 5.26 RETAIN Statement

```
Values at beginning of DATA step:
   CITY1= CITY2= CITY3= CITYPOP1=10000 CITYPOP2=50000 CITYPOP3=100000 YEAR=1987 TAXYEAR=1987 GAIN=. I=. _ERROR_=0 _N_=1
Values after adding GAIN to city populations:
   CITY1= CITY2= CITY3= CITYPOP1=15000 CITYPOP2=55000 CITYPOP3=105000 YEAR=1987 TAXYEAR=1987 GAIN=5000 I=4 _ERROR_=0
_N_=1
Values at beginning of DATA step:
   CITY1= CITY2= CITY3= CITYPOP1=15000 CITYPOP2=55000 CITYPOP3=105000 YEAR=1987 TAXYEAR=1987 GAIN=. I=. _ERROR_=0 _N_=2
Values after adding GAIN to city populations:
   CITY1= CITY2= CITY3= CITYPOP1=25000 CITYPOP2=65000 CITYPOP3=115000 YEAR=1987 TAXYEAR=1987 GAIN=10000 I=4 _ERROR_=0
_N_=2
Values at beginning of DATA step:
   CITY1= CITY2= CITY3= CITYPOP1=25000 CITYPOP2=65000 CITYPOP3=115000 YEAR=1987 TAXYEAR=1987 GAIN=. I=. _ERROR_=0 _N_=3
```

Note that the first PUT statement is executed three times, whereas the second PUT statement is executed only twice. The DATA step ceases execution when the INPUT statement has no more observations to read; that occurs after the first PUT statement executes in the third iteration of the DATA step.

Example 2: Selecting One Value from a Series of Observations

In this example, the data set TIMECARD contains several observations for each SSN value. Different observations for a particular SSN value may have different values of the variable GRADE. You want to create a new data set, WORKERS, containing one observation for each SSN value. The observation must have the highest GRADE value of all observations for that SSN in TIMECARD.

```
proc sort data=timecard;
   by ssn;
data workers;
   set timecard;
   by ssn;
   if first.ssn then highest=.;
   retain highest;
   highest=max(highest,grade);
   drop grade;
   if last.ssn then output;
```

The variable HIGHEST is created in an assignment statement. Since the RETAIN statement tells SAS not to set the value of HIGHEST to missing each time a new observation is read, the statement

```
highest=max(highest,grade);
```

compares the previous value of HIGHEST to the value of GRADE in the current execution of the DATA step and assigns the higher value as the current value of HIGHEST. Since you want the highest GRADE value for each different SSN, not the highest value in the entire data set, the statement

```
if first.ssn then highest=.;
```

sets HIGHEST to a missing value for each new SSN value.

Output 5.27 shows the contents of data sets TIMECARD and WORKERS.

Output 5.27 Data Sets before and after Highest Value Selected

```
               DATA SET TIMECARD--MULTIPLE OBSERVATIONS PER SSN                    1
                   OBS       SSN         GRADE

                    1     111442222        2
                    2     111442222        4
                    3     333115555        6
                    4     333115555        1
```

```
            WORKERS--ONE OBSERVATION PER SSN AND HIGHEST VALUE OF GRADE            2
                   OBS       SSN        HIGHEST

                    1     111442222        4
                    2     333115555        6
```

RETURN Statement

The RETURN statement tells the SAS System to stop executing statements at the current point in the DATA step and to return to a predetermined point before continuing execution. The point to which the SAS System returns depends on the situation in which the RETURN statement appears.

- When a LINK statement has been executed, a RETURN statement causes the SAS System to return to the statement immediately following the LINK and continue executing.
- In a HEADER= group of statements, a RETURN statement causes the SAS System to return to the statement immediately following the last statement executed prior to beginning a new page and continue executing. (See the **FILE Statement** for a description of the HEADER= option.)
- Elsewhere in the DATA step, a RETURN statement causes the SAS System to return to the beginning of the step for another execution of the DATA step.

When a RETURN causes a return to the beginning of the DATA step, SAS first writes the current observation to any new data sets (unless OUTPUT statements are used in the step). SAS also increments the automatic variable _N_ by 1 and releases input lines held by a trailing @. Every DATA step has an implied RETURN as its last executable statement.

The form of the RETURN statement is

RETURN;

Here is an example of a RETURN statement used in an IF-THEN statement:

```
data survey;
   input x y z;
   if x=y then return;
   x=y+z;
   a=x**2;
   cards;
data lines
;
```

When X equals Y, the RETURN statement is executed. The SAS System adds the observation to the data set and returns to the beginning of the DATA step. The two statements

```
x=y+z;
a=x**2;
```

are not executed.

When X is not equal to Y, the RETURN statement is not executed. The two assignment statements are executed before the observation is added to the data set.

The example below has a RETURN and an OUTPUT statement within an iterative DO group. The RETURN statement causes the SAS System to return to the beginning of the step when a particular condition is true, avoiding unnecessary iterations of the DO group.

```
data report;
   input a b c;
   do x=1 to 5;
      ax=a*x;
      if ax>b then return;
      output;
```

```
          end;
       cards;
    data lines
    ;
```

This DATA step produces multiple observations in SAS data set REPORT from each input line. In this example, up to 5 observations can be generated from each observation. The statements in the DO group multiply the value of A by X and test the result (variable AX) to see whether the value is greater than the value of B. As long as the value of AX is less than or equal to B, SAS outputs that observation and continues execution of the DO group (up to 5 iterations). As soon as the value of AX becomes greater than B, the IF condition is true and the RETURN statement is executed. SAS returns to the beginning of the DATA step for a new observation, regardless of the number of iterations of the DO group that have occurred. Thus, unnecessary executions of the DO group are avoided since once the value of AX becomes larger than the value of B, it remains larger than B for all subsequent iterations of the loop for that observation.

See the **GO TO Statement** and the **LINK Statement** earlier in this chapter for other examples using the RETURN statement.

SELECT Statement

The SELECT statement in the DATA step allows the SAS System to execute one of several statements or groups of statements.

The SELECT statement begins a SELECT group; within the SELECT group, each WHEN statement identifies a SAS statement to be executed when a particular condition is true. At least one WHEN statement must be present. An optional OTHERWISE statement specifies a statement to be executed if no WHEN condition is met. An END statement ends a SELECT group.

The general form of the SELECT statement is

SELECT [(*selectexpression*)];
   WHEN (*whenexpression*) *statement*;
   ...
   [**OTHERWISE** *statement*;]
END;

The following terms can appear in the SELECT statement:

selectexpression
> can be any valid SAS expression that evaluates to a single value. *Selectexpression* is optional.

whenexpression
> can be any valid SAS expression. The way a WHEN expression is used depends on whether a SELECT expression is present.
>
> If *selectexpression* is present, SAS first evaluates *selectexpression* and *whenexpression*. SAS then compares the two as though an equal sign connected them (performing a numeric-character or character-numeric conversion on the WHEN expression if necessary) and returns a value of true or false. If the comparison is true, *statement* (see below) is executed. When the comparison is false, execution proceeds to the next WHEN statement, if one is present, or the OTHERWISE statement, if one is present. If the result of all SELECT-WHEN comparisons is false and no OTHERWISE statement is present, SAS issues an error message.
>
> If no *selectexpression* is present, *whenexpression* is evaluated to produce a result of true or false. When the result is true, *statement* (see below) is executed. If more than one WHEN statement has a true WHEN expression, only the first WHEN statement is used. When the result is false, SAS proceeds to the next WHEN statement, if one is present, or the OTHERWISE statement, if one is present. (That is, omitting *selectexpression* causes SAS to perform the action indicated in the first true WHEN statement.) If the result of all WHEN expressions is false and no OTHERWISE statement is present, SAS issues an error message.

statement
> can be any executable SAS statement, including DO, SELECT, and null statements.
>
> You can use a null statement in a WHEN statement to cause SAS to recognize a condition as true without taking further action. For example, suppose a numeric variable A has a value of 1, 2, 3, or missing. This SELECT group leaves the value of X unchanged when A=2:

```
data new;
   set old;
   x=uniform(0);
   select (a);
      when (1) x=x*10;
      when (2);
```

244 Chapter 5

```
            when (3) x=x*100;
            otherwise x=1;
            end;
    run;
```

You can use a null statement in an OTHERWISE statement, as in

```
otherwise;
```

to prevent SAS from issuing an error message when all WHEN conditions are false.

The following example illustrates a SELECT statement with a SELECT expression:

```
data payroll;
   input id type salary hrlywage hrs;
   label type='10=SALARY, 20=HOURLY';
   select (type);
      when (10) amt=salary;
      when (20) do;
         amt=hrlywage*min(hrs,40);
         if hrs>40 then link overtime;
         end;
      otherwise link error;
      end;
   return;
   overtime: put 'CHECK TIMECARD ' _all_;
      return;
   error: amt=.;
      _error_=1;
      put 'PROBLEM OBSERVATION ' _all_;
      return;
   cards;
68852 10 5000   .    .
46960 20 .      3.50 35
58342 20 .      4.00 55
64439 11 5200   .    .
;
```

In this example TYPE is a numeric variable with values of 10 and 20. When the value of TYPE is 10, the SAS System assigns the value of the variable SALARY to the variable AMT. When the value of TYPE is 20, SAS performs the calculations in the DO group. If the value of TYPE is anything else, SAS executes the LINK ERROR statement and performs the work indicated for an error in the data.

This example illustrates a SELECT statement without a SELECT expression. You can use it to do range checking, which must be done in a SELECT statement without a SELECT expression or in an IF statement.

```
data _null_;
   do mon='JAN', 'FEB', 'MAR', 'APR', 'MAY', 'JUN', 'JUL',
      'AUG', 'SEP';
      select;
         when (mon='JUN' | mon='JUL' | mon='AUG') put 'SUMMER ' mon=;
         when (mon='MAR' | mon='APR' | mon='MAY') put 'SPRING ' mon=;
         otherwise put 'FALL OR WINTER ' mon=;
         end; /* End of select group*/
      end; /* End of do group */
run;
```

Since there is no SELECT expression, SAS executes the first PUT statement for which the WHEN expression is true. If neither WHEN expression is true, SAS executes the OTHERWISE clause.

What happens if you use a SELECT expression in this example? SAS compares the result of the WHEN expression (1 or 0) to the value of MON in the current execution of the loop. Thus, for example, when MON has a value of JUN, the comparison is JUN='1'; the result of the comparison is false and the statement

```
put 'SUMMER ' mon=;
```

is not executed.

This example uses nested SELECT statements with complex expressions in WHEN statements. The outer SELECT group does not contain an OTHERWISE statement.

```
data _null_;
   cent='19';
   do month='JAN', 'FEB', 'MAR';
      do day='MON', 'TUE', 'WED';
         do year='1984', '1985';
            select (year);
               when (cent||'84') do;
                  select (month||day);
                     when ('JANMON') put '1984 MON-JAN';
                     when ('FEBTUE') put '1984 TUE-FEB';
                     when ('MARWED') put '1984 WED-MAR';
                     otherwise      put '1984 ' month= day=;
                  end; /* Mon||day */
               end; /* Cent||84 */
               when (cent||'85') do;
                  select (month||day);
                     when ('JANWED') put '1985 WED-JAN';
                     when ('FEBTUE') put '1985 TUE-FEB';
                     when ('MARMON') put '1985 MON-MAR';
                     otherwise      put '1985 ' month= day=;
                  end; /* Month||day */
               end; /* Cent||85 */
            end; /* Select year */
         end; /* Do year */
      end; /* Do day */
   end; /* Do month */
run;
```

The WHEN expressions in the outer SELECT group are made up of the concatenated value of variable CENT and the characters '84' or '85'. You can also write the WHEN expressions as

```
when ('1984') do;
when ('1985') do;
```

The SELECT expressions in the inner SELECT groups are made up of the concatenated values of variables MONTH and DAY.

SET Statement

Introduction 246
Copying Data Sets 249
   Subsetting variables 249
   Subsetting observations 249
   Creating new variables 250
Concatenating Data Sets 250
   Same variables 250
   Different variables 250
   Different variable attributes 250
Interleaving Data Sets 251

Introduction

The SET statement tells the SAS System to read observations from one or more SAS data sets. Use SET when you want to read, subset, concatenate, or interleave observations from existing SAS data sets into a new data set. The SET statement brings in all variables from the SAS data sets listed unless otherwise directed by a DROP= or KEEP= data set option. For example, the statements below create data set TWO as a copy of data set ONE:

```
data one;
   input x y z;
   cards;
data lines
;
data two;
   set one;
```

The SET statement is flexible and has a variety of uses in SAS programming. The examples in this description illustrate some common uses of the SET statement; other applications include the use of more than one SET statement in a DATA step and direct access of SAS data sets by observation number.

The form of the SET statement is

SET [[*SASdataset* [(*dsoptions* **IN=***name*)]...] [*setoptions*]];

These terms and options can appear in the SET statement:

SASdataset
   names one or more existing SAS data sets from which to read observations each time the SET statement is executed. You can name up to 50 data sets in a SET statement. These are examples of valid SET statements:

- `set fitness;`
- `set work.fitness;`
- `set save.fitness;`
- `set health exercise well;`
- `set males in.females;`
- `set;`

If you omit the data set name entirely in the SET statement, the statement is equivalent to:

`set _last_;`

LAST is a special SAS data set name that refers to the most recently created SAS data set in your job.

See "SAS Files" for more information on using SAS data set names.

In general, SAS executes a SET statement by reading sequentially from the data sets listed. If more than one data set name is listed, SAS reads all observations from the first data set, then all from the second data set, and so on until all observations from all the data sets have been read. SAS thus treats all the data sets listed in the SET statement as one aggregate SAS data set. (See **Concatenating Data Sets** later in this section for more information.) You can cause SAS to process the observations from all data sets in sorted order by adding a BY statement (described in **Interleaving Data Sets** later in this section); you can cause SAS to process particular observations in the order you specify with the POINT= option, below.

(*dsoptions*)

specifies data set options in parentheses after each SAS data set name. For example,

```
data three;
   set one(firstobs=100);
```

These options include those described in "SAS Files" as well as the IN= data set option (described below), which is unique to the SET, MERGE, and UPDATE statements.

IN=*name*

creates a variable with the name given after the equal sign. Within the DATA step, the value of the variable is 1 if the data set contributed data to the current observation and 0 otherwise. The IN= data set option is most useful when the SET statement contains more than one data set name. By using the IN= option and a different variable name for each data set, you can tell which data set contributed the current observation. For example,

```
data four;
   set one(in=inone firstobs=100) two(in=intwo)
      three(in=inthree);
   if state=. then put state= inone= intwo= inthree=;
```

INONE has the value 1 when an observation is read in from ONE; otherwise, it has the value 0. The values of INTWO and INTHREE are determined similarly. Thus, you can see which data set contains the observation with a missing value for the variable STATE by examining the values of INONE, INTWO, and INTHREE.

IN= variables are not added to the data set being created.

setoptions

specifies the SET statement options described below.

POINT=*name*

creates a numeric variable whose value is the number of the observation in the input data set you want the current execution of the SET statement to process. You must specify the values of the POINT= variable (for example, by using the POINT= variable as the index variable in a DO statement). The POINT= variable is available anywhere in the DATA step, but it is not added to any new SAS data set. This form of reading input data sets is called direct (or random) access by observation number.

For example, the statements below create a subset of ALL that contains only observations 3, 5, 7, and 4 in that order. The STOP statement tells SAS to stop building the data set after the DO loop is complete:

```
data subset;
   do n=3,5,7,4;
      set all point=n;
      if _error_=1 then abort;
      output;
      end;
   stop;
```

Caution: when you use the POINT= option, you usually also include a STOP statement to stop processing the DATA step.

If you execute a random access SET statement with an invalid value of the POINT= variable, SAS sets the automatic variable _ERROR_ to 1. It is a good idea to check for this indication after a random access SET statement since it is more likely that your DATA step will go into an endless loop when this error goes undetected.

If more than one data set is listed in the SET statement, for example,

```
set hockey polo point=n;
```

the POINT= variable retrieves observations from all the data sets as though they are concatenated. If the value of the POINT= variable is greater than the total number of observations, SAS sets the automatic variable _ERROR_ to 1.

The POINT= option **cannot** be used with a BY statement.

NOBS=name

creates a variable with the name given after the equal sign whose value is the total number of observations in the input data set. If more than one data set is listed in the SET statement, the value of the NOBS= variable is the total number of observations in the data sets listed. SAS assigns the value of the NOBS= variable automatically at compilation time. Thus, the NOBS= variable can appear before the SET statement. The variable is available in the DATA step but is not added to the new data set.

END=name

creates a variable with the name given after the equal sign to contain an end-of-file indication. The variable, which is initialized to zero, is set to 1 when the SET statement reads the last observation of the input data set or concatenated data sets. This variable is not added to any new data set. If more than one data set is listed in the SET statement, the END= variable is set to 1 when the SET statement reads the last observation in the last data set listed.

This example uses the END= variable to write a message on the SAS log after the last observation of a concatenated series of SAS data sets has been read:

```
data new;
   set olda oldb end=last;
   if last then do;
      put 'LAST OBSERVATION' x= y=;
      end;
run;
```

Copying Data Sets

To make a new copy called B of a SAS data set named A, write

```
data b;
   set a;
```

This SET statement brings all variables in each observation of A into the DATA step to create SAS data set B.

Subsetting variables To make a copy containing a subset of variables, use DROP or KEEP specifications in any of three ways:

- Use a DROP= or KEEP= data set option in the SET statement:

```
data b;
   set a(keep=x y);
```

In this case the subset is formed before the data are brought into the DATA step. This method saves computer resources, particularly when the original data set is large and you need only a few variables for the current data set.

- Use a DROP or KEEP statement in the DATA step:

```
data b;
   set a;
   keep x y;
```

A DROP or KEEP statement controls which variables are output to SAS data sets; all variables in A are present in the DATA step and can be used in program statements, regardless of whether they are to be output to a data set. This method produces the same subset of variables in all output data sets.

- Use a DROP= or KEEP= option in the DATA statement:

```
data b(keep=x y) c(keep=y);
   set a;
```

This method allows you to output a different subset of variables to each data set specified. All variables in A are present in the DATA step and can be used in program statements.

Subsetting observations To make a copy containing a subset of observations, use program statements such as the subsetting IF, DELETE, or OUTPUT to control which observations are output to SAS data sets. For example, each of these DATA steps selects only the observations where the variable SEX has the value of M for the output data set:

```
data males;
   set people;
   if sex='M';

data males;
   set people;
   if sex='M' then output;

data males;
   set people;
   if sex^='M' then delete;
```

Creating new variables You can add program statements to create new variables as you copy a data set. For example, your original data set, MONTHLY, contains figures for several companies. The sales figures are represented by the variables MONTH1-MONTH12. You want to create a new variable to contain the total sales for the year for each company. You use a SET statement to tell SAS where to find the observations for the new data set and then create the new variable TOTAL with an assignment statement.

These SAS statements create a new data set YEARLY containing the same observations as MONTHLY plus a variable, TOTAL, which is the yearly sales figure.

```
data yearly;
   set monthly;
   total=sum(of month1-month12);
```

If you do not want the values of MONTH1-MONTH12 to be included in the YEARLY data set once you have created the total sales for the year, add a DROP statement to the DATA step. Data set YEARLY thus contains all the observations from data set MONTHLY, but excludes the monthly sales figures:

```
data yearly;
   set monthly;
   total=sum(of month1-month12);
   drop month1-month12;
```

Concatenating Data Sets

Concatenation is processing two or more data sets one after the other as though they were a single large data set. To concatenate two or more SAS data sets to create a new one, name them in a SET statement. The new data set contains all the observations in all the input data sets listed.

Same variables In the simplest case, all the input data sets contain the same set of variables, which also are the variables in the new data set.

For example, say you have two data sets, each containing the same variables. One is made up of data for 1984; the other, data for 1985. You want to combine them into a single data set containing all observations for 1984 and 1985 with these statements:

```
data bothyear;
   set y1984 y1985;
```

The number of observations in the new data set is the sum of the number of observations in the Y1984 data set and the number of observations in the Y1985 data set. The order of the observations in BOTHYEAR is all the observations of Y1984 followed by all the observations of Y1985. The new data set's variables are the same as those in the old data sets.

Different variables If the data sets in the SET statement contain different sets of variables, observations obtained from one data set have missing values for variables that are defined only in the other data set or data sets.

Different variable attributes Data sets listed in the SET statement may contain some of the same variables, but the variables may have different attributes. In that case SAS takes the action outlined in **Table 5.4**.

Table 5.4 Actions for Incompatible Variable Attributes

Action	Incompatible Attribute				
	Type	Length	Informat	Format	Label
SAS issues an error message	X				
An explicitly specified attribute for the variable overrides a default attribute, regardless of the position of the data set in the list.		text below	X	X	X

For numeric variables, an explicitly specified length overrides a default length, regardless of the position of the data set in the list. For character variables, SAS uses the length in the first data set listed that contains the variable.

To change an attribute in the data set you are creating, specify the attribute before the SET statement, for example,

```
data a;
   name='MARY';
   *Length of variable name is 4;
data b;
   name='SUZANNE';
   *Length of variable name is 7;
data c;
   length name $ 10;
   set a b;
   *Length of variable name is 10;
```

See the **LENGTH Statement** earlier in this chapter for more examples of changing variable lengths.

Interleaving Data Sets

Interleaving is an operation that combines data sets in sorted order. To interleave two or more data sets, use a BY statement as well as a SET statement. (Only one BY statement can accompany each SET statement. A BY statement applies only to the most recent SET statement.) The data sets listed in the SET statement must be sorted by the variables used in the BY statement. SAS reads all the observations in a given BY group from the first data set listed, then all the observations in that BY group from the second data set listed, and so on. The new data set contains all the observations in the input data sets in sorted order by the variables in the BY statement. SAS treats data sets with different variables and variables with different attributes in different data sets the same way that it does in a concatenation operation.

Suppose you have two data sets, one for each department in your company. You want to combine the two input data sets, interleaving observations from each one, to create a new data set sorted by the variable LASTNAME. The number of observations in the new data set is the sum of the number of observations in each of the original data sets. Each data set must be sorted by the variable LASTNAME. These statements perform the interleaving operation:

```
proc sort data=dept1;
   by lastname;
proc sort data=dept2;
   by lastname;
data allempl;
   set dept1 dept2;
   by lastname;
```

Note: although the term "merge" is often used to mean "interleave," SAS reserves merge for a matching operation described under the **MERGE Statement** later in this chapter.

STOP Statement

You can use the STOP statement to stop processing a SAS DATA step. The observation being processed when the STOP statement is encountered is not added to the SAS data set.

The form of a STOP statement is

STOP;

The STOP statement does not affect the execution of any subsequent DATA or PROC steps. Execution continues from the first DATA or PROC statement found after the STOP statement. (Use the ABORT statement if you want the SAS System to stop processing the entire SAS job.)

Here is an example:

```
data count1;
   input x y z;
   if _n_=250 then stop;
   cards;
more than 250 data lines
proc print;
```

The value of the automatic variable _N_ corresponds to the number of the current execution of the DATA step; thus, in this example the value of _N_ corresponds to the number of the observation being processed. During the 250th execution of the DATA step, the STOP statement is executed and SAS stops building the data set. SAS then executes the PROC PRINT step. Since the 250th observation was being processed when the STOP statement was encountered and was not added to the data set, data set COUNT1 contains 249 observations.

Sum Statement

Sum statements add the result of an expression to an accumulator variable. The form of a sum statement is

   variable **+** *expression*;

where

   variable   specifies the name of the accumulator variable. The variable must be a numeric variable; any valid SAS variable name can be used. The variable is automatically set to 0 before the first observation is read. Its value is retained from one execution to the next, just as if it had appeared in a RETAIN statement. To initialize a sum variable to a value other than 0, include it in a RETAIN statement with an initial value. (See the **RETAIN Statement** description for more information.)

   expression   is any valid SAS expression. The expression is evaluated and the result added to the accumulator variable. When the evaluation of the expression results in a missing value, it is treated as zero.

The sum statement is equivalent to using the SUM function and a RETAIN statement as shown below:

```
variable=sum(variable,expression,0);
retain variable 0;
```

Here is an example:

```
data accum;
   input x y z;
   if x=4 then n+1;
   if n=250 then stop;
   cards;
data lines
;
```

Each time the sum statement

```
n+1;
```

is executed, 1 is added to the value of N. When 250 observations with an X value of 4 have been read, the value of N is 250. The statement

```
if n=250 then stop;
```

tells SAS to stop building the data set when N equals 250.

More examples of sum statements are given below:

```
balance+(-debit);
```

This sum statement subtracts the DEBIT amount from BALANCE. The plus (+) is required in a sum statement; the statement

```
balance-debit;
```

is incorrect.

In the sum statement

```
sumxsq+x*x;
```

the result of X*X is added to SUMXSQ each time the sum statement is executed.
The following statements:

```
nx+x^=.;
nx+(x^=.);
```

show the use of the comparison operator. When the value of X is not missing, the expression is true (has the value 1). When X is missing, the expression's value is 0. Thus, NX contains the number of observations processed with a nonmissing X value. See "SAS Expressions" for more information about logical expressions.

UPDATE Statement

Introduction 256
Example 257
Updating Values to Missing 258

Introduction

The UPDATE statement combines observations from two SAS data sets in a manner similar to the MERGE statement, but UPDATE performs the special function of updating a master file by applying transactions. The UPDATE statement must be accompanied by a BY statement giving the name of an identifying variable by which to match observations in the two data sets. The data set containing the master file and the data set containing the transactions must both be sorted by this identifying variable or variables, and the master data set must not contain observations with duplicate values of the identifying variable. The new data set contains one observation for each observation in the master data set; if any transaction observations were not matched with master observations, these become new observations in the new data set as well. Note: when you specify more than one UPDATE statement, any successive BY statement is attached only to the UPDATE statement immediately preceding it. You can use only one BY statement with an UPDATE statement.

The form of the UPDATE statement is

UPDATE *masterdataset*[(*dsoptions* **IN**=*variable1*)] *transactiondataset*
  [(*dsoptions* **IN**=*variable2*)] [**END**=*variable*];

where

masterdataset
  names the SAS data set used as the master file. Only one observation in this data set can have each value of the variable(s) in the BY statement.

transactiondataset
  names the SAS data set containing transactions to be applied to the master. This data set must contain the BY variable(s), but multiple observations with the same BY value can occur.

dsoptions
  give SAS more information about the data set to which the data set options refer. See "SAS Files" for the data set options that are available.

IN=*variable*
  creates a variable with the name given after the equal sign. A different IN= variable should be associated with each data set. The UPDATE operation indicates which data sets contributed data to the current observation by setting values of this variable to 1 or 0. Specify IN= in parentheses after the names of the data sets in the UPDATE statement as shown below:

```
data three;
   update one(in=inone) two(in=intwo);
   by id;
```

INONE has the value 1 when information in the current observation comes from the master data set ONE; otherwise, it has the value 0. The value of INTWO is determined similarly. Both variables INONE and INTWO are equal to one if both data sets contribute information.

END=*name*
  is used optionally to create a variable with the name given after the equal sign to let you know when the last observation in the UPDATE

operation is being processed. The variable, which is initialized to zero, is set to 1 when the UPDATE statement is on the last observation. This variable is not added to any new data set.

Example

You have a SAS data set containing your master file and another SAS data set containing updates—your transaction file. There may be several transactions for each master observation. Usually, both data sets contain the same variables, but the transaction data set need not contain variables that will not be updated, and it may contain variables to be added to the master data set. If a variable is being updated in some, but not all of the observations, its value is missing in observations where it is not to be changed. Both data sets are sorted by the identifying variable. **Output 5.28** shows the input data sets.

Output 5.28 Master and Transaction Data Sets

```
                       DATA OLDMASTR                                        1

        OBS   ID   NAME     SEX   AGE   WEIGHT

         1    01   JONES     M     46   116.8
         2    04   MILLER    F     59   132.2
         3    30   PARKER    M     29   111.3
         4    49   SMITH     M     34   209.1
         5    87   WILSON    F     30    98.3
```

```
                       DATA TRANS                                           2

        OBS   ID   AGE   WEIGHT   NAME

         1    01   47       .
         2    30    .    108.4
         3    49   35    215.1
         4    87    .       .    CAMERON
         5    87    .    104.1
```

Since both data sets are sorted in order of ID, these statements perform the update:

```
data new;
   update oldmastr trans;
   by id;
```

Output 5.29 shows the resulting data set NEW.

Output 5.29 New Data Set

```
                        DATA NEW                                    3
         OBS   ID    NAME      SEX   AGE   WEIGHT
          1    01    JONES      M     47   116.8
          2    04    MILLER     F     59   132.2
          3    30    PARKER     M     29   108.4
          4    49    SMITH      M     35   215.1
          5    87    CAMERON    F     30   104.1
```

Note that

- since the variable SEX is not updated, it does not appear in the TRANS data set
- variables need not appear in the same order in the two data sets
- only values to be updated are specified in the transaction data set; missing values in TRANS do not change the original values in OLDMASTR
- multiple transaction records (as with ID 87) are all applied to the master before the record is output to NEW
- if a record is not to be updated, it need not appear in the transaction data set (see ID 04).

Updating Values to Missing

When the transaction data set contains one of the special missing values A through Z, the SAS System updates the variable in the master data set to that value. The special missing value underscore (_) in the transaction data set updates the variable with a regular missing value (.), while the missing value (.) in the transaction data set does not update the master data set. (See the **MISSING Statement** description or "Missing Values" for more information.)

For example, suppose data set MASTER is created with the first set of the following statements and data set TRANS with the second set:

```
data master;
   input x y;
   cards;
1 2
2 3
4 5
6 7
;
data trans;
   missing _ A;
   input x y;
   cards;
1 100
2 .
4 _
6 A
;
```

SAS Statements Used in the DATA Step

The following statements perform the update:

```
data new;
   update master trans;
   by x;
proc print;
   title 'Updating with Missing Values';
run;
```

As the following output shows, the underscore in data set TRANS updates the value 5 in data set MASTER to a missing value (.), while the missing value in data set TRANS has no effect and the value 3 remains unchanged. The SAS System allows the special missing value in data set TRANS to be updated. The results are shown in **Output 5.30**.

Output 5.30 Using the UPDATE Statement with Special Missing Values

```
                   Updating with Missing Values                    1
                       OBS     X      Y

                        1      1     100
                        2      2       3
                        3      4       .
                        4      6       A
```

WHERE Statement

WHERE Expressions 261
   Arithmetic Operators 261
   Comparison Operators 261
   Logical (Boolean) Operators 261
   Other Operators 262
   Restrictions on WHERE Expressions 262
Comparison of WHERE and Subsetting IF Statements 262
Examples 263
   Example 1: WHERE Statement with One Data Set 263
   Example 2: WHERE Statement with Two Data Sets 263
   Example 3: Combining WHERE and Subsetting IF Statements for Efficiency 264
   Example 4: Different Data Sets Produced by WHERE and Subsetting IF Statements 264

The WHERE statement allows you to select observations from an existing SAS data set that meet a particular condition before the SAS System brings observations into the DATA step. WHERE selection is the first operation the SAS System performs in each execution of a set, merge, or update operation. The WHERE statement is not executable; that is, you cannot use it as part of an IF-THEN statement.*

The WHERE statement in the DATA step is not a replacement for the subsetting IF statement. The two work differently and produce different output data sets in some cases. A single DATA step can use either statement, both, or neither. See **Comparison of WHERE and Subsetting IF Statements** later in this section for details.

The form of the WHERE statement is

WHERE *whereexpression*;

in which

> *whereexpression*   is an arithmetic or logical expression as defined in **WHERE Expressions**, below. WHERE expressions make comparisons using unformatted values of variables.

One WHERE statement can accompany each SET, MERGE, or UPDATE statement in a DATA step. A WHERE statement applies to all data sets in the preceding SET, MERGE, or UPDATE statement, and variables used in a WHERE statement must appear in all those data sets. (To select observations from individual data sets, apply a WHERE= data set option to each data set that needs a WHERE expression. The WHERE= data set option is discussed in Chapter 15, "SAS Files.") If a WHERE statement and a WHERE= data set option apply to the same data set, the SAS System uses the data set option and ignores the statement.

The WHERE statement takes effect immediately after the SAS data set options in a set, merge, or update operation. WHERE selection occurs after the SAS system options FIRSTOBS= and OBS= take effect and before BY groups are created.

---

* The SAS WHERE statement contains a subset of features from the ANSI SQL WHERE clause and some additional features that ensure compatibility with other SAS statements and expressions.

The following are examples of valid WHERE statements:

```
where score>50;
where date>='01jan87'd and time>='9:00't;
where state='Mississippi';
```

WHERE Expressions

A WHERE expression is a sequence of operands and operators. Operands include constants you supply, values of variables obtained from the SAS data set(s) to which the WHERE statement applies, and values created within the WHERE expression itself. You cannot use variables created within the DATA step (for example, FIRST., LAST., _N_, or variables created in assignment statements) in a WHERE expression.

A WHERE expression can use the operators listed below.

Arithmetic Operators

*	multiplication
/	division
+	addition
−	subtraction

Comparison Operators

= or EQ	equal to
^= or NE	not equal to*
> or GT	greater than
< or LT	less than
>= or GE	greater than or equal to
<= or LE	less than or equal to

You can use the colon modifier (:) with any of the comparison operators. See Chapter 3, "SAS Expressions," for a description of the colon modifier.

Logical (Boolean) Operators

& or AND	logical AND
| or OR	logical OR (if the symbol | is not available, use ¦ or !)
^ or NOT	logical NOT (if the symbol ^ is not available, use the symbol ~)

Names of numeric variables can stand alone in logical expressions; in that case, the SAS System treats values other than 0 or missing as true (having the value 1). A value of 0 or missing is false (that is, 0). For example, the following statements contain valid WHERE expressions:

```
where x;
where x and y;
```

---

* For compatibility with the ANSI SQL WHERE clause, you can also represent "not equal to" with the operator <>.

The first WHERE statement selects observations in which X has a value other than 0 or missing. The second statement selects observations in which both X and Y have values other than 0 or missing.

Names of character variables cannot stand alone in logical expressions. To select nonmissing character values, write the expression as either

```
where c^=' ';
```

or

```
where c is not missing;
```

The IS MISSING operator is described in **Other Operators**, below.

Other Operators

The WHERE expression can use the BETWEEN-AND operator, the IS MISSING or IS NULL operator, and the IN operator.

The BETWEEN-AND operator has the form

quantity **BETWEEN** *constant1* **AND** *constant2*

The BETWEEN-AND operator selects values that are between two constants, inclusively. It is equivalent to the expression

constant1 <= *quantity* <= *constant2*

The IS MISSING or IS NULL operator has the form

quantity **IS MISSING | IS NULL**

The IS MISSING operator selects all missing values. For numeric variables, IS MISSING is equivalent to

quantity <= .Z

For character variables, IS MISSING is equivalent to

quantity =' '

To select nonmissing values, combine the NOT operator with IS MISSING or IS NULL:

quantity **IS NOT MISSING | IS NOT NULL**

(You can also write the NOT operator before the word IS, if you prefer.)

The IN operator has the form

quantity **IN** (*constant*[,] . . .)

The IN operator compares a value to a series of numeric or character constants. Enclose character constants in quotes. The IN operator is equivalent to

quantity = *constant1* OR *quantity* = *constant2* OR *quantity* = *constant3* . . .

Restrictions on WHERE Expressions

A WHERE expression cannot use the DATA step operators for concatenation, minimum, and maximum, and it cannot contain a SAS function.

Comparison of WHERE and Subsetting IF Statements

The most important difference between the WHERE statement in the DATA step and the subsetting IF statement is that the WHERE statement works before observations are brought into the DATA step (that is, the program data vector), whereas the subsetting IF statement works on observations that are already in the DATA step. In addition, the WHERE statement is not executable, but the subsetting IF statement is. The WHERE statement uses the expressions described in **WHERE Expressions**, but the subsetting IF statement uses the expressions described in Chapter 3, "SAS Expressions." Finally, the WHERE statement operates only on observations in SAS data sets, whereas the subsetting IF statement can operate either on observations from an existing SAS data set or on observations created with an INPUT statement.

When a SET statement reads a single SAS data set or a concatenated series of data sets and a BY statement is not present, a WHERE statement with a given expression produces the same subset as a subsetting IF statement with that expression immediately following the SET statement. However, if a BY statement accompanies the SET statement, or in a merge or update operation, the WHERE statement produces a different data set from the subsetting IF statement in some cases. (**Examples**, below, shows a case in which the data sets are different.)

When a WHERE expression and a subsetting IF expression produce the same result, the WHERE statement is more efficient than the subsetting IF statement in almost all cases. For example, selecting a small subset of a large SAS data set is more efficient with the WHERE statement than with the subsetting IF statement because the SAS System does not have to move all observations from the large data set into the program data vector of the small SAS data set before making the selection.

If a DATA step contains both a WHERE statement and a BY statement, WHERE selection occurs before the SAS System assigns values to the FIRST. and LAST. variables. The first (or last) observation with a given BY value that is selected by the WHERE statement is assigned a FIRST. or LAST.*byvariable* value of 1, regardless of whether that observation was the first (or last) with the BY value in the original data set. In contrast, the subsetting IF statement selects observations after the FIRST. and LAST. values have been assigned.

If a DATA step contains both a WHERE statement and a MERGE statement, the SAS System applies the WHERE expression to each input data set before combining the current observations. In contrast, the subsetting IF statement selects observations after they have been combined. If a WHERE expression accepts the current observation in one input data set but not in the other(s), the current input observations that reach the MERGE statement are not the same as if all observations were being combined for selection by a subsetting IF statement later in the DATA step.

Examples

Example 1: WHERE Statement with One Data Set

In the following example, you use a WHERE statement to select observations with values of STATE equal to NC before the observations are brought into the DATA step:

```
data nccities;
   set in.cities;
   where state='NC';
run;
```

Example 2: WHERE Statement with Two Data Sets

The following example concatenates data sets WEATHER1 and WEATHER2 and selects only observations in which the variable RAIN has a value of true (that is, nonzero and nonmissing):

264　Chapter 5

```
data yearly;
   set weather1 weather2;
   where rain;
run;
```

Variable RAIN must appear in both data sets.

Example 3: Combining WHERE and Subsetting IF Statements for Efficiency

In the following example, a SAS data set named SAVE.BANKING contains an observation for every bank that does business in North Carolina (variable BANK). You need to produce a data set containing all banks that do business in Wake, Durham, Orange, or Franklin counties (variable COUNTY) and that are members of the Federal Deposit Insurance Corporation (identified by the letters FDIC in variable BANK). Here are values of BANK and COUNTY for some observations:

BANK	COUNTY
Metropolis Bank, Member FDIC	Wake
United Union Bank	Franklin
Amalgamated National Bank, Member FDIC	Chatham

To make the DATA step as efficient as possible, use a WHERE statement to select observations based on the value of COUNTY; only observations that pass the WHERE filter enter the DATA step. Then, because WHERE expressions cannot contain a SAS function, use a subsetting IF statement with the INDEX function to select FDIC members. The DATA step looks like this:

```
data temp;
   set save.banking;
   where county in ('Wake','Durham','Orange','Franklin');
   if index(bank,'FDIC');
run;
```

Example 4: Different Data Sets Produced by WHERE and Subsetting IF Statements

This example compares the results of merging data sets (without a BY statement) when you select observations with the WHERE statement and a subsetting IF statement. **Output 5.31** shows the resulting data sets.

```
data a;
   input id x;
   cards;
1 10
3 30
4 40
;
data b;
   input id y;
   cards;
1 100
2 200
4 400
;
```

```
data wherdata;
   merge a b;
   where id>2;
run;
data ifdata;
   merge a b;
   if id>2;
run;
proc print data=wherdata;
   title 'One-to-one Merge Using WHERE';
proc print data=ifdata;
   title 'One-to-one Merge Using Subsetting IF';
run;
```

Output 5.31 Comparison of Data Sets Produced by WHERE and Subsetting IF Statements

```
                 One-to-one Merge Using WHERE                    1

              OBS    ID      X      Y

               1      4     30    400
               2      4     40      .
```

```
              One-to-one Merge Using Subsetting IF               2

              OBS    ID      X      Y

               1      4     40    400
```

WINDOW Statement

Introduction 266
Defining Fields 268
Automatic Variables 271
Displaying Windows 271
Examples 272
 Example 1: simple WINDOW statement 272
 Example 2: window with two groups of fields 273
 Example 3: two windows at the same time 274
 Example 4: creating a SAS data set from a window 276
 Example 5: persisting and nonpersisting fields 277

Introduction

You can use the WINDOW statement in display manager, line-oriented, or non-interactive mode to create customized windows for your applications. Windows you create can display text and accept input; they have command and message lines, and the name of the window appears at the top of the window. You can use commands and function keys with windows you create.

You must define a window before you display it. Use the DISPLAY statement to display windows created with the WINDOW statement. See the description of the **DISPLAY Statement** earlier in this chapter.

A window definition remains in effect only for the DATA step containing the WINDOW statement.

Here is a simple WINDOW statement:

```
window start color=yellow
#5 @28 'WELCOME TO THE SAS SYSTEM' attr=highlight color=blue
#7 @8
'THIS PROGRAM CREATES TWO SAS DATA SETS AND USES THREE PROCEDURES'
#12 @30 'PRESS ENTER TO CONTINUE';
```

Window START is yellow and fills the entire screen. It displays three lines of text at the positions indicated by *#row @column*. For more information on START, including an illustration, see **Example 1: simple WINDOW statement** under **Examples** later in this section.

The form of the WINDOW statement is

WINDOW *windowname* [*windowoptions*] [*field* ...]
 [**GROUP=** *group* [*field* ...]] ...;

where

windowname
 names the window. *Windowname* is required.

windowoptions
 specify characteristics of the window as a whole. Specify all *windowoptions* before any field or GROUP= specifications. *Windowoptions* can include the following:

 COLOR=*color*
  specifies the color of the window background. If you do not specify a color, SAS uses black. *Color* can be one of the following:

WHITE	BLUE	YELLOW
GREEN	PINK	GRAY
RED	BLACK	BROWN
CYAN	MAGENTA	ORANGE

  The representation of colors may vary, depending on the monitor you use.

ROWS=*rows*
: specifies the number of rows (or lines) in the window, excluding borders. If you do not specify a number, the window fills all remaining rows in the screen; the number of rows depends on the type of monitor being used.

COLUMNS=*columns*
: specifies the number of columns in the window, excluding borders. If you do not specify a number, the window fills all remaining columns in the screen; the number of columns depends on the type of monitor being used.

IROW=*row*
: specifies the initial row (or line) within the screen at which the window is displayed. If you do not specify a number, SAS displays the window at row 1.

ICOLUMN=*column*
: specifies the initial column within the screen at which the window is displayed. If you do not specify a number, SAS displays the window at column 1.

KEYS=*filename*
: specifies the file containing the function key definitions for the window. To define function keys for a window, enter the display manager KEYS window, define the keys you want, and save the window with a file name. When you use the KEYS= option with that file name, SAS uses those function key definitions for the window. If you omit the KEYS= option, SAS uses the current function keys defined in the KEYS window.

field
: identifies and describes a variable or character string to be displayed in the window or group. A window or group can contain any number of fields, and you can define the same field in several groups or windows. The form of a field is given in **Defining Fields** below.

GROUP=*group*
: names a group of related fields. The GROUP= name must be a valid SAS name. When you refer to a group in a DISPLAY statement, write the name as *windowname.group*.

    A group contains all fields in a window that you want to display at the same time. You can display various groups of fields within the same window at different times by naming each group. Choose the group to appear by specifying *windowname.group* in the DISPLAY statement. If you omit the GROUP= specification, the window contains one unnamed group of fields.

    Specifying several groups within a window saves repeating window options that do not change and helps you to keep track of related displays. For example, if you are defining a window to check data values, you can arrange the display of variables and messages for most data values in the data set in a group named STANDARD and different messages in a group named CHECKIT that appears when data values meet the conditions you want to check.

If a WINDOW statement contains the name of a new variable, SAS adds that variable to the data set being created (unless you use a KEEP or DROP specification).

Defining Fields

Use a field to identify a variable or character string to be displayed, its position, and its attributes. Enclose character strings in quotes. The position of an item is its beginning row (or line) and column; attributes include color, whether you can enter a value into the field, and characteristics such as highlighting.

The form of a field definition is

[*row column*] *variable* [*format*] | '*text*' *options*

where

> *row*
> *column*
>> identify the position of the variable or literal. If you omit *row* (or *line*) in the first field of a window or group, SAS uses the first line of the window; if you omit *row* in a later field specification, SAS continues on the line from the previous field. If you omit *column*, SAS uses column 1 (the left border of the window). Although you can specify either *row* or *column* first, the examples in this book show the row first.
>>
>> SAS keeps track of its position in the window with a pointer. For example, when you tell SAS to write a variable's value in the third column of the second row of a window, the pointer is located at row 2, column 3. Use the following pointer controls to move the pointer to the position for an item:

Row pointer controls

> #*n*
>> specifies row *n* within the window; *n* must be a positive integer.
>
> #*pointvariable*
>> specifies the row within the window given by the value of *pointvariable*. The *pointvariable* must be a numeric variable; its values must be positive integers.
>
> #(*expression*)
>> specifies the row within the window given by the value of *expression*. The *expression* can contain both explicitly subscripted and implicitly subscripted array references and must evaluate to a positive integer. Enclose the *expression* in parentheses.
>
> /
>> moves the pointer to column 1 of the next line.

Column pointer controls

> @*n*
>> specifies column *n* within the window; *n* must be a positive integer.
>
> @*pointvariable*
>> specifies the column within the window given by the value of *pointvariable*. The *pointvariable* must be a numeric variable whose values are positive integers.
>
> @(*expression*)
>> specifies the row within the window given by the value of *expression*. The *expression* can contain both explicitly subscripted and implicitly subscripted array references and must evaluate to a positive integer. Enclose the *expression* in parentheses.

+*n*
: moves the pointer *n* columns; *n* must be a positive integer.

+*pointvariable*
: moves the pointer the number of columns given by the *pointvariable*. The *pointvariable* must be a numeric variable whose values are positive or negative integers.

variable
: names a variable to be displayed or to receive the value you enter at that position when the window is displayed. The *variable* can also be an explicitly or implicitly subscripted array reference. You can enter or change a variable value displayed in a field; to display a value only, use the PROTECT= option below. You can also protect an entire window or group for the current execution of the DISPLAY statement by specifying the NOINPUT option in the DISPLAY statement. See the **DISPLAY Statement** earlier in this chapter for more information.

format
: gives the format (and informat if needed) for the variable. If you do not specify *format*, SAS uses an informat and format specified elsewhere (for example, in an ATTRIB, INFORMAT, or FORMAT statement or permanently stored with the data set) or a SAS default informat and format. A format and informat in a WINDOW statement override an informat and format specified elsewhere.

  If a field only displays a variable (that is, you specify the PROTECT=YES option below), *format* can be any SAS format or a format you define with the FORMAT procedure. If a field can both display a variable and accept input, you must either specify the informat in an INFORMAT or ATTRIB statement or use a SAS format such as $CHAR. or TIME. that has a corresponding informat (because you can specify only one format or informat in a field).

'*text*'
: contains text to be displayed. The text must be enclosed in quotes. You cannot enter a value into a field containing text.

options
: can include the following:

  ATTR=*attribute*
  A=*attribute*
  : controls the following attributes of the field:

    BLINK
    : causes the field to blink.

    REV_VIDEO
    : displays the field in reverse video.

    HIGHLIGHT
    : displays the field at high intensity.

    UNDERLINE
    : underlines the field.

  To specify more than one attribute, use the form

  ATTR=(*attribute,...*)

  The attributes available depend on the type of monitor you use.

AUTOSKIP=*skip*
AUTO=*skip*
: controls whether the cursor moves to the next unprotected field of the current window or group when you have entered data in all positions of a field. If you specify AUTOSKIP=YES, the cursor moves automatically to the next unprotected field; if you specify AUTOSKIP=NO, the cursor does not move automatically. If you do not specify the AUTOSKIP= option, the cursor does not move automatically.

COLOR=*color*
C=*color*
: specifies a color for the variable or character string. If you do not specify a color, SAS uses white. *Color* can be one of the following:

WHITE	BLACK
GREEN	MAGENTA
RED	YELLOW
CYAN	GRAY
BLUE	BROWN
PINK	ORANGE

The representation of colors may vary, depending on the monitor you use.

DISPLAY=YES | NO
: controls whether the contents of a field are displayed. If you use DISPLAY=YES, the SAS System displays characters in a field as you type them in. If you use DISPLAY=NO, the SAS System does not display the characters as you enter them. The default is YES.

PERSIST=YES | NO
: controls whether a field is displayed by all executions of a DISPLAY statement in the same iteration of the DATA step until the DISPLAY statement contains the BLANK option. If you use PERSIST=NO, each execution of a DISPLAY statement displays only the current contents of the field. If you use PERSIST=YES, each execution of the DISPLAY statement displays all previously displayed contents of the field as well as those scheduled for display in the current execution. If the new contents overlap persisting contents, the persisting contents are no longer displayed. The PERSIST= option is most useful when the position of a field changes in each execution of a DISPLAY statement.

PROTECT=*protect*
P=*protect*
: controls whether information can be entered into a field. If you specify PROTECT=YES, you cannot enter information into a field. PROTECT=NO allows you to enter information. Use the PROTECT=option only for fields containing variables; fields containing text are automatically protected.

REQUIRED=YES | NO
: controls whether a field can be left blank. NO is the default. If you try to leave a field blank that was defined with REQUIRED=YES, the SAS System does not allow you to input values in any subsequent fields.

Automatic Variables

The WINDOW statement creates two automatic SAS variables:

CMD
: contains the last command from the window's command line that was not recognized by display manager. _CMD_ is a character variable of length 80; its value is set to ' ' before each execution of a DISPLAY statement. You can use _CMD_ to enter values that work like display manager commands.

MSG
: contains a message you specify to be displayed in the message area of the window. _MSG_ is a character variable with length 80; its value is set to ' ' after each execution of a DISPLAY statement.

For example, suppose a WINDOW statement contains two groups of fields called SHOW.REGULAR and SHOW.MORE. You need to see SHOW.REGULAR in each execution of the DATA step, and, occasionally, you need to see the additional information displayed by SHOW.MORE. You can place this statement in the DATA step:

```
if _cmd_='MORE' then display show.more;
```

When you enter MORE on the command line of SHOW.REGULAR, SAS assigns _CMD_ the value 'MORE'. The IF statement then becomes true, and the THEN statement displays SHOW.MORE.

This example tests for erroneous display manager commands in a window defined with the WINDOW statement:

```
if _cmd_ ne ' ' then _msg_='CAUTION: UNRECOGNIZED COMMAND '||_cmd_;
```

If you enter a command containing an error, SAS assigns the text of that command as the value of _CMD_. Since the value of _CMD_ is no longer blank, the IF statement is true. The THEN statement assigns _MSG_ the value created by concatenating 'CAUTION: UNRECOGNIZED COMMAND ' and the value of _CMD_ (up to a total of eighty characters). The next time a DISPLAY statement displays that window, the message line of the window displays

```
CAUTION: UNRECOGNIZED COMMAND command
```

where *command* is the erroneous display manager command.

Displaying Windows

The DISPLAY statement allows you to display windows. Once you display a window, the window remains visible until you display another window over it or until the end of the DATA step. When you display a window containing fields into which you can enter values, you must either enter a value or press ENTER at **each** unprotected field to cause SAS to proceed to the next display. You cannot skip any fields. While a window is being displayed, you can use commands and function keys to view other windows, change the size of the current window, and so on. SAS execution proceeds to the next display only after you have pressed ENTER in all unprotected fields.

A DATA step containing a DISPLAY statement continues execution until the last observation read by a SET, MERGE, UPDATE, or INPUT statement has been processed or until a STOP or ABORT statement is executed. (You can also enter END on the command line of the window to stop the execution of the DATA step.)

Examples

Example 1: simple WINDOW statement The following DATA step creates a window with a single group of fields. **Screen 5.1** shows the window.

```
data _null_;
   window start color=yellow
   #5 @28 'WELCOME TO THE SAS SYSTEM' attr=highlight color=blue
   #7 @8
   'THIS PROGRAM CREATES TWO SAS DATA SETS AND USES THREE PROCEDURES'
   #12 @30 'PRESS ENTER TO CONTINUE';
   display start;
   stop;
run;
```

The START window fills the entire screen. It is yellow; the first line of text is high-intensity blue; the other two lines are white at normal intensity. The text is centered on each line. The START window does not require you to input any values. However, you must press ENTER to cause SAS execution to proceed to the STOP statement. If you omit the STOP statement, the DATA step executes endlessly unless you enter END on the command line of the window. (Since this DATA step does not read any observations, SAS cannot detect an end-of-file to cause DATA step execution to cease.) If you add the NOINPUT option to the DISPLAY statement, the window is displayed quickly and removed.

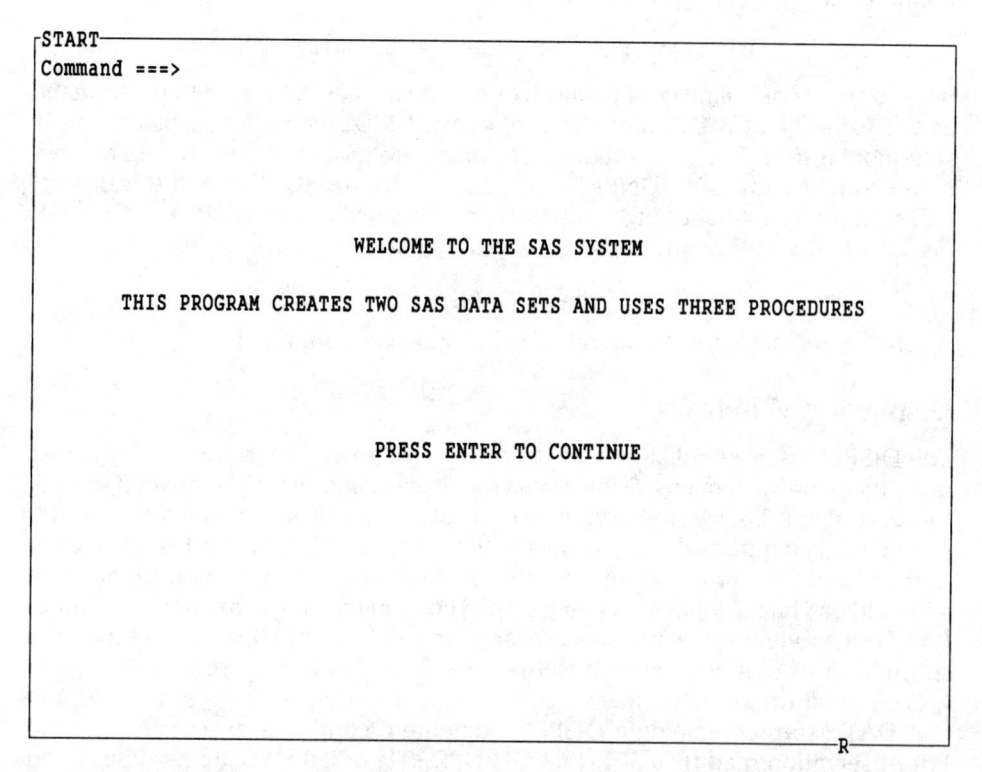

```
┌START─────────────────────────────────────────────────────────────┐
│Command ===>                                                      │
│                                                                  │
│                                                                  │
│                                                                  │
│                       WELCOME TO THE SAS SYSTEM                  │
│                                                                  │
│      THIS PROGRAM CREATES TWO SAS DATA SETS AND USES THREE PROCEDURES │
│                                                                  │
│                                                                  │
│                                                                  │
│                         PRESS ENTER TO CONTINUE                  │
│                                                                  │
│                                                                  │
│                                                                  │
│                                                                 R│
└──────────────────────────────────────────────────────────────────┘
```

Screen 5.1 Window with a Single Group of Fields

Example 2: window with two groups of fields In this DATA step, window CHECK occupies the right half of the screen. CHECK can display either of two sets of information, VARCK or BEGIN. CHECK.BEGIN is shown in **Screen 5.2**, and CHECK.VARCK is shown in **Screen 5.3**.

```
data sales;
   set in.revenue;
   window check irow=1 icolumn=40 rows=21 columns=38 color=red
      group=varck #3 @5 id protect=yes @15 'CHECK SALES' color=yellow
         +2 sales color=yellow
      group=begin #10 @5
         'READY--PRESS ENTER TO BEGIN';
   if _n_=1 then display check.begin;
   if sales=. then display check.varck blank;
run;
```

```
┌OUTPUT─────────────────────────────┐ ┌CHECK──────────────────────────────┐
│Command ===>                       │ │Command ===>                       │
│                                   │ │                                   │
│                                   │ │                                   │
│                                   │ │                                   │
│                                   │ │                                   │
│                                   │ │                                   │
│                                   │ │                                   │
│                                   │ │                                   │
│                                   │ │                                   │
│                                   │ │   READY--PRESS ENTER TO BEGIN     │
├LOG────────────────────────────────┤ │                                   │
│Command ===>                       │ │                                   │
│                                   │ │                                   │
│    8    if _n_=1 then display check.be│                                │
│    9    if sales=. then display check.│                                │
│   10    run;                      │ │                                   │
├PROGRAM EDITOR─────────────────────┤ │                                   │
│Command ===>                       │ │                                   │
│                                   │ │                                   │
│00001                              │ │                                   │
│00002                              │ │                                   │
│00003                              │ │                                 R │
└───────────────────────────────────┘ └───────────────────────────────────┘
```

Screen 5.2 Instructions at the Beginning of a DATA Step

```
┌OUTPUT─────────────────────┐ ┌CHECK──────────────────────┐
│Command ===>               │ │Command ===>               │
│                           │ │                           │
│                           │ │                           │
│                           │ │     0824      CHECK SALES .│
│                           │ │                           │
│                           │ │                           │
│                           │ │                           │
│                           │ │                           │
├LOG────────────────────────┤ │                           │
│Command ===>               │ │                           │
│                           │ │                           │
│    8   if _n_=1 then display check.be│                  │
│    9   if sales=. then display check.│                  │
│   10   run;               │ │                           │
├PROGRAM EDITOR─────────────┤ │                           │
│Command ===>               │ │                           │
│                           │ │                           │
│00001                      │ │                           │
│00002                      │ │                           │
│00003                      │ │                           │
└───────────────────────────┘ └───────────────────────────┘
```

Screen 5.3 Window for Correcting Missing Data Values

This DATA step allows you to examine the values for SALES during the execution of the DATA step and change missing values for SALES. When the DATA step begins execution, CHECK.BEGIN informs you that SAS has begun executing the DATA step. Although you do not enter any values into this display, pressing ENTER removes the display and allows execution to proceed. The BLANK option in the second DISPLAY statement removes the text in CHECK.BEGIN from the window before displaying the fields in CHECK.VARCK. Each time the value of SALES is missing, CHECK.VARCK displays the values of ID and SALES for that observation. Since the ID field is protected, you cannot change the value of ID; however, you can change the value of SALES. Press ENTER when you have entered the value. If you do not change the value, press ENTER to cause execution to continue. The window remains visible even when SAS is processing observations that do not have missing values for SALES. After SAS processes the last observation in IN.REVENUE, the window disappears.

Example 3: two windows at the same time Suppose you are a newspaper editor and you have a list of article topics you want to assign to reporters on your staff. The list is stored as variable ART in SAS data set IN.ARTICLE; you want to examine each topic, assign it to a writer, and create a new SAS data set named SAVE.ASSIGN containing the topics and reporters' names. You also want to be sure, while you are making the assignments, that you divide the topics evenly among the reporters. The following SAS program displays windows, shown in

SAS Statements Used in the DATA Step

Screen 5.4, that allow you to do this:

```
libname save '\misc\people' in '\misc\projects';
data save.assign;
   set in.article end=final;
   window assign irow=15 color=green
      #3 @10 'ARTICLE' +1 art protect=yes +2 name $8.;
   window showtot irow=1 rows=10 color=cyan
      group=subtot
      #3 @10 'BAGGETT HAS' +1 b
      #4 @10 'CRUM HAS' +1 b
      #5 @10 'FRIED HAS' +1 f
      #6 @10 'HART HAS' +1 h
      #7 @10 'KIENZLE HAS' +1 k
      group=lastmsg
      #9 @20 'ALL ARTICLES ASSIGNED. PRESS ENTER TO STOP PROCESSING';
   display assign blank;
   if name='BAGGETT' then b+1;
   else if name='CRUM' then c+1;
   else if name='FRIED' then f+1;
   else if name='HART' then h+1;
   else if name='KIENZLE' then k+1;
   display showtot.subtot blank noinput;
   if final then display showtot.lastmsg;
run;
```

```
┌─SHOWTOT────────────────────────────────────────┐
│Command ===>                                    │
│                                                │
│                                                │
│                                                │
│        BAGGETT HAS 4                           │
│        CRUM HAS 3                              │
│        FRIED HAS 2                             │
│        HART HAS 3                              │
│        KIENZLE HAS 4                           │
│                                                │
│                                                │
└────────────────────────────────────────────────┘
┌─ASSIGN─────────────────────────────────────────┐
│Command ===>                                    │
│                                                │
│                                                │
│        ARTICLE ELECTION   FRIED                │
│                                                │
│                                                │
│                                              R─│
└────────────────────────────────────────────────┘
```

Screen 5.4 Multiple Windows for Data Entry and Displaying Running Totals

276 Chapter 5

In window ASSIGN (which fills the bottom half of the screen) you see the name of the article and a field into which you enter the reporter's name. After you enter the first name, SAS displays group SHOWTOT.SUBTOT in the top half of the screen. SHOWTOT.SUBTOT shows you the number of articles assigned to each reporter (including the assignment you just made). As you continue to make assignments, SHOWTOT.SUBTOT contains the subtotal assigned to each reporter so far (because the group from the previous execution of the DATA step is displayed until after you make the new assignment). During the last execution of the DATA step, SAS displays group SHOWTOT.LASTMSG, which tells you that you are finished and what you should do to end the DATA step. The text in SHOWTOT.LASTMSG is displayed at the bottom of the last group of totals so that you can examine the totals (because the DISPLAY statement does not contain the BLANK option).

Example 4: creating a SAS data set from a window This example, shown in **Screen 5.5**, uses WINDOW and DISPLAY statements to create a SAS data set:

```
libname out '\store\inventry';
data out.inven;
   window stock color=red
   #5 a10 'Enter values as directed'
   #10 a5 'Item' a10 item $12. a25 'Number' a32 number
       a41 'Cases (c) or boxes (b)' a64 type $1.
   #19 a10
   'After you enter the last value, enter STOP on the command line'
   #20 a10 'instead of pressing ENTER'
   ;
   do while (upcase(_cmd_) ne 'STOP');
      display stock blank;
      output;
      item=' ';
      number=.;
      type' ';
      end;
   stop;
run;
```

In window STOCK you enter values for ITEM, NUMBER, and TYPE. SAS outputs each observation when you press ENTER after entering the last value in the window. When you enter STOP on the command line, SAS assigns the value STOP to the automatic variable _CMD_. The value of _CMD_ controls execution of the DO WHILE group. Since display manager does not translate values to uppercase unless you specify the CAPS option, using the UPCASE function ensures that the comparison is performed correctly. (Note: entering END on the command line at any point also causes the DATA step to stop; however, if you accidentally enter END before you press ENTER for the last field in a display, SAS does not add that observation to the data set. Using _CMD_ in the DO WHILE statement prevents this problem since the loop always completes execution.) The STOP statement causes the DATA step to cease execution.

```
┌─STOCK─────────────────────────────────────────────────────────┐
│Command ===>                                                    │
│                                                                │
│                                                                │
│                                                                │
│           Enter values as directed                             │
│                                                                │
│                                                                │
│                                                                │
│       Item notebooks      Number 15      Cases (c) or boxes (b) C │
│                                                                │
│                                                                │
│                                                                │
│                                                                │
│                                                                │
│       After you enter the last value, enter STOP on the command line │
│       instead of pressing ENTER                                │
│                                                              R─│
└────────────────────────────────────────────────────────────────┘
```

Screen 5.5 Window for Creating a SAS Data Set

Example 5: persisting and nonpersisting fields The following example illustrates the PERSIST= option.

```
data _null_;
   array row{3} r1-r3;
   array col{3} c1-c3;
   input row{*} col{*};
   window one color=white
      #1 @31 'Persisting Field' color=red
      #(row{i}) @(col{i}) 'Hello' color=red persist=yes;
   window two color=white
      #1 @31 'Non-Persisting Field' color=green
      #(row{i}) @(col{i}) 'Hello' color=green persist=no;
   do i=1 to 3;
      display one;
      end;
   do i=1 to 3;
      display two;
      end;
   cards;
5 10 15 5 10 15
;
```

The first window in **Output 5.32** shows a persisting field after the third iteration of the DO loop, and the second window shows a nonpersisting field.

Output 5.32 Persisting and Nonpersisting Fields

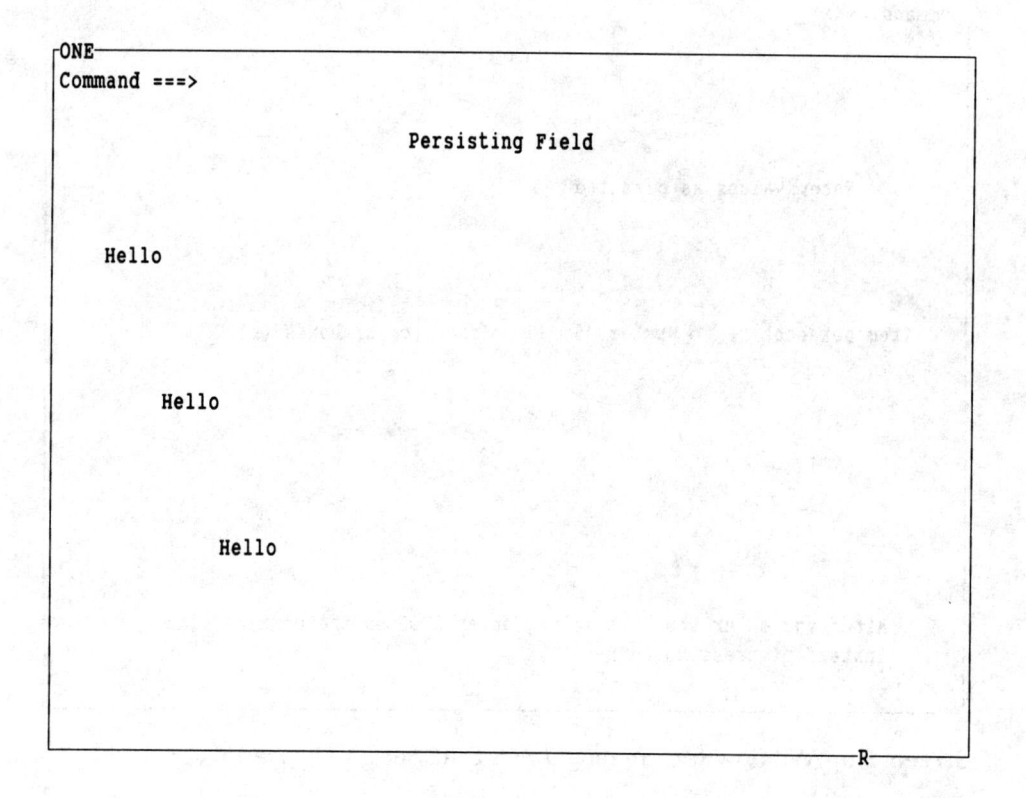

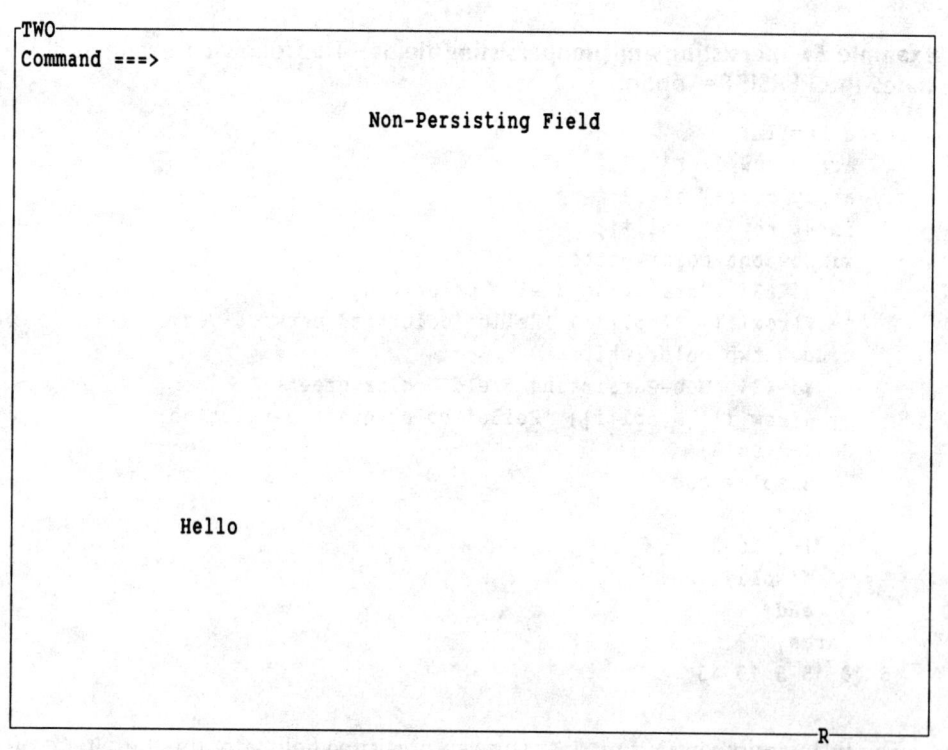

```
┌ONE─────────────────────────────────────────────────────────┐
│Command ===>                                                │
│                      Persisting Field                      │
│                                                            │
│                                                            │
│   Hello                                                    │
│                                                            │
│                                                            │
│       Hello                                                │
│                                                            │
│                                                            │
│            Hello                                           │
│                                                            │
│                                                            │
│                                                            │
│                                                            │
│                                                            │
│                                                          R │
└────────────────────────────────────────────────────────────┘

┌TWO─────────────────────────────────────────────────────────┐
│Command ===>                                                │
│                    Non-Persisting Field                    │
│                                                            │
│                                                            │
│                                                            │
│                                                            │
│                                                            │
│                                                            │
│                                                            │
│                                                            │
│            Hello                                           │
│                                                            │
│                                                            │
│                                                          R │
└────────────────────────────────────────────────────────────┘
```

Note that in both windows, the title field does not use the PERSIST=option. It is not needed because each execution of the DISPLAY statement displays the same text in the same position.

THE PROC STEP

Introduction

SAS® Statements Used in the PROC Step

Chapter 6
Introduction

INTRODUCTION 281
WHAT IS A PROC STEP? 281
PROC STEP STATEMENTS 281

INTRODUCTION

Once you have created a SAS data set with a DATA step, you can analyze and process it with SAS procedures. SAS procedures are programs that read SAS data sets, compute statistics, print results, and create other SAS data sets. In a DATA step you can do your own programming using SAS statements to manipulate your data and to describe the SAS data set being created. In a PROC step, you call a procedure by its name—the program is already written for you.

WHAT IS A PROC STEP?

A PROC step is a group of one or more SAS statements that begins with a PROC statement.

In the simplest PROC step,

- you want to process the most recently created SAS data set.
- you want all the variables processed and computations performed on all numeric variables.
- you want the entire data set processed at once rather than in subsets.

Since the SAS System handles this situation automatically, your PROC step is only a PROC statement to name the procedure you want:

```
proc program;
```

For other analyses, you can include options in the PROC statement, or you can add other statements and their options to the PROC step to specify the analysis you want in more detail.

For example, to process a data set other than the most recently created one, you can specify its name in the DATA= option in the PROC statement:

```
proc program data=SASdataset;
```

You can also add other statements to your PROC step to specify that the data should be processed in a special way. If you add a BY statement, the data are processed in BY groups:

```
proc program;
   by variables;
```

PROC STEP STATEMENTS

The SAS statements that can appear in a PROC step are procedure information statements and variable attribute statements. Other statements also available for use within a PROC step are listed in the "Introduction" to DATA AND PROC STEP FEATURES.

The statements that are shared by a number of SAS procedures are introduced here; many other statements are unique to different procedures. All procedure information statements that can be used with each procedure are also explained in detail in the individual procedure descriptions in the *SAS Procedures Guide, Release 6.03 Edition*. Commonly used procedure information statements are described below:

BY	specifies that the input data set is to be processed in groups defined by the BY variables.
CLASS	identifies any classification variables in the analysis.
FREQ	identifies a variable that represents frequency of occurrence.
ID	specifies one or more variables whose values identify observations in the printed output or SAS data set created by the procedure.
OUTPUT	gives information about an output data set created by the procedure.
VAR	identifies the variables to be analyzed by the procedure.
WEIGHT	specifies a variable whose values are relative weights for the observations.

The following is a list of commonly used variable attribute statements:

ATTRIB	specifies any of the attributes format, informat, label, and length for variables.
FORMAT	specifies formats for printing variable values.
LABEL	associates descriptive labels with variable names.

The variable attribute statements INFORMAT and LENGTH can also be used with a few SAS procedures.

You can use the DROP= and KEEP= data set options to identify variables to be excluded from or included in a data set or analysis. These options are available in the PROC step wherever data set names are used; see "SAS Files" for descriptions of these options. DROP and KEEP statements are not available in the PROC step.

Chapter 7
SAS® Statements Used in the PROC Step

ATTRIB Statement 284
BY Statement 285
CLASS Statement 287
FORMAT Statement 288
FREQ Statement 290
ID Statement 291
LABEL Statement 292
OUTPUT Statement 293
PROC Statement 294
QUIT Statement 295
VAR Statement 296
WEIGHT Statement 297
WHERE Statement 298

ATTRIB Statement

The ATTRIB statement in the PROC step allows you to specify the format, informat, label, and length of one or more variables in a single statement. An attribute specified in a PROC step is associated with the variable for that PROC step and in any output data sets the procedure creates that contain the variable.

The form of the ATTRIB statement is

ATTRIB variable [**FORMAT**=format] [**INFORMAT**=informat][**LABEL**='label']
  [**LENGTH**=[$]length]...;

You can specify the following terms in the ATTRIB statement:

variable
> names the variable to receive the attributes. *Variable* can be a single variable name, a list of names, or one of the variable lists described in the "Introduction" to USING THE SAS LANGUAGE, except for the special lists _NUMERIC_, _CHARACTER_, and _ALL_.

FORMAT=*format*
> specifies the format to associate with the preceding variables. The format can be either a SAS format or a format you have created with the FORMAT procedure. See the **FORMAT Statement** later in this chapter for more information on the format attribute, and see "SAS Informats and Formats" for descriptions of SAS formats.

INFORMAT=*informat*
> specifies the informat to associate with the preceding variables. See the **INFORMAT Statement** in "SAS Statements Used in the DATA Step" for information on the informat attribute, and see "SAS Informats and Formats" for descriptions of informats.

LABEL=*'label'*
> specifies a label to be associated with the preceding variables. See the **LABEL Statement** later in this chapter for information on variable labels.

LENGTH=[$]*length*
> specifies the length of the preceding variables. If the variables are character variables, put a dollar sign ($) in front of the length.

You can also assign variable attributes with FORMAT, INFORMAT, LABEL, and LENGTH statements. Any attribute that you have assigned with an ATTRIB statement can be changed in an individual statement and vice versa.

Here are examples of valid ATTRIB statements:

- `attrib x y z length=$4 label='SAMPLE VARIABLES';`

- `attrib holiday informat=mmddyy. format=worddate.;`

- `attrib month1-month12 length=3;`

- ```
  attrib day1-day7 label='DAY OF WEEK'
         week1-week4 label='WEEK OF MONTH'
         month1-month12 label='MONTH OF YEAR'
         sales informat=comma8.2 format=dollar10. label='TOTAL SALES';
  ```
  ```

BY Statement

You can use a BY statement in a PROC step when you want the SAS System to process the data set in groups. A BY statement is always used with the SORT procedure to define the order in which the data set should be sorted. When a BY statement is used with most other procedures that analyze SAS data sets, the procedure processes each BY group separately. See the **BY Statement** in "SAS Statements Used in the DATA Step" for a discussion of BY groups.

The BY statement has the form:

BY [**DESCENDING**] *variable* ... [**NOTSORTED**];

where

variable
: names the variable or variables that define the BY groups. The procedure processes the data set in the groups defined in the BY statement.

DESCENDING
: specifies that the data set is sorted in descending order by the variable that immediately follows the word DESCENDING in the BY statement.

NOTSORTED
: specifies that observations with the same BY values are grouped together, but the BY values are not necessarily sorted in alphabetical or numerical order. It may appear anywhere in the BY statement. The NOTSORTED option cannot be used with the SORT procedure.

If you do not specify either DESCENDING or NOTSORTED, SAS assumes that the data set is sorted in ascending order of the BY variables.

For example, the statement

```
by descending x y;
```

specifies that the data set is sorted in descending order of the values of X and, within each X value, in ascending order of Y. The statement

```
by descending x descending y;
```

specifies that the data set is sorted in descending order of the values of X, and within each X value, in descending order of Y.

In the following example, data set CLASS contains observations with a variable DAY whose values are the three-letter abbreviation for the day of the week. The observations with the same DAY values are grouped together in the data set, but the DAY values are in calendar order, not alphabetical order. The following statement can be used with a PROC statement to process the data set by DAY:

```
by day notsorted;
```

When a BY statement is used with a procedure to process the data in BY groups, the data set being processed need not have been previously sorted by the SORT procedure. However, the data set must be in the same order as though the SORT procedure had sorted it unless NOTSORTED is specified.

For example, below is a listing of SAS data set DEGREES. The data set is sorted by STATE, CITY within STATE, and MONTH within CITY.

STATE	CITY	MONTH	DEGDAYS
NC	CHARLOTTE	1	716
NC	CHARLOTTE	2	588
NC	CHARLOTTE	3	461
NC	RALEIGH	1	760
NC	RALEIGH	2	638
NC	RALEIGH	3	502
VA	NORFOLK	1	760
VA	NORFOLK	2	661
VA	NORFOLK	3	532
VA	RICHMOND	1	853
VA	RICHMOND	2	717
VA	RICHMOND	3	569

With the data set sorted in this order, the following statements cause SAS to print two listings—a separate listing for each state:

```
proc print;
   by state;
```

(The PRINT procedure has several options that allow enhanced BY-group processing when a BY statement is in effect. See "The PRINT Procedure" in the *SAS Procedures Guide, Release 6.03 Edition* for details.)

The following statements produce descriptive statistics in four separate reports—one for each combination of STATE and CITY values:

```
proc means;
   by state city;
   var degdays;
```

If you have used a FORMAT or ATTRIB statement to group a continuous variable into discrete groups, the BY statement creates BY groups based on the formatted values.

CLASS Statement

The CLASS (or CLASSES) statement is used by several SAS procedures to identify classification variables by which the analysis is to be performed.

The form of the CLASS statement is

    CLASS *variables*;

or

    CLASSES *variables*;

where

    variables specifies the classification variable(s) in the analysis. When more than one classification variable is allowed by the procedure, any form of variable list is allowed as described in the "Introduction" to USING THE SAS LANGUAGE.

FORMAT Statement

Introduction 288
Using FORMAT for Datetime Values 289

Introduction

You can use the FORMAT statement to associate formats with variables in PROC steps. The formats can be either SAS formats or formats you have defined with PROC FORMAT. You can give the same format to several variables or different formats to different variables with a single FORMAT statement. When the SAS System prints values of the variables, it uses the associated format to print the values.

A format specified in a PROC step is associated with the variable for the duration of that PROC step and in any output data sets the procedure creates that contain the variable.

You can associate formats with variables with the statement

FORMAT *variables* [*format*]...;

These terms are included in the FORMAT statement:

variables names the variable or variables you want to associate with a format.

format gives the format you want SAS to use for writing values of the variable or variables in the previous variable list. Every format name ends with a period (for example, SEXFMT.) or has a period between the width value and number of decimal places (for example, DOLLAR8.2).
See "SAS Informats and Formats" for more information on the types of SAS formats that are available. See "The FORMAT Procedure" in the *SAS Procedures Guide, Release 6.03 Edition* for information on how to define your own output formats.

If a variable appears in more than one FORMAT statement, the format given in the last FORMAT statement is used. A FORMAT statement used in a DATA step to associate one format with a variable can be overridden by a FORMAT statement in a later PROC step. The original format name remains stored with the variable in the data set. To disassociate a format from a variable, use the variable's name in a FORMAT statement with no format.

You can also assign formats with the ATTRIB statement. You can change a format assigned in a FORMAT statement with an ATTRIB statement and vice versa.

If you have used the FORMAT procedure to define your own formats, you need a FORMAT statement to associate the format with one or more variables:

```
proc format;
   value sexfmt 1='MALE'
                2='FEMALE';
proc print data=all;
   format sex sexfmt.;
```

The FORMAT procedure defines the SEXFMT. format. The FORMAT statement in the PROC step associates SEXFMT. with SEX, a variable in data set ALL. When the values of SEX are printed by the PRINT procedure, MALE and FEMALE are printed instead of the numbers 1 and 2.

To use some SAS procedures like FREQ, you may need to divide observations on continuous variables into distinct groups or categories. You can use the FORMAT procedure to define these categories or ranges of values. If you then use a FORMAT statement to associate the new format defined by PROC FORMAT with the variables, FREQ uses the formatted values to determine the category or group into which each observation falls.

Using FORMAT for Datetime Values

When you are using SAS datetime values in procedures, you must assign them a corresponding date, time, or datetime format in order for the values to be printed in an intelligible form. If you want to associate the format with the variable only for the duration of the procedure, use a FORMAT statement in the PROC step. For example,

```
proc print;
   var date farenht celsius;
   format date date7.;
   title 'HIGH TEMPERATURE FOR DAY';
```

The result of the PRINT procedure is a listing of each date in the data set in the form *ddMMMyy* (DATE7.) with the Fahrenheit and Celsius temperature values. Without the FORMAT statement, values of DATE appear as the number of days between January 1, 1960 and the value of the variable DATE, a large number that is difficult to interpret. See "SAS Informats and Formats" for more information on SAS date, time, and datetime values.

FREQ Statement

The FREQ statement is used with several procedures to identify a variable that represents the frequency of occurrence for the other values in the observation.

The form of the FREQ statement is

FREQ *variable*;

where

variable   names a numeric variable whose value represents the frequency of occurrence for the observation.

When a FREQ statement appears, the procedure treats the data set as though each observation appears *n* times, where *n* is the value of the FREQ variable for that observation.

If the value of the FREQ variable in an observation is less than one, the observation is not used in the analysis. If the value is not an integer, only the integer portion is used.

ID Statement

The ID statement is used by several SAS procedures to specify one or more variables whose values identify observations in the printed output or SAS data set created by the procedure.

The form of the ID statement is

ID *variables*;

where

> *variables* specifies the identifying variables.

For example, when an ID statement is used with the PRINT procedure, the observations are identified by the value of the ID variable; the observation number is not printed.

LABEL Statement

You can use a LABEL statement in a PROC step to give labels to variables. Most SAS procedures use these variable labels in writing the results of analyses. The LABEL statement is an attribute statement that can occur anywhere among the statements in a PROC step. Although the statement is available to all procedures that read SAS data sets, it is not described in any procedure description. When a LABEL statement is used in a PROC step, the labels are associated with the variables for the duration of the procedure step.

The form of the LABEL statement is

LABEL *variable*='*label*' ...;

where

    variable   names the variable to be labeled.

    label   specifies a label of up to forty characters, including blanks, for the variable. The label must be enclosed in either single or double quotes. When quotes are part of the label, they must be written as two quotes. When two quotes are used within a label to represent one quote, they are counted as one character.

Any number of variable names and labels can appear. Here is an example:

```
proc plot;
   plot x*y;
   label x='RESPONSE TIME' y='HOUR OF DAY';
```

In this example, labels rather than variable names are used to label the vertical and horizontal axes of the plot.

You can also assign variable labels with the ATTRIB statement.

OUTPUT Statement

The OUTPUT statement is used by several SAS procedures to tell the procedure to create a SAS data set as output.

Although the form of the OUTPUT statement may vary with each procedure, the general form is

OUTPUT [**OUT**=*SASdataset*] [*keyword*=*names*]...;

where

SASdataset
specifies the name of the new SAS data set to be created by the procedure.

keyword=names
names the output variables on the data set associated with keywords. Keywords vary with each procedure but are usually descriptive of a statistic or other value being output to the new data set.

For example, in the MEANS procedure step below:

```
proc means;
   var x;
   output out=outmean mean=meanx;
```

the MEAN= keyword specifies that the mean of X, calculated by the MEANS procedure, should be given the name MEANX in the new data set OUTMEAN.

PROC Statement

The PROC (or PROCEDURE) statement is used to begin a PROC step and to identify the procedure you want to use.

The form of the PROC statement is

PROC *program* [*options*]*;*

where

> *program*   names the SAS procedure you want to use.
>
> *options*   specifies one or more options for the procedure. See the individual procedure descriptions for options that can be specified in the PROC statement.

Three kinds of options are commonly used:

keyword
: is a single keyword that requests a feature of the procedure.

keyword=value
: specifies a keyword and value, where value is a number or character string.

keyword=SASdataset
: specifies an input or output SAS data set.

The options that can be specified with each procedure are described in detail in the individual procedure description.

QUIT Statement

The QUIT statement ends an interactive procedure. When a QUIT statement is submitted, all remaining statements for the interactive procedure are completed and output is displayed before the procedure ends. The form of the QUIT statement is

QUIT;

You can end an interactive procedure by submitting another DATA or PROC statement, a QUIT statement, an ENDSAS statement, or the display manager BYE command. You must end an interactive procedure with the QUIT statement in order to submit subsequent statements using the remote submit feature of the micro-to-host link.

The following example shows the use of the QUIT statement:

```
proc plot;
   plot x*y;
   title 'first plot';
run;
submit the statements and see the first plot
   plot x*z;
   title 'second plot';
submit the statements to create a second plot
quit;
see the second plot and end the interactive PLOT step
```

Until you end the PROC PLOT step, the PLOT procedure remains a part of the SAS session, and the letter R in the lower corner of the screen indicates that it is active.

Note that the SAS log reports the time elapsed since you entered the PROC statement in an interactive procedure, not the time used in executing the RUN groups.

See Chapter 9, "Starting and Running SAS Programs," for a discussion of interactive procedures.

VAR Statement

The VAR (or VARIABLES) statement is used by several SAS procedures to identify the variables to be analyzed.

The form of the VARIABLES statement is

VAR *variables*;

or

VARIABLES *variables*;

where

variables   identifies the variables in the data set you want analyzed by the procedure. Any valid form of variable list may be used. (See the "Introduction" to USING THE SAS LANGUAGE for details.)

WEIGHT Statement

The WEIGHT statement is used by several SAS procedures to specify a variable whose values are relative weights for the observations.

The form of the WEIGHT statement is

WEIGHT *variable*;

where

> *variable*   names the variable whose values contain the relative weights.

The WEIGHT statement is often used in analyses where the variance associated with each observation is different and the values of the weight variable are proportional to the reciprocals of the variances.

The WEIGHT statement should not be confused with the FREQ statement, which identifies a variable that represents frequency of occurrence for the observation. See the **FREQ Statement** description for more information.

298   Chapter 7

WHERE Statement

> *WHERE Expressions   298*
>   *Arithmetic Operators   299*
>   *Comparison Operators   299*
>   *Logical (Boolean) Operators   299*
>   *Other Operators   300*
>   *Restrictions on WHERE Expressions   300*
> *EXAMPLES   300*
>   *Example 1: Selecting One Value   300*
>   *Example 2: Selecting a List of Values   301*
>   *Example 3: Excluding Values   301*

The WHERE statement allows you to select observations from a SAS data set that meet a particular condition before the SAS System brings observations into the PROC step.*

The form of the WHERE statement is

WHERE *whereexpression*;

in which

> *whereexpression*   is an arithmetic or logical expression as defined in **WHERE Expressions**, below. WHERE expressions make comparisons using unformatted values of variables.

WHERE selection is performed immediately after SAS data set options take effect. Therefore, if you have used a RENAME= data set option, for example, you must use the new name in the WHERE statement. WHERE selection occurs after the FIRSTOBS= and OBS= system options take effect and before BY groups are created.

In the PROC step, a WHERE statement with a given expression selects the same subset as a subsetting IF statement with that expression used as the last statement in the DATA step that created the data set.

In procedures that use more than one SAS data set as input, the WHERE statement may apply to one or more of the input data sets. See the individual procedure descriptions for information on the input data set(s) to which the WHERE statement applies. Variables in a WHERE expression must appear in all input data sets to which the statement applies.

Note: in Release 6.03 you cannot use the WHERE statement with procedures in SAS/FSP software.

WHERE Expressions

A WHERE expression is a sequence of operands and operators. Operands include constants you supply, values of variables obtained from the SAS data sets to which the WHERE statement applies, and values created within the WHERE expression itself. The operators you can use in WHERE expressions are listed below:

---

* The SAS WHERE statement contains a subset of features from the ANSI SQL WHERE clause and some additional features that ensure compatibility with other SAS statements and expressions.

Arithmetic Operators

    *   multiplication
    /   division
    +   addition
    −   subtraction

Comparison Operators

   = or EQ   equal to
   ^= or NE   not equal to*
   > or GT   greater than
   < or LT   less than
   >= or GE   greater than or equal to
   <= or LE   less than or equal to

You can use the colon modifier (:) with any of the comparison operators. See Chapter 3, "SAS Expressions," for a description of the colon modifier.

Logical (Boolean) Operators

   & or AND   logical AND
   | or OR   logical OR (if the symbol | is not available, use ¦ or !)
   ^ or NOT   logical NOT (if the symbol ^ is not available, use the symbol ~)

Names of numeric variables can stand alone in logical expressions. In that case, the SAS System treats all values except 0 and missing as true (as having the value 1). A value of 0 or missing is false (that is, 0). For example, the following statements contain valid WHERE expressions:

```
where x;
where x and y;
```

The first WHERE statement selects observations in which X has a value other than 0 or missing. The second statement selects observations in which both X and Y have values other than 0 or missing.

Names of character variables cannot stand alone in logical expressions. To select nonmissing character values, write the expression as either

```
where c^=' ';
```

or

```
where c is not missing;
```

The IS MISSING operator is described in **Other Operators**, below.

---

* For compatibility with the ANSI SQL WHERE clause, you can also represent "not equal to" with the operator <>.

Other Operators

The WHERE expression can use the BETWEEN-AND operator, the IS MISSING or IS NULL operator, and the IN operator.

The BETWEEN-AND operator has the form

quantity **BETWEEN** *constant1* **AND** *constant2*

It selects values that are between two constants, inclusively. It is equivalent to the expression

constant1 <= *quantity* <= *constant2*

The IS MISSING or IS NULL operator has the form

quantity **IS MISSING | IS NULL**

It selects all missing values. For numeric variables, IS MISSING is equivalent to

quantity <= .Z

For character variables, IS MISSING is equivalent to

quantity =' '

To select nonmissing values, combine the NOT operator with IS MISSING or IS NULL:

quantity **IS NOT MISSING | IS NOT NULL**

(You can also write the NOT operator before the word IS, if you prefer.)

The IN operator has the form

quantity **IN** (*constant*[,] . . .)

It compares a value to a series of numeric or character constants. Enclose character constants in quotes. The IN operator is equivalent to

quantity=*constant1* OR *quantity*=*constant2* OR *quantity*=*constant3* . . .

Restrictions on WHERE Expressions

A WHERE expression cannot use the DATA step operators for concatenation, minimum, and maximum, and it cannot contain a SAS function.

Examples

Example 1: Selecting One Value

Suppose you have a SAS data set containing information about all the counties in North Carolina, and you want to print only the observations for Wake county. You can use the following statements:

```
proc print data=nc;
   where county='Wake';
   title 'Observations for Wake County';
run;
```

Example 2: Selecting a List of Values

If you want to print observations for Wake, Franklin, and Dare counties, use

```
proc print data=nc;
   where county in ('Wake','Franklin','Dare');
   title 'Wake, Franklin, and Dare Counties';
run;
```

Example 3: Excluding Values

To print all observations except those for Wake county, use

```
proc print data=nc;
   where county ^='Wake';
   title 'Counties Except Wake';
run;
```

DATA AND PROC STEP FEATURES

Introduction

Starting and Running SAS® Programs

SAS® Display Manager System

Error Handling

SAS® Output

SAS® Informats and Formats

Missing Values

SAS® Files

SAS® Global Options

SAS® Macro Facility

SAS® Statements Used Anywhere

Chapter 8
Introduction

This section of the manual describes SAS features that are applicable to both DATA and PROC steps. Topics discussed include SAS files, SAS informats and formats, missing values, SAS output, and SAS global options.

The following statements can be used anywhere in a SAS program, either outside or within either DATA or PROC steps:

comment	allows you to write comments with your SAS statements to document the program.
DM	allows you to issue display manager commands as SAS statements.
ENDSAS	causes SAS to terminate execution immediately.
FILENAME	defines a fileref for an external file.
FOOTNOTE	specifies footnote lines to be written with SAS output.
%INCLUDE	includes SAS source lines from external files.
LIBNAME	defines a libref for a SAS data library to be used as the first level of a two-word SAS file name.
OPTIONS	allows you to change SAS system options.
RUN	causes the previously entered SAS step to begin execution.
TITLE	specifies title lines to be written with SAS output.
X	is used to issue an operating system command within a SAS session.

Chapter 9
Starting and Running SAS® Programs

INTRODUCTION   307
STARTING A SAS SESSION OR PROGRAM   307
THREE MODES OF EXECUTION   308
   Interactive Display Manager Mode   308
      Interrupting Execution   309
   Interactive Line Mode   309
      Sample Sessions   309
   Noninteractive Mode   311
      Log and Output Files   311
      Invoking a Full-Screen or Graphics Procedure
         in Noninteractive Mode   312
SETTING OPTIONS AUTOMATICALLY   312
   CONFIG.SAS File   312
   PROFILE.SCT File   312
EXECUTING SAS STATEMENTS AUTOMATICALLY   313
   AUTOEXEC.SAS File   313
INTERACTIVE PROCEDURES   313
   Time Elapsed   314
   Interactive Procedures and the Micro-to-Host Link   314
   Error Handling   315

INTRODUCTION

This chapter discusses the SAS command, which starts a SAS program or session; the various ways you can execute SAS programs; techniques for automatically setting global options and automatically executing SAS statements at system initialization; and the use of interactive procedures in a SAS program or session.

   Throughout this chapter, examples of the SAS command are preceded by the DOS prompt, C:>, to emphasize that the SAS command is executed from DOS. SAS command examples are followed by the characters <ENTER> to remind you to press the ENTER key after you type the command.

STARTING A SAS SESSION OR PROGRAM

You start a SAS session or program by entering the SAS command from DOS. The form of the SAS command is

   SAS [*file_spec options*]

where

> *file_spec*   is the name of a file containing SAS programming statements. The file_spec is used for one type of execution, noninteractive mode, as explained later in this chapter.
>
> *options*   are SAS global options, either configuration options or SAS system options. Options can be specified for any type of execution. Refer to Chapter 16, "SAS Global Options," for information on global options and how they are specified in the SAS command.

The exact specifications you include in the SAS command depend on

- the execution mode you use
- the content of your CONFIG.SAS file.

These topics are discussed in the following sections.

THREE MODES OF EXECUTION

The term *modes of execution* refers to the environment you use to run SAS programs. Three modes of execution are possible in Release 6.03 of the SAS System:

- interactive display manager mode
- interactive line mode
- noninteractive mode.

Interactive Display Manager Mode

In interactive display manager mode, you execute SAS programs using the SAS Display Manager System, which is a full-screen facility with windows for editing and executing programming statements, displaying the SAS log, displaying procedure output, setting function keys, and more. See Chapter 10, "SAS Display Manager System," for a discussion of display manager.

Interactive display manager mode is invoked with the following form of the SAS command:

SAS [*options*]

where *options* are global options. The -DMS configuration option must be in effect to invoke display manager mode. Therefore, unless your CONFIG.SAS file includes the -DMS specification, you must include the -DMS option in the SAS command:

```
C:> sas -dms        <ENTER>
```

See **CONFIG.SAS File** later in this chapter for more information on setting options in the CONFIG.SAS file.

Other global options can also be specified in the SAS command, for example,

```
C:> sas -dms -nodate -profile      <ENTER>
```

Interrupting Execution

To interrupt SAS program execution in display manager execution mode, issue a *control-break signal* (sometimes referred to as an *attention* signal). You issue a control-break signal by pressing the CTRL and BREAK keys simultaneously.*

After you issue a control-break signal, a requestor panel is displayed that prompts you for input to determine what to do next. An example of such a requestor panel is shown in **Screen 9.1**. The panel in **Screen 9.1** presents three alternatives: cancel submitted statements, halt the current step, or continue. Some requestor panels displayed after a control-break have different alternatives, depending on what kind of procedure or program you interrupted. For example, if you issue a control-break when the micro-to-host link is active and a SIGNON, RSUBMIT, or SIGNOFF command is executing, the link's BREAK window appears and offers choices appropriate to link processing.

```
┌─BREAK─────────────────────────────────────────────┐
│  Press Y to cancel submitted statements, T to halt data │
│  step/proc, N to continue                         │
└───────────────────────────────────────────────────┘
```

Screen 9.1 Sample Control-Break Signal Requestor Panel

Interactive Line Mode

In line-mode execution, program statements are entered in sequence in response to prompts from the SAS System. DATA and PROC steps execute when a RUN statement is entered or when another DATA or PROC statement is entered. (Also see **INTERACTIVE PROCEDURES** later in this chapter.) The SAS log and output are displayed on the screen immediately following the programming statements. This mode of execution requires approximately 100K less memory than display manager mode.

Interactive line mode is invoked with a SAS command of the following form:

SAS [*options*]

where *options* are global options. The -NODMS configuration option must be in effect to invoke interactive line mode. Therefore, unless your CONFIG.SAS file includes the -NODMS specification, you must include the -NODMS option in the SAS command:

```
C:>sas -nodms        <ENTER>
```

See **CONFIG.SAS File** later in this chapter for more information on using the CONFIG.SAS file.

Other global options can also be specified in the SAS command, for example,

```
C:> sas -nodms -nodate -profile    <ENTER>
```

Sample Sessions

Screen 9.2 shows a sample line-mode SAS session. As you can see, the SAS System prompts you with a number and a question mark to enter SAS statements. (You can enter more than one SAS statement per line.) After you use a CARDS statement in a DATA step, the prompt changes to a number and a greater-than (>)

---

* On some keyboards the control key is labeled CNTL rather than CTRL.

symbol. This indicates that the SAS System expects you to enter data before you enter more SAS statements.

Also notice that notes from the SAS log and output from procedure steps are interspersed with the programming statements and data that you enter. Compare the log and procedure output in **Screen 9.2** and **Screen 9.3**. The DATA and PROC steps in **Screen 9.2** end with RUN statements. Therefore, one step executes before the next step begins, and the log and procedure output follow immediately after the statements that produced them. In **Screen 9.3**, the DATA step does not end with a RUN statement. Instead, the PROC PRINT statement indicates that the preceding DATA step has ended and a new step is beginning. The DATA step executes after the SAS System reads the PROC statement. This causes the log notes from the DATA step to print in the middle of the PROC PRINT step.

```
C:> sas -nodms

NOTE: Copyright(c) 1985, 86, 87 SAS Institute Inc.,
      Cary, NC 27511, U.S.A.
NOTE: SAS (r) Proprietary Software Release 6.03
      Licensed to SAS Institute 6.03, Site xxxxxxxxxxxx

NOTE: AUTOEXEC processing completed.

    1?data a;
    2?input @1 x 1. @3 y $5.;
    3?cards;
    4>1 cat
    5>2 dog
    6>3 bird
    7>4 cow
    8>run;

NOTE: The data set WORK.A has 4 observations and 2 variables.
NOTE: The DATA statement used 1.60 minutes.
    9?options nodate;
   10?proc print data=a;
   11?title 'Procedure Output in a Line-Mode SAS Session';
   12?run;

             Procedure Output in a Line-Mode SAS Session 1

                    OBS     X      Y

                     1      1     cat
                     2      2     dog
                     3      3     bird
                     4      4     cow
NOTE: The PROCEDURE PRINT used 30.00 seconds.
   13?
```

Screen 9.2 Sample Line-Mode Session with RUN Statements

```
*This is what happens if you don't use a RUN statement to execute
a step.;
   1?data a;
   2?input a1 x 1. a3 y $5.;
   3?cards;
   4>1 cat
   5>2 dog
   6>3 bird
   7>4 cow
   8>options nodate;
   9?proc print data=a;

NOTE: The data set WORK.A has 4 observations and 2 variables.
NOTE: The DATA statement used 1.60 minutes.
   10?
```

Screen 9.3 Sample Line-Mode Session without RUN Statements

Noninteractive Mode

In noninteractive execution, SAS program statements are stored in a DOS file. The statements in the file execute when you issue a SAS command referencing the file. The SAS log and output from the noninteractive program are written to DOS files; the log and output do not display on the screen. Noninteractive execution requires approximately 100K less memory than display manager execution mode.

Noninteractive mode is invoked with a SAS command of the following form:

SAS [*file_spec options*]

where *file_spec* is the name of a DOS file containing the SAS program you want to execute, including drive and path information if needed, and where *options* are global options.

The file containing SAS programming statements can have any extension or no extension at all. If the extension is .SAS, you do not need to specify the extension in the SAS command. For example, suppose you have a SAS program in a file called A:\SASPGMS\FINANCE.SAS. You can execute the program with this SAS command:

```
C:>sas a:\saspgms\finance     <ENTER>
```

Log and Output Files

The SAS log from a SAS program executed in noninteractive mode is written to a file with the same filename as the source file and .LOG as an extension. The output from a noninteractive program is written to a file with the same filename as the source file and .LST as an extension. By default, the .LOG and .LST files are written to the current directory.

For example, suppose the current directory is \MYDIR, and the name of the source file is \MYDIR\GLM.SAS. You execute the program with this SAS command:

```
C:>sas glm
```

The log and output files from the program are \MYDIR\GLM.LOG and \MYDIR\GLM.LST.

You can redirect the .LOG and .LST files with the -LOG and -PRINT configuration options, as described in Chapter 16, "SAS Global Options," or with PROC PRINTTO, as described in Chapter 26, "The PRINTTO Procedure," in the *SAS Procedures Guide, Release 6.03 Edition*.

Invoking a Full-Screen or Graphics Procedure in Noninteractive Mode

You can execute full-screen procedures or graphics procedures in a noninteractive program. Notes are written to the SAS log file, as they would be for any program. Output is displayed on the screen. When you end the procedure, you return to DOS.

SETTING OPTIONS AUTOMATICALLY

CONFIG.SAS File

Each time you start the SAS System (that is, each time you execute a SAS command), the SAS System looks for a file called CONFIG.SAS. The CONFIG.SAS file contains settings for the SAS global options known as *configuration options*. Configuration options affect how the SAS System initializes its interfaces with your computer hardware and the DOS operating system.

Configuration options can be specified in the SAS command. However, configuration options set in CONFIG.SAS do not have to be specified in the SAS command because they take effect automatically. Therefore, you can avoid repeatedly specifying configuration options in the SAS command by including the settings that you want to use in the CONFIG.SAS file.

For example, one important configuration option is the -DMS | -NODMS option. The setting of this option tells the SAS System whether to start an interactive display manager session (-DMS) or an interactive line-mode session (-NODMS). If you typically use display manager mode, you would include the -DMS specification in your CONFIG.SAS file. On the other hand, if you typically use line-mode execution, you would include the -NODMS specification in your CONFIG.SAS file.

Refer to Chapter 16, "SAS Global Options," for more information on the CONFIG.SAS file and descriptions of all SAS configuration options.

PROFILE.SCT File

You can also set many SAS system options automatically. A SAS system option is another kind of SAS global option. System options control the appearance of SAS output, SAS data set processing, and so on. Set system options automatically through your user profile catalog, PROFILE.SCT, and the PROFILE system option.

The SAS System always checks for a PROFILE.SCT file at system initialization time. If PROFILE.SCT includes a POPTIONS entry, the SAS System sets the system options according to the values in the POPTIONS entry. In order to save option settings in PROFILE.SCT, be sure that the PROFILE system option is in effect when you end a SAS session. If PROFILE is in effect, settings for many options are saved and are available the next time you run a SAS session or program.

Refer to Chapter 16, "SAS Global Options," for more information on the PROFILE option. Refer to Appendix 2, "User Profile Catalog," for information on PROFILE.SCT.

EXECUTING SAS STATEMENTS AUTOMATICALLY

AUTOEXEC.SAS File

As discussed in the preceding section, global options can be set automatically when the SAS System starts. You can also execute SAS statements automatically during SAS initialization by creating an AUTOEXEC.SAS file. Any SAS statement can be included in an AUTOEXEC.SAS file, and SAS display manager commands can be used if they are embedded in a DM statement.

Each time the SAS System is invoked, it looks for an AUTOEXEC.SAS file. The SAS System checks for AUTOEXEC.SAS first in the current directory, then in any directories specified by the DOS PATH command, and finally in the root directory. If your AUTOEXEC.SAS file is not stored in one of these locations, specify the correct location with the -AUTOEXEC configuration option. Refer to Chapter 16, "SAS Global Options," for a description of the -AUTOEXEC option.

One common use of the AUTOEXEC.SAS file is for setting SAS system options through the OPTIONS statement. For example, you may want to set the REMOTE= option for the micro-to-host link. Another common use of the AUTOEXEC.SAS file is to define librefs and filerefs that you use routinely. Include LIBNAME and FILENAME statements in AUTOEXEC.SAS to define librefs and filerefs. Here is a sample AUTOEXEC.SAS file:

```
options remote=irma;
libname mydata 'c:\account';
libname master 'c:\dept47';
filename out 'c:\saspgm\output';
data _null_;
   if weekday(date())=6 then
       put '******  Turn in your time report for this week.  ******';
run;
```

INTERACTIVE PROCEDURES

Some procedures in the SAS System are *interactive*. This means that the procedure step does not terminate after a RUN statement executes. Instead, the interactive procedure remains active, so you can enter additional statements for execution without repeating the PROC statement. You can continue to enter statements for that procedure as long as you like. The procedure does not terminate until you execute a QUIT statement or begin a new DATA or PROC step.

The interactive procedures in base SAS software are the CATALOG, DATASETS, and PLOT procedures. The rules governing each interactive procedure are discussed in that procedure's description.

Statements for interactive procedures are executed in *RUN groups*, that is, one or more statements followed by a RUN statement. Consider this example using the PLOT procedure. Begin execution of a PROC PLOT step with the PROC statement and other procedure statements, for example,

```
proc plot data=staff.times;
   by staffmem;
   plot month*hours;
run;
```

When the RUN statement executes, the PLOT procedure begins. Now you can keep entering PLOT statements:

```
    plot weeks*hours;
run;
    plot hours*projects;
run;
```

You can continue to enter procedure statements and RUN statements, executing substeps of the PLOT procedure. When you want to start a different step or a new PROC PLOT step, you can enter a QUIT statement

```
quit;
```

or another PROC or DATA statement.

Do not confuse interactive procedures with full-screen procedures. All full-screen procedures are interactive, but not all interactive procedures are full-screen. In addition, once you start a full-screen procedure, you control processing with procedure commands, not with groups of statements delimited by RUN statements. Full-screen procedures are terminated with an END command, not with the QUIT statement.

Time Elapsed

Release 6.03 of the SAS System reports the time elapsed for procedure step execution in the SAS log. Note that the time elapsed figure for an interactive procedure is for the entire step, not for individual RUN groups.

Interactive Procedures and the Micro-to-Host Link

There is an exception to the rule that an interactive procedure step is terminated by a new PROC or DATA statement. When you are using the SAS micro-to-host link, you cannot terminate an interactive procedure with a DATA or PROC step that is executed by the RSUBMIT command. You must end the interactive step with a QUIT statement first. For example, **do not attempt to do this**:

```
* This is the WRONG way to follow an interactive procedure step
  with a step executed by an RSUBMIT command;

* Execute the PLOT step's RUN groups with a SUBMIT command;

proc plot data=staff.times;
   by staffmem;
   plot month*hours;
run;
   plot weeks*hours;
run;
   plot hours*projects;
run;

* You must execute the following DOWNLOAD step with an RSUBMIT
  command.  However, the RSUBMIT fails because you did
  not QUIT the interactive procedure step first.;

proc download data=host.sasdata out=pc.sasdata;
run;
```

Starting and Running SAS Programs 315

Because the DOWNLOAD step must be executed with an RSUBMIT command, the program above does not work and an error message is issued. The correct way to run the program is to execute a QUIT statement (using the SUBMIT command or key) before the DOWNLOAD step. Then, issue the RSUBMIT command to execute the DOWNLOAD step.

```
* This is the RIGHT way to follow an interactive procedure step
  with a step executed by an RSUBMIT command;

* Execute the PLOT step's RUN groups and the QUIT statement
  with a SUBMIT command;

proc plot data=staff.times;
   by staffmem;
   plot month*hours;
run;
   plot weeks*hours;
run;
   plot hours*projects;
run;
quit;

* Now you can issue the RSUBMIT command to execute the
  DOWNLOAD step.;

proc download data=host.sasdata out=pc.sasdata;
run;
```

Error Handling

If an error is made in the PROC statement for an interactive procedure, the SAS System does not execute any statements in the procedure. If an error occurs in a statement after the PROC statement, the SAS System attempts to resolve the error. If the error can be resolved, processing of the current RUN group continues. If the error cannot be resolved, the SAS System terminates processing of the current RUN group and goes on to the next RUN group.

Chapter 10
SAS® Display Manager System

INTRODUCTION 319
SPECIAL KEYS 320
  Keyboard 320
  Function Keys 320
  Editing and Cursor Keys 320
  Other Special Keys 322
DISPLAY MANAGER COMMAND CONVENTIONS 322
  Command Syntax 322
  Executing Display Manager Window Commands 323
    Entering Command-Line Commands Directly 323
    Command-Line Commands with Options 324
    Executing Multiple Commands 324
    Executing Commands with Function Keys 324
    Function Keys and Multiple Commands 324
DISPLAY MANAGER GLOBAL COMMANDS 324
  Window Call Commands 325
    Primary Windows 325
    Special Windows 325
  Window Management Commands 326
  Window Position Commands 326
  Scrolling Commands 327
  COLOR Command 330
    Valid Field Types for All Windows 330
    Valid Field Types for Selected Windows 330
    Valid Colors 331
    Designing a Color Alternative: NEXT 331
    Valid Highlighting Attributes 331
  Micro-to-Host-Link Commands 331
  Cut and Paste Features 332
    Basic Commands 332
      Additional commands 333
      Where can you do what? 333
    Cut and Paste Global Commands 334
SAS TEXT EDITOR 337
  Using the Full-Screen Editor 337
    Entering Line Commands Directly 338
      Single line command 338
      Line command with option 338
      Line command requiring a target command 338
      Block line command 339
    Executing Line Commands without Line Numbers 339
  SAS Text Editor Commands 339
    Command-Line Command Definitions 340
    Line Command Definitions 349

PGM WINDOW: THE PROGRAM EDITOR   353
    Submitting SAS Programs   353
    Managing Your Files   354
    Ending Your SAS Session   356
    Commands   356
LOG WINDOW   357
    The SAS Log   357
    Commands   358
OUTPUT WINDOW   360
    Commands   362
CATALOG WINDOW   364
    Using Selection Fields   365
    Commands   366
DIR WINDOW   366
    Fields   367
        The Selection Field   367
    Commands   367
FILENAME WINDOW   368
    Commands   368
FOOTNOTES AND TITLES WINDOWS   368
    Commands   370
HELP WINDOW   370
    Commands   371
KEYS WINDOW   372
    Text Insert Feature   373
    Commands   373
LIBNAME WINDOW   375
    The Selection Field   376
    Commands   376
MENU WINDOW   376
    The MENU Command   378
    Commands   378
NOTEPAD WINDOW   379
    Commands   381
    Extended Keys   381
        Colors   382
        Highlighting Attributes   382
OPTIONS WINDOW   382
    Commands   383
SETINIT WINDOW   384
    Commands   385
VAR WINDOW   385
    Commands   386
SPECIAL TOPIC 1: SUBMITTING SAS STATEMENTS AT INITIALIZATION TIME   387
    Creating Your File of SAS Statements   387
SPECIAL TOPIC 2: CUSTOMIZING YOUR ENVIRONMENT   387
    Rearranging Windows   388
        Using the WDEF Command   388
        Using the Cursor Keys   390
    Changing Window Colors   392
    Customizing Windows with Function Keys   392
    Notes on Customizing Windows   393

INTRODUCTION

This chapter is a general introduction to the SAS Display Manager System and a complete reference guide for all keys, commands, and windows of display manager.

The SAS Display Manager System is a full-screen display and keyboard environment for your SAS session. It presents a set of windows corresponding to the various input and output parts of your SAS session. The three primary windows, as shown in **Screen 10.1**, are

- the PROGRAM EDITOR (PGM) window, where you enter and submit SAS statements and save SAS source files
- the LOG window, where you can browse and scroll the SAS log
- the OUTPUT window, where you can browse and scroll procedure output from your SAS session.

```
┌OUTPUT─────────────────────────────────────────────────────────────────┐
│Command ===>                                                           │
│                                                                       │
│                                                                       │
│                                                                       │
│                                                                       │
│                                                                       │
│                                                                       │
│                                                                       │
│                                                                       │
├LOG────────────────────────────────────────────────────────────────────┤
│Command ===>                                                           │
│                                                                       │
│NOTE: Copyright(c) 1985,86,87 SAS Institute Inc., Cary, NC 27512-8000, U.S.A.│
│NOTE: SAS (r) Proprietary Software Release 6.03                        │
│      Licensed to SAS Institute 6.03, Site 00000000.                   │
│                                                                       │
├PROGRAM EDITOR─────────────────────────────────────────────────────────┤
│Command ===>                                                           │
│                                                                       │
│00001                                                                  │
│00002                                                                  │
│00003                                                                  │
└───────────────────────────────────────────────────────────────────────┘
```

Screen 10.1 Default Initial Display Manager Screen Format

Display manager also has special windows that you can display on the screen to perform various functions for your SAS session. These are described briefly in **DISPLAY MANAGER GLOBAL COMMANDS** and in detail by individual window.

This chapter starts by describing some special keys and how to use them with the SAS Display Manager System. It continues with a description of command conventions and examples of executing commands in display manager windows. It lists and defines display manager global commands, which are commands that can be issued from any display manager window. It then lists and defines the text editing commands available through the full-screen editor.

Next the PGM, LOG, OUTPUT, and special windows are discussed. The discussion includes each window's role in your SAS session and the commands used in that window. The special topics sections describe how to submit SAS statements at initialization and how to modify display manager windows.

SPECIAL KEYS

Keyboard

Your PC's keyboard is divided into the following sections: function keys, typewriter keys, cursor control keys, and the numeric keypad. Each of these sections contains special keys to use with the SAS Display Manager System.

Function Keys

Each function key can be set to execute one or more display manager commands or can be defined as a character string. Default values are supplied for your function keys, although you can change the default settings with the KEYS window.

Editing and Cursor Keys

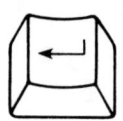

Press the ENTER key to execute a command typed on the command line or on a line number. Press the ENTER key by itself to move the cursor to the beginning of the next line of text. The key has additional uses in some windows; they are described with those windows.

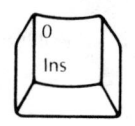

Press the INSERT key once to turn on insert mode; then position the cursor where you want to insert characters. The next key you press inserts its character before the cursor position, shifting characters to the right to make room. Press the INSERT key again to turn it off. The letter I is displayed on the bottom line of the screen to indicate insert mode.

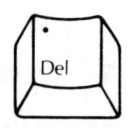

The DELETE key erases the character in the current cursor position, shifting any remaining characters to the left.

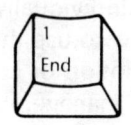

The END key erases all the characters from the cursor position to the end of a data entry line or, in some windows, the end of a field.

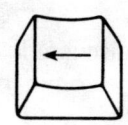

The BACKSPACE key moves the cursor backward, erasing characters as it moves.

SAS Display Manager System   321

The HOME key moves the cursor to the command line in the currently active window, which is the window containing the cursor.

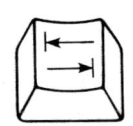

The TAB key moves the cursor to the beginning of the next unprotected field. Press the SHIFT and TAB keys to move the cursor to the beginning of the previous unprotected field.

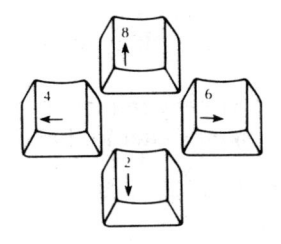

The CURSOR keys move the cursor one position to the right, left, up, or down.

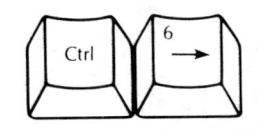

Press the CTRL and CURSOR RIGHT keys to move the cursor to the first character of the next word (delineated by blanks and special characters), scrolling the data if necessary. The cursor also stops at the beginning of each ensuing unprotected field.

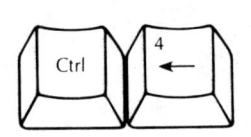

Press the CTRL and CURSOR LEFT keys to move the cursor to the first character of the previous word, scrolling the data if necessary. The cursor also stops at the beginning of each previous unprotected field.

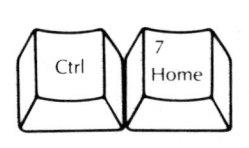

Press the CTRL and HOME keys to move the cursor to the far left text area of the window.

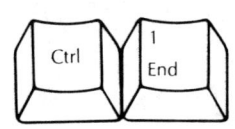

Press the CTRL and END keys to move the cursor to the right, one space beyond the last character of the last word on a line.

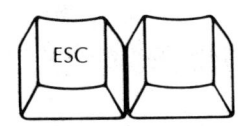

Use the ESC key in conjunction with a letter or number key to use color or highlighting attributes in the NOTEPAD window in the Display Manager System, in SAS/AF software, and in SAS/FSP software. See the **NOTEPAD WINDOW** section later in this chapter for more information.

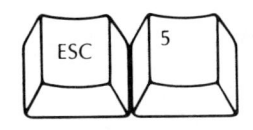

Press the ESC and number 5 keys to alter the cursor size.

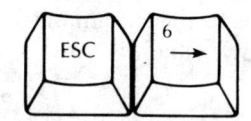

Press the ESC and number 6 keys to toggle the typematic rate from fast to slow.

Note that you must press the CTRL and SHIFT keys simultaneously with other keys and the ESC key before the letter or number keys.

Other Special Keys

A few keys can be used, like function keys, to execute commands. Unlike function keys, their values cannot be redefined.

The key on the left is equivalent to the command on the right. These commands are defined in **Scrolling Commands** and **SAS Text Editor Commands** later in this chapter.

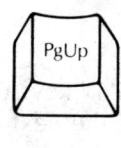

[PgUp]   BACKWARD PAGE

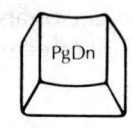

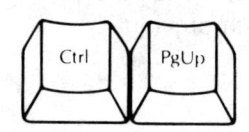

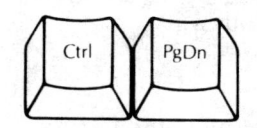

[PgDn]   FORWARD PAGE

[Ctrl][PgUp]   TOP

[Ctrl][PgDn]   BOTTOM

DISPLAY MANAGER COMMAND CONVENTIONS

Command Syntax

Descriptions of display manager window commands follow these conventions:

    COMMAND OPTION | *option*[OPTION | *option* | . . .]

where

    CAPITALIZATION
        indicates a keyword; you must use the same spelling and form as shown, although you can enter keywords in either uppercase or lowercase.

    lowercase italic
        indicates you supply the actual value.

vertical bar |
: means *or*; use only one of the terms separated by vertical bars.

brackets [ ]
: indicate optional information or keywords. Note that you do not type the brackets when you enter the command.

ellipses (. . .)
: mean that more than one of the terms preceding the ellipses can be optionally specified.

For example, the FIND command description looks like this:

FIND *characterstring* [NEXT | FIRST | LAST | PREV | ALL] [WORD | PREFIX | SUFFIX]

where

FIND
: is the command keyword.

characterstring
: is a user-supplied value. You type the string of characters you want to locate. It is not in brackets, so you are required to specify a character string.

[NEXT | FIRST | LAST | PREV | ALL]
: are five option keywords. The uppercase letters indicate that you enter each option exactly as written, although you can enter them in either uppercase or lowercase. The brackets indicate that these options are allowed but not required; the vertical bars indicate that you can specify only one of the five.

[WORD | PREFIX | SUFFIX]
: are three more option keywords. The uppercase letters indicate that you must enter each option exactly as written, although you can enter them in either uppercase or lowercase. The brackets indicate that these options are allowed but not required; the vertical bars indicate that you can specify only one of the three.

Executing Display Manager Window Commands

A special line called the command line is near the top of all windows. The command line is indicated in the display by

```
COMMAND ===>
```

Command-line commands can be typed on the command line or executed with function keys. To execute a command with a function key, you need to know the function key settings. Use the KEYS command to display the KEYS window and view or change your current function-key settings. (These commands can also be executed with the DM statement. For more information on the DM statement, see Chapter 18, "SAS Statements Used Anywhere.")

Entering Command-Line Commands Directly

To enter a command-line command directly, type the command on the command line and press the ENTER key. For example, to scroll backward, type

```
backward
```

on the command line and press ENTER. The BACKWARD command is an example of the most basic kind of command to enter; it requires only that you type a keyword and press ENTER.

Command-Line Commands with Options

The BACKWARD command also allows options to be specified. For example, to scroll backward the maximum amount, type

    backward max

on the command line and press ENTER.

Executing Multiple Commands

You can enter a series of commands on the command line by separating the commands with semicolons. For example, you can type the BACKWARD MAX scroll command and the FIND command on the command line, separated with a semicolon:

    backward max; find 'data one'

You can then execute both by pressing the ENTER key once.

Executing Commands with Function Keys

Executing a command with a function key can be as simple as pressing the function key instead of typing a command on the command line and pressing ENTER. To use a function key to execute a command with an option, you can either assign that function key the command with the option, such as BACKWARD MAX, or you can type the option MAX on the command line and press the BACKWARD function key.

Function Keys and Multiple Commands

You can also use the function key to submit multiple commands. For example, if you set a function key to execute the command BACKWARD MAX followed by a semicolon, as in

    backward max;

then you can enter

    find 'data one'

on the command line and execute both by pressing the key you set to execute the BACKWARD MAX command. The procedure executes the BACKWARD MAX command first and then the FIND command. You can also assign the function key to execute multiple commands; use a semicolon to separate them. For example,

    backward max; find 'data one'

DISPLAY MANAGER GLOBAL COMMANDS

The following groups of commands, called *global commands*, can be executed from the command line or with a function key in any window in the SAS Display Manager System. They are listed below, grouped by function:

window call commands
: display a window and move the cursor to it, making it active.

window management commands
: help you use windows efficiently.

window position commands
: alter the size and position of windows on the screen.

scrolling commands
: set the vertical and horizontal scroll amounts to scroll the window contents.

color commands
: change the color and highlighting attributes of selected portions of the window.

micro-to-host commands
: submit SAS statements for execution on a remote mainframe or minicomputer system.

cut and paste commands
: cut and paste text within windows, across window boundaries, and from one window to another.

Window Call Commands

These commands call up and make active a display manager window. The special windows are displayed only if needed. If the window is already displayed on your screen, a window call command moves the cursor to it, making it the currently active window.

Primary Windows

PGM
: is where you type SAS statements, make changes, and submit the statements for execution.

LOG
: displays the SAS log, which consists of SAS statements as they are processed along with notes and messages about your SAS session.

OUTPUT
: displays output from various SAS procedures and data steps.

Special Windows

AF
: displays applications developed with SAS/AF software and CBT courses.

CATALOG
: displays the directory of SAS catalogs and allows you to manage SAS catalogs and their entries or to create new catalogs.

DIR
: displays information about SAS data sets and SAS catalogs stored in a SAS data library.

FILENAME
: displays currently assigned filerefs and the name of the files to which they refer.

FOOTNOTES
: provides a menu for entering up to ten footnote lines to appear on procedure or data step output and then for browsing those footnotes.

HELP
: displays a help facility with information about the SAS System.

KEYS
: provides a facility for displaying, altering, and saving function key settings.

LIBNAME
: displays all currently assigned librefs and the path names to which they refer.

MENU
: displays the SAS Procedure Menu System, an application that uses a series of fill-in-the-blank panels to guide you through the procedures in the SAS System.

NOTEPAD
: allows you to create and store "notepads" of supporting documentation or information.

OPTIONS
: displays the current settings of SAS options, which you can change as well as browse.

SETINIT
: displays the currently licensed SAS software and expiration dates.

TITLES
: provides a menu for entering up to ten title lines to appear on procedure or data step output and then for browsing those titles.

VAR
: displays information about variables in a SAS data set.

Window Management Commands

In addition to the window call commands, window management commands help you use windows more efficiently. The window management commands are listed below:

BYE
: ends your SAS session. You can use this command interchangeably with the ENDSAS command.

CLOCK
: turns the clock on or off. The CLOCK command works like an on/off switch. The clock displays the time of day in the upper-right corner of the screen.

END
: removes a window from the screen. Unlike other global commands, the END command cannot be used in the LOG and OUTPUT windows. It is, however, the command you use most often to exit from a special window. In some cases, depending on the window, the END command closes and saves a file; in others, it simply allows you to exit the window and remove its display. See the description of each window for details on using the END command in that window.

  Note: a function key assigned to execute the SUBMIT command, an important command that can be used in the PGM, MENU, and AF windows, works like an END command in all special windows. The function key assigned to execute the SUBMIT command has ZOOM OFF preset.

ENDSAS
: ends your SAS session. This command is interchangeable with the BYE command.

NEXT [*windowname*]
: moves the cursor to the next window and activates that window; special windows must have already been made active. For example, the command

    next log

moves the cursor to the LOG window. Alternately, you can simply specify the name of a window to which you want to move the cursor. To move your cursor to the LOG window from the OUTPUT window, you can specify either

    log

or

    next

You must specify the displayed window name.

PREVCMD | ?
: recalls the last command entered on the command line of any window. You can repeatedly issue PREVCMD to recall previous commands (up to 128 characters are saved). This command is circular: after all previous commands have been recalled once, they are recalled again starting with the most recent. Note that a question mark (?) is an alias for PREVCMD.

RESHOW
: rebuilds the window currently displayed on the screen. For example, you can use RESHOW to remove messages from the operating system.

X ['dos command']
: executes the requested DOS command and then prompts you to press any key to return to the SAS System. If you enter X only, the SAS System puts you into PC DOS mode where you can enter commands in response to the DOS prompt. Type EXIT to return to the SAS System.

ZOOM [ON | OFF]
: causes the display of the active window to take over the entire screen, concealing the other windows. The ZOOM command works like an on/off switch: you can turn it off by entering the command again.
: Combining the ZOOM command and the NEXT command or a window call command is a convenient way of moving from window to window and viewing the contents of the new window easily. For example, after submitting a program from the PGM window, you can execute

    output; zoom

from the command line of the PGM window. The cursor moves to the OUTPUT window, and the window then occupies the entire screen, allowing you to view your output more easily. Execute ZOOM again to return to the previous window size.

Window Position Commands

You can customize your display manager window format by altering the position and size of windows on the screen. These commands are defined below. This topic is fully discussed in **SPECIAL TOPIC 2: CUSTOMIZING YOUR ENVIRONMENT.**

The WGROW, WSHRINK, and WMOVE commands work like on/off switches: you can turn them off by entering the command again.

WDEF *srow scol nrows ncols*
: redefines the window by moving it to a specified location on the screen
where

    srow
    : specifies the starting row for the window border.

    scol
    : specifies the starting column for the window border.

    nrows
    : specifies the number of rows inside the window, excluding the border.

    ncols
    : specifies the number of columns inside the window, excluding the border.

WGROW
: puts the screen in grow mode, allowing you to enlarge the active window by using cursor keys. Use the vertical cursors to make the window taller and the horizontal cursors to make it wider. The word GROW appears in the lower-right corner of the screen.

WMOVE
: sets the screen in move mode, allowing you to move the window with cursor keys while maintaining the current window dimensions. The word MOVE appears in the lower-right corner of the screen.

WSHRINK
: puts the screen in shrink mode, allowing you to decrease the size of the active window by using cursor keys. Use the vertical cursors to make the window shorter and the horizontal cursors to make the window narrower. The word SHRINK appears in the lower-right corner of the screen.

WSAVE*
: saves the position and color attributes of the window. If you do not execute WSAVE, the window maintains its new configuration only for the duration of the window. Window position and color attribute information is saved in SASUSER.PROFILE, a special SAS catalog. For more information, see Appendix 2, "User Profile Catalog."

Scrolling Commands

Use the following commands to scroll the contents of a window. You can scroll backward and forward, left and right, to the top and bottom, and to a specified line number. You can also set the horizontal and vertical scroll amounts with the HSCROLL and VSCROLL commands:

HSCROLL PAGE | HALF | MAX | *n*
: specifies the horizontal scroll amount for LEFT and RIGHT scrolling commands. The default HSCROLL amount is HALF. Specify one of the following:

    PAGE
    : the entire amount showing in the window

    HALF
    : half the amount showing in the window

    MAX
    : the leftmost or rightmost portion showing in the window

    n
    : *n* spaces.

---

* THE WSAVE command is available in all display manager windows except the HELP and MENU windows.

VSCROLL PAGE | HALF | MAX | *n*
> specifies the vertical scroll amount for FORWARD and BACKWARD commands. The default VSCROLL amount is HALF. Specify one of the following:
>
> PAGE   the entire amount showing in the window
>
> HALF   half the amount showing in the window
>
> MAX   the topmost or bottommost portion showing in the window
>
> *n*   *n* lines.

Scroll to a specific line number or in a specified direction with one of the following commands:

n
> scrolls line *n* to the top of the window, so that it is the first numbered line below the command line.

BACKWARD [PAGE | HALF | MAX | *n*]
FORWARD [PAGE | HALF | MAX | *n*]
> moves the contents of the window backward (toward the beginning) or forward (toward the end) the vertical scroll amount set by the VSCROLL command. You can also specify an amount to scroll backward or forward. Valid scroll amounts are
>
> PAGE   the entire amount showing in the window
>
> HALF   half the amount showing in the window
>
> MAX   the first line (BACKWARD) or the last line (FORWARD) to the top of the window
>
> *n*   *n* lines.
>
> For both the BACKWARD and FORWARD commands, when you specify PAGE, HALF, and *n*, the cursor stays on the command line. When you specify BACKWARD MAX, the cursor moves to the first character in the field; when you specify FORWARD MAX, the cursor is positioned after the last word in the text.

LEFT [PAGE | HALF | MAX | *n*]
RIGHT [PAGE | HALF | MAX | *n*]
> moves the contents of the window to the left or right the amount set by the HSCROLL command. You can also specify an amount to scroll left or right. Valid scroll amounts are
>
> PAGE   the entire amount showing in the window
>
> HALF   half the amount showing in the window
>
> MAX   to the left margin or the right margin, respectively
>
> *n*   *n* spaces.

TOP
BOTTOM
> scrolls to the first line in the window and moves the cursor to the first character or scrolls to the last line in the window and moves the cursor one space beyond the last character.

COLOR Command

You can change the color and highlighting of selected portions of a window. Use the COLOR command to specify the portion of the window you want to change, the color, and (optionally) a highlighting attribute.

The form of the COLOR command is

COLOR *fieldtype color* | NEXT [*highlight*]

Fieldtype is the area of the window or type of text you want to change. Note that support for color and highlighting attributes varies by terminals.

In all display manager windows except the NOTEPAD window, the COLOR command changes the default color and the color already displayed in the active window. In the NOTEPAD, SAS/AF, and SAS/FSP windows, the COLOR command changes only the default color.

See also the description of the COLOR MAP command in **SAS TEXT EDITOR** in this chapter.

Valid Field Types for All Windows

BACKGROUND
  background of the window
BANNER
  protected headings in the window including "Command===>"
BORDER
  lined border of the window and the window name
COMMAND
  unprotected field in the command line, where commands are entered
MESSAGE
  message line immediately below the command line.

Valid Field Types for Selected Windows

BYLINE
  BY statements in the OUTPUT window
DATA
  data lines in the OUTPUT window
ERROR
  error message lines in the LOG window
FOOTNOTE
  footnotes in the OUTPUT window
HEADER
  headings other than title headings in the OUTPUT window
NOTE
  note lines in the LOG window
NUMBERS
  line numbers in the PGM and NOTEPAD windows
SOURCE
  source lines in the LOG window
TEXT
  text areas of the PGM window
TITLE
  titles in the OUTPUT window.

Valid Colors

Color is the new color for the field. Valid colors* are

B blue	W white
R red	K black
G green	M magenta
C cyan	A gray | grey
P pink	N brown
Y yellow	O orange

Designing a Color Alternative: NEXT

Specifying NEXT instead of a color is an easy way to change the color of a field. The facility displays the field in a different color each time you execute the command, allowing you to choose among all available colors.

As an example, assign the following command to a function key:

```
color border next
```

Each time you press that function key, the command executes and the border of the window you are using changes to the next available color, one by one. Assign

```
color background next
```

to another function key to change the background color easily. You can do this with every field the COLOR command allows you to specify. Using NEXT with the COLOR command helps you design a new display combination quickly and easily.

Valid Highlighting Attributes

Highlight is the highlighting attribute for the field. With each new COLOR command, you must respecify a highlighting attribute; the previous attribute is not retained. Valid highlighting attributes are

H	highlight
U	underline
R	reverse video
B	blinking

Micro-to-Host-Link Commands

You can use micro-to-host-link commands to establish or discontinue a link between your PC and a remote mainframe or minicomputer system. For more information about establishing this link, see Appendix 1, "Micro-to-Host Link" and the *SAS Guide to the Micro-to-Host Link, Version 6 Edition*. Also, see RSUBMIT, a related command, in **PGM WINDOW: THE PROGRAM EDITOR**.

SIGNON [RLINK | *fileref* | '*actualfilename*']
establishes a link between the microcomputer you are using and a remote mainframe or minicomputer system. The SIGNON command

---

* Not all video devices support all colors, but an attempt is made to match a color to its closest counterpart.

requires a special file, called a script file, to establish the micro-to-host link. You can specify the script file to be used with the SIGNON command in one of three ways:

1. Omit the specification. This results in the default fileref (RLINK) being used to locate the script file. The RLINK fileref is defined as TSO.SCR by default in the AUTOEXEC.SAS file provided by SAS Institute.
2. Specify your own previously assigned fileref.
3. Enclose the actual name in quotes. This name can be a fully qualified path name or the name of a script file in your current directory.

No link is established if the SAS System cannot find the file. Use the SIGNOFF command to terminate the link.

SIGNOFF [RLINK | fileref | 'actualfilename']
terminates the link you established between your microcomputer and a remote mainframe or minicomputer system. The SIGNOFF command also requires a script file to terminate the link, and you can specify the script file with the SIGNOFF command in one of three ways:

1. Omit the specification. This results in the default fileref (RLINK) being used to locate the script file. The RLINK fileref is defined as TSO.SCR by default in the AUTOEXEC.SAS file provided by SAS Institute.
2. Specify your own previously assigned fileref.
3. Enclose the actual name in quotes. This name can be a fully qualified path name or the name of a script file in your current directory.

The Institute-supplied script files perform both SIGNON and SIGNOFF functions; therefore, you can use the same script file for both SIGNON and SIGNOFF commands. Ask your on-site SAS Software Consultant for information about how the script file applies to your site.

Cut and Paste Features

With display manager, you can cut and paste text within windows, across window boundaries, and from one window to another. By marking text—parts of lines, entire lines, blocks of text, or areas that cross window boundaries—you can copy information from one window to another and create independent files from many parts of a single window or from several windows at once.

Basic Commands

While other options and commands give you additional flexibility in manipulating and storing text, six basic commands form the core of the cut and paste features:

CUT
MARK
PASTE
SMARK
STORE
UNMARK

The MARK and SMARK commands identify the text you want to manipulate. Both the STORE and CUT commands store marked text in a temporary storage location called the *paste buffer*, which is in effect only for the current working SAS session. The STORE command copies the marked text into the paste buffer but leaves the original text intact and unmarks it. The CUT command deletes it from the window and copies it into the paste buffer. The PASTE command inserts marked text that you have previously stored in the paste buffer with the CUT or STORE command. The UNMARK command cancels the previous MARK command and allows you to restart the cut and paste operation. If you make a mistake or change your mind about a mark, use UNMARK and start over.

Additional commands Using additional commands and options, you can create more than one paste buffer, clear the contents of a paste buffer, and list existing paste buffers. See **Cut and Paste Global Commands**.

Where can you do what? You can copy and store information from all display manager windows, either for inserting in a window that permits editing or in a separate file for later use. Windows that permit editing, such as the PGM window in display manager and SAS procedure windows that use the SAS text editor, allow you to delete and insert text with the CUT and PASTE commands.

The commands that allow you to use the cut and paste features are listed by function and then defined below:

In all windows

to define and undefine information

MARK*
UNMARK
SMARK

to copy information and to place in paste buffer

STORE

to manage paste buffers

PCLEAR
PLIST

In the windows that use the SAS text editor, the PGM and NOTEPAD windows and various SAS/FSP and SAS/AF procedure windows

to delete information from window and
to place in paste buffer

CUT

to insert information

PASTE

---

* The MARK command is available in all display manager windows except the HELP and MENU windows. In those windows, use the SMARK command instead.

Cut and Paste Global Commands

CUT [APPEND][BUFFER=*pastebuffername*][LAST | ALL]

This command is available only in windows that use the SAS text editor. You can use it in the PGM and NOTEPAD windows of display manager and in SAS/AF and SAS/FSP procedure windows. See **SAS TEXT EDITOR** later in this chapter for more information.

MARK [CHAR | BLOCK]

identifies text so you can use it later with another command, such as CHANGE, CUT, FIND, or STORE.

If you want to look for a character or text string in a particular section of text, execute MARK to identify the area you want searched by the FIND or CHANGE command.

Also use the MARK command when you want to perform cut and paste operations. First indicate the text to be manipulated with the MARK command; then issue the CUT command to remove it from the display, or simply copy it with the STORE command and insert it elsewhere with the PASTE command.

How to mark information The easiest way to mark a string of text is to use a function key set to execute the MARK command. Position the cursor on the beginning of a text string and press the MARK function key. The first letter appears in reverse video. Move the cursor to the first position after the string and press the MARK key again. Now the whole string appears in reverse video. This mark is a character (CHAR) mark, the default. You can also mark text by first typing MARK on the command line. Then position your cursor at the beginning of a text string and press ENTER. Return your cursor to the command line and type MARK again. Move the cursor to the first position after the string and press ENTER again. Use the same procedure to execute other command-line commands.

To mark a block of text, set a function key to execute the MARK BLOCK command; indicate the top and bottom corners of the block. Position the cursor on the character you want to be the upper corner of the block, press MARK BLOCK, place it one position after the bottom corner, and press MARK BLOCK again. From any two corners, the SAS System calculates the desired block.

You can also have more than one marked string or block at a time. Simply remember that if you have more than one marked string or block of text when you execute a CUT or STORE command, you must specify either ALL (for all existing marks) or LAST (for only the mark last made).

Where can you mark? You can mark information displayed in a window, but not information that belongs to the descriptive format of a window, such as the command line and borders.

Use the MARK CHAR command to mark a continuous string of text spanning one line or more. **Screen 10.2** shows the result of using MARK CHAR, with the cursor positioned first on the first character of the SAS code and then to the right of the last character of the code.

Use the MARK BLOCK command to mark a rectangular block of text. **Screen 10.3** shows the result of using MARK BLOCK with the cursor positioned first on the first character of the SAS code and then to the right of the last character of code.

```
-PROGRAM EDITOR-
Command ===>

00001 data sales;
00002     input salesrep $ sales region $ machine $;
00003     cards;
00004 Stafer      9664    east      SM
00005 Young      22969    east      SM
00006 Stride     27253    east      SM
00007 Topin      86432    east      C
00008 Spark      99210    east      C
00009 Vetter     38928    west      C
00010 Curci      21531    west      SM
00011 Marco      79345    west      C
00012 Greco      18523    west      SM
00013 Ryan       32915    west      SM
00014 Tomas      42109    west      SM
00015 Thalman    94320    south     C
00016 Moore      25718    south     SM
00017 Allen      64700    south     C
00018 Stelam     27634    south     SM
00019 Farlow     32719    north     SM
00020 Smith      38712    north     SM
00021 Wilson     97214    north     C
                                                    -ZOOM-
```

Screen 10.2 Using the MARK CHAR command

```
-PROGRAM EDITOR-
Command ===>

00001 data sales;
00002     input salesrep $ sales region $ machine $;
00003     cards;
00004 Stafer      9664    east      SM
00005 Young      22969    east      SM
00006 Stride     27253    east      SM
00007 Topin      86432    east      C
00008 Spark      99210    east      C
00009 Vetter     38928    west      C
00010 Curci      21531    west      SM
00011 Marco      79345    west      C
00012 Greco      18523    west      SM
00013 Ryan       32915    west      SM
00014 Tomas      42109    west      SM
00015 Thalman    94320    south     C
00016 Moore      25718    south     SM
00017 Allen      64700    south     C
00018 Stelam     27634    south     SM
00019 Farlow     32719    north     SM
00020 Smith      38712    north     SM
00021 Wilson     97214    north     C
                                                    -ZOOM-
```

Screen 10.3 Using the MARK BLOCK command

336   Chapter 10

The MARK BLOCK command is especially useful for marking tabular data.

When is marked text unmarked?   Marked text is automatically returned to normal status when you execute a STORE command. The CUT command deletes the marked text and places it in a paste buffer so that it can be inserted elsewhere with a PASTE command. The STORE command simply copies the marked text and makes it available for later use with the PASTE command.

If you do not intend to execute a CUT or STORE command on marked text, you must return it to normal status yourself. Use the UNMARK command to free text you marked by mistake or text that you no longer need for use with the FIND and CHANGE commands.

A quick method   You can combine the execution of a second MARK command with a CUT or STORE command if only one string is marked. For example, use MARK to indicate the beginning of a text string. Then move the cursor to the character following the string and press the CUT or STORE function key instead of the MARK key. The end of the string is marked automatically, the CUT or STORE command is executed, and the string is unmarked.

PASTE [CHAR | BLOCK][BUFFER=*pastebuffername*]
This command is available in the PGM and NOTEPAD windows of display manager. See **SAS Text Editor Commands** later in this chapter for more information.

PCLEAR [BUFFER=*pastebuffername*]
clears the contents of any paste buffer. Execute

    pclear

to delete the contents of the default paste buffer. Use the BUFFER= option to clear a named paste buffer. For example,

    pclear buffer=taxpaste

clears the contents of a paste buffer named TAXPASTE.

PLIST
displays a list of the names of all current paste buffers in the LOG window.

SMARK
identifies an area on the screen that you want to copy later with the STORE command. SMARK is similar to the MARK command in that you use it to identify what you want to capture later with a STORE command. However, SMARK differs from the MARK command in two important ways:

1. SMARK identifies an area on the physical screen, rather than specific sections of text. When you later execute a STORE command, whatever information is displayed in that portion of the screen at the time the STORE is executed is copied, not what was displayed at the time you executed SMARK.
2. SMARK allows you to mark a screen area that includes all portions of a window, including nonscrollable sections. You can also cross window borders with SMARK.

How to identify a screen area with SMARK   SMARK works like the MARK BLOCK command. Identify the top corner with the cursor position and press a function key set to execute the SMARK command.

Then position the cursor one character after the bottom corner of the block and press the same function key and then ENTER. From any two corners, the SAS System calculates the desired block. You can also use the SMARK command-line command.

STORE [APPEND][BUFFER=*pastebuffername*][LAST | ALL]
copies marked text in the current window and stores the copy in a paste buffer. Remember that the paste buffer does not store information beyond your current working SAS session. The STORE command, unlike the CUT command, does not remove marked strings from their original location.

More than one mark If more than one mark exists when you execute a STORE command, you must specify ALL or LAST. If you specify LAST, only the most recently made mark is copied and all other marks are unmarked. If you want to store all current marks, specify ALL.

Add to existing buffer or replace? Specify APPEND if you want text to be added to information in an existing paste buffer; if you do not specify APPEND, the information being copied replaces any information currently in that buffer.

Naming paste buffers When you store text strings, copies are stored in the default paste buffer unless you specify a name. Because you can specify a paste buffer name, you can create additional paste buffers. To insert information stored in a named paste buffer, you must specify the buffer's name when you execute the PASTE command.

For example, if you create a paste buffer with the command

```
store buffer=buffer1
```

you must specify BUFFER1 in the PASTE command, as in

```
paste buffer=buffer1
```

to insert information stored in BUFFER1. Follow the same naming rules for your paste buffer as for SAS data sets and SAS variables: make it one to eight characters; start with a letter (A-Z); and continue with letters, numbers, or underscores.

See also the CUT, MARK, and PASTE commands.

UNMARK [ALL]
returns marked text to normal status. Position the cursor somewhere within a marked string or block of text to indicate which text to unmark, and execute UNMARK with a function key or from the command line. Specify ALL to unmark all marked text in the current window.

See the CUT, FIND, MARK, and STORE commands.

SAS TEXT EDITOR

The SAS text editor is a powerful full-screen editor available in the SAS Display Manager System and in SAS/FSP and SAS/AF software.

Using the Full-Screen Editor

In **Executing Display Manager Window Commands**, you have already seen how to execute command-line commands. With the SAS text editor, you can use command-line commands to scroll the contents of the window, to manage your files, to change the color of various fields in the window for easier viewing, to assign highlighting attributes, to search for text strings, and to move and store blocks of text.

To perform many text editing tasks, you can use line commands. You can use line commands to move, delete, copy, and insert data lines. You can execute these commands either by entering them directly—typing them over a line number and pressing ENTER—or by positioning the cursor and pressing a function key defined to execute that command. You can also type the command, preceded by a colon, on the command line, position the cursor, and type ENTER.

Entering Line Commands Directly

To enter a line command directly, type the command over a line number and press the ENTER key. To number or unnumber data entry lines, use the NUMBERS ON or NUMBERS OFF command. Type the command on the command line and press ENTER.

Examples below include single line commands, line commands with options, line commands requiring target commands, and block commands. Note the underscore (_) marking the cursor position in several of the examples.

Single line command   As an example, to insert a new line for entering text, type I, the insert line command, on any part of a line number:

```
0i 01 data line one
00002 data line two
00003 data line three
```

Press ENTER. One new line is inserted between the first and second lines:

```
00001 data line one
00002 _
00003 data line two
00004 data line three
```

Line command with option   Some line commands, for example, the I line command, allow you to specify an option for which you supply the value, such as a number. To specify how many lines to insert, follow the I line command with a number, such as 3, and a blank space:

```
i3 01 data line one
00002 data line two
00003 data line three
```

Press ENTER. Three new lines are inserted between the first and second lines:

```
00001 data line one
00002 _
00003
00004
00005 data line two
00006 data line three
```

Line command requiring a target command   The following example shows how to use the M (move) and A (after) line commands:

```
m0001 Move the first line
a0002 after the second line
00003 with the m (move) and a (after) line commands.
```

The first line is moved to the second line:

```
00001 after the second line
00002 Move the first line
00003 with the m (move) and a (after) line commands.
```

Block line command You can also use line commands to affect blocks of lines. The following example shows how to use the MM (move) and A (after) line commands to move a block of text:

```
mm001 Move the first two lines
mm002 after the third line
a0003 with the mm (move block) and a (after) line commands.
```

The third line becomes the first line:

```
00001 with the mm (move block) and a (after) line commands.
00002 Move the first two lines
00003 after the third line
```

Executing Line Commands without Line Numbers

If your data lines are not numbered, you can still execute line and block line commands without having to use the NUMBERS ON command to display line numbers. Type the line command, preceded by a colon (:), on the command line; then use the CURSOR keys to position the cursor on the line you want to be affected by the line command, and press ENTER. You can also execute a line command with a function key when line numbers are not displayed. Position the cursor where you want the command to take effect, and press a function key that is set to execute the line command. Use the KEYS command to find out which function keys are set to which commands. The line command must be preceded by a colon (:).

SAS Text Editor Commands

Valid SAS text editor commands are listed below by function; command definitions follow.

Command-line commands

General editing	File management	Cut and Paste
AUTOADD	FILE	CUT
AUTOFLOW	INCLUDE	MARK*
AUTOWRAP		PASTE
BOUNDS		PCLEAR*
CAPS	**Scrolling**	PLIST*
CHANGE	BACKWARD	SMARK*
CLEAR	BOTTOM	STORE*
COLOR	FORWARD	UNMARK*
CURSOR	HSCROLL	
FILL	LEFT	
FIND	*n*	
INDENT	RIGHT	
NUMBERS	TOP	
RCHANGE	VSCROLL	
RESET		
RFIND		*(continued on next page)*

---

* These commands are global and can be used in all display manager windows. They are defined in **DISPLAY MANAGER GLOBAL COMMANDS** earlier in this chapter.

(continued from previous page)

Line commands

Single line commands	Block commands
A,B	CC
C[n]	CCL
CL	CCU
CU	DD
D[n]	JJC[n]
I[n] | IA[n] | IB[n]	JJL[n]
JC[n]	JJR[n]
JL[n]	MM
JR[n]	>>[n]
M[n]	<<[n]
>[n]	RR[n]
<[n]	
O	**Special line commands**
R[n]	COLS
TF[n]	MASK
TS[n]	TABS, TA[n]

Command-Line Command Definitions

AUTOADD [ON | OFF]
    controls the automatic insertion of new lines as you scroll forward past existing text. If AUTOADD is off, you must execute another command, such as the I (insert) line command, to insert new data lines. If you do not specify ON or OFF, AUTOADD works like an on/off switch; type it once to turn it on and again to turn it off.
    See also the I (insert) line command.

AUTOFLOW [ON | OFF]
    controls the automatic flowing of text as you bring it into the text editor with an INCLUDE or PASTE command. If you do not specify ON or OFF, AUTOFLOW works like an on/off switch.
    When text is flowed, the left and right boundaries are determined by previous executions of the INDENT and BOUNDS commands.
    See also the BOUNDS, INCLUDE, INDENT, and PASTE commands described below.

AUTOWRAP [ON | OFF]
    controls whether text that cannot fit on one line is automatically moved (wrapped) to the next line. If you do not specify ON or OFF, AUTOWRAP works like an on/off switch.
    AUTOWRAP ON allows you to enter text continuously without moving the cursor to the next line. It also allows you to use the INCLUDE command to bring a file with a longer line length into the text editor without truncating any text. When INDENT is set to on, you can "wrap" text that is indented and keep the indention.
    See also the INCLUDE and INDENT commands described below.

BACKWARD [PAGE | HALF | MAX | *n*]
: moves the contents of the text editor backward (toward the beginning) the amount set by the VSCROLL command. You can also specify an amount to scroll backward. Valid scroll amounts are

    PAGE the entire amount showing in the window
    HALF half the amount showing in the window
    MAX   the first line to the top of the window
    n   *n* lines.

    See the FORWARD and VSCROLL commands described below.

BOTTOM
: scrolls to the last line of text and positions the cursor to the right of the last character.

BOUNDS *n1 n2*
: identifies the left- and right-hand boundaries of the section of the window that you want to be affected when text is flowed, by either the TF (text flow) or AUTOFLOW command.

    For example, if you want the text flowed between columns 10 and 60, inclusive, execute

    ```
    bounds 10 60; indent off
    ```

    Each time text is flowed after this BOUNDS command is executed, it is flowed between spaces 10 and 60, inclusive, until you issue another BOUNDS or INDENT command. If INDENT is set on, you must turn it off for the left boundary to be in effect. To determine the current bounds setting, specify BOUNDS without an argument.

    See also the TF (text flow) line command and the AUTOFLOW and INDENT commands.

CAPS [OFF | ON]
: With CAPS ON, all text entered or lines modified afterward are translated into uppercase letters when you press either ENTER or a function key or when you move the cursor from the line. Character strings for the FIND and CHANGE commands are also translated into uppercase. Enclose your character string in quotes for the FIND or CHANGE command if you do not want lowercase letters in the string translated into uppercase. All text is interpreted as entered when CAPS OFF is in effect.

    The CAPS setting remains in effect for a window until the session ends or until it is changed by another CAPS command. If you execute the CAPS command without specifying ON or OFF, it works like an on/off switch.

    To change the case of previously typed text, see the CL, CU, CCL, and CCU line commands.

CHANGE *'string1' 'string2'* [NEXT | FIRST | LAST | PREV | ALL]
    [WORD | SUFFIX | PREFIX]
: changes one or more occurrences of *string1* to *string2*. Follow the CHANGE command with a string of characters to be changed, a space, and then the new string, or type the strings on the command line and press the CHANGE function key.

    When text is marked If any text has been marked with the MARK command, the CHANGE command searches for and alters only the marked text. *String2* can be longer than *string1* if the resulting block of text is no longer than the marked space. Remove all marks if you want to search the rest of the file.

Search order You can specify in the CHANGE command that the SAS System search for and alter the next occurrence of the specified string after the current cursor location, the first or last occurrence of the string in the file regardless of current cursor location, or the previous occurrence, which depends upon the current cursor position. If you specify ALL, you receive a message that reports how many times the string occurs in the entire file, and each occurrence is changed. By default, the CHANGE command searches for and changes the next occurrence of the specified string after the current cursor location.

Context You can also specify one of the following options: PREFIX, SUFFIX, or WORD. If you do not specify one of these, *string1* is changed to *string2*, regardless of context. In the CHANGE command, as in the FIND command, a WORD is one or more symbols preceded and followed by a delimiter. A delimiter is any symbol other than an uppercase letter, a lowercase letter, a digit, or an underscore.

Special characters and embedded blanks Remember to use single or double quotes to enclose strings with special characters or embedded blanks. Single word strings require no quotation marks, for example,

```
c your my
c 'your data set' 'my data set'
```

Also enclose your string in single or double quotes if you have specified CAPS ON and you do not want lowercase letters in the string translated into uppercase letters. For example,

```
c 'Bob' 'Bill'
```

If your string contains a single quote, such as

```
c "Bob's" "Bill's"
```

enclose the string in double quotes.

You can combine the use of the CHANGE command (without the ALL option) and RFIND function key (or command). For example, after you enter a CHANGE command, you can press the RFIND function key to locate the next occurrence of *string1* before pressing RCHANGE to change it to *string2*.

Also see the FIND, RCHANGE, and RFIND commands described below.

CLEAR
  removes the contents of all text lines.

COLOR MAP *fromcolor* [*fromhighlight*] *tocolor* [*tohighlight*]
  searches all text to find all occurrences of the first color and/or highlighting attributes specified and changes them to the second color and/or highlighting attributes specified.
  Note: in the SAS Display Manager System, COLOR MAP is valid only in the NOTEPAD window. It is available in SAS/FSP and SAS/AF facilities that store color and highlighting information, such as edit mode of the FSLETTER procedure, screen customization mode of the FSEDIT procedure, and building entries in the BUILD procedure.

COLOR NUMBERS | TEXT | MTEXT *color* [*highlight*]
  sets the color or color and highlighting attributes for the three fields

below in addition to the fields available in the global COLOR command:

- NUMBERS — line numbers in the text editor.
- TEXT — text displayed in the text editor. Note that this option sets new default color and highlighting attributes, as well as the settings for existing text in the PGM window. In the NOTEPAD window it sets only the new default color and highlighting attributes.
- MTEXT — marked string or block of text. COLOR MTEXT is valid only in the NOTEPAD window and in SAS/AF and SAS/FSP facilities that store color and highlighting information, such as edit mode of the FSLETTER procedure and screen customization mode of the FSEDIT procedure.

CURSOR
: moves the cursor to the command line. The CURSOR command is designed to be executed with a function key. You can also press the HOME key to move the cursor to the command line.

CUT [APPEND][BUFFER=*pastebuffername*][LAST | ALL]
: removes marked text strings in the current window and stores them in a paste buffer.

   More than one mark If more than one mark exists when you execute a CUT command, you must specify ALL or LAST. If you specify LAST, only the most recently made mark is cut and all other marks are unmarked. If you want to cut all current marks, specify ALL.

   Add to an existing buffer or replace? Specify APPEND if you want text to be added to information in an existing paste buffer; if you do not specify APPEND, the information being cut replaces any information currently in that buffer.

   Naming paste buffers When you cut text strings, they are stored in the default paste buffer unless you specify a name. Because you can specify a paste buffer name, you can create additional paste buffers. To insert information stored in a named paste buffer, you must specify the buffer's name when you execute the PASTE command.

   For example, if you create a paste buffer with the command

   ```
   cut buffer=buffer1
   ```

   you must specify BUFFER1 in the PASTE command, as in

   ```
   paste buffer=buffer1
   ```

   to insert information stored in BUFFER1.

   A quick method If only one piece of text is marked with the MARK command, you can use this quick method of executing MARK and STORE or CUT commands. Use MARK to indicate the beginning of the text string; when you position the cursor after the last character in the string, press the STORE or CUT function key instead of the MARK key a second time. The text is marked automatically, the STORE or CUT command is executed, and the string is unmarked.

   Cut and paste features The special cut and paste facility includes several important global commands that you can use in all display manager windows. See the related commands MARK, SMARK, STORE, and UNMARK in **DISPLAY MANAGER GLOBAL COMMANDS** earlier in this chapter. Also see the PASTE text editor command below.

FILE [*fileref* | '*actualfilename*'][TABS]
: writes the entire contents of the text editor into an external file.

How to specify a file You can specify a previously assigned fileref or an actual file name. If you specify an actual file name, you must enclose it in single or double quotes. You can specify either a file name in your current working directory or a fully qualified path name. If you do not specify a fileref or a file name, the file in the previous INCLUDE or FILE command is used. Note that if the file already exists, the FILE command overwrites it.

Sending text to a printer To send text from the window directly to a printer attached to your PC, execute the command

```
file 'prn:'
```

TABS option By default, the text editor stores spacing between text in a file "as is." Specify TABS if you want the text editor to compress a file by storing spacing in the text as "tabs." Storing this spacing as tabs can save considerable storage space when the file is stored on disk.

FILL ['*fill-character*'][*n*]
places fill-characters beginning at the current cursor position. By default, the space is filled with underscores from the current cursor position either to the end of a line or to the space before the next nonblank character, whichever occurs first.

You can specify a fill-character other than the default underscore (_) by specifying it after the command and enclosing it in single quotes. Once you specify a new fill-character, it remains in effect until you specify another. For example,

```
fill '?'
```

places a ? as the fill-character at the cursor location. You can also specify an exact number of fill-characters. The command

```
fill 5
```

places five underscores (the default) at the cursor location.

FIND *characterstring* [NEXT | FIRST | LAST | PREV | ALL]
          [WORD | PREFIX | SUFFIX]
searches for a specified string of characters. Enclose the string in single or double quotes if it contains embedded blanks or special characters. You can execute the FIND command by typing it on the command line or by typing the character string on the command line and pressing the FIND function key.

When text is marked If text is marked, the FIND command searches only the marked text. Remove all marks if you want to search the rest of the file.

Search order You can specify in the FIND command that the SAS System search for the next occurrence of the specified string after the current cursor location, the first or last occurrence of the string in the file regardless of your current cursor location, or the previous occurrence, which depends on the current cursor position. If the cursor is on the command line, the NEXT option starts at the top of the current screen and the PREV option at the end of the last line of the current screen. If you specify ALL, you receive a message that reports how many times the string occurs in the entire file. By default, the FIND command searches for the next occurrence of the specified string after the current cursor location.

Context You can also specify PREFIX, SUFFIX, or WORD. If you do not specify one of these options, the SAS System searches for each occurrence of the string, regardless of context.

In the FIND command, a WORD is one or more symbols preceded and followed by a delimiter. A delimiter is any symbol other than an uppercase letter, a lowercase letter, a digit, or an underscore. For example,

```
abc123
```

is a word, but

```
abc$123
```

is two words separated by the delimiter $. The option PREFIX or SUFFIX is treated just as its grammatical definition. In the first example, ABC123, you can specify ABC as a prefix and 123 as a suffix. In the second example, ABC$123, ABC and 123 are words, not a prefix and a suffix.

Special characters and embedded blanks   Use single or double quotes to enclose strings with special characters or embedded blanks. The first example requires no quotation marks:

```
f your
```

The second example does:

```
f 'your data set'
```

Also enclose your string in quotes if you have executed the command CAPS ON and you do not want lowercase letters in the string translated into uppercase letters. For example, if you have specified CAPS ON, the following command finds the next occurrence of BOB instead of Bob:

```
f Bob
```

If your string contains a single quote, such as

```
f 'Bob''s'
```

enclose the string in double quotes:

```
f "Bob's"
```

See also the CHANGE, RCHANGE, and RFIND commands described in this section.

FORWARD [PAGE | HALF | MAX | n]
  moves the contents of the text editor forward (toward the end) the amount set by the VSCROLL command. You can also specify an amount to scroll forward. Valid scroll amounts are

  PAGE   the entire amount showing in the window

  HALF   half the amount showing in the window

  MAX   the last line to the top of the window; positions the cursor after the last word in the text

  n   n lines.

  See the BACKWARD and VSCROLL commands.

HSCROLL PAGE | HALF | MAX | n
  specifies the default horizontal scroll amount for the LEFT and RIGHT scrolling commands. Specify one of the following:

  PAGE   the entire amount showing in the window

  HALF   half the amount showing in the window

MAX   the leftmost or rightmost portion showing in the window

n   n horizontal spaces.

INCLUDE [fileref | 'actualfilename'] [NOTABS]

allows you to bring an external file into the text editor. The lines of the file brought in are inserted at the end of the text currently displayed or wherever you specify with an A or B line command.

How to specify a file   You can specify a previously assigned fileref or an actual file name. If you specify an actual file name, you must enclose it in single quotes. You can specify either a file name in your current working directory or a fully qualified path name. If you do not specify a fileref or a file name, the file specified in the previous INCLUDE or FILE command is used. See the FILE command earlier in this chapter.

File with a long line length   If you bring in lines from a file that has a longer line length than the text editor, one of two things occurs, depending on the AUTOWRAP setting. With AUTOWRAP OFF, the lines are truncated. With AUTOWRAP ON, excess words are printed on a new line. See the AUTOWRAP command.

NOTABS option: Specify NOTABS to prevent the automatic expansion of tab characters in the file. The text editor, by default, uses a standard eight-character tab.

Automatic text flowing   If you want text automatically flowed when you bring a file into the text editor with the INCLUDE command, execute AUTOFLOW ON before you execute the INCLUDE command. Use the BOUNDS and INDENT commands to indicate the right and left text boundaries and how you want indented text to be treated. See the AUTOFLOW, BOUNDS, and INDENT commands.

INDENT [ON | OFF]

allows indentation at the left margin to remain when text is flowed or automatically wrapped to the next line.

The INDENT command works like an on/off switch. You can also specify ON or OFF.

See the AUTOFLOW, AUTOWRAP, and BOUNDS commands and the TF line command.

LEFT [PAGE | HALF | MAX | n]

moves the contents of the text editor left the amount set by the HSCROLL command. You can also specify an amount to scroll left. Valid scroll amounts are

PAGE   the entire amount showing in the window

HALF   half the amount showing in the window

MAX   to the left margin

n   n horizontal spaces.

See the RIGHT and HSCROLL commands.

MARK [CHAR | BLOCK]

identifies text you want to manipulate. See **DISPLAY MANAGER GLOBAL COMMANDS** earlier in this chapter for a complete description.

n

scrolls line n to the top of the window.

NUMBERS [ON | OFF]

turns on or off line numbers for data lines in the PGM and NOTEPAD windows in display manager and also in SAS/AF and SAS/FSP windows.

If your window already contains text, all data are shifted to the right, and the line numbers appear on the left. When line numbers are displayed, you can use them to execute line commands. Execute NUMBERS OFF to remove line numbers and shift text back to the left. If you do not specify ON or OFF, the NUMBERS command works like an on/off switch.

See also the RESET command and the line commands, and the section **Entering Line Commands Directly** in this chapter.

PASTE [CHAR | BLOCK] [BUFFER=*pastebuffername*]

inserts at the cursor location text stored in the default paste buffer or in the paste buffer you specify.

How information is inserted   If you specify

```
paste
```

with no options, the contents of the default paste buffer are inserted as a text string or a block, depending on which you specified when you marked it. For example, if you marked it with the command

```
mark char
```

a text string is inserted. If you marked it with the command

```
mark block
```

a block of text is inserted. You can, however, insert information using either option with the PASTE command, regardless of how you marked it.

Using the two PASTE options   The following example shows the text before the paste operation:

```
00001 HERE IS TEXT._MORE TEXT IS HERE.
00002 HERE IS TEXT. MORE TEXT IS HERE.
```

When you execute

```
paste char
```

the default paste buffer, a text string, is inserted at the cursor location. Any text that followed the insert location is moved to the right. Any excess text is placed on the next line.

In this example, the cursor is positioned between the two sentences; the results are

```
00001 HERE IS TEXT. paste line one.
00002 paste line two. MORE TEXT IS HERE.
00003 HERE IS TEXT. MORE TEXT IS HERE.
```

When you execute

```
paste block
```

a block of text is inserted at the cursor location. Information currently displayed is moved to the right. Should this cause truncation, the PASTE command is not executed and you receive an error message. Here are the results:

```
00001 HERE IS TEXT. paste line one. MORE TEXT IS HERE.
00002 HERE IS TEXT. paste line two. MORE TEXT IS HERE.
00003
```

Inserting a named paste buffer Because you can name paste buffers, many paste buffers can exist at any one time. To insert a named paste buffer, instead of the default, follow the PASTE command (or the type of paste if one is specified) with BUFFER= and the name of that paste buffer.

Cut and paste features The special cut and paste facility includes several important global commands that you can use in all display manager windows. See the related commands MARK, SMARK, STORE, and UNMARK in **DISPLAY MANAGER GLOBAL COMMANDS**. Also see the CUT text editor command above.

PCLEAR
   clears the contents of a paste buffer. See **DISPLAY MANAGER GLOBAL COMMANDS** for a complete description.

PLIST
   displays a list of current paste buffers in the LOG window. See **DISPLAY MANAGER GLOBAL COMMANDS** for a complete description.

RCHANGE
   continues to find and change a string of characters specified in the previous CHANGE command.
      See also the CHANGE, FIND, and RFIND commands.

RESET
   removes any pending line commands.

RFIND
   continues the search for a string of characters previously specified in a FIND command.
      See also the FIND, CHANGE, and RCHANGE commands.

RIGHT [PAGE | HALF | MAX | n]
   scrolls the contents of the text editor right the amount set by the HSCROLL command. You can also specify an amount to scroll right. Valid scroll amounts are

   PAGE   the entire amount showing in the window
   HALF   half the amount showing in the window
   MAX   to the right margin
   n   n horizontal spaces.

   See the LEFT and HSCROLL commands.

SMARK
   identifies an area on the screen that you want to copy later with the STORE command. See **DISPLAY MANAGER GLOBAL COMMANDS** for a complete description.

STORE [APPEND] [BUFFER=*pastebuffername*][LAST | ALL]
   copies marked text in the current window and stores the copy in a paste buffer. See **DISPLAY MANAGER GLOBAL COMMANDS** for a complete description.

TOP
   scrolls to the first line in the window and moves the cursor to the first character.

UNMARK [ALL]
   returns marked text to normal status. See **DISPLAY MANAGER GLOBAL COMMANDS** for a complete description.

SAS Display Manager System

VSCROLL PAGE | HALF | MAX | n
: specifies the default vertical scroll amounts for the BACKWARD and FORWARD scroll commands. Specify one of the following:

　　PAGE　the entire amount showing in the window

　　HALF　half the amount showing in the window

　　MAX　the topmost or bottommost portion showing in the window

　　n　n lines.

Line Command Definitions*

A,B
: *After* and *Before*: mark the target position of one or more lines being moved or copied with a C, M, CC, MM, or INCLUDE command. Indicate an A (after) on the number of the line you want the source line(s) to follow. Use a B (before) to mark the line you want the source line(s) to precede.

C[n]
: *Copy:* copies one or more lines to another location in the file indicated by a target line command. Indicate C on the number of the line to be copied. Then indicate an A on the number of the line you want the copied line to follow, a B on the number of the line you want it to precede, or an O on the line you want it to overlay. You can also specify n number of lines to be copied by following C with a number and a blank space.

CC
: *Copy (block):* copies a block of lines to another location in the file indicated by a target line command. Indicate CC on the line numbers of the first and last lines of the block of lines to be copied.

CCL
: *Case Lower (block):* sets all characters in a designated block of lines to lowercase. Indicate CCL on the line numbers of the first and last lines of the block of lines to be converted to lowercase.

CCU
: *Case Upper (block):* sets all characters in a designated block of lines to uppercase. Indicate CCU on the line numbers of the first and last lines of the block of lines to be converted to uppercase.

CL
: *Case Lower:* sets all characters on a designated line to lowercase.

COLS
: *Columns:* displays a line that marks the horizontal spaces (columns) in the text editor. Use the RESET command or the D (delete) line command in the first column position to remove the COLS line.**

CU
: *Case Upper:* sets all characters on a designated line to uppercase.

---

* You cannot issue a line command when text is marked.

** Now a line command, the COLS command was previously a global command.

D[*n*]   *Delete*: deletes one or more lines. Indicate D on the line number of the line to be deleted. By default, one line is deleted. To delete more than one line, follow D with a number and a blank space.

DD   *Delete* (block): deletes a block of lines. Indicate DD on the line numbers of the first and last lines of the block of lines to be deleted.

I[*n*] | IA[*n*]   *Insert After*: inserts one or more new lines. By default, one line is inserted after the line on which you execute the I or IA command. To insert more than one line, follow I with a number and a blank space. See also the IB command below.
    See the MASK command below to insert lines with a defined content other than a blank line.

IB[*n*]   *Insert Before*: inserts one or more lines before the line on which you enter the IB command. By default, only one line is inserted. To insert more than one line, follow I with with a number. See also the I and IA commands.

JC[*n*]   *Justify Center*: centers line of text. You can specify a number to indicate a position other than the center of the line to be used for centering the text.

JJC[*n*]   *Justify Center* (block): centers the text on a designated block of lines. Indicate JJC on the line numbers of the first and last lines of the block of lines to be centered. You can specify a number to indicate a position, other than the center of the line to be used for centering the text.

JJL[*n*]   *Justify Left* (block): aligns a designated block of text at the left margin. Indicate JJL on the line numbers of the first and last lines of the block of lines to be left-aligned. You can specify *n* to indicate a left boundary other than the margin of the window.

JJR[*n*]   *Justify Right* (block): aligns a designated block of text at the right margin. Indicate JJR on the line numbers of the first and last lines of the block of lines to be right-aligned. You can specify *n* to indicate a right boundary other than the margin of the window.

JL[*n*]   *Justify Left*: aligns a line of text at the left margin. You can specify *n* to indicate a left boundary other than the margin of a window.

JR[*n*]   *Justify Right*: aligns a line of text at the right margin. You can specify *n* to indicate a right boundary other than the margin of a window.

M[*n*]   *Move*: moves one or more lines to another location in the file indicated by a target line command. Indicate M on the line number of the line to be moved. If you move more than one line, follow M with a number and a blank space. Then specify an A on the number of the line you want the moved line to follow, a B on the line you want it to precede, or an O on the line you want it to overlay.

MASK *Mask*: defines the initial contents of a new line. Type MASK over a line number and press ENTER. Then type on the MASK line whatever characters you want to repeat. After you define a MASK, a line with the contents of the MASK line is inserted each time you use the I (insert), IA (insert after), or IB (insert before) line commands.

    The MASK line remains in effect for the text editor in the procedure you are using until you change it. To redefine it, simply type over the text on the MASK line. To return to the default (a blank line), blank out any characters on the MASK line, and use the RESET command or the D (delete) line command in column 1 to remove the display of the MASK line. The MASK remains in effect even when it is not displayed.

MM *Move* (block): moves a block of lines to another location in the file, indicated by a target line command. Indicate the block to be moved with an MM line command on the first and last line numbers of the block.

>[n] *Shift Right*: shifts text one or more spaces to the right. Indicate > or > followed by a number and a blank space on the number of the line to be shifted. Note that a text shift command allows no loss of text. The default is one space.

<[n] *Shift Left*: shifts text one or more spaces to the left. Indicate < or < followed by a number and a blank space on the number of the line to be shifted. Note that a text shift command allows no loss of text. The default is one space.

>>[n] *Shift Right* (block): shifts a block of lines one or more spaces to the right. Indicate >> or >> followed by a number and a blank space on the number of the first line of the block to be shifted and another >>n or >> on the last line number of the block. Note that a text block shift command allows no loss of text. The default is one space.

<<[n] *Shift Left* (block): shifts a block of lines one or more spaces to the left. Indicate << or << followed by a number and a blank space on the number of the first line of the block to be shifted and another <<n or << on the last number of the block. Note that a text block shift command allows no loss of text. The default is one space.

O *Overlay*: marks the target position for a C, M, CC, or MM line command. Indicate the O (overlay) line command on the line number that you want the source line, or the moved or copied line, to overlay. Characters from the source line overlay blank or null spaces on the target line, the line marked with the O line command.

If any characters occupy the same positions on the source and target lines, the characters on the target line remain, and characters from the source line do not appear. If you are executing the M (move) command, you receive an error message and the line intended to be moved remains in its original position.

R[n] *Repeat:* repeats one or more times the line on which the command is executed. To repeat a line more than once, follow R with a number and a blank space.

RR[n] *Repeat* (block): repeats a block of lines. Indicate RR on the numbers of the first and last lines of the block of lines to be repeated. RR followed by a number and a blank space repeats the block *n* times. You can specify *n* on the first or last RR command or on both.

TABS *Tabs:* allows you to indicate tab settings. When
TAn   you execute TABS, a tabs line is displayed. Position the cursor and type a T to indicate each tab stop.

If you want to indicate tab stops at regular intervals, you can use the TA line command followed by a number and a blank space. For example, execute

```
ta15
```

to display the tab settings line with tab stops set every 15 spaces. You can then make any further alterations, such as deleting or adding tab stops or changing the position of one or more tabs.

When tabs are set, use the TAB key to move from one tab stop to another. (The TAB key also moves the cursor to the beginning of the next or previous unprotected field.) You can also assign a function key to execute TABS.

To remove the tab settings line, use the RESET command. You can also use the D (delete) line command. The tab settings remain in effect until you change them and whether or not the tabs line is displayed.

TF[n] *Text Flow:* flows a paragraph by removing trailing blanks from each line until the next blank line. You can use the TF (text flow) line command to move text into wasted space left at ends of lines, especially after performing insertions and deletions. Either type TF on a line number, position the cursor where you want the text flowing to begin, and press ENTER, or position the cursor and press the :TF function key.

You can follow the TF command with a number and a blank space to specify the right boundary. This right boundary specification temporarily overrides the one set by the BOUNDS command, which otherwise affects the right boundary used by the TF command. The INDENT command also affects the TF command. If the INDENT feature is on, any left boundary indentations remain intact when text is flowed. See the BOUNDS and INDENT commands.

TS[n] *Text Split*: moves text following the current cursor position to another line and inserts an extra blank line for insertion of new text. Either type TS on a line number, position the cursor where you want the text to split, and press ENTER, or position the cursor and press the :TS function key. Follow TS with a number and a blank space to insert more than one blank line when the text is split. See the I (insert) line command for inserting space between lines rather than within the text of a line.

PGM WINDOW: THE PROGRAM EDITOR

You have already seen in the previous section how the SAS text editor provides you with full-screen editing capabilities. The PGM window, shown in **Screen 10.4**, is the SAS PROGRAM EDITOR window, where you can use all of the SAS text editor commands. You can use it to enter and edit your program statements, to submit program statements to the SAS System for execution, and to manage your files. You can save the contents of the PGM window to a file. You can also copy an existing file containing SAS program statements or data into the PGM window. After you have entered and edited your program, submit your job to the SAS System for execution using the SUBMIT command.

Submitting SAS Programs

Submitting a SAS program to the SAS System for execution is as simple as issuing one command or pressing one function key. When you are satisfied with your program statements, type

    submit

on the command line and press ENTER or press a function key set to execute the SUBMIT command.

Note: in the PGM window, the SUBMIT and END commands do the same thing; they submit statements to the SAS System for execution.

The SAS log is displayed in the LOG window, and output is displayed in the OUTPUT window. If you want a better view of your SAS log or output, move the cursor to the appropriate window (or execute the LOG or OUTPUT command on the command line or with a function key) and use the ZOOM command to make the window occupy the full-screen area.

```
┌PROGRAM EDITOR──────────────────────────────────────┐
│Command ===>                                        │
│                                                    │
│00001 data sales;                                   │
│00002    input salesrep $ sales region $ machine $; │
│00003    cards;                                     │
│00004 Stafer     9664    east      SM               │
│00005 Young     22969    east      SM               │
│00006 Stride    27253    east      SM               │
│00007 Topin     86432    east      C                │
│00008 Spark     99210    east      C                │
│00009 Vetter    38928    west      C                │
│00010 Curci     21531    west      SM               │
│00011 Marco     79345    west      C                │
│00012 Greco     18523    west      SM               │
│00013 Ryan      32915    west      SM               │
│00014 Tomas     42109    west      SM               │
│00015 Thalman   94320    south     C                │
│00016 Moore     25718    south     SM               │
│00017 Allen     64700    south     C                │
│00018 Stelam    27634    south     SM               │
│00019 Farlow    32719    north     SM               │
│00020 Smith     38712    north     SM               │
│00021 Wilson    97214    north     C                │
│                                              ─ZOOM─│
└────────────────────────────────────────────────────┘
```

Screen 10.4 PGM Window

To resubmit a SAS job, type

```
recall
```

on the command line and press ENTER or press a function key set to execute the RECALL command. This recalls your statements to the program editor. You can then edit and resubmit the statements.

Managing Your Files

The FILE command, a text editor command already described, allows you to save your program statements without removing them from the window so that you can then submit them for execution. To save a program you have entered in the PGM window, use the FILE command, specifying the file and, optionally, the extension in which you want the contents of the PGM window stored (see **Screen 10.5**). All lines in the window are saved, not just those currently displayed. If you want to store the file in a directory other than the one to which you currently have access, specify a directory name and a backslash before the file name and extension, as shown below:

```
file '\directory\filename.extension'
```

Note that if the file already exists, the FILE command overwrites the file with the contents of the PGM window.

To bring the contents of an existing file into the PGM window, use the INCLUDE command, again specifying the file and, optionally, the extension. If you want to include a file from a directory other than the one to which you currently have access, specify a directory name and backslash before the file name and extension, as also required for the FILE statement. For example,

```
include 'pgm2.sas'
```

copies the file called PGM2.SAS from the current directory to the PGM window. The contents of file PGM2.SAS are added to the bottom of the data lines currently in the window, shown in **Screen 10.6**.

```
┌PROGRAM EDITOR─────────────────────────────────────────────────────┐
│Command ===> file 'salepgm.sas'                                    │
│                                                                   │
│00011  Marco       79345    west      C                            │
│00012  Greco       18523    west      SM                           │
│00013  Ryan        32915    west      SM                           │
│00014  Tomas       42109    west      SM                           │
│00015  Thalman     94320    south     C                            │
│00016  Moore       25718    south     SM                           │
│00017  Allen       64700    south     C                            │
│00018  Stelam      27634    south     SM                           │
│00019  Farlow      32719    north     SM                           │
│00020  Smith       38712    north     SM                           │
│00021  Wilson      97214    north     C                            │
│00022  run;                                                        │
│00023                                                              │
│00024                                                              │
│00025                                                              │
│00026                                                              │
│00027                                                              │
│00028                                                              │
│00029                                                              │
│00030                                                              │
│00031                                                              │
│                                                            ─ZOOM─ │
└───────────────────────────────────────────────────────────────────┘
```

Screen 10.5 Saving Contents of PGM Window

To send your SAS program directly to a printer attached to your PC, type

```
file 'prn:'
```

```
┌PROGRAM EDITOR─────────────────────────────────────────┐
│Command ===> include 'pgm2.sas'                        │
│                                                       │
│00011 Marco       79345     west      C                │
│00012 Greco       18523     west      SM               │
│00013 Ryan        32915     west      SM               │
│00014 Tomas       42109     west      SM               │
│00015 Thalman     94320     south     C                │
│00016 Moore       25718     south     SM               │
│00017 Allen       64700     south     C                │
│00018 Stelam      27634     south     SM               │
│00019 Farlow      32719     north     SM               │
│00020 Smith       38712     north     SM               │
│00021 Wilson      97214     north     C                │
│00022 run;                                             │
│00023 proc print;                                      │
│00024 run;                                             │
│00025 proc freq;                                       │
│00026     tables region*machine;                       │
│00027 run;                                             │
│00028 proc sort; by machine;                           │
│00029 run;                                             │
│00030 proc means; by machine;                          │
│00031 run;                                             │
│                                                 ZOOM──│
└───────────────────────────────────────────────────────┘
```

Screen 10.6 Bringing a File into the PGM Window

Ending Your SAS Session

To end your SAS session, submit the statement

   endsas;

from a data line of the PGM window or execute the BYE or ENDSAS command from the command line of the PGM window.

Commands

In addition to global commands and text editor commands, you can use the following commands in the PGM window:

RECALL
RSUBMIT
SUBMIT
SUBTOP

RECALL
   brings back to the PGM window the most recently submitted block of statements since you entered display manager. The system adds the recalled lines to the top of the PGM window in front of any other lines already displayed. After you have used the RECALL command once, you can enter it again to recall the next most recent block.

RSUBMIT ['*SASstatement;*']
: submits SAS program statements from the PGM window to a remote mainframe or minicomputer system for execution. To use the RSUBMIT command, you must first establish a micro-to-host link. You can submit a SAS program that uses SAS software available only on the remote operating system. See the SIGNON and SIGNOFF system link commands described earlier in **DISPLAY MANAGER GLOBAL COMMANDS**.

    You can also submit a SAS program statement directly from the command line. Follow the RSUBMIT command with one or more SAS statements, each ending with a semicolon, and enclose the whole string in quotes.

SUBMIT ['*SASstatement;*']
: submits SAS program statements from the data lines of the PGM window.

    You also can submit a SAS program statement directly from the command line with the SUBMIT command. Follow the SUBMIT command with one or more SAS statements, each ending with a semicolon, and enclose the whole string in quotes.

SUBTOP
: submits only the first line in the PGM window to the SAS System for execution. This command is useful when you have a window full of statements and you may want to alter later statements, depending on the results of the first statements submitted. It also is useful if you want to use SUBMIT for the first statement and RSUBMIT for the remainder.

LOG WINDOW

The SAS Log

When you submit SAS statements from the PGM window, the SAS log is displayed in the LOG window. The LOG window is an easy-to-use browsing window that allows you to view, save, or send to the printer the SAS log created when you submit a job to the SAS System. **Screen 10.7** shows the log produced by the DATA step shown in the previous example.

To help you locate the information you need, you can scroll the contents of the window, issue a FIND command, and alter the color of different areas in the window and specific types of text lines. For example, you can alter the color of SAS source lines in the log to make locating them easier. In the LOG window, execute the command

```
color source red
```

to display SAS source lines in red. (For more information on the COLOR commands, see **COLOR Command** earlier in this chapter.)

358   Chapter 10

```
┌LOG─────────────────────────────────────────────────────────────┐
│Command ===>                                                    │
│                                                                │
│NOTE: Copyright(c) 1985,86,87 SAS Institute Inc., Cary, NC 27512-8000, U.S.A.│
│NOTE: SAS (r) Proprietary Software Release 6.03                 │
│      Licensed to SAS Institute 6.03, Site 00000000.            │
│                                                                │
│  1    data sales;                                              │
│  2       input salesrep $ sales region $ machine $;            │
│  3       cards;                                                │
│  22   run;                                                     │
│NOTE: The data set WORK.SALES has 18 observations and 4 variables.│
│NOTE: The DATA statement used 21.00 seconds.                    │
│                                                                │
│                                                        ─ZOOM─  │
└────────────────────────────────────────────────────────────────┘
```

Screen 10.7 LOG Window

Commands

In addition to global commands, you can use the commands listed and defined below in the LOG window. Note that you can use many of the same commands in the PGM and OUTPUT windows.

> AUTOSCROLL *n*
> CAPS
> CLEAR
> FILE
> FIND *characterstring*
> RFIND

> AUTOSCROLL *n*
>> sets the automatic forward scroll amount in the LOG window. When the LOG window receives a line of data, you are scrolled automatically to the end of the data stream. As more lines are received, they are displayed in the window. When the bottom of the window is reached, it automatically scrolls forward one line. If you want to scroll forward five lines when the bottom of the window is reached, execute AUTOSCROLL 5. You can stop automatic scrolling by executing AUTOSCROLL 0.

> CAPS [OFF | ON]
>> With CAPS ON, character strings following a FIND/RFIND command are translated into uppercase. Enclose your character string in quotes if you do not want lowercase letters in the string translated into uppercase letters. All text is interpreted as entered when CAPS OFF is in effect. The CAPS command is in effect for the remainder of the SAS session or until changed by another CAPS command. If you execute the CAPS command without specifying ON or OFF, it works like an on/off switch.

CLEAR
  removes the contents of the window. Execute the FILE command before executing CLEAR if you want to store the information for later reference.

FILE [*fileref* | '*actualfilename*'] [TABS]
  writes the entire contents of the window to an external file or to the printer attached to your PC without removing text from the LOG window. Type

```
file 'prn:'
```

  to send the contents to a printer. You can specify a previously assigned fileref or an actual file name. If you specify an actual file name, you must enclose it in single or double quotes. You can specify either a file name in your current directory or a fully qualified path name. If you do not specify a fileref or a file name, the file in the previous FILE command is used. Note that if the file already exists, the FILE command overwrites it with the contents of the LOG window.

FIND *characterstring* [NEXT | FIRST | LAST | PREV | ALL]
  [WORD | PREFIX | SUFFIX]
  searches for a specified string of characters. Enclose the string in single or double quotes if it contains embedded blanks or special characters. You can execute the FIND command by typing it on the command line or by typing the character string on the command line and pressing the FIND function key.

  Search order You can specify in the FIND command that the SAS System search for the next occurrence of the specified string after the current cursor location, the first or last occurrence of the string in the file regardless of your current cursor location, or the previous occurrence, which depends on the current cursor position. If the cursor is on the command line, the NEXT option starts at the top of the current screen and the PREV option at the end of the last line of the current screen. If you specify ALL, you receive a message that reports how many times the string occurs in the entire file. By default, the FIND command searches for the next occurrence of the specified string after the current cursor location.

  Context You can also specify PREFIX, SUFFIX, or WORD. If you do not specify one of these options, the SAS System searches for each occurrence of the string regardless of context.

  In the FIND command, a WORD is one or more symbols preceded and followed by a delimiter. A delimiter is any symbol other than an uppercase letter, a lowercase letter, a digit, or an underscore. For example,

```
abc123
```

  is a word, but

```
abc$123
```

  is two words separated by the delimiter $. The option PREFIX or SUFFIX is treated just as its grammatical definition. In the first example, ABC123, you can specify ABC as a prefix and 123 as a suffix. In the second example, ABC$123, ABC and 123 are words, not a prefix and a suffix.

  Special characters and embedded blanks Use single or double quotes to enclose strings with special characters or embedded blanks. The following example requires no quotation marks:

```
f your
```

This example does:

```
f 'your data set'
```

Also, enclose your string in quotes if you have executed the CAPS ON command and you do not want lowercase letters in the string translated into uppercase letters. For example, if you have specified CAPS ON, the following command finds the next occurrence of BOB instead of Bob:

```
f Bob
```

If your string contains a single quote, such as

```
f Bob's
```

enclose the string in double quotes:

```
f "Bob's"
```

RFIND
allows you to continue the search for a string of characters previously specified in a FIND command.

OUTPUT WINDOW

The OUTPUT window is an easy-to-use browsing window, much like the LOG window. Output is saved for your SAS session so you can scroll backward and forward, viewing current output as well as output produced by a previously executed PROC step. Note that the OUTPUT window is automatically cleared after 32,000 lines have been produced. Use the FILE command to save the information stream of the OUTPUT window if you want to store it for future use or to print it on your attached printer. To send the entire contents of the OUTPUT window to the printer attached to your PC, type

```
file 'prn:'
```

When you submit SAS statements from the PGM window, output produced by a PROC step is displayed in the OUTPUT window. For example, suppose you create a data set called SALES. You submit the statements

```
proc print data=sales;
run;
```

from the PGM window. Then type the commands

```
output; zoom
```

from the command line to move to the OUTPUT window and allow it to occupy the full screen, as shown in **Screen 10.8**.

```
┌OUTPUT─────────────────────────────────────────────────────────────────┐
│Command ===>                                                           │
│                                                                       │
│                          SAS       10:51 Friday, August 21, 1987    1 │
│                                                                       │
│           OBS    SALESREP   SALES    REGION   MACHINE                 │
│                                                                       │
│            1     Stafer      9664    east     SM                      │
│            2     Young      22969    east     SM                      │
│            3     Stride     27253    east     SM                      │
│            4     Topin      86432    east     C                       │
│            5     Spark      99210    east     C                       │
│            6     Vetter     38928    west     C                       │
│            7     Curci      21531    west     SM                      │
│            8     Marco      79345    west     C                       │
│            9     Greco      18523    west     SM                      │
│           10     Ryan       32915    west     SM                      │
│           11     Tomas      42109    west     SM                      │
│           12     Thalman    94320    south    C                       │
│           13     Moore      25718    south    SM                      │
│           14     Allen      64700    south    C                       │
│           15     Stelam     27634    south    SM                      │
│           16     Farlow     32719    north    SM                      │
│           17     Smith      38712    north    SM                      │
│                                                                ZOOM───┘
```

Screen 10.8 OUTPUT Window

To help you locate the information you need, you can issue a FIND command. For example, to locate the first occurrence of EAST in the OUTPUT window, from the command line execute

    find east

The cursor moves to the first occurrence of EAST in the window (see **Screen 10.9**).

You can also use a command-line command to alter the color of different areas of the window and specific types of text lines. For example, to alter the color of SAS data lines in the OUTPUT window, from the command line, execute the command

    color data red

to display all data lines in red.

```
┌OUTPUT─────────────────────────────────────────────────────────┐
│Command ===>                                                   │
│                                                               │
│                          SAS      10:51 Friday, August 21, 1987   1│
│                                                               │
│         OBS   SALESREP   SALES   REGION   MACHINE             │
│                                                               │
│          1    Stafer     9664    east     SM                  │
│          2    Young      22969   east     SM                  │
│          3    Stride     27253   east     SM                  │
│          4    Topin      86432   east     C                   │
│          5    Spark      99210   east     C                   │
│          6    Vetter     38928   west     C                   │
│          7    Curci      21531   west     SM                  │
│          8    Marco      79345   west     C                   │
│          9    Greco      18523   west     SM                  │
│         10    Ryan       32915   west     SM                  │
│         11    Tomas      42109   west     SM                  │
│         12    Thalman    94320   south    C                   │
│         13    Moore      25718   south    SM                  │
│         14    Allen      64700   south    C                   │
│         15    Stelam     27634   south    SM                  │
│         16    Farlow     32719   north    SM                  │
│         17    Smith      38712   north    SM                  │
│                                                         ─ZOOM─┤
└───────────────────────────────────────────────────────────────┘
```

Screen 10.9 Executing a FIND Command

Commands

In addition to global commands, you can use the commands listed and defined below in the OUTPUT window. Note that you can use many of the same commands in the LOG and PGM windows.

AUTOSCROLL *n*
CAPS
CLEAR
FILE
FIND *characterstring*
PAGE
RFIND

AUTOSCROLL *n*
: sets the automatic forward scroll amount in the OUTPUT window. When the OUTPUT window receives a line of data, you are scrolled automatically to the end of the data stream. As more lines are received, they are displayed in the window. When the bottom of the window is reached, it automatically scrolls forward one line. If you want to scroll forward five lines when the bottom of the window is reached, execute AUTOSCROLL 5. You can also stop automatic scrolling by executing AUTOSCROLL 0.

CAPS [OFF | ON]
: With the CAPS ON command, character strings following a FIND command are translated into uppercase. Enclose your character string in quotes if you do not want lowercase letters in the string translated into uppercase letters. All text is interpreted as entered when CAPS OFF is in effect. The CAPS command is in effect for the remainder of the SAS

session or until changed by another CAPS command. If you execute the CAPS command without specifying ON or OFF, it works like an on/off switch.

CLEAR
removes the contents of the window. Execute the FILE command before you execute CLEAR if you want to store the output for later reference.

FILE [*fileref* | '*actualfilename*'] [TABS]
writes the entire contents of the window into an external file or to the printer attached to your PC. Type

```
file 'prn:'
```

to send the contents to a printer. You can specify a previously assigned fileref or an actual file name. If you specify an actual file name, you must enclose it in single or double quotes. You can specify a file name in your current working directory or a fully qualified path name. If you do not specify a fileref or a file name, the file in the previous FILE command is used. Note that if the file already exists, the FILE command overwrites it with the contents of the OUTPUT window.

FIND *characterstring* [NEXT | FIRST | LAST | PREV | ALL]
[WORD | PREFIX | SUFFIX]
searches for a specified string of characters. Enclose the string in single or double quotes if it contains embedded blanks or special characters. You can execute the FIND command by typing it on the command line or by typing the character string on the command line and pressing the FIND function key.

Search order You can specify in the FIND command that the SAS System search for the next occurrence of the specified string after the current cursor location, the first or last occurrence of the string in the file regardless of your current cursor location, or the previous occurrence, which depends on the current cursor position. If the cursor is on the command line, the NEXT option starts at the top of the current screen and the PREV option at the end of the last line of the current screen. If you specify ALL, you receive a message that reports how many times the string occurs in the entire file. By default, the FIND command searches for the next occurrence of the specified string after the current cursor location.

Context You can also specify PREFIX, SUFFIX, or WORD. If you do not specify one of these options, the SAS System searches for each occurrence of the string, regardless of context.

In the FIND command, a WORD is one or more symbols preceded and followed by a delimiter. A delimiter is any symbol other than an uppercase letter, a lowercase letter, a digit, or an underscore. For example,

```
abc123
```

is a word, but

```
abc$123
```

is two words separated by the delimiter $. The option PREFIX or SUFFIX is treated just as its grammatical definition. In the first example, ABC123, you can specify ABC as a prefix and 123 as a suffix. In the second example, ABC$123, ABC and 123 are words, not a prefix and a suffix.

Special characters and embedded blanks Use single or double quotes to enclose strings with special characters or embedded blanks. The following example requires no quotation marks:

```
f your
```

This example does:

```
f 'your data set'
```

Also enclose your string in single quotes if you have executed the CAPS ON command and you do not want lowercase letters in the string translated into uppercase letters. For example, if you have specified CAPS ON, the following command finds the next occurrence of BOB instead of Bob:

```
f Bob
```

If your string contains a single quote, such as

```
f Bob's
```

enclose the string in double quotes:

```
f "Bob's"
```

PAGE [ON | OFF]
　　specifies whether scrolling should or should not be sensitive to page breaks. With PAGE OFF, a page break is displayed in the OUTPUT window as a dashed line, and more than one page's data may appear in the window at one time.
　　With PAGE ON, scrolling commands are sensitive to page breaks, and the window is filled with blank lines when a page break is encountered.
　　If you do not specify ON or OFF, the PAGE command functions like an on/off switch.

RFIND
　　continues the search for a string of characters previously specified in a FIND command.

CATALOG WINDOW

Use the CATALOG window to manage entries in SAS catalogs. While in the CATALOG window, you can

- browse the list of entries in a catalog
- rename, delete, and copy entries in the current catalog
- copy entries into the current catalog from another catalog.

To use the CATALOG window, enter

```
catalog  [libref] [.catalog]
```

from any command line, where *libref* names a SAS library and *catalog* names a catalog in that library. CATALOG can be abbreviated to CAT. If you do not specify *libref* and/or *catalog*, you can enter them in the fields provided at the top of the window. Press ENTER to display that catalog's entries. The CATALOG window is shown in **Screen 10.10**.

```
┌OUTPUT─────────────────┬─CATALOG──────────────────────────────────────
│Command ===>           │Command ===>
│                       │
│                       │Libref : SASHELP
│                       │Catalog: BASE
│                       │
│                       │   Name      Type     Description
│                       │
│                       │ _ APPEND    HELP     APPEND Procedure (17)    SASH
│                       │ _ AUTOADD   HELP     AUTOADD command (6)
│                       │ _ AUTOFLOW  HELP     AUTOFLOW command (6)
├LOG────────────────────┤ _ AUTOWRAP  HELP     AUTOWRAP command (5)
│Command ===>           │ _ BACKWARD  HELP     BACKWARD command (12)
│                       │ _ BOTTOM    HELP     BOTTOM command (4)
│NOTE: Copyright(c) 1985,86,│ _ BOUNDS HELP     BOUNDS command (8)
│NOTE: SAS (r) Proprietary S│ _ CALENDAR HELP   CALENDAR Procedure (52)   S
│      Licensed to SAS Insti│ _ CAPS   HELP     CAPS command (15)
│                       │ _ CATALOG   HELP     CATALOG Procedure (44)    S
├PROGRAM EDITOR─────────┤ _ CHANGE    HELP     CHANGE command (25)
│Command ===>           │ _ CHART     HELP     CHART Procedure (84)      S
│                       │ _ CIMPORT   HELP     CIMPORT Procedure (24)
│00001                  │ _ CLEAR     HELP     CLEAR command (6)
│00002                  │ _ COLOR     HELP     COLOR command (40)
│00003                  │ _ COMPARE   HELP     COMPARE Procedure (55)   SASH
└───────────────────────┴──────────────────────────────────────────────
```

Screen 10.10 CATALOG Window

You can also use the LIBNAME and DIRECTORY windows to specify a *libref* and *catalog*:

1. Enter the LIBNAME window by typing LIB on a command line. Select a libref from the list shown in the window. You are taken to the DIRECTORY window.
2. Select a catalog from the list shown in the DIR window. You are taken to the CATALOG window.

When you enter the CATALOG window, a list of entries for the specified catalog is displayed. Use selection-field commands or command-line commands to copy, rename, or delete entries.

Note: if you specify a catalog that does not exist, a message asks if you want to create the catalog you specified. If you answer yes, an empty catalog is created. If you answer no, you receive a CATALOG NOT FOUND message. If the catalog exists but cannot be opened for update, it is opened in browse mode and you cannot make any modifications.

Using Selection Fields

You can use one-letter commands in the window's selection field to execute commands, or you can use command-line commands (documented in **Commands**, below).

To use a selection field command, move the cursor to the selection field of the entry you want. Then type a command letter and press ENTER. The command letters are

      D   Delete this entry. When you press ENTER, a message asks you if you really want to delete the entry. To verify, type V in the selection field, and then press ENTER. To cancel the deletion, press ENTER without entering V. There is no way to restore a catalog entry once you have deleted it.

R Rename this entry. When you press ENTER, the NAME and DESCRIPTION fields are highlighted. Just type the new name and/or description over the old one, and then press ENTER.

Commands

In addition to all global commands, you can use the following in the CATALOG window:

COPY *from-spec* [*to-spec*]
: copies an entry. *From-spec* is the entry from which you want to copy. You can copy entries from other catalogs by specifying a three- or four-level name (remember, an entry is fully specified as *libref.catalog.name.type*). You must specify at least *name.type*. You can leave out *to-spec* if you are copying from another catalog. The new entry is given the same name it had in the other catalog.

  To-spec is the entry to which you want to copy. You can only copy to the current catalog, so you specify *name.type*. The entry types of *from-spec* and *to-spec* must match. (If you leave *type* out of the *to-spec*, the type is made the same as that in the *from-spec*.)

  You always use the CATALOG window to enter a catalog and then to copy entries into it. You cannot copy entries from the current catalog to an outside catalog.

DELETE *entry.type*
: deletes an entry. DELETE can be abbreviated to DEL. This command deletes the entry immediately without asking for verification. There is no way to restore a catalog entry once you have deleted it.

END
: removes the CATALOG window from the screen.

You cannot delete a catalog from a SAS library in the CATALOG window. To delete a catalog, you must use the DATASETS procedure.

DIR WINDOW

When you want to display a listing of SAS files, use the DIR command to display the DIR window. **Screen 10.11** shows the window displayed when you issue the DIR command. You can also enter the DIR window from the LIBNAME window by selecting the libname of the SAS data library whose contents you want to display in the DIR window.

To display the names of SAS data sets and SAS catalogs, enter the libref and SAS file type and press ENTER. Then, for example, you can select a SAS data set (a SAS file of type DATA), which automatically displays a VAR window showing the variables belonging to that SAS data set, or you can select a SAS catalog to display its catalog entries. To choose a file, simply place the cursor on the underscore to the left of the SAS file you want and type in any character; then press ENTER.

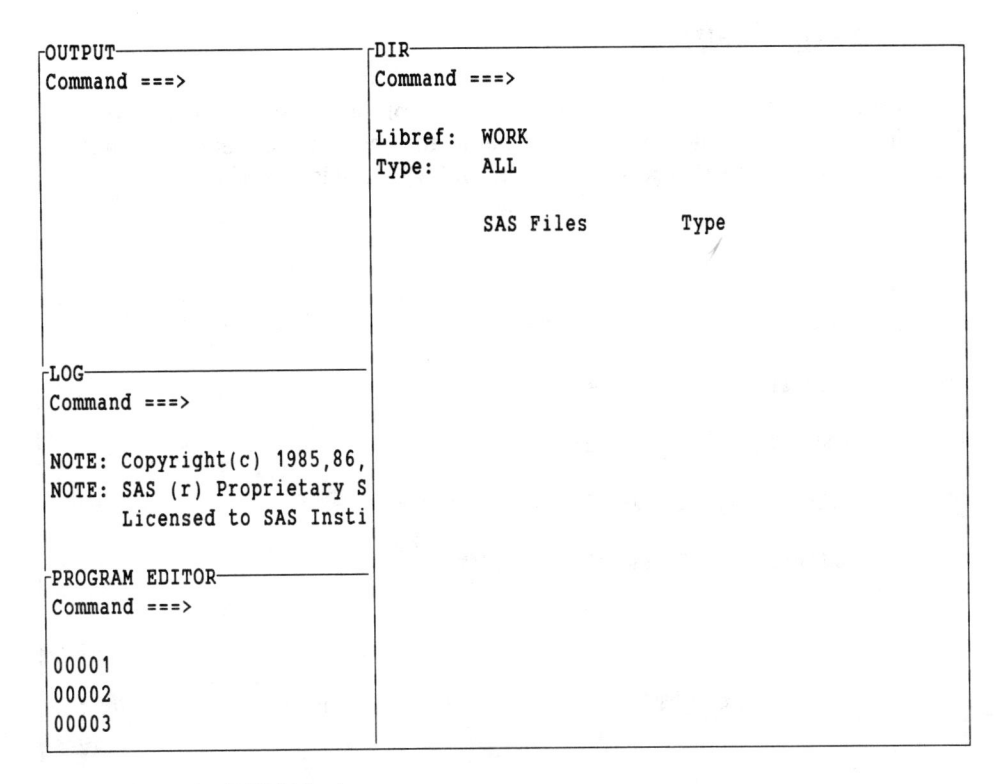

```
┌OUTPUT─────────────────┐┌DIR──────────────────────────────────┐
│Command ===>           ││Command ===>                         │
│                       ││                                     │
│                       ││Libref:   WORK                       │
│                       ││Type:     ALL                        │
│                       ││                                     │
│                       ││          SAS Files        Type      │
│                       ││                                     │
│                       ││                                     │
│                       ││                                     │
│                       ││                                     │
├LOG────────────────────┤│                                     │
│Command ===>           ││                                     │
│                       ││                                     │
│NOTE: Copyright(c) 1985,86, │                                 │
│NOTE: SAS (r) Proprietary S │                                 │
│      Licensed to SAS Insti │                                 │
│                       ││                                     │
├PROGRAM EDITOR─────────┤│                                     │
│Command ===>           ││                                     │
│                       ││                                     │
│00001                  ││                                     │
│00002                  ││                                     │
│00003                  ││                                     │
└───────────────────────┘└─────────────────────────────────────┘
```

Screen 10.11   DIR Window

Fields

If you enter the DIR window directly rather than through the LIBNAME window, WORK appears in the LIBREF field by default and ALL appears in the TYPE field.

LIBREF   specifies the libref of the SAS data library for which you want the SAS files listed. The libref must have been previously assigned to that SAS data library in a LIBNAME statement. Specify WORK if you want a listing of the temporary SAS files created during your current session.

TYPE   specifies the type of SAS files you want displayed. ALL appears here by default. Press ENTER to display SAS files of all types in the specified SAS data library, or enter DATA for SAS data sets or CATALOG for SAS catalogs. For more information on SAS files, see Chapter 15, "SAS Files."

The Selection Field

Place any character in the selection field preceding a SAS data set (a SAS file of type DATA) to display the VAR window showing the variable names, their types, and labels. Select a SAS file of type catalog to display a CATALOG window listing its entries.

Commands

You can use all global commands in the DIR window. Use the END command to remove the DIR window from the screen.

FILENAME WINDOW

Use the FILENAME window to display a listing of all currently assigned filerefs. The fileref and the complete host file name to which it has been assigned are displayed. **Screen 10.12** shows a sample FILENAME window.

```
┌FILENAME─────────────────────────────────────────────────────────┐
│Command ===>                                                     │
│                                                                 │
│         Fileref        Host File Name                           │
│                                                                 │
│         MONTHLY        A: TEMP.DAT                              │
│                                                                 │
│         RLINK          C: SAS603 SASLINK TSO.SCR                │
│                                                                 │
│         SALEDAT        C: SAS603 MYDATA.DAT                     │
│                                                                 │
│                                                                 │
│                                                                 │
│                                                                 │
│                                                                 │
│                                                                 │
│                                                         ─ZOOM─  │
└─────────────────────────────────────────────────────────────────┘
```

Screen 10.12 Example of a FILENAME Window

Commands

You can use all global commands in the FILENAME window. Use the END command to remove the FILENAME window from the screen.

FOOTNOTES AND TITLES WINDOWS

The FOOTNOTES and TITLES windows function identically. The FOOTNOTES window is used to specify up to ten footnotes to appear on output from SAS procedures; the TITLES window is used to specify titles for output; the default title is SAS. The two windows are shown in **Screens 10.13** and **10.14**.

```
┌─OUTPUT─────────────────────────────────────────────────────────────┐
│ Command ===>                                                       │
│                                                                    │
│          ┌─FOOTNOTES──────────────────────────────────┐            │
│          │ Command ===>                               │            │
│          │                                            │            │
│          │ Footnote Description                       │            │
│          │     1     Sales Amount                     │            │
│          │     2                                      │            │
│┌─LOG─────│     3                                      │──────────┐ │
││ Command │     4                                      │          │ │
││         │     5                                      │          │ │
││ NOTE: Co│     6                                      │   U.S.A. │ │
││ NOTE: SA│     7                                      │          │ │
││      Li│     8                                      │          │ │
││         │     9                                      │          │ │
│┌─PROGRAM─│    10                                      │          │ │
││ Command └────────────────────────────────────────────┘          │ │
││                                                                 │ │
││ 00001                                                           │ │
││ 00002                                                           │ │
││ 00003                                                           │ │
└─────────────────────────────────────────────────────────────────────┘
```

Screen 10.13 FOOTNOTES Window

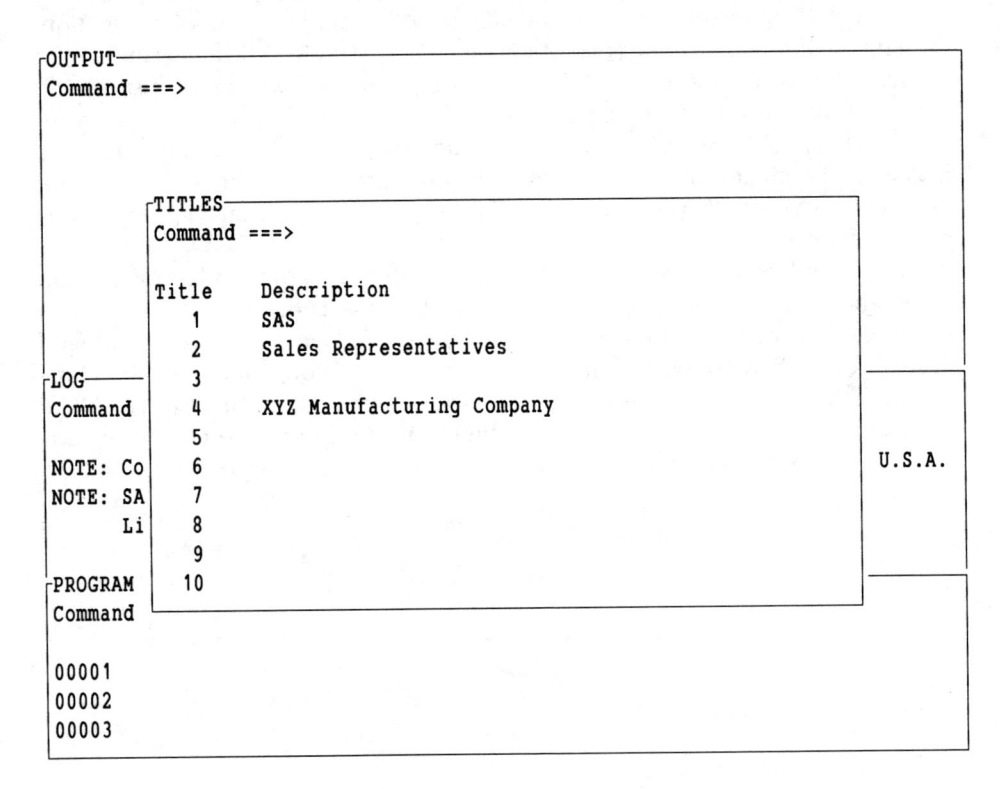

```
┌─OUTPUT─────────────────────────────────────────────────────────────┐
│ Command ===>                                                       │
│                                                                    │
│          ┌─TITLES─────────────────────────────────────┐            │
│          │ Command ===>                               │            │
│          │                                            │            │
│          │ Title    Description                       │            │
│          │   1      SAS                               │            │
│          │   2      Sales Representatives             │            │
│┌─LOG─────│   3                                        │──────────┐ │
││ Command │   4      XYZ Manufacturing Company         │          │ │
││         │   5                                        │          │ │
││ NOTE: Co│   6                                        │   U.S.A. │ │
││ NOTE: SA│   7                                        │          │ │
││      Li│   8                                        │          │ │
││         │   9                                        │          │ │
│┌─PROGRAM─│  10                                        │          │ │
││ Command └────────────────────────────────────────────┘          │ │
││                                                                 │ │
││ 00001                                                           │ │
││ 00002                                                           │ │
││ 00003                                                           │ │
└─────────────────────────────────────────────────────────────────────┘
```

Screen 10.14 TITLES Window

When you want to add footnotes or titles to the output produced by SAS procedures, you can invoke the FOOTNOTES or TITLES window and enter the text beside the corresponding numbers in the window. Conversely, you can add TITLE or FOOTNOTE statements to the program statements you enter in the PGM window. After you submit and run your program, the footnotes or titles appear in the appropriate window.

After you have entered footnotes or titles, issue the END or SUBMIT command to submit them to the SAS System. The footnotes or titles are then added to subsequent output produced during the session.

Any FOOTNOTE or TITLE statements submitted to the SAS System as SAS statements are automatically added to the FOOTNOTES and TITLES windows if those windows are closed. They override previous entries, starting with the footnote or title number being changed. For example, suppose you have titles 1 through 7, and you change title 6. Titles 1 through 5 remain unchanged, title 6 is changed, and title 7 is deleted. The same rules apply to the FOOTNOTES window.

Commands

You can use all global commands in the FOOTNOTES and TITLES windows. Use END to submit any new titles or footnotes to the SAS System and remove the window from the screen. You can also use the CLEAR command to delete all defined footnotes or titles from the window.

HELP WINDOW

Use the HELP command to display the HELP window and view help information. The HELP window has two types of panels: menu panels and help panels. You can scroll backward and forward to browse help information (see **Screen 10.15**).

When you execute the HELP command from one of the three primary windows, the SAS SYSTEM HELP, which is an on-line, menu-driven help facility, is displayed. It contains information about all of the products in the SAS System for personal computers. If you execute HELP from one of the special windows, information about using that window is displayed.

Type a number or name of a specific option on the command line of a menu panel, and press ENTER to make a selection. Use the END command to return to the previous panel. If you are on the primary menu panel, the END command closes the HELP window. When you are on a menu, you select specific HELP by typing the number or name of what you want to view. You can also type HELP followed by the name of a procedure to view specific procedure HELP from any window except the HELP window.

```
┌OUTPUT─────────────────────────────────────────────────────────────┐
│Command ===>                                                       │
│ ┌HELP─────────────────────────────────────────────────────────────┤
│ │Command ===>                                                     │
│ │                                                                 │
│ │                    Editing and Cursor Keys                      │
│ │                                                                 │
│ │   ENTER:CR    carriage return (CR) executes any commands on command line
│ │               or moves the cursor to beginning of next line.    │
│ │   INSERT      inserts characters in a field.                    │
│ │   DELETE      deletes characters from a field.                  │
│L│   END         erases all the characters from the cursor position to the end
│C│               of the data entry line or, on some windows, the end of a fiel
│ │   BACKSPACE   moves the cursor back, erasing characters as it moves.
│N│   HOME        moves the cursor to the entry area of the command line
│N│               on the window currently active.                   │
│ │                                                                 │
│ └─────────────────────────────────────────────────────────────────┤
│                                                                   │
┌PROGRAM EDITOR─────────────────────────────────────────────────────┐
│Command ===>                                                       │
│                                                                   │
│00001                                                              │
│00002                                                              │
│00003                                                              │
└───────────────────────────────────────────────────────────────────┘
```

Screen 10.15 Sample Help Panel

Commands

In addition to all global commands except the MARK and WSAVE commands, you can use the commands listed below when viewing information in the HELP window.

END
: returns you to the previous panel. If you are on the primary menu, you are returned to the previous window.

=
: returns you to the primary HELP menu.

FIND *characterstring*
BFIND *characterstring*
: searches for a specified string of characters. Enclose the string in quotes if it contains special characters, embedded blanks, or lowercase letters. You can execute the FIND command by entering it directly or by typing the character string on the command line and pressing the FIND function key.

Searching backward Use BFIND instead of FIND if you want to search from the cursor position backward to the top of the panel rather than forward to the end.

name
> **MENU panels only** selects an entry from the current menu panel. If the entry is not found in the current menu panel, the submenu panels are searched for a match.

n
> **MENU panels only** selects an entry from the current menu panel.

=*n*[.*n* . . .]
> displays a specified help panel from the primary menu. You can use an equal sign (=) followed by numbers or names separated by periods (. . .). For example, the command
>
>   =fsp.fsedit
>
> goes to the primary menu, selects option FSP, and then selects option FSEDIT on the next menu.
>
> Note that if you make an invalid selection, an error message is displayed and the invalid menu selection item is displayed on the command line.

=X
> lets you exit the HELP window and removes it from the display. You can use this command from any help panel.

KEYS WINDOW

The KEYS window lets you display and alter your function key definitions. You can view the keys without making any changes and exit the window. You can change your key definitions and save your changes. If you make mistakes and want to return to your original key settings, you can enter CANCEL on the command line to cancel any changes. **Screen 10.16** shows the KEYS window with the default function key settings.

If you alter a key definition, you must execute a SAVE or END command to put the new settings into effect before you exit the KEYS window. Using a SAVE command allows you to put new key settings into effect while leaving the KEYS window on the screen for easy reference. The new key settings are stored automatically in the catalog SASUSER.PROFILE.

SAS Display Manager System

```
┌OUTPUT─────────────────────────────────┐┌KEYS <DMKEYS>──────────────┐
│Command ===>                           ││Command ===>               │
│                                       ││                           │
│                                       ││Key       Description      │
│                                       ││F1        help             │
│                                       ││F2        keys             │
│                                       ││F3        log              │
│                                       ││F4        output           │
│                                       ││F5        next             │
│                                       ││F6        pgm              │
│                                       ││F7        zoom             │
┌LOG────────────────────────────────────┤│F8        subtop           │
│Command ===>                           ││F9        recall           │
│                                       ││F10       zoom off; submit │
│NOTE: Copyright(c) 1985,86,87 SAS Institute Inc│SHF F1    mark      │
│NOTE: SAS (r) Proprietary Software Release 6.03│SHF F2    unmark    │
│      Licensed to SAS Institute 6.03, Site 0000│SHF F3    cut       │
│                                       ││SHF F4    store            │
┌PROGRAM EDITOR─────────────────────────┤│SHF F5    paste            │
│Command ===>                           ││SHF F6                     │
│                                       ││SHF F7    left             │
│00001                                  ││SHF F8    right            │
│00002                                  ││SHF F9    back             │
│00003                                  ││SHF F10   forward          │
└───────────────────────────────────────┘└───────────────────────────┘
```

Screen 10.16 KEYS Window with Default Settings

Text Insert Feature

In addition to defining a function key to execute a SAS command, you can define a function key as a text string and then insert that text string by positioning the cursor where you want it to appear and pressing the function key. When you define a function key to insert a text string, precede the string with a tilde (~). The tilde must appear in the first column of the key definition field. For example, define SHF F6 as the character string

```
~/*new DATA step begins here*/
```

as shown in **Screen 10.17**. You can then go to the PGM window, position the cursor on a data line, and press SHF F6 to insert this line of text wherever you want it to appear.

Commands

In addition to global commands, you can use the following commands in the KEYS window:

CANCEL
: cancels any changes you have made to the current key settings and returns the screen to the previous window.

```
┌KEYS <DMKEYS>─────────────────────────────────────────────┐
│Command ===>                                              │
│                                                          │
│Key        Description                                    │
│F1         help                                           │
│F2         keys                                           │
│F3         log                                            │
│F4         output                                         │
│F5         next                                           │
│F6         pgm                                            │
│F7         zoom                                           │
│F8         subtop                                         │
│F9         recall                                         │
│F10        submit                                         │
│SHF F1     mark                                           │
│SHF F2     unmark                                         │
│SHF F3     cut                                            │
│SHF F4     store                                          │
│SHF F5     paste                                          │
│SHF F6     -/*new DATA step begins here*/                 │
│SHF F7     left                                           │
│SHF F8     right                                          │
│SHF F9     back                                           │
│SHF F10    forward                                        │
│                                                   ─ZOOM─┘
```

Screen 10.17 Defining a Function Key to Insert Text

COPY [*name*]
: brings a previously created set of function key definitions into the KEYS window. You can follow the COPY command with the name of a set of function key definitions you have stored with the SAVE command. The name must conform to SAS naming conventions. Note that you must execute a SAVE command to put the new key definitions into effect.

    Executing COPY without specifying a name cancels whatever changes have been made and returns the current key settings. Because you can specify another name with the COPY and SAVE commands, you can create as many different sets of function key definitions as you want.

END
: saves any changes you have made to the current key settings, puts the new settings into effect, and removes the KEYS window from the screen.

SAVE [*name*]
: stores your function key settings in SASUSER.PROFILE. Use the SAVE command instead of the END command when you want to leave the KEYS window on the screen. Note that when you alter function key settings, you must execute a SAVE command to put the new settings into effect if you remain in the KEYS window.

    Whether or not you specify a name, the SAS System automatically stores the function key settings for you in the catalog SASUSER.PROFILE and displays the name. If you want to create more than one set of function key definitions, you can specify a valid SAS name with the SAVE command; additional key settings are stored in SASUSER.PROFILE under the specified name. Because you can specify a name with the COPY and SAVE commands, you can create as many different sets of function key definitions as you want.

VERIFY ON | OFF
: determines whether or not you want the KEYS window to verify that commands assigned to function keys are valid SAS commands when entered in the KEYS window. VERIFY ON checks for valid SAS commands. Execute VERIFY OFF if you do not want the function keys checked.

LIBNAME WINDOW

Use the LIBNAME window to display a listing of all currently assigned librefs. The libref and the complete host path name of the SAS data library to which it has been assigned are displayed. **Screen 10.18** shows a sample LIBNAME window.

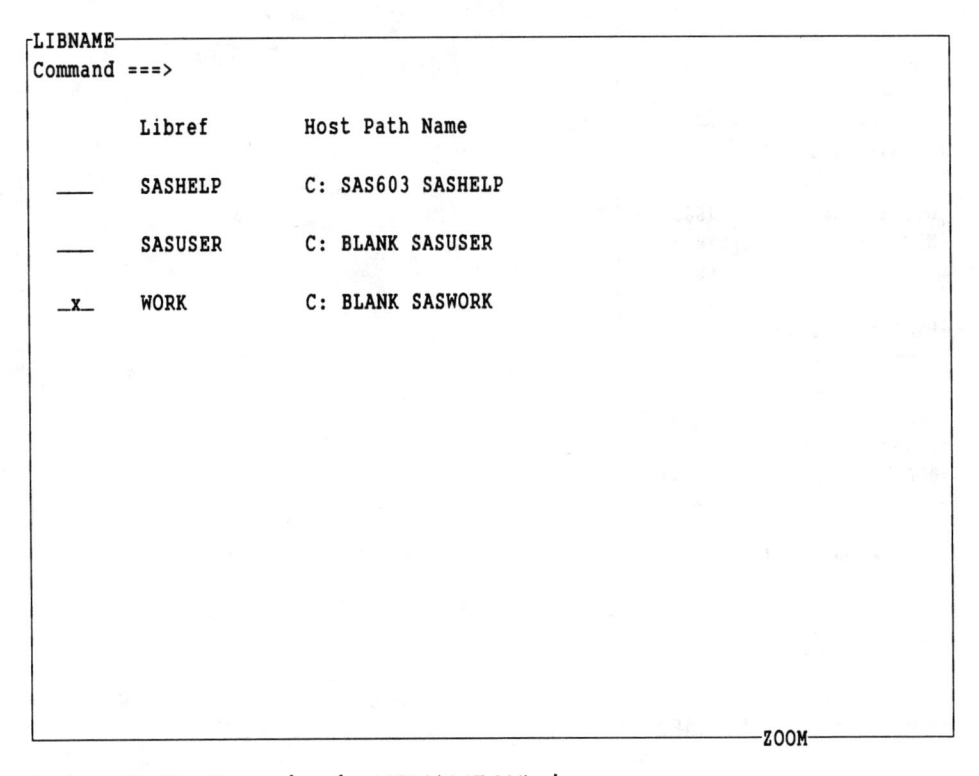

```
┌LIBNAME─────────────────────────────────────────────────────┐
│Command ===>                                                │
│                                                            │
│          Libref        Host Path Name                      │
│                                                            │
│  ___     SASHELP       C: SAS603 SASHELP                   │
│                                                            │
│  ___     SASUSER       C: BLANK SASUSER                    │
│                                                            │
│  _x_     WORK          C: BLANK SASWORK                    │
│                                                            │
│                                                            │
│                                                            │
│                                                            │
│                                                            │
│                                                            │
│                                                   ─ZOOM─   │
└────────────────────────────────────────────────────────────┘
```

Screen 10.18 Example of a LIBNAME Window

The LIBNAME, DIR, CATALOG, and VAR windows are interactive. If you select a libref in the LIBNAME window, a DIR window displaying the SAS files in that data library is shown. In the DIR window, you can select a SAS data set to display a VAR window showing the variables belonging to that SAS data set or you can select a SAS catalog to display a CATALOG window showing its entries.

The Selection Field

Place any letter in the selection field preceding a libref and press the ENTER key to display the DIR window for that SAS data library. In **Screen 10.18** the WORK library, the library that contains all temporary SAS files created during the current session, has been chosen. **Screen 10.19** shows the resulting DIR window.

```
┌OUTPUT─────────────────┬─DIR──────────────────────────────────┐
│Command ===>           │Command ===>                          │
│                       │                                      │
│                       │Libref:  WORK                         │
│                       │Type:    ALL                          │
│                       │                                      │
│                       │         SAS Files      Type          │
│                       │  ___    SALES          DATA          │
│                       │  ___    SASST0         CATALOG       │
│                       │                                      │
│                       │                                      │
├LOG────────────────────┤                                      │
│Command ===>           │                                      │
│                       │                                      │
│NOTE: Copyright(c) 1985,86,                                   │
│NOTE: SAS (r) Proprietary S                                   │
│      Licensed to SAS Insti                                   │
├PROGRAM EDITOR─────────┤                                      │
│Command ===>           │                                      │
│                       │                                      │
│00001                  │                                      │
│00002                  │                                      │
│00003                  │                                      │
└───────────────────────┴──────────────────────────────────────┘
```

Screen 10.19 Displaying the DIR Window for WORK Library

Commands

You can use all global commands in the LIBNAME window. Use the END command to remove the LIBNAME window from the screen.

MENU WINDOW

Use the MENU window to display applications that are shipped with the SAS System. **Screen 10.20** shows a sample MENU window.

```
┌─SAS PROCEDURE MENU SYSTEM──────────────────────────────────┐
│Select Option ===>                                          │
│         S A S   P R O C E D U R E   M E N U   S Y S T E M │
│         BASE              UTILITIES          REMOTE LINK   │
│                                                            │
│         CALENDAR          APPEND             DOWNLOAD      │
│         CHART             CATALOG   (use 1)  UPLOAD        │
│         CORR              CIMPORT            SIGNON   (use 3) │
│         FORMS             COMPARE            SIGNOFF  (use 4) │
│         FREQ              CONTENTS                         │
│         MEANS             COPY                             │
│         PLOT              CPORT              OTHER SAS PRODUCTS │
│         PRINT             DATASETS                         │
│         RANK              DBF                SAS/STAT  (use STAT) │
│         STANDARD          DIF                SAS/GRAPH (use GRAPH)│
│         SUMMARY           FORMAT             SAS/FSP   (use FSP)  │
│         TABULATE          OPTIONS   (use 2)  SAS/AF    (use 5)    │
│         TIMEPLOT          PRINTTO                          │
│         TRANSPOSE         SORT                             │
│         UNIVARIATE                           TYPE H FOR HELP │
│                                                            │
│                                                            │
│                                                            │
│                                                   ──ZOOM── │
└────────────────────────────────────────────────────────────┘
```

Screen 10.20 MENU Window

The MENU window displays the SAS Procedure Menu System, a tool that provides a series of fill-in-the-blank panels to guide you through the procedures in the SAS System.

To use the System, select a procedure or software product by typing the appropriate name or indicated number on the select option line and press ENTER. The statements needed to execute the procedure are displayed. You simply specify the statements you want to see and then issue the SUBMIT or END command to submit your statements to the SAS System for execution.

When you work with a procedure screen, you can request a selection list of data sets or catalogs in a library or a selection list of variables in a data set by typing a question mark (?) in the field and pressing ENTER. To select from the list that appears, use the cursor keys to move the cursor to the item you want to select and press ENTER. The selection is then highlighted. If you change your mind, you can "unselect" an item by positioning the cursor on a highlighted item and pressing ENTER. Once you have made your selection, type END on the command line and press ENTER or use the END key to close the list.

If the selected items appear on the screen, you can also change the selection by retyping the line.

You can use the CANCEL command to exit the procedure screen without submitting statements and the END command to exit the procedure screen and submit the procedure statements to the SAS System for execution. Your output from the submitted statements appears in the OUTPUT window, and any messages resulting from the procedure are written to the LOG window.

You can use the MENU command to display entries that are provided with the SAS System.

The MENU Command

MENU *options*

AUTOSAVE=YES | NO
determines whether or not the SAS System automatically saves user input when the screen is closed. See also the SAVE command described below.

AUTOREC=YES | NO
determines whether or not the SAS System automatically recalls user input values when the screen is displayed. See also the RECALL command described below.

start-location
specifies a menu selection to display when the application begins. This option allows you to move quickly to a specific screen in an application you use frequently. For example, MENU FSP.FSEDIT displays the FSEDIT program screen first.

Commands

In addition to all global commands except the MARK and WSAVE commands, you can use the following commands in the MENU window:

CANCEL
cancels any changes you have made in the MENU window and removes the currently displayed entry from the display. If you are "filling in the blanks" in a program screen, any SAS statements generated are not submitted to the SAS System. The MENU window remains active unless you issue CANCEL from the primary menu; if you issue CANCEL from the primary window, you return to the display manager window from which you invoked the MENU window.

CLEAR
clears all data entry fields on a screen.

END
removes the displayed entry from the screen. If you are "filling in the blanks" in a program screen, any SAS statements generated are submitted to the SAS System for execution. If END is issued from the primary menu, you return to the display manager window from which you invoked the MENU window.

FIND *characterstring*
BFIND *characterstring*
searches for a specified string of characters. Enclose the string in quotes if it contains special characters, embedded blanks, or lowercase letters. You can execute the FIND command by entering it directly or by typing the character string on the command line and pressing the FIND function key.

Searching backward Use BFIND instead of FIND if you want to search from the cursor position backward to the top of the panel rather than forward to the end.

=*selection*
displays the specified selection.

=
displays the primary menu.

QCAN
: "quick cancel" cancels the current screen and closes the current MENU window; it does not send pending SAS statements to the SAS System. It then returns you to the display manager window from which you invoked the MENU window.

QEND
: "quick end" closes the current MENU window and ends the screen, submitting any statements in it to the SAS System. It then returns you to the display manager window from which you invoked the MENU window.

RECALL
: recalls information to data entry fields if you have specified SAVE or AUTOSAVE=YES.

SAVE
: saves the values of the data entry fields. The next time you invoke the MENU window, you can use the RECALL command to restore the values on the screen from a previous execution of the same screen. See also the AUTOSAVE=option on the MENU command.

NOTEPAD WINDOW

The NOTEPAD window provides you with a full-screen editor for entering and altering text and allows you to save information from session to session. To display the NOTEPAD window, type NOTEPAD on the command line of any display manager or full-screen window and press ENTER. When you invoke the NOTEPAD window, it displays the contents of your most recent notepad. **Screen 10.21** shows the NOTEPAD window as it appears if you invoke it from the LOG, OUTPUT, or PGM window.

You can use the NOTEPAD window for many purposes. For example, you can use it to store comments about a particular program or data set. You can also use it to enter and save information you want to refer to often. It provides extended color and highlighting attributes that allow you to accent individual letters, words, or complete lines or blocks of text.

As with all other windows, you can use the ZOOM command to make using the NOTEPAD window more convenient. You can enter text and then execute the SAVE command to store the information.

As shown in **Screen 10.22**, the command

```
save n_sales
```

creates a notepad named N_SALES.NPAD. The SAVE command does not require that you specify a notepad name. If you issue the SAVE command alone, the SAS System automatically stores a notepad for you under the reserved name SCRATCH.NPAD in the catalog SASUSER.PROFILE. This notepad remains stored after your current SAS session.

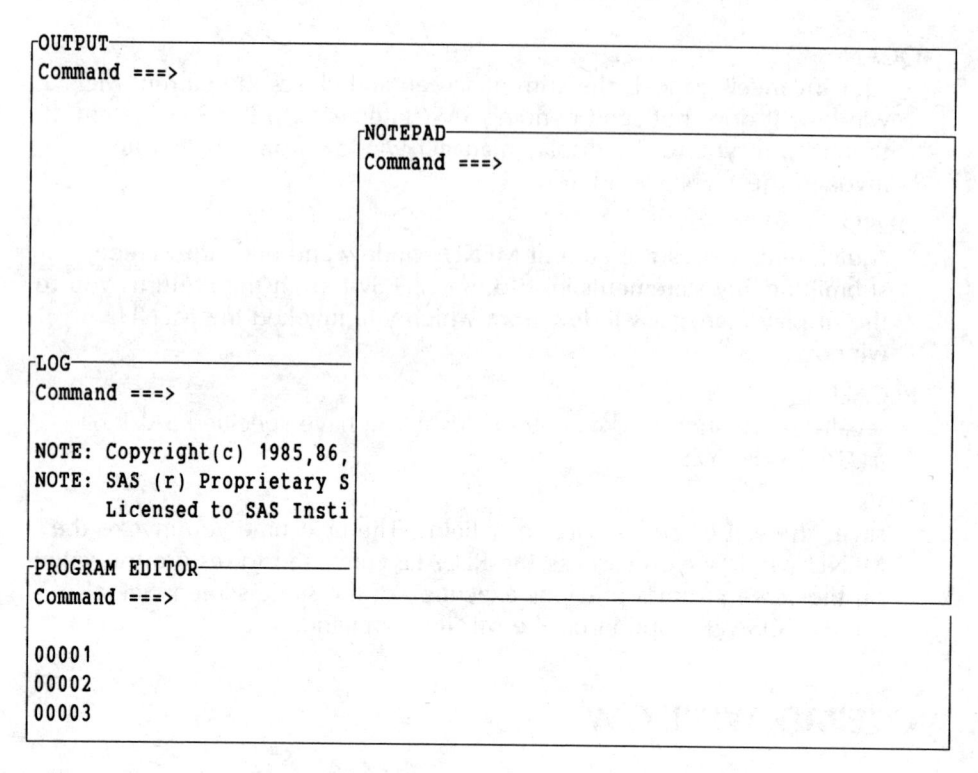

```
┌─OUTPUT─────────────────────────────────────────────┐
│ Command ===>                                       │
│                                                    │
│                  ┌─NOTEPAD──────────────────────┐  │
│                  │ Command ===>                 │  │
│                  │                              │  │
│                  │                              │  │
│                  │                              │  │
│                  │                              │  │
│─LOG──────────────│                              │──│
│ Command ===>     │                              │  │
│                  │                              │  │
│ NOTE: Copyright(c) 1985,86,                     │  │
│ NOTE: SAS (r) Proprietary S                     │  │
│       Licensed to SAS Insti                     │  │
│─PROGRAM EDITOR───│                              │──│
│ Command ===>     │                              │  │
│                  └──────────────────────────────┘  │
│ 00001                                              │
│ 00002                                              │
│ 00003                                              │
└────────────────────────────────────────────────────┘
```

Screen 10.21 NOTEPAD Window

```
┌─NOTEPAD────────────────────────────────────────────┐
│ Command ===>                                       │
│                                                    │
│ NOTE for SALES data set                            │
│ created 8/20/87                                    │
│ creates a temporary data set                       │
│ program source lines are stored in DIR1 SALESPGM.SAS│
│                                                    │
│ See Gordon about YEAR-TO-DATE and YEAR-END reports.│
│ Send copy of PRINTOUT to marketing--8-21-87.       │
│                                                    │
│                                                    │
│                                                    │
│                                                    │
│                                                    │
│                                                    │
│                                                    │
│                                                    │
│                                              ZOOM──│
└────────────────────────────────────────────────────┘
```

Screen 10.22 Creating and Storing a Notepad

Commands

In addition to all global and text editor commands, you can use the following commands in the NOTEPAD window.

CANCEL
> cancels any changes you have made and removes the NOTEPAD window from the screen.

COMMAND
> toggles the command banner on and off.

COPY [*notepadname*]
> copies the contents of a stored notepad into the NOTEPAD window. If you do not specify a name, a notepad with the default name SCRATCH.NPAD is brought into the window. Note that it replaces text currently displayed in the NOTEPAD window.

DELETE *notepadname*
> deletes the specified stored notepad.

DES '*description*'
> assigns a description of up to forty characters to be saved with the notepad. Issue the DES command and then the SAVE command. Note that this command works only with new entries; it does not work with the default.

END
> saves the contents of the NOTEPAD window in a notepad named SCRATCH.NPAD and removes the window from the screen.

NTITLE *title*
> changes the displayed title of the window. Enclose the title in quotes if blanks or special characters are used. Titles can be up to fifteen characters long.

SAVE [*notepadname*]
> stores the contents of the NOTEPAD window in the SASUSER.PROFILE catalog under the name you specify. If you do not specify a name, it is stored under the reserved name SCRATCH.NPAD. Note that it replaces text already stored in that catalog. For a listing of notepads, go to the CATALOG window and specify SASUSER.PROFILE.

With the FILE and INCLUDE commands, use the ATTR option to store the color and highlighting attributes in a text file or to include them in the NOTEPAD window. The syntax for the FILE command is

```
file [fileref|'actualname'][attr|notabs]
```

Note that if you use the FILE command with the ATTR option, you must use the INCLUDE command with it. If you use the FILE command without the ATTR option, you must use the INCLUDE command without it.

Extended Keys

Extended color and highlighting attribute keys are available for the NOTEPAD window. Press the ESC key and the indicated letter or number key to turn a color or highlighting attribute on or off. With this feature, you can alter the color of or assign a highlighting attribute to entire lines or individual words or letters. Valid colors and highlighting attributes and the keys you use to implement them are listed below.

Colors

You can press the letter key in either uppercase or lowercase.

ESC B	blue	ESC W	white
ESC R	red	ESC M	magenta
ESC P	pink	ESC O	orange
ESC G	green	ESC K	black
ESC C	cyan	ESC N	brown
ESC Y	yellow	ESC A	gray

Highlighting Attributes

ESC 0	turns off all highlighting attributes
ESC 1	turns on highlight
ESC 2	turns on underline (monochrome screens only)
ESC 3	turns on reverse video
ESC 4	turns on blinking.

Note that the global COLOR text command overrides the escape sequences. All other COLOR commands have no effect.

OPTIONS WINDOW

You invoke the OPTIONS window by typing the OPTIONS command on the command line of any display manager window and pressing ENTER. With the OPTIONS window, you can

- list the current settings of all SAS system options
- alter system option settings.

The OPTIONS window combines the functions of the OPTIONS procedure, which lists current option values, and the OPTIONS statement, which alters system option values. See Chapter 16, "SAS Global Options," and Chapter 18, "SAS Statements Used Anywhere," in this book and Chapter 23, "The OPTIONS Procedure," in the *SAS Procedures Guide, Release 6.03 Edition* for more information.

The OPTIONS window is shown in **Screen 10.23**. The left column, labeled Option, lists all of the system options in alphabetical order. You cannot type in the Option column. The right column, labeled Value, lists the current setting for each system option. To change an option setting, type over the value in the Value column. Omit the equal sign for options that take character or numeric strings as arguments. Use the values ON and OFF to change the value of positive or negative options.

```
┌OPTIONS─────────────────────────────────────────────────────┐
│Command ===>                                                │
│                                                            │
│Option           Value                                      │
│CENTER           ON                                         │
│CHARCODE         OFF                                        │
│DATE             ON                                         │
│DEVICE                                                      │
│ERRORS           20                                         │
│FIRSTOBS         1                                          │
│FORMCHAR         |----|+|---+=|-/ <>*                       │
│KANJI            OFF                                        │
│LINESIZE         78                                         │
│MISSING          .                                          │
│MPRINT           OFF                                        │
│MTRACE           OFF                                        │
│NEWS                                                        │
│NOTES            ON                                         │
│NUMBER           ON                                         │
│OBS              MAX                                        │
│OVP              OFF                                        │
│PAGENO           0                                          │
│PAGESIZE         21                                         │
│PROBSIG          0                                          │
│                                                      ZOOM──┘
```

Screen 10.23 OPTIONS Window

Changes to option values take effect immediately; you do not need to exit the OPTIONS window for the new options to take effect. The settings remain in effect throughout your current session unless you change them through the OPTIONS window or the OPTIONS statement. If the PROFILE option is in effect, settings for some options are saved after you end the SAS session. (See the description of the PROFILE system option in Chapter 16, "SAS Global Options," for a list of options that are saved.)

If the OPTIONS window is active and you reset a system option with the OPTIONS statement, the new setting is not displayed in the OPTIONS window automatically. You must close and reopen the OPTIONS window for settings specified by the OPTIONS statement to be displayed.

Commands

In addition to global commands, you can use the following commands in the OPTIONS window:

CANCEL
: cancels any changes you have made to the current options settings and returns the screen to the previous window.

END
: saves any changes you have made to the current settings and removes the OPTIONS window from the screen.

SETINIT WINDOW

Use the SETINIT window to display or alter site license information. Consult your SAS Installation Representative if you have questions about license information. You can invoke the SETINIT window by typing SETINIT on the command line and pressing ENTER.

The DATA panel is the first of four panels displayed when you invoke the SETINIT window. Also known as the SITEINFO panel, the DATA panel contains information pertinent to site licensing of SAS Institute-supplied software. **Screen 10.24** shows the SETINIT window with the DATA panel displayed.

```
┌SETINIT-DATA─────────────────────────────────────────────────────┐
│Command ===>                                                      │
│                                                                  │
│                                                                  │
│   SAS Version Number:       6.03                                 │
│   Customer Name:            SAS Institute 6.03                   │
│   Customer Number:                   1                           │
│   License Expiration Date:  ddmmmyy                              │
│   Customer Password:                                             │
│                                                                  │
│                                                                  │
│      Product         Trial              Product        Trial     │
│                                                                  │
│      Base              *                SAS/QC           *       │
│      SAS/STAT          *                NEWPDT01                 │
│      SAS/GRAPH         *                NEWPDT02                 │
│      SAS/ETS           *                NEWPDT03                 │
│      SAS/FSP           *                NEWPDT04                 │
│      SAS/OR            *                NEWPDT05                 │
│      SAS/AF            *                NEWPDT06                 │
│      SAS/IML           *                NEWPDT07                 │
│                                                                  │
│   Enter the "CBT" command to get to the CBT screen.              │
│                                                                  │
│                                                            ZOOM──┘
```

Screen 10.24 SETINIT Window

The SAS Version Number, the Customer Name (also on the log), and the Customer Number (also on the log) are included on the DATA panel. The License Expiration Date is the date after which you have 60 days to renew your site license. The Customer Password field appears blank until renewal; it is then usually completed by the SAS Installation Representative. This field can be completed only if you enter the window via the -SETINIT option when you invoke the SAS System. Note that the SAS Version Number and Customer Number fields cannot be changed. You must use the password corresponding to your site number and to Release 6.03 when updating this screen. Otherwise, the password is rejected.

The remaining dates on the DATA panel are expiration dates for add-on software products. An asterisk (*) beside a product name means that the expiration date is the same as the base expiration date. Any other date is a trial date used when your site is in the trial period to determine if licensing is desired.

Note that the presence of product names on this panel does not mean that the product is available. All possible software releases for Release 6.03 have been placed on this panel for future use. The designation NEWPDT in the Product column indicates that products may be introduced and names are not currently assigned.

The SEC panel contains secondary SETINIT information. All information on this panel is optional. The SAS Installation Representative may identify your copy of the SAS System with this panel. If so, pertinent information is shown in the USER IDENTIFICATION fields. If these fields are completed, the information is displayed in the SAS log. The representative may also choose to enter contact information in the FURTHER INFORMATION fields. This information is contained only in the SEC panel. The SITE REPRESENTATIVE CODE field is completed by the representative when initializing your copy of the system. None of the information on this panel can be changed without that code.

The CBT panel contains additional product expiration dates.

The REQUIRED panel contains text that is displayed when the SAS System is initialized (after the SAS command is entered). The text, if any, is provided by SAS Institute before product shipment. Most often, there is none. This text cannot be altered or deleted by any user, including the SAS Installation Representative.

Commands

In addition to global commands, you can use the following commands in the SETINIT window:

COPY
> copies current site data into the panel.

CBT
> displays the panel containing information on CBT product expiration dates.

DATA
> displays the panel containing site data.

END
> saves any changes you have made and removes the SETINIT window from the screen.

REQUIRED
> displays the panel containing text displayed when the SAS System is initialized.

SAVE
> saves site data on the panel when used with the SAS SETINIT command.

SEC
> displays secondary site data information.

VAR WINDOW

Use the VAR window to display information about variables in a specified SAS data set. The VAR window, shown in **Screen 10.25**, displays the variable names, type, and label.

The VAR window provides a quick and easy way to check the contents of a SAS data set.

386   Chapter 10

```
┌OUTPUT─────────────────┬VAR──────────────────────────────
│Command ===>           │Command ===>
│                       │
│                       │Libref:    work
│                       │Data Set:  sales
│                       │
│                       │  Name       Type    Label
│                       │  SALESREP   $
│                       │  SALES
│                       │  REGION     $
│                       │  MACHINE    $
│                       │
├LOG────────────────────┤
│Command ===>           │
│                       │
│NOTE: Copyright(c) 1985,86,
│NOTE: SAS (r) Proprietary S
│      Licensed to SAS Insti
│                       │
├PROGRAM EDITOR─────────┤
│Command ===>           │
│                       │
│00001                  │
│00002                  │
│00003                  │
└───────────────────────┴─────────────────────────────────
```

Screen 10.25 VAR Window Displaying SAS Data Set Information

Like the LIBNAME and DIR windows, the VAR window is interactive. In the DIR window you can select a SAS data set (a SAS file of type DATA) to display a VAR window showing the variables belonging to that SAS data set. If you enter the VAR window directly, the libref and data set fields are blank. You must enter the libref and the name of a SAS data set. If you want to display information about a temporary data set, specify WORK in the LIBREF field.

Once you have accessed the VAR window, you can continue to specify SAS data sets for which you want information. Move the cursor to the Data Set field and specify the name of another SAS data set, for example

```
data set: sales2
```

and press ENTER to display information about a SAS data set named SALES2.

When you have finished using the VAR window, use the END command to remove it from the display.

Commands

You can use all global commands in the VAR window. Use the END command to remove the VAR window from the screen.

SPECIAL TOPIC 1: SUBMITTING SAS STATEMENTS AT INITIALIZATION TIME

You can execute a list of SAS statements stored in an external file automatically at initialization time. When you enter the SAS System, it looks for a file named AUTOEXEC.SAS (or another file named in the -AUTOEXEC configuration option). If the SAS System finds such a file, the statements are submitted to the SAS System automatically.

By executing a series of SAS statements stored in an external file, you can save time and decrease the possibility of errors. You can submit DATA steps, PROC steps, or DM statements. A DM statement is a special SAS statement that allows you to execute command-line commands as part of a series of SAS statements. Suppose you want a series of commands executed each time you enter display manager. For example, you can specify commands that

- alter the default colors of various areas of a window
- execute statements that make SAS data libraries or external files available to your session
- establish a link to a remote mainframe system.

The AUTOEXEC.SAS file provided by SAS Institute contains the default RLINK fileref definition used by the SIGNON and SIGNOFF commands with respect to the micro-to-host link.

Creating Your File of SAS Statements

The SAS statements you want to be executed at initialization time must be stored in an external file, not a SAS data set. For information on this file, see the -AUTOEXEC configuration option in Chapter 16, "SAS Global Options." Use the SAS DM statement to enter any display manager commands. If you use a window call command in a DM statement to activate a window, list only commands that are valid in that window. See Chapter 18, "SAS Statements Used Anywhere," for more information on the DM statement.

SPECIAL TOPIC 2: CUSTOMIZING YOUR ENVIRONMENT

For some applications, you may want to change the position and colors of the windows in the SAS Display Manager System. You can design the placement and color of any window by using commands and cursor keys. For example, you can recall the default initial screen configuration of the SAS Display Manager System as shown in **Screen 10.26**.

388 Chapter 10

```
┌OUTPUT─────────────────────────────────────────────────────────┐
│Command ===>                                                   │
│                                                               │
│                                                               │
│                                                               │
│                                                               │
│                                                               │
│                                                               │
│                                                               │
┌LOG────────────────────────────────────────────────────────────┐
│Command ===>                                                   │
│                                                               │
│NOTE: Copyright(c) 1985,86,87 SAS Institute Inc., Cary, NC 27512-8000, U.S.A.
│NOTE: SAS (r) Proprietary Software Release 6.03                │
│      Licensed to SAS Institute 6.03, Site 00000000.           │
┌PROGRAM EDITOR─────────────────────────────────────────────────┐
│Command ===>                                                   │
│                                                               │
│00001                                                          │
│00002                                                          │
│00003                                                          │
└───────────────────────────────────────────────────────────────┘
```

Screen 10.26 Default Initial Display Manager Screen Format

Rearranging Windows

Using the WDEF Command

Suppose that you want to rearrange the windows on the screen so that the three windows are in the positions shown in **Screen 10.27**. There are two ways to change the position of windows. First, you can use the WDEF command to define the position on the screen where the window is to be placed. (See **Window Management Commands** in this chapter for complete information on the WDEF command.)

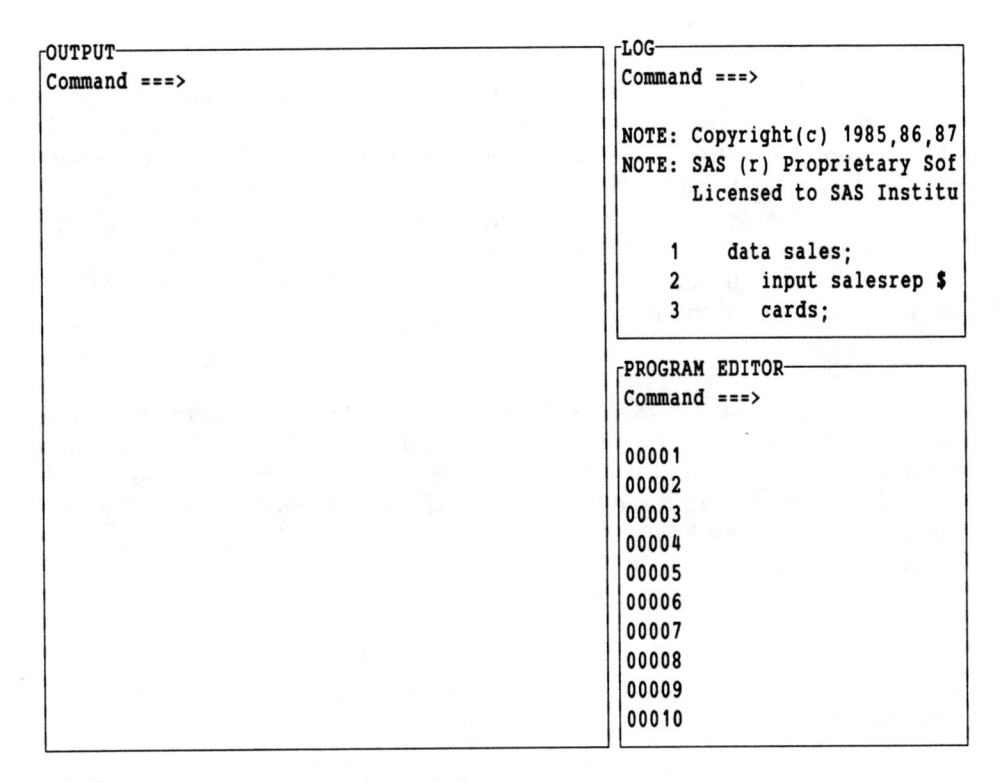

```
┌OUTPUT─────────────────────────┐  ┌LOG──────────────────────────┐
│Command ===>                   │  │Command ===>                 │
│                               │  │                             │
│                               │  │NOTE: Copyright(c) 1985,86,87│
│                               │  │NOTE: SAS (r) Proprietary Sof│
│                               │  │      Licensed to SAS Institu│
│                               │  │                             │
│                               │  │   1     data sales;         │
│                               │  │   2        input salesrep $ │
│                               │  │   3     cards;              │
│                               │  └─────────────────────────────┘
│                               │  ┌PROGRAM EDITOR───────────────┐
│                               │  │Command ===>                 │
│                               │  │                             │
│                               │  │00001                        │
│                               │  │00002                        │
│                               │  │00003                        │
│                               │  │00004                        │
│                               │  │00005                        │
│                               │  │00006                        │
│                               │  │00007                        │
│                               │  │00008                        │
│                               │  │00009                        │
│                               │  │00010                        │
└───────────────────────────────┘  └─────────────────────────────┘
```

Screen 10.27 Altered Screen Format

For example, suppose the PGM window shown in **Screen 10.26** is the active window. Enter the command

   wdef 12 50 12 29

on the command line and press ENTER. The PGM window moves to the screen location specified by the four numbers following WDEF: the starting row of the window border is row 12; the starting column of the window border is column 50; the window consists of 12 rows and 29 columns, excluding the borders.

Next, move the cursor to the command line of the LOG window. Enter the command

   wdef 1 50 9 29

and press ENTER. The LOG window now begins at row 1, column 50; it contains 9 rows and 29 columns, excluding the borders.

Finally, move the cursor to the command line of the OUTPUT window and enter the command

   wdef 1 1 23 47

and press ENTER. The OUTPUT window now occupies the left portion of the screen; it begins at row 1, column 1 and contains 23 rows and 47 columns, excluding the borders.

If you would like some or all of the windows to remain in this arrangement during future SAS sessions, enter

   wsave

on the command line of the window you want to save and press ENTER. Repeat the command for each window you want to save; when you display that window in future SAS sessions, the SAS System displays it in the position you saved.

Using the Cursor Keys

The second method of changing windows is to design by appearance instead of by calculating positions. To do this, place the active window into grow, shrink, or move mode, and use the cursor keys on the numeric keypad to move the window to the location you want.

For example, suppose you want to arrange the windows as shown in **Screen 10.27**. Assuming that the screen shows the default window arrangement, you can work as follows. You want to make the PGM window taller and shift it right. On the command line of the PGM window, enter

```
wgrow
```

and press ENTER. The word GROW appears in the lower-right corner of the window, indicating that it is in grow mode. In grow mode, the cursor keys push the borders of the window in the direction of the arrow on each key. Press the UP cursor key repeatedly to make the window taller (see **Screen 10.28**). When the window is the desired height (temporarily covering the LOG window), reenter WGROW to end grow mode.

```
┌OUTPUT─────────────────────────────────────────────────────┐
│Command ===>                                                │
│                                                            │
│                                                            │
│                                                            │
│                                                            │
│                                                            │
│                                                            │
│                                                            │
├PROGRAM EDITOR─────────────────────────────────────────────┤
│Command ===>                                                │
│                                                            │
│00001                                                       │
│00002                                                       │
│00003                                                       │
│00004                                                       │
│00005                                                       │
│00006                                                       │
│00007                                                       │
│00008                                                       │
│00009                                                       │
│00010                                                       │
│                                                   ─GROW─  │
└────────────────────────────────────────────────────────────┘
```

Screen 10.28 Using Grow Mode

To make the PGM window fit in the right corner of the screen, enter

```
wshrink
```

on the command line, and press ENTER to place it in shrink mode. In shrink mode, each cursor key pulls the far border of the window in the direction the arrow points, shrinking the window. To shrink the left border of the PGM window toward the right, press the RIGHT cursor key repeatedly until the left border of the window reaches the correct position; then reenter WSHRINK to end shrink mode. The PGM window is now finished (see **Screen 10.29**).

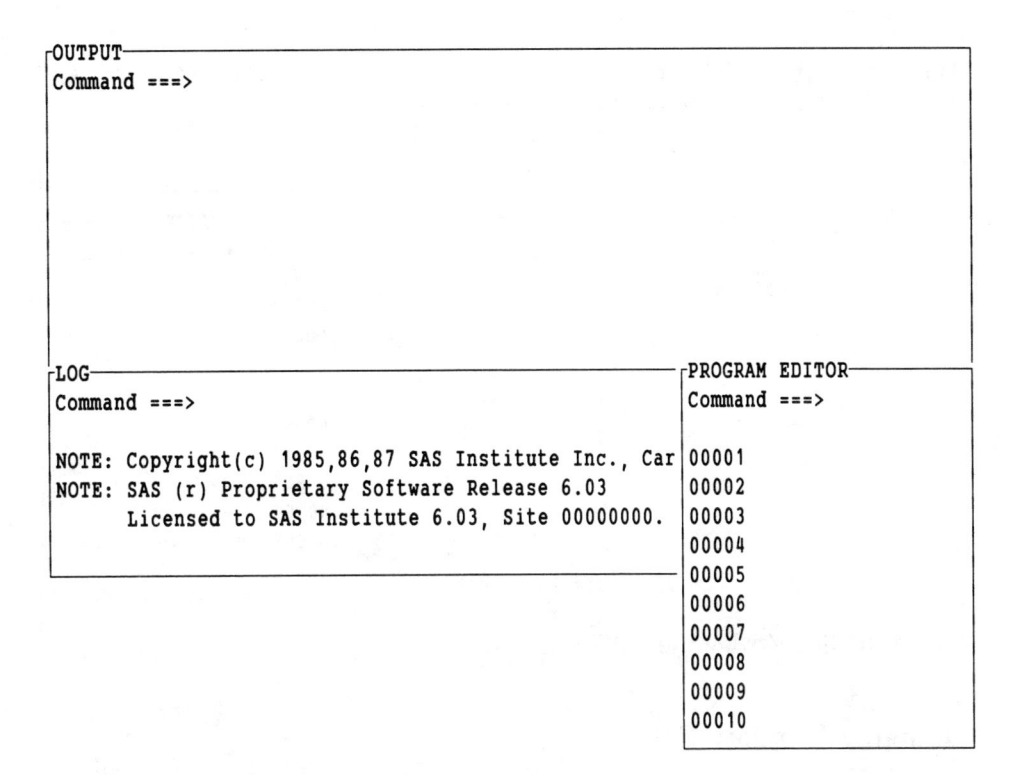

```
┌OUTPUT─────────────────────────────────────────────────────────────────┐
│Command ===>                                                           │
│                                                                       │
│                                                                       │
│                                                                       │
│                                                                       │
│                                                                       │
│                                                                       │
│                                                                       │
│┌LOG──────────────────────────────────────────┐┌PROGRAM EDITOR─────────┤
││Command ===>                                 ││Command ===>           │
││                                             ││                       │
││NOTE: Copyright(c) 1985,86,87 SAS Institute Inc., Car│00001            │
││NOTE: SAS (r) Proprietary Software Release 6.03     │00002            │
││      Licensed to SAS Institute 6.03, Site 00000000.│00003            │
││                                             ││00004                  │
│└─────────────────────────────────────────────┘│00005                  │
│                                               │00006                  │
│                                               │00007                  │
│                                               │00008                  │
│                                               │00009                  │
│                                               │00010                  │
└───────────────────────────────────────────────┴───────────────────────┘
```

Screen 10.29 New PGM Window Position

Since the PGM window now covers part of the LOG window, you need to move the LOG window so that none of it is hidden behind the PGM window; you also need to make the LOG window taller and move it to the right. Move the cursor to the command line of the LOG window (it temporarily overlays the PGM window) and type

    wmove

and press ENTER. The word MOVE appears in the lower-right corner of the screen, indicating that the window is in move mode. In move mode, each cursor key pulls the window in the direction of the arrow. Press the UP cursor key repeatedly to move the LOG window up until its bottom edge rests on the top edge of the PGM window; then reenter WMOVE to end move mode (see **Screen 10.30**). Now you can enter grow and shrink modes as before to fit the LOG window into the upper-right corner of the screen.

Finally, you need to make the OUTPUT window occupy the left part of the screen. Place the cursor on the command line of the OUTPUT window and enter shrink mode; then use the LEFT cursor key to shrink the right border of the window toward the left until it appears next to the border of the LOG and PGM windows. Then end shrink mode and enter grow mode; use the DOWN cursor key to push the bottom edge of the OUTPUT window to the bottom of the screen. When you end grow mode, the screen is finished.

To save one or more of the windows, enter WSAVE on the command line of each window you want to save.

```
┌OUTPUT─────────────────────────────────────────────────────────────────┐
│Command ===>                                                           │
│                                                                       │
├─LOG───────────────────────────────────────────────────────────────────┤
│Command ===>                                                           │
│                                                                       │
│NOTE: Copyright(c) 1985,86,87 SAS Institute Inc., Cary, NC 27512-8000, U.S.A.│
│NOTE: SAS (r) Proprietary Software Release 6.03                        │
│      Licensed to SAS Institute 6.03, Site 00000000.                   │
│                                                                       │
└───────────────────────────────────────────────────────────────────────┘
                                              ┌─PROGRAM EDITOR──────────┐
                                              │Command ===>             │
                                              │                         │
                                              │00001                    │
                                              │00002                    │
                                              │00003                    │
                                              │00004                    │
                                              │00005                    │
                                              │00006                    │
                                              │00007                    │
                                              │00008                    │
                                              │00009                    │
                                              │00010                    │
                                              └─────────────────────────┘
```

Screen 10.30 Moving the LOG Window

Changing Window Colors

You can also customize windows by assigning colors to parts of the window. For example, to make the background of the PGM window red, enter

    color background red

on the command line of the PGM window.
  To make messages on the LOG window yellow, enter

    color message yellow

on the command line of the LOG window.
  You can also alter the color of other parts of the window. Colors available are WHITE, GREEN, RED, CYAN, BLUE, BLACK, MAGENTA, YELLOW, GREY, ORANGE, BROWN, and PINK. For more information on assigning colors, see **COLOR Command** in this chapter.

Customizing Windows with Function Keys

You can customize windows and issue other commands more conveniently by assigning commands to function keys. First display the KEYS window by typing

    keys

on the command line of any window and pressing ENTER. The KEYS window appears. Then type the command next to the function key you want to use. Separate multiple commands on a line with a semicolon; a semicolon is not required after the last command. For example, to use the SHIFT and F1 keys to color the background of the LOG window red, type

    log; color background red

on the SHF F1 line of the KEYS window. The LOG command makes the LOG window the active window, and the COLOR command colors the background.

To save the new key definitions, enter SAVE on the command line of the KEYS window; to save them and remove the display of the KEYS window, enter the END command.

Notes on Customizing Windows

- Default keys are available for the WGROW, WSHRINK, and WMOVE commands. Pressing one of these function keys places the active window into that mode; if it is already in that mode, pressing the key ends the mode. You can also use the function keys to go directly from one mode to another (for example, grow to shrink) without having to leave the previous mode.
- Text that disappears when you shrink a window or move another window over it reappears when you move or enlarge the window again.
- You cannot move or enlarge a window past the edge of the screen.
- You can save only one version of a window at a time with the WSAVE command. To create multiple versions of a window (for example, a large OUTPUT window at some times and a small one at other times), use the commands that create each version in a series of SAS DM statements, and save each group of DM statements in a separate file. You can then use the INCLUDE command to bring the contents of the external file to the PGM window and then execute the SUBMIT command to create the desired window arrangement. See **The DM Statement** in Chapter 18, "SAS Statements Used Anywhere."

You can also assign the commands to create each version to a different function key; pressing the function key creates the arrangement you want.

Chapter 11
Error Handling

INTRODUCTION 395
REQUESTOR PANELS AND PROMPTS 395
OUT-OF-MEMORY CONDITION 396
DOS CRITICAL ERRORS 396

INTRODUCTION

This chapter describes features of the 6.03 Release of the SAS System for PCs that help you handle error conditions. It also recommends actions to take when you encounter serious problems, such as insufficient memory or a DOS critical error.

REQUESTOR PANELS AND PROMPTS

The SAS System for PCs uses a *requestor panel* or *requestor prompt* to handle some error conditions and user decision points. A sample requestor panel is shown in **Screen 11.1**.

```
┌─ BREAK ─────────────────────────────────────────────┐
│    Press Y to cancel submitted statements, N to continue │
└─────────────────────────────────────────────────────┘
```

Screen 11.1 Sample Requestor Panel

The purpose of a requestor panel or prompt is to get input from you to resolve a specific situation. For example, some scripts for the SAS micro-to-host link use requestor panels to prompt you to input your host ID and host password.

The requestor panel or prompt is used throughout the PC SAS System. If you are running a display manager session or a full-screen product like SAS/FSP software, the requestor panel appears. If you are running a line-mode session, a requestor prompt appears.

These are some of the conditions that cause a requestor panel or prompt to display:

- when you issue the ENDSAS statement in a display manager session while an interactive procedure is still active
- when you request a catalog that does not exist in the CATALOG window of display manager
- when you use SAS/GRAPH software without specifying a device name
- when your machine is out of memory
- when you issue a control-break signal
- when a DOS critical error has occurred.

OUT-OF-MEMORY CONDITION

When you try to use a SAS procedure or feature in the display manager and you do not have enough memory for it, a requestor panel is displayed. The requestor panel tells you there is not enough memory and asks you how you want to solve the problem. Several alternatives are offered:

- A   automatic clean-up of memory for this occurrence of the problem. If you choose this alternative, the SAS System deletes all active auxiliary windows, paste buffers, functions, and formats.

- G   automatic clean-up of memory for this occurrence and future occurrences of the problem. If you choose this alternative, the SAS System deletes all active auxiliary windows, paste buffers, functions, and formats every time you run out of memory. If you select this alternative, this requestor panel is not displayed again during your SAS session.

- S   selective clean-up of memory. Your choices are to delete
  - all windows
  - all paste buffers
  - all functions and formats (that are not currently in use).

  Typically, deleting auxiliary windows results in the largest reduction in memory use.

- N   do not delete anything. If you select this alternative, the SAS procedure or feature attempts to continue processing.

If you are running the SAS System for PCs in any other mode and run out of memory, the SAS System stops processing the step.

DOS CRITICAL ERRORS

The SAS System for PCs uses requestor panels or prompts to help you resolve DOS critical errors. DOS critical errors include

- when you designate drive A: but have not inserted a diskette. The requestor panel or prompt tells you to insert a diskette.
- when a printer or plotter is not on-line when the system is ready to send output to it. Requestor panels prompt you to load paper in the printer and turn the device on.
- when you run out of disk space in the middle of a program or application. When this happens, a requestor panel displays a message indicating the problem and giving you two choices:

1. You can exit to DOS SUBSET mode and delete files to make space on the disk. When you have finished deleting files, you return to your SAS session and continue processing.
2. You can end the program you were executing. If you choose this alternative, the step terminates abnormally but does not end your SAS session abnormally. If the error occurs during execution of a command that writes to the disk, such as the display manager FILE command, the command writes as much as it can to the disk. The file then is closed and the step ends.

Chapter 12
SAS® Output

INTRODUCTION 399
SAS LOG 399
   Destination of the Log 400
   Structure of the SAS Log 400
   Writing on the Log 401
   Suppressing All or Part of the Log 402
PRINTED RESULTS OF SAS PROCEDURES 402
   Procedure Output Destination 403
   Titles 403
   Printing Values 403
   Printing Variable Names 403
   Page and Line Sizes 404
   Page Numbering 404
   Date and Time 404
   Centering Output 404
ERRORS 404
   Syntax Errors 405
   Programming Errors 407
   Data Errors and Other Warning Messages 408
   Return Codes 410

INTRODUCTION

The SAS System produces printed output in the form of the SAS log (a description of the SAS session) and the results of SAS procedures. This chapter discusses these forms of printed SAS output and how you can tailor them to meet your specific needs. The last section describes SAS errors and error messages.

   Important Note: the SAS Display Manager System provides another method of displaying the SAS log and procedure output. Refer to the "SAS Display Manager System" chapter for details.

SAS LOG

The SAS log includes information about the processing of the SAS program: what statements were executed; what data sets were created and how many variables and observations they contain; how much time each step in the program required. The log is also used by some of the SAS procedures that perform SAS or utility functions, such as DATASETS. Messages are written on the log by certain PUT statements.

   The SAS log is necessary and important documentation that gives a journal of the processing, and it can help you solve problems that arise during the session.

400 Chapter 12

Destination of the Log

Using the Default

The default destination of the log depends on the mode of execution you use:

- For interactive full-screen sessions, the log appears in the LOG window of display manager.
- For interactive line-mode sessions, the log appears on your screen as each step executes.
- For noninteractive SAS programs, the log is written to a disk file. By default, that file is written to your current directory and is called *name*.LOG, where *name* is the first level or filename portion of the source file that was input to the SAS System.

You can also use the PRINTTO procedure to define the destination for your procedure output and to change the destination of the SAS log. For further information, see "The PRINTTO Procedure" in the *SAS Procedures Guide, Release 6.03 Edition*.

Redirecting the Log

You can redirect the destination of the log for a noninteractive SAS program by specifying the configuration option –LOG either in the CONFIG.SAS file or on the command line when you invoke the SAS System. The option specified on the command line overrides the option specified in the CONFIG.SAS file.

To terminate the option, simply specify it on the command line with no argument.

Structure of the SAS Log

Each line in your SAS program containing SAS statements is printed and numbered on the log; for example, the small number 1 printed to the left of the DATA statement in the example below means that it was the first line in the program.

Interspersed with your SAS statements are messages from the SAS System. These messages sometimes begin with the word NOTE, the word ERROR, or an error number. They sometimes refer to a SAS statement by its line number on the log.

Output 12.1 is a sample SAS log. The numbered items shown on the log are explained in the list following the output.

Output 12.1 Sample SAS Log

```
NOTE: Copyright(c) 1985, 86, 87 SAS Institute Inc. Cary, N.C. 27512-8000, U.S.A.   ❶ 10:30  Tuesday, December 8, 1987
NOTE: SAS (r) Proprietary Software Release 6.03    ❷   ❸  ❹
      Licensed to SAS Institute Inc., Site 00000000.
1      ❺ data htwt;
2           input name $ 1-10 sex $ 12 age 14-15 height 17-18 weight 20-22;
3           list;
4           cards;
RULE:      ----+----1----+----2----+----3----+----4----+----5----+----6----+----7
5          ALFRED     M 14 69 112
6          ALICE      F 13 56 84
7          BARBARA    F 14 62 102
```

(continued on next page)

(continued from previous page)

```
8          BERNADETTE  F  13  65   98
9          HENRY       M  14  63  102
10         JAMES       M  12  57   83
11         JANE        F  12  59   84
12         JANET       F  15  62  112
13         JEFFREY     M  13  62   84
14         JOHN        M  12  59   99
15         JOYCE       F  11  51   50
16         JUDY        F  14  64   90
17         LOUISE      F  12  56   77
18         MARY        F  15  66  112
19         PHILIP      M  16  72  150
20         ROBERT      M  12  64  128
21         RONALD      M  15  67  133
22         THOMAS      M  11  57   85
23         WILLIAM     M  15  66  112
NOTE: The data set WORK.HTWT has 19 observations and 5 variables. ❽
NOTE: The DATA statement used   26.00 seconds.

24
24         proc print;
25
NOTE: The PROCEDURE PRINT used   17.00 seconds. ❽

26
26         proc plot;
30             plot height*weight=sex;
NOTE: The PROCEDURE PLOT used   12.00 seconds. ❽

NOTE: SAS Institute Inc., SAS Circle, PO Box 8000, Cary, N.C. 27512-8000  ❾
```

1. Date and time the program was run.
2. The SAS System release used to run this program.
3. Name of the computer installation where the program was run.
4. The computer installation site number. (The site number is used by SAS Institute to identify the installation given in 3.)
5. SAS statements for each DATA or PROC step in the program.
6. For each external file of data read or written in a DATA step, information about the file, including the number of lines read or written (not illustrated in **Output 12.1**).
7. For each SAS data set created, its name, the number of observations and variables, and the number of observations that can be stored in one track of disk space (not illustrated in **Output 12.1**).
8. Computer time used by the step.
9. The name and address of SAS Institute Inc. When you see this note, you know that your program or session has completed.

Writing on the Log

In addition to the information that SAS automatically writes to the log, you can have other information printed there. You can tell SAS to write to the log in two ways: the LIST statement automatically prints the current data line on the log and PUT statements can be directed to the log. **Output 12.2** is the log of a SAS program that uses a LIST statement and a PUT statement directed to the log. (Note that in this DATA step FILE LOG is assumed since no FILE statement is present.)

Output 12.2 Writing on the Log

```
NOTE: Copyright(c) 1985, 86, 87 SAS Institute, Inc., Cary, N.C. 27512-8000 U.S.A.
NOTE: SAS (r) Proprietary Software Release 6.03
      Licensed to SAS Institute Inc., Site 00000000.
1          data one;
2             input id $ x y;
3             list;
4             if x=y then put 'X AND Y ARE EQUAL ' x=;
5             cards;
RULE:      ----+----1----+----2----+----3----+----4----+----5----+----6----+----7
6          A01 1.2 3
7          A21 2.4 4
8          A02 2   2
X AND Y ARE EQUAL X=2
9          B01 3   0
10         B21 3   3
X AND Y ARE EQUAL X=3
11         B02 1   .
12         C01 .   5
NOTE: The data set WORK.ONE has 7 observations and 3 variables.
NOTE: The DATA statement used  16.00 seconds.

13         ;
14         PROC PRINT;
NOTE: The PROCEDURE PRINT used  15.00 seconds.

NOTE: SAS Institute Inc., SAS Circle, PO Box 8000, Cary, N.C. 27512-8000
```

Suppressing All or Part of the Log

When you have large SAS programs that you run on a regular basis without changes, you may want to suppress the listing of your SAS statements on the log. You can use the system option NOSOURCE in an OPTIONS statement at the beginning of your program to suppress these lines.

Sometimes you may want to suppress the notes that SAS prints on the log. You can use the system option NONOTES to prevent SAS from printing any of the messages beginning with NOTE. **Do not** use this option until your program is error-free. The notes that SAS prints are required for debugging.

When data errors occur in your SAS program, SAS prints error messages for up to *n* errors where *n* is the value of the system option ERRORS=. Normally, the default value is ERRORS=20, and SAS prints messages for up to 20 data errors. You can set the value of ERRORS= to another number to specify the maximum number of error messages you want printed on your log. If ERRORS=0, no error messages are printed. (Note that the ? or ?? message modifiers in the INPUT statement also affect the printing of error messages. See the **INPUT Statement** for more information.)

For more information about these and other system options, see the chapter "SAS Global Options."

PRINTED RESULTS OF SAS PROCEDURES

The display manager OUTPUT window contains the results of PROC steps as well as reports printed by DATA steps using the PUT and FILE statements routed to the PRINT file. These results and reports appear in the same order as the corresponding DATA and PROC steps that appeared in the program, and notes on the log tell which output pages were produced by which DATA or PROC step.

Each SAS procedure produces a different form of output. Consult the procedure descriptions in the *SAS Procedures Guide* for examples of output from SAS procedures. You can tailor SAS printouts using certain SAS statements and system options.

Procedure Output Destination

Using the Default

The default destination of your procedure output depends on the mode of execution you use:

- For interactive full-screen sessions, procedure output appears in the OUTPUT window of the SAS Display Manager System.
- For interactive line-mode sessions, procedure output appears on your screen as each step executes.
- For noninteractive SAS programs, procedure output is written to a disk file. By default, that file is written to your current directory and is called *name*.LST, where *name* is the first level or filename portion of the SAS source file that was input to the SAS System.

Redirecting Your Output

You can redirect the destination of the output for a noninteractive SAS program by specifying the configuration option –PRINT either in the CONFIG.SAS file or as a command option when you invoke the SAS System. The command option overrides the CONFIG.SAS file option. To terminate the option, simply specify it with no argument.

Titles

SAS prints the title

```
SAS
```

at the top of each page of output unless you specify your own titles with one or more TITLE statements.

Printing Values

You have some control over the way SAS prints values in procedure output. For example, by default SAS prints a single dot (.) as a missing value for a numeric variable. To have SAS print some other character for a missing value, use the SAS system option MISSING= in an OPTIONS statement. For example, if you specify

```
options missing='B';
```

when the value of a numeric variable is missing, the letter B is printed instead of a single period.

You can use FORMAT or ATTRIB statements to associate formats with variables. This format is then used to print the values of variables. The SAS formats available are described in "SAS Informats and Formats."

You can define your own formats using the FORMAT procedure. This procedure gives you a great deal of flexibility in printing the results of procedures.

See the descriptions of the **FORMAT Statement** and the **ATTRIB Statement** in this manual and "The FORMAT Procedure" in the *SAS Procedures Guide, Release 6.03 Edition* for more information.

Printing Variable Names

For most SAS procedures, if a LABEL statement has been specified in the DATA step used to create the data set being analyzed or in the current PROC step, the label rather than the variable name is printed. The label can be up to forty characters long, thus giving a more descriptive name to the variable. See the **LABEL Statement** descriptions for more information.

Page and Line Sizes

The default number of lines per page (page size) and characters per line (line size) are determined by the values of the SAS system options PAGESIZE= (or PS) and LINESIZE= (or LS). You can reset these options to your own values with the OPTIONS statement.

For example, suppose you are planning to photo-reduce your output to fit on an 8.5" x 11" page. Instead of the default values of 60 lines per page and 132 characters per line, you will be able to fit 76 lines per page but only 100 characters per line. If you use the OPTIONS statement below in your SAS program, output printed uses 76 lines per page and 100 characters per line.

```
options pagesize=76 linesize=100;
```

The values you use for LINESIZE= and PAGESIZE= can affect the output produced by some SAS procedures. For example, the default set of descriptive statistics printed by the MEANS procedure is dependent on the line size in effect at the time. The appearance of the output from procedures changes slightly for different line sizes.

Page Numbering

SAS numbers the output pages at the top of the page, beginning with page 1.

If you do not want page numbers printed on your output, use the SAS system option NONUMBER. For example, you can specify this OPTIONS statement as the first statement in your SAS program to suppress page numbering:

```
options nonumber;
```

Date and Time

The date and time that the program was run appear on the printout. These values become important when you are running a program several times.

If you do not want the time and date values to appear, you can use the system option NODATE. For example, this OPTIONS statement causes SAS to leave off the current date and time from each page of output:

```
options nodate;
```

Centering Output

SAS normally centers titles and procedure output on the pages. If you want the output left aligned rather than centered, you can use the system option NOCENTER:

```
options nocenter;
```

See the chapter "SAS Global Options" for more information about SAS system options.

ERRORS

SAS can detect three kinds of errors: syntax errors, programming errors, and data errors. SAS finds syntax errors as it compiles each SAS step before the statements are executed. Data errors and some programming errors are discovered when your SAS program is being executed.

Syntax Errors

If you misspell a SAS keyword, forget a semicolon, or make similar mistakes, SAS prints the word ERROR followed by an error message. Some errors are explained fully by the message that SAS prints, but other error messages are not as easy to interpret. For example, because SAS statements are free-format and can begin and end anywhere, when you fail to end a SAS statement with a semicolon, SAS does not always detect the error. Here is an example:

```
data a;
   input x y
   z+x+y;
   list;
   cards;
1 2
2 3
4 5
6 7
;
proc print;
   title 'THE EFFECT OF A MISSING SEMICOLON';
```

The log from the program above shows that the missing semicolon in the INPUT statement is not detected as an error by SAS. (See **Output 12.3**.)

Output 12.3 A Syntax Error SAS Did Not Detect

```
NOTE: Copyright(c) 1985,86,87 SAS Institute Inc., Cary, NC 27512-8000 U.S.A.
NOTE: SAS (r) Proprietary Software Release 6.03
      Licensed to SAS Institute Inc. Site 00000000.
    1    data a;
    2       input x y
    3       z+x+y;
    4       list;
    5       cards;
RULE:----+----1----+----2----+----3----+----4----+----5----+----6----+----7----+----8----+----9----+----0
    7 2 3
    9 6 7
   10    ;
NOTE: SAS went to a new line when INPUT statement reached past the end of a line.
NOTE: The data set WORK.A has 2 observations and 3 variables.
NOTE: The DATA statement used 3.00 seconds.
   11    proc print;
   12       title 'THE EFFECT OF A MISSING SEMICOLON';
```

The sum statement is considered part of the INPUT statement. The message

```
NOTE: SAS went to a new line when INPUT statement reached
      past the end of a line.
```

is often an indication that your data lines are not being read as you expected. When the LIST statement is executed, the current record is the second in each group of two lines. The PRINT procedure prints the data set created (see **Output 12.4**).

406 Chapter 12

Output 12.4 The Output from PROC PRINT Reveals the Error

```
                    THE EFFECT OF A MISSING SEMICOLON                          1
              OBS     X      Y      Z
                1     2      2      .
                2     6      5      .
```

Below is a DATA step in which a semicolon was left off the DATA statement. Again, SAS did not detect the error (see **Output 12.5**):

```
data a
    input x y;
    z= x + y;
    list;
    cards;
1 2
3 4
5 6
7 8
;
proc print;
    title 'A MISSING SEMICOLON IN THE DATA STATEMENT';
```

Output 12.5 SAS Did Not Detect the Missing Semicolon

```
NOTE: Copyright(c) 1985,86,87 SAS Institute Inc., Cary, NC 27512-8000, U.S.A.
NOTE: SAS (r) Proprietary Software Release 6.03
      Licensed to SAS Institute Inc., Site 00000000.
      1    data a
      2        input x y;
      3        z= x+ y;
      4        list;
      5        cards;
NOTE: Variable X is uninitialized.
NOTE: Variable Y is uninitialized.
NOTE: Missing values were generated as a result of performing an operation on missing values.
      Each place is given by: (Number of times) at (Line):(Column).
      1 at 3:7
NOTE: The data set WORK.A has 1 observations and 3 variables.
NOTE: The data set WORK.INPUT has 1 observations and 3 variables.
NOTE: The data set WORK.X has 1 observations and 3 variables.
NOTE: The data set WORK.Y has 1 observations and 3 variables.
NOTE: The DATA statement used 5.00 seconds.
      6    1 2
      7    3 4
      8    5 6
      9    7 8
     10    ;
     11    proc print;
     12        title 'A MISSING SEMICOLON IN THE DATA STATEMENT';
```

The INPUT statement was assumed to be part of the DATA statement. Thus, SAS was prepared to build four data sets: A, INPUT, X, and Y. One observation was written to each data set when the DATA step was executed.

The messages on the SAS log indicate that four data sets were created—WORK.A, WORK.INPUT, WORK.X, and WORK.Y—each with one observation.

This is your clue that an error occurred. Since no INPUT statement was executed, X and Y were assumed to be missing in the assignment statement, and the LIST statement had no record to write. The resulting PROC PRINT is shown in **Output 12.6**.

Output 12.6 PROC PRINT Shows the Results of the Missing Semicolon

```
                A MISSING SEMICOLON IN THE DATA STATEMENT                    1
                     OBS    Z    X    Y
```

When SAS finds a syntax error, it does not run the step in which the error occurred. To warn you, it prints:

```
NOTE:  SAS stopped processing this step because of errors.
```

Programming Errors

The execution-time errors that cause your SAS program to fail are called *programming errors*. For example, if your program processes an array and SAS encounters a value of the array's subscript that is out of range, SAS prints an error message and stops.

Below is an example. The DATA step defines an array with ten elements. Variable I contains the value of the subscript for the current execution of the DATA step. The value of I is read with an INPUT statement before the array is processed in a programming statement. A miscoded I value results in an error message.

```
data a;
   array all(10) x1-x10;
   input i measure;
   if measure>0 then all(i)=measure;
   cards;
1 1.5
. 3
2 4.5
;
proc print;
```

See **Output 12.7**.

Output 12.7 A Miscoded Value Causes an Error Message to Be Printed

```
NOTE: Copyright(c) 1985,86,87 SAS Institute Inc., Cary, NC 27512-8000, U.S.A.
NOTE: SAS (r) Proprietary Software Release 6.03
      Licensed to SAS Institute Inc., Site 00000000.
    1     data a
    2        input x y;
    3        z= x+ y;
    4        list;
    5        cards;
NOTE: Variable X is uninitialized.
NOTE: Variable Y is uninitialized.
NOTE: Missing values were generated as a result of performing an operation on missing values.
      Each place is given by: (Number of times) at (Line):(Column).
      1 at 3:7
NOTE: The data set WORK.A has 1 observations and 3 variables.
NOTE: The data set WORK.INPUT has 1 observations and 3 variables.
NOTE: The data set WORK.X has 1 observations and 3 variables.
NOTE: The data set WORK.Y has 1 observations and 3 variables.
NOTE: The DATA statement used 5.00 seconds.
    6     1 2
    7     3 4
    8     5 6
    9     7 8
   10     ;
   11     proc print;
   12        title 'A MISSING SEMICOLON IN THE DATA STATEMENT' ;
   13     data a;
NOTE: The PROCEDURE PRINT used 4.73 minutes.
   14        array all{10} x1-x10;
   15        input i measure;
   16           if measure >0 then all{i}=measure;
   17        cards;
ERROR: Array subscript out of range at line 16 column 33.
RULE:----+----1----+----2----+----3----+----4----+----5----+----6----+----7----+----8----+----9----+----0
   19  . 3
X1=. X2=. X3=. X4=. X5=. X6=. X7=. X8=. X9=. X10=. I=. MEASURE=3 _ERROR_=1 _N_=2
   21     ;
NOTE: The data set WORK.A has 1 observations and 12 variables.
NOTE: The DATA statement used 4.00 seconds.
   22     proc print;
```

Data Errors and Other Warning Messages

Like programming errors, data errors are detected during the execution of the program. However, unlike programming errors, data errors do not cause execution to stop. SAS warns you of the data errors on the SAS log.

The DATA step below reads seven data lines:

```
options ls=80;
data one;
    input id $ x y;
    z=x/y;
    lg=log(x);
    cards;
a01 1.2 3
a21 2.4 4
a02 0   2
b01 3   0
b21 A   3
b02 1   .
c01 .   5
;
proc print;
```

The SAS log produced when the program is run contains several warning messages; however, the program ran to completion. Notice that data lines following a CARDS statement are numbered along with the log statements (see **Output 12.8**).

Output 12.8 Warning Messages Are Printed When SAS Encounters Data Errors

```
NOTE: Copyright(c) 1985,86,87 SAS Institute Inc., Cary, NC 27512-8000, U.S.A.
NOTE: SAS (r) Proprietary Software Release 6.03
      Licensed to SAS Institute Inc., Site 00000000.
     1     options ls=80;
     2     data one;
     3        input id $ x y;
     4        z=x/y;
     5        lg=log(x);
     6        cards;
NOTE: Invalid argument to function LOG at line 5 column 11.
RULE:----+----1----+----2----+----3----+----4----+----5----+----6----+----7----+
     9 a02 0   2
ID=a02 X=0 Y=2 Z=0 LG=. _ERROR_=1 _N_=3
ERROR: Division by zero detected at line 4 column 6.
    10 b01 3   0
ID=b01 X=3 Y=0 Z=. LG=1.0986122887 _ERROR_=1 _N_=4
NOTE: Invalid data for X in line 11 5-5.
    11 b21 A   3
ID=b21 X=. Y=3 Z=. LG=. _ERROR_=1 _N_=5
    14 ;
NOTE: Mathematical operations could not be performed at the following places.
      The results of the operations have been set to missing values.
      Each place is given by: (Number of times) at (Line):(Column).
      1 at 5:11
      1 at 4:6
NOTE: Missing values were generated as a result of performing an operation on
      missing values.
      Each place is given by: (Number of times) at (Line):(Column).
      3 at 4:6
      2 at 5:11
NOTE: The data set WORK.ONE has 7 observations and 5 variables.
NOTE: The DATA statement used 13.00 seconds.
    15    proc print;
```

The first data error occurs when X is 0. Zero is an invalid argument to the LOG function. The error causes SAS to print several types of information. They are

- the warning message, which in this case is

  NOTE: Invalid argument to function LOG at line 5 column 11.

- for the first error, the RULE, which gives the column numbers referred to in this and later messages.
- the current record in the input buffer (usually the line in error).
- the current values of all the variables.

  For each subsequent error that occurs while SAS is executing the DATA step, SAS prints the warning message, the line in error, and the current values of the variables.

At the end of the step, SAS prints a summary of the operations that could not be performed because of invalid arguments or divisors. The number of times a missing value was the result of an operation is also given. The operations that resulted in missing values are summarized in the form:

(Number of times) at (Line):(Column)

For example, the SAS log above summarizes the number of times that missing values were generated as a result of performing operations on missing values:

3 at 4:6   2 at 5:11

This note tells you that missing values resulted three times at line 4, column 6 of the SAS log—the location of the variable X in the assignment statement

z=x/y;

and two times at line 5, column 11 of the SAS log in the statement

lg=log(x);

where the LOG function appears.

Return Codes

Each execution of the SAS command sets a return code. A return code of 0 indicates that the session ended normally. If you are using PC DOS, you can check the value of the return code with the IF and ERRORLEVEL PC DOS commands within a BAT file. For more information, consult your SAS Software Consultant.

Chapter 13
SAS® Informats and Formats

INTRODUCTION 411
   Reading and Writing Binary Data 412
USING SAS INFORMATS 413
   Informat Descriptions: Numeric 415
   Informat Descriptions: Character 422
USING SAS FORMATS 425
   Format Descriptions: Numeric 428
   Format Descriptions: Character 435
USING SAS DATE, TIME, AND DATETIME INFORMATS AND FORMATS 437
   Duration vs. Date 439
   Date, Time, and Datetime Informat Descriptions 441
   Date, Time, and Datetime Format Descriptions 444

INTRODUCTION

At times you must give the SAS System directions for reading or writing a value in a certain way. For example, the value

   1,000,000

in a data line is not usually acceptable as a number because it contains commas. However, you can tell the SAS System to ignore the commas and read the value as

   1000000

Likewise, you can tell the SAS System to display the value 1000000 as

   1,000,000
   $1,000,000

and in other ways.

   A set of directions for reading a value is an *informat*. For example, to read 1,000,000 use the COMMA. informat. A set of directions for writing a value is a *format*. The formats used above to display 1000000 are the COMMA. and DOLLAR. formats, respectively.

   The SAS System provides many informats and formats for use with numeric and character data and with date, time, and datetime values. In addition, you can define your own formats with the FORMAT procedure.

   In the SAS System there are several ways to use informats and formats for reading and writing data values. **Table 13.1** illustrates the techniques available for using SAS informats and formats in particular situations.

Table 13.1 Techniques for Using SAS Informats and Formats

	Techniques	Associate Informats/ Formats with Variables Using...	Use Informat/ Format Directly in...
Reading Values	SAS informats (including date, time, and datetime informats)	INFORMAT statement ATTRIB statement	INPUT statement INPUT function
Writing Values	SAS formats (including date, time, and datetime formats)	FORMAT statement ATTRIB statement	PUT statement PUT function
	Formats you define with PROC FORMAT		

SAS informats and formats have the form

informatw.d
formatw.d

where *informat* or *format* is the name of the informat or format, *w* is a width value (the number of columns in the input or output field), and *d* is an optional decimal scaling factor. If you omit the *w* and *d* values from the informat or format, SAS uses a default *w* value. However, you **must** use a period after the informat or format name.

Reading and Writing Binary Data

Different computers store numeric binary data in different forms. IBM 370, Hewlett-Packard 9000, Data General Eclipse, and PRIME computers store bytes in one order. IBM-compatible microcomputers and VAX computers store bytes in a different order called byte-reversed. The SAS System provides a number of informats for reading binary data and corresponding formats for writing binary data. Some of these informats and formats read and write data in native mode, that is, using the byte-ordering system that is standard for the machine. Other informats and formats force the data to be read and written by the IBM 370 standard, regardless of the native mode of the machine. The informats and formats that read and write in native mode are IB., PD., PIB., and RB. . The informats and formats that read and write in IBM 370 mode are S370FIB., S370FPD., S370PIB., and S370FRB. .

If a SAS program that reads and writes binary data will be run on only one type of machine, you can use the native mode informats and formats. However, if you want to write SAS programs that can be run on multiple machines using different byte-storage systems, use the IBM 370 formats and informats. The purpose of the IBM 370 informats and formats is to allow you to write SAS programs that can be run in any SAS environment, no matter what the standard for storing numeric data.

For example, suppose you have a program that writes data with the PIB. format. You execute the program on a microcomputer, so the data are stored in byte-reversed mode. Then, you run another SAS program on the microcomputer that uses the PIB. informat to read the data. The data are read correctly because both programs are run on the microcomputer, using byte-reversed mode. However, you cannot upload the data to a Hewlett-Packard 9000-series machine and read them correctly, because they are stored in a form native to the microcomputer but foreign to the Hewlett-Packard 9000. To avoid this problem, use the S370PIB. format to write the data; even on the microcomputer, this will cause the data to be stored in IBM 370 mode. Then, read the data using the S370PIB. informat; regardless of what type of machine you use when reading the data, they are read correctly.

USING SAS INFORMATS

The simplest way to associate a variable with an informat is to follow the variable with the informat in an INPUT statement. For example, the following INPUT statement uses the *w.* and *w.d* informats, respectively:

```
input @15 style 3. @21 price 5.2;
```

You can also associate an informat with a variable in an INFORMAT or ATTRIB statement like these:

```
data b;
   informat birthdat intervw date.;
   attrib income informat=comma.;
   input @20 birthdat intervw @50 income;
```

SAS uses the INFORMAT or ATTRIB statement to determine the variable's type (numeric or character) but uses it to determine the length only when it is a character variable. See Chapter 5, "SAS Statements Used in the DATA Step," for more information on the INFORMAT and ATTRIB statements.

Note: if you use an informat that is not compatible with the variable's value (for example, alphabetic characters in a numeric field), SAS prints an error message on the SAS log describing the problem and sets the variable's value to missing. See **Illegal Characters in Input Data** in Chapter 14, "Missing Values," for more information.

Table 13.2 lists the numeric and character informats described in this section; additional informats are described in **USING SAS DATE, TIME, AND DATETIME INFORMATS AND FORMATS** later in this chapter.

Table 13.2 SAS Numeric and Character Informats

SAS Numeric Informats

Informat	Description	Width Range	Decimal Range	Default Width
w.	standard numeric	1-32		
w.d			0-31	
BZw.d	blanks are zeros	1-32	0-31	1
COMMAw.d	commas in numbers	1-32	0-31	1
Ew.d	scientific notation	7-32	0-31	12
HEXw.	numeric hexadecimal	1-16		8
IBw.d	integer binary	1-8	0-10	4
MRBw.d	Microsoft BASIC real binary	2-8	0-10	4
PDw.d	packed decimal	1-16	0-10	1
PIBw.d	positive integer binary	1-8	0-10	1
PKw.d	unsigned packed decimal	1-16	0-10	1
RBw.d	real binary (floating point)	2-8	0-10	4
S370FIBw.d	IBM 370 integer binary	1-8	0-10	4
S370FPDw.d	IBM 370 packed decimal	1-16	0-10	1
S370FRBw.d	IBM 370 real binary	2-8	0-10	6
S370FPIBw.d	IBM 370 positive integer binary	1-8	0-10	4

SAS Character Informats

Informat	Description	Width Range	Default Width
$w.	standard character	1-200	1 or length of variable
$CHARw.	characters with blanks	1-200	1 or length of variable
$CHARZBw.	characters with binary zeros as blanks	1-200	1 or length of variable
$EBCDICw.	EBCDIC to ASCII	1-200	1
$HEXw.	character hexadecimal	1-200	2
$VARYINGw.	varying-length values	1-200	8 or length of variable

Informat Descriptions: Numeric

W.d informat: standard numeric data
range: 1-32

The standard SAS numeric informat *w.d* can read standard numeric data values (one digit per byte), where

> *w*   is a number giving the length, in columns, of the field containing the value.
>
> *d*   is an optional number giving the number of digits to the right of the decimal point in the value.

The *w.d* informat can read numeric values located anywhere in the field; blanks can precede or follow the value. A minus sign precedes negative values, without a blank between the sign and the value. Values read with the *w.d* informat can include decimal points. Values in scientific E-notation can be read with either the *w.d* informat or the E. informat, described below. The *w.d* informat interprets a period as a missing value.

Include a *d* value in the *w.d* informat when you want the SAS System to insert decimal points in numeric input values entered without decimal points. When an informat includes a *d* value and the data value does not include a decimal point, the value is divided by 10^d. (However, a decimal point already in the data value remains in its original position.)

Note that with the *w.d* informat, trailing blanks are not the same as trailing zeros. (If you want trailing blanks to be read as zeros, use the BZ. informat, below.)

Example 1   The following DATA step shows several representations of the number 23, all of which can be read with the numeric informat 6.:

```
data a;
   input @1 x 6.;
   cards;
23           left-aligned
    23       right-aligned
  23         in the middle
  23.0       with decimal point
  2.3E1      in scientific notation
   -23       negative value
```

Example 2   The data lines below show four representations of the number 23, each of which can be read with the informat 6.2:

```
data a;
   input @1 x 6.2;
   cards;
  2300       right-aligned
2300         left-aligned
 -2300       negative value
    23.      explicit decimal point
```

Using column input is equivalent to using a pointer control and a *w.d* informat. For example, the statement

```
input x 1-6 .2;
```

is equivalent to

```
input @1 x 6.2;
```

BZw.d informat: blanks are zeros
range: 1-32
default: 1

Sometimes data are entered without punching embedded and trailing zeros. For example, say that the value 340 is entered in columns 2-4; however, instead of a zero in column 4, there is a blank. Some languages translate the blank to zero; however, the *w.* and *w.d* SAS informats read the value as 34.

To read the value as 340, use the BZ. (**B**lanks are **Z**eros) informat. The BZ. informat is identical to the standard *w.d* informat except that it treats blanks other than leading blanks as zeros.

Example 1 X's value is 340 but is entered as 34 followed by a blank.

ASCII hex: 33 34 20
input data: 34
informat: BZ3.

```
input @10 x bz3.;
```

Example 2 Y's value is −200 but is entered as '−2 '.

ASCII hex: 2D 32 20 20
input data: −2
informat: BZ4.

```
input @5 y bz4.;
```

Do not use the BZ. informat in an INFORMAT or ATTRIB statement within a DATA step if the INPUT statement uses list input because SAS interprets blanks between values in the data line as delimiters rather than zeros. For example, do not use statements like the following:

```
informat x bz5.;
input x y z;
```

COMMAw.d informat: embedded characters
range: 1-32
default: 1

The COMMA. informat removes embedded commas, blanks, dollar signs, percent signs, and parentheses from input data. Left parentheses at the beginning of a field are converted to minus signs.

Example 1 X's value is 1000000, but it is entered with a comma separating each three digits.

ASCII hex: 31 2C 30 30 30 2C 30 30 30
input data: 1,000,000
informat: COMMA9.

```
input @10 x comma9.;
```

Example 2 Y's value is −500 but it is entered with parentheses indicating a negative value.

ASCII hex: 28 35 30 30 29
input data: (500)
informat: COMMA5.

```
input @10 comma5.;
```

**Ew.d informat: scientific notation
range: 7-32
default: 12**

You can read values of numeric variables in scientific notation using the E. informat. However, the E. informat is normally not needed since the standard w.d numeric informat can read numbers in scientific notation.

Example X's value is 1.257E3, stored in columns 10-16 of a data line.

ASCII hex: 31 2E 32 35 37 45 33
input data: 1.257E3
informat: E7.

```
input @10 x e7.;
```

**HEXw. informat: converts hex representation of a positive binary number to fixed or floating point binary
width range: 1-16
default width: 8**

The HEXw. informat converts the hexadecimal representation of positive binary numbers to floating point binary. The width value of the HEXw. informat determines whether the input represents an integer (fixed point) or real (floating point) binary number. When you specify a width of 1 through 15, the input hexadecimal represents an integer binary number. When you specify 16 for the width value, the input hexadecimal represents a floating point value. Note that the HEXw. informat cannot read negative values, so it treats the input value as unsigned (positive).

The HEXw. informat expects input that is not byte-reversed, that is, not in PC form. (The IBw., PIBw., and RBw. informats for binary numbers expect the bytes to be reversed.) This means that you can use the HEXw. informat to read hex literals from SAS programs created in another environment.

For example, in most environments the hex representation of the decimal integer 2 is 0002, with the least significant hex digit as the digit on the extreme right. (The PC stores the same value with the bytes reversed, that is, as 0200.) Therefore, the HEX4. informat reads 0002 and stores it as a floating point number.

To read hex literals in PC form (with reversed bytes), you need to read the value as a hex character string with the $HEXw. informat and then read the resulting character variable with an informat for binary numbers (IBw., PIBw., or RBw.). For example, suppose you want to read a PC memory dump that contains the byte-reversed hex representation of the decimal value 2 (02000000). The first step is to read in the byte-reversed hex value with the $HEX8. informat. The $HEXw. informat converts the input hex digits that occupy one byte each into a character variable with each byte containing two hex digits. You can then use the INPUT function to read the resulting hex value (still in byte-reversed form) with the IB4. informat, as shown below:

```
input x $hex8.;
/* x='02000000'x */
y=input(x,ib4.);
/* y=2 */
```

**IBw.d informat: integer binary
range: 1-8
default: 4**

The IB. informat reads fixed-point binary values. Negative values are represented in two's complement notation. If the informat includes a *d* value, the number is divided by 10^d. It is usually impossible to key in binary data directly from a console, though many programs write data in binary. The notation for integer binary in several programming languages is as follows:

SAS	IB2.	IB4.
FORTRAN	INTEGER*2	INTEGER*4
PC assembler	DW	DD
C	int	long

Refer to **Reading and Writing Binary Data** for more information on this informat.

Example 1 The value 128 is stored as a 4-byte integer binary number in columns 20-23 of a data line.

hex: 00 00 00 80
informat: IB4.

```
input @20 x ib4.;
```

Example 2 The value −255 is stored in columns 20-23 of the data line:

hex: FF FF FF 01
informat: IB4.

```
input @10 x ib4.;
```

**MRBw.d informat: Microsoft BASIC real binary (floating point) number width
range: 2-8
default width: 4**

The MRB. informat reads a numeric value stored in Microsoft BASIC floating point form. When you specify a *d* value, the number is divided by 10^d.

For example, the statement

```
input @20 x mrb8.;
```

reads the value 1 in Microsoft BASIC floating point notation

00 00 00 00 00 00 00 81 .

PDw.d informat: packed decimal
range: 1-16
default: 1

Each byte contains two digits in packed decimal data. The value's sign is in the first bit of the first byte. Although it is usually impossible to key in packed decimal data directly from a console, many programs write data in packed decimal.

Example 1 The value 128 is stored in packed decimal form in columns 4-7 of a data line.

hex: 00 00 01 28
informat: PD4.

```
input @4 x pd4.;
```

Example 2 You have a packed decimal date value from which you want to create a SAS date variable:

```
data new;
   input mnth pd4.;
   date=input(put(mnth,6.),mmddyy6.);
```

The PUT function converts the packed decimal value to standard numeric—the way it looks when printed. Then the INPUT function uses the MMDDYY. informat to read that value as a SAS date value.

PIBw.d informat: positive integer binary
range: 1-8
default: 1

Positive integer binary values are the same as integer binary (see the IB. informat, above), except that all values are treated as positive.

If the informat includes a d value, the data value is divided by 10^d.

If you are planning to test the bits of a byte, read the value with the PIB1. informat. Another way is to read it with the $CHAR1. informat.

When you want the decimal equivalent of one of the 128 ASCII characters, read the character with the PIB. informat. For example, the hex code for the letter A is 41 in ASCII with a decimal equivalent of 65. The statements

```
data x;
   input char pib1.;
   put char;
   cards;
a
;
```

produce 65.

Refer to **Reading and Writing Binary Data** for more information on this informat.

Example The value 12 is stored as a 1-byte positive integer binary value in column 43 of a data line.

hex: 0C
informat: PIB1.

```
input @43 x pib1.;
```

PKw.d informat: unsigned packed decimal
width range: 1-16
default width: 1

The PK. informat reads values stored as unsigned packed decimal data. Because there is no sign nibble, each byte contains two digits. When you specify a *d* value, the number is divided by 10^d.

The following example shows how the value 1234 is stored in packed decimal and unsigned packed decimal.

Decimal Value	Packed Decimal (Hex)	Unsigned Packed Decimal (PK2.) (Hex)
1234	001234	1234
−1234	801234	1234 (not valid with unsigned)

RBw.d informat: real binary (floating point)
range: 2-8
default: 4

Numeric data for scientific calculations are often stored in floating-point representation. (The SAS System stores all numeric values in floating-point.) A floating-point value consists of two parts: a mantissa giving the value and an exponent giving the value's magnitude. It is usually not possible to key in floating-point binary data directly from a console, though many programs write data in floating point binary. This table compares the names of floating-point notation in several languages:

	4 bytes	8 bytes
SAS	RB4.	RB8.
FORTRAN	REAL*4	REAL*8
PC assembler	DD	DQ
C	single	double

Refer to **Reading and Writing Binary Data** for more information on this informat.

Example The value 128 as an 8-byte floating point value is stored in columns 10-17 of a data line.

hex: 40 60 00 00 00 00 00 00
informat: RB8.

```
input @10 x rb8.;
```

S370FIBw.d informat: mainframe integer binary
width range: 1-8
default width: 4

The S370FIB. informat reads integer binary (fixed point) values stored in IBM 370 form. Negative values are represented in two's complement notation.

The following table shows the equivalent integer binary notation for several IBM 370 program languages:

SAS	S370FIB2.	S370FIB4.
PL/I	FIXED BIN(15)	FIXED BIN(31)
FORTRAN	INTEGER*2	INTEGER*4
COBOL	COMP PIC 9(4)	COMP PIC 9(8)
assembler	H	F
C	short	long

Refer to **Reading and Writing Binary Data** for more information on this informat.

S370FPD w.d informat: mainframe packed decimal
width range: 1-16
default width: 1

The S370FPD. informat reads packed decimal numbers in IBM 370 form. The PC and mainframe store packed decimal values differently. On the PC, the first byte indicates the sign: a 00 for positive numbers and an 80 for negative numbers. On the mainframe, the last nibble of the last byte indicates the sign: a C or F for positive numbers and a D for negative numbers.

Packed decimal data (in either environment) contains two digits per byte, except for the byte that contains the sign indicator bit. A d value specified in the informat means that the number is to be divided by 10^d.

The following table shows the equivalent packed decimal notation for several IBM 370 program languages:

SAS	S370PD4.
PL/I	FIXED DEC(7,0)
COBOL	COMP-3 PIC S9(7)
assembler	PL4

Refer to **Reading and Writing Binary Data** for more information on this informat.

S370FPIB w.d informat: mainframe positive integer binary
width range: 1-8
default width: 4

The S370FPIB. informat reads positive integer binary numbers in IBM 370 form. Positive integer binary values are the same as integer binary (see the S370FIB. informat, above), except that all values are treated as positive. If the informat includes a d value, the number is divided by 10^d.

Refer to **Reading and Writing Binary Data** for more information on this informat.

S370FRB w.d informat: mainframe real binary
width range: 2-8
default width: 6

The S370FRB. informat reads real binary numbers in IBM 370 form. Numeric data for scientific calculations are commonly represented in floating point. The SAS System stores all numeric values in SAS data sets in floating point. The following table shows the equivalent floating point notation for several IBM 370 programming languages.

	4 bytes	8 bytes
SAS	S370FRB4.	S370FRB8.
PL/I	FLOAT BIN(21)	FLOAT BIN(53)
FORTRAN	REAL*4	REAL*8
COBOL	COMP-1	COMP-2
assembler	E	D
C	float	double

Refer to **Reading and Writing Binary Data** for more information on this informat.

Informat Descriptions: Character

$w. informat: standard character data
range: 1-200
default: 1 if the length of the variable is not yet defined;
         otherwise, the length of the variable.

Use the SAS informat $w. to read character data. The *w* value gives the number of columns in the field containing the character value. The $w. informat trims leading blanks before storing values; that is, it automatically left aligns when reading values. In addition, the $w. informat converts a period (.) to a blank because it interprets the period as a missing value.

Example 1 Columns 10-12 of the input data line contain the value 'ABC'.

ASCII hex: 41 42 43
informat: $3.

The statement

```
input @10 name $3.;
```

reads the value as

```
'ABC'
```

This statement is equivalent to

```
input name $ 10-12;
```

Example 2 Columns 21-25 of an input data line contain the value ' XYZ'.

ASCII hex: 20 20 58 59 5A
informat: $5.

The statement

```
input @21 name $5.;
```

reads the value as

'XYZ '

$CHARw. informat: leading and trailing blanks
range: 1-200
default: 1 if the length of the variable is not yet defined;
otherwise, the length of the variable

The $CHAR. informat is identical to the $w. informat above except that $CHAR. does not trim leading blanks. This table compares the SAS informat $CHAR8. with notation in other languages:

SAS	$CHAR8.
FORTRAN	A8
PC assembler	DB 8 DUP (?)
C	char [8]

Example The value ' ABC' with one leading blank is in columns 7-10 of the data line.

ASCII hex: 20 41 42 43
informat: $CHAR4.

The statement

```
input @7 name $char4.;
```

reads this value as

' ABC'

Do not use the $CHAR. informat in an INFORMAT or ATTRIB statement within a DATA step if the INPUT statement uses list input because SAS interprets blanks between values in the data line as delimiters. For example, do **not** use statements like the following:

```
informat x $char12.;
input x y z;
```

$CHARZBw. informat: binary zeros as blanks
range: 1-200
default: 1 if the length of the variable is not yet defined;
    otherwise, the length of the variable

The $CHARZB. informat is identical to the $CHAR. informat except that $CHARZB. reads the specified input area and changes any byte of binary zero (X'00') to a blank character (X'20').

Example The value 'SMITH, JOHN   ' is in a data record at offset +42 with trailing binary zeros instead of blanks.

ASCII hex: 53 4D 49 54 48 2C 20 4A 4F 48 4E 00 00 00 00 00 00 00 00 00
informat: $CHARZB20.

The statement

```
input @43 name $charzb20.;
```

reads this value as

```
'SMITH, JOHN
```

$EBCDICw. informat: converts EBCDIC to ASCII
width range: 1-200
default width: 1

The $EBCDIC. informat converts character data from IBM 370 EBCDIC into ASCII. The following table shows the EBCDIC representation for several character values and the corresponding ASCII representation that the $EBCDIC. informat converts them to:

Value	EBCDIC	ASCII
abc	818283	616263
ABC	C1C2C3	414243
();	4D5D5E	28293B

$HEXw. informat: character hexadecimal
range: 1-200
default: 2

The $HEX. informat is like the HEX. informat in that it reads values in which each hex digit occupies 1 byte. Use the $HEX. informat to encode binary information into a character variable when your input data are limited to printable characters.

Example Columns 21-24 contain the value C1C2.

ASCII hex: 43 31 43 32
informat: $HEX4.

```
input @21 name $hex4.;
```

In the SAS data set, the character variable NAME has a length of 2, even though the w. value in the informat is 4, since SAS stores the 4 hex digits C1C2 in 2 bytes.

$VARYINGw. informat: varying-length values
range: 1-200
default: 8 or length of variable

Use the $VARYING. informat when the length of a character value differs from record to record. Typically, the character value's length in the current record is given in a numeric field in the record (or implicitly by the fact the character variable occupies the entire varying portion of a variable-length record). A numeric *w* value specifying the character variable's maximum length usually follows the $VARYING. informat.

With the $VARYING. informat, SAS first determines the character value's length in the current observation from a numeric length variable. It can obtain the value of the length variable in several ways, such as by reading a field described in the same INPUT statement as the character variable, by reading the length field in another INPUT statement, or by calculating the value. SAS then reads the character value for that observation from the number of columns specified. The variable's value is padded with blanks if necessary to equal the maximum length specified by *w* before being stored.

The $VARYING. informat **must** include a length variable. If the length variable's value is 0 or negative (including missing values) for a given observation, SAS assigns it a length of 1. If the length variable's value is greater than 0 but less than the *w* value, SAS reads the number of columns specified by the length variable and pads the value with trailing blanks to the maximum length. If the value of the length variable is equal to or greater than the *w* value, SAS uses the *w* value for the character variable's length. The length variable cannot be an array reference.

The SAS System always associates a *w* value with the $VARYING. informat. If you do not specify a value for *w*, SAS assigns a length to the character variable and uses that length as the value of *w*. SAS assigns the character variable's length with the same rules it uses when assigning lengths to character variables in other situations: if you have given the variable a length earlier (for example, with a LENGTH statement) it uses that length; if you have not given the variable a specific length, it uses a length of 8.

The pointer's position after reading a data value with the $VARYING. informat is the first column after the value.

Example DSNAME is a character variable whose length can vary from one to forty-four characters.

In the input lines, the LENVAR variable contains DSNAME's length, in bytes, for the current line. The INPUT statement first reads the LENVAR variable and then uses it after the $VARYING44. informat to give the current length of the DSNAME value, up to a maximum of forty-four characters:

```
data test;
   input lenvar pib1. dsname $varying44. lenvar;
```

USING SAS FORMATS

The simplest way to associate a format with a variable is to follow the variable with a format in the PUT statement. The following example uses the DOLLAR. format to write numeric values as dollar amounts:

```
data money;
   amount=1145.32;
   put amount dollar10.2;
```

The statements above produce the value

```
$1,145.32
```

In DOLLAR10.2, the *w* value of 10 and the *d* value of 2 indicate a maximum of 10 columns for the value, with two of these columns for the decimal part of the value, one for the decimal point, and seven reserved for the minus sign (if the value is negative), dollar sign, comma, and dollar part of the value.

A FORMAT or ATTRIB statement also associates a format with a variable. However, there is a difference between using a format in the PUT statement as opposed to specifying the format in a FORMAT or ATTRIB statement. A format in the PUT statement preserves leading blanks, whereas a FORMAT or ATTRIB statement trims leading blanks.

If you want to associate a format with a variable permanently so that later PROC and DATA steps use the format, you **must** specify the variable and format in a FORMAT or ATTRIB statement in a DATA step. For example,

```
data wholeyr;
   input sales1-sales12;
   salesyr=sum(of sales1-sales12);
   format sales1 sales7 sales12 salesyr dollar10.;
proc print;
   var sales1 sales7 sales12 salesyr;
```

The PRINT procedure prints the variables SALES1, SALES7, SALES12, and SALESYR preceded by dollar signs and with commas separating each three columns of figures.

If you want to associate a format with a variable only for the duration of a procedure, use a FORMAT or ATTRIB statement in the PROC step. For example, the statements

```
proc print data=products;
   format price dollar8.2;
   var style color price;
```

print the values of PRICE with dollar signs, commas, and two decimal places.

If a variable is specified in more than one FORMAT or ATTRIB statement, the format given in the last statement is used. To delete a variable's format, use the variable name in a FORMAT or ATTRIB statement without a format. You can also change or delete formats with PROC DATASETS. See "The DATASETS Procedure" in the *SAS Procedures Guide, Release 6.03 Edition* for more information.

If the value of a variable does not fit into the width of the format you are using, SAS tries to squeeze the value into the space available. Character formats truncate values on the right. Numeric formats sometimes revert to the BEST. format. The SAS System prints asterisks if it is not possible to represent the value.

The preceding information on SAS formats applies both to SAS formats and those created with PROC FORMAT.

Formats created with PROC FORMAT can be stored for use in later jobs.

Note: storing formats is an important consideration when you are associating formats with variables for permanent SAS data sets, especially when the data sets are shared with other users. SAS produces an error message if it cannot find the format associated with a variable. To avoid losing information in formats you have created, always give directions for accessing the stored formats with directions for accessing the data set. Or, if you give a diskette containing a SAS data set with user-created formats to another SAS user, be sure that one file on the diskette contains the formats.

Table 13.3 lists the numeric and character formats described in this section; additional formats are described in **USING SAS DATE, TIME, AND DATETIME INFORMATS AND FORMATS** later in this chapter.

Table 13.3 SAS Numeric and Character Formats

	SAS Numeric Formats				
Format	Description	Width Range	Decimal Range	Default Width	Alignment
w.	standard numeric	1-32			right
w.d			d<w		
BESTw.	SAS chooses best notation	1-32		12	right
COMMAw.d	commas in numbers	2-32	0 or 2	6	right
DOLLARw.d	dollar sign, commas	2-32	0 or 2	6	right
Ew.	scientific notation	7-32		12	right
HEXw.	numeric hexadecimal	1-16		8	left
IBw.d	integer binary	1-8	0-10	4	left
MRBw.d	Microsoft real BASIC binary	2-8	0-10	4	
PDw.d	packed decimal	1-16	0-10	1	left
PIBw.d	positive integer binary	1-8	0-10	1	left
PKw.d	unsigned packed decimal	1-16	0-10	1	
RBw.d	real binary (floating point)	2-8	0-10	4	left
ROMANw.	Roman numerals	2-32		6	left
SSNw.	social security numbers	11		11	
S370FIBw.d	IBM 370 integer binary	1-8	0-10	4	
S370FPDw.d	IBM 370 packed decimal	1-16	0-101	1	

continued on next page

428 Chapter 13

Table 13.3 *continued*

SAS Numeric Formats

Format	Description	Width Range	Decimal Range	Default Width	Alignment
S370FRB*w.d*	IBM 370 real binary	2-8	0-10	6	
S370FPIB*w.d*	IBM 370 positive integer binary	1-8	0-10	4	
Z*w.d*	print leading zeros	1-32		1	right

SAS Character Formats

Format	Description	Width Range	Default Width	Alignment
$*w*.	standard character	1-200	1 or length of variable	left
$CHAR*w*.	characters with blanks	1-200	1 or length of variable	left
$EBCDIC*w*.	EBCDIC to ASCII	1-200	1	
$HEX*w*.	character hexadecimal	1-200	2	left
$VARYING*w*.	varying-length character values	1-200	8 or length of variable	left

Format Descriptions: Numeric

W.d format: standard numeric data
range: 1-32

You can use the *w.d* format to write values in a field *w* positions wide, with *d* positions to the right of the decimal point. If *d* is 0 or if it is omitted, the value is written without a decimal point.

Numbers written with the *w.d* format are rounded to the nearest number that can be represented in the output field. If the number is too large to fit, the BEST. format, described below, is used instead. Negative numbers are printed with a leading minus sign.

In choosing a *w* value, allow enough space to write the value, the decimal point, and a minus sign if necessary.

Example   The statements

```
data test;
   x=23.45;
   put x 6.3;
```

produce the line

```
23.450
```

Using column output is equivalent to using a pointer control and a *w.d* format. For example, the statement

```
put x 1-8 .2;
```

is equivalent to

```
put @1 x 8.2;
```

BESTw. format: SAS chooses best notation
range: 1-32
default: 12
alignment: right

The BEST. format is the default when a format is not specified. SAS chooses the notation that gives the most information about the value that will fit into the number of columns available. SAS continues to store the complete value.

Example 1 X's value is 1257000, and you want to write it in the six columns 10-15. Since seven columns are needed to represent the value exactly, SAS squeezes the value into E-notation to get it into six columns: the statement

```
put @10 x best6.;
```

prints the value

```
1.26E6
```

Example 2 X's value is 1257000, and you want to write it in columns 10-12. The SAS System puts the most information possible into three columns: the statement

```
put @10 x best3.;
```

prints the value

```
1E6
```

Although part of the value is not displayed, the value still prints. If you give only two columns to print this value, SAS prints asterisks instead of trying to represent the value.

COMMAw.d format: commas
range: 2-32
default: 6
alignment: right

The COMMA. format is like the DOLLAR. format, below, except that it does not print a dollar sign in front of the value. You may use DOLLAR. to print a total and use COMMA. to print the detail lines. The *d* value, if specified, must be either 0 or 2. If the value is too large for the field, the BEST. format is used instead.

Example SALES' value is 23451.23, and you want to print it in columns 24-33 of the output lines. The statement

```
put @24 sales comma10.2;
```

prints the value

```
23,451.23
```

DOLLARw.d format: dollar sign, commas, and decimal point
range: 2-32
default: 6
alignment: right

You can print numeric values as dollar amounts with the DOLLAR. format. A dollar sign precedes the value, commas separate every three digits, and if the format includes a decimal value, two decimal digits representing cents are printed following a decimal point.

The *d* value, if specified, must be either 0 or 2. If the value is too large for the field, the BEST. format is used instead.

Example NETPAY's value is 1254.71, and you want to print it in columns 53-62 of the output line. The statement

```
put a53 netpay dollar10.2;
```

prints the value

```
$1,254.71
```

Ew. format: scientific notation
range: 7-32
default: 12
alignment: right

You can write numeric variable values in scientific notation using the E. format.

Example X's value is 1257, and you want to write it in columns 10-19 of the output line in scientific notation. The statement

```
put a10 x e10.;
```

prints the value

```
1.257E+03
```

Column 10 is blank because it is reserved for a minus sign.

HEXw. format: converts floating point to hexadecimal
width range: 1-16
default width: 8
alignment: left

The HEX*w*. format converts a real (floating point) binary number to its hexadecimal representation. When you specify a width value of 1 through 15, the real binary number is truncated to a fixed point integer before being converted to hex. When you specify 16 for the width, the floating point value of the number is used; in other words, the number is not truncated.

The HEX*w*. format does not reverse the bytes when it writes output values; that is, the least significant hex digit is the rightmost digit. (The other formats for binary numbers write values with the bytes reversed.) This means that you can use the HEX*w*. format to write hex literals that can be read in SAS programs in other environments. Therefore, if you want to write hex values in PC byte-reversed form, you need to write the decimal value with the PUT function and a format for binary numbers. You can then convert the resulting byte-reversed value to a hex character string with the $HEX*w*. format, as shown below:

```
/* y=2 */
x=put(y,ib4.);
/* x='02000000'x */
put x $hex8.;
```

The $HEX8. format in the PUT statement creates a hex output string of 02000000. If you used only the PUT statement with the HEX8. format, the output value would be 00000002.

IBw.d format: integer binary
range: 1-8
default: 4
alignment: left

Integers are stored in integer-binary, or fixed-point, form. For example, the number 2 is stored as 00000002. If the format includes a *d* value, the number is divided by 10^d. The following table compares integer-binary notation in several languages:

SAS	IB2.	IB4.
FORTRAN	INTEGER*2	INTEGER*4
PC assembler	DW	DD
C	short	long

Refer to **Reading and Writing Binary Data** for more information on this format.

Example You want to write the numeric variable X's value of 128 in columns 20-23 of the output line:

```
put @20 x ib4.;
```

MRBw.d format: Microsoft BASIC real binary (floating point) number
width range: 2-8
default width: 6
alignment: left

The MRB. format converts a SAS numeric value to a Microsoft BASIC floating point numeric value. If *w* is 3 or 4, the Microsoft value is single precision; if *w* is 5 to 8, the Microsoft value is double precision. When you specify a *d* value in the MRB. format, the value is multiplied by 10^d.

For example, if X's value, 1, is stored by the SAS System as 000000000000F03F, the statement

```
put x mrb8.;
```

writes the value in the Microsoft BASIC double-precision floating point form

0000000000000000081

PDw.d format: packed decimal
range: 1-16
default: 1
alignment: left

In packed decimal data, each byte contains two digits. The *w* value represents the number of bytes, not the number of digits. The value's sign is in the first bit of the first byte.

Refer to **Reading and Writing Binary Data** for more information on this format.

Example X's value is 128, and you want to store it in packed decimal form in columns 4-7 of an output line.

```
put @4 x pd4.;
```

PIBw.d format: positive integer binary
range: 1-8
default: 1
alignment: left

Positive integer binary values are the same as integer binary (see the IB. format, above) except that all values are treated as positive. Thus, the high-order bit is part of the value rather than the value's sign.

If a *d* value is specified in the PIB. format, the data value is divided by 10^d.

Refer to **Reading and Writing Binary Data** for more information on this format.

Example X's value is 12, and you want to write it as a 1-byte positive integer binary value in column 43 of an output line:

```
put @43 x pib1.;
```

PKw.d format: unsigned packed decimal
width range: 1-16
default width: 1
alignment: left

The PK. format converts SAS numeric values to unsigned packed decimal values. Because there is no sign nibble, each byte contains two digits. When you specify a *d* value in the PK. format, the value is multiplied by 10^d.

The following example shows how the PK. format converts the numeric value 1234 to unsigned packed decimal values:

Decimal Value	Packed Decimal (Hex)	Unsigned Packed Decimal (PK2.) (Hex)
1234	001234	1234
−1234	801234	1234 (not valid with unsigned)

RBw.d format: real binary (floating point)
range: 2-8
default: 6
alignment: left

Numeric data for scientific calculations are commonly represented in floating point. (SAS stores all numeric values in floating point.) A floating-point value consists of two parts: a mantissa giving the value and an exponent giving the value's magnitude.

Real binary is the most efficient format for representing numeric values since SAS already represents numbers this way and no conversion is needed. This table compares the names of floating-point notation in several languages:

	4 bytes	8 bytes
SAS	RB4.	RB8.
FORTRAN	REAL*4	REAL*8
PC assembler	DD	DQ
C	single	double

Refer to **Reading and Writing Binary Data** for more information on this format.

Example The numeric variable X's value is 128, and you want to write it in columns 10-17 of the output line:

```
put @10 x rb8.;
```

ROMANw. format: Roman numerals
range: 2-32
default: 6
alignment: left

The ROMAN. format prints numeric values as Roman numerals. Noninteger values are truncated to integers before printing.

Example X's value is 1982, and you want to print it in columns 25-35 of the output line. The statement

```
put @25 x roman10.;
```

prints the value

```
MCMLXXXII
```

SSNw. format: social security numbers
range: 11
default: 11

The SSN. format prints 9-digit numeric values as U.S. social security numbers, with dashes between the third and fourth digits and between the fifth and sixth digits. If the value is missing, SAS prints nine single periods with dashes between the third and fourth periods and between the fifth and sixth periods. If the value contains fewer than nine digits, SAS aligns the value on the right and pads the value with zeros on the left. If the value has more than nine digits, it is set to missing.

Example ID's value is 263878439, and you want to print it in columns 21-31 of the output line:

```
put @21 id ssn11.;
```

prints the value

```
263-87-8439
```

S370FIBw.d format: IBM 370 integer binary
width range: 1-8
default width: 4
alignment: left

Integer values are stored in integer-binary, or fixed-point, form. The following table shows the equivalent integer binary notation for several IBM 370 programming languages:

SAS	S370FIB2.	S370FIB4.
PL/I	FIXED BIN(15)	FIXED BIN(31)
FORTRAN	INTEGER*2	INTEGER*4
COBOL	COMP PIC 9(4)	COMP PIC 9(8)
assembler	H	F
C	short	long

Refer to **Reading and Writing Binary Data** for more information on this format.

S370FPDw.d format: IBM 370 packed decimal
width range: 1-16
default width: 1
alignment: left

The IBM PC and mainframe store packed decimal data in different forms. Each byte (except the last) of packed decimal data contains two digits. The sign for an IBM 370 packed decimal value is in the last half of the last byte: a C or F indicates a positive value and a D indicates a negative value. PC packed decimal data have the sign in the first byte: 00 indicates a positive value and 80 indicates a negative value. Depending on the number stored, a value may require one more byte on a PC than on a mainframe.

The S370FPD*w.d* format writes packed decimal values stored on the PC in IBM 370 format. If you specify a *d* value in the format, the number is multiplied by 10^d.

The following table shows the equivalent packed decimal notation for several IBM 370 programming languages:

SAS	S370PD4.
PL/I	FIXED DEC(7,0)
COBOL	COMP-3 PIC S9(7)
assembler	PL4

Refer to **Reading and Writing Binary Data** for more information on this format.

S370FPIBw.d format: IBM 370 positive integer binary
width range: 1-8
default width: 4
alignment: left

The S370FPIB. format converts SAS numeric values to positive integer binary, IBM 370 form. Positive integer binary values are the same as integer binary (see the S370FIB. format, above), except that all values are treated as positive.

If a *d* value is specified in the S370FPIB. format, the data value is multiplied by 10^d.

Refer to **Reading and Writing Binary Data** for more information on this format.

S370FRBw.d format: real binary (floating point)
width range: 2-8
default width: 6
alignment: left

The SAS System stores all numeric values in real binary, also called floating point, form.

The S370FRB. format writes real binary values in IMB 370 real binary form. If you specify a *d* value in the S370FRB. format, the data value is multiplied by 10^d.

A floating point value consists of two parts: a mantissa giving the value and an exponent giving the value's magnitude. Since the SAS System stores all numbers in floating point, formats that write values as real binary are the most efficient because they eliminate the need for conversion.

The following table shows the equivalent floating point notation for several IBM 370 programming languages:

	4 bytes	8 bytes
SAS	S370FRB4.	S370FRB8.
PL/I	FLOAT BIN(21)	FLOAT BIN(53)
FORTRAN	REAL*4	REAL*8
COBOL	COMP-1	COMP-2
assembler	E	D
C	float	double

Refer to **Reading and Writing Binary Data** for more information on this format.

Zw.d format: print leading zeros
range: 1-32
default: 1
alignment: right

The Z. format fills in zeros rather than blanks to the left of the data value.

Example SEQNUM's value is 1350, and you want to print it in columns 73-80 of the output line, with zeros in the columns before the value. The statement

```
put @73 seqnum z8.;
```

prints the value

```
00001350
```

Format Descriptions: Character

To write a character variable, you must use a character format. Character formats begin with a dollar sign ($).

$w. format: standard character data
range: 1-200
default: 1 if length of variable not yet defined; otherwise,
      the length of the variable
alignment: left

To write character data, use the SAS format $w. The w value gives the number of columns used to write the character value.

Example NAME's value is 'ABC', and you want to write it in columns 10-12 of the output line. Each of the statements

```
put @10 name $3.;
```

or

```
put name $ 10-12;
```

or

```
put name 10-12;
```

writes the value

```
'ABC'
```

You can omit the dollar sign in a PUT statement since SAS knows that NAME is a character variable.

$CHARw. format: leading blanks
range: 1-200
default: 1 if length of variable not yet defined; otherwise,
       the length of the variable
alignment: left

The $CHAR. format is identical to the $w. format above except that $CHAR. does not trim leading blanks. This table compares the $CHAR. format to notation in some other languages:

SAS	$CHAR8.
FORTRAN	A8
PC assembler	DB 8 DUP (?)
C	char[8]

Example NAME's value is ' ABC', with one leading blank, and you want to write it in columns 7-10 of an output line:

```
put @7 name $char4.;
```

$EBCDICw. format: converts ASCII to EBCDIC
width range: 1-200
default width: 1
alignment: left

The $EBCDIC. format converts character data from ASCII into IBM 370 EBCDIC. The following table shows the ASCII representation for several character values and the corresponding EBCDIC representation to which the $EBCDIC. format converts them.

Value	EBCDIC	ASCII
abc	616263	818283
ABC	414243	C1C2C3
();	28293B	4D5D5E

$HEXw. format: character hexadecimal
range: 1-200
default: 2
alignment: left

The $HEX. format is like the HEX. format in that it converts a character value to hexadecimal, with each byte requiring two columns.

Example The character variable NAME's value is 'AB', and you want to print its hex equivalent in columns 21-24. Note that 4 columns are required for the output value.

```
put @21 name $hex4.;
```

$VARYINGw. format: varying-length values
range: 1-200
default: 8 or length of variable
alignment: left

Use the $VARYING. format when the length of a character value differs from record to record. Typically, the character value's length in the current record is given in a numeric field in the record (or implicitly, by the fact that the character variable occupies the entire varying portion of a variable-length record). A numeric *w* value specifying the variable's maximum length usually follows the $VARYING. format.

With the $VARYING. format, SAS ascertains the character value's length to determine how long the printed value is to be. The length variable is not printed. The $VARYING. format **must** include a length variable.

If the length variable's value is 0 or negative (including missing values) for a given observation, SAS assigns it a length of 1. If the length variable's value is greater than 0 but less than the *w* value, SAS prints the length specified by the length variable. If the value of the length variable is equal to or greater than the *w* value, SAS uses the *w* value for the character variable's length. The length variable cannot be an array reference.

The SAS System always associates a *w* value with the $VARYING. format. If you do not specify a value for *w*, SAS assigns a length to the character variable and uses that length as the value of *w*. SAS assigns the character variable's length with the same rules that it uses when assigning lengths to character variables in other situations. If you have given the variable a length earlier (for example, with a LENGTH statement) it uses that length; if you have not given the variable a specific length, it uses a length of 8. Note: do not use the $VARYING. format in a FORMAT statement within a PROC step because you may get unexpected results.

The pointer's position after printing a value with the $VARYING. format is the first column after the value.

Example CITY is a variable in your data set whose length ranges from 1 to 30 characters, although it is stored with a length of 30. LEN is another variable in the data set giving the actual length of CITY for the current observation. You want to write the CITY value beginning in column 10; the pointer's position after writing the value should be the first column after the actual CITY value:

```
put @10 city $varying30. len;
```

Note that the LEN variable in this statement is part of the $VARYING30. format.

USING SAS DATE, TIME, AND DATETIME INFORMATS AND FORMATS

A special case in which you need to assign an informat and format to a variable occurs when the variable's value represents a SAS date, time, or datetime value. To work with these values, you need to understand how the SAS System stores them.

- The SAS System stores a date value as the number of days between January 1, 1960 and the date. For example, March 3, 1962 is stored as 792; August 24, 1985 is stored as 9367; and July 4, 1776 is stored as −67019.
- Similarly, the SAS System stores a time value as the number of seconds since midnight. The time value 9:54 is stored as 35640; the value 15:23 (or 3:23 PM) is stored as 55380.

- A datetime value is stored as the number of seconds between midnight, January 1, 1960 and the date and time. For example, the datetime value 27APR85:17:49:45 is stored as 799091385.

This method of storing date, time, and datetime values is useful because you can obtain the interval between values by subtraction and because the values are easy to sort. The standard is also internationally recognizable. However, if you use the default informat and format for date, time, or datetime values, you must enter and read large numbers like those shown above. To enter and read values in a recognizable form, specify a SAS date, time, or datetime informat and format for the variable.

For example, consider the date July 4, 1982. Suppose that this date is written in an input data line as 7-4-82. To read the value as a SAS date value, use the date informat MMDDYY8., which reads 7-4-82 and converts it to the number of days between January 1, 1960 and July 4, 1982: 8220 days.

```
data days;
   input birthday mmddyy8.;
   cards;
7-4-82
;
```

After the INPUT statement executes, BIRTHDAY's value is 8220, and if you print it with the statement

```
put birthday;
```

the value 8220 appears.

In order to print 8220 as a date, you must assign a format to the variable BIRTHDAY. There are several formats available that print the date. One is DATE., which prints the date as the day of the month, followed by the first three letters of the month, and then the year. So the statement

```
put birthday date7.;
```

prints the line

```
04JUL82
```

You can associate a format with the value for the duration of the session with a FORMAT or ATTRIB statement in the DATA step. For example, both of these statements:

```
format birthday date7.;
attrib birthday format=date7.;
```

print the BIRTHDAY value as 04JUL82 for the remainder of the session.

SAS dates are valid back to A.D. 1582 and ahead to A.D. 20,000, and leap year, century, and fourth-century adjustments are handled properly. However, leap seconds are ignored, and the SAS System does not adjust for daylight saving time.

If the width of your informat is not sufficient to read all the columns containing the date, time, or datetime value in your data lines, you will get unexpected results. (Remember that blanks or special characters between the day, month, year, or time add to the length of the value.) For example, if you use the informat DATE8. to read these values:

```
01/JAN/82
3/MAR/1955
```

SAS assigns date values corresponding to 01JAN08 and 03MAR19, respectively. If the width is such that the last column SAS reads is a special character, SAS produces an invalid data message.

If the width of a date, time, or datetime format is not sufficient to write all the information about the value, SAS truncates the value on the right. In some formats SAS abbreviates the name of the month, the name of the weekday, or both, in order to print as much information as possible. If the format specifies more columns than necessary, the value is right aligned.

If you give a two-digit year value, SAS assumes that the year is in the 1900's.

Duration vs. Date

When you are working with date and datetime values, it is important to remember the associated units when you work with the values.

For example, suppose you want to calculate the ages of employees from their birth dates. You read the birth dates with a date informat (say DATE7.), and use the function TODAY to assign today's date to a variable. To find the employees' ages, subtract BIRTHDAY from TODAY:

```
data emplage;
   input id birthday date7.;
   today=today();
   age=today-birthday;
```

The value of AGE is the number of days between the employees' birthdays and today, representing a duration in days rather than in years.

As an example, suppose an employee's birthday is December 1, 1959. The internal representation of that date is −31. Today's date is January 15, 1986; the internal representation of that date is 9511. Subtracting −31 from 9511 gives 9542, which is the number of days between today and December 1, 1959. This number is **not** a SAS date value since it represents a duration that is not based on January 1, 1960. To print the value in a form that makes sense (such as the employees' ages in years), you must calculate how many years are in 9542 days:

```
ageyears=age/365.25;
```

Table 13.4 lists the date, time, and datetime informats and formats available in the SAS System.

Table 13.4 SAS Date, Time, and Datetime Informats and Formats

SAS Date, Time, and Datetime Informats

Informat	Description	Width Range	Default Width
DATE*w*.	dates of form ddMMMyy	7-32	7
DATETIME*w.d*	date-time values	13-40	18
DDMMYY*w*.	date values	6-32	8
JULIAN*w*	Julian dates	5-32	5
MMDDYY*w*.	date values	6-32	8
MONYY*w*.	month and year	5-32	5
NENGO*w*	Japanese dates	7-32	10
TIME*w.d*	time values	5-32	8
YYMMDD*w*.	date values	6-32	8
YYQ*w*.	year and quarter	4-32	4

SAS Date, Time, and Datetime Formats

Format	Description	Width Range	Default Width
DATE*w*.	dates of form ddMMMyy	5-9	7
DATETIME*w.d*	date-time values	7-40	16
DDMMYY*w*.	date values	2-8	8
HHMM*w.d*	hour and minutes	2-20	5
HOUR*w.d*	hour	2-20	2
JULIAN*w*	Julian dates	5-7	5
MMDDYY*w*.	date values	2-8	8
MMSS*w.d*	minutes and seconds	2-20	5
MONYY*w*.	month and year	5-7	5
NENGO*w*	Japanese dates	2-10	10
TIME*w.d*	time values	2-20	8
TOD*w*.	time-of-day	2-20	8
WEEKDATE*w*.	date values	3-37	29
WEEKDATX*w*.	date values	3-37	29
WORDDATE*w*.	date values	3-32	18
WORDDATX*w*.	date values	3-32	18
YYMMDD*w*.	date values	2-8	8
YYQ*w*.	year and quarter	4-6	4

Date, Time, and Datetime Informat Descriptions

DATEw. informat: ddMMMyy
range: 7-32
default: 7

The DATE. informat reads values in the form *ddMMMyy*, where *dd* is the day of the month, 01-31; *MMM* is the first three letters of the month name; and *yy* or *yyyy* is the year. Blanks and other special characters can be placed before and after the date and also between the day, month, and year values.

Example The statements

```
data dates;
   input day1 date10.;
   cards;
1jan1982
01 jan 82
1 jan 82
1-jan-1982
;
```

read each of these values as a SAS date value corresponding to 01JAN82.

DATETIMEw.d informat: date and time
range: 13-40
default: 18

Datetime values are those that include both a date and a time, written as the date first and then the time. The date must be in the form *ddMMMyy*, followed by a blank or special character, and the time must be in the form *hh:mm*, with an optional part *ss.ss* representing seconds and decimal fractions of seconds. The value of *hh* ranges from 00 to 23. You must give both a value for date and a value for time.

Example These fields are read with the DATETIME. informat as SAS datetime values corresponding to 10:03:17.2 a.m., December 23, 1976:

```
23DEC76:10:03:17.2
23DEC1976/10:03:17.2
```

DDMMYYw. informat: day-month-year
range: 6-32
default: 8

You can use the DDMMYY. informat to read a value in *ddmmyy* form, where *dd* is the day of the month, *mm* the month, and *yy* the year. Blanks can be placed before and after the date. The month, day, and year fields can be separated by blanks or special characters. However, if any of these fields are separated by blanks or special characters, all of them must be separated by blanks or special characters.

Example If you use the informat DDMMYY8., the values below are read as SAS date values corresponding to 15OCT82:

```
151082
15/10/82
15 10 82
```

JULIANw. informat: Julian dates (YYDDD or YYYYDDD)
width range: 5-32
default width: 5

The JULIAN. informat reads Julian dates, which are in the form of a year followed by a number from 1-365 (366 for a leap year). The Julian date must be a string of contiguous numbers, which means that zeros must pad any space between the year and day value. For example, the ninety-first day of 1987 (01APR87) must be represented as 87091, not 87 91. The year can be two or four digits. The SAS System assumes the twentieth century if the year value is two digits.

MMDDYYw. informat: month-day-year
range: 6-32
default: 8

The MMDDYY. informat reads a value in *mmddyy* form, where *mm* is the month, *dd* the day of the month, *yy* the year. Blanks can be placed before and after the date. The month, day, and year fields can be separated by blanks or special characters. However, if any of these fields are separated by blanks or special characters, all of them must be separated by blanks or special characters.

Example The values below are read as the SAS date value corresponding to 01JAN81 if you use the informat MMDDYY8.:

```
010181
1/1/81
01 1 81
```

MONYYw. informat: month and year
range: 5-32
default: 5

The MONYY. informat reads values in the form *MMMyy*, where *MMM* is the first three letters of the month name and *yy* or *yyyy* is the year. The *MMM* and *yy* or *yyyy* values cannot be separated by blanks.

A value read with the MONYY. informat results in a SAS date value corresponding to the first day of the specified month.

Example The statement

```
input month monyy5.;
```

reads the field JUN81 and produces a SAS date value corresponding to

```
01JUN81
```

NENGOw. informat: Japanese dates (R.YYMMDD)
width range: 7-32
default width: 10

The NENGO. informat reads Japanese date values in the form *r.yymmdd*, where

r	is a letter representing an emperor's reign. In chronological order, *r* can be M, T, or S for Meiji, Taisho, or Showa.
.	is an optional period.
yy	is the year within the reign.
mm	is the month.
dd	is the day of the month.

The year, month, and day fields can be separated by blanks or any non-numeric character; however, either the fields must have no separators or they must all be delimited with separators.

TIMEw.d informat: hours, minutes, and seconds
range: 5-32
default: 8

The TIME. informat reads values in the form *hh:mm:ss.ss*, where *hh* is the hour, *mm* the minute, and *ss.ss* an optional fractional part representing seconds and hundredths of seconds. If you do not give a value for seconds, SAS assumes a value of 0 seconds.

Example These SAS statements read a value for the variable BEGIN:

```
data timedata;
   input begin time8.;
   cards;
14:22:25
;
```

YYMMDDw. informat: year-month-day
range: 6-32
default: 8

The YYMMDD. informat can be used to read a value in *yymmdd* form, where *yy* is the year, *mm* the month, and *dd* the day of the month. Blanks can be placed before and after the date, and the month, day, and year fields can be separated by blanks or special characters. However, if any of these fields are separated by blanks or special characters, all of them must be. The YYMMDD. informat also accepts a four-digit year value.

Example 1 The data values in the example below are read as SAS date values corresponding to 1JAN76:

```
data newyear;
   input beg yymmdd8.;
   cards;
760101
76 1 1
76-01-01
76/1/1
19760101
;
```

Example 2 The first value below is read as the SAS date value for 01JAN1952; the second is read as 16OCT1884.

```
data a;
   input date yymmdd10.;
   cards;
19520101
1884/10/16
;
```

YYQw. informat: quarters of year
range: 4-32
default: 4

The YYQ. informat reads values in the form *yyQq* or *yyyyQq*, where *yy* or *yyyy* is the year, Q is the letter Q, and *q* is the quarter of the year (1, 2, 3, or 4). The year value, the letter Q, and the quarter value cannot be separated with blanks.

A value read with the YYQ. informat produces a SAS date value corresponding to the first day of the specified quarter.

Example The statement

```
input entered yyq4.;
```

reads the value 82Q2 and gives ENTERED a value of 1APR1982.

Date, Time, and Datetime Format Descriptions

DATEw. format: ddMMMyy
range: 5-9
default: 7

The DATE. format writes SAS date values in the form *ddMMMyy*, where *dd* is the day of the month, 01-31; *MMM* is the first three letters of the month name; and *yy* or *yyyy* is the year.

Example

Format	Value Printed
date5.	12SEP
date6.	12SEP
date7.	12SEP79
date8.	12SEP79
date9.	12SEP1979

DATETIMEw.d format: date and time
range: 7-40
default: 16

Datetime values are those that include both a date and a time, with the date followed by the time. The DATETIME. format prints SAS datetime values as *ddMMMyy:hh:mm:ss.s*. When the field width is 18, the *d* value can be 1. When the field width is greater than 18, the *d* value can be 2.

Example The statement

```
put event datetime18.;
```

prints the value

```
23DEC81:10:03:17.2
```

Format	Value Printed
datetime7.	12SEP79
datetime8.	12SEP79
datetime9.	12SEP79
datetime10.	12SEP79:03
datetime11.	12SEP79:03
datetime12.	12SEP79:03
datetime13.	12SEP79:03:19
datetime14.	12SEP79:03:19
datetime15.	12SEP79:03:19
datetime16.	12SEP79:03:19:43
datetime17.	12SEP79:03:19:43
datetime18.	12SEP79:03:19:43
datetime18.1	12SEP79:03:19:43.2
datetime19.2	12SEP79:03:19:43.22
datetime20.2	12SEP79:03:19:43.22
datetime21.2	12SEP1979:03:19:43.22
datetime22.2	12SEP1979:03:19:43.22

DDMMYYw. format: day-month-year
range: 2-8
default: 8

You can use the DDMMYY. format to write a SAS date value in *ddmmyy* form, where *dd* is the day of the month, *mm* the month, and *yy* the year.

When the field width is from 2 to 5, as much of the month and day values as possible prints. When the width is 7, the date prints with a two-digit year without slashes, and the value is right-aligned in the output field.

Example The DDMMYY6. format writes the date as *ddmmyy*: for example, 251282. The DDMMYY8. format writes the date as *dd/mm/yy*: for example, 25/12/82.

JULIANw. format: Julian dates (YYDDD or YYYYDDD)
width range: 5-7
default width: 5

The JULIAN. format converts a SAS date value into a Julian date. When you specify a width value (*w*) of 5, the Julian date is written with a two-digit year. When *w* is 6, the date is padded on the left with a blank. When *w* is 7, the Julian year value is four digits. For example, the JULIAN. format converts the SAS date value 9952 (01APR87) to a Julian date form corresponding to the *w* value as shown below:

Format	Julian Date Form
julian5.	87091
julian6.	87091
julian7.	1987091

When converting a non-twentieth century SAS date value, always specify a *w* value of 7 (that is, JULIAN7). Otherwise, the SAS System produces only a two-digit year that implies the twentieth century. For example, the JULIAN. format converts 01JAN1899 to 99001 (the Julian form of 01JAN1999). To convert 01JAN1899 to its Julian equivalent, 1899001, requires the JULIAN7. format.

HHMMw.d format: hours and minutes
range: 2-20
default: 5

The HHMM. format prints the hours and minutes of a SAS time value and is similar to the TIME. format except that seconds do not print. If the optional *d* value is given, decimal fractions of minutes print. The SAS System rounds minutes and hours based on the value of the seconds in the SAS time value.

Example 1 The statements

```
data new;
   time='12:34:56't;
   put time hhmm.;
```

print

```
12:35
```

Example 2 The statements

```
data new;
   time='12:59:56't;
   put time hhmm.;
```

print

```
13:00
```

HOURw.d format: hours and decimal fractions of hours
range: 2-20
default: 2

The HOUR. format writes only the hour part of a SAS time value. If the optional *d* value is given, decimal fractions of the hour print. SAS rounds hours based on the value of the minutes in the SAS time value.

Example The statements

```
data _null_;
   time='11:30:00't;
   put time hour4.1;
```

print

```
11.5
```

MMDDYYw. format: month-day-year
range: 2-8
default: 8

The MMDDYY. format writes a SAS date value in *mmddyy* form, where *mm* is the month, *dd* the day of the month, *yy* the year.

Example The MMDDYY6. format writes the date as *mmddyy*: for example, 122582. The MMDDYY8. format writes the date as *mm/dd/yy*: for example, 12/25/82.

Format	Value Printed
mmddyy2.	09
mmddyy3.	09
mmddyy4.	0912
mmddyy5.	09/12
mmddyy6.	091279
mmddyy7.	091279
mmddyy8.	09/12/79

MMSSw.d format: minutes and seconds
range: 2-20
default: 5

The MMSS. format converts a SAS time value to the number of minutes and seconds since midnight. If the optional d value is specified, fractional seconds print as decimals.

Example The statements

```
data _null_;
   time='1:15:30't;
   put time mmss.;
```

write on the SAS log

```
75:30
```

MONYYw. format: month and year
range: 5-7
default: 5

The MONYY. format writes SAS date values in the form *MMMyy*, where *MMM* is the first three letters of the month name and *yy* or *yyyy* is the year.

Example The statement

```
put acquired monyy7.;
```

prints

```
JUN1981.
```

NENGOw. format: Japanese dates (R.YYMMDD)
width range: 2-10
default width: 10

The NENGO. format writes Japanese date values in the form *r.yymmdd*, where

- *r* is a letter representing an emperor's reign. In chronological order, *r* can be M, T, or S, for Meiji, Taisho, or Showa.
- *.* is an optional period.
- *yy* is the year within the reign.
- *mm* is the month.
- *dd* is the day of the month.

448 Chapter 13

The values that the NENGO. format produces depend on the width value (w) that you specify. For example, the NENGO. format converts the date 15OCT86 (1986 converts to Showa 60) according to the following width values:

Format	Japanese Date Produced
nengo2.	60
nengo3.	S60
nengo4.	S.60
nengo5.	S6010
nengo6.	S60/10
nengo7.	S601015
nengo8.	S.601015
nengo9.	S60/10/15
nengo10.	S.60/10/15

TIMEw.d format: hours, minutes, and seconds
range: 2-20
default: 8

The TIME. format writes SAS time values in the form *hh:mm:ss.ss*, where *hh* is the hour, *mm* the minute, and *ss* the seconds, with an optional fractional part representing hundredths of seconds.

Example The statement

    put begin time.;

prints a value of BEGIN as

    16:24:43

TODw. format: time portion of datetime values
range: 2-20
default: 8

The TOD. format converts a SAS time value to a duration from midnight of the day in a datetime value so that you can print the time portion of datetime values.

Example Suppose you read the datetime value 29APR82:3:24:00 into the variable BDTIME. This value is stored internally as the number of seconds between 1JAN60:00:00 and 29APR82:3:24:00. To print just the time part of the value (from midnight, 29APR82), use the TOD. format. The statement

    put bdtime tod7.;

prints the line

    3:24:00

WEEKDATEw. format: day of week and date
range: 3-37
default: 29

The WEEKDATE. format writes a SAS date value in the form *day-of-week, monthname dd, yyyy*. If the value of *w* is too small to write the complete day of the week and the month, SAS abbreviates as needed.

Example The statement

```
put beg weekdate.;
```

writes the line

MONDAY, NOVEMBER 27, 1979

Format	Value Printed
weekdate3.	WED
weekdate9.	WEDNESDAY
weekdate15.	WED, SEP 12, 79
weekdate17.	WED, SEP 12, 1979
weekdate23.	WEDNESDAY, SEP 12, 1979
weekdate29.	WEDNESDAY, SEPTEMBER 12, 1979

WEEKDATXw. format: day of week and date
range: 3-37
default: 29

The WEEKDATX. format writes a SAS date value in the form *day-of-week, dd monthname yyyy*. If the value of *w* is too small to write the complete day of the week and the month, SAS abbreviates as needed.

Example The statement

```
put beg weekdatx.;
```

writes the line

MONDAY, 27 NOVEMBER 1979

WORDDATEw. format: date with name of month written as word
range: 3-32
default: 18

The WORDDATE. format writes a SAS date value in the form *monthname dd, yyyy*.

Example The statement

```
put term worddate.;
```

writes the value of TERM as

SEPTEMBER 30, 1980

Format	Value Printed
worddate3.	SEP
worddate9.	SEPTEMBER
worddate12.	SEP 12, 1979
worddate18.	SEPTEMBER 12, 1979
worddate20.	SEPTEMBER 12, 1979

WORDDATXw. format: date with name of month written as word
range: 3-32
default: 18

The WORDDATX. format writes a SAS date value in the form *dd monthname yyyy*.
   Example   The statement

   `put term worddatx.;`

writes the value of TERM as

   `30 SEPTEMBER 1980`

YYMMDDw. format: year-month-day
range: 2-8
default: 8

You can use the YYMMDD. format to write a SAS date value in *yymmdd* form, where *yy* is the year, *mm* the month, and *dd* the day of the month.
   Example   The statement

   `put day yymmdd2.;`

writes January 1, 1983 as 83. The statement

   `put day yymmdd.;`

writes March 18, 1982 as 82-03-18.

Format	Value Printed
yymmdd2.	79
yymmdd3.	79
yymmdd4.	7909
yymmdd5.	79-09
yymmdd6.	790912
yymmdd7.	790912
yymmdd8.	79-09-12

YYQw. format: quarters of year
range: 4-6
default: 4

The YYQ. format writes SAS date values in the form *yyQq* or *yyyyQq* where *yy* or *yyyy* is the year, Q is the letter Q, and *q* is the quarter of the year (1, 2, 3, or 4).
   Example   The statement

   `put acquired yyq4.`

prints any value of ACQUIRED between 1OCT82 and 31DEC82 as

   `82Q4`

Chapter 14
Missing Values

INTRODUCTION *451*
MISSING VALUES IN INPUT DATA LINES *451*
    Blanks for missing values *451*
    Periods for missing values *452*
    Other ways to represent missing values *452*
    Special missing values *452*
    MISSING statement *453*
    Illegal characters in input data *453*
WORKING WITH MISSING VALUES *453*
    Missing initial values *453*
    Magnitudes of missing values *454*
    Specifying missing constants *454*
    Missing values in comparison operations *455*
    Missing values in logical operations *455*
    Printing missing values *455*
MISSING VALUES GENERATED BY THE SAS SYSTEM *456*
    Missing values used in arithmetic calculations *456*
    Illegal operations *456*
    Illegal character-to-numeric conversions *456*

INTRODUCTION

Most collections of data include missing values. For example, if a respondent in a survey fails to answer a given question, an analyst may classify that data item as missing. Sales figures for various products may include a missing value for last year's sales of a product introduced this year. In addition, errors in entering data can produce unidentifiable values.

Values like these can be recognized as missing at the time the SAS System reads them. Other missing values can be produced during the DATA step. You can use program statements to assign missing values to variables, and the SAS System can automatically generate missing values for variables when certain conditions arise.

MISSING VALUES IN INPUT DATA LINES

Blanks for missing values You can represent missing values on data lines for numeric and character variables with either blanks or single periods. If you are not using list input, the easiest way to indicate a missing value is simply to leave blank the columns that the value would occupy if it were not missing. When SAS reads the data line, it sets the value to missing.

For example, say your data values are pre- and post-test scores for students. If Susan is absent the day of the post-test, you simply leave Susan's POSTTEST field blank on the input lines:

```
data testscor;
   input name $ 1-6 pretest 8-9 posttest 11-12;
   cards;
ANN    92 96
SUSAN  84
BILL   81 95
more data lines
;
```

Periods for missing values You can also use a single period (.) to represent a missing value. When SAS sees a single period in the columns corresponding to a variable value, it sets the value to missing. (To read a single period as the value of a character variable without having SAS consider the value missing, use the $CHAR. informat.)

If you are using list input, you **must** use periods rather than blanks to represent missing values. With list input, SAS begins reading the next data value at the next nonblank column, so you must use the period to prevent SAS from reading the value of the following variable in place of the value that is missing. (See the **INPUT Statement** in "SAS Statements Used in the DATA Step" for more information about list input.)

For example, say you are using list input to read the test scores in the example above. Use a single period to represent Susan's POSTTEST value:

```
data testscor;
   input name $ pretest posttest;
   cards;
ANN    92 96
SUSAN  84 .
BILL   81 95
more data lines
;
```

Other ways to represent missing values You can also use 9s, 99s, or other values clearly out of the expected range to represent missing values. Although SAS does not automatically read values like these as missing values, you can use program statements to convert them to missing.

For example, say you are reading values of the variable SCORE. The values range from 0 to 7; a value of 9 indicates a missing value. You can use this SAS statement to convert all values of 9 in SCORE to a SAS missing value:

```
if score=9 then score=.;
```

Special missing values At times you may want to differentiate among classes of missing values. For example, in a survey one missing value may mean that the respondent refused to answer a given question, whereas another missing value may mean that the respondent gave an invalid answer.

For numeric variables only, you can designate up to twenty-seven special missing values (the uppercase letters A through Z and the special character underscore (_)) when you want to differentiate among missing values. In the survey example you could use the uppercase letter R to indicate that the person refused to respond to a question and the uppercase letter X to indicate that the response is invalid.

See **WORKING WITH MISSING VALUES** later in this chapter for information on using special missing values to cause SAS to distinguish between different classes of missing data values.

MISSING statement   When your data lines contain characters in numeric fields that you want SAS to interpret as special missing values, you **must** include a MISSING statement. (See the **MISSING Statement** in "SAS Statements Used in the DATA Step.") For example, in the survey above, you may create a data set like this one:

```
data survey;
   missing r x;
   input id questn1;
   cards;
8401 2
8402 R
8403 1
8404 X
8405 2
more data lines
;
```

in which the letters R and X in the MISSING statement indicate that values of R and X in the input data lines are to be considered special missing values rather than invalid numeric data values.

Illegal characters in input data   In addition to blanks or periods and special missing values, you may find that numeric values in your data lines contain illegal characters such as letters or underscores not identified in a MISSING statement, other special characters, or embedded blanks. When SAS encounters these values, it prints a warning message and sets each invalid data value to missing (.).

WORKING WITH MISSING VALUES

Missing initial values   At the beginning of each execution of the DATA step, SAS sets the value of each variable you create in the DATA step with an INPUT or assignment statement to missing (except for variables named in a RETAIN statement or created in a SUM statement). SAS then replaces the missing values as it encounters values you assign to the variables. Thus, if you use program statements to create new variables, their values in each observation are missing until you assign the values in an assignment statement.

For example, consider these statements:

```
data new;
   input x;
   if x=1 then y=2;
   cards;
4
1
3
1
;
```

When X equals 1, Y's value is set to 2. But since there are no assignment statements that set Y's value when X is not equal to 1, Y remains missing for those observations where X does not equal 1.

When variables are read with a SET, MERGE, or UPDATE statement, SAS sets the values to missing only before the first execution of the SET, MERGE, or UPDATE statement for a given data set (or before the first execution of the statement for each BY group, if a BY statement is present). Thereafter, the variables retain their values until new values become available (for example, through an assignment statement or through the next execution of the SET, MERGE, or UPDATE statement).

When a data set in a match-merge operation (with a BY statement) exhausts its observations, variables it contributes to the output data set retain their values as described above. That is, as long as the BY value in effect when the data set exhausted its observations does not change, the variables it contributes to the output data set retain their values from the final observation. When the BY value changes, the variables are set to missing and remain missing because the data set contains no more observations to provide replacement values. When a data set in a one-to-one merge operation (without a BY statement) exhausts its observations, variables it contributes to the output data set are set to missing and remain missing. See the **MERGE Statement** in "SAS Statements Used in the DATA Step" for examples; see the "Introduction" to THE DATA STEP for more information on the program data vector and how variable values are retained.

Magnitudes of missing values Within the SAS System, a missing value for a numeric variable is smaller than all numbers. If you sort your data set by a numeric variable, observations with missing values for that variable appear first in the sorted data set. For numeric variables, you can compare the special missing values described in **Special Missing Values** above with numbers and with each other as shown in this table. From smallest to largest, the order of magnitude for SAS missing values for numeric variables is

```
 _
 .
 A
 B
 ↓
 Z
numbers
```

Missing values of character variables are smaller than any printable character value. However, some usually unprintable characters (for example, machine carriage-control characters, real or binary numeric data that have been read in error as character data) have values less than the blank. Thus, when you sort a data set by a character variable, observations with missing (blank) values of the sorting variable may not appear first in the sorted data set, but they always appear before observations in which values of the sorting variable contain only printable characters.

Specifying missing constants When your input data lines contain special missing values, enter the values without periods in front of them. However, when you use a special missing value in an expression or in an assignment statement, put a period before the letter or underscore so that SAS will identify it as a missing value instead of a variable name.

For example, suppose that you are checking the ages that people report for themselves in a survey by subtracting their date of birth from the date of the interview and comparing that with their answer to the question on age. If the subtraction gives a different age than they report, you assign a value of .D (for discrepancy) to AGE:

```
data survey;
   input survdate birthdat age;
   if (survdate-birthdat) ^=age then age=.d;
   cards;
data lines
;
```

When SAS prints a special missing value, it prints only the letter or underscore.

Missing values in comparison operations   To check for missing values in your data, you can use statements like the following:

```
if xxx=. then do;
```

for numeric variables, or

```
if xxx=' ' then do;
```

where ' ' is a blank literal for character variables. In each case, SAS checks to see if XXX's value in the current observation is equal to the missing value specified. If it is, SAS executes the DO group.

Note that, for numeric variables, the first statement checks only for missing values represented by a period (.); it does not check for special missing values such as A or _. If your data contain special missing values, you can check for all missing values of a variable with the following statement:

```
if xxx<=.z then do;
```

Since Z is the largest missing value, if any missing values for XXX are present, SAS executes the DO group. To produce a data set containing no observations that have missing values for XXX, use:

```
if xxx>.z;
```

You can set values to missing within your DATA step with program statements. For example, the statement

```
if age<0 then age=.;
```

sets the value of AGE to missing if AGE has a value less than 0. Note that if you already have special missing values for AGE, you are resetting them to (.). To avoid resetting them use:

```
if .z<age<0 then age=.;
```

Missing values in logical operations   Missing values and zero have a value of "false" when you use them with logical operators such as AND or OR. All other values have a value of "true." (See "SAS Expressions" for more information on logical operators.)

Printing missing values   SAS prints a period (.) for a missing value of a numeric variable; however, if you have special missing values for numeric variables, it prints the letter or the underscore. For character variables, SAS prints a series of blanks equal to the length of the variable.

You can ask SAS to substitute another character for numeric missing values if you do not want a period (.) printed; however, SAS continues to store the number as (.). Use the SAS option MISSING to define the character you want. For example, to print a blank instead of (.) for numeric missing values, use this statement before the step that prints the values:

```
options missing=' ';
```

The MISSING option does not affect special missing values; for example, the value .A appears as A in printed output even if you specify another value with the MISSING option. To change special missing values, you must use program statements.

MISSING VALUES GENERATED BY THE SAS SYSTEM

In addition to the missing values that are present in your data and that you assign in program statements, the SAS System can assign missing values to protect you from problems arising in three common computing situations: using missing values in calculations, performing illegal operations, and converting character values to numeric ones when the character variable contains non-numeric information.

Missing values used in arithmetic calculations If you use a missing value in an arithmetic calculation, SAS sets the result of that calculation to missing. Then, if you use that result in another calculation, the next result is also missing. This action is called *propagation of missing values*. Propagation of missing values is important because the SAS System continues working at the same time that it lets you know, via warning messages, which arithmetic expressions have missing values and at what point it created them.

If you do not want missing values to propagate in your arithmetic expressions, you can use the sample statistic functions described in "SAS Functions" to omit missing values from the computations. For example, consider the DATA step below:

```
data text;
   x=.;
   y=5;
   a=x+y;
   b=sum(x,y);
run;
```

X's value is missing; Y's value is 5. Adding X and Y together in an expression produces a missing result, so A's value is missing. However, using the SUM function to add X and Y produces the value 5 since the SUM function ignores missing values.

Illegal operations If you try to perform an illegal operation (for example, dividing by zero or taking the logarithm of zero), SAS prints a warning message and assigns a missing value to the result.

Illegal character-to-numeric conversions The SAS System automatically converts character values to numeric values if a character variable is used in an arithmetic expression. If a character value contains non-numeric information and SAS tries to convert it to a numeric value, SAS prints an error message and sets the result of the conversion to missing. (For more information about character-to-numeric conversion of data values, see "SAS Expressions.")

Chapter 15
SAS® Files

INTRODUCTION 457
KINDS OF SAS FILES 458
NAMING SAS FILES 458
   The Libref 459
      Reserved Librefs 460
      Names for Permanent SAS Files 460
         The USER Libref 460
      Names for Temporary SAS Files 461
THE SAS DATA LIBRARY 461
   The WORK Library 462
   Duplicate Names 462
SAS FILE MANAGEMENT 462
   Replacing SAS Files 463
   Documenting the Contents of SAS Data Libraries 463
   Copying SAS Data Libraries 463
   Uploading and Downloading SAS Data Sets 463
   Renaming and Deleting SAS Files 463
SAS DATA SETS 464
   Definition 464
   Further Notes on SAS Data Set Names 464
      Specifying _NULL_ 464
      Omitting a Name 464
      The _LAST_ Data Set 464
   Advantages of Permanent SAS Data Sets 465
   Calculating the Size of a SAS Data Set 465
   SAS Data Set Options 465
      TYPE= CORR Data Sets 469
SAS CATALOGS 469
   Definition 469
   Further Notes on Catalog Entry Names 470
   Entry Types 470
   Storing Catalog Entries 471
   Managing Catalog Entries 471
   Transporting and Converting Version 5 Catalogs 473
   Converting Release 6.01/6.02 Catalogs to Release 6.03 Format 473

INTRODUCTION

To analyze and process information with most SAS procedures, you must first put the information in a *SAS file*. The SAS System can create and process two kinds of SAS files for specialized purposes. When you store a number of SAS files in the same place, you have a *SAS data library*. The first three sections of this chapter describe the kinds of SAS files, how they are created and named, and how they are managed in a SAS data library. The remaining sections of the chapter focus on the *SAS data set*, the most frequently used of the SAS files, and SAS catalogs.

    Important Note: in many computing environments the terms *file* and *data set* are used interchangeably. However, this discussion does not equate *SAS file* with

SAS data set. In this context, a *SAS data set* is a particular kind of *SAS file*. In other words, all SAS data sets are SAS files, but not all SAS files are SAS data sets.

KINDS OF SAS FILES

The SAS System uses specially structured files called *SAS files*. The special characteristics of SAS files make them more convenient and efficient for SAS programs to use. SAS files are different from *external files*. External files can be processed by other programming languages, as well as by the DATA step's INFILE and FILE statements, the %INCLUDE statement, and several SAS utility procedures. SAS files can be processed only by SAS programs.

The most commonly used SAS file is the *SAS data set*, which contains *observations* for which *variable values* have been recorded. SAS data sets are used with DATA, SET, MERGE, and UPDATE statements and with most SAS procedures.

The other kind of SAS file is a catalog, which contains *entries*. A catalog entry may be any of the wide variety of utility items for use in SAS programming, including a screen for use with the FSEDIT procedure, function key settings for display manager sessions, a format or informat created with the FORMAT procedure, and more. Refer to the **Entry Types** section later in this chapter for a list of the possible entries for catalogs.

Note that the operating system's extension to the file's name indicates what type of SAS file it is. The extensions are

- SSD (SAS data set)
- SCT. (SAS catalog)

SAS files can be temporary (used in only one program) or permanent (stored on disk to be used repeatedly). The name of a SAS file determines whether it is temporary or permanent, as discussed in the next section.

NAMING SAS FILES

See the discussion of SAS naming conventions in the "Introduction" to USING THE SAS LANGUAGE for rules governing names used in SAS programs.

A SAS file is named at the time it is created. For example, a SAS data set created in a DATA step is given a name in the DATA statement. A SAS file created in a PROC step is usually given a name in the PROC statement or an OUTPUT statement. You can name a SAS file explicitly, or the SAS System can assign a default name.

Once created, a SAS file is accessed in subsequent DATA or PROC steps by specifying its name. You usually specify the name explicitly, although under certain circumstances, SAS can supply a default name. For example, to use an existing SAS data set in a DATA step, specify the name in a SET, MERGE, or UPDATE statement. To use an existing SAS file in a PROC step, specify its name in the PROC statement.

A SAS file's complete name consists of two words separated by a period, for example, FOOD.PRICES. The first word is called the *first-level name* or *libref*; it identifies the library where the file is stored. The second word, the *second-level name*, identifies the specific file (PRICES).

The libref of a SAS file can be from one to eight characters long. Second-level names are also one to eight characters long.

The Libref

A SAS file's libref (short for "SAS data library reference") is a name that is associated with a storage location, or *directory*.

When you create a new SAS file, the libref points to the directory where the file is to be stored. When you reference an existing SAS file, the libref indicates the directory where SAS should look for the file.

For example, when this statement executes:

```
data employ.dept1;
```

SAS writes a file called DEPT1 in the directory referenced by the name EMPLOY. Suppose that another SAS program uses a PROC PRINT step to print the same SAS file:

```
proc print data=employ.dept1;
```

When the PROC statement executes, SAS looks for the SAS file DEPT1 in the directory referenced by the name EMPLOY.

The SAS System knows which directory a libref references because you associate the libref with the directory using the SAS LIBNAME statement. Associating a libref with a storage location is also called *defining a libref*. In general, a libref must be defined to be used in a SAS program (exceptions are noted where appropriate). Once defined, the libref can be used repeatedly throughout a program and remains associated with the directory until the program ends (or you issue another LIBNAME statement reassigning the libref).

Use the SAS statement LIBNAME to associate a libref with the name of the directory in which you want to store or have stored a SAS file. For example, suppose you are creating the SAS data set called PRICES and you decide to store it in a directory called \SURVEY\STORES in your current directory. Before the DATA step that creates PRICES, enter a LIBNAME statement:

```
libname food '\survey\stores';
data food.prices;
   input ... ;
more SAS statements
```

Similarly, if you want to access an existing SAS file, you use the LIBNAME statement to associate a libref with the directory in which the file is stored. For example,

```
libname food '\survey\stores';
data suprmart;
   set food.prices;
   if store= ... ;
more SAS statements
```

A directory does not have to be referred to by the same libref all the time. A different libref could be associated with a directory in every SAS program using the directory.

To create a permanent SAS file or read an existing permanent SAS file, you must define and use a libref other than WORK. The SAS System uses WORK as a default libref for files for which no other libref is defined. All SAS files with a libref of WORK are *temporary files* and are deleted at the end of the SAS session.

Reserved Librefs

The SAS System reserves a number of names for particular files or kinds of files. You should not use these reserved names as librefs, except as intended. The reserved names are

LIBRARY
SASxxxx
USER
WORK

Names for Permanent SAS Files

To read or write a permanent SAS file, you usually specify both the first- and second-level names in the SAS statement that requests the file (such as a DATA or PROC statement).

For instance, suppose you want to create a permanent SAS data set with the second-level name PRICES. First, you decide where to store the PRICES data set (that is, in which directory). Next, you use the LIBNAME statement to define a libref; you choose FOOD as the libref. Then, you name the SAS data set in a DATA statement:

```
data food.prices;
```

When the DATA step executes, a SAS data set named PRICES is stored in the directory referenced by the libref FOOD. To read FOOD.PRICES in a subsequent DATA or PROC step in the same SAS program, specify both names again. For example,

```
proc sort data=food.prices;
   by item;
```

Since the libref FOOD was defined earlier in the program, it does not need to be redefined. However, if you want to read the PRICES data set in a different program, you need to include a libref definition again.

The USER Libref

There is an exception to the rule that you must specify both a libref and a second-level name to read or write a permanent SAS file. If you define USER as a libref, you need only specify a second-level name to access permanent SAS files stored in the directory referenced by USER.

For example, if you use this LIBNAME statement:

```
libname user '\food\data';
```

you can specify only the second-level name of any SAS file stored in the \FOOD\DATA directory. When SAS encounters a one-level file name, it automatically uses \FOOD\DATA to read or write the file.

Specifying the default libref USER does not mean that files from other directories cannot be accessed. However, only those files in the USER directory can be referenced using one name.

Note that USER overrides the SAS System's default libref, which is WORK. To create temporary SAS files while the USER libref is assigned, specify a two-level name with WORK as the libref. (WORK does not need to be defined as a libref because SAS assumes that WORK refers to temporary storage.)

Names for Temporary SAS Files

To create or read a temporary SAS file (one that exists only for the duration of the program), you usually specify only one name, the second-level name of the file. SAS automatically uses WORK for the libref. WORK is the SAS System's default libref, and it indicates that the file is stored temporarily and will be deleted at the end of the SAS program.

For example, if your DATA statement is

```
data sales;
```

the new SAS data set's complete name is WORK.SALES. Similarly, to read an existing temporary file, specify only the second-level name:

```
set coupons;
```

When the SET statement executes, SAS reads the file WORK.COUPONS.

Remember that you do not need to define the libref WORK; it is defined automatically when you invoke SAS.

The only time that specifying one name results in a permanent file is when you have defined the default libref USER.

THE SAS DATA LIBRARY

All of the SAS files in a given directory are members of one *SAS data library*. A directory can contain external (non-SAS) files as well as SAS files, but only the SAS files are members of the SAS data library.

As discussed in the earlier section, **The Libref**, a SAS file's libref is a name associated with the directory in which the file is stored. All of the SAS files in a directory belong to the same SAS data library; therefore, all of the SAS files in a directory can be referenced by one libref.

The SAS data library is a logical concept, not a physical entity. **Figure 15.1** depicts the relationship among a SAS data library, SAS files, and the elements of the SAS files. Notice that the library corresponds to a directory, and a SAS file corresponds to a file within the directory.

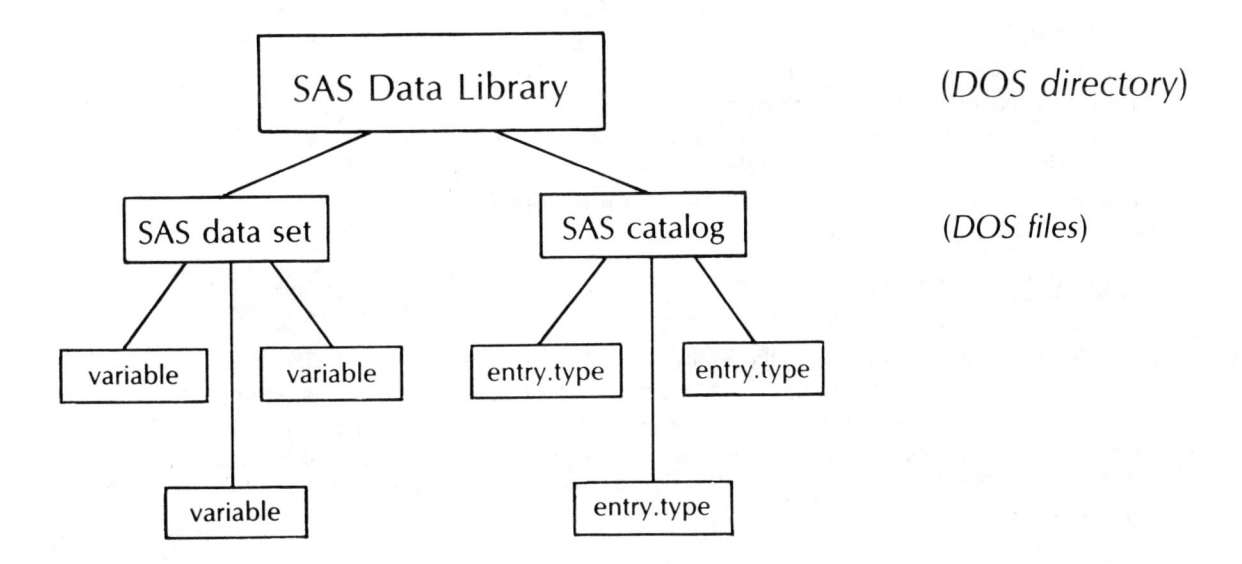

Figure 15.1 SAS Data Library Structure

There is no limit to the number of SAS files in a SAS data library, and you can have different kinds of SAS files (SAS data sets and catalogs) in one library.

When multiple SAS files are members of one library, processing those files with the CONTENTS, COPY, and DATASETS procedures is convenient. That is, you can process more than one member at a time simply by referencing the library. Suppose you have two SAS data sets named LIBONE.SCORES and LIBTWO.COURSES. The libref is different for the two files, so you know that they are not members of the same library. To process both files with PROC CONTENTS, you need two PROC steps:

```
proc contents data=libone.scores;
proc contents data=libtwo.courses;
```

If you had stored the files as members of one library, for example, MYSASLIB.SCORES and MYSASLIB.COURSES, you could use one PROC step:

```
proc contents data=mysaslib._all_;
```

Another advantage of storing multiple SAS files as members of a SAS data library is that they are logically connected by sharing a common name (their libref). This makes management and tracking of your SAS files easier.

The WORK Library

WORK is the libref of the default SAS data library, which is a temporary library. The WORK library is necessary for the operation of SAS. In any SAS session, a number of temporary files (WORK files) are used. Some WORK files you create explicitly, such as WORK SAS data sets. Other WORK files are internally generated by the SAS System, and you may not be aware of their existence.

Typically, the WORK library is deleted automatically at the end of a SAS session. A new WORK library is defined automatically at the beginning of a SAS session.

Duplicate Names

You can assign the same second-level name to more than one SAS file in a SAS data library, as long as the files are of different types. For example, suppose you have a SAS data library with the libref LIB2 and you are creating a SAS data set and a SAS catalog that will be stored in LIB2. You could give both files the same second-level name, for example, ADDRESS. The SAS System distinguishes the files from each other by checking their types.

We do not recommend that you duplicate names within a library. However, if you do, be careful when using the COPY, CONTENTS, and DATASETS utility procedures so that you know which files are being processed.

SAS FILE MANAGEMENT

The SAS utility procedures available for SAS file management are designed to allow you to work with more than one SAS file at a time, as long as the files belong to the same SAS data library. Therefore, we often discuss file management in terms of SAS data libraries, whether the library contains one or many SAS files. Refer to the *SAS Procedures Guide, Release 6.03 Edition* for information on utility procedures.

Replacing SAS Files

If you are creating a SAS file that has the same name as an existing file of the same type in your SAS data library, the original file is deleted by default after the new file is written successfully. However, if errors occur before the new file is finished, the original file is preserved. Note that the disk must have enough free space to hold a copy of the SAS data set being replaced since the original data set is deleted only **after** the new data set has been written completely with no errors.

You can allow or disallow replacement of a permanent file with the REPLACE | NOREPLACE system option. REPLACE is the default value; if you do not want files to be automatically replaced, specify NOREPLACE as a system option.

In addition, for SAS data sets only, you can override the REPLACE | NOREPLACE system option with the REPLACE= data set option. For example, the NOREPLACE system option is in effect in the SAS job shown below, but it is temporarily overridden for the FOOD.MEAT SAS data set:

```
options noreplace;
data food.milk;
    set food.dairy;
    if product=milk;
data food.meat (replace=yes);
    set food.meat;
    if date>'1JUL84'd;
```

Documenting the Contents of SAS Data Libraries

PROC CONTENTS gives you complete documentation on the contents of the SAS data library and the files it contains. The type of each SAS file is shown; also, PROC CONTENTS displays variable names and labels, the number of observations, and other information for SAS data sets. See "The CONTENTS Procedure" in the *SAS Procedures Guide, Release 6.03 Edition* for complete information.

Copying SAS Data Libraries

PROC COPY can be used to copy SAS data libraries. It is especially designed for backups of SAS files. See "The COPY Procedure" in the *SAS Procedures Guide, Release 6.03 Edition* for a complete description.

Uploading and Downloading SAS Data Sets

There are two SAS procedures that allow you to copy SAS data sets to and from a remote mainframe or minicomputer system: PROC UPLOAD and PROC DOWNLOAD. See these procedures in the *SAS Procedures Guide for Personal Computers* for more information. These procedures are part of the SAS System's micro-to-host link, which is described in Appendix 3.

Renaming and Deleting SAS Files

You can use PROC DATASETS to rename SAS files, delete SAS files, and systematically rename a group of functionally related files in the same SAS data library. DATASETS also allows you to rename and relabel variables in SAS data sets. See "The DATASETS Procedure" in the *SAS Procedures Guide, Release 6.03 Edition* for more information.

SAS DATA SETS

Definition

SAS data sets are the most frequently used type of SAS file. They are created and read in the DATA step and by SAS procedures.

A *SAS data set* is a file of data packaged in a convenient way for SAS software to use. SAS data sets contain *observations* for which *variable values* (data) have been recorded and descriptor information on the variables. SAS data sets can be permanent or temporary.

SAS data sets differ from external files in the way they store data and because they automatically maintain descriptive information about the data set. The data are arranged in a rectangular table with the rows of the table representing the observations and the columns representing the variables. The descriptor information is at the beginning of each SAS data set and includes the names and certain attributes of the variables in the data set. The attributes stored for each variable are

- name (from one to eight characters in length)
- type (character or numeric)
- length (the number of bytes used to store a variable)
- position (the location of the variable within an observation)
- informat name (for reading the variable values)
- format name (for printing the values)
- label (a variable descriptor consisting of from one to forty characters).

Whether you intend to store a SAS data set permanently or temporarily, you must have your data in a SAS data set in order to use most SAS procedures. SAS relies on the information in the descriptor section to process variable values correctly.

Further Notes on SAS Data Set Names

Specifying _NULL_

If you want to execute a DATA step but do not want to create a SAS data set, you can specify _NULL_ in the DATA statement rather than a SAS data set name:

```
data _null_;
```

For example, if you are writing a report based on the values in a SAS data set, you probably do not want to create another SAS data set containing the same information. Using _NULL_ means that SAS executes the DATA step just as if it were creating a new SAS data set, but it does not write any observations. This can be an efficient use of computer resources.

Omitting a Name

If you do not specify a SAS data set name or _NULL_ in the DATA statement, a temporary SAS data set is created. The temporary data set's name is WORK.DATA*n*, where *n* is the number of the data set. For example, the first such SAS data set created is WORK.DATA1, the second is WORK.DATA2, and so on.

The _LAST_ Data Set

The SAS System uses a special automatic variable called _LAST_ to keep track of the most recently created SAS data set in a SAS program. The value of _LAST_ is null initially, but each time a new SAS data set is created, the value of the _LAST_ variable changes to the name of the newest data set.

When you execute a SAS procedure without specifying a SAS data set, SAS, by default, uses the _LAST_ data set. For example,

```
data food.dairy;
   set food.prices;
   if dept='DAIRY';
proc print;
```

After the DATA step executes, the value of the _LAST_ variable is FOOD.DAIRY. The PROC PRINT statement does not specify a SAS data set name, so SAS uses FOOD.DAIRY (the _LAST_ data set) by default.

The SAS system option _LAST_= allows you to assign a value to the _LAST_ variable explicitly. The value you assign with the _LAST_= option remains the value of the _LAST_ variable until a new SAS data set is created.

You may use the _LAST_ option when, for example, you want to run a number of PROC steps using an existing permanent SAS data set. By using _LAST_=, you avoid the need to specify a SAS data set name in each PROC statement.

Advantages of Permanent SAS Data Sets

There are several advantages to storing your data in a permanent SAS data set rather than leaving them in an external file or recreating a temporary data set in every SAS job:

- You leave reading the data to SAS; you need not be concerned about format, and you do not need to execute INPUT statements each time a SAS data set is used.
- SAS automatically documents the SAS data set, and you can keep track of its contents easily. Using SAS utility procedures, you can always find out which variables the data set contains, their lengths and formats, and other information that often gets lost for undocumented files.
- No data conversion is necessary since data are stored in the form in which SAS uses them.

Calculating the Size of a SAS Data Set

The formula for calculating the size of a SAS data set is

$$(218 + (v*106)) + (nobs*(tvl + 4))$$

where v is the number of variables, $nobs$ is the number of observations, and tvl is the total of all variable lengths. For example, suppose you have a data set with 2 variables ($v=2$), each of which has a length of 8 ($tvl=16$), and 10 observations ($nobs=10$). The size of the data set is

$$(218 + (2*106)) + (10*(16 + 4)) = 628 \text{ bytes}$$

SAS Data Set Options

Data set options are those that appear after SAS data set names. They specify actions that are applicable only to the processing of the SAS data set with which they appear and let you perform such operations as:

- giving a descriptive label to a SAS data set
- specifying variables to be included or dropped in later processing
- selecting only the first or last *n* observations for processing.

SAS data set options apply only to SAS data sets, not to SAS catalogs.

Data set options are specified in parentheses after the SAS data set name in DATA step or PROC statements, for example,

```
data new(drop=year);
```

The DROP= option specifies that a variable called YEAR be dropped from the SAS data set called NEW.

To specify two or more options, leave at least one space between them in the parenthesized list. For example,

```
data new(drop=year label='SALES BY REGION');
```

Some data set options are valid only when a SAS data set is created; for example, they can appear in a DATA statement but not in a SET statement. Other options are valid only when an existing data set is being read, as in a SET, MERGE, or UPDATE statement. Some options can be used in both situations.

The data set options are listed below. The accompanying explanation gives the circumstances under which the option can be specified.

DROP=*variables*
: causes the specified variables to be omitted from the SAS data set that is being created or during the processing of the data set. If the DROP= option appears in a DATA statement and only one data set is being created, DROP= functions exactly as the DROP program statement does. If the DATA statement specifies several data sets, the DROP= option can be used to control which variables appear in which data sets. For example, consider the following statements:

    ```
    data hischool(drop=collname collcode)college;
       input yrs_educ hsname $ collname $ collcode;
       if yrs_educ<=12 then output hischool;
       if yrs_educ>12 then output college;
    ```

    The SAS data set COLLEGE contains all the variables in the INPUT statement; the data set HISCHOOL includes all the variables except COLLNAME and COLLCODE.

    The DROP= option is useful with the OUT= option in a PROC statement. The DROP= option can also appear when an existing SAS data set is being processed. The listed variables are not available to SAS during the processing. This could be useful if, for example, you want to update only some of the variables of a data set. Variables that are not to be updated could be excluded from the update operation with a DROP= option:

    ```
    data new;
       update old(drop=paycode) ups;
       by ssn;
    ```

FIRSTOBS=*n*
: causes processing to begin with the *n*th observation. The *n* value must be a positive integer. For example, the statement

    ```
    proc print data=study(firstobs=20);
    ```

    results in printing observations beginning with number 20. This option is valid only when reading an existing SAS data set.

IN=*variable*
: names a new variable in a SET, MERGE, or UPDATE statement that contains values indicating the data set from which an observation

comes. The variable's value is 1 if values in the current observation were taken from that data set, and it is 0 otherwise. The IN= option is specified in parentheses after a SAS data set name in the SET, MERGE, or UPDATE statement, for example,

```
merge food.dairy(in=indairy) food.meat;
```

Values of IN= variables are available to program statements during the DATA step, but the variables are not included in the SAS data set being created.

KEEP=*variables*

causes only the listed variables to be retained for processing or output to the SAS data set. If KEEP= appears when a SAS data set is created, only the listed variables appear in the new data set. KEEP= is useful when several data sets are created with one DATA statement: it can specify which variables are to be included in which data sets.

If the KEEP= option is used when an existing data set is read, only the variables listed are available to SAS during processing; however, the variables not listed are still in the data set.

LABEL=*'label'*

specifies a label for the SAS data set, which is stored with the data set and printed whenever the CONTENTS procedure is used to print the data set's contents. The label consists of up to 40 characters and should be enclosed in quotes. If the label characters include single quotes, write them as two single quotes, and enclose the entire label in single quotes. For example,

```
data w2(label='1976 W2 INFO, HOURLY');
data new(label='DAVE''S LIST');
data sales(label='SALES FOR MAY(NE)');
```

The LABEL= option is used only when a data set is created.

OBS=*n*

specifies the last observation of the SAS data set that will be processed. (Note OBS= does not specify how many observations should be processed.) The *n* value must be a positive integer. This option is valid only when reading an existing data set.

RENAME=(*oldname*=*newname*...)

changes the name of a variable. If RENAME= is specified when a data set is created, the new name is permanent. If RENAME= is specified at any other time, the new name exists only for the duration of the procedure. For example, the statements

```
data new(rename=(x=keys));
   set old;
```

create the SAS data set NEW. NEW contains the same variable values as data set OLD; however, the variable named X in data set OLD is named KEYS in data set NEW.

Several variables can be renamed with one RENAME option, for example,

```
data new(rename=(x=keys y=locks));
```

If RENAME= is used and either DROP= or KEEP= is also used, DROP= and KEEP= are applied before RENAME=. Thus, use the *oldname* in the KEEP= or DROP= option.

You cannot use an abbreviated variable list (for example, X1-X10) with the RENAME= option.

REPLACE=YES
REPLACE=NO

is used to override the REPLACE|NOREPLACE system option allowing replacement of permanent SAS data sets.

TYPE=DATA
TYPE=CORR

specifies the SAS data set type for input data.

Most SAS data sets are TYPE=DATA; however, there are several specially structured SAS data sets that are used by some SAS/STAT procedures. These SAS data sets contain special variables and observations, and they are usually created by SAS statistical procedures. You can also use a DATA step to create a special SAS data set in the proper format, in which case you use the TYPE= data set option to indicate the data set's type to SAS. Since most of the special SAS data sets are used with SAS/STAT software, they are described in the *SAS/STAT User's Guide, Release 6.03 Edition.* TYPE=CORR data sets, which are output by PROC CORR, are described below.

WHERE=(*whereexpression*)

is available for use with SAS data sets in SET, MERGE, and UPDATE statements in the DATA step. (This option cannot be used with data sets in a PROC step.) The WHERE= option allows you to select observations from a SAS data set that meet a particular condition before the SAS System brings observations into the DATA step (that is, into the program data vector). WHERE selection is the first operation the SAS System performs in each execution of the DATA step.

The form of the WHERE= option is

WHERE=(*whereexpression*)

in which *whereexpression* is an arithmetic or logical expression. WHERE expressions make comparisons using unformatted values of variables. Refer to the description of the WHERE statement in Chapter 5, "SAS Statements Used in the DATA Step," for details on WHERE expressions.

For example, the WHERE= data set option in the DATA step below selects only those observations from data set IN.CITIES that have NC for the STATE variable:

```
data nccities;
   set in.cities (where=(state='NC'));
run;
```

Like any SAS data set option, the WHERE= option applies only to the data set whose name it follows. It does not apply to all data sets accessed in the DATA step. Any variables specified in the WHERE expression must be part of the data set to which the WHERE= option applies.

You cannot use both the WHERE= option and a WHERE statement with a SET, MERGE, or UPDATE statement. If you do use both, the WHERE statement is ignored and no warning is issued.

Refer to the description of the WHERE statement in Chapter 5, "SAS Statements Used in the DATA Step," for more information on WHERE processing, including a comparison of the WHERE statement with the subsetting IF statement.

TYPE=CORR Data Sets

A TYPE=CORR data set contains a correlation matrix along with the variable means, standard deviations, the number of observations in the original SAS data set from which the correlation matrix was computed, and possibly other statistics (depending on which procedure created the SAS data set).

Using PROC CORR with an output data set specification automatically produces a TYPE=CORR data set. You can also create a TYPE=CORR data set from input data that contain a correlation matrix. In this case, TYPE=CORR must be specified as a data set option.

TYPE=CORR data sets can be used as input for PROC FACTOR, PROC REG, and other SAS/STAT procedures.

The variables in a TYPE=CORR data set are

- BY variables, if a BY statement was used with PROC CORR
- _TYPE_, containing the types of the observations (MEAN, STD, N, CORR, SUMWGT)
- _NAME_, identifying the variable with which a given row of the correlation matrix is associated
- variables from the data set analyzed by PROC CORR.

For the first observation, which contains the variable mean, the _TYPE_ variable's value is 'MEAN'; for the second observation, containing standard deviations, _TYPE_'s value is 'STD'; for the third observation, containing the number of observations, _TYPE_'s value is 'N'. If a WEIGHT statement was used there is also an observation containing the sum of the weights for each variable with a _TYPE_ value of SUMWGT. The _NAME_ variable's value is blank for these first four observations.

The first four observations are produced when PROC CORR creates the TYPE=CORR data set. However, if you create the TYPE=CORR data set, the data set need not contain these four observations.

Following the first three observations are the observations containing the correlation matrix; one for each row of the matrix. _TYPE_'s value for each of these observations is 'CORR'. _NAME_'s value for each observation is the variable name associated with that observation (row). See the *SAS/STAT User's Guide, Release 6.03 Edition* for more details on TYPE=CORR data sets and examples.

SAS CATALOGS

Definition

A SAS catalog is a kind of SAS file that contains *entries*. The entries in a catalog serve a variety of utility purposes. For example, the function key settings that you use in a display manager session are stored in a KEYS entry. Catalogs are created by SAS procedures or the CATALOG window. The entries within a catalog are created in various ways, depending on the type of entry.

Note: in previous releases of SAS software, there were multiple kinds of catalogs. For example, in the Version 5 SAS System there were full-screen catalogs (MEMTYPE=CAT) and graphics catalogs (MEMTYPE=GCAT). Now, in Release 6.03, there is only one kind of catalog. Its member type (MEMTYPE=) is CATALOG.

Further Notes on Catalog Entry Names

Like other SAS files, SAS catalogs have two-level names:

libref.catalog

where the first-level name, the *libref*, is a name assigned to the SAS data library to which the catalog belongs, and the second-level name, *catalog*, is the name of the catalog file.

A completely qualified catalog entry name is a four-level name:

libref.catalog.entry.entrytype

where *libref* and *catalog* are as described above, *entry* is the name of the entry, and *entrytype* is a keyword specifying the type of entry. Entry types are explained later in this chapter.

Generally, you do not need to specify all four levels of an entry's name to access the entry; most of the time you specify only the last two levels. The syntax required for entry names is dependent on the SAS procedure or facility you are using. See individual procedure descriptions for details.

Entry Types

There are many types of catalog entries, and you can store entries of different types in one catalog. The list below gives entry type keywords and descriptions for the types that you can create and manipulate. Note that the SAS System creates some additional types for internal purposes. These specialized entries include the types AFCBT, AFGO, AFPGM, RLINKLL. Although you may notice these entries in your user profile catalog, you cannot access them; therefore, they are not described below.

AFMACRO	contains the macros defined with a ### macro block in a Version 5 program screen. An AFMACRO entry is created when a Version 5 SAS/AF program screen is converted to Release 6.03 format.
BTREE	contains a SAS data set index created by the INDEX command in SAS/IML software.
CBT	contains the text, including questions and possible responses, of an application created with the SAS/AF software BUILD procedure.
CMAP	contains a color map created by the GREPLAY procedure in SAS/GRAPH software.
EDPARMS	contains attributes of your editing environment in SAS/FSP and SAS/AF software.
FONT	contains a software font created by the GFONT procedure in SAS/GRAPH software and used in graphics output containing text.
FORM	contains printer information for SAS/AF and SAS/FSP software.
FORMAT	contains a user-written numeric format created by the FORMAT procedure.
FORMATC	contains a user-written character format created by the FORMAT procedure.
GRSEG	contains a graph created by SAS/GRAPH software.
HELP	contains help information for applications developed with the BUILD procedure in SAS/AF software.

INFMT   contains a user-written numeric informat created with the FORMAT procedure.

INFMTC   contains a user-written character informat created with the FORMAT procedure.

IMOD   contains a module or subroutine created and used by SAS/IML software.

KEYS   contains function-key settings for any of a variety of full-screen procedures and features, including display manager.

LETTER   contains text created, edited, and output with the FSLETTER procedure in SAS/FSP software.

LIST   contains a screen that lists the values used by an application created by the BUILD procedure in SAS/AF software.

MATRIX   contains a matrix created and used by SAS/IML software.

MENU   contains SAS/AF software menu screens.

NPAD   contains a notepad saved from the NOTEPAD window in display manager.

PBUFFER   contains the contents of a paste buffer created with the CUT and PASTE facility in display manager.

POPTION   contains settings for SAS system options saved in your user profile catalog. System option settings are saved when the PROFILE option is in effect.

PROGRAM   contains SAS/AF software program screen created by the BUILD procedure.

SCREEN   contains a screen created by the FSEDIT procedure and used by FSEDIT and FSBROWSE in SAS/FSP software.

TEMPLATE   contains a template or layout created with the GREPLAY procedure for graphs displayed with SAS/GRAPH software.

WSAVE   contains window and associated attributes from display manager window commands.

Storing Catalog Entries

You can store a mixture of entry types in a catalog. Which types you store in a given catalog and how many entries you store in a catalog depend on the applications you have for catalogs and entries. For example, user-written formats and informats must be stored in a catalog called LIBRARY.FORMATS. You can store other types of entries in LIBRARY.FORMATS, but you may prefer to reserve this catalog for formats and informats. Similarly, there are two types of entries associated with any FSLETTER procedure application: LETTER and FORM entries. You may want to create a separate catalog for each FSLETTER application you have, or you may want to store all entries with types LETTER and FORM in one catalog. It depends on what is most convenient for you.

Managing Catalog Entries

There are several features to help you manage the entries in catalogs. One is the CATALOG procedure, a part of base SAS software. Another is the CATALOG window in display manager. Finally, a catalog directory screen for managing entries is included in a number of full-screen procedures in SAS/AF, SAS/FSP, and SAS/GRAPH software.

The CATALOG procedure is similar to the DATASETS procedure. However, PROC DATASETS operates on SAS files, the members of a SAS data library; PROC CATALOG operates on entries, the members of a catalog. Use the CATALOG procedure to perform these catalog management functions:

- copying entries to another catalog
- deleting entries from a catalog
- listing the entries in a catalog, and writing the list to a SAS data set or external file
- renaming entries
- exchanging entry names.

See Chapter 7, "The CATALOG Procedure," in the *SAS Procedures Guide, Release 6.03 Edition* for details on the syntax and use of PROC CATALOG.

The CATALOG window is a display manager window you can bring up at any time in a display manager session. The window displays the name, type, descriptions, and date of last update for each entry in the specified catalog. CATALOG window commands allow you to

- rename entries
- delete entries
- copy entries from another catalog to the current catalog.

Refer to Chapter 10, "SAS Display Manager System," for details on the CATALOG window.

Catalog directories are available in these full-screen procedures:

FSBROWSE (SAS/FSP software)
FSEDIT (SAS/FSP software)
FSLETTER (SAS/FSP software)
BUILD (SAS/AF software)
GREPLAY (SAS/GRAPH software)
GDEVICE (SAS/GRAPH software).

A catalog directory is a specialized screen that lists the same kind of information that the CATALOG window provides: entry name, type, description, and date of last update. The management functions you can perform on entries depend on what procedure the directory is used with and the kind of entries that procedure uses. Most directories allow you to

- browse entries
- edit entries
- delete entries
- rename entries
- scroll through the directory
- search the directory for specific information.

Additional capabilities are available for some directories. See the description of each full-screen procedure for details on the catalog directory for that procedure.

The feature you choose for catalog management depends on what you want to do and what execution mode you are using. PROC CATALOG can be accessed in any execution mode: display manager, line-mode interactive, or noninteractive. The CATALOG window is available only in display manager or with full-screen procedures in interactive line-mode sessions. Catalog directories are available only within certain full-screen procedures.

Transporting and Converting Version 5 Catalogs

Full-screen catalogs created under Version 5 SAS software can be moved to and used with Version 6 SAS software. Note that you cannot transport a 6.03 catalog to a Version 5 environment.

If you want to use Version 5 full-screen catalogs (MEMTYPE=CAT) under Release 6.03, you must convert them.

In order to convert a Version 5 full-screen catalog, you must first download the catalog to your PC from the computer running the Version 5 SAS System. You must have communications hardware that allows the transfer of files between machines. You must also have communications software that allows the transfer of files. If you have a CMS, TSO, or VMS host running the Version 5 SAS System, you can use the SAS micro-to-host link and download the file with the DOWNLOAD procedure. If you have an AOS/VS, PRIMOS, or VSE host running the Version 5 SAS System, you must have some other kind of communications software because the SAS micro-to-host link is not supported for these hosts.

To download via the SAS micro-to-host link, follow these steps:

1. From a CMS, TSO, or VMS host running Version 5 of the SAS System, execute PROC CPORT and write the transport catalog to disk.
2. From the PC running Release 6.03, start the SAS link, and use the DOWNLOAD procedure to download the transport catalog as an external file (that is, using the INFILE= and OUTFILE= options). You must specify the BINARY option in the PROC DOWNLOAD statement.
3. Once the catalog is downloaded to the PC, execute the CIMPORT procedure on the PC, specifying one of the conversion options, OPT or NOOPT.

For more details on converting Version 5 catalogs to Release 6.03 form, see Part II of Technical Report P-173, *Transporting and Converting Version 5 Full-Screen Catalogs to a Release 6.03 System*.

Once the catalog is transported to the 6.03 machine, execute the CIMPORT procedure under Release 6.03, specifying one of the conversion options, OPT or NOOPT.

Converting Release 6.01/6.02 Catalogs to Release 6.03 Format

Important: catalogs created under Release 6.01 or 6.02 of the SAS System must be converted to 6.03 form to be used with the 6.03 Release. Release 6.01/6.02 catalogs and Release 6.03 catalogs can be readily distinguished because they have different extensions. The extension for 6.01/6.02 catalogs is .SFS. The extension for 6.03 catalogs is .SCT.

Converting Release 6.01/6.02 catalogs is easy: simply execute PROC CATALOG with the CONVERT option specified in the COPY statement. Refer to "The CATALOG Procedure" in the *SAS Procedures Guide, Release 6.03 Edition* for a complete description of the CATALOG procedure.

For example, suppose you have a catalog created under Release 6.02 called \MYDIR\MYCAT.SFS. To convert it for use under Release 6.03, you could use this PROC CATALOG step:

```
libname track 'c:\mydir';
proc catalog catalog=track.mycat;
   copy out=track.newcat convert;
run;
quit;
```

The converted catalog is \MYDIR\NEWCAT.SCT. Notice that the SAS System gives the new catalog the 6.03 extension, .SCT, automatically.

If you have used the 6.01 or 6.02 Releases of the SAS System for PCs, you will probably want to convert your user profile catalog, PROFILE.SFS, to Release 6.03 form. For example, suppose your 6.02 user profile catalog is \OLDDIR\SASUSER\PROFILE.SFS., and you want to store the converted profile catalog in \NEWDIR\SASUSER\PROFILE.SCT. You can use a PROC CATALOG program like this one to convert the profile catalog:

```
libname lib602 '\olddir\sasuser';
libname lib603 '\newdir\sasuser';
proc catalog catalog=lib602.profile;
   copy out=lib603.profile convert;
run;
quit;
```

Chapter 16
SAS® Global Options

INTRODUCTION 475
CONFIGURATION OPTIONS 476
    Specifying Configuration Options 476
    Finding Out What Option Settings Are in Effect 476
    Descriptions of Configuration Options 477
SAS SYSTEM OPTIONS 488
    Specifying SAS System Options 488
    SAS System Option Syntax 489
    Finding Out What Option Settings Are in Effect 490
    Descriptions of SAS System Options 490
SUMMARY OF SAS GLOBAL OPTIONS 498

INTRODUCTION

This chapter describes the *SAS global options* available with Release 6.03 of the SAS System.

SAS software uses two other kinds of options in addition to the global options:

- *SAS data set options* (such as RENAME= and KEEP=), which are specified in parentheses following a SAS data set's name and affect only that SAS data set
- *statement options* (such as HEADER= for the FILE statement), which are specified only in a given SAS statement or statements and affect only that statement or step.

Global options are SAS options that are in effect for the duration of your SAS session or program. Unlike statement options and data set options, global options are effective throughout a program or session.

There are two categories of SAS global options: configuration options and SAS system options.

- *Configuration options* are those that affect features of SAS System initialization, the SAS System's interface with your computer hardware, and the SAS System's interface with the operating system. Because they interact with the hardware and operating system, configuration options must be set when the SAS System begins a session or program. They cannot be changed dynamically; that is, they cannot be changed in the middle of a session or program.
- *SAS system options* are those that affect the appearance of SAS output, handling of some of the files used by the SAS System, use of system variables, processing of observations in SAS data sets, and so on. SAS system options can be set or reset at any time in a SAS session or program.

This chapter discusses how to specify and check the settings of configuration options and system options. It also includes complete descriptions of configura-

476   Chapter 16

tion options and system options. At the end of this chapter there is a table summarizing SAS global options: their names, the category to which they belong, where they can be specified, and their defaults.

CONFIGURATION OPTIONS

Specifying Configuration Options

SAS configuration options can be specified in two places: in a CONFIG.SAS file or in the SAS command.

- A CONFIG.SAS file is a DOS file containing SAS global options. For example, a CONFIG.SAS file can contain the following options:

```
-dms
-filebuffers 5 512
-msg \sas\sasmsg
-path \sas\sasexe\base
-sashelp \sas\sashelp
-work \saswork
```

By default, each time the PC SAS System is invoked, the SAS System checks for a CONFIG.SAS file. It looks first in the current directory, then in any directories indicated by the DOS PATH command, and finally in the root directory. When the SAS System finds a CONFIG.SAS file, it uses the settings specified in that file for configuration options. Although you can have multiple CONFIG.SAS files in different directories, SAS software does not use more than one CONFIG.SAS file per session.

We recommend that you have a CONFIG.SAS file in the directory from which you execute SAS programs or sessions. If you execute SAS from a variety of directories, store a CONFIG.SAS file in each of those directories.

- You can also specify any configuration option in the SAS command. For example, the following SAS command includes three configuration option specifications:

```
sas -nodms -profile -fsdevice sasxdicx
```

If you specify the same configuration option in the SAS command and in a CONFIG.SAS file, the setting established with the SAS command overrides the setting in the CONFIG.SAS file. Where you specify configuration options is up to you. If you use the same option settings frequently, it is convenient to specify the options in CONFIG.SAS.

Finding Out What Option Settings Are in Effect

You can display the current settings of configuration options by using the -VERBOSE configuration option. If you specify -VERBOSE, a listing of the options and their settings is displayed when the SAS System begins initialization. The list is displayed on the DOS screen before your SAS session starts. Initialization processes pause so that you can read the listing. Initialization resumes when you press the ENTER key.

If you want to change one of the configuration options listed on the DOS screen, you must edit the CONFIG.SAS file and specify the new values. These values do not take effect until the next time you invoke the SAS System. You may want to examine the contents of the CONFIG.SAS file before invoking the SAS System to ensure that the options you prefer are included.

Descriptions of Configuration Options

-AUTOEXEC *filename*
: specifies the file name for your AUTOEXEC.SAS file. AUTOEXEC.SAS is a file containing SAS statements that are executed automatically whenever the SAS System is invoked. AUTOEXEC.SAS can contain any SAS statements you like. For example, you can include LIBNAME statements for SAS data libraries you access routinely in SAS sessions.

  The SAS System looks for an AUTOEXEC.SAS file whenever it is invoked. By default, it looks first in the current directory, next in any directories specified by a DOS PATH command, and finally in the root directory. Therefore, if you store AUTOEXEC.SAS in the current directory, a directory specified in a DOS PATH command, or the root directory, you need not use this option. However, there are three cases when you must specify the -AUTOEXEC option:

  1. when you store your AUTOEXEC.SAS file in a directory that is not one of the default directories.
  2. when you have multiple AUTOEXEC.SAS files, one of which is stored in a directory that is higher in the search order than the one you want to use. For example, suppose you have two AUTOEXEC.SAS files, one in the current directory and one in the root directory. If the -AUTOEXEC option is not specified, the SAS System uses the default search order described above, and the AUTOEXEC.SAS file in the current directory is selected. If you want to use the one in the root directory, you must specify the -AUTOEXEC option:

     ```
     -autoexec \autoexec.sas
     ```

  3. when you give the file a name other than AUTOEXEC.SAS.

-CONFIG *filename*
: specifies the complete file name for your CONFIG.SAS file. CONFIG.SAS is a file of SAS global options that are executed automatically whenever the SAS System is invoked. There is a default CONFIG.SAS file in the \SAS directory, but you can create your own CONFIG.SAS file and store it in the directory of your choice.

  We recommend that you have a CONFIG.SAS file in the directory from which you execute SAS programs or sessions. If you execute the SAS System from a variety of directories, store a CONFIG.SAS file in each of those directories.

  The SAS System looks for a CONFIG.SAS file whenever it is invoked. By default, it looks first in the current directory, next in any directories specified by a DOS PATH command, and finally in the root directory. Therefore, if you store CONFIG.SAS in the current directory, a directory specified in a DOS PATH command, or the root directory, you need not use this option. However, there are three cases when you must specify the -CONFIG option:

  1. when you store your CONFIG.SAS file in a directory that is not one of the default directories.
  2. when you have multiple CONFIG.SAS files, one of which is stored in a directory that is higher in the search order than the one you want to use. For example, suppose you have two CONFIG.SAS files, one in the current directory and one in the root directory. If the -CONFIG option is not specified, the SAS System uses the default search order described above, and the CONFIG.SAS file in

the current directory is selected. If you want to use the one in the root directory, you must specify the -CONFIG option:

```
-config \config.sas
```

3. when you give the file a name other than CONFIG.SAS.

Note: the -CONFIG option can be specified only in the SAS command, not in a CONFIG.SAS file. If you specify this option in the CONFIG.SAS file, it is ignored.

-DMS | -NODMS

specifies what kind of interactive SAS session is initiated. If -DMS is specified, a SAS display manager session begins. If -NODMS is specified, a line-mode session begins. -DMS is the default.

-ECHO 'textstring'
-ECHO CLS

specifies a message to be displayed when the SAS System is invoked, where *textstring* is the message you want to display and CLS clears the screen. The message must be enclosed in quotes and should fit on a single line. For example, to clear the screen and display this message:

```
For assistance with SAS software questions, call 555-9898.
```

you specify the -ECHO option like this:

```
-echo cls
-echo 'For assistance with SAS software questions, call 555-9898.'
```

Note that the message is displayed on your DOS screen before the SAS session actually begins. It is not written to the SAS log.

-EMS *n*
-EMS ALL

specifies the amount of expanded memory you want the SAS System to use, where *n* is an integer value representing the number of 16K pages of expanded memory to be used. (A 2-megabyte expanded memory board has 128 16K-pages.) ALL means the SAS System will use as much memory as it needs (up to 2 megabytes). There is no default setting for the -EMS option. The recommended setting is

```
-ems all
```

In order to use the -EMS option, your machine must have an expanded memory board (EMS) or enhanced expanded memory board (EEMS) installed. The board must conform to the LIM Specification 3.0 or later.* The SAS System supports use of any EMS or EEMS board conforming to LIM 3.0+, including AST Research Inc.'s RAMpage™ board and Intel Corporation's Above™ Board.

Specifying the -EMS option increases your machine's capacity to execute memory-intensive SAS procedures and to process SAS data sets with large numbers of variables. The option works as follows.

When you execute SAS programs without the -EMS option, the SAS supervisor is loaded into the PC's conventional memory.** The supervisor uses approximately 350K of memory. If you begin a SAS

---

* The LIM Specification is the Lotus-Intel-Microsoft Specification, a widely accepted standard for the features and performance of expanded memory boards.

** The SAS supervisor is the core of the SAS System. All procedures, DATA step features, and other facilities in the SAS System rely on the supervisor.

session with 450K of free memory, this means that about 100K are available for other parts of the SAS System, such as procedures, and for data. This amount of memory may not be sufficient for certain SAS procedures or for processing large SAS data sets.

When you specify the -EMS option, the SAS System loads as much of the SAS supervisor into the allotted expanded memory area as possible. This means that larger amounts of conventional memory are available for loading and executing SAS procedures and processing SAS data sets.

If the SAS programs you are running involve many SAS procedures, using the -EMS option increases performance. When you use the -EMS option, the SAS supervisor and many SAS procedures become EMS memory resident. Thus, the SAS System can avoid reloading these key components from disk.

Depending on the application you are running, there can be a significant amount of overhead caused by memory management when using an expanded memory board. This overhead can decrease the speed with which applications execute. On the other hand, the expanded memory board allows you to execute programs requiring large amounts of memory, and you may not be able to run these programs at all without the expanded memory board and -EMS option. If you set the option to 4 pages (64K)

```
-ems 4
```

you increase the available memory without incurring much memory management overhead.

-FILEBUFFERS n_buffers s_buffer

specifies the number of file buffers you want the SAS System to use and the size of those file buffers, where n_buffers is the number of buffers, and s_buffer is the size of each buffer, in bytes. The n_buffers value must be an integer between 1 and 50. The s_buffer value must be an integer between 256 and 64512.

The -FILEBUFFERS parameters are positional parameters; you must specify n_buffers first and s_buffer second. You must specify both parameters except when you are turning off file buffering. To turn off file buffering, specify only the option keyword:

```
-filebuffers
```

The purpose of the -FILEBUFFERS option is to enhance the speed of the SAS System. -FILEBUFFERS improves performance by reducing the number of read and write disk accesses when you access

- a SAS data set
- an external file in a SAS procedure; the INFILE, FILE, or %INCLUDE statements; or the FILE or INCLUDE display manager commands.

The -FILEBUFFERS option works as follows.

Typically, two kinds of buffers are involved in reading and writing SAS data sets and external files. One kind of buffer is a DOS buffer, managed by the DOS operating system. DOS buffers are 512 bytes in size. You establish how many DOS buffers are defined in memory with the BUFFERS= parameter in the CONFIG.SYS file. The other kind of buffer is the SAS input buffer (for reading files) or output buffer (for writing files). SAS input/output buffers are managed by the SAS System. A SAS input/output buffer is equal in size to the maximum record length of the file with which it is associated. The SAS System sets up one input buffer for each file opened for read access and one output buffer for each file opened for write access.

By default, each time a SAS program reads a record from a SAS data set or external file, a disk access must be made to transfer the data from the physical disk to the DOS buffer. Similarly, each output operation passes data from the DOS buffer to the physical disk and performs a disk write access.

Disk accesses are relatively slow. It is faster to read or write large blocks of data than to repeatedly read or write small records from the disk. The -FILEBUFFERS option allows the SAS System to use DOS buffers more efficiently to read and write large chunks of data.

For example, suppose you are creating a new external file. Each record in the file is 20 bytes in length. Also suppose that you have specified the -FILEBUFFERS option as

```
-filebuffers 5 500
```

meaning that you want the SAS System to use 5 file buffers, each of which is 500 bytes in size. Each time your program writes to the new file, a 20-byte record is written from the SAS output buffer to the file buffer. The records accumulate in the file buffer until it is full. Each record is 20 bytes long, so 25 complete records can be written to the file buffer. When the file buffer is full, its contents are written to the disk file. Therefore, disk access occurs only once for every 25 records, instead of for every record. It is this reduction in the number of disk accesses that saves time in your SAS programs.

You should be aware of the following points when using the -FILEBUFFERS option:

- The recommended values for the -FILEBUFFERS option are

    ```
    -filebuffers 10 512
    ```

    or

    ```
    -filebuffers 5 512
    ```

- The -FILEBUFFERS option offers the biggest performance enhancements in programs that involve a lot of read/write operations on files with relatively short records. Savings decrease if read/write activity is low or if records are long.
- The SAS System does not use a file buffer if the buffer's size is less than the size of a single record. In other words, a file's record length must be less than the buffer size.
- The SAS System uses one file buffer for each file that is open. If there are more files open than there are buffers, the last file(s) opened do not use file buffers. File buffers used for files referenced by the %INCLUDE statement, FILE command, or INCLUDE command are freed as soon as the statement or command executes. Therefore, the file buffer becomes available for another file.
- Although the -FILEBUFFERS option can improve the speed of a SAS program, it increases memory requirements. Each file buffer you define requires some memory. The amount of memory is equal to the number of buffers times the size of the buffers; for instance, if you specify

    ```
    -filebuffers 10 512
    ```

the file buffers occupy 5,120 bytes of memory. You must balance the costs of greater memory use with the benefits of increased speed.

-FILECACHE *path n*
specifies a directory and the number of files in that directory that can be "cached," where *path* is the directory from which files are cached and *n* is an integer value from 1 to 50.

Caching a file means that when the file is opened, it is listed in a special table, the filecache table. At the point in the SAS program where the file would typically be closed, it is "logically" closed by SAS rather than "physically" closed by DOS. When the same file is referenced subsequently in the SAS session, the SAS System can find and open the file more quickly because it has not been physically closed. Therefore, the -FILECACHE option increases the speed of the SAS System by reducing the overhead involved in opening files. File caching is most effective with executable files and is less effective with data files.

You can specify as many -FILECACHE options as you need. For example, if you specify these -FILECACHE settings

```
-filecache \sas\sasexe\base 10
-filecache \sas\sasmsg 5
```

the SAS System sets up a filecaching table with ten entries reserved for files from \SAS\SASEXE\BASE and five for \SAS\SASMSG.

You can turn off the filecaching facility by specifying the option keyword only:

```
-filecache
```

Do not specify a given directory in more than one -FILECACHE option. The SAS System searches the filecache table from top to bottom and only uses the entries created by the first specification. Entries created as a result of multiple specifications for a directory are not used and, therefore, waste memory.

For the best performance, the total number of table entries across all directories to be cached should not exceed the value of the FILES= parameter in the CONFIG.SYS file. This is because the FILES= parameter determines how many files can be open at one time, and the SAS System cannot override the DOS limit. If you try to cache more files than are allowed to be open by DOS, you waste memory.

The -FILECACHE option increases speed, but also uses up some memory. Filecaching uses 16 bytes for each entry in the table.

-FSDEVICE *driver specifications*
specifies the device driver for your PC's monitor and optional specifications affecting the display. If you have an IBM PC-compatible machine, you normally do not need to specify the -FSDEVICE option. For IBM-compatible machines, use this option only if you want to change specifications, such as colors or the Typo-matic rate.

When the SAS System is invoked and -FSDEVICE is not specified, the SAS System checks an internal flag that indicates whether the machine is an IBM-compatible device. If your machine is not IBM-compatible, you must specify the -FSDEVICE option to run full-screen SAS features, including display manager and any full-screen procedure.

If you have a device that is not IBM compatible, select the appropriate driver for the device from the list below.

482 Chapter 16

> **Caution:** be very careful in specifying a device driver. If you select an inappropriate driver, the results are unpredictable. Do not experiment with the option if you are not sure about what it should be set to. Call your local SAS Software Consultant for assistance.

Valid values for *driver* are

SASXDICA	for IBM AT with CGA card and compatibles
SASXDICX	for IBM XT with CGA card and compatibles
SASXDIMA	for IBM AT with monochrome monitor and compatibles
SASXDIMX	for IBM XT with monochrome monitor and compatibles
SASXDNCA	for IBM 3270 PC, AT-compatible and compatibles
SASXDNCX	for IBM 3270 PC, XT-compatible and compatibles
SASXDIEA	for IBM AT with EGA card and compatibles
SASXDIEX	for IBM XT with EGA card and compatibles
SASXDWGM	for Wang with monochrome monitor
SASXDWGC	for Wang with color monitor
SASXDCPA	for COMPAQ with plasma display
SASXDVCA	for Hewlett-Packard Vectra with color monitor
SASXDASY	for all other non-IBM-compatible machines that use the ANSI.SYS driver.

The optional specifications you can use depend on the driver you use. **Table 16.1** lists the specifications supported for each device driver. These specifications are described in detail after **Table 16.1**.

Table 16.1 Available Options for Device Drivers

Driver Specification	BORDER=	COLOR1=	LINEnn	MODE=	NOWAIT	TYPExxx
SASXDICA		X		X	X	X
SASXDICX		X		X	X	
SASXDIMA						X
SASXDIMX						
SASXDNCA		X		X		X
SASXDNCX		X		X		
SASXDIEA		X	X	X		X
SASXDIEX		X	X	X		
SASXDWGM	X					
SASXDWGC	X					
SASXDCPA		X		X		X
SASXDVCA		X		X		X
SASXDASY	X	X				

SAS Global Options 483

The optional specifications for the -FSDEVICE option are

BORDER= *b1, b2, b3, b4, b5, b6*
: specifies characters to be used for borders of windows in display manager, where

  b1 is the top left corner
  b2 is the horizontal dimension
  b3 is the top right corner
  b4 is the vertical dimension
  b5 is the bottom left corner
  b6 is the bottom right corner.

  The values specified for *b1, b2,* and so on must be decimal ASCII values separated by commas with no embedded spaces. The default values are

  ```
  border=43,45,43,124,43,43
  ```

  which produce the characters +-+ ¦ ++.

color1 = *color2*
: specifies that color settings should be changed, where *color1* and *color2* are valid SAS color names. This specification changes *color1* to *color2* in display manager, whether it is a default color for a window or field, or a color specified in the WINDOW statement or COLOR window.

  For example, if you specify

  ```
  gray=blue
  ```

  all references to gray become blue. Features such as the LOG window, which is ordinarily gray, are displayed in blue. You can change as many colors as needed.

  This specification is useful for devices that allow only eight colors; these devices display several color settings as the same color. In this case, you might have foreground text displayed in the same color as the background (making it not visible). This specification allows you to define alternate values for colors that cannot be correctly displayed.

LINES*nn*
: specifies the number of rows on the screen, where *nn* is 25 for 25 lines and 43 for 43 lines.

MODE=BW40 | BW80 | CO40 | CO80
: specifies whether you want the monitor to use color or black-and-white mode and whether you want to use a 40-column or 80-column mode. This specification performs the same action as the DOS MODE command for setting display modes.

  - Use MODE=BW40 for black-and-white, 40-column display.
  - Use MODE=BW80 for black-and-white, 80-column display.
  - Use MODE=CO40 for color, 40-column display.
  - Use MODE=CO80 for color, 80-column display.

NOWAIT causes SAS screens to refresh faster because the SAS System does not wait for the hardware's horizontal retrace. Note: on some machines, using this specification causes a snowy effect on the screen.

TYPExxxx specifies whether the Typo-matic rate (the rate at which keys repeat) is fast or slow. To request the fast rate, use TYPEFAST. To request the slow rate, use TYPESLOW.

Recommended device drivers and specifications for various machines are listed in **Table 16.2**.

Table 16.2 Recommended Device Drivers and Specifications

Machine and Device	Recommended Specifications
IBM AT with CGA	`-fsdevice SASXDICA`
IBM XT with CGA	`-fsdevice SASXDICX`
IBM AT monochrome	`-fsdevice SASXDIMA`
IBM XT monochrome	`-fsdevice SASXDIMX`
IBM AT with 3270	`-fsdevice SASXDNCA`
IBM XT with 3270	`-fsdevice SASXDNCX`
IBM AT with EGA	`-fsdevice SASXDIEA`
IBM XT with EGA	`-fsdevice SASXDIEX`
Wang monochrome	`-fsdevice SASXDWGM`
Wang color	`-fsdevice SASXDWGC`
COMPAQ-AT color	`-fsdevice SASXDICA NOWAIT`
COMPAQ with plasma display	`-fsdevice SASXDCPA`
Hewlett-Packard Vectra	`-fsdevice SASXDVCA`
Leading Edge XT	`-fsdevice SASXDICX`
AT&T color	`-fsdevice SASXDICX`
AT&T monochrome	`-fsdevice SASXDICX MODE=BW80 GRAY=BLACK BLACK=WHITE`
Non-IBM-compatible supporting ANSI.SYS monochrome (when no other driver available)	`-fsdevice SASXDASY`

-IBM AT | XT | NO
: overrides an internal flag indicating whether your PC is compatible with an IBM PC. **Caution: if this option is set incorrectly, unpredictable results can occur. Do not experiment with this option if you are not sure about what it should be set to. Call your local SAS Software Consultant for assistance.**

The SAS System is designed to run optimally on IBM-compatible machines. Many microcomputers that are IBM-compatible have an internal flag that indicates compatibility; however, some machines, such as the Leading Edge, do not use the flag. The SAS System checks this flag when attempting to perform some actions, for example, when you invoke a SAS/GRAPH procedure. If you are using a machine that is supposed to be IBM-compatible, but the SAS System cannot verify that it is compatible, you will not be able to run SAS/GRAPH unless you use the -IBM option. In this case, specify IBM AT or IBM XT, depending upon which type of device you have.

For some non-IBM-compatible device drivers, such as the one for Wang machines, you must specify -IBM NO as well as specifying the appropriate value for the -FSDEVICE option.

-LOG *filename*
: specifies a file to which the SAS log should be written when executing SAS programs in noninteractive mode. By default, the SAS log from a noninteractive SAS program is written to a file in the current directory with the same filename as the SAS source file and an extension of .LOG. You can override this default with the -LOG option by indicating a specific file for the log. For example, if you want to write the log to \MYLOGS\PRG1.LOG, specify the -LOG option as follows:

```
-log \mylogs\prg1.log
```

-MSG *pathname*
: specifies the path name for the directory containing the SAS error message file. This option is set in the installation process and is not normally changed after installation. The default value is

```
-msg \sas\sasmsg
```

-NEWS *filename*
: specifies the name of a file that contains a message to be printed in the LOG window after the SAS logo. This option provides the same function as the NEWS system option, described later in this chapter.

-PATH *pathname* . . .
: specifies path information for a directory containing SAS executable modules. The default settings are

```
-path \sas\sasexe\core
-path \sas\sasexe\base
-path \sas\sasexe\stat
-path \sas\sasexe\iml
-path \sas\sasexe\af
-path \sas\sasexe\fsp
-path \sas\sasexe\graph
```

You can set up paths for multiple directories of executable files by using more than one -PATH option. Note that the paths are searched in the order you specify the -PATH options; therefore, specify the products you run most frequently at the top of the list.

-PRINT *filename*
: specifies the file to which the SAS output should be written when executing SAS programs in noninteractive mode. By default, the SAS output from a noninteractive SAS program is written to a file in the current directory with the same filename as the SAS source file and an extension of .LST. You can override this default with the -PRINT option by indicating a specific file for the output. For example, if you want to write the output to \MYPRINT\PRG1.LST, specify the -PRINT option as follows:

```
-print \myprint\prg1.lst
```

-SASHELP *pathname*
: specifies the path name for the directory containing the SAS help files. This option is set in the installation process and is not normally changed after installation. The default value is

```
-sashelp \sas\sashelp
```

-SASUSER *pathname*
: specifies the path name for the directory to contain the SAS user profile catalog (PC DOS file PROFILE.SCT). The directory and catalog are created automatically by the SAS System; you do not have to create them explicitly. The default value is

```
-sasuser sasuser
```

For information on the SAS user profile catalog, see Appendix 2, "User Profile Catalog."

-SET SASROOT *pathname*
: specifies the root directory of the SAS System. The root directory of the SAS System is where the main executable file SAS.EXE exists and where all other subdirectories of the SAS System are defined. The default value for this option is

```
-set sasroot \sas
```

This option allows the SAS System to be installed in a directory other than the default \SAS directory. The -SET SASROOT option must be the first option in the CONFIG.SAS file; it is required for executing the SAS System.

The default path names for the subdirectories of the SAS System are defined in the CONFIG.SAS file as follows:

```
-sashelp  !sasroot\sashelp
-sasuser  !sasroot\sasuser
-work     !sasroot\saswork
-msg      !sasroot\sasmsg
-path     !sasroot\sasexe\core
-path     !sasroot\sasexe\base
-path     !sasroot\sasexe\stat
-path     !sasroot\sasexe\iml
-path     !sasroot\sasexe\af
-path     !sasroot\sasexe\fsp
-path     !sasroot\sasexe\graph
```

When you invoke the SAS System, the !SASROOT value in each of these path names is replaced by the *pathname* you assign with the -SET SASROOT option. Note: all of the examples in this documentation assume that the -SET SASROOT option has been set as follows:

```
-set sasroot \sas
```

-SYSIN *filename*
specifies a file containing a SAS program. This option is applicable only when you are using noninteractive SAS execution mode and can be specified only in the SAS command. For example, if you want to execute a SAS program stored in the DOS file \SASPGMS\REPORT1.SAS, you can use this SAS command:

```
sas -ems 4  -sysin \saspgms\report1.sas
```

Note that it is not necessary to precede the file specification with the -SYSIN option if the file specification immediately follows the keyword SAS, for example,

```
sas \saspgms\report1.sas -ems 4
```

-SYSPRINT *device* | *filename*
specifies a destination for printed output, where *device* is one of the following printer specifications

- prn
- lpt1
- lpt2
- com1
- com2

and *filename* is a file. If you use a file specification, the output is written to the file indicated, and the file contains control characters necessary for printing.

You must use the -SYSPRINT option when running SAS/AF and SAS/FSP software in noninteractive mode. You can also use the -SYSPRINT option to set a default output device for output from procedures other than SAS/AF and SAS/FSP, but in this case, you must also specify a FILENAME statement. If you specify a FILENAME statement in the format

```
filename fileref printer ''
```

the file indicated by *fileref* is routed to the printer specified in the -SYSPRINT option. You can override the default printer set by the -SYSPRINT option by specifying a FILENAME statement in the format

```
filename fileref printer 'device'
```

where *device* is a different value than the value for *device* in the -SYSPRINT option. Refer to **The FILENAME Statement** in Chapter 13, "SAS Statements Used Anywhere," for more information.

-USER *pathname*
specifies the path name for the directory containing your default permanent SAS data library. If this option is specified, you can use one-level names to reference permanent SAS files in SAS statements. The SAS System assumes that files referenced with one name belong in the -USER directory.

488 Chapter 16

-VERBOSE
: lists the settings of all options in the CONFIG.SAS file and the name of the CONFIG.SAS file (including path information). The list of settings is written to the DOS screen, not to the SAS log. Execution pauses so that you can read the list, and you must press ENTER in order for execution to resume.

-WORK *pathname*
: specifies the path name for the directory to contain the SAS WORK library. The library will be created if it does not already exist. The default is

```
-work saswork
```

-XWAIT ON
-XWAIT OFF
: indicates whether or not the SAS System waits for you to press a key after a DOS command executes in order to resume SAS processing. By default, the SAS System does not automatically resume execution after processing a DOS command that produces output. Instead, it waits for you to press any key. This allows time for you to read the DOS response to the command. However, if you are running noninteractive SAS programs, this feature can be inconvenient. By specifying XWAIT OFF, you override the wait feature and SAS execution resumes with no intervention from you.

SAS SYSTEM OPTIONS

Specifying SAS System Options

SAS system options can be specified in four places: in the user profile catalog, in the SAS command, in an OPTIONS statement, or in the display manager OPTIONS window.

- The user profile catalog, PROFILE.SCT, is a utility catalog containing entries that tailor the SAS System to your needs. A number of the entries in the PROFILE.SCT are POPTIONS entries. POPTIONS entries contain settings for system options. When you specify the PROFILE option in a SAS session and terminate the SAS session with PROFILE in effect, the current settings of most of the SAS system options are stored in various POPTIONS entries. The next time you invoke a SAS session, the settings in POPTIONS are used as defaults.

  For more information on which options are stored in the user profile catalog, see the description of the PROFILE option later in this chapter. For more information on the SAS user profile catalog, see Appendix 2, "User Profile Catalog."

- SAS system options can also be specified in the SAS command by prefixing the option name with a hyphen. For example, the following SAS command specifies the DATE system option:

  ```
  sas -date
  ```

  You can combine specification of configuration options and SAS system options in a SAS command, as in the command below:

  ```
  sas -nodate -filebuffers 10 1024
  ```

- Within a SAS program or during a SAS session you can specify SAS system options in an OPTIONS statement, for example,

  ```
  options nodate center linesize=75;
  ```

  You can specify an OPTIONS statement at any time during a session or program. Settings remain in effect throughout the session or program unless reset with another OPTIONS statement or changed in the OPTIONS window.

  For details on the OPTIONS statement, see **The OPTIONS Statement** in Chapter 18, "SAS Statements Used Anywhere."

- During a SAS display manager session you can also specify SAS system options in the OPTIONS window. Any settings changed in the OPTIONS window take effect immediately and remain in effect throughout the session, unless reset with an OPTIONS statement or changed in the OPTIONS window.

  For details on the OPTIONS window, see its description in Chapter 10, "SAS Display Manager System."

You can specify the same SAS system option in more than one place. The order of precedence determining which setting takes effect is as follows:

- a system option specified through any of the methods just described overrides the default for the option.
- settings specified in the SAS command override settings specified in PROFILE.SCT.
- settings specified in an OPTIONS statement or the OPTIONS window override settings specified on the SAS command. The order of execution determines if settings specified through the OPTIONS window or OPTIONS statement are in effect.
- whatever is specified last overrides an earlier specification.

SAS System Option Syntax

The syntax used to specify system options varies depending on where you specify the option. The rules for syntax are

- Any system option specified in the SAS command must be preceded by a dash:

  ```
  sas -nodate -firstobs 500
  ```

  However, you must not include the dash when specifying the option in other contexts.

- Options taking a character or numeric value require use of an equal sign when specified in the OPTIONS statement, for example,

  ```
  options firstobs=500 linesize=140 remote=irma;
  ```

  However, the equal sign is omitted if the option is specified in the OPTIONS window or the SAS command, for example,

  ```
  sas -firstobs 500 -linesize 140 -remote irma
  ```

- Positive/negative options are specified as xxxxxxx | NOxxxxxxx in the SAS command and in the OPTIONS statement. They are specified as xxxxxxx ON | xxxxxxx OFF in the OPTIONS window, for example:

  ```
  date|nodate   (SAS command, OPTIONS statement form)
  date on|date off   (OPTIONS window form)
  ```

  ```
  charcode|nocharcode   (SAS command, OPTIONS statement form)
  charcode on|charcode off   (OPTIONS window form)
  ```

Finding Out What Option Settings Are in Effect

You can check the current settings of all SAS system options at any time in a SAS program by executing the OPTIONS procedure:

```
proc options;
run;
```

The output from the OPTIONS procedure is a list of all of the system options and their current settings.

If you are running a display manager session, you can also check option settings by activating the OPTIONS window. The window lists all of the options and their current settings, in addition to providing fields in which you can specify new settings. Refer to **The OPTIONS Window** in Chapter 10, "SAS Display Manager System," for more information.

Descriptions of SAS System Options

This section lists the SAS system options in alphabetical order.

CENTER | NOCENTER (OPTIONS statement form)
CENTER ON | CENTER OFF (OPTIONS window form)
  controls whether SAS procedure output is centered. The default value for this option is CENTER or CENTER ON.

CHARCODE | NOCHARCODE (OPTIONS statement form)
CHARCODE ON | CHARCODE OFF (OPTIONS window form)
  activates the ability to substitute some alternative character combinations for characters you may not have on your keyboard. If you do not have a vertical bar, underscore character, logical not sign, square brackets, backslash, backquote, or braces on your keyboard, you can substitute the following character combinations for these symbols:

  ?/   for the vertical bar (|)
  ?-   for the underscore (_)
  ?=   for the logical not sign (^)
  ?(for the left square bracket ([)
  ?)   for the right square bracket (])
  ?,   for the backslash (\)
  ?:   for the backquote (`)
  ?<   for the left brace ({)
  ?>   for the right brace (}).

  If NOCHARCODE or CHARCODE OFF is specified, you cannot use the substitutes. If CHARCODE or CHARCODE ON is specified, you can use the substitutes. The default value is NOCHARCODE or CHARCODE OFF.

DATE | NODATE (OPTIONS statement form)
DATE ON | DATE OFF (OPTIONS window form)
  controls whether the current date is printed at the top of each page of the SAS log, the standard SAS print file, and any file with the PRINT attribute. If NODATE is specified, the date is omitted from the first title line of each page. The default for this option is DATE or DATE ON.

SAS Global Options

DBCS | NODBCS (OPTIONS statement form)
DBCS ON | DBCS OFF (OPTIONS window form)
 specifies whether or not responses to fill-in-the-blank questions in CBT courses are converted to uppercase before being compared to answers. The DBCS and KANJI options have the same effect. If DBCS or DBCS ON is specified, responses are converted to uppercase. If NODBCS or DBCS OFF is specified, responses are not converted. The default is NODBCS or DBCS OFF.

DEVICE=name (OPTIONS statement form)
DEVICE name (OPTIONS window form)
 specifies a terminal device name designation. SAS/GRAPH software uses this option. There is no default value.

ERRORS=n (OPTIONS statement form)
ERRORS n (OPTIONS window form)
 specifies the maximum number of observations for which complete error messages are printed. If data errors are detected in more observations than the number specified, processing continues, but error messages do not print for the additional errors. The default value is 20.

FIRSTOBS=n (OPTIONS statement form)
FIRSTOBS n (OPTIONS window form)
 specifies the number of the first observation that the SAS System is to process. Normally, the SAS System begins with the first observation in a data set. For example, if FIRSTOBS=50, the SAS System begins processing with the 50th observation of the data set.

 Note that this option applies to every data set used in a job. Thus, in this example,

```
options firstobs=11;
data a;
   set old; /* 100 observations */
data b;
   set a;
data c;
   set b;
```

 data set OLD has 100 observations, data set A has 90, B has 80, and C has 70. To avoid decreasing the number of observations in successive data sets, reset FIRSTOBS=1 at an appropriate point in your SAS statements.

 If the SAS System is processing a file of raw data, the FIRSTOBS= option specifies the first line of data that the SAS System should process.

 FIRSTOBS= specified as either a data set option or an INFILE statement option takes precedence over the FIRSTOBS= system option. (See Chapter 15, "SAS Files," for a discussion of the FIRSTOBS= data set option.) The default value is 1.

FORMCHAR='formatting characters' (OPTIONS statement form)
FORMCHAR 'formatting characters' (OPTIONS window form)
 specifies the output *formatting characters* for your output device. Formatting characters are used to construct tabular output outlines and dividers.

 The value given for *formatting characters* is any string or list of strings of characters up to 64 bytes long. If fewer than 64 bytes are specified, the value is padded with blanks on the right. The first eleven characters define the two bar characters, vertical and horizontal, and the nine corner characters: upper left, upper middle, upper right, middle left, middle middle (cross), middle right, lower left, lower middle, and lower right. In addition to these eleven characters, nine other characters are used:

Character	Use
12	starting or ending character for an event line
13	fill character for an event line
14	no special use
15	no special use
16	separation character for variables in event line label
17	no special use
18	left arrow for continuing an event line
19	right arrow for continuing an event line
20	highlighting character for holiday name

The standard values for these characters are the following:

|----|+|---+=|-/\<>*

You can substitute any character or hexadecimal string to customize the table. If standard printers at your installation do not include the vertical bar (|), you can substitute the capital letter I for each vertical bar in the standard string of characters. Note: if you change any value for a character with the OPTIONS statement, you must specify all the characters. You can use a FORMCHAR option in the FREQ, TABULATE, and CALENDAR procedures if you want to change a single character value.

Specifying all blanks,

```
formchar= ' '
```

produces output with no outlines or dividers.

KANJI | NOKANJI (OPTIONS statement form)
KANJI ON | KANJI OFF (OPTIONS window form)
  specifies whether or not responses to fill-in-the-blank questions in CBT courses are converted to uppercase before being compared to answers. The DBCS and KANJI options have the same effect. If KANJI or KANJI ON is specified, responses are converted to uppercase. If NOKANJI or KANJI OFF is specified, responses are not converted. The default is NOKANJI or KANJI OFF.

LAST=SASdataset (OPTIONS statement form)
LAST SASdataset (OPTIONS window form)
  specifies the _LAST_ data set name. After a SAS data set has been created in a SAS job, the value of _LAST_ is the name of the most recently created SAS data set. The default value is _NULL_.

LINESIZE | LS=width (OPTIONS statement form)
LINESIZE | LS width (OPTIONS window form)
  specifies the printer line width for the SAS log and the standard SAS print file used by the DATA step and procedures. LINESIZE values can range from 64 to 256. The default value is 78.

MISSING='*character*' (OPTIONS statement form)
MISSING '*character*' (OPTIONS window form)
: specifies the character to be printed for missing numeric variable values. The default value is '.'.

MPRINT | NOMPRINT (OPTIONS statement form)
MPRINT ON | MPRINT OFF (OPTIONS window form)
: specifies whether SAS statements generated by macro execution are displayed in an easy-to-read form. Specifying MPRINT causes the statements to appear with macro variable references and macro functions resolved, each statement to begin on a new line, and one space to appear between words. The default is NOMPRINT or MPRINT OFF.

MTRACE | NOMTRACE (OPTIONS statement form)
MTRACE ON | MTRACE OFF (OPTIONS window form)
: specifies whether the macro processor displays messages that trace its execution. If the MTRACE option is in effect and the macro processor encounters a macro invocation, the macro processor displays messages that identify the beginning of macro execution, the values of macro parameters at that point, the execution of each macro program statement, whether each %IF condition is true or false, and the ending of macro execution. The default is NOMTRACE or MTRACE OFF.

NEWS=*filename* (OPTIONS statement form)
NEWS *filename* (OPTIONS window form)
: specifies the name of a file that contains a message to be printed in the LOG window after the SAS logo. If you set the NEWS option in a SAS session and save the option by setting the PROFILE option on, the news message will be displayed the next time you invoke the SAS System. Refer to the description of the PROFILE option for more information on how to save system options. Note: this option provides the same function as the -NEWS configuration option, described earlier in this chapter.

NOTES | NONOTES (OPTIONS statement form)
NOTES ON | NOTES OFF (OPTIONS window form)
: controls whether notes are printed on the SAS log. (These messages usually begin with NOTE:.) If the NONOTES option is specified, informative messages are not printed on the SAS log. NOTES must be specified on SAS jobs that are sent to SAS Institute for problem determination and resolution; SAS Institute cannot help with program or system problems if notes are not printed. The default value for this option is NOTES or NOTES ON.

NUMBER | NONUMBER (OPTIONS statement form)
NUMBER ON | NUMBER OFF (OPTIONS window form)
: controls whether the page number prints on the first title line of each SAS printed output page. The default value for this option is NUMBER or NUMBER ON.

OBS=n | MAX (OPTIONS statement form)
OBS n | MAX (OPTIONS window form)
: specifies the **last** observation that the SAS System is to process from a data set. Normally, the SAS System processes all the observations in a data set. For testing purposes you can select the first n observations of each SAS data set or the first n lines of a raw data file with the OBS= option.

For example, specifying

```
options obs=50;
```

as the first statement of a SAS job causes the SAS System to read only through the 50th observation when reading a SAS data set. Analysis of SAS data sets in PROC steps is also controlled by the OBS= option, so in this example, only the first 50 observations of any data set would be analyzed in a subsequent PROC step.

If the SAS System is processing a file of raw data, the OBS= option specifies how many lines of data to read. SAS counts a line of input data as one observation even if the raw data for several SAS data set observations are on a single line.

You can check the syntax of SAS statements in a job by specifying

```
options obs=0 noreplace;
```

as the first statement in a job. However, since the SAS System actually executes each DATA and PROC step in the job (using no observations), SAS can take certain actions even when the OBS=0 and NOREPLACE options are in effect. For example, SAS executes procedures that process the directories of SAS data sets (such as CONTENTS, DELETE, and DATASETS). External files are also opened and closed. Thus, even if you specify OBS=0 when your job writes to an external file with a PUT statement, an end-of-file mark is written, and any existing data in the file are deleted.

You can use the FIRSTOBS= and OBS= options together to process a set of observations from the middle of a data set. For example, to process only observations 1000 through 1100, specify

```
options firstobs=1000 obs=1100;
```

OBS= specified as either a data set option or an INFILE statement option takes precedence over the OBS= system option. See Chapter 15, "SAS Files," for a discussion of the OBS= data set option. The default value is MAX, which has the value of 2,147,483,647.

OVP | NOOVP (OPTIONS statement form)
OVP ON | OVP OFF (OPTIONS window form)
controls whether SAS-printed output lines can be overprinted. For example, when the SAS System encounters an error in a SAS statement, it prints underscores beneath the word in error if OVP is in effect. If NOOVP is in effect, the SAS System prints dashes on the next line below the error. Note: when displaying output on a screen, OVP is overridden and changed to NOOVP. The default value for this option is NOOVP or OVP OFF.

PAGENO=n (OPTIONS statement form)
PAGENO n (OPTIONS window form)
specifies a beginning page number for the next page of output produced by the SAS System. This option allows you to reset page numbering to one (or any other value) in the middle of a SAS session. The default value is 1.

SAS Global Options 495

PAGESIZE | PS=*n* (OPTIONS statement form)
PAGESIZE | PS *n* (OPTIONS window form)
  specifies the number of lines that can be printed per page of SAS output. The default value is 21.

PROBSIG=*n* (OPTIONS statement form)
PROBSIG *n* (OPTIONS window form)
  controls the formatting of *p*-values in some statistical procedures. When PROBSIG=0, *p*-values are printed with four decimal places and truncated at .0001. The default value is 0.

  PROBSIG=1 guarantees that *p*-values are printed with at least one significant digit; that is, values greater than .000095 are printed with four decimal places, but values less than .000095 are printed in E-notation.

  PROBSIG=2 guarantees at least two significant digits so that values greater than .0000995 are printed with five decimal places, and smaller values are printed in E-notation.

PROFILE | NOPROFILE (OPTIONS statement form)
PROFILE ON | PROFILE OFF (OPTIONS window form)
  controls whether system option settings are saved from one session to the next. The default value is NOPROFILE or PROFILE OFF.

  If you specify PROFILE or PROFILE ON, the settings of certain system options are saved in your user profile catalog, PROFILE.SCT as POPTIONS entries. Any option settings in effect when you end a SAS session are saved. Note that option settings are saved only if you exit from the SAS session normally with the BYE command or ENDSAS statement. Settings are not saved if your session ends abnormally. For more information on the user profile, see Appendix 2, "User Profile Catalog."

  The following options can be saved in the user profile catalog:

```
CENTER | NOCENTER or CENTER ON | CENTER OFF
CHARCODE | NOCHARCODE or CHARCODE ON | CHARCODE OFF
DATE | NODATE or DATE ON | DATE OFF
DBCS | NODBCS or DBCS ON | DBCS OFF
DEVICE= or DEVICE
FIRSTOBS= or FIRSTOBS
FORMCHAR= or FORMCHAR
KANJI | NOKANJI or KANJI ON | KANJI OFF
LINESIZE= or LINESIZE
MISSING= or MISSING
NEWS= or NEWS
NUMBER | NONUMBER or NUMBER ON | NUMBER OFF
OVP | NOOVP or OVP ON | OVP OFF
PAGESIZE= or PAGESIZE
PROBSIG= or PROBSIG
REMOTE= or REMOTE
SOURCE2 | NOSOURCE2 or SOURCE2 ON | SOURCE2 OFF
STIMER | NOSTIMER or STIMER ON | STIMER OFF
```

496   Chapter 16

The following options are not saved in the user profile, regardless of the setting of the PROFILE option:

ERRORS= or ERRORS
LAST= or _LAST_
MPRINT | NOMPRINT or MPRINT ON | MPRINT OFF
MTRACE | NOMTRACE or MTRACE ON | MTRACE OFF
NOTES | NONOTES or NOTES ON | NOTES OFF
OBS= or OBS
PAGENO= or PAGENO
PROFILE | NOPROFILE or PROFILE ON | PROFILE OFF
REPLACE | NOREPLACE or REPLACE ON | REPLACE OFF
SOURCE | NOSOURCE or SOURCE ON | SOURCE OFF
SYMBOLGEN | NOSYMBOLGEN or SYMBOLGEN ON | SYMBOLGEN OFF

REMOTE=*device* (OPTIONS statement form)
REMOTE *device* (OPTIONS window form)

specifies the kind of adapter you are using with the SAS micro-to-host link, where *device* is a keyword that indicates what kind of adapter your machine has.

This option must be specified in two places to start the link:

1. in your local PC SAS session. Typically, specification in the SAS session is made to happen automatically via the OPTIONS statement or the user profile catalog. An OPTIONS statement submitted in the SAS session can be included in the AUTOEXEC.SAS file, and, therefore, REMOTE= for the PC is set automatically each time the SAS System is invoked. Alternatively, you can save the setting in your user profile catalog (see Appendix 2). If you do not specify the REMOTE= option in your AUTOEXEC.SAS file or user profile, you have to type and submit the OPTIONS statement before executing a SIGNON command.

2. in the SAS command executed to invoke the SAS System on the host. The SAS command for the host is included in the script that starts the link, and, therefore, REMOTE= for the host is set automatically when the script executes. If you do not specify REMOTE= in the SAS command in the script you use, an error message is issued and the link terminates.

Valid values for the *device* specification are shown in **Table 16.3**. Note that some of the values are used only in the SAS command invoking the host SAS System, and the other values are used only in the OPTIONS statement executed in the SAS session.

Table 16.3 Values for the REMOTE= Option Device Specification

Connection Type	PC SAS OPTIONS Statement REMOTE= Specification	Comments	Host SAS Command REMOTE= Specification	Comments
Asynchronous	ASYNC*n*	*n* is 1 or 2, depending on whether you use COM1 or COM2 port; 1 is the default	ASYNC	no *n* value is specified
CXI	CXI		PCLINK	
Forte PJ™ ForteGraph™	FORTE		PCLINK	
IRMA™	IRMA		PCLINK	
3270 PC	PC3270*x*	*x* is the alphabetic character indicating the host session; E is the default.	PC3270	no *x* value is specified
3278/3279	PC7879		PCLINK	

Forte PJ, ForteGraph, and IRMA are trademarks of Digital Communication Associates, Inc.

REPLACE | NOREPLACE (OPTIONS statement form)
REPLACE ON | REPLACE OFF (OPTIONS window form)
    controls the replacement of permanently stored SAS data sets. If NOREPLACE is specified, a permanently stored SAS data set cannot be replaced with one of the same name. This prevents the inadvertent replacement of existing SAS data sets.
    The REPLACE= data set option takes precedence over the REPLACE | NOREPLACE system option. See Chapter 15, "SAS Files," for a discussion of the REPLACE= data set option. The default value for this option is REPLACE or REPLACE ON.

SOURCE | NOSOURCE (OPTIONS statement form)
SOURCE ON | SOURCE OFF (OPTIONS window form)
    controls whether SAS source statements are printed on the SAS log. The default value for this option is SOURCE or SOURCE ON.

SOURCE2 | NOSOURCE2 (OPTIONS statement form)
SOURCE2 ON | SOURCE2 OFF (OPTIONS window form)
    controls whether secondary source statements from files included by %INCLUDE are printed on the SAS log. The default value for this option is NOSOURCE2 or SOURCE2 OFF.

STIMER | NOSTIMER (OPTIONS statement form)
STIMER ON | STIMER OFF (OPTIONS window form)
    controls whether the SAS log includes notes reporting the amount of time required to execute DATA and PROC steps. If the option is set as STIMER or STIMER ON, the time notes are displayed. The default value is STIMER or STIMER ON.

498 Chapter 16

SYMBOLGEN | NOSYMBOLGEN (OPTIONS statement form)
SYMBOLGEN ON | SYMBOLGEN OFF (OPTIONS window form)
specifies whether the macro processor displays the result of resolving macro variable references. If SYMBOLGEN is in effect when the macro processor resolves a macro variable reference, the macro processor writes the message

    Macro variable name resolves to value

The default value is NOSYMBOLGEN or SYMBOLGEN OFF.

SUMMARY OF SAS GLOBAL OPTIONS

			Specified in				
Option	Type	Default	CONFIG. SAS	PROFILE. SCT	SAS cmd.	OPTIONS stmt.	OPTIONS window
-AUTOEXEC	C	autoexec.sas	X		X		
CENTER	S	ON CENTER		X	X	X	X
CHARCODE	S	OFF NOCHARCODE		X	X	X	X
-CONFIG	C	config.sas			X		
DATE	S	ON DATE		X	X	X	X
DBCS	S	OFF NODBCS		X	X	X	X
DEVICE=	S	none		X	X	X	X
-DMS	C	-dms	X		X		
-ECHO	C	none	X		X		
-EMS	C	none	X		X		
ERRORS=	S	20			X	X	X
-FILEBUFFERS	C	none	X		X		
-FILECACHE	C	none	X		X		
FIRSTOBS=	S	1		X	X	X	X
FORMCHAR=	S	|----|+|---+ =|-/\\<>*		X	X	X	X
-FSDEVICE	C	none	X		X		
-IBM	C	none	X		X		

(continued on next page)

(continued from previous page)

			Specified in			
Option	Type	Default	CONFIG. SAS	PROFILE. SCT	SAS cmd.	OPTIONS stmt.	OPTIONS window
KANJI	S	OFF NOKANJI		X	X	X	X
LAST=	S	_NULL_			X	X	X
LINESIZE=	S	78		X	X	X	X
-LOG	C	_____.log	X		X		
MISSING=	S	.		X	X	X	X
MPRINT	S	OFF NOMPRINT			X	X	X
-MSG	C	\sas\sasmsg	X		X		
MTRACE	S	OFF NOMTRACE			X	X	X
-NEWS	C	none	X		X		
NEWS=	S	none		X	X	X	X
NOTES	S	ON NOTES			X	X	X
NUMBER	S	ON NUMBER		X	X	X	X
OBS=	S	MAX			X	X	X
OVP	S	OFF NOOVP		X	X	X	X
PAGENO=	S	1			X	X	X
PAGESIZE=	S	21		X	X	X	X
-PATH	C	refer to option description	X		X		
-PRINT	C	_____.lst	X		X		
PROBSIG=	S	0		X	X	X	X
PROFILE	S	OFF NOPROFILE			X	X	X
REMOTE=	S	none		X	X	X	X

(continued on next page)

(continued from previous page)

| | | | \multicolumn{5}{c|}{Specified in} |
Option	Type	Default	CONFIG. SAS	PROFILE. SCT	SAS cmd.	OPTIONS stmt.	OPTIONS window
REPLACE	S	ON REPLACE			X	X	X
-SASHELP	C	\sas\sashelp	X		X		
-SASUSER	C	sasuser	X		X		
-SET SASROOT	C	\sas	X				
SOURCE	S	ON SOURCE			X	X	X
SOURCE2	S	OFF NOSOURCE2		X	X	X	X
STIMER	S	STIMER STIMER ON		X	X	X	X
SYMBOLGEN	S	OFF NOSYMBOLGEN			X	X	X
-SYSIN	C	none	X		X		
-SYSPRINT	C	none	X		X		
-USER	C	none	X		X		
-VERBOSE	C	none	X		X		
-WORK	C	saswork	X		X		
-XWAIT	C	ON	X		X		

Chapter 17
SAS® Macro Facility

MACRO VARIABLES 501
MACRO PROGRAM STATEMENTS 502
MACRO FUNCTIONS 503
DATA STEP INTERFACES 503

The SAS macro facility is a tool for extending and customizing the SAS System and for reducing the amount of text you must enter to do common tasks.

The following features are available in the SAS macro facility in Release 6.03. For documentation and sample applications, see the *SAS Guide to Macro Processing, Version 6 Edition*.

MACRO VARIABLES

Macro variables include those you create and those created by the macro processor (known as *automatic macro variables*). The automatic macro variables in base SAS software are listed below. Some other products in the SAS System also provide automatic macro variables; those variables are described with the product that uses them.

SYSBUFFR
: receives text entered in response to a %INPUT statement that the macro processor cannot match with any variable in the statement.

SYSCMD
: contains the last command from the command line of a macro window that was not recognized by display manager.

SYSDATE
: gives the date on which the SAS job started execution.

SYSDAY
: gives the day of the week the SAS job or session started execution.

SYSDEVIC
: gives the name of the current graphics device.

SYSDSN
: gives the name of the most recently created SAS data set as two words left-aligned in eight-character fields.

SYSENV
: returns FORE if the SAS program was entered from the keyboard and BACK if input does not come from the keyboard or if the macro executes in noninteractive mode.

SYSERR
: contains the return code set by SAS procedures.

SYSINDEX
: gives the number of macros that have started execution so far in the current SAS job or session.

SYSINFO
: contains return code information provided by some SAS procedures.

502 Chapter 17

SYSJOBID   gives the name of the currently executing batch job or the userid that invoked the current SAS session on a host computer. In Version 6 of SAS software for personal computers, the value is null (0 characters).

SYSLAST   gives the name of the most recently created SAS data set in the form *libref.datasetname*.

SYSMENV   gives the currently active macro execution environment.

SYSMSG   contains a message you specify to be displayed in the message area of a macro window.

SYSSCP   returns the abbreviation for your operating system.

SYSTIME   gives the time the SAS program started execution.

SYSVER   gives the version of SAS software you are using.

MACRO PROGRAM STATEMENTS

The following macro program statements are available in Release 6.03:

%*comment   places comments in a macro.

%DISPLAY   displays a macro window.

%DO   treats text and program statements as a unit until a matching %END statement appears.

iterative %DO   executes a portion of a macro repetitively based on the value of an index variable.

%DO %UNTIL   executes the statements in a loop repetitively until a condition becomes true.

%DO %WHILE   executes a group of statements repetitively while a condition holds.

%END   ends a %DO group.

%GLOBAL   creates global macro variables.

%GOTO | %GO TO   causes macro execution to branch to the label specified.

%IF-%THEN/%ELSE   execute a portion of a macro conditionally.

%INPUT   supplies values to macro variables during macro execution.

%*label*:   identifies a portion of a macro to which execution branches when a %GOTO statement is executed.

%LET   creates a macro variable and assigns it a value or changes the value of an existing macro variable.

%LOCAL   creates local macro variables.

macro invocation   causes the macro processor to begin executing a macro.

%MACRO   begins the definition of a macro, assigns the macro a name, and optionally includes a parameter list of macro variables.

%MEND	ends a macro definition.
%PUT	writes text to the SAS log.
%WINDOW	defines a macro window.

MACRO FUNCTIONS

The following macro functions are available in Release 6.03:

%BQUOTE	quotes unanticipated special characters in a resolved value.
%EVAL	evaluates arithmetic and logical expressions.
%INDEX	finds the first occurrence of a string.
%LENGTH	finds the length of an argument.
%NRBQUOTE	quotes unanticipated special characters including & and % in a resolved value.
%NRQUOTE	quotes a resolved value including % and &.
%NRSTR	quotes constant text including % and &.
%QUOTE	quotes a resolved value.
%SCAN	scans for "words."
%STR	quotes constant text.
%SUBSTR	substrings a string.
%UNQUOTE	undoes quoting.
%UPCASE	translates lowercase characters to uppercase.

DATA STEP INTERFACES

The DATA step interfaces described below allow you to create macro variables, assign them values, and retrieve macro variable values during DATA step execution rather than when the DATA step is being constructed:

SYMGET function	returns the value of a macro variable during DATA step execution.
SYMPUT routine	either creates a macro variable whose value is information from the DATA step or assigns a DATA step value to an existing macro variable.

Chapter 18
SAS® Statements Used Anywhere

Comment Statement 506
DM Statement 507
ENDSAS Statement 508
FILENAME Statement 509
FOOTNOTE Statement 511
%INCLUDE Statement 512
LIBNAME Statement 514
OPTIONS Statement 516
RUN Statement 519
TITLE Statement 520
X Statement 522

Comment Statement

The comment statement can be used anywhere in your SAS job to document the purpose of the job, to explain any unusual segments of the program, or to describe the steps in a complex program or calculation. The form of the comment statement is

*message;

where

> message   explains or documents the job. The message can be any length, although it cannot contain semicolons.

You can use any number of comment statements in a job. The comment statement **must** end in a semicolon. These statements are valid comments:

```
*This code finds the number in the by group;
*Test run;
*proc print;
    *var inspectr lot;
```

Drawing a box around comments is a useful way to document your SAS job:

```
*-------------------------------------------------------------------*
|                         This is a box-style                       |
|                             comment                               |
*-------------------------------------------------------------------* ;
```

Comments of the form

/*message*/

can also be used. They can appear within SAS statements anywhere a single blank can appear and can contain semicolons. Do not nest comments of this type.

For example, this statement is a valid SAS statement:

```
proc sort /* Sort the data set */;
```

You can also use comments to eliminate parts of an existing SAS program. The following example eliminates some BY variables for the current execution of the job:

```
proc sort;
    by region state /* County city */;
```

This example eliminates a DATA and a PROC step:

```
data all;
    set in.old;
proc print;
        /*
data subset;
    set all;
    if state='NC';
proc print;
        */
run;
```

To run the complete program, remove the comment symbols.

DM Statement

The DM statement allows you to submit SAS display manager commands as SAS statements. The syntax of the statement is

DM '*displaymanagercommand;...*' [*window*];

where

displaymanagercommand
is any valid display manager command as described in Chapter 10, "SAS Display Manager System."

window
is the window where the cursor is left after the commands are executed (known as the active window). If you omit *window*, the cursor returns to the PROGRAM EDITOR window. The *window* option is most useful for specifying the MENU and AF windows.

If you specify either MENU or AF as the active window and have other SAS statements following the DM statement (for example, in an AUTOEXEC.SAS file), those statements are submitted to the SAS System when control returns to display manager. Statements following the DM statement are executed before statements submitted from the AF or MENU window.

Do not issue the DM statement from within an interactive procedure.

An example of the DM statement is shown below:

```
dm 'log;color source red';
```

This SAS statement makes the log the active window and changes all source statements to red as soon as it is submitted. After the DM statement is executed, the PGM window becomes the active window.

In addition to using the DM statement to change features of display manager during a SAS session, the SAS System can also execute DM statements stored in the AUTOEXEC.SAS file as soon as you get into the system. See "Starting and Running SAS Programs" for information on AUTOEXEC.SAS.

The following example illustrates the use of the *window* option used with DM statements stored in an AUTOEXEC.SAS file. Suppose you set up an AUTOEXEC.SAS file that submits the following statements when you initiate a SAS session:

```
data a;
   x=1;
run;
dm 'menu';
```

When the AUTOEXEC.SAS runs, data set A is created and the MENU window is displayed, but the cursor returns to the PGM window.

However, suppose you set up an AUTOEXEC.SAS file that submits the following statements:

```
data a;
   x=1;
run;
dm 'menu' menu;
```

When the AUTOEXEC.SAS runs, data set A is created, the MENU window is made active, and the cursor remains in the MENU window. You can now fill out procedure panels and submit them. If the AUTOEXEC.SAS file contains any further statements (for example, a PROC PRINT statement), those statements are not executed until control returns to display manager (for example, when you submit a PROC step from the menu). The statements remaining in the file are executed just before the PROC step from the menu.

ENDSAS Statement

The ENDSAS statement causes a SAS job or session to terminate at the end of the current DATA or PROC step.

The form of the ENDSAS statement is

ENDSAS;

FILENAME Statement

Specifying a Device Type   510
Routing to Output Devices   510

The FILENAME statement associates a SAS *fileref* (a file reference name) with an external file's complete name (directory plus file name). The fileref is then used as a shorthand reference to the file in the SAS programming statements that access external files (INFILE, FILE, and %INCLUDE). Associating a fileref with an external file is also called *defining* the file. Use the FILENAME statement to define a file before using a fileref in an INFILE, FILE, or %INCLUDE statement.

The association between a fileref and a file name lasts only for the duration of the SAS session or until you change it by specifying another FILENAME statement. You can change the fileref for a file as often as you want.

The form of the FILENAME statement is

FILENAME *fileref* [*devicetype*] '*pathname*';

where

fileref is the name you use to refer to the external file. The fileref must follow the rules for SAS names. A fileref can refer to only one file. If you are accessing more than one file from the same directory, each file must be assigned a unique fileref.

devicetype specifies the type of output device. Valid values are PRINTER and TERMINAL.

pathname is the name of the file. If the file is in another directory, use the complete path name. If the file is in the current directory, you need to specify only the file name. If you specify a *devicetype*, *pathname* can take on special values. (See **Routing to Output Devices** below.)

The following program reads data lines from a file in your current directory identified with the fileref FOOD and creates a temporary SAS data set:

```
filename food 'shopping.dat';
data market;
   infile food;
   input day mmddyy8. meat groc dairy;
run;
```

The difference between the FILENAME statement and the LIBNAME statement is that the FILENAME statement defines a fileref for an external file to be used in a SAS FILE, INFILE, or %INCLUDE statement, whereas the LIBNAME statement defines a libref that your program uses to read or create permanent SAS files, such as SAS data sets.

This example reads data from a file with fileref GREEN and creates a permanent SAS data set stored in a directory with libref SAVE:

```
filename green '\misc\myveg.dat';
libname save 'allveg';
data save.vegetabl;
   infile green;
   input lettuce cabbage broccoli;
run;
```

If a fileref is used in a FILE or INFILE statement without having been defined, SAS uses the word specified as the fileref for a file name in your current default directory. For example, if you use this INFILE statement:

```
infile student;
```

without first defining STUDENT as a fileref, SAS looks for a file called STUDENT in your current directory.

If an undefined fileref appears in a %INCLUDE statement, SAS searches for a file named *fileref*.sas in your current directory.

Specifying a Device Type

In Release 6.03, you can use the FILENAME statement to route output to a printer or other output device. If you specify the device type PRINTER, the associated output file is assumed to be a printer. Note that this is not necessarily the case. You can specify PRINTER as a device type and route output to a disk file. Output is written to a disk file as if it were a printer, perhaps with special control characters. Also note that specifying PRINTER allows you to append data to a file that already exists.

If you specify the device type TERMINAL, output is written to the screen (print file CON:) no matter what is specified as the path name.

Routing to Output Devices

With device type PRINTER, you can route output to any printer destination identified to your system. When using the PRINTER option, the following values are valid for *destination*:

- *printername* routes output to the specified printer. The destination can be any printer specification that is identified to your system.
- *pathname* routes output to the disk file specified.
- blank routes output to the device specified in the SYSPRINT option (See Chapter 16, "SAS Global Options," for more details.) If SYSPRINT is not specified, output goes to the default system printer.

For example, the following FILENAME statement defines a fileref 'plot' to route output to a printer connected to your serial port COM1:

```
filename plot printer 'com1';
```

Note that by using the FILENAME statement for this purpose, it is possible to route SAS output to several devices during the same session.

With the device type TERMINAL, SAS output can be routed to the screen. If you are using the SAS Display Manager System, routing output to the terminal causes the display manager screens to be replaced with a blank screen to which your directed output is written. When the SAS System once again needs to write to a display manager screen, you are prompted to press a key to return to display manager mode. Output written to the screen in this fashion is not saved. When you return to the SAS System, output that was written to the screen is lost.

The following example defines a fileref SCREEN that routes output to the terminal:

```
filename screen terminal '';
```

Note: the quotes at the end of the statement must be included.

FOOTNOTE Statement

Use the FOOTNOTE statement to print lines at the bottom of the page. FOOTNOTE statements can be used to produce up to ten lines.

The FOOTNOTE statement has the form:

FOOTNOTE[n] ['text'];

where

> n   specifies the relative line to be occupied by the footnote. For footnotes, lines are "pushed up" from the bottom. The FOOTNOTE statement with the highest number appears on the bottom line. N can range from 1 to 10; if you omit n, SAS assumes a value of 1.
>
> 'text'   specifies the text of the footnote.

Once you use a FOOTNOTE statement, the text is printed on all pages until the SAS System encounters another FOOTNOTE statement for that line. When a FOOTNOTE statement is specified for a given line, it cancels the previous FOOTNOTE statement for that line and for all lines below it. To cancel all existing footnotes, specify

```
footnote;
```

%INCLUDE Statement

Introduction 512
 Variable in a TITLE or FOOTNOTE statement 513

Introduction

The %INCLUDE (or %INC) statement is used to include SAS statements and data lines from external files.

A %INCLUDE statement must begin at a statement boundary. That is, it must be the first statement in a SAS job or immediately follow a semicolon ending another statement. A %INCLUDE statement cannot immediately follow a CARDS statement; however, you can include data lines by making the CARDS statement the first item in the file containing the data lines. You must include an entire external file; you cannot selectively include lines. A %INCLUDE statement can be a statement in a file that is %INCLUDEd. The maximum level of nesting is 50 %INCLUDE statements.

The difference between the %INCLUDE statement and the INCLUDE command in the display manager program editor is that the %INCLUDE statement sends the included statements to the SAS System for immediate execution, while the INCLUDE command brings the included lines into the program editor screen. You must issue a display manager SUBMIT command to send those lines to the SAS System for execution.

The form of the %INCLUDE statement is

%INCLUDE *fileref* | *'filename'* [/ *option*];

or

%INC *fileref* | *'filename'* [/ *option*];

where

> *fileref* is the fileref of an external file you want to include. Assign the fileref to the external file in a FILENAME statement before you use the fileref in the %INCLUDE statement. If you use a fileref in a %INCLUDE statement without assigning it in a FILENAME statement, SAS searches for a file named *fileref*.sas in your current directory. See the **FILENAME Statement** for more information.
>
> *'filename'* is the name of a PC DOS file. Enclose *filename* in quotes.

and where *option* can be

> SOURCE2 causes the SAS log to show the source statements that are being included in your SAS program. This can also be accomplished using the system option SOURCE2. The statement option overrides the system option for that statement.

The two methods of referring to files in %INCLUDE statements are equivalent; use whichever method is more convenient for you.

The following examples illustrate including SAS statements stored in a file named A:\SALES\EAST.DAT. The first example assigns a fileref to the file and uses the fileref in the %INCLUDE statement:

```
filename e 'a:\sales\east.dat';
%include e;
```

The second example uses the file name in the %INCLUDE statement:
```
%include 'a:\sales\east.dat';
```

Suppose you regularly create and print a SAS data set containing variables X, Y, Z, and MONTH. You can store the SAS statements for the DATA and PROC steps in a file for later execution. The file, named \MISC\MONTH.RPT, contains:

```
filename new '\m1\report.fig';
data monthly;
   infile new;
   input x y z month $;
proc print;
run;
```

To execute this group of statements, assign a fileref (for example, IN1) to the file in a FILENAME statement and use that name in the %INCLUDE statement:

```
filename in1 '\misc\month.rpt';
%include in1;
```

You can also omit the FILENAME statement and write the %INCLUDE statement as

```
%include '\misc\month.rpt';
```

Variable in a TITLE or FOOTNOTE statement You can include the value of a variable in a SAS TITLE or FOOTNOTE statement using the %INCLUDE statement. The statements below first create a variable named NOW containing the current date and LASTWK containing the date a week ago. Then the PUT statements write a TITLE and a FOOTNOTE statement to an external file in your current directory with fileref NEW. In the PROC step, the %INCLUDE statement reads the file containing the TITLE and FOOTNOTE statements.

```
filename new 'tf.dat';
data _null_;
   now=today();
   lastwk=now-7;
   file new;
   put 'title ''DAILY REPORT FOR ' now date. ''';';
   put 'footnote ''SUMMARIZING ACTIVITY SINCE ' lastwk date. ''';';
run;
proc print date=anydata;
   %include new;
run;
```

Note: you can also write the PUT statements as follows:

```
put 'title "DAILY REPORT FOR ' now date. '";';
put 'footnote "SUMMARIZING ACTIVITY SINCE ' lastwk date. '";';
```

In this method the PUT statements use the single quotes, and the TITLE and FOOTNOTE statements in file NEW contain the double quotes (quotation marks).

You can use the method shown in this example to write SAS programs that generate and execute other SAS programs.

LIBNAME Statement

The LIBNAME statement defines one or more directories (or path names) to be used by your SAS program. If you want to read or create a permanent SAS file, you must define the directory to be used in a LIBNAME statement. The LIBNAME statement associates a *libref* (short for "library reference") with a directory name. Then, you specify the libref in SAS statements to refer to the directory. You must include the LIBNAME statement before a SAS statement that specifies the libref.

Refer to "SAS Files" for information on different types of SAS files and how they are logically grouped to form a SAS data library within a directory.

Use the LIBNAME statement to define directories that your program accesses to read or create SAS files, including SAS data sets. If your program reads and creates external files (for example, in INFILE and FILE statements), use the FILENAME statement to define the file. See the **FILENAME Statement** earlier in this chapter.

The form of the LIBNAME statement is

LIBNAME *libref* [**SASV5XPT**] *'path'*...;

where

- *libref* is a name associated with a directory and then used in SAS statements to refer to the directory. The libref must follow the rules for SAS names (as described in the "Introduction" to USING THE SAS LANGUAGE). A libref can refer to only one directory.

- SASV5XPT specifies that the file contains a Version 5 transport-format data library. This option allows you to read transport-format data sets imported from a Version 5 SAS System. You can also write transport-format data sets to be exported to a Version 5 SAS System.

- *'path'* is the name of a directory or file to be accessed by the SAS program. If you specify SASV5XPT in the LIBNAME statement, the *path* must be a file name; otherwise, *path* is a directory name. The directory or file name must be enclosed in quotes and must include any necessary characters to separate elements in the directory or file name.

The association between the libref and the directory or file remains in effect until you change it with another LIBNAME statement or until the end of your session. You can either create or read a permanent SAS file once you have defined the directory in a LIBNAME statement. The following program creates a permanent SAS data set:

```
libname store1 '\inventry';
data store1.mar;
   input day mmddyy8. mean groc dairy;
   cards;
data lines
;
```

The LIBNAME statement associates the libref STORE1 with directory INVENTRY, and then STORE1 is used as the first level of the permanent SAS data set name in the DATA statement. When this program executes, the permanent SAS data set MAR.SSD is stored in INVENTRY.

You can define more than one libref in one LIBNAME statement. The following DATA step reads a permanent SAS data set from one directory and creates a permanent SAS data set in another directory. One LIBNAME statement defines both librefs:

```
libname stock '\misc1' food '\data2\eat';
data stock.apples;
   set food.fruit;
   if item='GRANNY' | item='TOSH' then output;
```

Once the association between libref and directory is made, you can access any SAS file in the directory by using the libref as the first level of a permanent SAS file name. For example, suppose you want to append one SAS file to another SAS file in the same directory. First, use the LIBNAME statement to associate the libref with the appropriate directory. Then, invoke the APPEND procedure, as follows:

```
libname sales '\saledata';
proc append base=sales.yr1985 data=sales.feb;
```

This program appends the SAS file FEB to the SAS file YR1985. Since both files are located in the directory referenced by SALES, the first-level name of both permanent SAS files is the same.

516 Chapter 18

OPTIONS Statement

Introduction 516
Options 516
   Options for Data Sets 516
   Output Formatting Options 517
   Other Options 517
   Source List Options 518

Introduction

The OPTIONS statement temporarily changes one or more SAS system options from the default value. SAS system options are one kind of global option. System options can be specified through the OPTIONS window, the SAS command, and your user profile catalog, as well as in an OPTIONS statement. For complete details on SAS system options, see Chapter 16, "SAS Global Options."

The form of the OPTIONS statement is

OPTIONS *option...;*

where

   option   specifies one or more SAS system options you want to change.

The changes made by an OPTIONS statement are in effect for the duration of the SAS session or until they are changed by another OPTIONS statement. (But note that some option settings can be saved from one SAS session to another by using the PROFILE option. For more information, see Chapter 16.)

For example, suppose you want to suppress the date normally printed on SAS output pages and left align the output on the page. You can use this OPTIONS statement:

```
options nodate nocenter;
```

An OPTIONS statement can be entered at any place in a SAS program. An OPTIONS statement entered within a DATA step or PROC step is effective for the execution of the entire DATA or PROC step, as well as for the duration of the SAS job, even if you enter the OPTIONS statement **after** all other statements (except the RUN statement) of the step. The following list gives a brief description of system options. These options are described more fully in Chapter 16.

Options

System options can also be specified through the OPTIONS window in the SAS display manager and in the SAS command. When you specify a system option in an OPTIONS statement, you use different syntax than you use to specify the option in the OPTIONS window or SAS command. The correct syntax for the OPTIONS statement is shown in the following list. Note: if a negative form of the option is presented below the command, use this form to achieve the opposite effect of the use described.

Options for Data Sets

FIRSTOBS=
   specifies first observation to be processed from SAS data sets.
LAST=
   specifies the name of the most recently created SAS data set.

OBS=
: specifies last observation to be processed from SAS data sets.

REPLACE
NOREPLACE
: replaces permanently allocated SAS data sets with others of the same name.

Output Formatting Options

CENTER
NOCENTER
: centers SAS procedure output.

CHARCODE
NOCHARCODE
: allows alternative character combinations for characters not on the keyboard.

DATE
NODATE
: prints the date at the top of the page.

FORMCHAR=
: specifies the output formatting characters for your output device.

LINESIZE=
: gives print line width for log and procedure output.

MISSING=
: specifies the character the SAS System prints for missing numeric variable values.

NOTES
NONOTES
: prints notes on the SAS log.

NUMBER
NONUMBER
: prints page numbers on SAS output.

OVP
NOOVP
: overprints SAS output.

PAGENO=n
: specifies a beginning page number for the next page of output.

PAGESIZE=
: gives number of lines printed per page of SAS output.

STIMER
NOSTIMER
: prints notes reporting the amount of time required to execute DATA and PROC steps on the SAS log.

Other Options

DBCS
NODBCS
: converts user responses to fill-in-the-blank questions in CBT courses to uppercase before the responses are compared to answers.

DEVICE=
: specifies a device name designation.

ERRORS=
: specifies the maximum number of observations for which complete error messages are printed.

KANJI
NOKANJI
: See DBCS|NODBCS description.

MPRINT
NOMPRINT
: specifies whether SAS statements generated by macro execution are displayed in an easy to read format.

MTRACE
NOMTRACE
: specifies whether the macro processor displays messages that trace its execution.

NEWS=*filename*
: specifies the name of a file that contains a message to be printed in the LOG window after the SAS logo.

PROBSIG=*n*
: controls the formatting of the *p*-values in all statistical procedures.

PROFILE
NOPROFILE
: saves some option settings from one SAS session to another. See the description of the PROFILE option in Chapter 16.

REMOTE=*device*
: specifies the adapter you are using with the SAS micro-to-host link.

SYMBOLGEN
NOSYMBOLGEN
: causes the macro processor to display the result of resolving macro variable references.

Source List Options

SOURCE
NOSOURCE
: lists SAS source statements on the SAS log.

SOURCE2
NOSOURCE2
: lists secondary source statements from files included by %INCLUDE on the SAS log.

RUN Statement

The RUN statement causes the previously entered SAS step to be executed; the SAS System is then ready to begin a new DATA or PROC step. In an interactive procedure, the RUN statement causes the previously entered group of statements to be executed, but SAS remains within that PROC step. Each interactive procedure contains a method (usually a QUIT statement) for ending the current PROC step; beginning a new DATA or PROC step also ends the step. See the individual procedure descriptions for details.

The form of the RUN statement is

RUN [**CANCEL**];

where

> **CANCEL** causes the SAS System to end the current step without executing it. SAS prints a message indicating that the step was not executed.

This example uses two RUN statements:

```
title 'USING PROC MEANS FOR ANALYSIS';
proc means data=anydata min max;
   var x y z;
run;
title 'USING PROC PLOT FOR ANALYSIS';
proc plot data=anydata;
   plot x*y;
run;
```

The first RUN statement causes the SAS System to execute the PROC MEANS step before reading the second TITLE statement. Without the first RUN statement, the SAS System executes the PROC MEANS step after it reads the PROC PLOT statement. In that case, the second TITLE statement replaces the first TITLE statement, and the output of both procedures contains the title for the PLOT procedure.

Output 18.1 illustrates the use of the CANCEL option. SAS attempts to execute the first DATA step but not the second one.

Output 18.1 RUN Statement with CANCEL Option

```
NOTE: Copyright(c) 1985, 86, 87 SAS Institute Inc., Cary, N.C. 27512-8000, U.S.A.
NOTE: SAS (r) Proprietary Software Release 6.03
      Licensed to SAS Institute Inc., Site 00000000.
1          data circle;
2             input radius;
3             c=2*4.13*radius;
4             *Incorrect value for PI;
5          run;

ERROR: No CARDS or INFILE statement.
NOTE: SAS stopped processing this step because of errors.

6          data circle;
7             input radius;
8             c=2*4.13*radius;
9             *Incorrect value for PI;
10         run cancel;

NOTE: Data step not executed at user's request.

NOTE: SAS Institute Inc., SAS Circle, PO Box 8000, Cary, N.C. 27512-8000
```

TITLE Statement

Introduction 520
Associating a Title with a Particular Step 520

Introduction

The TITLE statement is used to specify up to ten title lines to be printed on each page of the SAS print file and other SAS output.

The form of the TITLE statement is

TITLE[*n*] ['*title*'];

where

- *n*   immediately follows the word TITLE, with no intervening blank, to specify the number of the title line. For example the statement

    ```
    title3 'THIS IS THE THIRD TITLE LINE';
    ```

    specifies a title for the third line from the top of the page. *N* can range from 1 to 10. For the first title line, either TITLE or TITLE1 may be specified.

    Omitting some values of *n* indicates that those lines are to be blank. For example, if TITLE1 and TITLE3 statements appear, a blank line appears between the two titles on the SAS output.

- '*title*'   gives a title of up to 132 characters that you want printed. If a title longer than the current line size is specified, it is split across multiple lines. Enclose the title in quotes.

Here are examples of valid TITLE statements:

```
title 'FIRST DRAFT';
title2 'YEAR''S END REPORT';
title5 "PROJECTED SALES FIGURES";
```

Once you specify a title for a line, it is used for all subsequent output until you cancel the title or define another title for that line. A TITLE statement for a given line cancels the previous TITLE statement for that line and for all lines with larger *n* values. To cancel all existing titles, specify

```
title;
```

To suppress the *n*th and later titles, use

```
titlen;
```

Associating a Title with a Particular Step

If you want a title associated with a given PROC step, include the title

- after a RUN statement for the previous step, if one is present, **or**
- anywhere after the PROC statement and before the next DATA, PROC, or RUN statement.

For example, the statements

```
proc print;
   title 'TITLE FOR FIRST PROC';
proc means;
```

print the title on the output for both the PRINT and the MEANS procedures.

These statements

```
proc print;
run;
   title 'TITLE FOR SECOND PROC';
proc means;
run;
```

print the title only on the PROC MEANS output.

These statements

```
proc print;
proc means;
   title 'TITLE FOR SECOND PROC';
```

also print the title only on the output pages from MEANS. See the **RUN Statement** earlier in this chapter for additional examples of associating titles with particular PROC steps.

X Statement

You can use the X statement to issue a PC DOS command from within a SAS session. The SAS System executes the X statement as soon as you enter it.

The form of the X statement is

X *'command'*;

where

> *'command'*   specifies the PC DOS command.

For example, suppose you decide during a SAS session that you need a new directory in which to store a permanent SAS data set named MONDAY. These statements create the subdirectory WEEK in your current working directory and store MONDAY in it:

```
x 'mkdir week';
libname save 'week';
data save.monday;
   more SAS statements
```

You can also use an X statement without specifying a PC DOS command to establish a PC DOS subsession (also called subset mode). For example, the statement

```
x;
```

puts you into a PC DOS subsession. To return to the SAS session, enter

```
exit
```

at the PC DOS prompt. (You can also enter a PC DOS subsession by entering the X command on the command line of the program editor in display manager. See Chapter 10, "SAS Display Manager System.")

Changing the default directory while in subset mode does not affect your session when you return to SAS. You can give the EXIT command from the new directory; you do not have to return to your original directory to issue the EXIT command. In references to files that are created in a SAS session, the complete path name to the file (or SAS data library) is used, so changing the default directory will not change the area referenced.

Note, however, that if you establish a libref or fileref without specifying the full path name to the library, the library is created in the current default directory. If you go into subset mode and change directories and then go back into the SAS System and establish another libref, the two librefs refer to SAS data libraries in different directories.

APPENDICES

Version 6 Changes and Enhancements to
Base SAS® Software: Language

User Profile Catalog

SAS® Micro-to-Host Link

SAS® Installation Details

Appendix 1
Version 6 Changes and Enhancements to Base SAS® Software: Language

USING THE SAS LANGUAGE   525
   SAS Variables   525
THE DATA STEP   525
   SAS Expressions   525
   SAS Functions   526
   SAS Statements Used in the DATA Step   527
THE PROC STEP   529
   SAS Statements Used in the PROC Step   529
FEATURES FOR BOTH DATA AND PROC STEPS   529
   SAS Display Manager   529
   SAS Output   529
   SAS Informats and Formats   529
   SAS Files   531
   SAS Global Options   531
   SAS Statements Used Anywhere   531

USING THE SAS LANGUAGE

SAS Variables

There are two new special variables: _CMD_ and _MSG_. _I_ is no longer available.
   The length of numeric variables can range from 3 to 8 bytes.

THE DATA STEP

SAS Expressions

The IN operator compares a value produced by an expression on the left to a list of values on the right; it allows you to process SAS expressions more efficiently.

526   Appendix 1

Two operators used in SAS expressions are indicated with different symbols on minicomputers (for example, Hewlett-Packard 9000-series and VAX) and microcomputers than are used with IBM mainframes.

The logical NOT operator is ^ (the caret) rather than the ¬ symbol. The logical OR operator is either ¦ (broken bar) or ! (exclamation point) rather than the | symbol.

SAS Functions

The new functions are listed below:

Arithmetic functions

HBOUND	returns the upper bound of an array.
LBOUND	returns the lower bound of an array.
TRUNC	returns a truncated numeric value of a particular length.

Financial functions

COMPOUND	calculates compounded value parameters.
DACCDB	calculates accumulated declining balance depreciation.
DACCDBSL	calculates accumulated declining balance converting to straight-line depreciation.
DACCSL	calculates accumulated straight-line depreciation.
DACCSYD	calculates accumulated sum-of-years'-digits depreciation.
DACCTAB	calculates accumulated depreciation from specified tables.
DEPDB	calculates declining balance depreciation.
DEPDBSL	calculates declining balance converting to straight-line depreciation.
DEPSL	calculates straight-line depreciation.
DEPSYD	calculates sum-of-years'-digits depreciation.
DEPTAB	calculates depreciation from specified tables.
INTRR	calculates internal rate of return as a fraction.
IRR	calculates internal rate of return as a percentage.
MORT	calculates mortgage loans.
NETPV	calculates net present value as a fraction.
NPV	calculates net present value with rate expressed as a percentage.
SAVING	calculates future value of periodic saving.

Quantile functions

CINV	gives a quantile for the chi-square distribution.
FINV	gives a quantile for the *F* distribution.
TINV	gives a quantile for the *t* distribution.

Character functions
- BYTE — returns a character in the ASCII collating sequence.
- RANK — returns the position of a character in the ASCII collating sequence.

Special functions
- DIF n — calculates the first difference for the n lag.
- LAG n — calculates the nth lagged value.
- SOUND — generates a sound of a specified frequency and duration. Use the SOUND function with the CALL statement.
- SYMGET — returns the value of a macro variable.

System functions are not available.

SAS Statements Used in the DATA Step

ABORT
  The ABEND and RETURN options function differently than in Version 5.

ARRAY
  Explicitly subscripted arrays, implicitly subscripted arrays, and multidimensional arrays are available. You can specify the upper and lower bound for each dimension of an array, and you can set initial values for array elements.

ATTRIB
  allows you to specify the format, informat, label, and length for a list of variables.

BY
  must immediately follow the SET, MERGE, or UPDATE statement to which it refers. In a DATA step with more than one SET statement, a BY statement can follow each SET statement; the BY statement affects only the SET statement it follows.

CALL
  can be used with additional routines.

DISPLAY
  displays a window defined with the WINDOW statement.

ERROR
  is not available.

FILE
  writes only to standard external files, not to special output files such as DA, DLI, PUNCH, and VSAM. There are several new options available.

FORMAT
  You can specify a default format with the new DEFAULT= option.

INFILE
  There are new options available.

INFORMAT
  You can specify a default informat with the new DEFAULT= option.

INPUT
  There are six new pointer controls.

Column pointer controls

@(expression)
: moves the pointer to the column given by the value of *expression*. The *expression* must evaluate to a positive integer.

@'characterstring'
: moves the pointer to the first nonblank column after *characterstring* in the input line.

@characterstring
: locates the series of characters in the input line given by the value of *charactervariable* and moves the pointer to the first nonblank column after that series of characters.

@(characterexpression)
: locates the series of characters in the input line given by the value of *characterexpression* (a SAS expression containing one or more literals or character variables) and moves the pointer to the first nonblank column after the series.

+(expression)
: moves the pointer the number of columns given by *expression*. The *expression* can evaluate to a positive or negative integer.

Line pointer controls

#(expression)
: moves the pointer to the line given by the value of *expression*. The *expression* must evaluate to a positive integer.

LENGTH
: accepts a length of 3 to 8 bytes for a numeric variable.

PUT
: contains three new pointer controls:

@(expression)
: moves the pointer to the column given by the value of *expression*. The *expression* must evaluate to a positive integer.

+(expression)
: moves the pointer the number of columns given by *expression*. The *expression* must evaluate to a positive or negative integer.

#(expression)
: moves the pointer to the line given by the value of *expression*. The *expression* must evaluate to a positive integer.

WHERE
: subsets observations from a SAS data set before they are brought into a DATA step.

WINDOW
: creates customized windows that can display text and accept input.

THE PROC STEP

SAS Statements Used in the PROC Step

PARMCARDS
: is not available.

PARMCARDS4
: is not available.

QUIT
: is used to end interactive procedures.

WHERE
: subsets observations from a SAS data set before they are brought into a PROC step.

FEATURES FOR BOTH DATA AND PROC STEPS

SAS Display Manager

The SAS Display Manager System offers several added or changed features. Its new text editor is a powerful full-screen editor available in the PROGRAM EDITOR and NOTEPAD windows of display manager and in SAS/AF and SAS/FSP software.

Several special windows are now available:

- The CATALOG window displays the directory of SAS catalogs and allows you to manage catalogs or to create new ones.
- The OPTIONS window displays the current settings of SAS options.
- The SETINIT window displays the currently licensed software and expiration dates.

In addition, the former AF window is now called the MENU window. The current MENU window displays the SAS Procedure Menu System, and the current AF window displays applications developed with SAS/AF software and CBT courses.

Display manager's new cut and paste facility allows you to cut and paste within windows, across window boundaries, and from one window to another. Global commands include MARK, PCLEAR, SMARK, STORE, and UNMARK; text editor commands are CUT and PASTE.

Finally, the full-screen editing features of the NOTEPAD window have been enhanced. Like the PROGRAM EDITOR window, it uses the text editor.

SAS Output

The primary mode of execution for SAS programs is the SAS Display Manager System; line-mode and noninteractive execution are also available.

SAS Informats and Formats

There are new informats and formats.
New informats are as follows:

$EBCDICw.
: reads mainframe-form (EBCDIC) character data.

JULIANw.
: reads Julian dates.

MRBw.d
: reads a numeric value stored in Microsoft Corporation's BASIC floating point form.

NENGOw.
: reads Japanese dates.

PKw.d
: reads unsigned packed decimal data.

S370FIBw.d
: reads IBM 370 integer binary data.

S370FPDw.d
: reads IBM 370 packed decimal data.

S370FPIBw.d
: reads IBM 370 positive integer binary data.

S370FRBw.d
: reads IBM 370 real (floating point) binary data.

New formats are as follows:

$EBCDICw.
: writes PC ASCII character data in mainframe EBCDIC characters.

JULIANw.
: converts SAS date values to Julian form.

MRBw.d
: converts a SAS numeric value to a Microsoft BASIC floating point number.

NENGOw.
: converts SAS date values to Japanese date format.

PKw.d
: converts a SAS numeric value to an unsigned packed decimal number.

S370FIBw.d
: writes PC integer binary values (byte-reversed form) in IBM 370 integer binary form.

S370FPDw.d
: writes PC packed decimal data in IBM 370 packed decimal data form.

S370FPIBw.d
: writes PC positive integer binary data in IBM 370 positive integer binary data form.

S370FRBw.d
: writes PC real (floating point) binary data in IBM 370 real binary form.

WEEKDATXw.
: writes a date value in the form *day-of-week, dd monthname yyyy*.

WORDDATXw.
: writes a date value in the form *dd monthname yyyy*.

SAS Files

In Release 6.03 of the SAS System there are a number of important changes to SAS catalogs:

- There is only one kind of catalog.
- There are many new entry types for the catalog.
- Catalogs created under Version 5 must be converted to be used under Release 6.03.

SAS Global Options

There are many new configuration and SAS system options, and additional ways to specify them.

SAS Statements Used Anywhere

DM
: allows you to submit SAS display manager commands as SAS statements.

FILENAME
: You can specify a device as well as a file.

RUN
: allows you to end a SAS step without executing it by using the CANCEL option; the QUIT option is no longer available.

    In an interactive procedure, the RUN statement causes the previously entered group of statements to be executed, but SAS remains within that PROC step after execution has completed. Each interactive procedure has a method of ending the current PROC step. Beginning a new DATA or PROC step also ends the current PROC step.

X
: allows you to specify a DOS command in quotes or to activate a DOS subsession without ending your SAS session.

Appendix 2
User Profile Catalog

INTRODUCTION 533
CONTENTS OF A USER PROFILE CATALOG 533
CREATING A USER PROFILE CATALOG 534
  Converting User Profiles from Release 6.01 or 6.02 534
  Re-creating the Default User Profile 534
USING A USER PROFILE CATALOG 535

INTRODUCTION

The SAS user profile is a SAS catalog containing entries that allow you to tailor features of the SAS System for your needs. For example, you can store your own defaults for function key settings and window attribute settings in the user profile catalog. The user profile catalog is stored in the SASUSER directory defined in your CONFIG.SAS file. By default, the user profile catalog is stored in

current directory\SASUSER\PROFILE.SCT

This appendix describes the contents and use of the user profile catalog. Refer to Chapter 15, "SAS Files," for general information on SAS catalogs and catalog entries.

CONTENTS OF A USER PROFILE CATALOG

The user profile catalog can include entries for

- function key settings for any feature, procedure, or product using function keys (entry type KEYS). KEYS entries are stored in the user profile catalog when you change key settings and execute an END command or any time you execute a SAVE command in a KEYS window.
- window attribute settings (entry type WSAVE). WSAVE entries are stored in the user profile catalog when you execute a WSAVE command in display manager.
- defaults for SAS system options (entry type POPTIONS). POPTIONS entries are stored in the user profile catalog when the PROFILE system option is in effect at the end of a PC SAS session. Use the OPTIONS window or the OPTIONS statement to set the system options. Be sure to set the PROFILE system option to on so the other system options are saved.
- notepads (entry type NPAD). NPAD entries are stored in the user profile catalog when you execute an END or SAVE command in a NOTEPAD window.

KEYS, WSAVE, POPTIONS, and NPAD entries are those that you store in the user profile catalog. In addition, the SAS System automatically stores some other entries in the user profile catalog. These are entry types that the SAS System uses for utility purposes. Do not attempt to alter these entries. The additional entries include

- AFCBT type
- AFGO type
- AFPGM type
- RLINKLL type.

CREATING A USER PROFILE CATALOG

A directory containing the user profile catalog is created automatically by the SAS System in your first SAS session. By default, this directory is named SASUSER and is created as a subdirectory of the current directory.

For example, suppose this is the first time you have used the SAS System. When you invoke the SAS System, it looks in the current directory for a SASUSER subdirectory. If there is no such subdirectory, SASUSER is created automatically as a subdirectory of the current directory. If you call the display manager KEYS window, alter some function key settings in the window, and then issue a SAVE command, the PROFILE catalog, including the KEYS entry, is written to the new SASUSER subdirectory.

All entry types except POPTIONS entries are saved immediately when you issue a SAVE or END command from the appropriate window. POPTIONS entries are saved at the end of the SAS session if the PROFILE system option is on.

Converting User Profiles from Release 6.01 or 6.02

User profiles created in the 6.01 and 6.02 releases of the SAS System are called PROFILE.SFS. As with all 6.01/6.02 catalogs, PROFILE.SFS must be converted to be used under Release 6.03. Use the CONVERT option on the COPY statement of the CATALOG procedure to convert the catalog.

Re-creating the Default User Profile

The default settings originally provided with the SAS System for the KEYS and POPTIONS entries are stored in the SASHELP directory. The CORE catalog in the SASHELP directory contains the original display manager keys and system options. The FSP catalog in the SASHELP directory contains entries for the key settings of other full-screen products. If you do not make any changes to key settings or system options, the SAS System uses the default settings in the CORE and FSP catalogs in the SASHELP directory. When you change a key setting or a system option, the SAS System creates an entry in the user profile catalog of the SASUSER directory. The key settings and system options in the user profile are then used instead of the default values stored in SASHELP.

If you want to restore the settings in your user profile to the ones originally defined in the SASHELP catalogs, use the CATALOG procedure or the CATALOG window to delete the entry that you want to change from the user profile catalog. You can then allow the SAS System to use the corresponding entry in the SASHELP catalogs, or you can copy the corresponding entry from CORE or FSP in SASHELP to SASUSER. Refer to Chapter 7, "The Catalog Procedure," in the *SAS Procedures Guide, Release 6.03 Edition* and Chapter 10, "SAS Display Manager System," for information on how to delete and copy entries in a catalog.

Note: some restored settings, such as POPTIONS entries, do not take effect until the next SAS session. To restore settings for KEYS entries immediately, follow the steps described above and then display the KEYS window. On the command line of the KEYS window, enter COPY. The keys definitions are restored and a message is displayed indicating the new definitions.

USING A USER PROFILE CATALOG

Once you have stored something in your user profile catalog, the SAS System automatically uses it. For example, SAS first checks the user profile catalog in the SASUSER directory for function key settings (KEYS entries) and system option settings (POPTIONS entry).

You can create more than one user profile catalog. To specify a different user profile catalog,

- change the path name specified in the -SASUSER option of the CONFIG.SAS file
- or specify a different path name with the -SASUSER option when you invoke the SAS System.

If no user profile catalog exists in the directory named in the SAS command or in the CONFIG.SAS file, the SAS System creates a PROFILE.SCT in that directory.

Appendix 3
SAS® Micro-to-Host Link

INTRODUCTION 537
WHAT IS THE MICRO-TO-HOST LINK? 537
    Capabilities 538
    Overview 538
NEW SCRIPT STATEMENTS IN RELEASE 6.03 539
    BREAK Statement 539
    EOPCHAR Statement 539
    XTIME Statement 539

INTRODUCTION

This appendix provides an overview of the SAS micro-to-host link and describes some enhancements to the link facility that are available as of Release 6.03 of the SAS System for PCs.

The SAS micro-to-host link was available in the 6.01 and 6.02 Releases of the SAS System for personal computers and was documented in SAS Technical Report P-144. Next, an enhanced 6.02 Release of the link became available that provided support for more adapters and the ability to copy external files between host and PC. The enhanced 6.02 Release is documented in the *SAS Guide to the Micro-to-Host Link, Version 6 Edition*, which replaced P-144.

Now, with Release 6.03 of the SAS System for PCs, additional capabilities have been added to the SAS link:

- the addition of a TRANSFER STATUS window to he DOWNLOAD and UPLOAD procedures. See Chapter 22, "The DOWNLOAD Procedure," and Chapter 38, "The UPLOAD Procedure," in the *SAS Procedures Guide, Release 6.03 Edition* for a description and examples of this new window.
- three new script statements. The new script statements are documented later in this appendix.

With the exception of documentation for the new 6.03 features, the *SAS Guide to the Micro-to-Host Link, Version 6 Edition* continues to be the primary documentation of the SAS link.

WHAT IS THE MICRO-TO-HOST LINK?

The SAS System's micro-to-host link is a facility that allows communication between a PC SAS session on a microcomputer and a SAS session on another, larger computer—the *host*.* The SAS link gives you access to the files and SAS

---

  * In other SAS documentation, the term "host" is synonymous with "operating system"; however, in this context, host refers to the larger computer in a link setup.

software on the host computer at the same time that you are running a PC SAS session.

Capabilities

The SAS link is more than an emulation package that allows you to use your microcomputer as a terminal connected to the host. With the SAS micro-to-host link, you have the ability to communicate with two SAS sessions: one on the host and one on the PC. Therefore, you can distribute SAS processing to either machine in order to use your computing resources to their best advantage. SAS data sets and external files stored on the PC can be copied to the host computer, and SAS data sets and external files stored on the host can be copied to the PC. SAS programs can be executed on the host computer's SAS System from a PC SAS display manager session.

Some typical applications of the SAS link include

- developing and testing programs for the host on the PC
- backing up PC files on the host
- using the host as a central place from which to distribute files to many PC workstations
- downloading collections of host files to the PC
- easily accessing host data sets too large to store on your PC.

Overview

The SAS link is easy to use. With a few SAS display manager commands, SAS system options, and the DOWNLOAD and UPLOAD procedures, you can start the link, communicate with the host system, and terminate the link connection when you are finished.

To start and stop the SAS link, you invoke the SIGNON and SIGNOFF commands to execute a script. A *script* is a DOS file containing special SAS statements that control the link. You can use one of the sample scripts provided by SAS Institute, a script furnished by your computing installation, or a script you write on your own.

There are five basic steps to starting the SAS link:

1. Start DOS.
2. Invoke your terminal emulator or control program.
3. Log on to the host system.
4. Invoke the PC SAS System.
5. Execute the SIGNON command.

Hardware and software configurations and the capabilities of the script you use determine which of these steps you perform.

Once you have started the link, you can execute programs on the host with the RSUBMIT (remote submit) command, and you can send files between the PC and the host with the DOWNLOAD and UPLOAD procedures.

- To execute SAS programs on the host system from a PC SAS session, use the RSUBMIT command. RSUBMIT is a PC SAS display manager command. Log and procedure output from SAS programs executed by the RSUBMIT command are displayed in your PC SAS display manager windows even though the program executes on the host system.
- To transfer files over the SAS link, use the DOWNLOAD and UPLOAD procedures. Sending a file from the host to the PC is *downloading*; sending a file from the PC to the host is *uploading*.

When you have finished using the SAS link, terminate the link with the SIGNOFF command. SIGNOFF is a PC SAS display manager command that you issue from any PC display manager window. The SIGNOFF command executes a script containing statements that terminate the link.

NEW SCRIPT STATEMENTS IN RELEASE 6.03

There are three new script statements for those who need to write or modify a script. The new statements are

- BREAK statement
- EOPCHAR statement
- XTIME statement.

BREAK Statement

Connection type: asynchronous

The BREAK statement specifies the duration (in seconds) of an asynchronous break signal sent over the link by a TYPE script statement. (The TYPE statement can send a break signal by specifying the ASCII code 'A9'X or by specifying the mnemonic BREAK.) The form of the BREAK statement is

BREAK *n* **SECOND | SECONDS**

where *n* is the duration of the signal. The default is 0.220 seconds.

EOPCHAR Statement

Connection type: asynchronous

The EOPCHAR statement specifies the end-of-packet character for packets going from the PC to the host. The form of the EOPCHAR statement is

EOPCHAR *character*;

where *character* is the ASCII character used by the host to signal the end of a terminal input message. You can specify *character* in one of the following forms:

- a literal character enclosed in quotes, such as '?'
- a hex constant enclosed in quotes, such as '0D'X
- an ASCII mnemonic, such as CR. *

The default is CR (carriage return).

The end-of-packet character cannot be an alphanumeric character, a period (.), a slash (/), or the same character used for the start-of-packet character.

XTIME Statement

Connection type: 3270

The XTIME statement specifies how long the PC waits after the host's X clock symbol disappears. The PC waits the specified time before sending input to the host or reading output from the host. Normally, the X clock appears when you send an AID key to the host (for example, the ENTER key) and disappears after the host responds. Sometimes the X clock reappears when the host updates a 3270 screen in a line-mode host session; this is most likely to happen during the host's start-up activities. If the X clock appears when you are not expecting it,

---

* See the information on ASCII control character mnemonics in the description of the TYPE script statement in the *SAS Guide to the Micro-to-Host Link, Version 6 Edition*.

it may interfere with link processing. This statement allows you to specify the minimum time the PC waits after the X clock disappears in order to reduce problems caused by unexpected display of the X clock.

The form of the XTIME statement is

XTIME n **SECOND | SECONDS**

where n specifies the amount of time the PC should wait after the X clock disappears. The default is 0.

The XTIME statement is not commonly used in scripts. It is not necessary to include XTIME in a script unless you are having problems with the X clock display.

Appendix 4
SAS® Installation Details

INTRODUCTION 541
FILES AND DIRECTORIES NEEDED BY THE SAS SYSTEM
*   FOR PERSONAL COMPUTERS 541*
*   Where Does the SAS System Reside? 541*
*   Subdirectories of the SAS System 541*
*   Files Used by the SAS System for Personal Computers 542*
RESERVED FILE NAME EXTENSIONS 543
RECOMMENDATIONS FOR SETTING UP DIRECTORIES 543
OTHER RECOMMENDATIONS 544
YOUR SAS SOFTWARE CONSULTANT 544

INTRODUCTION

This appendix discusses the DOS files that make up the SAS System on your microcomputer and some recommendations for using DOS with SAS software. Refer to DOS documentation for general questions about creating and using DOS files.

FILES AND DIRECTORIES NEEDED BY THE SAS SYSTEM FOR PERSONAL COMPUTERS

This section describes where you can install the SAS System, the subdirectories created when you install the system, and the files used when you install and run the SAS System.

Where Does the SAS System Reside?

When you install the SAS System for personal computers, the installation process asks you to identify where you want to install the system. The default directory is \SAS, but that name is not required.
The documentation for Release 6.03 of the SAS System for personal computers uses \SAS to represent the directory where the SAS System is stored.

Subdirectories of the SAS System

A number of subdirectories of the \SAS directory are created when the SAS System for personal computers software is installed. The subdirectories include:

- **\SAS\SASEXE** for the executable SAS software files.
- **\SAS\SASHELP** for the SAS help files.
- **\SAS\SASINST** for the installation process software.
- **\SAS\SASLINK** for portions of the micro-to-host link software.

- **\SAS\SASMSG** for the SAS message files.
- **\SAS\SASUSER** for the SAS user-profile catalog.
- **\SAS\SASWORK** for storing temporary SAS files during execution.

Except for programs stored in the SASUSER directory, you should not store any personal files in a \SAS directory or its subdirectories. You avoid destroying files accidentally by storing personal files in a personal directory.

Files Used by the SAS System for Personal Computers

The SAS System for personal computers uses several files to set up the environment to run the SAS System. Some of these are PC files that you may already have defined; others are used exclusively by the SAS System.

The PC files used by the SAS System are

- **CONFIG.SYS** is a file with DOS configuration parameters that are required for the SAS System for personal computers. (You may already have a CONFIG.SYS file on your machine.) To run the SAS System, your CONFIG.SYS file must include this line:

    ```
    files=50
    ```

    This is the minimum acceptable value for the FILES parameter.

- **AUTOEXEC.BAT** is a file with DOS commands that are executed automatically when your computer is started. (You may already have an AUTOEXEC.BAT file on your machine.) If you want to be able to execute the SAS System without being in the directory that contains the SAS System, include the following command in your AUTOEXEC.BAT file:

    ```
    path c:\;c:\sas
    ```

    where \SAS is the directory where the SAS System is stored.

    If your personal computer does not have a clock card, you need the DATE and TIME commands in your AUTOEXEC.BAT file. If the commands are not already in your file, add

    ```
    date
    time
    ```

The files used exclusively by the SAS System are

- **CONFIG.SAS** is a file containing special SAS configuration options. The CONFIG.SAS file is shipped with default option settings in it, but you can edit the file to change the option settings. This file is described in more detail in Chapter 16, "SAS Global Options." (Note: do not confuse this file with the CONFIG.SYS file. The CONFIG.SYS file contains DOS configuration information.) The CONFIG.SAS file is installed in the \SAS directory. You should copy this file to the directory from which you will invoke the SAS System.

- **AUTOEXEC.SAS** is a file containing SAS statements that execute automatically when the SAS System is invoked. The file is shipped with default statements in it, but you can edit the file so that it contains whatever SAS statements you like. See the description of the -AUTOEXEC configuration option in Chapter 16, "SAS Global Options," for more information on AUTOEXEC.SAS. (Note: do not confuse this file with the AUTOEXEC.BAT file.) The AUTOEXEC.SAS file is installed in the \SAS directory. You should copy this file to the directory from which you will invoke the SAS System.

RESERVED FILE NAME EXTENSIONS

The SAS System produces or uses a number of different types of DOS files denoted by the file name extension. For files with the extensions listed below for your reference, the SAS System supplies the file name extension automatically; you should not create files with these extensions:

.EXE	executable SAS System module
.LOG	SAS log output
.LST	SAS procedure listing
.MSG	SAS message file
.SSD	SAS data set
.SCT	SAS catalog
.SSP	SAS stored program

Files with the extensions above are created by the SAS System. The extensions listed below are recommended for the names of DOS files that you create to use with the SAS System:

.SAS	SAS program statements (used with %INCLUDE)
.DAT	data (used with INFILE)
.DIF	data interchange format files (for example, Lotus® 1-2-3,® VisiCalc™)
.DBF	dBASE II® and dBASE III® files

RECOMMENDATIONS FOR SETTING UP DIRECTORIES

- Modify your AUTOEXEC.BAT file to include the \SAS directory in your PATH command. This allows you to access the SAS System from any current directory. For example,

    ```
    path c:\;c:\sas
    ```

- Do not store files in your SAS root directory. It is best to leave only the files that were installed with your SAS System in the SAS root directory.
- Set up separate directories for each user and each project. For example, you may have two users with two projects each, as shown in **Figure A3.1**.

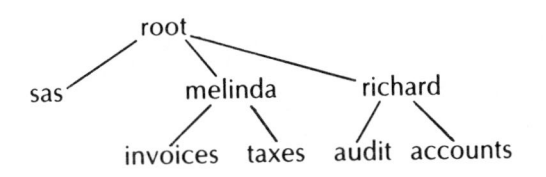

```
            root
          /  |   \
        sas melinda richard
            / \    / \
      invoices taxes audit accounts
```

Figure A3.1 Example Directories for Multiple Users and Projects

It is convenient for each project subdirectory to contain any related data files with a .DAT extension as well as relevant SAS program files with a .SAS extension.
- Tailor the AUTOEXEC.SAS file to meet your needs. You can use this file to customize your SAS initialization process. For example, you may want to include LIBNAME statements to set up certain librefs at the outset, DM statements to customize your screen layout, and X statements for DOS commands. For example, one way to create the AUTOEXEC.SAS file is shown below:

```
c>cd \melinda

c>copy con: autoexec.sas

libname invoices 'invoices';

libname taxes 'taxes';

CTRL-Z

c>sas
```

OTHER RECOMMENDATIONS

Other steps for managing your DOS files for use with the SAS System are included below:

- You **must** set the correct date before entering the SAS System.
- Delete files you do not need and use the DOS command CHKDSK occasionally to recover unusable storage on your fixed disk. The more your disk contains, the more storage may be fragmented.

YOUR SAS SOFTWARE CONSULTANT

See your SAS Software Consultant for more information on using the SAS System on your microcomputer most efficiently. This person will also be able to give you specific local recommendations for your particular SAS applications.

Index

A

ABEND option
   ABORT statement   108
ABORT statement   108, 527
ABS function   49
addition operator (+)   31
AF window
   DM statement   507
AFMACRO entry   470
ALL specification
   PUT statement   224
ampersand (&)
   INPUT statement   179-180
AND keyword   33
ARCOS function   49
arithmetic operators   31
ARRAY statement   109-121, 527
   specifying bounds   114-115
   specifying more than one dimension   113
arrays   109-121
   bounds   113
   explicitly subscripted   109-116
   implicitly subscripted   117-121
   multidimensional explicitly subscripted   113
   multidimensional implicitly subscripted   120-121
   processing with DO groups   111
   subscripts   109
ARSIN function   49
assignment statement   122
   length attribute of result variable   123
   type attribute of result variable   122
asterisks (*) or (**)   31
at-sign pointer control (@)
   INPUT statement   182-185
ATAN function   50
attention signal   309
ATTR= option
   more than one attribute   270
   WINDOW statement   269
ATTRIB statement   527
   DATA step   124
   PROC step   284
AUTOADD command
   SAS text editor   340
-AUTOEXEC configuration option   313, 477
AUTOEXEC.BAT file   542
AUTOEXEC.SAS file   313, 477, 542
AUTOFLOW command
   SAS text editor   340
automatic macro variables   501-502
automatic special variables   13
automatic variables
   _N_   253
AUTOREC= option
   MENU command   378

AUTOSAVE= option
   MENU command   378
AUTOSCROLL command
   LOG window   358
   OUTPUT window   362
AUTOSKIP= option
   WINDOW statement   270
AUTOWRAP command
   SAS text editor   340

B

BACKWARD command
   SAS text editor   341-342
   window scrolling   329-330
bars   30
batch execution   311
BELL option
   DISPLAY statement   141
BESTw. format   429
BETAINV function   50
BETWEEN-AND operator   262, 300
BFIND command
   HELP window   371
   MENU window   378
binary data   412-413
bit testing   35-36
BLANK option
   DISPLAY statement   141
blanks
   in SAS names   4
   representing in data lines   451-452
   using to represent missing values   451-452
bold type in statement descriptions   5
Boolean operators   33
BOTTOM command
   SAS text editor   341
   window scrolling   329
BOUNDS command
   SAS text editor   341
brackets in statement descriptions   5
BREAK statement   539
BTREE entry   470
BY groups   126
BY statement   125-131, 527
   MERGE statement   128
   PROC step   285-286
   SET statement   128-129
   UPDATE statement   128
BYE command   326
BYTE function   50, 527
byte-reversed data   412-413
BZw.d informat   415

C

CALL statement   132-133, 527

546 Index

CALL subroutines 47
    compared to random number functions 47
CANCEL command
    KEYS window 373
    MENU window 378
    NOTEPAD window 381
    OPTIONS window 383
CANCEL option
    RUN statement 519
CAPS command
    LOG window 358
    OUTPUT window 362-363
    SAS text editor 341
carats (^) 30
CARDS statement 134
CARDS4 statement 134-135
CATALOG procedure 313, 472
CATALOG window 364-366, 472
    commands 366
    using selection fields 365-366
catalogs
    converting to Release 6.03 format 473
    converting to Version 6 form 472
    directories 472
    entries 469-472
    managing 471-472
    names 469
    Release 6.03 473-474
    storing entries 471
    transporting 473
    Version 5 469, 473
CBT command
    SETINIT window 385
CBT entry 470
CEIL function 51
CENTER SAS system option 490
CHANGE command
    SAS text editor 341-342
changing variable lengths 199-200
character comparisons 32-33
character constants 28-29
character data 191
character strings 28
character-to-numeric conversion 36
CHARCODE SAS system option 490
$CHARw. format 436
$CHARw. informat 423
$CHARZBw. informat 424
CIMPORT procedure 473
CINV function 51, 526
CLASS statement 287
classification variables 287
CLEAR command
    LOG window 359
    MENU window 378
    OUTPUT window 363
    SAS text editor 342
CLOCK command 326
CMAP entry 470
CMD automatic variable 271
CMD special variable 525
COLLATE function 51-
colons (:)
    format modifier 179-180
    with comparison operators 33

COLOR= option
    WINDOW statement 266, 270
color attribute keys
    NOTEPAD window 382
COLOR command 330-332
    designing color alternatives 331
    SAS text editor 342
    valid colors 331
    valid field types for all windows 330
    valid field types for selected windows 330
    valid highlighting attributes 331
color commands
    display manager global commands 325
COLOR MAP command
    SAS text editor 342
COLOR NUMBERS command
    SAS text editor 342-343
column input 175-176
column output
    PUT statement 224-225
column pointer controls 182-186
COLUMN= option
    FILE statement 151-152
    INFILE statement 165
COLUMNS= option
    WINDOW statement 267
COMMAND command
    NOTEPAD window 381
command specification
    X statement 522
COMMAw.d format 429
COMMAw.d informat 416
comment statements 506
    within SAS statements 10, 506
comparison operators 31-33
COMPOUND function 52, 526
COMPRESS function 53
concatenating SAS data sets 250
    when variables have different attributes 250
    with different variables 250
concatenation operator (||) 34
-CONFIG configuration option 477
CONFIG.SAS file 312, 476, 477, 542
CONFIG.SYS file 542
configuration options 475-481
    CONFIG.SAS file 312
constants 28
CONTENTS procedure 463
control-break signal 309
COPY command
    CATALOG window 366
    KEYS window 374
    NOTEPAD window 381
    SETINIT window 385
copying data sets 249-250
    creating new variables 250
    subsetting observations 249
CORR procedure
    output data sets 469
correlation matrix 469
COS function 53
COSH function 53
CPORT procedure 473
CSS function 53-54

CURSOR command
  SAS text editor 343
customizing the display manager
    environment 387-393
  WDEF command 388
cut and paste features 332-336
  basic commands 332
  display manager global commands 325
  global commands 334
CUT command 332
  cut and paste global command 334
  SAS text editor 343-344
CV function 54

D

DACCDB function 54, 526
DACCDBSL function 55, 526
DACCSL function 55, 526
DACCSYD function 55-56, 526
DACCTAB function 56, 526
data, missing 451-456
DATA command
  SETINIT window 385
data lines, signaling end 219
data set options 136-137, 465
data sets
  See SAS data sets
DATA statement 136-140
DATA step 17-25
  action statements 20-21
  control statements 21
  creating SAS data sets from existing SAS
    data sets 19
  definition 5
  file-handling statements 20
  information statements 21-22
  input data on disk 18
  input in the job stream 18
  interfaces to macro facility 503
  number of times executed 24
  report writing 19
  statements 19-22
  two input sources, example 25
data values 6
DATA SAS data set name 137
DATAn naming convention 137
DATASETS procedure 313
DATE command 542
date constant (D) 29
DATE function 56-57
DATE SAS system option 490
DATEJUL function 57
DATEPART function 57-58
datetime constant (DT) 29
DATETIME function 58
DATETIMEw.d format 444-445
DATETIMEw.d informat 441
DATEw. format 444
DATEw. informat 441
DAY function 58-59
DBCS SAS system option 491
DDMMYYw. format 445
DDMMYYw. informat 441
decimal points 28

default destination
  procedure output 403
  SAS log 400
DEFAULT= option
  LENGTH statement 196
defining directories
  LIBNAME statement 514-515
defining files 509
DELETE command
  CATALOG window 366
  NOTEPAD window 381
DELETE statement 140
DELIMITER= option
  INFILE statement 166
DEPDB function 59, 526
DEPDBSL function 59, 526
DEPSL function 60, 526
DEPSYD function 60, 526
DEPTAB function 60-61, 526
DES command
  NOTEPAD window 381
DESCENDING option
  BY statement 125
DEVICE= SAS system option 491
device drivers 481
DHMS function 61
DIF function 61-63, 527
DIGAMMA function 63
DIM function 63
DIR window 366-367
  commands 367
  fields 367
directories 459-460
display manager 317-393, 529
  CATALOG window 364-366
  command conventions 322-324
  customizing the environment 387-393
  DIR window 366-367
  editing and cursor keys 320-322
  executing window commands 323-324
  FILENAME window 368
  FOOTNOTES and TITLES windows
    368-370
  function keys 320
  global commands 324
  HELP window 370-372
  interrupting execution 309
  KEYS command 323
  KEYS window 372-375
  LIBNAME window 375-376
  LOG window 357-360
  MENU window 376-379
  NOTEPAD window 379-382
  OPTIONS window 382-383
  OUTPUT window 360-364
  PGM window 353-357
  SAS text editor 337-353
  SETINIT window 384-385
  special keys 320-322
  starting a session 307-308
  window call commands 325-326
display manager command conventions
  command syntax 322-323
  command-line commands 323
  command-line commands with options
    324

display manager command conventions
    (continued)
  commands with function keys 324
  function keys 324
  multiple commands 324
DISPLAY statement 141, 527
division operator (/) 31
DM statement 313, 507, 531
-DMS configuration option 308, 309, 478
DO groups 142-147
DO statement 142-147
  compared to GO TO statement 160
  iterative 142-145
  simple 142
DO UNTIL statement 146-147
DO WHILE statement 146
dollar signs ($)
  INPUT statement 175
DOLLARw.d format 430
DOS critical errors 396-397
DOS extensions
  See extensions
DOS files 541
double trailing at-sign (@@) 188
DOWNLOAD procedure 463, 537
DROP statement 148
DROP= data set option 466, 467

E

E-notation 28
$EBCDICw. format 436
$EBCDICw. informat 424
-ECHO configuration option 478
editing and cursor keys 320-322
EDPARMS entry 470
ELSE statement 162
-EMS configuration option 478
END command 314
  CATALOG window 364-366
  HELP window 370-372
  KEYS window 372-375
  MENU window 376-379
  NOTEPAD window 379-382
  OPTIONS window 382-384
  SETINIT window 384-385
  window management 326
END statement 142, 149
  SELECT groups 243
END= option
  INFILE statement 166
  MERGE statement 210-211
  SET statement 248
  UPDATE statement 256-257
ENDSAS command
  window management 326
ENDSAS statement 508
entries
  managing 471-472
  names of 470
  storing 471
  types of 470-471
EOF= option
  INFILE statement 166-167
EOPCHAR statement 539

EQ keyword 31
equal to operator (=) 31
ERF function 64
ERFC function 64
error handling 395-397
ERROR statement 527
errors 404-410
  data 408-409
  programming 407-408
  syntax 405-407
ERRORS= SAS system option 491
evaluation of expressions
  operator priority 30-31
Ew. format 430
Ew.d informat 417
executing
  programs 308
  SAS statements automatically 313
EXP function 64
exponentiation operator (**) 31
expressions 27-37
  evaluating 30
  IN operator 525
extensions 543
  .LOG 311-312
  .LST 311-312
  .SAS 311-312
external files 458
  %INCLUDE statement 512-513
  identifying for INPUT statement 164
  uploading and downloading 538

F

fields
  WINDOW statement 267
FILE command
  LOG window 359
  OUTPUT window 363
  SAS text editor 343-344
file name extensions 543
file names
  FILE statement 150-155
  %INCLUDE statement 512
FILE statement 150-155, 527
  description 150
  more than one 154-155
  print files 155
file transfer
  See link
-FILEBUFFERS configuration option 479
-FILECACHE configuration option 481
FILENAME statement 509-510, 531
FILENAME window 368
  commands 368
filerefs 150
  associating with external files 509
files
  See external files; SAS files
FILL command
  SAS text editor 344
FIND command
  HELP window 371
  LOG window 359
  MENU window 378

FIND command (*continued*)
    OUTPUT window   363-364
    SAS text editor   344-345
FIND *characterstring* command
    OUTPUT window   363
FINV function   64-65, 526
FIPNAME function   65
FIPNAMEL function   65
FIPSTATE function   65
FIRST.*byvariables*   127
first-level names
    SAS files   458, 460
FIRSTOBS= option
    data set option   466, 475
    INFILE statement   167
    SAS system option   491
floating point numbers   36-37
FLOOR function   66
FLOWOVER option
    INFILE statement   167
FONT entry   470
FOOTNOTE statement   511
    inserting variable values   513
FOOTNOTES window   368-370
    commands   370
FORM entry   470
FORMAT entry   470
format modifiers   179-180
FORMAT statement   156-158, 288-289, 527
    SAS datetime values   289
FORMAT= specification
    ATTRIB statement   124, 284
FORMATC entry   470
formats   411-450
    definition   8
    new   529
    SAS character   435-437
    SAS character, table   428
    SAS date, time, and datetime   437-440, 444-450
    SAS date, time, and datetime, table   440
    SAS numeric   428-435
    SAS numeric, table   427-428
    using   425-437
formatted input   178
formatted output
    PUT statement   226-227
    variable and format lists   226-227
FORMCHAR= SAS system option   491-492
FORWARD command   329
    SAS text editor   345
fractional values   36-37
FREQ statement   290
    problem with calculated values   37
-FSDEVICE configuration option   481
full-screen procedures   312, 314
function keys   320-322
functions   39-106
    arithmetic   42
    calling random-number   27
    character   45
    date and time   45-46
    financial   44, 49
    hyperbolic   43
    mathematical   42
    new   526

probability   43
quantile   43
random-number   44, 46-48, 132
sample statistic   43-44, 46
special   46
state and ZIP code   46
system   42
trigonometric   43
truncation   42
FUZZ function   66

G

GAMINV function   66
GAMMA function   66-67
GE keyword   31
global options   475-488
    CONFIG.SAS file   312
    PROFILE.SCT file   312-313
    table   498
GO TO statement   159-160
    compared to DO statement   160
    compared to LINK statement   159, 201
graphics procedures   312
greater than operator (>)   31
greater than or equal to operator (>=)   31
GROUP= option
    WINDOW statement   267
GROUPFORMAT option
    BY statement   125, 129-131
GRSEG entry   470
GT keyword   31

H

HBOUND function   67, 526
HEADER= option
    FILE statement   151
HELP entry   470
HELP window
    commands   371-372
hexadecimal constants
    character   35
    numeric   35
HEXw. format   430-431
$HEXw. format   436
$HEXw. informat   424
HEXw. informat   417
HHMMw.d format   446
highlighting attribute keys
    NOTEPAD window   382
HMS function   67-68
host processing   537
HOUR function   68
HOURw.d format   446
HSCROLL command   328
    SAS text editor   345-346

I

I line command   350
-IBM configuration option   485

IBMw.d format   431
IBw.d informat   418
ICOLUMN= option
    WINDOW statement   267
ID statement   291
IF statement   161-163
    conditional   161
    subsetting   163
IF-THEN statement   161-163
IF-THEN/ELSE statement   161-163
IMOD entry   471
IN operator   262, 300, 525
    equal to one in a list   32
IN= option
    data set option   466-467
    MERGE statement   210
    SET statement   247
    UPDATE statement   256
in-stream data   134
INCLUDE command
    compared to %INCLUDE statement   512
    SAS text editor   346
%INCLUDE statement   512-513
incrementing
    using iterative DO statement   143-144
INDENT command
    SAS text editor   346
INDEX function   68
index variables
    iterative DO statement   143-144
INDEXC function   69
INFILE statement   164-170, 527
    CARDS fileref   165
    file names   165
    filerefs   165
    more than one external file   164
INFILE specification
    PUT statement   224
infix operators   29
INFMT entry   471
INFMTC entry   471
INFORMAT= specification
    ATTRIB statement   124, 284
INFORMAT statement   171-172, 527
informats   411-447
    definition   8
    new   529
    SAS character   422-425
    SAS character, table   414
    SAS date, time, and datetime   437-441
    SAS date, time, and datetime, table   440
    SAS datetime   441-444
    SAS numeric   415-422
    SAS numeric, table   414
input data files, identifying   164-170
INPUT function   69
INPUT statement   173-192
    arrays   192
    column input   175-176
    end of file   192
    format modifiers   179-180
    formatted input   178-180
    grouped format lists   178-179
    invalid data   191-192
    list input   176-177
    named input   181-182

pointer controls   182-190
question (?) format modifier   189
questions (??) format modifier   189-190
INT function   37, 69-70
INTCK function   70-71
interactive display manager mode   308-309
    See also display manager
interactive line mode   309
interactive mode
    RUN statement   519
interactive procedures   313-314
    error handling   315
interleaving SAS data sets   251-252
interrupting execution   309
INTNX function   71-72
INTRR function   72, 526
IROW= option
    WINDOW statement   267
IRR function   72, 526
IS MISSING operator   262, 300
IS NULL operator   262, 300
italic in statement descriptions   5
iterative DO statement   142-145
    array processing   145
    incrementing   143-144
    multiple clauses, evaluating   144
    starting values   143
    stopping values   143
    UNTIL clause   144
    WHILE clause   144

J

JULDATE function   73
JULIANw. format   445
JULIANw. informat   442

K

KANJI SAS system option   492
KEEP statement   193
    with RENAME statement   193
KEEP= data set option   467
KEYS entry   471
KEYS window   372-375
    commands   373-374
    text insert feature   373
KEYS= option
    WINDOW statement   267
keywords   4
KURTOSIS function   73

L

LABEL= data set option   467
LABEL= specification
    ATTRIB statement   124, 284
label attributes   8
LABEL statement   194
    PROC step   292
labels, statement   195
labels, variable   292

LAG function 73-75, 527
LAST.byvariables 127
LAST SAS data set name 138, 246, 464-465
LAST variable 464-465
LAST= SAS system option 465, 492
LBOUND function 75-76, 526
LE keyword 31
LEFT command 329
   SAS text editor 346
LEFT function 76
LENGTH= option
   INFILE statement 167
LENGTH= specification
   ATTRIB statement 124, 284
length
   produced by various expressions 123
   truncation 197-198
length attributes 8
LENGTH function 76
LENGTH statement 196-200, 528
less than operator (<) 31
less than or equal to operator (<=) 31
LETTER entry 471
LGAMMA function 76
LIBNAME statement 459, 460, 514-515
LIBNAME window 321, 375-376
   commands 376
   selection field 376
librefs 458-461
   defining 459
   permanent files 459, 460
   reserved 460
   temporary files 459, 461
LINE= option
   FILE statement 152
   INFILE statement 167
line hold specifiers 187-188
line pointer controls 186-187
line-mode execution 309-311
LINESIZE= option
   FILE statement 152
   INFILE statement 167-168
   SAS system option 492
LINESLEFT= option
   FILE statement 152
link 537
   capabilities 538
   new features 537
   script statements 539
LINK statement 201-203
   compared to GO TO statement 159, 201
LIST entry 471
list input 176-177
list output
   PUT statement 225-226
LIST statement 204-205
literals 28
LL= option
   FILE statement 152
log
   See SAS log
-LOG configuration option 485
.LOG extension 311
LOG function 76-77

LOG specification
   FILE statement 150
LOG window 319, 321, 357-360
   commands 358-360
   SAS log 357
logical operators 33-34
LOG2 function 77
LOG10 function 77
LOSTCARD statement 206-209
LRECL= option
   FILE statement 152
   INFILE statement 168
LS= option
   FILE statement 152
.LST extension 311
LT keyword 31

M

macro facility 501-503
macro functions 503
macro program statements 502-503
macro variables
   automatic 501-503
   handling from inside SAS programs 132
MARK command
   cut and paste global command 332-334
   SAS text editor 346
master files, updating 256
match-merging 212-217
MATRIX entry 471
MAX function 77-78
MAX keyword 34
maximum operator (<>) 34
MDY function 78
MEAN function 78
memory usage
   noninteractive mode 311
MENU command
   AUTOREC= option 378
   AUTOSAVE= option 378
   start-location option 378
MENU entry 471
MENU window
   commands 378-379
   DM statement 507
   options 372
MERGE statement 210-217
   with RETAIN statement 211
merging observations
   comparison of one-to-one 217
   match-merging 212-217
   one-to-one 211-212
   table lookup 215-216
micro-to-host link
   interactive procedures 314
   see link 537
micro-to-host link commands 331
   display manager global commands 325
MIN function 78
MIN keyword 34
minimum operator (><) 34
minus sign (−) 28, 29
MINUTE function 79
missing constants 454-455

MISSING statement 218, 453
missing values 451-456
  arithmetic calculations 456
  character 29
  comparison operations 455
  DATA step, at beginning of 453-454
  illegal character-to-numeric conversions 456
  illegal characters in input data 453
  illegal operations 456
  in arithmetic expressions 31
  logical operations 455
  magnitudes 454
  MISSING option 455-456
  MISSING statement 218, 453
  numeric 28
  printing 455-456
  propagation of 456
  representing in data lines 451-456
  representing in program statements 453-456
  special 452
  updating 258-259
MISSING= SAS system option 493
MISSOVER option
  INFILE statement 168
MMDDYYw. format 446-447
MMDDYYw. informat 442
MMSSw.d format 447
MOD function 79
MOD option
  FILE statement 152
modes of execution 308-312
MONTH function 79-80
MONYYw. format 447
MONYYw. informat 442
MORT function 80, 526
MPRINT SAS system option 493
MRBw.d format 431
MRBw.d informat 418
-MSG configuration option 485
MSG automatic variable 271
MSG special variable 525
MTRACE SAS system option 493
multiplication operator (*) 31

N

N= option
  FILE statement 152-153
  INFILE statement 168
N function 80-81
n command
  HELP window 372
n option
  ABORT statement 108
_N_ automatic variables 24, 253
name command
  HELP window 372
named input 181-182
names 4
NE keyword 31
negative sign (−) 28, 29
NENGOw. format 447-448
NENGOw. informat 442-443

NETPV function 81, 526
NEWS= SAS system option 493
-NEWS configuration option 485
NEXT option
  COLOR command 326-327
NEXT [windowname] command
  window management 327
NMISS function 81
NOBS= option
  SET statement 248
NOINPUT option
  DISPLAY statement 141
noninteractive mode 311
nonstandard-form data 174
NOPAD option
  FILE statement 154
NOPRINT option
  FILE statement 153
NORMAL function 81-82
not equal operator (^=) 31
NOT keyword 33
NOT operator 526
not sign (^) 30
NOTEPAD window 321, 379-382
  color attribute keys 382
  commands 381
  extended keys 381
  highlighting attribute keys 382
NOTES SAS system option 493
NOTITLES option
  FILE statement 153
NOTSORTED option
  BY statement 125
NPAD entries 471
NPV function 82, 526
NTITLE command
  NOTEPAD window 381
null statement (;) 134, 219
  WHEN statement 243
NULL SAS data set name 138, 464
NUMBER SAS system option 493
numbers, precision of machine storage 36-37
NUMBERS command
  PGM window 346
  SAS text editor 346
numeric constants 28
numeric data 174, 190-191
numeric-to-character conversion 36

O

OBS= option
  data set option 467
  INFILE statement 168-169
  SAS system option 493-494
observations 6, 464
  choosing an ID 291
  counting n times 290
  creating several from one input line 220-221
  maximum number 6
OLD option
  FILE statement 153
one-to-one merging 211-212

Index 553

operating systems
  executing commands from inside a SAS program 132
operators 29-34
  IN 525
  logical NOT 526
  logical OR 526
  priority of 30-31
options
  See also global options; SAS system options
  in statement descriptions 5
  SAS data set 465-469
OPTIONS procedure 490
OPTIONS statement 488, 516-518
  specifying SAS system options 489
OPTIONS window 382, 383, 488
  commands 383
  specifying SAS system options 489
OR keyword 33
OR operator 526
order of operations 30-31
OTHERWISE statement
  SELECT groups 243
out-of-memory condition 396
output
  See procedure output; SAS output
output files, specifying external 150
OUTPUT statement 220-222, 293
OUTPUT window 319, 360-364
  commands 362-364
output, procedure
  See procedure output; SAS output
overprinting output lines 230-231
OVP SAS system option 494

P

PAD option
  FILE statement 154
  INFILE statement 169
PAGE command
  OUTPUT window 364
PAGE specification
  PUT statement 230
PAGENO= SAS system option 494
PAGESIZE specification
  N= option 152-153
PAGESIZE= option
  FILE statement 154
  SAS system option 495
parentheses in expressions 30
PARMCARDS statement 529
PARMCARDS4 statement 529
PASTE command
  cut and paste global command 332, 336
  SAS text editor 347
-PATH configuration option 485
PBUFFER entry 471
PCLEAR command
  cut and paste global command 336
  SAS text editor 348
PDw.d format 431
PDw.d informat 419

periods (.)
  using to represent missing values 452
PGM window 352-357
  commands 356-357
  ending SAS sessions 356
  managing your files 354-355
  program editor 353-357
  submitting SAS programs 353-354
PIBw.d format 432
PIBw.d informat 419
PKw.d format 432
PKw.d informat 420
PLIST command
  cut and paste global command 336
  SAS text editor 348
PLOT procedure 313
plus signs (+) 29
plus sign pointer control (+)
  INPUT statement 185
POINT= option
  SET statement 247-248
pointer controls
  going past end of output line 232
  location after writing 232
  output 227-234
  WINDOW statement 268-269
POISSON function 82
POPTION entries 312, 471, 488
pound sign pointer control (#)
  INPUT statement 186-187
powers, raising to 31
prefix operators 29
PREVCMD? command
  window management 327
-PRINT configuration option 485
print files
  FILE statement 155
PRINT option
  FILE statement 154
PRINT specification
  FILE statement 151
printed output 399-410
PROBBETA function 82-83
PROBBNML function 83
PROBCHI function 83
PROBF function 84
PROBGAM function 84
PROBHYPR function 84-85
PROBIT function 85
PROBNEGB function 85-86
PROBNORM function 86
PROBSIG= SAS system option 495
PROBT function 86
PROC statement 294
PROC step 5, 281-282
  excluding variables 282
  including variables 282
  interactive 295
procedure output 399, 402-404
  centering 404
  date values 404
  default destination 403
  page and line sizes 404
  page numbering 404
  printing values 403
  printing variable names 403-404

554 Index

procedure output (*continued*)
   redirecting 403
   time values 404
PROCEDURE statement 294
procedures
   full-screen 314
   interactive 313-314
PROFILE SAS system option 312, 495-496
PROGRAM EDITOR (PGM) window 319
PROGRAM entry 471
programs
   execution modes 308-312
   interactive procedures 313-314
   interrupting 309
   starting and running 307-314
   time elapsed 314
propagation of missing values 456
PUT function 86-87
PUT statement 223-235, 528
   description 223
   formatted output 226-227
   list output 225-226
   named output 234
   null 224
   pointer controls 227-234
   writing array elements 234
   writing character constants 233
   writing the current input line 233-234
   writing values of all variables 234

Q

QCAN command
   MENU window 378
QEND command
   MENU window 379
QTR function 87
question (?) format modifier
   INPUT statement 189
QUIT statement 295, 313-314, 529
quotes
   character constants 28-29

R

RANBIN function 87
RANCAU function 87-88
random number functions
   CALL statement 132
   compared to CALL subroutines 47-48
RANEXP function 88
RANGAM function 88-89
RANGE function 89
RANK function 90, 527
RANNOR function 90
RANPOI function 90
RANTBL function 91
RANTRI function 91-92
RANUNI function 92
RBw.d format 432-433
RBw.d informat 420
RCHANGE command
   PGM window 348
   SAS text editor 348

rearranging windows 388
RECALL command
   MENU window 379
   PGM window 356
RECFM= option
   FILE statement 154
   INFILE statement 169
records, combining 221-222
REMOTE SAS system option 496
remote submit command 538
RENAME statement 235
RENAME= data set option 467-468
REPEAT function 92
REPLACE SAS system option 497
REPLACE= data set option 463, 468
requestor panels 395
requestor prompts 395
REQUIRED command
   SETINIT window 385
RESET command
   PGM window 348
   SAS text editor 348
RESHOW command
   window management 327
RETAIN statement 236-240
retaining values 237-240
   table 237
RETURN option
   ABORT statement 108
RETURN statement 201, 241-242
   with GO TO statement 159
REVERSE function 92
RFIND command
   LOG window 360
   OUTPUT window 364
   PGM window 348
   SAS text editor 348
RIGHT command 329
   SAS text editor 348
RIGHT function 92
ROMANw. format 433-434
ROUND function 37, 93
ROWS= option
   WINDOW statement 267
RSUBMIT command 314, 538
   PGM window 357
RUN groups 313
RUN statement 519, 531
   interactive procedures 313
   line mode execution 309

S

SAS catalogs
   See catalogs
SAS command 307
   configuration options 476
   display manager 308
   line mode execution 309
   noninteractive execution 311
   specifying SAS system options 489
   syntax 307
SAS data libraries 457, 461-463
   copying 463
   documenting 463

Index 555

librefs 462
  managing 462-463
  structure 461-462
SAS data library references
  See librefs 459
SAS data set options 465-469
SAS data sets 6, 136, 457-458
  compared to SAS files 457-458
  copying 463
  creating 18-19, 293
  creating more than one in a single DATA
    step 138, 221
  definition 464
  documenting 463
  downloading 538
  first-level names 137
  labels 467
  librefs 137
  names 137-138, 464-465
  omitting name 464
  options 465-469
  permanent 465
  second-level names 137
  special types 468
  uploading 538
  variable attributes 464
  variables 464
SAS datetime values 289
SAS directory 541
SAS Display Manager System
  See display manager
SAS expressions 27-37
.SAS extension 311
SAS files 457-474
  catalogs 469-474
  changes 531
  compared to SAS data sets 457-458
  copying 463
  documenting 463
  duplicating names 462
  first-level names 458, 460
  librefs 458-461
  managing 462-463
  naming 458-461
  permanent 459, 460
  saving 459
  second-level names 458, 460
  storage locations 459
  temporary 459-460, 461
  types 458
SAS global options 475-482
  table 498-500
SAS keywords 4
SAS language 3
SAS link
  See link
SAS log 399-402
  default destination 400
  display manager 309
  line mode execution 309
  noninteractive execution 311
  redirecting 400
  structure 400-401
  suppressing 402
  writing on 401

SAS names 4
SAS operators 29-34
SAS output 399-410
  display manager 309
  line mode execution 309
  noninteractive execution 311
SAS programs
  See also programs
  definition 3
  steps 5
  writing 9-11
SAS root directory 541, 543
SAS source file 311
SAS statements
  creating files of 387
  definition 3
  executing automatically 313
  submitting initialization time 387
SAS system options 475, 488
  See also configuration options 312
  PROFILE.SCT file 312
  syntax 489
SAS text editor 337
  command-line command definitions 340
  command-line commands, table 339
  commands 339-349
  entering line commands directly 338
  executing line commands without line
    numbers 339
  line command definitions 349
  line commands, table 340
  using the full-screen editor 337
-SASHELP configuration option 486
-SASUSER configuration option 486
SAVE command
  KEYS window 374
  MENU window 379
  NOTEPAD window 381
  SETINIT window 385
SAVING function 93, 526
SCAN function 94
scientific notation 28
SCREEN entry 471
script statements 539
scripts 538
scrolling commands
  display manager global commands 325
SEC command
  SETINIT window 385
SECOND function 94
second-level names
  SAS files 458, 460
SELECT statement 243-245
  range checking 244
semicolons (;) 219
  in comment statements 506
  in data lines 134-135
-SET SASROOT configuration option 486
SET statement 246-252
SETINIT window 384
  commands 385
setting options automatically 312
SIGN function 94
SIGNOFF command 332, 539
SIGNON command 331
SIN function 95

556   Index

SINH function   95
SKEWNESS function   95
slash operator (/)   30
slash pointer control (/)
   INPUT statement   187
SMARK command   332
   cut and paste global command   336
   SAS text editor   348
SOUND function   95, 527
SOUND routine
   CALL statement   132
source file
   See SAS source file
SOURCE SAS system option   497
SOURCE2 SAS system option   497
spacing in SAS programs   9
special characters   4
special keys   320
special variables
   CMD   525
   MSG   525
SQRT function   96
SSNw. format   433
standard-form data   174
start-location option
   MENU command   378
START= option
   INFILE statement   169
starting SAS programs   307
   setting global options   312
statement labels   195
   GO TO statement   159
   LINK statement   201
statistics
   saving calculations   293
STD function   96
STDERR function   96
STFIPS function   96
STIMER SAS system option   497
STNAME function   97
STNAMEL function   97
STOP statement   253
   with POINT= option of SET statement   248
STOPOVER option
   INFILE statement   170
STORE command   332
   cut and paste global command   337
   SAS text editor   348
strings, character   28
SUBMIT command
   PGM window   357
subsetting IF statement   163
   compared to WHERE statement   262
SUBSTR function   97-98
SUBTOP command
   PGM window   357
subtraction operator (−)   31
SUM function   98
sum statement   254-255
SYMBOLGEN SAS system option   498
SYMGET function   98, 527
SYMPUT routine
   CALL statement   132
syntax   3
-SYSIN configuration option   487

-SYSPRINT configuration option   487
SYSTEM routine
   CALL statement   132
S370FIBw.d format   433
S370FIBw.d informat   421
S370FPDw.d format   434
S370FPDw.d informat   421
S370FPIBDw.d format   434
S370FPIBw.d informat   421
S370FRBw.d format   434-435
S370FRBw.d informat   422

T

TABS option
   INFILE statement   170
TAN function   98
TANH function   99
TEMPLATE entry   471
TIME command   542
time constant (T)   29
time elapsed for procedure step   314
TIME function   99
TIMEPART function   99-100
TIMEw.d format   448
TIMEw.d informat   443
TINV function   100, 526
TITLE statement   520
   inserting variable values   513
   with a particular PROC step   520
TITLES window   368
   commands   370
TODAY function   100
TODw. format   448
TOP command   329
   SAS text editor   348
trailing at-sign (@)   187
transaction files, updating   256
TRANSFER STATUS window   537
TRANSLATE function   101
TRIM function   101-102
TRUNC function   102, 526
truncation   197-198
TYPE= data set option   468
TYPE=CORR data set   468-469
types of variables
   definitions   7-8

U

UNBUFFERED option
   INFILE statement   170
underscores in SAS names (_)   4
UNIFORM function   102
UNMARK command   332
   cut and paste global command   337
   SAS text editor   348
UNTIL clause
   iterative DO statement   144
UPCASE function   102
UPDATE statement   256
updating files   256
   example   257
UPLOAD procedure   463, 537

Index

-USER configuration option   487
user profile catalog   488
   PROFILE.SCT file   312
USS function   103

V

VAR function   103
VAR statement   296
VAR window   385
   commands   386
variable values   464
variables
   at beginning of DATA step execution   22
   attributes   7
   automatic special   13
   changing length   199
   character variable length   198
   choosing for analysis   296
   definition   7
   dropping   466
   label   292
   labeling   194
   lists   10
   retaining values   237
   table of attributes   7
   types   7-8
VARIABLES statement
   See VAR statement
$VARYINGw. format   437
$VARYINGw. informat   425
-VERBOSE configuration option   476, 488
VERIFY command
   KEYS window   374
VERIFY function   103
vertical bars   30
   in statement descriptions   5
VSCROLL command   328
   SAS text editor   349

W

$w. format   435-436
$w. informat   422-423
w.d format   428-429
w.d informat   415
WDEF command   388
   window position   328
WEEKDATEw. format   448-449
WEEKDATXw. format   449
WEEKDAY function   104
WEIGHT statement   297
WGROW command
   window position   328
WHEN statement
   SELECT groups   243
WHERE expressions
   DATA step   261
   PROC step   298
WHERE statement   260, 529
   compared to WHERE= data set option   260
   compared to subsetting IF statement   262-263
   DATA step   260
   PROC step   298
WHERE= data set option   468
   compared to WHERE statement   260
WHILE clause
   iterative DO statement   144
window call commands   325
   display manager global commands   324
window management commands   326
   display manager global commands   324
window placement
   rearranging with cursor keys   389
   rearranging with WDEF command   388
window position commands   327
   display manager global commands   324
   WDEF command   328
   WGROW command   328
   WMOVE command   328
   WSAVE command   328
   WSHRINK command   328
window scrolling commands   328-329
window specification
   DISPLAY statement   141
   DM statement   507
WINDOW statement   266-280, 528
   pointer controls   268
windows, TRANSFER STATUS   537
WMOVE command
   window position   328
WORDDATEw. format   449
WORDDATXw. format   450
-WORK configuration option   488
WORK files   462
writing data values   223
WSAVE command
   window position   328
WSAVE entry   471
WSHRINK command
   window position   328

X

X ['dos command'] command
   window management   327
=X command
   HELP window   372
X statement   522, 531
XTIME statement   539
-XWAIT configuration option   488

Y

YEAR function   104
YYMMDDw. format   450
YYMMDDw. informat   443
YYQ function   104
YYQw. format   450
YYQw. informat   444

Z

ZIPFIPS function   105

ZIPNAME function   105
ZIPNAMEL function   105
ZIPSTATE function   105
ZOOM command
   window management   327
Zw.d format   435

Special Characters

| |
   concatenation operator   31
=
   equal to operator   31
= command
   MENU window   378
= *n* command
   HELP window   372
= *selection* command
   MENU window   378
<=
   less than or equal to operator   31
<>
   maximum operator   34
<
   less than operator   31
>=
   greater than or equal to operator   31
>
   greater than operator   31
+
   addition operator   31
−
   subtraction operator   31
^
   not equal to operator   31
(><)
   minimum operator   34
*
   multiplication operator   31
**
   exponentiation operator   31
/
   division operator   31
:
   colon operator   33

Your Turn

If you have comments about SAS software or the *SAS Language Guide for Personal Computers, Release 6.03 Edition*, please send us your ideas on a photocopy of this page. If you include your name and address, we will reply to you.

Please return to the Publications Division, SAS Institute Inc., SAS Campus Drive, Cary, NC 27513